On Exhibit

✿

ART LOVER'S

TRAVEL GUIDE

TO

AMERICAN MUSEUMS

2002

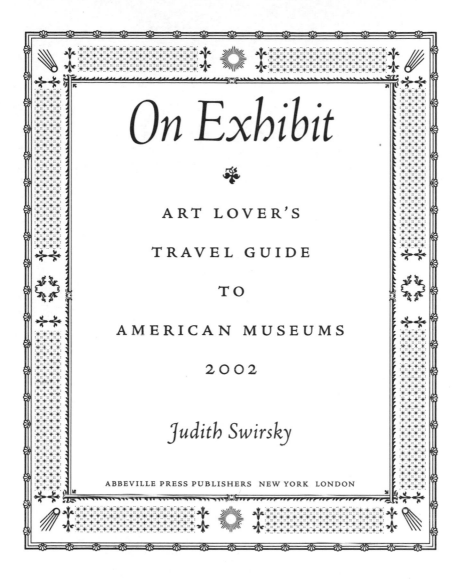

On Exhibit

ART LOVER'S

TRAVEL GUIDE

TO

AMERICAN MUSEUMS

2002

Judith Swirsky

ABBEVILLE PRESS PUBLISHERS NEW YORK LONDON

Copyright © 2001 Patti Sowalsky & Judith Swirsky.
All rights reserved under international copyright conventions.
No part of this book may be reproduced or utilized in any form
or by any means, electronic or mechanical,
including photocopying, recording,
or by any information storage and retrieval system,
without permission in writing from the publisher.
Inquiries should be directed to Abbeville Publishing Group,
22 Cortlandt Street,
New York, NY 10007.
The text of this book was set in Adobe Jenson.
Designed by Misha Beletsky
Printed and bound in the United States.

ISBN 0-7892-0747-8

First Edition

10   9   8   7   6   5   4   3   2   1

Library of Congress Cataloging-in-Publication Data
available upon request.

THE 2002 ISSUE OF

ON EXHIBIT'S

ART LOVER'S TRAVEL GUIDE

TO

AMERICAN MUSEUMS

IS DEDICATED

TO DR. LEO J. SWIRSKY

AND

MARJORIE SWIRSKY ZELNER.

THEY MADE DREAMS

INTO REALITY

AND

WILL FOREVER BE

MY INSPIRATION.

Contents

❧

Acknowledgments

❧

Even in the somewhat solitary process of writing a book, the help, counsel, and encouragement of others is essential. I owe a debt of thanks to Marjorie and Larry Zelner, who have solved numerous technical problems for us with their expertise.

In the years to come, On Exhibit promises to continue providing the art-loving traveler—and art professional—with the most factual, timely, and comprehensive guide available to the hundreds of treasure houses that preserve America's artistic heritage. I thank the thousands of art lovers and hundreds of participating museums who have enthusiastically supported our effort.

Introduction

❧

Celebrating its ninth successful year of annual publication, On Exhibit's *Art Lover's Travel Guide to American Museums* is the comprehensive guide to art museums nationwide. Easy to use, up to date, and completely reliable, it is the ultimate museum reference.

Written for those who travel on business or for pleasure and love to explore interesting art museums, On Exhibit's annual travel guides allow you to "know before you go" with complete assurance. With this guide in hand, you will never again miss a "little gem" of a museum or an important exhibition for lack of information.

I encourage you to join the thousands of art lovers who are loyal fans of On Exhibit. Like them, you are certain to be completely delighted with this quick, yet comprehensive overview of America's artistic riches.

Important Information on How to Use This Guide

The On Exhibit *Art Lover's Travel Guide* has been designed to be reader-friendly.

All museums are listed alphabetically by state, and then by city within each state.

Most permanent collection and museum facility information is expressed in easily recognized standard abbreviations. These are explained in the front of the book—and, for your convenience, on the back of the enclosed bookmark.

Note the exclamation point ("!"). This is the symbol used to remind you to call or check for information or any other verification.

All museums offering group tours require some advance notice. It is suggested that arrangements be made well in advance of your visit. When calling be sure to check on group size requirements and fee information. A group tour phone number is only included in cases where it is different from the regular museum number.

As a reminder, it is recommended that students and seniors always present proper I.D.'s in order to qualify for museum fee discounts wherever they are offered (age requirements for both vary!).

Admission and/or advance ticket requirements are included in the listings for certain special exhibitions.

Please note that exhibitions at most college and university museums are only scheduled during the academic year. Due to the constraints of space, student or faculty exhibits are rarely listed.

Some museums that have no exhibition listings simply did not have the information available at press time, others did not respond to our request for information, and therefore have abbreviated listings.

Every effort has been made to check the accuracy of all museum information, as well as exhibition schedules, at the time of publication. All hours, fees, days closed, and especially exhibitions, including those not already marked as tentative, are nonetheless subject to change at any time. We strongly suggest that you call to confirm any exhibition you wish to see.

If you find any inaccuracies, please accept our apologies—but do let us know. Finally, if we have inadvertently omitted your favorite museum, a letter to us would be most appreciated, so we can include it in the 2003 edition.

Explanation of Codes

❦

The coding system we have developed for this guide is made up primarily of standardized, easy to recognize abbreviations. All codes are listed under their appropriate categories.

MAIN CATEGORIES

Am   American

Af   African

An/Grk   Ancient Greek

An/R   Ancient Roman

As   Asian

Brit   British

Byz   Byzantine

Ch   Chinese

Cont   Contemporary

Du   Dutch

Egt   Egyptian

Eur   European

Fl   Flemish

Fr   French

Ger   German

It   Italian

Ind   Indian

Impr   Impressionist

Jap   Japanese

Lat/Am   Latin American

Mex   Mexican

Med   Medieval

Nat/Am   Native American

Oc   Oceanic

OM   Old Masters

Or   Oriental

P/Col   Pre-Columbian

P/Raph   Pre-Raphaelite

Reg   Regional

Ren   Renaissance

Russ   Russian

Sp   Spanish

MEDIUM

Cer   Ceramics

Dec/Art   Decorative Arts

Drgs   Drawings

Gr   Graphics

Per/Rms   Period Rooms

Phot   Photography

Post   Posters

Ptgs   Paintings

Sculp   Sculpture

W/Col   Watercolors

SUBJECT MATTER

Ab   Abstract

Ant   Antiquities

Arch   Architectural

Cart   Cartoon

Exp   Expressionist

Eth   Ethnic

Fig   Figurative

Folk   Folk Art

Ldscp   Landscape

Prim   Primitive

St/Lf   Still Life

REGIONS

E   East

Mid/E   Middle East

N   North

S   South

W   West

Perm/Coll Permanent Collection

The punctuation marks used for the permanent collection codes denote the following:

The colon (":") is used after a major category to indicate sub-listings with that category. For example, "Am: ptgs, sculp" indicates that the museum has a collection of American paintings and sculpture.

The semi-colon (";") indicates that one major category is ending and another major category listing is beginning. For example, "Am: ptgs; Sp: sculp; Du; Af" indicates that the museum has collections that include American paintings, Spanish sculpture, and works of Dutch and African origin.

A number added to any of the above denotes century, i. e., "Eur: ptgs 19,20" means that the collection contains European painting of the nineteenth and twentieth centuries.

Museum Services

❧

! Call to confirm or for further information

Y Yes

P Parking

♿ Handicapped Accessibility; "yes" means facility is completely accessible

❙❙ Restaurant Facilities

ℂ Not to be Missed

* Please Note

Adm Admission

Sugg/Cont. Suggested Contribution—Pay What You Wish, But You Must Pay Something

Vol/Cont. Voluntary Contribution—Free Admission, Contribution Requested

F Free

Sr Cit Senior Citizen, with I.D. (Age may vary)

GT Group Tours

DT Drop-in Tours

Mus/Sh Museum Shop

H/B Historic Building

S/G Sculpture Garden

TBA To Be Announced

Tent! Tentatively Scheduled

ATR! Advance Tickets Required—Call

Cat Catalog

WT Exhibition Will Travel—see index of traveling exhibitions

HOLIDAYS

Acad! Academic Holidays—Call For Information

Leg/Hol! Legal Holidays—Call For Information

Thgv Thanksgiving

Mem/Day Memorial Day

Lab/Day Labor Day

Mo Monday

Tu Tuesday

We Wednesday

Th Thursday

Fr Friday

Sa Saturday

Su Sunday

Museums & Exhibitions by State

❧

ALABAMA

BIRMINGHAM

Birmingham Museum of Art
2000 8th Ave. North, Birmingham, AL 35203

205-254-2565 www.artsBMA.org
Open: 10-5 Tu-Sa, 12-5 Su *Closed:* Mo, 1/1, Thgv, 12/25
& P *Museum Shop* ¶: Terrace cafe
Group Tours: 205-254-2318 *Docents Tour times:* 11:30 & 12:30 Tu-Fr; 2:00 Sa, Su *Sculpture Garden*
Permanent Collection: Am: ptgs; Eur: ptgs; Or; Af; P/Col; Dec/Art; Phot; Cont; glass; Ren: Kress Coll.

The Birmingham Museum of Art, with over 21,000 works in its permanent collection, is the largest municipal museum in the Southeast. In addition to the most extensive Asian art collection in the Southeast, the museum houses the finest collection of Wedgewood china outside of England. ℂ Multi-level outdoor Sculpture Garden featuring a waterwall designed by sculptor Elyn Zimmerman and two mosaic lined pools designed by artist Valerie Jaudon; Hitt Collection of 18th-c French paintings & decorative arts; Beeson Collection of Wedgewood finest outside of England; Contemporary Glass; Kress Collection of Renaissance Art.

ON EXHIBIT 2002

10/06/2001 to 06/02/2002 *Perspectives 6: Lawrence Weiner*
A site specific installation by one of the foremost conceptual artists of the 1960s. The work is titled "A Basic Assumption" *Brochure*

10/14/2001 to 01/06/2002 *In the Presence of Spirits: Selections from the National Museum of Ethnology, Lisbon*
Art from Angola, Mozambique, and Guinea Bissau used during initiation rituals. Many will be on exhibit in the U.S. for the first time. *Will Travel Brochure*

11/14/2001 to 01/06/2002 *Gracious Splendor: The Bequest of Susan Mabry and William Hansell Hulsey*
Collectors of European art, particularly of Marie Laurencin. This is the most complete collection of Laurencin's works in this country. Also included are works by Degas, Vlaminck, and Luce. *Catalog*

01/20/2002 to 04/07/2002 *Methods and Media: Drawings from the Birmingham Museum of Art*
The purpose of the exhibition is to ask viewers to discover how and why the artists use drawing as their medium. Works from the 16th-20th centuries include van Ostade, Cavedone, Guardi, Cole, Bellows, and Lewitt. *Catalog*

02/01/2002 to 04/09/2002 *European Masterpieces: Six Centuries of Painting from the National Gallery of Victoria, Australia*
Old master and modern paintings from the 14th to the 20th century will be shown including El Greco, Rembrandt, Van Dyck, Gainsborough, Pissaro, Monet, Picasso, Hockney, and others. *Catalog Will Travel*

05/05/2002 to 01/01/2002 *Avant-Garde Glass from Vienna Secession to the Bauhaus: The Torsten Brohan Collection from the Museo National de Artes Decortivas, Madrid*
One hundred eighty exquisite glass works showcasing the transitions from central European design to the highly ornamental Vienna Secession and the Weiner Werkstatt to the functional Bauhaus period. *Catalog Will Travel*

09/20/2002 to 01/05/2003   *The Stuff of Dreams/Matieres de Reves: Masterworks from the Paris Musee des Arts Decoratifs*
One hundred masterpieces of French design in silver, ivory, porcelain, jewelry, and furniture from the Middle Ages to the present day.   *Will Travel*

DAPHNE

American Sport Art Museum and Archives
Affiliate Institution: U.S. Sports Academy
One Academy Dr., Daphne, AL   36526

334-626-3303   www.asama.org
Open: 10-2 Mo-Fr   *Closed:* Sa, Su, Leg/Hol, Acad!
&   P: Free   *Museum Shop*
Group Tours: 334-626-3303   *Docents   Tour times:* Available upon request
Permanent Collection: ptgs, sculp, gr all on the single theme of American sports heros

One of the largest collections of sports art in the world may be found at this museum which also features works highlighting an annual sport artist of the year. Of special interest is the two-story high mural on an outside wall of the Academy entitled "A Tribute to the Human Spirit." Created by world-renowned Spanish artist Cristobal Gabarron, the work pays tribute to Jackie Robinson on the 50th anniversary of his breaking the color barrier in major league baseball. Works by former "Sport Artists of the Year" are on display daily. ℂ "The Pathfinder," a large sculpture of a hammerthrower by John Robinson where the weight of the ball of the hammer is equal to the rest of entire weight of the body of the figure.

DOTHAN

Wiregrass Museum of Art
126 Museum Ave., Dothan, AL   36302-1624

334-794-3871   www.wiregrassmuseumoart.org
Open: 10-5 Tu-Sa, 1-5 Su   *Closed:* Mo, Leg/Hol!
Sugg./Contr.: Yes, $1 per person
&   P: At the Dothan Civic Center parking lot and adjacent to the Museum   *Museum Shop   Group Tours*
Historic Building: Located in former 1912 electric plant on National Register of Historic Places
Permanent Collection: Reg

Featured on the main floor galleries of this regional visual arts museum are a variety of works that reflect the ever changing world of art with emphasis on solo exhibits showcasing important emerging artists of the south. The museum, located in the South East corner of Alabama, approximately 100 miles from Montgomery, recently renovated four galleries for the display of decorative arts, African art and works on paper. ℂ ARTventures, a "hands on" gallery for children, schools, & families

ON EXHIBIT 2002

01/12/2002 to 04/28/2002   *Voices Rising: Alabama Women at the Millennium*

01/26/2002 to 07/28/2002   *Rites of Passage: African Art*

03/30/2002 to 05/26/2002   *The Photographs of P. H. Polk*

05/04/2002 to 07/07/2002   *Nall: Retrospective*

09/14/2002 to 11/03/2002   *Francis de la Rosa*

Fayette Art Museum
530 Temple Ave. N., Fayette, AL   35555

205-932-8727
Open: 9-noon & 1-4 Mo, Tu, Th, Fr, and by appointment   *Closed:* We, Sa, Su, Le/Hol!
Vol./Contr.: Yes
&.   P: Free   *Group Tours   Docents   Drop-In Tours:* daily during museum hours   *Historic Building*
Permanent Collection: Am: ptgs 20; Folk

Housed in a 1930s former school house, this collection consists mostly of 3,600 works of 20th-century American art. Six folk galleries, opened in 1996. ❰ One of the largest collections of folk art in the Southeast

Gadsden Museum of Art
2829 W. Meighan Blvd., Gadsden, AL   35904

205-546-7365
Open: 10-4 Mo-We & Fr, 10-8 Th, 1-5 Su   *Closed:* Sa, Leg/Hol
Vol./Contr.: Yes
&.   P: Free   *Group Tours   Docents*
Permanent Collection: Eur: Impr/ptgs; Cont; Dec/Art

Historical collections and works by local and regional artists are housed in this museum.

Huntsville Museum of Art
300 Church Street South, Huntsville, AL   35801

256-535-4350   www.hsu.museum.org
Open: 10-5 Tu-Sa, 1-5 Su   *Closed:* Mo, Leg/Hol!
Free Day: Th eve   *Adm: Adult:* $5.00 special adm for some exh   *Children:* under 12 Free
Students: $4.00 with ID   *Seniors:* $4.00 over 60
&.: Totally accessible with wheelchairs available   P: Paid parking in garage across the street
Museum Shop   Docents   Tour times: selected S afternoons
Permanent Collection: Am: ptgs, drgs, phot, sculp, folk, dec/art, reg 18-20; Eur: works on paper; Or; Af

Focusing on American paintings and graphics from the 18th through the 20th century, as well as works by regional artists, the Huntsville Museum promotes the recognition and preservation of artistic heritage in its own and other Southeastern states, and serves as the leading visual arts center in North Alabama. Major touring exhibtions are scheduled each year.

Mobile Museum of Art
4850 Museum Dr. Langan Park, Mobile, AL   36608

334-343-2667   www.mobilemuseumofart
Open: 10-5 Mo-Sa, 1-5 Su   *Closed:* Mo, Thgv, 12/25
&.   P: Free   *Museum Shop*
Docents   Tour times: unguided, guides by res.   *Sculpture Garden*
Permanent Collection: Am: 19; Af; Or; Eur; Dec/Art; Cont/Crafts

Beautifully situated on a lake in the middle of Langan Park, this museum offers the visitor an overview of 2,000 years of culture represented by more than 6,000 pieces in its permanent collection. ❰ Boehm porcelain bird collection; 20th-century decorative arts collection

ON EXHIBIT 2002

09/06/2002 to 01/12/2003   *Picturing French Style: Three Hundred Years of Art and Fashion*
Eight themes will weave the period from the 1700s to today: Frivolity and Folly; An ordered Fashion; Romance of the Exotic; Courting the Middle Class;Legend of the Milliner; The Theatrical Milieu; Constructing Modernism; and Quoting Traditions   *Catalog*

Mobile Museum of Art Downtown
300 Dauphin St., Mobile, AL   36602

251-208-5200   www.mobilemuseumofart
Open: 10-5 Mo-Sa, 1-5 Su
   P: Metered and lot parking available.   *Museum Shop   Group Tours   Drop-In Tours*

A renovated early 1900s hardware store is home to this downtown art museum gallery.

MONTGOMERY

Montgomery Museum of Fine Arts
One Museum Dr. P.O. Box 230819, Montgomery, AL   36123

334-244-5700   www.mmfa.org
Open: 10-5 Tu-Sa, till 9 Th, Noon-5 Su   *Closed:* Mo, Leg/Hol!
   P: Free   *Museum Shop*   ¶: Tu-Sa 11-2
Docents   Tour times: 1 Sa, Su; 6:30 Th
Permanent Collection: Am: ptgs, gr, drgs 18-20; Eur: ptgs, gr, sculp, dec/art 19; Cont/Reg; Blount Collection of Am Art

Set in a picturesque, English-style park, the Museum is noted for its holdings of 19th- and 20th-century American paintings in the Blount Collection, its Southern regional art, and its Old Master prints. ¶ "A Peaceable Kingdom with Quakers Bearing Banners" by Edward Hicks, "New York Office" by Edward Hopper, interactive gallery for children

ON EXHIBIT 2002

11/03/2001 to 02/03/2002   *The Art of the Goldsmith: Masterworks from the Buccelatti Foundation*
Producing finely crafted objets de art and jewelry since the mid-18th century, these are from the family's private collection.

11/03/2001 to 02/03/2002   *ArtNow: Keiji Shinohara*
Shinohara is a printmaker working in the traditional woodcut medium ukiyo-e. Included are wook blocks he carves to create the printed images.

02/23/2002 to 05/05/2002   *Brush with History: Paintings from the National Portrait Gallery*
75 paintings from the Smithsonian which is under renovation include works by Stuart, Sargent, Degas, Eakins, Benton, Elaine de Kooning, Neel, Katz, Warhol, and others   *Will Travel*

05/18/2002 to 08/04/2002   *Hubert Shuptrine*
Shuptrine started as an abstract painter and then turned to representational watercolors in "Jerico: The South Beheld." He paints people, houses, Native Americans, and pets emphasizing their dignity and spirit.

05/18/2002 to 09/01/2002   *Red Grooms: Selections from the Complete Graphic Work, 1956–2000*
A career retrospective of the artist's work in folk idiom and narrative themes. He plays on regional resources and the larger history of art.   *Will Travel*

09/15/2002 to 10/21/2002   *Engravings and Woodcuts by Albrecht Dürer*
An exploration of this most influential artist's work in the collection of the Museum.

11/02/2002 to 01/05/2003   *Artful Teapots*
250 teapots from the Kamm collection acquired from all over the world and reflecting all styles and subjects

ALASKA

ANCHORAGE

Anchorage Museum of History and Art
121 W. Seventh Avenue, Anchorage, AK   99519-6650

907-343-4326
Open: 9-6 Mo-Su mid May-mid Sept; 10-5 Tu-Sa rest of year   *Closed:* Mo, Winter, 1/1 Thgv, 12/25
Adm: Adult: $5.00   *Children:* Free under 18   *Seniors:* $4.50
Museum Shop   ¶: Café   *Group Tours:* 907-343-6187   *Drop-In Tours:* 10, 11, 1, 2, Alaska Gallery summer
Permanent Collection: Eth

The Anchorage Museum of History and Art is dedicated to the collection, preservation, and exhibition of Alaskan ethnology, history, and art.

KETCHIKAN

Totem Heritage Center
Affiliated Institution: Ketchikan Museums
601 Deermount, Ketchikan, AK   99901

907-225-5900   www.city.ketchikan.ak.us
Open: 8-5 Daily (5/1-9/30); 1-5 Tu-Fr (10/1-4/30: no adm fee)   *Closed:* 1/1, Easter, Veteran's Day,
Thgv, 12/25
Adm: Adult: $4.00   *Children:* Free under 6
&   P   *Museum Shop*   *Group Tours:* 907-225-5900   *Drop-In Tours*
Permanent Collection: Eth

The Totem Heritage Center houses a world-renowned collection of original, unrestored totem poles, recovered from abandoned Tlingit and Haida villages near Ketchikan. These poles give silent testimony to the skill and artistry of 19th-century Native carvers. The Center also features changing exhibits of Northwest Coast Native arts, interpretive panels, classes in Northwest Coast Native Art traditions, and special cultural programs throughout the year.   ¶ A new Pole, "Honoring Those who Give" carved by Tlingit carver Nathan Jackson to commemorate the founding of the Totem Heritage Center was dedicated in 1999 and visitors will see it at the entrance to the Center in 2000.

ARIZONA

MESA

Mesa Southwest Museum
53 N. Macdonald, Mesa, AZ   85201

480-644-2230   www.ci.mesa.azus/parkspec/msm/index.html
Open: 10-5 Tu-Sa, 1-5 Su   *Closed:* Mo, Leg/Hol!
Adm: Adult: $6.00   *Children:* $3.00 (3-12)   *Students:* $5.00   *Seniors:* $5.00
&   P: Street parking in front of the museum & covered parking directly behind the museum on the first level of the parking garage. Handicapped spaces located in front of the museum.
Museum Shop   *Group Tours:* 480-644-3553 or 3071   *Drop-In Tours:* Reserved in advance
Historic Building: Sirrine House (1896)
Permanent Collection: Eth; P/Col; Cer

The Museum explores the Southwest's history from before the time of the dinosaurs to today. The expansion, opening May 27, 2000 treats visitors to an eye-popping, mind-expanding multi-sensory experience.

Heard Museum
2301 North Central Avenue, Phoenix, AZ   85004

602-252-8840   www.heard.org
Open: 9:30-5 daily   *Closed:* Leg/Hol!
Adm: *Adult:* $7.00   *Children:* Free under 4, 4-12 $3.00   *Seniors:* $6.00
&   P: Free   *Museum Shop* ¶¶   *Group Tours:* 602-251-0230   *Drop-In Tours:* Many times daily!
Sculpture Garden
Permanent Collection: Nat/Am; Eth; Af; Or; Oc; S/Am

The collection of the decorative and fine arts of the Heard Museum, which spans the history of Native American Art from the pre-historic to the contemporary, is considered the most comprehensive collection of its kind in the entire country. Named after the Heards who founded the museum based on their great interest in the culture of the native people of Arizona, the museum is housed in the original structure the Heards built in 1929 adjacent to their home called Casa Blanca. *A new branch of the museum called Heard Museum North is now open at the Boulders Resort in Scottsdale (phone 602-488-9817 for information). ℂ Experience the cultures of twenty-one Native American tribes with the interactive exhibit "We are America's First People"

ON EXHIBIT 2002

11/03/2001 to 04/01/2003   *Masterworks from the Heard Museum*
Three exhibitions will showcase Native American fine and cultural art in all media including pottery, basketry, jewelry, beadwork, sculpture, and fine art by contemporary artists. "We Are America's First People"

01/01/2002 to 01/31/2002   *Brilliant Navajo Germantown and Eyedazzler Textiles*
This is one of the most innovative periods in Navaho weaving. It will be accompanied by interpretive text by Navajo weaver Marylou Schultz.

02/09/2002 to 01/01/2003   *8th Annual American Fine Art Invitational*
Eight cutting edge Native artists from the United States and Canada. A competitive juried exhibition and important forum.

Phoenix Art Museum
1625 N. Central Ave., Phoenix, AZ   85004-1685

602-257-1880   www.phxart.org
Open: 10-5 Tu-Su, till 9pm Th, Fr   *Closed:* Mo, I/1, 7/4, Thgv, 12/25
Free Day: Th   *Adm:*   *Adult:* $7.00   *Children:* $2.00 6-18   *Students:* $5.00 full time   *Seniors:* $5.00
&   P   *Museum Shop* ¶¶: Art Museum Café
Group Tours: 602-257-4356   *Drop-In Tours:* 2:00 daily & 6:00 on Th; Gallery Talks 12:00 daily
Permanent Collection: Am: Western, cont; As; Eu: 18-19; Cont Lat/Am; Fashion

The new 160,000-sq ft. Phoenix Art Museum is double its former size. The classically progressive design of the Museum integrates art and architecture with the southwestern landscape, accommodating large traveling exhibitions, a collection of over 100,000 works and a growing arts audience. Visitors enjoy an audiovisual orientation theater, an interactive gallery for children, a restaurant, a museum store, and an audioguide to the collection. ℂ "Artworks Gallery" for children and their families; Thorne miniature rooms of historic interiors.

Phippen Museum Art of the American West
Affiliated Institution: Art of the American West
4701 Hwy 89 N, Prescott, AZ   86301

520-778-1385   www.phippenmuseum.org
Open: open daily in summer !   *Closed:* 1/1, Thgv, 12/25
Adm: *Adult:* $3.00   *Children:* Free under 12   *Students:* $2.00   *Seniors:* $2.00
& P: Free   *Museum Shop   Group Tours   Drop-In Tours*
Permanent Collection: Ptgs, Sculp

The Phippen is dedicated to excellence in exhibitions, and presents several stellar exhibits each calendar year featuring art of the American West. ℂ 3-foot-high bronze of Father Kino by George Phippen; spectacular view and historic wagons in front of the museum

Fleischer Museum
17207 N. Perimeter Dr., Scottsdale, AZ   85255

408-585-3108   www.fleischer.org
Open: 10-4 Daily   *Closed:* Leg/Hol!
Vol/Contr.: yes   & P: Free   *Museum Shop*
Group Tours: 480-563-6292   *Drop-In Tours:* Tu-Fr; 10-4 by reservation only   *Sculpture Garden*
Permanent Collection: Am/Impr; ptgs, sculp (California School)

Located in the 261 acre Perimeter Center, the Fleischer Museum was the first museum to feature California Impressionist works. More than 80 highly recognized artists represented in this collection painted in "plein air" from the 1880s-1940s, imbuing their landscape subject matter with the special and abundant sunlight of the region. Russian & Soviet Impressionism from the Cold War era are represented in the permanent collection as well. ℂ "Mount Alice at Sunset" by Franz A. Bischoff, "Mist Over Point Lobos" by Guy Rose, "Spanish Boats" by Arthur G. Rider, "In the Orchard. c.1915-1917" by Joseph Raphael.

Scottsdale Museum of Contemporary Arts
7380 E. Second St., Scottsdale, AZ   85251

602-994-2787   www.scottsdalearts.org
Open: 10-5 Tu-Sa; till 9 Th, 12-5 Su   *Closed:* Mo, Leg/Hol!
Free Day: Tu   *Adm:*   *Adult:* $5.00   *Children:* Free under 15   *Students:* $3.00
& P: Free   *Museum Shop*
Group Tours: 602-874-4641   *Drop-In Tours:* 1:30 Su Oct-Apr, 3:00 Su (outdoor sculp) Nov-Apr
Sculpture Garden
Permanent Collection: Cont; Reg

Four exhibition spaces and a beautiful outdoor sculpture garden are but a segment of this community oriented multi-disciplinary cultural center. The opening of a new museum called Gerard L. Cafesjian Pavilion will open a new and exciting concept with walls extending to the very limits of the city under the auspices of Scottsdale Museum of Contemporary art. ℂ "The Dance" a bronze sculpture (1936) by Jacques Lipchitz; "Ambient Landscape" by Janet Taylor; "Time/Light Fusion" sculpture (1990) by Dale Eldred

Sylvia Plotkin Judaica Museum
10460 N. 56th St., Scottsdale, AZ   85253

480-951-0323   www.TempleBethIsrael.com and www.sylviaplotkinjudaicamuseum.org
Open: 10-3 Tu-Th, 12-3 (most) Su; open after Fr evening services   *Closed:* Mo, Fr, Sa, Leg/Hol!;
Jewish Hol! Jul
Sugg/Contr.: Yes   *Adm:*   *Adult:* $2.00
& P: In front & side of building   *Museum Shop*
Group Tours: 480-443-4150   *Drop-In Tours:* by appt   *Sculpture Garden*
Permanent Collection: Jewish Art and Ceremonials; Tunisian Synagogue Period Room; Biblical Garden

Considered to be one of the most important centers of Jewish art and culture in the Southwest, the Sylvia Plotkin Judaica Museum has artifacts spanning 5000 years of Jewish history and heritage. The Museum hosts 3 special exhibitions a year, features guest speakers, Lecture Series, and interactive programs. It is advised to call ahead for summer hours. ❤ Reconstructed Tunisian Synagogue; To-scale Replica of a portion of the Western Wall in Jerusalem

ON EXHIBIT 2002

01/01/2002 to 03/15/2002   *Lloyd Wolf & Paula Wolfson, Jewish Mothers, Photo Exhibition*
"Jewish Mothers" celebrates the strength, traditions, and accomplishments of American Jewish women.

03/15/2002 to 05/15/2002   *Birth of Tuvo Durn*

TEMPE

ASU Art Museum
Affiliated Institution: Arizona State University
Nelson Fine Arts Center & Ceramics Research Center, Tempe, AZ   85287-2911

602-965-2787   http://asuam.fa.asu.edu
Open: Sept-May: 10-9 Tu, 10-5 We-Sa, 1-5 Su; Summer: 10-5 Tu-Sa, 1-5 Su   *Closed:* Mo, Leg/Hol!
Vol/Contr.: Yes
& P: Metered parking or $3.00 lot weekdays till 7; Free Tu after 7 and weekends; physically-challenged parking in front of Nelson Center on Mill Ave.   *Museum Shop*
Group Tours: 602-965-2787   *Drop-In Tours*
Historic Building: Award winning new building by Antoine Predock
Permanent Collection: Am: ptgs, gr; Eur: gr 15-20; Am: crafts 19-20; Ceramics; Lat/Am: ptgs, sculp; Cont; Af; Folk

For more than forty years the ASU Art Museum, founded to broaden the awareness of American visual arts in Arizona, has been a vital resource within the valley's art community. The ASU Art Museum consists of both the Nelson Center and the Ceramics Research Center. ❤ Significant ceramics collection—important and challenging collections and exhibitions of contemporary art.

TUCSON

Center for Creative Photography
Affiliated Institution: University of Arizona
Tucson, AZ   85721-0103

520-621-7968   www.ccparizona.edu/ccp.html
Open: 9-5 Mo-Fr; 12-5 Sa, Su   *Closed:* Most Leg/Hol!
Vol/Contr.: Yes   *Sugg/Contr.:* $2.00
& P: Pay parking in the Visitors' Section of the Park Avenue Garage on NE corner of Speedway & Park with direct pedestrian access under Speedway to the Center's front door.   *Museum Shop*
Group Tours: education dept

With more than 60,000 fine prints in the permanent collection, the singular focus of this museum, located on the campus of the University of Arizona, is on the photographic image, its history, and its documentation.

Tucson Museum of Art and Historic Block
140 N. Main Ave., Tucson, AZ   85701

520-624-2333   www.tucsonarts.com
Open: 10-4 Mo-Sa, 12-4 Su   *Closed:* (Mo Mem-Lab/Day), Leg/Hol!
Free Day: Su   *Adm:*   *Adult:* $5.00   *Children:* Free 12 & under   *Students:* $3.00   *Seniors:* $4.00 60+
& P: Free lot on north side of building; pay lot on east side of building; commercial underground
parking garage under city hall across street   *Museum Shop*   ₦: Café a La C'Art Mo-Fr 11-3
Group Tours: 520-696-7450   *Drop-In Tours:* Daily Historic tours except Mo !
Historic Building: Located on the site of the original Spanish Presidio - 5 historic properties
Sculpture Garden
Permanent Collection: P/Col; Am: Western; Cont/SW; Sp: colonial; Mex

Past meets present in this museum and historic home complex set in the Plaza of the Pioneers.
The contemporary museum building itself, home to more than 5,000 works in its permanent
collection, is a wonderful contrast to five of Tucson's most prominent historic homes that are all
situated in an inviting parklike setting. One, the historic 1860s Edward Nye Fish House on
Maine Ave., has recently opened as the museum's John K. Goodman Pavilion of Western Art.
*1. Tours of the Historic Block are given at 11am We & Th from 10/1 through 5/1. 2. Free art
talks are offered at 1:30 on Mo & Th in the Art Education Building.   ₡ Contemporary &
modern collections

ON EXHIBIT 2002

11/17/2001 to 01/13/2002   *Directions: Barbara Rogers: Natural Facts/Unnatural Acts*
Paintings associated with garden decay, death, rebirth, and renewal

11/17/2001 to 01/13/2002   *Iron Maidens: Cast Metal and Steel Sculpture by Bella Feldman, Mary
Bates-Neubauer, and Kim Cridler*

01/12/2002 to 03/17/2002   *Overt Voyeurism: Shu Minlin*

01/19/2002 to 02/02/2002   *Ready, Set, D'Art*

02/16/2002 to 04/21/2002   *Threads of the World: Folk Costumes*

02/16/2002 to 04/28/2002   *American Spectrum: Paintings and Sculpture from the Smith College
Museum of Art*

02/24/2002 to 03/24/2002   *Western Artists of America: Branding Iron Show*

University of Arizona Museum of Art
Olive and Speedway, Tucson, AZ   85721-0002

520-621-7567   artmuseum.arizona.edu
Open: mid Aug-mid May: 9-5 Mo-Fr & 12-4 Su; mid May-mid Aug: 10-3:30 Mo-Fr & 12-4   *Closed:* Sa,
Leg/Hol!, Acad
& P: $1.00 per hour in the UA garage at the NE corner of Park and Speedway (free parking Su only).
Museum Shop   Group Tours   Drop-In Tours: Upon request
Permanent Collection: It: Kress Collection 14-19; Cont/Am: ptgs, sculp; Cont/Eu: ptgs, sculp; Or: gr; Cont:
gr; Am: ptgs, gr

With one of the most complete and diverse university collections, the Tucson based
University of Arizona Museum of Art features Renaissance, later European and American
works in addition to outstanding contemporary creations by Lipchitz, O'Keeffe, and
Zuñiga.   ₡ Sixty-one plaster models & sketches by Jacques Lipchitz; 26-panel retablo
of Ciudad Rodrigo by Gallego (late 15th century); Georgia O'Keeffe's "Red Canna"; Audrey
Flack's "Marilyn"

ARKANSAS

Fort Smith Art Center
423 North Sixth St., Fort Smith, AR   72901

501-784-2787   www.ftsartcenter.com
Open: 9:30-4:30 Tu-Sa   *Closed:* Su, Mo, Easter, 7/4, Thgv, 12/21-1/1
&: To lower floor   P: Free   *Museum Shop*
Group Tours   Historic Building: Pilot House for Belle Grove Historic District
Permanent Collection: Cont/Am: ptgs, gr, sculp, dec/arts; Phot; Boehm Porcelains

Located mid-state on the western border of Oklahoma, the Fort Smith Art Center, housed in a Victorian Second Empire home, features regional and nationally recognized artists in changing monthly exhibits ☾ Large Boehm Porcelain Collection

Arkansas Arts Center
9th & Commerce, MacArthur Park, Little Rock, AR   72203

501-372-4000   www.arartscenter.org
Open: 10-5 Mo-Sa, till 8:30 Fr, 12-5 Su   *Closed:* 12/25
Vol/Contr.: $2.00
& P: Free   *Museum Shop*   ¶
Group Tours   Historic Building: The Decorative Arts Museum is housed in a 1840 Greek Revival building
Sculpture Garden
Permanent Collection: Am: drgs 19-20; Eu: drgs; Am: all media; Eu: all media; Or; Cont/Crafts

The state's oldest and largest cultural institution, features a permanent collection of over 10,000 objects that includes a nationally recognized collection of American and European drawings, contemporary American crafts and objects of decorative art.   ☾ "Earth," a bronze sculpture by Anita Huffington

Arts & Science Center for Southeast Arkansas
701 Main St., Pine Bluff, AR   71601

870-536-3375
Open: 8-5 Mo-Fr, 1-4 Sa, Su   *Closed:* 1/1, Easter, 7/4, Thgv, 12/24, 12/25
& P   *Group Tours   Drop-In Tours   Theater*
Permanent Collection: Eu: ptgs 19; Am: ptgs, gr 20; Om: drgs; Cont/Eu: drgs, Delta Art; Reg

The Museum, whose new building opened in Sept. '94, is home to a more than 1,000-piece collection of fine art that includes one of the country's most outstanding permanent collections of African American artworks. The museum also contains a noted collection of American drawings (1900 to the present) which are always on view.   ☾ Collection of African/American art by Tanner, Lawrence, Bearden, and others; Art Deco & Art Nouveau bronzes

CALIFORNIA

BAKERSFIELD

Bakersfield Museum of Art
1930 , Bakersfield, CA   93301

661-323-7219
Open: 10-4 Tu-Sa, 12-4 Su   *Closed:* Mo, Leg/Hol!
Free Day: 3rd Fr each month, 12-4   *Adm:*   *Adult:* $4.00   *Children:* Free under 12   *Students:* $1.00
Seniors: $2.00
&   P: Free   *Museum Shop   Group Tours*
Permanent Collection: Ptgs; Sculp; Gr; Reg

Works by California regional artists are the main focus of the collection at this museum, a facility which is looking forward to the results of an expansion project due to start in early 1999. Besides the sculptures and flowers of the museum's gardens where, with 3 days notice, box lunches can be arranged for tour groups, visitors can enjoy the 7-9 traveling exhibitions and 1 local juried exhibitions presented annually.

BERKELEY

Judah L. Magnes Museum
2911 Russell St., Berkeley, CA   94705

510-549-6950   www.magnesmuseum.org
Open: 10-4 Su-Th   *Closed:* Jewish & Leg/Hols
Sugg/Contr.: Yes   *Adm:*   *Adult:* $5.00
&.: Most galleries, restroom   P: Free   *Museum Shop*
Group Tours: 510-549-6938 (by appt.)   *Drop-In Tours:* 10-4 Su-Th
Historic Building: 1908 Berkeley landmark building (Burke Mansion)   *Sculpture Garden*
Permanent Collection: Fine Arts; Jewish Ceremonial Art, Rare Books & Manuscripts; Archives of Western U.S. Jews

Founded in 1962, the Judah L. Magnes Museum soon became the first Jewish museum to be accredited by the American Association of Museums. Thousands of prints, drawings and paintings by scores of Jewish artists of the past few centuries are represented in the permanent collection, which also includes ceremonial and folk pieces and textiles from antiquity to the present, from around the world, as well as rare books and manuscripts, and western U.S. Jewish history documents. The Museum aims to increase intercultural dialogue, and understanding through its collections and exhibits. ℂ "The Jewish Wedding" by Trankowsky; ceremonial objects 16-20th century.

ON EXHIBIT 2002

05/07/2000 to 05/01/2002   *Telling Time: To Everything There is a Season*
"Telling Time" is structured around the seasons of the year and the seasons of life. Objects range from the sacred and the secular, to the provocative and the whimsical. Highlights include the treasures from Jewish ceremonial and folk art, rare books and manuscripts, contemporary and traditional fine art, video, photography, and cultural kitsch. Interactive features in the exhibition offer new opportunities for guests to share their cultures, by writing or recording favorite rituals, traditions, and commemorative dates. The exhibition also features a Resource Room where guests are greeted by "Faces in Time," a portrait gallery featuring eleven prominent Jewish writers, scientists, and philosophers. Special programs and events offered throughout the exhibition include "Family Day," June 18; "Summer Talks," May 23, June 27, July 25, August 22; and children's workshops and school programs.

University of California Berkeley Art Museum & Pacific Film Archive

Affiliated Institution: University of California
2626 Bancroft Way, Berkeley, CA   94720-2250

510-642-0808   www.bampfa.berkeley.edu
Open: 11-5 We-Su, 11-9 Th   *Closed:* Leg/Hol!
Free Day: Th 11-9   *Adm:*   *Adult:* $6.00   *Children:* Free under 12   *Students:* $4.00, 12-18   *Seniors:* $4.00
& P: Parking next to the museum on Bancroft Way, on Bowditch between Bancroft and Durant, and at
Berkeley Public Parking, 2420 Durant Ave.   *Museum Shop   Group Tours   Sculpture Garden*
Permanent Collection: Am: all media 20; Visual Art; As; Ch: cer, ptgs; Eu: Ren-20

The UC Berkeley Art Museum is the principal visual arts center for the University of California at Berkeley. Since its founding in the 1960s with a bequest of 45 Hans Hoffman paintings, the BAM has become one of the largest university art museums in the US. International in scope, the Museum's 13,000 work collection emphasizes twentieth-century painting, sculpture, photography, and conceptual art, with especially significant holdings in Asian art. ℭ Contemporary collection including masterpieces by Calder, Cornell, Frankenthaler, Still, Rothko, and others

ON EXHIBIT 2002

early October 2001 to late January 2002   *The Lady in the Window: Figure Painting in the Quig Dynasty*
The ideal *mei ren* (beautiful woman), beggars, and street vendors all appear in this exploration of the ways Chinese painters presented the human figure. A small group of Song Dynasty (960–1368) will also be shown.

11/18/2001 to 01/13/2002   *Thomas Scheibitz/Matrix 195*
A first exhibition of the work of this East German painter in the U.S. The works appear to be familiar objects-flowers, landscape settings but a closer look reveals abstract arrangements of bright 70s style colors without patterns or grids.

12/12/2001 to 03/10/2002   *Ansel Adams in the University of California Collections*
A rich and unusual selection including inspirational scenes of the California wilderness to photographs of the UC Berkeley campus and images he produced while working as a commercial photographer

01/16/2002 to 03/24/2002   *Migrations: Photographs by Sebastiao Salgado*
Salgado recorded the plight of whole communities set adrift from their homelands along with what happens to them en route and where they end up.

01/27/2002 to 03/10/2002   *Sowon Kwon/Matrix 196*
Kwon works mostly in digital media to address the production of physical, gendered, and psychological spaces and the limits and restrictions of particular domestic spaces.

mid-February 2002 to mid-June 2002   *The Work of a Lifetime: Highlights from the Cahill Family Collections*
Sixty paintings spanning 800 years collected by University Professor Cahill who drew attention to Song dynasty painters of the Yuan (1279–1368), Ming (1368–1644), and early Qing (1644–1911) dynasties.   *Catalog   Will Travel*

02/06/2002 to 08/25/2002   *Micropainting: The Practice of Portrait Miniature in England and France*
With its roots in manuscript illumination techniques, portrait miniature painting declined with the rise of daguerrotype and photography in the mid-1800s.

03/20/2002 to 05/26/2002   *Marion Brenner: The Subtle Life of Plants and People*
Two recent series of work include nearly abstract black and white photographs that capture the life of a variety of plants as they stir and shift during a long single exposure. The new series uses the same technique for large-format portraits.

03/24/2002 to 05/12/2002   *Sanford Biggers/Matrix 197*
Biggers uses conventional African American references, 1970s process art, race politics, world religions, and hip-hop to explore and extend issues of urban culture, technology, ethnography, and Black history.

04/10/2002 to 07/14/2002   *Komar & Melamid's Asian Elephant Art and Conservation Project*
This exhibition presents paintings created by elephants formerly employed in the Thai logging industry. It questions the concepts of individual creativity, abstract expressionism, and the workings of the art market in general.

05/28/2002 to 07/14/2002   *Yehudit Sasportas/Matrix 198*
An installation artist whose work fuses drawing, painting, sculpture, and architecture

07/28/2002 to 09/15/2002   *Vince Fecteau/Matrix 199*
Fecteau uses simple materials like aluminum foil, cardboard, paperclips, and matboard to create miniaturized sculptures as microcosms for the large, formal architectural basis of contemporary society.

09/29/2002 to 11/17/2002   *T. J. Wilcox/Matrix 200*
Labor intensive films pieced together frame by frame from vintage and new film clips and animation. He then copies them to video, transfers them back again to 16mm and gets a grainy, low tech version.

10/23/2002 to 12/29/2002   *Beyond Preconceptions: The Sixties Experiment*
Twenty-one artists from 3 continents whose work reflects the dramatic social, political, and cultural change of the 60s

CLAREMONT

Pomona College Museum of Art: formerly Montgomery Gallery
Affiliated Institution: Pomona College
30 N. College Way, Claremont, CA   91711-6344

909-621-8283   www.pomona.edu/montgomery
Open: 12-5 Tu-Fr; 1-5 Sa & Su   *Closed:* Acad!, Leg/Hol!, Summer
&   P: Free, street   *Group Tours*
Permanent Collection: Kress Ren: ptgs; Gr; Drgs, Phot; Nat/Am: basketry, cer, beadwork

Important holdings include the Kress Collection of 15th- and 16th-century Italian panel paintings; over 5,000 examples of Pre-Columbian to 20th-century American Indian art and artifacts, including basketry, ceramics, and beadwork; and a large collection of American and European prints, drawings, and photographs.

ON EXHIBIT 2002

Fall 2001 to Spring 2002   *Art and Labor in the 1930s (working title)*

Fall 2001 to Spring 2002   *Dorothea Lange, Photographs (working title)*

Fall 2001 to Spring 2002   *Japanese Paintings from the Sanso Collection (working title)*

Fall 2001 to Spring 2002   *Post-Landscape: Between Nature and Culture (working title)*

Fall 2001 to Spring 2002   *Preparatory Drawings: Orozco's Prometheus (working title)*

Fall 2001 to Spring 2002   *Project Series 11: Edgar Arcenaux (working title)*

Fall 2001 to Spring 2002   *Project Series 12: Charles Labelle (working title)*

DAVIS

Richard L. Nelson Gallery & The Fine Arts Collection, UC Davis
Affiliated Institution: University of California
Davis, CA 95616

530-752-8500 http:a>t.ucdavis.edu/nelson/
Open: 12-5 Mo-Fr, 2-5 Su *Closed:* Sa, Leg/Hol! Acad/Hol; Summer!
Vol/Contr.: Yes
& P: On campus lots 1, 2, 5, 6 (Handicapped), & 10; $4.00 parking fee charged weekdays
Museum Shop Group Tours Sculpture Garden
Permanent Collection: Drgs, Gr, Ptgs 19; Cont; Or; Eu; Am; Cer

The gallery, which has a 2,500-piece permanent collection acquired primarily through gifts donated to the institution since the 1960s, presents an ongoing series of changing exhibitions. ⊄ "Bookhead" and other sculptures by Robert Arneson; Deborah Butterfield's "Untitled" (horse)

DOWNEY

Downey Museum of Art
10419 Rives Ave., Downey, CA 90241

562-861-0419
Open: 12-5 We-Sa *Closed:* Mo, Tu, Su, Leg/Hol!
Vol/Contr.: Yes
& P: Ample free off-street parking *Group Tours*
Permanent Collection: Reg: ptgs, sculp, gr, phot 20; Cont

With over 400 20th century and contemporary works by Southern California artists, the Downey Museum has been the primary source of changing exhibits of art in this region for over 43 years.

FRESNO

Fresno Art Museum
2233 N. First St., Fresno, CA 93703

559-441-4220 fresnoartmuseum.com
Open: 10-5 Tu-Fr; Noon-5 Sa, Su *Closed:* Leg/Hol!
Free Day: Tu *Adm:* Adult: $4.00 *Children:* Free 15 & under *Students:* $2.00 *Seniors:* $2.00
& P: Free *Museum Shop* ¶: ! Th only 12-2:00 *Group Tours:* 559-485-4810 *Sculpture Garden*
Permanent Collection: P/Col; Mex; Cont/Reg: Am: gr, sculp

In addition to a wide variety of changing exhibitions, pre-Columbian Mexican ceramic sculpture, French Post-impressionist graphics, and American sculptures from the permanent collection are always on view. ⊄ Hans Sumpfsumpf Gallery of Mexican Art containing pre-Columbian ceramics through Diego Rivera masterpieces.

Fresno Metropolitan Museum
1555 Van Ness Ave., Fresno, CA 93721

559-441-1444 www.fresnomet.org
Open: 11-5 Tu-Su, 11-8 Th *Closed:* Mo, Leg/Hol
Free Day: 5-8 Th *Adm:* Adult: $6.00 *Children:* Free 2 & under *Students:* $3.00 *Seniors:* $3.00
& P: Ample parking in free lot adjacent to the museum *Museum Shop*
¶: boxed lunches available during select exhibitions
Group Tours Drop-In Tours: 9-4 daily during most exhibitions *Historic Building*
Permanent Collection: Am: st/lf 17-20; Eu: st/lf 17-20; Eu: ptgs 16-19; Phot (Ansel Adams)

Located in the historic "Fresno Bee" building, the Fresno Metropolitan Museum is the largest cultural center in the central San Joaquin Valley. ⊄ Oscar & Maria Salzar collection of American & European still-life paintings 17th-early 20th century

ON EXHIBIT 2002

01/26/2002 to 05/12/2002   *A T-Rex Named Sue*
A massive 45-foot articulated skeletal cast of this T-Rex, along with video footage, freestanding interactive panels, colorful graphics, and touchable casts of dinosaur bones

05/25/2002 to 07/31/2002   *Masterworks from the Albertina*
Drawings including Rembrandt, Rubens, Michelangelo, Raphael, Tiepolo, Fragonard, and others

HANFORD

Ruth and Sherman Lee Institute for Japanese Art at the Clark Center
15770 Tenth Avenue, Hanford, CA   93230

559-582-4915   www.shermanleeinstitute.org
Open: Tu-Sa 1-5   *Closed:* Su, Mo; July, Aug, Mar 2, Leg/Hols!
Sugg/Contr.: Y
  P   *Group Tours   Drop-In Tours:* Sa 1   *Theater*
Permanent Collection: Buddhist ptg; sculp, Edo ptg, folding screens (byohu)

California Japanese art Institute named for Ruth and Sherman Lee. The announcement of The Ruth & Sherman Lee Institute for Japanese Art was made at a dinner in NY hosted by the center founders, Willars and Elizabeth Clark. 4 special exhibitions per year are planned.

IRVINE

Irvine Museum
18881 Von Karman Ave. 12th Floor, Irvine, CA   92612

949 476 2565   www.ocartenet.org/irvinemuseum
Open: 11-5 Tu-Sa   *Closed:* Su, Mo, Leg/Hol!
  P: Free parking with validation   *Group Tours:* 949-476-0294   *Drop-In Tours:* 11:15 Th   *Theater*
Permanent Collection: CA Impr Art 1890-1930

Opened in 1993, this museum places its emphasis on the past by promoting the preservation and display of historical California art with particular emphasis on the school of California Impressionism (1890–1930).

LA JOLLA

Museum of Contemporary Art, San Diego
700 Prospect St., La Jolla, CA   92037-4291

858-454-3541; DT619-234-1001   www.mcasandiego.org
Open: 11-5 Mo & Tu; 11-8 Th; Summer: 11-8 Mo, Tu, Th, & Fr; 11-5 Sa & Su   *Closed:* We, 1/1, Thgv, 12/25
Free Day: 1st Su & 3rd Tu of every month   *Adm: Adult:* $4.00   *Children:* Free under 12
Students: $2.00   *Seniors:* $2.00
  P: 2 hour free street parking at La Jolla; validated $2.00 2 hour parking at America Plaza garage for downtown location during the week plus some metered street parking and pay lots nearby.
Museum Shop   ¶: Museum Cafe (at La Jolla location) 858-454-3945
Group Tours: ex 151   *Drop-In Tours:* 2:00 Tu; 6-8 Th; 2-4 Sa & Su
Historic Building: Former Ellen Scripps Browning Home—Irving Gill Architecture   *Sculpture Garden*
Permanent Collection: Cont: ptgs, sculp, drgs, gr, phot

Perched on a bluff overlooking the Pacific Ocean, this 50-year-old museum recently underwent extensive renovation and expansion, the results of which New York Times architecture critic, Paul Goldberger, describes as an "exquisite project". Under the direction of noted architectural wizard, Robert Venturi, the original landmark Scripps house, built in 1916, was given added prominence by being cleverly integrated into the design of the new building. Additional exhibition space, landscaping that accommodates outdoor sculpture, a café, and an expanded bookstore are but a few of the Museum's new features. Both this and the downtown branch at 1001 Kettner Blvd. at Broadway in downtown San Diego (phone: 619-234-1001) operate as one museum with 2 locations where contemporary art (since the 1950s) by highly regarded national and international artists as well as works by emerging new talents may be seen. * 1. Self-guided "Inform" audio tours of the Museum's permanent collection are available to visitors free of charge. 2. Downtown admission fees: Free admission Downtown

ON EXHIBIT 2002

09/16/2001 to 01/13/2002   *Cross References: Works from the Permanent Collection by Stuart Collection Artists*
Fifteen site-specific commissioned works from this collection

09/16/2001 to 01/13/2002   *Lateral Thinking: Art of the 1990s*
The Museum's nontraditional approach to collection building is focused on here. It attempts to develop a new axis of the contemporary art world running north and south through North, Central, and South America.

10/06/2001 to 01/15/2002   *Alexis Smith and Amy Gerstler: The Sorcerers Apprentice*
A collaborative sculptural installation based on the fairy tale.

01/27/2002 to 04/21/2002   *Indivisible: Stories of American Community*

01/27/2002 to 05/19/2002   *Wolfgang Laib: A Retrospective*
Laib shows his deeply religious spiritual relationship with nature and commitment to eastern philosophies of purity and simplicity.

06/02/2002 to 09/08/2002   *Out of the Ordinary: The Architecture and Design of Robert Venturi, Denise Scott Brown and Associates*
These architects have changed the direction of "post-modernism" which was identified with their influence in ideas.   *Will Travel*

LAGUNA BEACH

Laguna Art Museum
307 Cliff Drive at Coast Highway, Laguna Beach, CA   92651-9990

949-494-8971   www.lagunaartmuseum.org
Open: 11-5 Tu, Th-Su   *Closed:* Mo, We, 12/25, 1/1
Free Day: 1st Th 5-9 pm   *Adm:*   *Adult:* $5.00   *Children:* Free under 12   *Students:* $4.00   *Seniors:* $4.00
   P: metered and non-metered street parking   *Museum Shop*
Group Tours: ext 218   *Drop-In Tours:* 2pm daily
Historic Building: oldest museum in Orange County, built 1918
Permanent Collection: Cont & Hist CA art

An independent nonprofit museum with an emphasis on American Art and particularly the art of California. Temporary exhibitions change quarterly.

ON EXHIBIT 2002

January 2002   *California Holiday: E. Gene Crain Collection*
This spectacular and focused collection of California art is the best in private hands. Eighty-five works will show the period from 1930–1990 and also includes work by later generations of watercolor painters.

07/29/2002 to 10/14/2002   *Surf Culture*
The history of the modern surfboard linking it to Pacific rim culture and technology.

mid-November 2002 to mid-January 2003   *In and Out of California: Travels of American Impressionists*
Many painters working in California also had successful careers in the mid-west, east coast and Europe. The work they produced makes an interesting comparison with those painted in California. Among those are Childe Hassam, Frieseke, and Miller.   *Catalog*

LANCASTER

Lancaster Museum/Art Gallery
44801 North Sierra Hwy., Lancaster, CA   93534

661-723-6250
Open: 11-4 Tu-Sa, 1-4 Su   *Closed:* Mo, Leg/Hol! & 1-2 weeks before opening of each new exhibit!
&: Wheelchair accessible   P: Ample and free   *Museum Shop   Group Tours*
Permanent Collection: Reg; Phot

About 75 miles north of Los Angeles, in the heart of America's Aerospace Valley, is the Lancaster Museum, a combined history and fine art facility that serves the needs of one of the fastest growing areas in southern California. The gallery offers eight to nine rotating exhibitions annually.

LONG BEACH

University Art Museum
Affiliated Institution: California State University, Long Beach
1250 Bellflower Blvd., Long Beach, CA   90840

562-985-5761   www.csulb.edu/~uam
Open: 12-8 Tu-Th, 12-5 Fr-Su: Call for Summer Hours   *Closed:* Mo, Acad/Hol!
Sugg/Contr.: Yes   *Adult:* $3.00   *Students:* $1.00
&: located in North Campus Center   P: Free   *Museum Shop*
¶: on campus   *Group Tours:* 562-985-7601   *Drop-In Tours:* res req   *Sculpture Garden*
Permanent Collection: Cont: drgs, gr; Sculp

Walking maps are available for finding and detailing the permanent site-specific Monumental Sculpture Collection located throughout the 322-acre campus of this outstanding university art facility.   ℂ Extensive collection of contemporary works on paper

LOS ANGELES

Autry Museum of Western Heritage
4700 Western Heritage Way, Los Angeles, CA   90027-1462

323-667-2000   www.autry-museum.org
Open: 10-5 Tu-Su and some Mo hols: Th until 8! Free Th 4-8pm   *Closed:* Mo, Thgv, 12/25
Free Day: 2nd Tu each month; Th 4-8   *Adm:*   *Adult:* $7.50   *Children:* $3.00 (2-12)   *Students:* $5.00
Seniors: $5.00
&   P: Free   *Museum Shop*   ¶: Golden Spur Cafe for breakfast & lunch (9am-4pm)   *Group Tours*
Permanent Collection: Fine & Folk Art

Fine art is but one aspect of this multi-dimensional museum that acts as a showcase for the preservation and understanding of both the real and mythical historical legacy of the American West.   ℂ The McCormick Tribune Family Foundation Family Discovery Children's Gallery; Spirit of Imagination

California African-American Museum
600 State Drive, Exposition Park, Los Angeles, CA   90037

213-744-7432   www.caam.ca.gov
Open: 10-5 Tu-Su   *Closed:* Mo, 1/1, Thgv, 12/25
&.: Restrooms, parking, ramps   P: Limited ($5.00 fee) next to museum   *Museum Shop   Group Tours*
Permanent Collection: Benjamin Bannister: drgs; Turenne des Pres: ptgs; Gafton Taylor Brown: gr; Af:
masks; Af/Am: cont; *The permanent collection is not on permanent display!

The primary goal of this museum is the collection and preservation of art and artifacts documenting the Afro-American experience in America. Exhibitions and programs focus on contributions made to the arts and various other facets of life including a vital forum for playwrights and filmmakers. The building itself features a 13,000 square foot sculpture court through which visitors pass into a spacious building topped by a ceiling of tinted bronze glass.

Gallery 825/Los Angeles Art Association
Affiliated Institution: Los Angeles Art Association
825 N. La Cienega Blvd., Los Angeles, CA   90069

310-652-8272   LAAA.org
Open: Noon-5 Tu-Sa   *Closed:* Su, Mo, Leg/Hol!
Sugg/Contr.: $5.00 for workshops and lectures
&.   P: rear of building   *Theater*

Gallery 825/Los Angeles Art Association is a nonprofit visual arts organization committed to supporting Southern California contemporary artists in furthering and achieving their diverse artistic visions. We provide exposure, education, and resources as well as foster public awareness through our unique and collaborative environment. Founded in 1925, Gallery 825/LAAA has launched many stellar careers of a wide variety of celebrated artists and played a central role in the formation of LA's now thriving art community.

Getty Center
1200 Getty Center Drive, Los Angeles, CA   90049-1681

310-440-7360   www.getty.edu
Open: 10-6 Tu-Th, Su; 10-9 Fr, Sa   *Closed:* Mo, Leg/Hol !
&.   P: Parking reservations required weekdays before 4pm. There is a $5.00 per car charge. For information call 310-440-7300.   *Museum Shop*   ¶   *Group Tours   Drop-In Tours:* On the hour   *Theater*
Permanent Collection: An/Grk; An/R; Eur: ptgs, drgs, sculp; Dec/Art; Am: phot 20; Eur: phot 20;
Illuminated Manuscripts

The Museum Complex, situated on one of the great public viewpoints in Los Angeles, consists of 6 buildings, designed by Richard Meier. These are joined by a series of gardens, terraces, fountains, and courtyards. An electric tram transports visitors from the parking area up the hill to the central plaza where a grand staircase welcomes their arrival. The collections span the history of art and will be amplified by special exhibitions.   ℭ "Irises" by Vincent Van Gogh, 1889; Pontormo's "Portrait of Cosimo I de Medici" c1537; "Bullfight Suerte de Varas" by Goya, 1824 (recently acquired)

ON EXHIBIT 2002

11/13/2001 to 02/03/2002   *Devices of Wonder: From the World in a Box to Images on a Screen*
Long before cyberspace, mirrors, microscopes, magic lanterns, automata, dioramas, panoramas, perspective theaters, and metamorphic toys expanded human perception. Included are the beautiful and bizarre works and works by contemporary artists including Samaras, Sherman, Wall, Holmes and Turrell

11/13/2001 to 02/17/2002   *Manuel Alvarez Bravo Optical Parables*
Alvarez Bravo's works from the 1930s combining Surrealist overtones and documentary reality

12/18/2001 to 03/10/2002   *Artful Reading in Medieval and Renaissance Europe*
Chartered here are the major technological changes in how the written word has been communicated over time.

12/21/2001 to 03/24/2002   *Exploding Landscape: Naples and Vesuvius on the Grand Tour*
Naples is explored as a tourist destination during the period when Sir William Hamilton served as the British Ambassador there.

01/08/2002 to 08/11/2002   *Rome on the Grand Tour*
The 18th-century grand tour was the way young British travelers learned taste, noble ideas, and moral value.

02/05/2002 to 05/12/2002   *Drawing Italy for the Grand Tour*
Visitors were guided through Venetian back streets by Canaletto and antique ports by Piranesi.

03/05/2002 to 06/23/2002   *Railroad Vision*
By the 1830s to the 1950s photography and railroads were interrelated.

03/26/2002 to 07/07/2002   *Images of Violence in the Middle Ages*
Seventeen illuminated manuscripts depicting violence as an aspect of life

04/16/2002 to 07/07/2002   *Framing the World (working title)*
Perspective as seen by Alberti, Dürer, Canaletto, Sergio, and Montagny is examined.

04/16/2002 to 07/07/2002   *The Sacred Spaces of Pieter Saenredam*
He spent his career immortalizing the churches of 17th century Holland.

05/28/2002 to 08/25/2002   *Dutch Drawings of the Golden Age (working title)*
The great age of Dutch drawing in the 1600s is shown.

07/09/2002 to 09/29/2002   *Gustave Le Gray (working title)*
A most important French photographer of the 19th century known for his imagination and technical innovations

07/23/2002 to 10/13/2002   *The Medieval Bestseller: Illuminated Books of Hours (working title)*

08/17/2002 to 09/29/2002   *Danube Exodus: The Rippling Currents of a River*
Multimedia interactive installation by Peter Forgacs including the exodus of Jewish refuges in 1939 and stories of displacement

09/10/2002 to 12/01/2002   *18th Century French Drawings (working title)*
The century which opened with the Rococo works of Watteau and closed with David's Neoclassical subjects

09/10/2002 to 12/01/2002   *Bill Viola: Works from the Passions Series (working title)*
This installation will use flat screen monitors, some looking like small altarpieces of the late Middle Ages and Renaissance.

09/10/2002 to 12/01/2002   *Greuze: The Draftsman*
Sixty works on paper from many institutions and 20 from St. Petersburg which have rarely left there. The exhibition will show viewers what a unique and thoroughly modern artist Greuze was.   *Catalog   Will Travel*

09/10/2002 to 12/01/2002   *Greuze: The Painter*
The paintings span his career and delve into his approach to painting.

Laband Art Gallery
Affiliated Institution: Loyola Marymount University
7900 Loyola Blvd., Los Angeles, CA   90045

310-338-2880   www.lmu.edu/colleges/cfa/art/laband
Open: 11-4 We-Fr, Noon-4 Sa   *Closed:* Su, Mo, Tu, Jun-Aug; Leg/Hol, Acad/Hol, Religious/Hol
Vol/Contr.   &   ¶: The Lair (cafeteria), Lion's Den (coffee bar)   *Group Tours*
Permanent Collection: Fl: om; It: om; Drgs; Gr

The Laband Art Gallery usually features exhibitions relating to Latin and Native American subjects, current social and political issues, Jewish and Christian spiritual traditions, and contemporary representational art.

Los Angeles County Museum of Art
5905 Wilshire Blvd., Los Angeles, CA   90036

323-857-6000   www.lacma.org
Open: 12-8 Mo, Tu, Th; 12-9 Fr; 11-8 Sa, Su   *Closed:* We, 1/1, Thgv, 12/25
Free Day: 2nd Tu each month   *Adm:*   *Adult:* $7.00   *Children:* $1.00 6-17, Free under 5
Students: $5.00   *Seniors:* $5.00
& P: Paid parking available in lot at Spaulding and Wilshire directly across the street from the entrance
to the museum (Free after 6pm).   *Museum Shop*
¶: Plaza Café and Pentimento   *Group Tours:* 323-932-5831   *Drop-In Tours:* Frequent & varied !
Sculpture Garden
Permanent Collection: An/Egt: sculp, ant; An/Grk: sculp, ant; An/R: sculp, ant; Ch; ptgs, sculp, cer; Jap:
ptgs, sculp, cer; Am/Art; Eu/Art; Dec/Art

The diversity and excellence of the collections of the Los Angeles Museum offer the visitor to this institution centuries of art to enjoy from ancient Roman or pre-Columbian art to modern paintings, sculpture, and photography. Recently the Museum completed the first phase of the reorganization and reinstallation of major portions of its renowned American, Islamic, South & Southeast Asian and Far Eastern galleries, allowing for the display of many works previously relegated to storage. Always striving to become more user accessible, the Museum's hours of operation have been changed to create a better "business-and-family-friendly" schedule. ℂ George de La Tour's "Magdelene with the Smoking Flame," 1636-1638; "Under the Trees" by Cézanne.

ON EXHIBIT 2002

09/23/2001 to 01/06/2002   *Jasper Johns to Jeff Koons: Four Decades of Art from the Broad Collection*
The Los Angeles based collection includes pieces by the most prominent artists of the 20th century including Warhol, Twombly, Ruscha, and Lichtenstein   *Catalog   Will Travel*

09/27/2001 to 01/13/2002   *Contemporary Projects 6: Los Carpinteros Transportable City*
Ten tents creating a moveable group of architectural forms. Particularly important for artists working in Havana

11/04/2001 to 01/20/2002   *Luca Giordano*
A prolific painter of the baroque era

11/18/2001 to 09/08/2002   *Seeing*
A 2nd project of the Boone Children's Gallery, a research and development unit at the Museum. Nine artists are asked to create participatory environments that address ways of seeing.

12/13/2001 to 04/07/2002   *The Kindness of Friends: Notable Gifts of Drawings and Prints, 1920–2001*
Works by Homer, Redon, Archipenko, Leger, and Marcoussis

02/14/2002 to 07/07/2002   *Spanish Pieta: A Masterpiece of the Eighteenth Century*
A spectacularly painted and gilded almost life-size Pieta

03/10/2002 to 06/02/2002   *Central European Avant-Gardes: Exchange and Transformation, 1910–1930*
Comparative analysis of avant-garde from Czech Republic, Germany, Hungary, Poland, Romania, and former Yugoslavia

04/04/2002 to 06/30/2002   *Munakata Shiko (1903–1975)*
One of the greatest Japanese artists of the 20th century painting in oils and traditional Japanese pigments

06/30/2002 to 09/22/2002   *Bartolome Esteban Murillo (1617–1682) Paintings from American Collections*
Described as the greatest religious painter of the late 17th century

07/21/2002 to 10/06/2002   *William Kentridge*
Animated films, drawings, and theater productions focusing on the violent history of his native South Africa   *Will Travel*

09/12/2002 to 12/15/2002   *Donald Blumberg*
The manner in which photographs function as social documents, formal remnants, and statements

11/10/2002 to 02/02/2003   *Noh and Kyogen Theater in Japan*
Carved wood masks, woven silk and gold costumes, painted fans, and lacquered instruments used in Noh, Japan's oldest continuing professional theater

Los Angeles Municipal Art Gallery
Affiliated Institution: Barnsdall Art Park
4800 Hollywood Blvd., Los Angeles, CA   90027

213-485-4581   www.lacity.org/cad
Open: 12:30-5 We-Su, till 8:30 Fr   *Closed:* Mo, Tu, 1/1, 12/25
Adm: *Adult:* $1.50
&: handicapped parking   P: Free, in Park   *Museum Shop*
Drop-In Tours: house only $2.00 adult:1.00 Sr; We-S 12, 1, 2, 3
Historic Building: 1921 Frank Lloyd Wright Hollyhock House closed to 2004 for renovation*
Permanent Collection: Cont: S/Ca art

The Los Angeles Municipal Art Gallery in the Barnsdall Art Park is but one of several separate but related arts facilities. Gallery and park are closed till mid-2002!

Museum of African American Art
4005 Crenshaw Blvd., 3rd Floor, Los Angeles, CA   90008

213-294-7071
Open: 11-6 Th-Sa, Noon-5 Su   *Closed:* Mo-We, 1/1, Easter, Thgv, 12/25
&: Elevator to third floor gallery location   P: Free   *Museum Shop   Group Tours   Theater*
Permanent Collection: Af: sculp, ptgs, gr, cer; Cont/Am: sculp, ptgs, gr; Harlem Ren Art

Located on the third floor of the Robinsons May Department Store, this museum's permanent collection is enriched by the "John Henry Series" and other works by Palmer Hayden. Due to the constraints of space these works and others are not always on view. The museum requests that you call ahead for exhibition information.   ℂ "John Henry Series" and other works by Palmer Hayden

Museum of Contemporary Art, Los Angeles
250 S. Grand Ave., Los Angeles, CA   90012

213-626-6222   www.MOCA-LA.org
Open: 11-5 Tu, We, Fr-Su; 11-8 Th   *Closed:* Mo, 1/1, Thgv, 12/25
Adm: *Adult:* $6.00   *Children:* Free under 12   *Students:* $4.00   *Seniors:* $4.00
&: wheelchairs available   P: For California Plaza Parking Garage (enter from Lower Grand Ave): weekday parking fee of $2.75 every 20 minutes charged before 5pm & $4.40 flat rate after 5pm weekdays and weekends; for The Music Center Garage (enter Grand Ave. between Temple & 1st.)
Museum Shop   ¶: Cafe 8:30-4 Tu-Fr; 11-4:30 Sa, Su
Group Tours: 213-621-1751   *Drop-In Tours:* 12, 1 & 2 daily; 6:00 Th
Historic Building: First American building commission by Arata Isozaki   *Theater*
Permanent Collection: Cont: all media

The Museum of Contemporary Art (MOCA) is the only institution in Los Angeles devoted exclusively to art created from 1940 to the present by modern-day artists of international reputation. The museum is located in two unique spaces: MOCA at California Plaza, the first building designed by Arata Isozaki; and The Geffen Contemporary at MOCA (152 North Central Ave., Los Angeles, CA 90013) a former warehouse redesigned into museum space by architect Frank Gehry.

UCLA Hammer Museum

10899 Wilshire Blvd., Los Angeles, CA   90024-4201

310-443-7000   hammer.ucla.edu
Open: 11-7 Tu, We, Fr, Sa; 11-9 Th; 11-5 Su   *Closed:* Mo, 1/1, 7/4, Thgv, 12/25
Free Day: Th   *Adm:*   *Adult:* $4.50   *Children:* Free under 17   *Students:* free w/ ID   *Seniors:* $3.00
&   P: Museum underground paid visitor parking available at $2.75 for the first three hours with a
museum stamp, $1.50 for each additional 20 minutes, and a flat $3.00 rate after 6:30 Th. Parking for the
disabled is available, on levels P1 & P3.   *Museum Shop*
Group Tours: 310-443-7041   *Drop-In Tours:* Call to arrange   *Sculpture Garden*
Permanent Collection: Eur: 15-19

With the largest collection of works by Honore Daumier in the country (more than 10,000)
plus important collections of Impressionist and Post-Impressionist art, the UCLA Hammer
Museum is considered a major U.S. cultural resource. Opened in 1990, the museum is now part
of UCLA. It houses the collections of the Wight Art Gallery and the Grunwald Center for the
Graphic Arts (one of the finest university collections of graphic arts in the country with 35,000
works dating from the Renaissance to the present).   ❰ Five centuries of Masterworks: over 100
works by Rembrandt, van Gogh, Cassatt, Monet, and others; The UCLA Franklin D. Murphy
Sculpture Garden, one of the most distinguished outdoor sculpture collections in the country
featuring 70 works by Arp, Calder, Hepworth, Lachaise, Lipchitz, Matisse, Moore, Noguchi,
Rodin and others.

USC Fisher Gallery

Affiliated Institution: University of Southern California
823 Exposition Blvd., Los Angeles, CA   90089-0292

213-740-4561   www.usc.edu/FisherGallery
Open: 12-5 Tu-Sa (closed during summer)   *Closed:* Mo, Leg/Hol! Summer
&   P: Visitor parking on campus for $6.00 per vehicle and metered parking on street
¶: on USC campus   *Group Tours:* 213-740-5537
Permanent Collection: Eur: ptgs, gr, drgs; Am: ptgs, gr, drgs; Ptgs 15-20, Armand Hammer Coll; Elizabeth
Holmes Fisher Coll

Old master paintings from the Dutch and Flemish schools, as well as significant holdings
of 19th-century British and French art are two of the strengths of USC Fisher Gallery.
*The permanent collection is available to museums, scholars, students, and the public by
appointment.

Watts Towers Arts Center

1727 E. 107th St., Los Angeles, CA   90002

213-847-4646
Open: Art Center: 10-4 Tu-Sa, Noon-4 Su   *Closed:* Mo, Leg/Hol!
&   P: Visitors parking lot outside of Arts center   *Museum Shop*
Permanent Collection: Af; Cont; Watts Tower

Fantastic lacy towers spiking into the air are the result of a 33 year effort by the late Italian
immigrant visionary sculptor Simon Rodia. His imaginative use of the "found object" resulted
in the creation of one of the most unusual artistic structures in the world. *Due to earthquake
damage, the towers, though viewable, are enclosed in scaffolding for repairs that are scheduled
to be completed by the April 2001.   ❰ Watts Towers "Day of the Drum Festival" and Jazz
Festival (last weekend in Sept.)

Frederick R. Weisman Museum of Art

Affiliated Institution: Pepperdine Center for the Arts, Pepperdine University
24255 Pacific Coast Highway, Malibu, CA   90263

310-456-4851   www.pepperdine.edu
Open: 11-5 Tu-Su   *Closed:* Mo, Leg/Hol!, 12/25-1/1
& P: Free   *Group Tours:* 310-317-7257   *Drop-In Tours:* call for specifics!   *Sculpture Garden*
Permanent Collection: Ptgs, Sculp, Gr, Drgs, Phot 20

Opened in 1992, this museum's permanent collection and exhibitions focus primarily on 19th-
& 20th-century art.   ℭ Selections from the Frederick R. Weisman Art Foundation

Monterey Museum of Art

559 Pacific St. Location 2 -720 Via Mirada, Monterey, CA   93940

831-372-5477 Loc. 2 831-372-3689   www.montereyart.org
Open: 11-5 We-Sa, 1-4 Su, till 8pm 3rd Th of the month   *Closed:* Mo, Tu, Leg/Hol
Free Day: 1st Su of month   *Adm:* Adult: $3.00   *Children:* Free under 12
& P: Street parking and paid lots nearby to main museum   *Museum Shop*
Drop-In Tours: 2 Su; 1 Sa & Su for La Mirada   *Historic Building*
Permanent Collection: Reg/Art; As; Pacific Rim; Folk; Eth; Gr; Phot

With a focus on its ever growing collection of California regional art, the Monterey Museum
has added a modern addition to its original building, La Mirada, the adobe portion of which
dates back to the late 1700s when California was still under Mexican rule. *The admission fee
for La Mirada, located at 720 Via Mirada, is $3.00.   ℭ Painting and etching collection of works
by Armin Hansen

Hearst Art Gallery

Affiliated Institution: St. Mary's College
Box 5110, Moraga, CA   94575

925-631-4379   http://galleryt.stmarys-ca.edu
Open: 11-4:30 We-Su   *Closed:* Mo, Tu, Leg/Hol!
Vol/Contr.: Yes   *Sugg/Contr.:* $2.00
& P: Free   *Museum Shop*   ¶: Café   *Group Tours:* 925-631-4069
Permanent Collection: Am: CA Ldscp ptgs 19-20; It: Med/sculp; Eur: gr; An/Cer; Christian Religious Art
15-20

Contra Costa County, not far from the Bay Area of San Francisco, is home to the Hearst Art
Gallery, located on the grounds of St. Mary's College, one of its most outstanding collections
consists of many cultures and centuries. *The museum is closed between exhibitions.   ℭ 150
paintings by William Keith (1838–1911), noted California landscape painter

Orange County Museum of Art, Newport Beach

850 San Clemente Dr., Newport Beach, CA   92660

949-759-1122   www.ocma.net
Open: 11-5 Tu-Su   *Closed:* Mo, 1/1, Thgv, 12/25, 7/4, Easter
Free Day: Tu   *Adm:*   Adult: $5.00   *Children:* Free under 16   *Students:* $4.00   *Seniors:* $4.00
& P: Free   *Museum Shop*   ¶: 11:00-3:00 Tu-Fr
Group Tours: 949-759-1122, ext 204   *Drop-In Tours:* 1:00 Tu-Su   *Sculpture Garden*
Permanent Collection: Reg: Post War Ca. art

With an emphasis on historical and contemporary art, the Orange County Museum of Art, with its late 19th and 20th century collection of California art, is dedicated to the enrichment of cultural life of the Southern California community through providing a comprehensive visual arts program that includes a nonstop array of changing exhibitions and stimulating education programs. Additional exhibitions are on view at the Museum's South Coast Plaza Gallery, 3333 Bristol Street in Costa Mesa (open free of charge, 10-9 Mo-Fr, 10-7 Sa & 11-6:30 Su)

OAKLAND

Oakland Museum of California
Oak & 10th Street, Oakland, CA   94607-4892

510-238-2200 or 888-625-6873   www.museumca.org.
Open: 10-5 We-Sa; 12-5 Su; 10-9 first Fr of each month   *Closed:* Mo, Tu, 1/1, 7/4, Thgv, 12/25
Free Day: 2nd Su   *Adm:*   *Adult:* $6.00   *Children:* Free 5 & under   *Students:* $4.00, 6-17
Seniors: $4.00 over 65
& P: Entrance on Oak & 12th St. small fee charged   *Museum Shop* ‖
Group Tours: 510-238-3514   *Drop-In Tours:* weekday afternoons on request; 12:30 weekends
Historic Building: Arch by Kevin Roche   *Sculpture Garden*
Permanent Collection: Reg/Art; Ptgs; Sculp; Gr; Dec/Art

The art gallery of the multi-purpose Oakland Museum of California features works by important regional artists that document the visual history and heritage of the state. Of special note is the Kevin Roche–John Dinkaloo designed building itself, a prime example of progressive museum architecture complete with terraced gardens. ☾ California art; Newly installed "On-line Museum" database for access to extensive information on the Museum's art, history, and science collections (open for public use 1:00-4:30 T).

ON EXHIBIT 2002

10/31/2001 to 01/13/2002   *Wrapped in Pride: Ghanian Kente and African American Identity*
Exhibition of Asante strip-woven cloth, or kente, the most popular and best known of all African textiles, linked to royalty in Africa and to black racial pride in the U.S. Focuses on the history and use of kente in Africa as well as contemporary kente and its manifestations.   *Catalog Will Travel*

11/03/2001 to 01/13/2002   *Grand Lyricist: The Art of Elmer Bischoff*
The most comprehensive retrospective to date of the work of Elmer Bischoff, who played an important role with Richard Diebenkorn and David Park in launching the Bay Area Figurative movement. The exhibition of 50 paintings and 20 works on paper traces the evolution of Bischoff's career, from his early abstract-surrealist efforts to the non-objective acrylics of the 1980s, with special emphasis on the distinctive figurative paintings that brought him acclaim.

11/17/2001 to 04/14/2002   *Native Grandeur: Preserving California's Vanishing Landscapes*
Fifty superb 19th- and 20th-century landscapes including Wendt, Redmond, Dixon, Hill, Grimm, and Rose. A narrative surveys the conservation movement and the challenges which still face it.

02/23/2002 to 05/12/2002   *Oakland Artists*
Paintings, sculpture, photography, and crafts by 45 contemporary artists from Oakland

06/15/2002 to 09/22/2002   *Joseph Raphael: American Impressionist at Home and Abroad*
Included are his dark and dramatic works done in France and the Netherlands, gardens and fields of Belgium, and views of Yosemite.

06/29/2002 to 09/22/2002   *Ansel Adams: Impact and Influence*
A works mostly from the collection of the Museum showing the photographers who influenced him, his colleagues, and students.

10/12/2002 to 11/24/2002   *Dias de los Muertos: Days of the Dead (working title)*
Altars created by artists, community groups, and students

11/02/2002 to 01/26/2003   *Arte Latino: Treasures from the Smithsonian American Art Museum*
Two hundred years of Latino art from across the U.S. Most of the work is contemporary (from 1950) with earlier work from colonial eras included to provide context.   *Catalog   Will Travel*

OXNARD

Carnegie Art Museum
424 S. C St., Oxnard, CA   93030

805-385-8157   www.vcnet.com/carnart
Open: 10-5 Th-Sa, 1-5 Su (Museum closed between exhibits)   *Closed:* Mo-We, Mem/Day, Lab/Day, Thgv, 12/25
Sugg/Contr.: Yes   *Adm:*   *Adult:* $4.00   *Children:* Free under 6   *Students:* $2.00   *Seniors:* $2.00
P: Free parking in the lot next to the museum   *Group Tours:* 805-385-8171   *Historic Building*
Permanent Collection: Cont/Reg; Eastwood Coll

Originally built in 1906 in the neo-classic style, the Carnegie, located on the coast just south of Ventura, served as a library until 1980. Listed NRHP ℂ Collection of art focusing on California painters from the 1920s to the present.

PALM SPRINGS

Palm Springs Desert Museum
101 Museum Drive, Palm Springs, CA   92262

760-325-7186   www.psmuseum.org
Open: 10-5 Tu-Sa, 12-5 Su   *Closed:* Mo, Leg/Hol!
Free Day: 1st Fr of each month, and some special events   *Adm:*   *Adult:* $7.50   *Children:* Free 5 & under
Students: $3.50   *Seniors:* $6.50
&: North entrance outdoor elevator   *P:* Free parking in the north and south Museum lots, both with handicap parking; Free parking in the shopping center lot across the street from the museum.
Museum Shop   ¶: Toor Gallery Café open Tu-Sa 10-5, Su 12-5, closed until Sept. 5, 2000
Group Tours   Drop-In Tours: 2 Tu-Su (Nov-May)
Historic Building: Architectural landmark   *Sculpture Garden   Theater*
Permanent Collection: Cont/Reg

Contemporary American art with special emphasis on the art of California and other Western states is the main focus of the 4,000 piece fine art and 2000 object Native American collection of the Palm Springs Desert Museum. The museum, housed in a splendid modern structure made of materials that blend harmoniously with the surrounding landscape, recently added 25,000 square feet of gallery space with the opening of the Steve Chase Art Wing and Education Center.   ℂ William Holden and George Montgomery Collections and Leo S. Singer Miniature Room Collection

ON EXHIBIT 2002

08/26/2001 to 03/03/2002   *Stars at Play: Photography by Bill Anderson*
A view of Palm Springs as it was in the 50s and 60s with all the major stars

09/01/2001 to 02/28/2002   *After the Dinosaurs*
Robotic animals that move, roar, breathe, and blink

Palo Alto Art Center
1313 Newell Rd., Palo Alto, CA   94303

650-329-2366   www.city.palo-alto.ca.us/artcenter
Open: 10-5 Tu-Sa, 7-9 Th, 1-5 Su   *Closed:* Mo, 1/1, 7/4, 12/25
Sugg/Contr.: $1.00 per person
&   P   *Museum Shop   Group Tours:* 650-329-2370   *Drop-In Tours:* call for information   *Sculpture Garden*
Permanent Collection: Cont/Art; Hist/Art

Located in a building that served as the town hall from the 1950s to 1971, this active community art center's mission is to present the best contemporary fine art, craft, design, special exhibitions, and new art forms.

Norton Simon Museum
411 W. Colorado Blvd., Pasadena, CA   91105

626-449-6840   www.nortonsimon.org
Open: 12-6 Mo, We, Th, Sa, Su; 12-9 Fr   *Closed:* Tu, 1/1 Thgv, 12/25
Adm: Adult: $6.00   *Children:* Free under 18   *Students:* Free   *Seniors:* $3.00
&   P: Free   *Museum Shop*   ¶: Garden Café   *Group Tours:* ex 245   *Sculpture Garden*
Permanent Collection: Eu: ptgs 15-20; sculp 19-20; Ind: sculp; Or: sculp; Eu/Art 20; Am/Art 20

Thirty-eight galleries with 1,000 works from the permanent collection that are always on display plus a beautiful sculpture garden make the internationally known Norton Simon Museum home to one of the most remarkable and renowned collections of art in the world. The seven centuries of European art on view from the collection contain remarkable examples of work by Old Master, Impressionist, and important modern 20th-century artists.   (Impr & Post/Impr Collection including a unique set of 71 original master bronzes by Degas

ON EXHIBIT 2002

11/16/2001 to 02/11/2002   *Lewis Baltz Tract House Photographs, 1969–1971*
Known for his detached views of natural and urban landscapes, this early series describes the details of a housing site under construction.

11/16/2001 to 02/11/2002   *Pop Culture!*
One of the most significant artistic movements of the 20th century, Pop Art challenged the standards with depictions of common objects. Drawn from the museum's permanent collection, included are Warhol, Oldenburg, Lichtenstein, Ruscha, and Thiebaud.

12/14/2001 to 04/08/2002   *Richard Diebenkorn*
Fourteen rarely seen gouache drawings are shown with oils from his famed "Berkeley" series

03/08/2002 to 07/08/2002   *Art in Ferment: Russian Paintings, Sculpture, and Works on Paper, 1890–1940*
In the midst of great social conflict and breakdown of traditional views, Russia produced brilliant talents. Works by Archipenko, Gotcharova, Jawlensky, Kandinsky, and Lissitzky are included.

Pacific Asia Museum
46 N. Los Robles Ave., Pasadena, CA   91101

626-449-2742   www.westmuse.org/Pacasiamuseum
Open: 10-5 We-Su; 10-8 Th   *Closed:* Mo, Tu, 1/1, Mem/Day, 7/4, Thgv, 12/25, 12/31
Free Day: 3rd Sa of each month   *Adm: Adult:* $5.00   *Children:* Free under 12   *Students:* $3.00
Seniors: $3.00
&   P: Free parking   *Museum Shop   Group Tours:* 626-449-2742   *Drop-In Tours   Historic Building:*
California State Historical Landmark, National Register of Historic Places   *Sculpture Garden*
Permanent Collection: As: cer, sculp; Ch: cer, sculp; Or/Folk; Or/Eth; Or/Phot

The Pacific Asia Museum, which celebrated its 25th anniversary in '96, is the only institution in Southern California devoted exclusively to the arts of Asia. The collection, housed in the gorgeous Chinese Imperial Palace style Nicholson Treasure House built in 1925, features one of only two authentic Chinese style courtyard gardens in the U.S. open to the public. ℂ Chinese courtyard garden, Carved Jade, Ceramics, Japanese paintings

RIVERSIDE

Riverside Art Museum
3425 Mission Inn Ave., Riverside, CA 92501

909-684-7111
Open: 10-4 Mo-Sa *Closed:* Su, Last 2 Weeks Aug; Leg/Hol!
Sugg/Contr.: Yes *Adm:* *Adult:* $2.00
♿: Access to lower floors only P: Limited free parking at museum; metered street parking
Museum Shop 🍴: Open weekdays *Group Tours* *Drop-In Tours:* daily upon request
Historic Building: 1929 building designed by Julia Morgan, architect of Hearst Castle
Permanent Collection: Ptgs, Sculp, Gr

Julia Morgan, the architect of the Hearst Castle, also designed this handsome and completely updated museum building. Listed on the NRHP, the museum is located in the Los Angeles and Palm Springs area. Aside from its professionally curated exhibitions, the museum displays the work of area students during the month of May.

UCR/California Museum of Photography
Affiliated Institution: University of California, Riverside
3824 Main St., Riverside, CA 92521

909-784-FOTO www.cmp.ucr.edu
Open: 11-5 Tu-Su *Closed:* Mo, 1/1, Thgv, 12/25
♿ P: Street parking and several commercial lots and garages nearby. *Museum Shop*
Group Tours: 909-787-4787 *Drop-In Tours* *Historic Building:* former Kress Dimestore, Art Deco
Permanent Collection: Phot 19-20; Camera Collection

Converted from a 1930s Kress dimestore into an award winning contemporary space, this is one of the finest photographic museums in the country. In addition to a vast number of photographic prints the museum features a 10,000 piece collection of photographic apparatus, an internet gallery, a community media lab, and digital studio. ℂ Junior League of Riverside Family Interactive Gallery; Internet Gallery, Permanent Collections room.

ON EXHIBIT 2002

10/19/2001 to 01/06/2002 ***The Legacy of the Panthers: A Photographic Exhibition***
Photographs conveying the substance and spirit of this historic group of young, urban, black people engaged in the country's civil rights struggle

11/10/2001 to 02/03/2002 ***Andy Warhol: Queering the City***
Following Warhol in his photographic promenades through the urban landscapes of New York

11/10/2001 to 02/03/2002 ***Beyond Decorum: The Photography of Ike Ude***
Nigerian born Ike Ude questions the production and circulation of images of race and gender as spectacles in popular visual culture.

02/23/2002 to 05/19/2002 ***Mel Edelman Photographs***
Edelman will build three small houses in an interactive gallery installation. The audience will discover the narrative and history of the house's fictional inhabitant.

06/08/2002 to 10/13/2002   *Natalie Jeremijenko*
A design engineer and technoartist whose installations use digital technologies to explore sensory perceptions within specific environments

10/26/2002 to 02/02/2003   *Warren Neidich*
Neidich links the discovery of photography to the birth of neurophysiology to explore constructions of culture. In his installation "The Cultured Brain" audience members will navigate a CD-ROM of images at their own pace.

SACRAMENTO

Crocker Art Museum
216 O St., Sacramento, CA   95814

916-264-5423   www.crockerartmuseum.org
Open: 10-5 Tu-Su, till 9 Th   *Closed:* Mo, 12/25, Thgv, 1/1
Adm: Adult: $6.00   Children: $3.00 7-17, Free under 6   *Students:* $3.00 with valid ID   *Seniors:* $4.00
&   P: On-site metered parking & city parking lots   *Museum Shop*
Group Tours: 916-264-5537   *Drop-In Tours:* Tu-Fr 10-2; Th 5-7; 12-4 Sa, 12-3 Su, on the hour
Historic Building: Over 120 years old
Permanent Collection: Ptgs: Ren-20; Om/Drgs 15-20; Cont; Or; Sculp

This inviting Victorian Italianate mansion, the oldest public art museum in the West, was built in the 1870s by Judge E. B. Crocker. It is filled with his collection of more than 700 European and American paintings displayed throughout the ballroom and other areas of the original building. Contemporary works by Northern California artists are on view in the light-filled, modern wing whose innovative facade is a re-creation of the Crocker home. Of special interest are two paintings, created by Charles Christian Nahl, that were commissioned for the spaces they still occupy. Both "Fandango" and "Sunday Morning in the Mines" are in their original frames (designed by I. Magnin of department store fame) and are so elaborate that one actually includes a high relief depiction of a pan of gold dust.   ℂ Early California painting collection

SAN DIEGO

Mingei International Museum
1439 El Prado Balboa Park - Plaza de Panama, San Diego, CA   92122

619-239-0003   www.mingei.org
Open: 10-4 Tu-Su   *Closed:* Mo, Leg/Hol!
Free Day: 3rd Tu of each month   *Adm:* Adult: $5.00   Children: $2.00 (6-17)   *Students:* $2.00
Seniors: $5.00
&   P: Parking a short distance from the museum in the Balboa Park lots   *Museum Shop*
Group Tours   Drop-In Tours: by appt
Permanent Collection: Folk: Jap, India, Af, & over 100 other countries; Pal Cost; Pre/Col

Six galleries of dynamic changing exhibitions dedicated to furthering the understanding of world folk art, traditional and contemporary. The museum shows the innate creative potential of all people.

ON EXHIBIT 2002

10/2001 to 05/2002   *I Hear America Singing*

2002   *Africa: Featuring the Permanent Collection of Mingei International*

2002   *China: The Permanent Collection of Mingei International, The Phila McDaniel Collection*

Winter 2002   *George Nakashima, Woodworker*   Will Travel

07/22/2001 to 01/06/2002   *Venine: Glass and Design in a World Perspective*

2002 to 01/01/2002   *Pre-Columbian Marine Animals; Mingei International Greaves Collection*

Museum of Photographic Arts
1649 El Prado, Balboa Park, San Diego, CA   92101

619-238-7559   www.mopa.org
Open: 10-5 Daily   *Closed:* Leg/Hol!
Free Day: 2nd Tu of every month   *Adm:*   *Adult:* $6.00   *Children:* Free under 12   *Students:* $4.00
Seniors: $4.00
  ♿   P: Free in Balboa Park   *Museum Shop*   *Group Tours:* ext. 301   *Drop-In Tours:* 1:00 Su
Historic Building   Theater
Permanent Collection: Phot

The Museum of Photographic Arts, dedicated exclusively to the care and collection of photographic works of art and film, is housed in Casa de Balboa, a structure built in 1915 for the Panama-California Exposition located in the heart of beautiful Balboa Park (designated as the number one urban park in America). The museum's major areas of strength are in modern and contemporary work, specifically in social documentary photography and photojournalism. ❮Film series in the state-of-the-art Joan Irwin Jacobs Theater. Call 619-238-7559 and press 3 for schedule.

ON EXHIBIT 2002

10/07/2001 to 01/06/2002   *Photography in Context (working title)*
The third in "The Visual Classroom Exhibition Series" examines images including 19th-century daguerrotypes, stereocards, and the work of Adams, Newman, Moore, and ParkeHarrison. It explores the significance of photographs within the larger context of history, science, and culture.

10/28/2001 to 01/06/2002   *Bill Brandt A Retrospective*
Assembled from vintage prints from the 40s thru 60s. Included is "Perspective of Nudes" series demonstrating the relationship of photography to sculpture and modernist abstraction.

01/13/2002 to 03/17/2002   *Double Vision: The Strauss Collection*
Offering a diverse group of photographers, traditional themes of portraiture and landscape by Man Ray and August Sandor are seen side by side with radical postmodernism of Cindy Sherman and Hans Bellmer.

San Diego Museum of Art
1450 El Prado, Balboa Park, San Diego, CA   92101

619-232-7931   www.sdmart.com
Open: 10-4:30 Tu-Su   *Closed:* Mo, 1/1, Thgv, 12/25
Free Day: 3rd Tu in month   *Adm:*   *Adult:* $8.00; military (w/ I.D.) $6   *Children:* $3.00 (6-17)
Students: $6.00   *Seniors:* $6.00
  ♿   P: Parking is available in Balboa Park and in the lot in front of the museum.   *Museum Shop*
❙❙: Sculpture Garden Cafe 10-3 Tu-Fr; 9-4:30 Sa, Su (619-696-1990)   *Drop-In Tours:* Many times daily
Historic Building: Built in 1926, the facade is similar to one at Univ. of Salamanca   *Sculpture Garden*
Permanent Collection: It/Ren; Sp/Om; Du; Am: 20 Eu; ptgs, sculp 19; As; An/Egt; P/Col

Whether strolling through the treasures in the sculpture garden or viewing the masterpieces inside the Spanish Colonial style museum building, a visit to this institution, located in San Diego's beautiful Balboa Park, is a richly rewarding and worthwhile experience. The museum also features the Image Gallery, interactive multimedia access to the permanent collection. ❮ Frederick R. Weisman Gallery of California art; world-renowned collection of South Asian paintings

ON EXHIBIT 2002

11/10/2001 to 01/13/2002   *The Frame in America: 1860–1960*
The tools, materials and methods used in gilding and frame manufacturing. Included are Whistler's reed frames, Renaissance frames by Stanford White, and painted frames by American Modernists John Marin and Lee Gatch.

2002   *High Societies: Psychedelic Rock Posters of Haight-Ashbury*
An examination of American culture and consciousness   *Catalog   Will Travel*

2002   *Jose Clemente Orozco in the United States 1927–1934*
A crucial period in Orozco's work in the period of the American depression   *Catalog   Will Travel*

Timken Museum of Art
1500 El Prado, Balboa Park, San Diego, CA   92101

619-239-5548   www.timkenmuseum.org
Open: 10-4:30 Tu-Sa, 1:30-4:30 Su   *Closed:* Mo, Leg/Hol!; Month of Sept
Vol/Contr.: Yes
& P   *Group Tours   Drop-In Tours:* 10-12 Tu-Th, and as arranged
Permanent Collection: Eu: om/ptgs 13-19; Am: ptgs 19; Russ/Ic 15-19; Gobelin Tapestries

Superb examples of European and American paintings and Russian icons are but a few of the highlights of the Timken Museum of Art located in beautiful Balboa Park, site of the former 1915–16 Panama California Exposition. Treasures displayed within the six galleries and the rotunda of this museum make it a "must see."   ℂ "Saint Bartholemeo" by Rembrandt; "The Magnolia Flower" by Martin Johnson Heade

ON EXHIBIT 2002

May 2002 to August 2002   *The Portraits of Bartolomeo Veneto*
The first exhibition ever devoted to this Renaissance master

October 2002 to February 2003   *In the Library: Still Life and Representation in 19th-Century America*
An investigation of the subject of books and libraries in 19th-century American art

SAN FRANCISCO

Asian Art Museum *(the Museum will be closed for most of 2002 for construction)*
Affiliated Institution: The Avery Brundage Collection
200 Larkin Street, San Francisco, CA   94102

415-379-8800   www.asianart.org
Permanent Collection: As: arts; Mid/E: arts; Brundage Collection (80% of holdings of the museum)

The Asian Art Museum-Chung Moon Lee Center for Asian Art and Culture is one of the largest museums in the Western World devoted exclusively to Asian Art. Opened in 1966 as a result of a gift to the city by industrialist Avery Brundage, its holdings include more than 12,000 objects spanning 6,000 years of history representing the countries and cultures throughout Asia. *The museum will be closed from October 7, 2001 until Fall 2002 in its new expanded facility at San Francisco's civic center.

Cartoon Art Museum
814 Mission St., San Francisco, CA   94103

415-CAR-TOON
Open: 11-5 We-Fr, 10-5 Sa, 1-5 Su   *Closed:* Mo, Tu, 1/1, 7/4, Thgv, 12/25
Adm: Adult: $5.00   *Children:* $2.00 (6-12)   *Students:* $3.00   *Seniors:* $3.00
&.: Sidewalk ramps & elevator; museum all one level   P: Fifth & Mission Garage   *Museum Shop*
Group Tours: 415-227-8671   *Drop-In Tours:* Upon request if available
Permanent Collection: Cartoon Art; Graphic Animation

The Cartoon Art Museum, founded in 1984, is located in a new 6,000 square foot space that includes a children's and an interactive gallery. With a permanent collection of 11,000 works of original cartoon art, newspaper strips, political cartoons, and animation cells, this is one of only 3 museums of its kind in the country and the only West Coast venue of its kind. *Children under 5 are admitted free of charge.

Coit Tower
1 Telegraph Hill, San Francisco, CA

415-362-0808
Open: Winter: 10-6 daily; Summer: 10-7 daily
Adm: Adult: $3.75   Children: 6-12 $1.50   *Seniors:* over 65 $2.50
&: parking lot in tower base   P: very limited timed parking   *Group Tours*
Permanent Collection: murals

Though not a museum, art lovers should not miss the newly restored Depression-era murals that completely cover the interior of this famous San Francisco landmark. Twenty-five social realist artists working under the auspices of the WPA participated in creating these frescoes that depict rural and urban life in California during the 1930s. Additional murals on the 2nd floor may be seen only at 11:15am on Sa. The murals, considered one of the city's most important artistic treasures, and the spectacular view of the city are a "must see" in San Francisco.

Fine Arts Museums of San Francisco
Affiliated Institution: M. H. de Young Memorial Museum & California Palace of Legion of Honor
Calif. Palace of the Legion of Honor, Lincoln Park, San Francisco, CA   94118-4501

415-863-3330   www.thinker.org
Open: 9:30-5 Tu-Su   *Closed:* Mo, Leg/Hol: Most holidays fall on Mo, when the museum is regularly closed
Free Day: Palace 2nd Tu   *Adm:* Adult: $8.00   Children: $5.00 (12-17)   *Students:* $10 Annual Pass
Seniors: $6.00
&   P: Free parking in the park   *Museum Shop*   ǁ: Cafe open 10am-4pm (Legion)
Group Tours: 425-750-3638   *Drop-In Tours:* Tu-Su (Palace)!
Historic Building: Calif. Palace of Legion of Honor modeled on Hotel de Salm in Paris   *Theater*
Permanent Collection: DeYoung: Ptgs, Drgs, Gr, Sculp; Am: dec/art; Brit: dec/art; An/Egt; An/R; An/Grk;
Af; Oc. CA Palace of Legion of Honor: Eu: 13-20; Ren; Impr: drgs, gr

The de Young Museum: Situated in the heart of Golden Gate Park, the deYoung features the largest collection of American art on the West Coast ranging from Native American traditional arts to contemporary Bay Area art. The California Palace of the Legion of Honor: One of the most dramatic museum buildings in the country, the recently renovated and reopened Palace of the Legion of Honor houses the Museum's European art, the renowned Achenbach graphic art collection, and one of the world's finest collections of sculpture by Rodin. *Children under 12 are admitted free at both facilities. The hours for each museum are as follows: de Young: hours 9:30-5 We-Su, open till 8:45 with free adm. 1st We of the month Palace of the Legion of Honor: hours 9:30-5:00 Tu-Su with free adm. 2nd We of month.   ℂ Rodin's "Thinker" & The Spanish Ceiling (Legion of Honor)

ON EXHIBIT 2002

01/19/2002 to 04/14/2002   *Richard Diebenkorn: Clubs and Spades*

08/10/2002 to 11/03/2002   *The Eternal Egypt: Egyptian Antiquities from the British Museum*
The exhibition will span the entire pharonic period from 3000 B.C. to 4th Century A.D. with many large scale works represented.   *Catalog   Will Travel*

Friends of Photography, Ansel Adams Center
655 Mission St., San Francisco, CA   94105-4126

415-495-7000
Open: 11-5 Tu-Su, 11-8 1st Th of the month   *Closed:* Mo, Leg/Hol!
Adm: Adult: $5.00   Children: $2.00 (12-17)   *Students:* $3.00   *Seniors:* $2.00
&: Restrooms, ramp (front of bldg), wheelchair lift (side of bldg)
P: Several commercial parking facilities
located nearby   *Museum Shop   Group Tours   Drop-In Tours:* 1:15 & 2 Sa   *Theater*
Permanent Collection: Phot; Collection of 125 Vintage Prints by Ansel Adams Available for study only

Founded in 1967 by a group of noted photographers including Ansel Adams, Brett Weston, and Beaumont Newhall, the non-profit Friends of Photography is dedicated to expanding public awareness of photography and to exploring the creative development of the media.

Mexican Museum

Affiliated Institution: Fort Mason Bldg. D.
Laguna & Marina Blvd., San Francisco, CA   94123

415-202-9700   www.mexicanmuseum.org
Open: 11-5 We-Su   *Closed:* Mo, Tu, Leg/Hol!
Free Day: 1st We of month   *Adm:*   *Adult:* $4.00   *Children:* Free under 10   *Students:* $3.00   *Seniors:* $3.00
&   P: Free   *Museum Shop*
Historic Building: Fort Mason itself is a former military site in Golden Gate Rec. Area
Permanent Collection: Mex; Mex/Am; Folk; Eth; Latin Ameican Modern Pre-Conquest : More Than 300
objects from the Nelson Rockefeller Collection of Mex/Folk Art (over 10,000 pieces in total)

With more than 10,000 objects in its collection, the Mexican Museum, founded in 1975, is
the first institution of its kind devoted exclusively to the art and culture of Mexico, Latin
America, and its people. Plans are underway to open in a new museum building in the Yerba
Buena Gardens district in 2002. This 66,000 square foot facility will house the most extensive
collection of Mexican and Mexican-American art in the U.S.   ("Family Sunday," a hands-on
workshop for children offered once per exhibition (quarterly) (call 415-202-9721 to reserve).

Museo Italoamericano

Ft. Mason Center, Bldg. C, San Francisco, CA   94123

415-673-2200   www.well.com/~museo
Open: Noon-5 We-Su, till 7pm 1st We of the month   *Closed:* Mo, Tu, Leg/Hol!
Free Day: 1st We of month   *Adm:*   *Adult:* $2.00   *Children:* Free   *Students:* $1.00   *Seniors:* $1.00
&   P: Free   *Museum Shop   Group Tours*
Permanent Collection: It & It/Am: ptgs, sculp, phot 20

This unique museum, featuring the art of many contemporary Italian and Italian-American
artists, was established in 1978 to promote public awareness and appreciation of Italian art and
culture. Included in the collection are works by such modern masters as Francesco Clemente,
Sandro Chia, and Luigi Lucioni.   ("Tavola della Memoria," a cast bronze sculpture from 1961
by Arnaldo Pomodoro

San Francisco Art Institute Galleries

800 Chestnut St,, San Francisco, CA   94133

415-771-7020   www.sfa.edu
Open: 10-5 Tu-Sa, till 8 Th, 12-5 Su   *Closed:* Mo, Leg/Hol
&   P: Street parking only   ¶: Café, separate from Gallery

Founded in 1871, the Art Institute is the oldest cultural institution on the West Coast, and one
of San Francisco's designated historical landmarks. The main building is a handsome Spanish
colonial style structure designed in 1926 by architect Arthur Brown. Featured in the
Walter/Bean Gallery are exhibitions by artists from the Bay Area and across the nation. The
views of San Francisco and the Bay are among the best.   (Mural by Diego Rivera

San Francisco Craft & Folk Art Museum

Landmark Building A, Fort Mason, San Francisco, CA   94123-1382

415-775-0990   www.mocfa.org
Open: 11-5 Tu-Sa, till 7pm 1st We of the month   *Closed:* Mo, 1/1, Mem/Day, 7/4, Lab/Day, Thgv, 12/25
Free Day: 10-2 every Sa, 1st We of month   *Adm:*   *Adult:* $3.00, fam $5.00   *Students:* $1.00   *Seniors:* $1.00
&: Limited to first floor only   P: Free   *Museum Shop*
¶: Right next door to famous Zen vegetarian restaurant, Greens
Group Tours: 415-775-0991   *Drop-In Tours:* 1:30 1st We, 2nd Fr, 3rd Sa of month
Historic Building: Building served as disembarkation center during WW II & Vietnam
Permanent Collection: non-collecting institution

Six to ten witty and elegant exhibitions of American and international contemporary craft and
folk art are presented annually in this museum, part of a fascinating, cultural waterfront center
in San Francisco. *Group tours are free of charge to those who make advance reservations.

ON EXHIBIT 2002

01/10/2002 to 04/07/2002   *Emblems of Passage, Rituals of Collecting: The Art of Africa, Oceania, and the Americas   Catalog*

04/18/2002 to 06/16/2002   *Findings: The Jewelry of Ramona Solberg*
Solberg's collection of jewelry from around the world

06/27/2002 to 09/01/2002   *Sirens and Snakes*

06/27/2002 to 09/01/2002   *Unwearable Art: Clothing in New Media*

09/12/2002 to 11/24/2002   *Fusing Traditions: Native American Artists Working in Glass*

12/05/2002 to 12/29/2002   *Third Annual Craft Showcase*

San Francisco Museum of Modern Art
151 Third St., San Francisco, CA   94103-3159

415-357-4000   www.sfmoma.org
Open: 11-6 Th-Tu, till 9 Th, Mem/Day to Lab/Day 10-6   *Closed:* We, 1/1, 7/4, Thgv, 12/25
Free Day: 1st Tu of month, half price Th 6-9pm   *Adm:*   *Adult:* $10.00   *Children:* Free under 12 with adult
Students: $6.00   *Seniors:* $7.00
&   P: Pay garages at Fifth & Mission, the Moscone Center Garage (255 3rd St), and the Hearst Garage
at 45 3rd St.   *Museum Shop*   ¶: Caffé Museo open 10-6 daily (except We), till 9pm Th
Group Tours: 415-357-4191   *Drop-In Tours:* daily (call 415-357-4096) or inquire in lobby
Permanent Collection: Am: ab/exp ptgs; Ger: exp; Mex; Reg; Phot; Fauvist: ptgs; S.F. Bay Area Art; Video Arts

A trip to San Francisco, if only to visit the new home of this more than 60-year-old museum, would be worthwhile for any art lover. Housed in a light filled architecturally brilliant and innovative building designed by Mario Botta, the museum features the most comprehensive collection of 20th century art on the West Coast. It is interesting to note that it is also the second largest single facility in the United States devoted to modern art. *1. Admission is half price from 6-9 on Thursday evenings; 2. Spotlight tours are conducted every Thursday; 3. Special group tours called "Modern Art Adventures" can be arranged (415-357-4191) for visits to Bay Area private collections artists' studios, and a variety of museums and galleries in the area. ◖ "Woman in a Hat" by Matisse, one of 30 superb early 20th c. works from the recently donated Elise Haas Collection.

ON EXHIBIT 2002

08/03/2001 to 01/13/2002   *Ansel Adams at 100*
The exhibition offers an aesthetic reappraisal of Adams as an artist and working photographer presenting a look at some of his lesser known works.

Yerba Buena Center for the Arts
701 Mission St., San Francisco, CA   94103-3138

415-978-ARTS (2787)   www.YerbaBuenaArts.org
Open: 11-6 Tu-Su, till 8pm Th-Fr   *Closed:* Leg/Hol!
Free Day: 1st Th of month 5-8 pm   *Adm:*   *Adult:* $5.00   *Children:* $3.00   *Students:* $3.00
Seniors: $3.00 Fr, Th
&   P: There is a public parking garage at 5th and Mission Sts., one block away from the Center.
¶: Café on 1st floor   *Group Tours:* ex 115   *Drop-In Tours:* 1, Sa: 6:30, Th
Permanent Collection: No permanent collection

Opened in 1993 as part of an arts complex that includes the San Francisco Museum of Modern Art, the Cartoon Art Museum, and the Ansel Adams Center for Photography, this fine arts and performance center features theme-oriented and solo exhibitions by a diverse cross section of Bay Area artists. *Admission for Seniors is free on Thursdays. ◖ The building itself designed by prize-winning architect Fumihiko Maki to resemble a sleek ocean liner complete with porthole windows.

Egyptian Museum and Planetarium
Rosicrucian Park, 1342 Naglee Ave., San Jose, CA   95191

408-947-3636   www.rosicrucian.org
Open: 10-5 Tu-Fr; 11-6 Sa, Su   *Closed:* Mo, 1/1, Thgv, 12/25, 12/31
Adm: Adult: $9.00   *Children:* $5.00 (5-10)   *Students:* $7.00   *Seniors:* $7.00 over 55
P: Free   *Museum Shop*
Group Tours: 408-947-3632   *Drop-In Tours:* rock tomb only periodically during day !
Permanent Collection: Ant: ptgs, sculp, gr

Without question the largest Egyptian collection in the West, the Rosicrucian is a treasure house full of thousands of objects and artifacts from ancient Egypt. Even the building itself is styled after Egyptian temples and, once inside, the visitor can experience the rare opportunity of actually walking through a reproduction of the rock tombs cut into the cliffs at Beni Hasan 4,000 years ago.   ❢ A tour through the rock tomb, a reproduction of the ones cut into the cliffs at Beni Hasan 4,000 years ago; Egyptian gilded ibis statue in Gallery B

ON EXHIBIT 2002

06/15/2002 to August 2002   *The Last Filipino Tribes: Artifacts and Historical Photographs*
Historically important archival photographs from 12 major institutions. This as the first definitive detailed account of the disappearing lifestyle of the Filipino Hill Tribes.

San Jose Museum of Art
110 S. Market St., San Jose, CA   95113

408-294-2787   www.sjmusart.org
Open: 11-5 Tu-Su, till 10pm Fr   *Closed:* Mo, Leg/Hol
Ġ.   P: Paid public parking is available underground at the Museum and at several locations within 3 blocks of the museum.   *Museum Shop*   ¶: The Museum Café at SJMA
Group Tours: 408-271-6840, 408-291-5393 school tours   *Drop-In Tours:* 12:30 & 2:30 Tu-Su
Historic Building: 1892 Richardsonian Romanesque Historic Wing; 1991 New Wing designed by Skidmore, Owings, & Merrill   *Sculpture Garden*
Permanent Collection: Am: 19-21; Nat/Am; Cont

Contemporary art is the main focus of this vital museum. Housed in a landmark building that once served as a post office/library, the museum added 45,000 square feet of exhibition space in 1991 to accommodate the needs of the cultural renaissance now underway in San Jose. * Signed tours for the deaf are given at 12:30 on the 2nd Sa of the month.

ON EXHIBIT 2002

10/13/2001 to 02/10/2002   *Object Lessons: Deborah Orapallo*
Orapallo expresses profound themes of time, memory, domesticity, survival and escape through the commonplace, mundane things—clocks, train tracks, inner tubes, toys, houses, tickets, and pennies which take on unusual symbolic power in her work.

10/14/2001 to 01/27/2002   *An American Diary: Paintings by Roger Shimomura*
Translations of his Grandmother's wartime diaries during the years she spent at an internment camp for the Japanese. Each painting is accompanied by its corresponding diary entry.

11/03/2001 to 01/20/2002   *Catherine Wagne : Cross Sections*
Wagner's current work examines life from the inside out. Employing modern imaging technology, she focuses on microscopic representations of organic images to investigate the fundamental nature of life.

12/08/2001 to 02/25/2002   *First Impressions: The Paulson Press*
The first museum showing of prints from the Paulson Press

02/08/2002 to 06/30/2002   *The Art of Nathan Oliveira*
A major retrospective of the work of this painter and printmaker. He explores the human form that brings to mind the work of Giacometi.   *Catalog   Will Travel*

03/30/2002 to 06/23/2002   *Tashio Shibata*
Large scale black and white photographs of dams and man-made structures   *Will Travel*

06/01/2002 to 09/22/2002   *Hard Candy*
Artists in various media take "cute" objects and change them to become menacing weapons and disturbing issues of power and sexuality.   *Brochure*

07/13/2002 to 11/03/2002   *Art/Women/California: Parallels and Intersections, 1950–2000*
Work produced by women artists living in CA during the last half of the century, highlighting the role that the cultural climate of California played in the development of their art.   *Book*

S A N   M A R I N O

Huntington Library, Art Collections and Botanical Gardens
1151 Oxford Rd., San Marino, CA   91108

626-405-2141   www.huntington.org
Open: 12-4:30 Tu-Fr, 10:30-4:30 Sa, Su; May 29-Sept 2: 10:30-4:30   *Closed:* Leg/Hol!
Free Day: 1st Th of each month   *Adm:*   *Adult:* $10.00   *Children:* Free under 12
Students: $7.00 (12-18) or w/ ID   *Seniors:* $8.50 over 65
& P: ample free parking   *Museum Shop*
¶: 1-4 Tu-Fr; 11:30-4:00 Sa, Su; Eng. Tea Noon-3:45 Tu-Fr; 10:45-3:45 Sa, Su
Group Tours: 626-405-2215   *Drop-In Tours:* Garden Tours at noon at posted intervals
Historic Building: 1910 estate of railroad magnate, Henry E. Huntington   *Sculpture Garden   Theater*
Permanent Collection: Brit: ptgs, drgs, sculp, cer 18-19; Eu: ptgs, drgs, sculp, cer 18; Fr: ptgs, dec/art, sculp 18; Ren: ptgs; Am: ptgs, sculp, dec/art 18-20

The multi-faceted Huntington Library, Art Collection & Botanical Gardens makes a stop at this complex a must! Known for containing the most comprehensive collections of British 18th- and 19th-century art outside of London, the museum also houses an outstanding American collection as well as one of the greatest research libraries in the world. A new installation of furniture and decorative arts, designed by California architects Charles & Henry Greene, opened recently in the Dorothy Collins Brown Wing which had been closed for refurbishing for the past three years. The Christopher Isherwood Archive is now at the Huntington. (not an exhibition; only available to researchers, exhibit planned for 2004) ❲ "Blue Boy" by Gainsborough; "Pinkie" by Lawrence; Gutenberg Bible; 12-acre desert garden; Japanese garden

ON EXHIBIT 2002

10/23/2001 to 01/20/2002   *Eye of the Storm: The Civil War Drawings of Robert Knox Sneden*   *Book*

02/03/2002 to 05/05/2002   *Great British Paintings from American Collections*
Seventy of the finest paintings including Van Dyck, Gainsborough, Constable, and Turner. A look at painting in Britain from the 16th century to the present   *Will Travel*

Summer 2002 to TBA   *Art Education in America*

Fall 2002 to TBA   *George Romney Retrospective*

09/15/2002 to 12/01/2002   *George Romney Retrospective (working title)*

S A N   S I M I O N

Hearst Castle
750 Hearst Castle Rd., San Simion, CA   93452-9741

800-444-4445   www.hearst-castle.org
Open: 8:20-3:20 (to reserve a tour call toll free 1-800-444-4445)   *Closed:* 1/1, Thgv, 12/25
Adm: *Adult:* $14.00 experience ticket   *Children:* $7.00 (6-17); children under 6 = free
&: Call 805-927-2070 to arrange for wheelchair-accessible tours   P: Free   *Museum Shop* ¶
Group Tours: 1-800-401-4775   *Historic Building   Sculpture Garden*
Permanent Collection: It/Ren: sculp, ptgs; Med: sculp, ptgs; Du; Fl; Sp; An/Grk: sculp; An/R: sculp; An/Egt: sculp

One of the prize house museums in the state of California is Hearst Castle, the enormous (165 rooms) and elaborate former estate of American millionaire William Randolph Hearst. The sculptures and paintings displayed throughout the estate, a mixture of religious, secular art, and antiquities, stand as testament to the keen eye Mr. Hearst had for collecting. *A 10% discount for groups of 12 or more (when ordered in advance for any daytime tour) has recently been implemented. Evening Tours are available for a fee of $25 for adults and $13 for children ages 6-12 (hours vary according to the sunset). There are 4 different daytime tours offered. All last approximately 1 hour & 50 minutes, include a walk of 1/2 mile, and require the climbing of 150 to 400 stairs. All tickets are sold for specific tour times. Be sure to call 1-800-444-4445 to reserve individual tours. For foreign language tours call 805-927-2020 for interpreters when available. Hours of operation may vary according to the season! ❬ Antique Spanish ceilings; a collection of 155 Greek vases; New IWERKS Theater presentation at the Visitor Center shows the 40-minute film "Hearst Castle: Building the Dream" on a 5-story high screen.

SANTA ANA

Bowers Museum of Cultural Art
2002 N. Main Street, Santa Ana, CA   92706

714-567-3600   www.bowers.org
Open: 10-4 Tu-Su   *Closed:* Mo, 1/1 Thgv, 12/25, 7/4
Free Day: 2nd Tu each month, except for ticketed exhibits and events   *Adm:*   *Adult:* $10.00
Children: $6.00 5-12, free under 5   *Students:* $8.00   *Seniors:* $8.00
&   P: Parking in lot on 20th St.   *Museum Shop*   ❙❙: Tangata Restaurant
Group Tours: 714-567-3680   *Drop-In Tours:* Call, times vary   *Theater*
Permanent Collection: Af: Pac/Oc: Pre/Col: Cal artifacts and Cal Plein Air Af; Pac/Oc; Pre/Col; California artifacts and Plein Air paintings

This museum was founded for the preservation, study, and exhibition of the fine arts of indigenous peoples. It focuses on artworks of pre-Columbian, Oceanic, Native American, African, and Pacific Rim cultures. ❬ In depth collection of William and Alberta McClosky

ON EXHIBIT 2002

10/06/2001 to 01/09/2002   *Exploring the Holy Land: The Prints of David Roberts and Beyond*
The focus is on the past two centuries and the changes which have taken place in the Holy Land.

SANTA BARBARA

Santa Barbara Museum of Art
1130 State St., Santa Barbara, CA   93101-2746

805-963-4364   www.sbmuseart.org
Open: 11-5 Tu-Sa, 11-9 Fr, 12-5 Su   *Closed:* Mo, 1/1, Thgv, 12/25
Free Day: Th & 1st Su of month   *Adm:*   *Adult:* $5.00   *Children:* Free under 6   *Students:* $2.00
Seniors: $3.00
&   P: 2 city parking lots each one block away from the museum   *Museum Shop*   ❙❙
Group Tours: 805-884-6489   *Drop-In Tours:* 2:00 daily, overview of collection ; daily at noon special exhibitions
Permanent Collection: An/Grk; An/R; An/Egt; Am; As; Eu: ptgs 19-20; Cont; Phot; CA:reg

The Santa Barbara Museum offers a variety of collections that range from antiquities of past centuries to contemporary creations of today. *In addition to a rich variety of special programs such as free Family Days, the museum offers a monthly bilingual Spanish/English tour. ❬ Collection of representative works of American Art

University Art Museum, Santa Barbara

Affiliated Institution: University of California
Santa Barbara, CA   93106-7130

805-893-2951   www.uamucsb.edu
Open: 12-8 Tu, We-Su 12-5   *Closed:* Mo, Leg/Hol!
&: Wheelchair accessible   P: Lot 23 for nominal fee   *Museum Shop*
Group Tours: 805-893-4320   *Drop-In Tours:* for groups of 12 or less no appointment required; architectural drawing collection by appt only 805-893-2724
Permanent Collection: It: ptgs; Ger: ptgs; Fl: ptgs; Du: ptgs; P/Col; Arch/Drgs; Gr; Om: ptgs; Af

Outstanding among the many thousands of treasures in the permanent collection is one of the world's finest groups of early Renaissance medals and plaquettes.   ◖ 15th- through 17th-century paintings from the Sedgwick Collection; Architectural Drawings; Cont Art

SANTA CLARA

deSaisset Museum

Affiliated Institution: Santa Clara University
500 El Camino Real, Santa Clara, CA   95053-0550

408-554-4528   www.scu.edu/deSaisset
Open: 11-4 Tu-Su   *Closed:* Leg/Hol!
&   P: Free in front of museum, parking permit available at front gate   *Group Tours*
Historic Building: adjacent to Mission Santa Clara
Permanent Collection: Am: ptgs, sculp, gr; Eu: ptgs, sculp, gr 16-20; As: dec/art; Af; Cont: gr, phot, It/Ren: gr

Serving Santa Clara University and the surrounding community, the deSaisset, since its inception in 1955, has been an important Bay Area cultural resource. *It is wise to call ahead as the museum may have limited hours between rotating exhibitions.   ◖ California history collection

Triton Museum of Art

1505 Warburton Ave., Santa Clara, CA   95050

408-247-3754   www.TritonMuseum.org
Open: 10-5 We-Su, till 9pm Tu   *Closed:* Mo, Leg/Hol
Vol/Contr.: $2.00
&   P: Free   *Museum Shop*   *Group Tours:* ext 14   *Drop-In Tours:* by appointment
Historic Building: Jamison-Brown House   *Sculpture Garden*
Permanent Collection: Am: 19-20; Reg; Nat/Am; Cont/Gr

Located in a seven-acre park adjacent to the City of Santa Clara, the Triton has grown by leaps and bounds to keep up with the cultural needs of its rapidly expanding "Silicon Valley" community. The museum is housed in a visually stunning building that opened its doors to the public in 1987.   ◖ The largest collection in the country of paintings by American Impressionist Theodore Wores; Austen D. Warburton Collection of American Indian Art and Artifacts

SANTA CRUZ

Museum of Art and History at the McPherson Center

705 Front St., Santa Cruz, CA   95060

831-429-1964   www.santacruzmah.org
Open: 11-5 Tu-Su; 11-7 Th   *Closed:* Mo, Leg/Hol!
Free Day: 1st Fr of month   *Adm:*   *Adult:* $4.00   *Children:* Free   *Students:* $2.00   *Seniors:* $2.00
&   P: Adjacent parking lot   *Museum Shop*   ¶: Indoor courtyard/cafe
Group Tours: ext 10   *Drop-In Tours:* Noon usually 1st Fr
Historic Building: Museum store is housed in historic Octagon Building   *Theater*
Permanent Collection: Cont

Presenting visual and cultural experiences focused on regional history and modern art; art and history exhibitions from the permanent collection; changing exhibitions from the permanent collection; changing exhibitions of nationally and internationally renowned artists; group exhibitions that demonstrate various art techniques, mediums, crafts, and historic periods.

ON EXHIBIT 2002

01/26/2002 to 04/07/2002   *Richard Deutsch: Sculpture*
Sculpture, abstract for private and public viewing, shaped by a visual play with man-made engineered objects from architecture and industry.

02/02/2002 to 04/21/2002   *Saving the Redwoods! 100 Years in Big Basins Tate Park*
Early views of Big Basin taken by Andrew P. Hill and contemporary views by regional photographers

04/27/2002 to 08/04/2002   *Out of the Earth: Frank Galuszka and Bob Kinzie*
Galuszka has created a monumental series of paintings (about 7 x 8 feet) exploring the fusion of mica crystals and canvas. Kinzie is a ceramist using clay as in ancient vessel making but creates modern works.

SANTA MONICA

Santa Monica Museum of Art
2525 Michigan Ave. Building G1, Santa Monica, CA   90404

310-586-6488   www.smmoa.org
Open: 11-6 Tu-Sa, 12-5 Su   *Closed:* Mo, Leg/Hols
Sugg/Contr.: Yes   *Adm:*   Adult: $3.00   *Students:* $2.00   *Seniors:* $2.00
&   P: Free at Bergamot Arts Center; on-site parking for the disabled   *Museum Shop*   *Group Tours*
Historic Building: Located in a renovated trolley station
Permanent Collection: non-collecting institution

Located in the historic Bergamont Station Arts Center area, this museum, devoted to the display of art by emerging and established living artists.

SANTA ROSA

Sonoma County Museum
425 Seventh St., Santa Rosa, CA   95401

707-579-1500
Open: 11-4 We-Su   *Closed:* Mo, Tu, Leg/Hol!
Adm: Adult: $2.00   *Children:* Free under 12   *Students:* $1.00   *Seniors:* $1.00
&   P: Free   *Museum Shop*   *Group Tours*   *Historic Building:* 1910 Federal Post Office
Permanent Collection: Am: ptgs 19 ; Reg

The museum is housed in a 1909 Post Office & Federal Building that was restored and moved to its present downtown location. It is one of the few examples of Classical Federal Architecture in Sonoma County.   ℂ Collection of works by 19th century California landscape painters

STANFORD

Iris and B. Gerald Cantor Center for Visual Arts at Stanford University
Affiliated Institution: Stanford University
Stanford, CA   94305-5060

650-723-4177   www.stanford.edu/dept/ccva/
Open: 11-5 We-Su; 11-8 Th   *Closed:* Mo, Tu, 1/1, 7/4, Thgv, 12/25
Vol/Contr.: Y
&   P: Metered parking at the Museum, free weekends, after 4 pm weekdays   *Museum Shop*   ¶
Group Tours: 650-723-3469   *Drop-In Tours:* Many tours call for info!   *Sculpture Garden*
Permanent Collection: Phot; Ptgs; Sculp (Rodin Collection); Dec/Art; Gr; Drgs; Or; Cont/Eu

The Iris and Gerald Cantor Center for Visual Arts includes the beautifully restored historic museum building, a new 42,000-sq ft wing with spacious galleries, an auditorium, café, and bookshop, an enhanced Rodin sculpture garden and new gardens for 20th- and 21st-century sculpture. With diverse collections and a superb schedule of special exhibition, educational programs, and events. The Cantor Arts Center is a major cultural resource for the campus and community. There is also a large collection of outdoor art throughout the campus which includes sculpture by Calder, Segal, Moore, and other artists as well as the Papua, New Guinea Sculpture Garden. (Largest Rodin sculpture collection outside the Musee Rodin in Paris.

ON EXHIBIT 2002

10/10/2001 to 01/06/2002   *Liberated Voices: Contemporary Art from South Africa*
Sixty-five works by 13 ethnically diverse artists made since Apartheid's end in 1994. It begins with Resistance art and explores major trends since the change in government.

10/10/2001 to 01/27/2002   *Paul Di Marinis: The Messenger*
Visitors can examine relationships between communications technology, art, and language in hand-held contraptions.

10/17/2001 to 01/06/2002   *Art of the Ndebele (working title)*
Beadwork, painting, adornment, and photographs from the Ndebele of South Africa

10/31/2001 to 02/10/2002   *Men at Work: Kristina Branch (working title)*
Paintings and studies of people at work

01/30/2002 to 04/21/2002   *Aerial Muse: The Art of Yvonne Jacquette*
The relationships between the artist's landscape painting and works on paper   *Catalog*

02/13/2002 to 05/12/2002   *The Southern Metropolis: Pictorial Art in 17th-Century Nanjing*
Paintings and wood-block printed books and document exploring the cosmopolitan area of 17th-century Nanjing.

May 2002 to Sept 2002   *Hannelore Baron: Works from 1969–1987*
Small scale sculpture and works on paper using collage   *Will Travel*

05/08/2002 to 08/11/2002   *A Rare and Admirable Collection: Masterworks of Native American Art from the Peabody Essex Museum*
A rediscovery of the oldest and most extensive collections of Native American Art in the United States.   *Catalog   Will Travel*

09/18/2002 to 12/29/2002   *Salviati at Stanford (working title)*
One hundred twenty Venetian glass vessels given to the museum in 1903 by the Salviati firm. It includes all of the techniques which have made Murano famous since the Renaissance.

10/09/2002 to 01/12/2003   *Wright Morris (working title)*
Photographs of mid-west America during the 1940s   *Catalog*

STOCKTON

Haggin Museum
1201 N. Pershing Ave., Stockton, CA   95203

209-462-1566   www.hagginmuseum.org
Open: 1:30-5 Tu-Su; Open to groups by advance appt!   *Closed:* Mo, 1/1, 11/28, 11/29, 12/24, 12/25
Free Day: 1st Tu of month   *Adm: Adult:* $5.00   *Children:* under 10 w/ adult Free   *Students:* $2.50
Seniors: $2.50
&: Call in advance to arrange for use of elevator, ground level entry   P: Free street parking where available
Museum Shop   Group Tours: 209-940-6315   *Drop-In Tours:* 2.00 Sa, Su
Permanent Collection: Am: ptgs 19; Fr: ptgs 19; Am: dec/art; Eu: dec/art

Wonderful examples of 19th-century French and American paintings from the Barbizon, French Salon, Rocky Mountain, and Hudson River Schools are displayed in a setting accented by a charming array of decorative art objects. ℂ "Looking up Yosemite Valley" and "Sunset in Yosemite Valley" by Bierstadt; "Gathering for the Hunt" by Rosa Bonheur

ON EXHIBIT 2002

02/09/2002 to 03/31/2002   *The 71st Annual Robert T. McKee Student Exhibition*

04/28/2002 to 07/14/2002   *Stephen's Brothers, Builders of Beautiful Boats*
A salute to Stockton's yacht-making family

05/05/2002 to 06/23/2002   *The Buffalo Soldier: The African American Soldier in the U.S. Army, 1866–1912*   *Catalog*   *Will Travel*

VENTURA

Ventura County Museum of History & Art
100 E. Main St., Ventura, CA   93001

805-653-0323
Open: 10-5 Tu-Su, till 8pm Th   *Closed:* Mo, 1/1, Thgv, 12/25
Adm: *Adult:* $3.00   *Children:* Free under 16   *Students:* $3.00   *Seniors:* $3.00
&   P: No charge at adjacent city lot   *Museum Shop*   *Group Tours*   *Drop-In Tours:* 1:30 Su
Permanent Collection: Phot; Cont/Reg; Reg

Art is but a single aspect of this museum that also features historical exhibitions relating to the history of the region. ℂ 3-D portraits of figures throughout history by George Stuart. Mr. Stuart has created nearly 200 figures which are rotated for viewing every 4 months. He occasionally lectures on his works (call for information)!

COLORADO

ASPEN

Aspen Art Museum
590 N. Mill St., Aspen, CO   81611

970-925-8050   www.aspenartmuseum.org
Open: 10-6 Tu-Sa, 12-6 Su, till 7pm Th   *Closed:* Mo, 1/1, Thgv, 12/25, 7/4, Mem/Day, Lab/Day, Pres/Day
Free Day: Sa, Free reception and gallery tour each Th 5-7 during exhibitions   *Adm:*   *Adult:* $3.00
Children: Free under 12   *Students:* $2.00   *Seniors:* $2.00
&   P   *Museum Shop*   *Group Tours*   *Drop-In Tours*
Historic Building: The museum is housed in a former hydroelectric plant (c.1855)   *Sculpture Garden*
Permanent Collection: Sculp

Located in an area noted for its natural beauty and access to numerous recreational activities, this museum, with its emphasis on contemporary art, offers the visitor a chance to explore the cultural side of life in the community with world class exhibitions. *The galleries may occasionally be closed between exhibits!

ON EXHIBIT 2002

12/14/2001 to 01/27/2002   *Thomas Demand*
Photographer Demand investigates the nature and process of the work looking for places such as Jackson Pollock's barn/studio or Dahmer's hallway.   *Catalog*

02/15/2002 to 04/07/2002   *Bamboo Masterpieces: Japanese Baskets from the Lloyd Cotsen Collection*

06/07/2002 to 07/28/2002   *Vito Acconci: Acts of Architecture*
In 1980 after years as a poet, photo-conceptualist, videographer, and installation artist he began to design unique "public art" patterned after sculptures and furniture.   *Catalog*   *Will Travel*

CU Art Galleries
Affiliated Institution: University of Colorado/Boulder
Campus Box 318, Boulder, CO   80309

303-492-8300   www.colorado.edu/cuartgalleries
Open: 8-5 Mo-Fr, till 8 Tu, 11-4 Sa; Summer:10-4:30 Mo-Fr, 12-4 Sa   *Closed:* Su
Vol/Contr.: Yes   *Sugg/Contr.:* $3.00
& P: Paid parking in Euclid Auto Park directly south of the building   ll: within walking distance
Group Tours: 303-735-2368
Permanent Collection: Ptgs 19-20; Gr 19-20; Phot 20; Drgs 15-20; Sculp 15-20

The visual arts museum of the University of Colorado at Boulder includes in the permanent collection more than 5,000 objects ranging from medieval illuminated manuscripts to contemporary prints. ℂ Works from the permanent collection

Leanin' Tree Museum of Western Art
6055 Longbow Dr., Boulder, CO   80301

1-800-777-8716 ext 299   www.leanintree.com
Open: 8-4:30 Mo-Fr, 10-4 Sa, Su   *Closed:* Leg/Hol!
Vol/Contr.: Yes
& P: Free   *Museum Shop   Group Tours:* 303-530-1442 ext 299   *Drop-In Tours:* 8-4:30 Mo-Fr, 10-4 Sa, Su
Permanent Collection: Western: sculp, ptgs, reg; Cont/Reg; Largest collection of ptgs by actualist Bill Hughes (1932–1993) in the country

This unusual fine art museum, just 40 minutes from downtown Denver, is housed in the corporate offices of Leanin' Tree, producers of greeting cards. With 200 original oil paintings and 75 bronze sculptures by over 90 artists Leanin' Tree is home to the largest privately owned collection of contemporary cowboy and western art on public view in America.

Colorado Springs Fine Arts Center
Affiliated Institution: Taylor Museum For Southwestern Studies
30 W. Dale St., Colorado Springs, CO   80903

719-634-5581   www.csfineartscenter.org
Open: 9-5 Mo-Sa, 1-5 Su   *Closed:* Leg/Hol!
Free Day: Sa 9-5   *Adm: Adult:* $4.00   *Children:* $2.00 (6-12)   *Students:* $2.00   *Seniors:* $2.00
& P   *Museum Shop   ll:* 11:30-3:00 Mo-Fr (summer only)
Group Tours: 719-475-2444   *Drop-In Tours:* by arrangement   *Historic Building   Sculpture Garden*
Permanent Collection: Am: ptgs, sculp, gr 19-20; Reg; Nat/Am: sculp; Cont: sculp

Located in an innovative 1930s building that incorporates Art Deco styling with a Southwestern Indian motif, this multi-faceted museum is a major center for cultural activities in the Pikes Peak region. ℂ Collection of Charles Russell sculpture and memorabilia; hands-on tactile gallery called "Eyes of the Mind"; New sculpture acquisitions: "The Family" by William Zorach, "Hopi Basket Dancers" by Doug Hyde, "Resting at the Spring" by Allan Houser, "Prometheus" by Edgar Britton

ON EXHIBIT 2002

December 2001 to February 2002   *Modernist Paintings (from the Phoenix Art Museum)*

01/18/2002 to April 2002   *Frida Kahlo Unmasked: Portraits by Various Photographers*

01/18/2002 to 04/21/2002   *Colorado 2002: A Juried Exhibition of Contemporary Art*

01/26/2002 to 04/01/2002   *The Enduring Word: The Art of Printing*

April 2002 to August 2002   *The Wyeth Family Exhibition: Delections from the Delaware Museum of Art*

June 2002 to August/Sept 2002   *A Covenant of Seasons: Joellyn Duesberry*

June 2002 to August/Sept 2002   *Natural Interests: The Photographs of Andrea Modica*

09/27/2002 to 01/04/2003   *Lateral Thinking: A Contemporary Collection*

09/28/2002 to 11/18/2002   *Senga Nengudi*
A solo group installation

Gallery of Contemporary Art
Affiliated Institution: University of Colorado Springs
1420 Austin Bluffs Pkwy (Shipping, Mail P.O. Box 1730), Colorado Springs, CO   80918

719-262-3567   harpy.uccs.edu/gallery/framesgallery.html
Open: 10-4 Mo-Fr, 1-4 Sa   *Closed:* Leg/Hol!
Adm: Adult: $1.00   Children: Free under 12   Students: $0.50   Seniors: $0.50
& P: pay parking in adjacent lot   ¶: adjacent plaza   *Group Tours   Drop-In Tours*
Permanent Collection: non-collecting institution

This non-collecting university art gallery, one of the most outstanding contemporary art centers in the nation, concentrates on cutting edge exhibitions of contemporary art with approximately sixexhibitions throughout the year. Attached to the second floor of the University science building, this is the only museum in the Colorado Springs (Pikes Peak) region to focus solely on contemporary art.

DENVER

Denver Art Museum
100 West 14th Ave. Pkwy., Denver, CO   80204

720-856-5000   www.denverartmuseum.org
Open: 10-5 Tu-Sa, 10-9 We, 12-5 Su   *Closed:* Mo, Leg/Hol!
Adm: Adult: $6.00   Children: Free under 12   Students: $4.50   Seniors: $4.50
& P: Public pay lot located south of the museum on 13th St.; 2 hour metered street parking in front of the museum   *Museum Shop*
¶: Palettes Tu-Sa 10-5; We 10-9, 12-3 Su; Palettes Express open 10-5 Tu-Sa, We till 8, Su 12-5
Group Tours: 720-913-0075   *Drop-In Tours:* 1:30 Tu-Su, 11 Sa, 12 and 1 We & Fr
Historic Building: Designed by Gio Ponti in 1971   *Sculpture Garden*
Permanent Collection: Arch; Design; Graphics, As, Modern & Cont, Nat Am (with famed Am Ind Coll); New World (P/Col & Sp colonial; Ptg, Sculp (Am, Eur, Western)

With over 40,000 works featuring 19th century American art, a fine Asian and Native American collection, and works from the early 20th century Taos group, in addition two newly renovated floors house the European, American, and Western Paintings, sculpture, design, and textiles. *The Museum offers many free family related art activities on Saturday. Call 720-913-0049 for specifics! Some special exhibitions have ticketed and timed entry. ❨ The outside of the building itself is entirely covered with one million Corning Glass tiles.

ON EXHIBIT 2002

03/24/2001 to 03/17/2002   *China Meets the Southwest*
Pottery from opposite sides of the globe. Native American pieces paired with ancient Chinese examples from the Sze Hong Collection

09/01/2001 to 01/06/2002   *Giants of Melanesia: Monumental Art from the South Pacific*
A diverse and compelling range of material from the museum's Oceanic collection

Fall 2001 to 01/06/2002   *Sunken Treasures: Ming Dynasty Ceramics from a Chinese Shipwreck*
Thirty ceramics from the cargo of the San Isidro, a Chinese ship which sank off the Philippine coast in the 16th century

10/27/2001 to 01/20/2002   *The Impressionism of Cos Cob: Impressionists on the Connecticut Shore*
Artist colonies sprang up in scenic spots on both coasts but primarily in the East. Sixty Impressionist works from Cos Cob, Connecticut, including Childe Hassam, Theodore Robinson, J. Alden Weir, and John Twactman.   *Admission Fee*

12/22/2001 to 06/16/2002   *Cultural Coatings: Coats from Different Cultures*
Coats from regional dress to high fashion-spanning high fashion to the present day

02/23/2002 to 05/26/2002   *US Design, 1975–2000 (title tentative)*
Covering fields of decorative design, architecture, graphics, and industrial design, the genius of American designers is explored.   *Admission Fee*

03/02/2002 to 05/26/2002   *Art and Home: Dutch Interiors in the Age of Rembrandt*
A rare opportunity to sample artistic riches from 1610–1700, it also showcases an outstanding selection of old master paintings, furniture, ceramics, silver, and other decorative arts.   Will Travel   *Admission Fee*

06/29/2002 to 09/29/2002   *An American Century of Photography: From Dry-Plate to Digital—The Hallmark Photographic Collection*
The depth and breadth of American photography from 1880 to the mid-1990s. Included are Stieglitz, Adams, Evans, Weston, Callahan, and Robert Adams.   *Will Travel*

06/29/2002 to 11/10/2002   *Woven Harmony: The Tapestries of Rebecca Bluestone*
Richly textured wools and silk in the colors of the sky and desert of the Southwest, Bluestone explores the relationship of color, light, music, and geometry in her tapestries.

08/17/2002 to 03/23/2003   *Yoruba Renaissance: New Forms, Old Images*
A juxtaposition of a contemporary African art with that of the old masters of Africa to demonstrate continuity and change

11/02/2002 to 01/12/2003   *Renaissance of Botanical Art: The Shirley Sherwood Collection*
The collection contains work of artists from from 17 countries and is a exceptional opportunity to see the scope of botanical illustration.

Museo de las Americas
861 Santa Fe Drive, Denver, CO   80204

303-571-4401
Open: 10-5 Tu-Sa   *Closed:* Su, Mo, 1/1, 7/4, Thgv, 12/25
Adm: *Adult:* $3.00   *Children:* Free under 10   *Students:* $1.00   *Seniors:* $2.00
& P   *Museum Shop   Group Tours:* Call to arrange for certain exhibitions
Historic Building: Housed in a former J.C. Penny store built in 1924
Permanent Collection: Sp Colonial Art; Cont Lat/Am

The Museo de las Americas, opened in 7/94, is the first Latino museum in the Rocky Mountain region dedicated to showcasing the art, history, and culture of the people of the Americas from ancient times to the present. *Bilingual tours are available with admission price—call ahead to reserve.

ENGLEWOOD

Museum of Outdoor Arts
7600 E. Orchard Rd. #160 N., Englewood, CO   80111

303-741-3609
Open: 8:30-5:30 Mo-Fr; some Sa from Jan-Mar & Sept-Dec!   *Closed:* Leg/Hol!
Sugg/Contr.: $3.00 adults, guided tour $2.00
& P   *Group Tours:* 303-741-3609, ext 290   *Sculpture Garden*
Permanent Collection: Sculp

Fifty-five major pieces of sculpture ranging from contemporary works by Colorado artists to pieces by those with international reputations are placed throughout the 400 acre Greenwood Plaza business park, located just south of Denver, creating a "museum without walls." A color brochure with a map is provided to lead visitors through the collection.

Sangre dellCristo Arts & Conference Center & Buell Children's Center
210 N. Santa Fe Ave., Pueblo, CO   81003

719-543-0130
Open: 11-4 Mo-Sa   *Closed:* Su, Leg/Hol!
Adm: *Adult:* $4.00   *Children:* $3.00   *Students:* $3.00   *Seniors:* $3.00
& P: 2 free lots   *Museum Shop*   ¶ *Group Tours*   *Sculpture Garden*
Permanent Collection: Am: Regional Western 19-20; Reg: ldscp, cont

The broad range of Western Art represented in the collection covers works from the 19th and early 20th century through contemporary Southwest and modern regionalist pieces as well as changing exhibitions   ℂ Francis King collection of Western Art; Art of the "Taos Ten"

A. R. Mitchell Memorial Museum of Western Art
150 E. Main St., P.O. Box 95, Trinidad, CO   81082

719-846-4224
Open: early Apr-through Sept: 10-4 Mo-Sa; Oct-Mar by appt   *Closed:* Su, 7/4
Vol/Contr.: Yes
&: Main floor and restrooms   P: Street parking on Main St; parking in back of building   *Museum Shop*
Group Tours   *Drop-In Tours:* often available upon request   *Historic Building*
Permanent Collection: Am: ptgs; Hisp: folk; Am: Western

Housed in a charming turn-of-the-century building that features its original tin ceiling and wood floors, the Mitchell contains a unique collection of early Hispanic religious folk art and artifacts from the old West, all of which is displayed in a replica of an early Penitente Morada. The museum is located in southeast Colorado just above the New Mexico border.   ℂ Two hundred fifty works by Western artist/illustrator Arthur Roy Mitchell

CONNECTICUT

Discovery Museum
4450 Park Ave., Bridgeport, CT   06604

203-372-3521   www.discoverymuseum.org
Open: 10-5 Tu-Sa, 12-5 Su (Open 10-5 Mo during Jul & Aug)   *Closed:* Mo!, Leg/Hol!
Adm: *Adult:* $7.00   *Children:* $5.50   *Students:* $5.50   *Seniors:* $5.50
& P: Free on-site parking   *Museum Shop*   ¶: Cafeteria   *Group Tours*   *Theater*
Permanent Collection: Am: ptgs, sculp, phot, furniture 18-20; It/Ren & Baroque: ptgs (Kress Coll)

18th- to 20th-century American works provide the art focus in this interactive art and science museum.   ℂ Fourteen unique hands-on exhibits that deal with color, line, and perspective in a studio-like setting.

Housatonic Museum of Art
900 Lafayette Blvd., Bridgeport, CT   06608-4704

203-332-5000   www.hctc.com
Open: Mo-Fr 8:30-5:30, Th til 7; 9-3 Sa   *Closed:* Su, Leg/Hol! Acad!
Vol/Contr.: Yes   *Sugg/Contr.:* $7.00
& P: Free parking in student lot; call ahead to arrange for handicapped parking.   ¶: college cafeteria
Group Tours: 203-332-5062   *Drop-In Tours*   *Sculpture Garden*
Permanent Collection: Am 19-20; Eu: 19-20; Af; Cont: Lat/Am; Cont: reg; As; Cont: Hispanic

With a strong emphasis on contemporary and ethnographic art, the Housatonic Museum displays works from the permanent collection and from changing exhibitions.

New England Center for Contemporary Art, Inc.
Route 169, Box 302, Brooklyn, CT   06234

860-774-8899
Open: (Open from 4/15-12/15 only) 10-5 Tu-Fr; Noon-5 Sa, Su   *Closed:* Mo, Thgv
& P: Free and ample   *Museum Shop   Sculpture Garden*
Permanent Collection: Am: cont/ptgs; Cont/Sculp; Or: cont/art

In addition to its sculpture garden, great emphasis is placed on the display of the contemporary arts of China in this art center which is located on the mid-east border of the state near Rhode Island. ℂ Collection of contemporary Chinese art; Collection of artifacts from Papua, New Guinea

Bush-Holley Historic Site
Affiliated Institution: The Historical Society of the Town of Greenwich
39 Strickland Rd., Cos Cob, CT   06807

203-869-6899   www.hstg.org
Open: 12-4 We-Su   *Closed:* Mo, Tu, 1/1 Thgv, 12/25
Free Day: Visitor's Center is always free, chg for house tour   *Adm:*   Adult: $6.00
Children: Free under 12   *Students:* $4.00   *Seniors:* $4.00
&; but quite limited!   P   *Museum Shop   Group Tours:* ext. 10   *Drop-In Tours*
Historic Building: Located in 18th-century Bush-Holley House, Home of CT first Am Impr art colony
Permanent Collection: Dec/Art 18-19; Am: Impr/ptgs

American Impressionist paintings are the important fine art offerings of the c.1730 Bush-Holley House. It was in this historical house museum, location of the first Impressionist art colony, that many of the artists in the collection resided while painting throughout the surrounding countryside. ℂ "Clarissa" by Childe Hassam

Hill-Stead Museum
35 Mountain Rd., Farmington, CT   06032

860-677-4787
Open: May-Oct: 10-5 Tu-Su; Nov-Apr: 11-4, Tu-Su   *Closed:* Mo, Leg/Hol!
Adm: Adult: $7.00   *Children:* $4.00 (6-12)   *Students:* $6.00   *Seniors:* $6.00
&; 1st floor only   P   *Museum Shop   Group Tours:* 860-677-2940
Drop-In Tours: hour long tours on the hour & half hour (last one one hour before closing)
Historic Building: National Historical Landmark
Permanent Collection: Fr: Impr/ptgs; Gr:19; Or: cer; Dec/Art

Hill-Stead, located in a suburb just outside of Hartford, is a Colonial Revival home that was originally a "gentleman's farm." Designed by daughter Theodale Pope with McKim, Mead and White at the turn of the century, the museum still houses her father's magnificent collection of French and American Impressionist paintings, Chinese porcelains, Japanese woodblock prints hung in situ with original furnishings. ℂ Period furnishings; French Impressionist paintings, Sunken garden, woodland trails and distant vistas

GREENWICH

Bruce Museum
Museum Drive, Greenwich, CT 06830-7100

203-869-0376
Open: 10-5 Tu-Sa, 1-4 Su *Closed:* Leg/Hol! Mo except during school vacations
Adm: *Adult:* $3.50 *Children:* Free under 5 *Students:* $2.50 *Seniors:* $2.50
♿ P *Museum Shop* *Group Tours*
Historic Building: original 1909 Victorian manor is part of the museum *Theater*
Permanent Collection: Am: ptgs, gr, sculp 19; Am: cer, banks; Nat/Am; P/Col; Ch: robes

In addition to wonderful 19th-century American works of art, the recently restored and renovated Bruce Museum also features a unique collection of mechanical and still banks, North American and pre-Columbian artifacts, and an outstanding department of natural history. Housed partially in its original 1909 Victorian manor, the museum is just a short stroll from the fine shops and restaurants in the charming center of historic Greenwich. ☾ Two new acquisitions: namely, "The Kiss," a 23 1/2" bronze sculpture by Auguste Rodin, and an oil painting entitled "The Mill Pond, Cos Cob, CT.," by Childe Hassam.

HARTFORD

Wadsworth Atheneum Museum of Art
600 Main Street, Hartford, CT 06103-2990

860-278-2670 www.wadsworthatheneum.org
Open: 11-5 Tu-Su, till 8 on some 1st Th of month *Closed:* Mo, 1/1, 7/4, Thgv, 12/25
Free Day: Th all day, Sa 11-12 *Adm:* *Adult:* $7.00 Some exhibitions have an additional admission fee.
Children: $3.00 6-17: Free under 6 *Students:* $5.00 *Seniors:* $5.00
♿: wheelchairs thru Avery entrance on Atheneum Square P: limited metered street parking, Free Parking Travelers outdoor lot #7, Sa and Su only. Commercial lots nearby *Museum Shop*
🍴: Lunch Tu-Sa, Brunch Su, dinner till 8 1st Th (860-728-5989 to reserve) Coffee wine bar daily till 4:30
Group Tours: ext 3046 *Drop-In Tours:* We 12:30: Sa, Su 1, 2:30 *Historic Building* *Sculpture Garden*
Permanent Collection: Am: ptgs, sculp, drgs, dec/art; Fr: Impr/ptgs Sp, It; Du: 17; Ren, Cer, Eur: Om 16-17: Eur: dec/art

Founded in 1842, the Wadsworth Atheneum is the oldest museum in continuous operation in the country. In addition to the many wonderful and diverse facets of the permanent collection, a gift in 1994 of two important oil paintings by Picasso: namely, "The Women of Algiers" and "The Artist," makes the collection of works by Picasso one of the fullest in New England museums. The museum is also noted for its collection of Hudson River School landscape paintings, collection of Thomas Cole, Caravaggio, Salvador Dali, Joan Miro, Piet Mondrian, and many others. ☾ Caravaggio's "Ecstasy of St. Francis," Wallace Nutting collection of pilgrim furniture, Colonial Period rooms; African-American art (Fleet Gallery); Elizabeth B. Miles English Silver Collection; Hudson River School collection; 4 Sol Lewitt Wall drawings. It continues to collect contemporary art in a variety of media.

ON EXHIBIT 2002

06/16/2001 to 01/20/2002 *Birmingham Totem (working title)*
This exhibition is the last in a four part series exploring the changing definitions of freedom throughout the history of African-Americans.

10/06/2001 to 01/06/2002 *Francis Alys/Phone Labyrinth/Matrix 145*
A conceptual artist who describes this as an "audio space for wanderings"

10/19/2001 to 01/06/2002 *Images from the World Between: The Circus in Twentieth-Century American Art*
A multi-media exhibition including Arbus, Bitner, Calder, Curry, Demuth, Evans, Gremillion, Kuhn, Mark, Marsh, Segal, Schinn, and others, describing the Circus as more than a popular entertainment. *Catalog* *Will Travel*

12/01/2001 to September 2002   *Reinventing Art*
Experimental artists in the 1960s and 70s developed "non-compositional" approaches. Included are Acconci, Andre, Bernd, Becker, Bocher, Boetti, Hesse, Kelly Lozano, Warhol, and others.

02/02/2002 to 04/28/2002   *Unstudio/Matrix 146*
This Amsterdam based studio combines imagination with computer technology to create "digital architecture."

02/02/2002 to 05/26/2002   *Hairitage*
Hairstyles in African American culture are looked at through painting, sculpture, photography, advertising, and artifacts.

02/09/2002 to 04/21/2002   *Sisters Collecting: Selections from the Cone and Adler Collections of the Baltimore Museum of Art (working title)*
These two pairs of sisters collected modernist paintings in the first half of the 20th century. Included are 50 works by Matisse, Picasso, Renoir, Bonnard, Kandinsky, Klee, Pollock, and van Gogh among others.

03/16/2002 to 08/18/2002   *The Art of French Fashion*
Colonial America looked to France for sumptuous style and fabrics which stopped with the Revolutions in both countries. This all began again with Worth, Pingat, Paquin, Lanvin, and Vionnet.

05/18/2002 to 09/01/2002   *Sam Durant/Matrix 147*
Inspired by the history of radical artistic practice within the context of social history

06/01/2002 to 08/11/2002   *The Stuff of Dreams/Matieres de Reves: Masterworks from the Paris Musee des Arts Decoratifs*
One hundred masterpieces of French design in silver, ivory, porcelain, jewelry, and furniture from the Middle Ages to the present day.   *Will Travel*

06/15/2002 to 01/19/2003   *Fresh Faces*
Twentieth century and contemporary African American artists portrays children and teenagers with empathy, dignity, and wonderment. Included are Savage, Waring, Lee-Smith, Crite, White, Simpson, and Bey.

09/07/2002 to 02/09/2003   *Textile Exhibition*

09/20/2002 to 12/01/2002   *Michael Sweerts, 1624–1664*
Not as wellknown as Vermeer and de Hooch, Sweerts was the most original and famous painter working in 17th-century Holland. This is the first ever exhibition in America.   *Will Travel*

11/01/2002 to Mid 2003   *Wallace Nutting*
A minister turned photographer, author, and furniture maker, he was influential in the early 20th century.

MIDDLETOWN

Davison Art Center
Affiliated Institution: Wesleyan University
301 High St., Middletown, CT   06459-0487

860-685-2500   www.wesleyan.edu/dac/home.html
Open: 12-4 Tu-Su (Sept-early May); closed June-August   *Closed:* Mo, Acad! Leg/Hol!
Vol/Contr.: Yes   P: On street   *Group Tours   Historic Building:* Historic 1830s Alsop House
Permanent Collection: Gr 15-20; Phot 19-20; Drgs

The Davison Art Center on the grounds of Wesleyan University is attached to a fine permanent collection of prints, photographs, and drawings.

New Britain Museum of American Art
56 Lexington St., New Britain, CT   06052

860-229-0257
Open: 1-5 Tu-Fr, 10-5 Sa, 12-5 Su   *Closed:* Mo, 1/1, Easter, 7/4, Thgv, 12/25
Adm: Adult: $3.00   *Children:* Free under 12   *Students:* $2.00   *Seniors:* $2.00
&: Entrance, elevators, restrooms   P: Free on street parking   *Museum Shop   Group Tours   Theater*
Permanent Collection: Am: ptgs, sculp, gr 18-20

The New Britain Museum, only minutes from downtown Hartford, and housed in a turn-of-the-century mansion, is one of only five museums in the country devoted exclusively to American art. The collection covers 250 years of artistic accomplishment including the nation's first public collection of illustrative art. A recent bequest by Olga Knoepke added 26 works by Edward Hopper, George Tooker, and other early 20th-century Realist artworks to the collection. *Tours for the visually impaired are available with advance notice.   ℂ Thomas Hart Benton murals; Paintings by Child Hassam and other important American Impressionist masters.

Silvermine Guild Art Center
1037 Silvermine Rd., New Canaan, CT   06840

203-966-5617
Open: 11-5 Tu-Sa, 1-5 Su   *Closed:* 1/1, 7/4, 12/25 & Hol. falling on Mo
Adm: Adult: $2.00
&: Ground level entries to galleries   P: Ample and free   *Museum Shop   Group Tours*
Historic Building: The Silvermine Guild was established in 1922 in a barn setting   *Sculpture Garden*
Permanent Collection: Prts: 1959-present

Housed in an 1890s barn, and established as one of the first art colonies in the country, the vital Silvermine Guild exhibits works by well-known and emerging artists. Nearly 30 exhibitions are presented yearly.

ON EXHIBIT 2002

01/06/2002 to 02/03/2002   *Aleksandr Razin*

03/10/2002 to 03/17/2002   *Bruce Dunbar; Alex McFarlane; Bob Keating*

03/24/2002 to 04/21/2002   *Paul Cadmus (tentative); Rain Kiernan*

05/10/2002 to 06/14/2002   *53rd Art of the Northeast*

06/23/2002 to 07/21/2002   *Silvermine Artists Group Exhibition*

08/04/2002 to 08/30/2002   *12th Annual Juried Competition*

09/08/2002 to 10/06/2002   *Drew Klotz; Mitch Kunzman; Joan Wheeler; Chandler Davis*

10/13/2002 to 11/10/2002   *24th National Print Biennial*

11/17/2002 to 12/22/2002   *Craft USA 2002*

Yale Center for British Art
Affiliated Institution: Yale University
1080 Chapel St, New Haven, CT   06520-8280

203-432-2800   www.yale.edu/ycba
Open: 10-5 Tu-Sa, 12-5 Su   *Closed:* Mo, Leg/Hol!
&   P: Parking lot behind the Center and garage directly across York St.   *Museum Shop*
Group Tours: 203-432-2858   *Drop-In Tours:* by appt: Thu, Sa and some Su   *Historic Building*
Permanent Collection: Brit: ptgs, drgs, gr 16-20

With the most comprehensive collection of English paintings, prints, drawings, rare books, and sculpture outside of Great Britain, the Center's permanent works depict British life and culture from the 16th century to the present. The museum, celebrated its 20th anniversary in 1998, is housed in the last building designed by the late great American architect, Louis Kahn.   ℂ "Golden Age" British paintings by Turner, Constable, Hogarth, Gainsborough, Reynolds

ON EXHIBIT 2002

01/25/2002 to 03/17/2002   *Painted Ladies: Women at the Court of Charles II, 1660–1685*
The court was characterized by splendor, excess, exuberance, and glamour. From royal brides and daughters to actresses and mistresses they were praised for beauty and despised for the political power they had.   *Catalog   Will Travel*

04/18/2002 to 06/30/2002   *Paula Rego: Celestina's House*

06/15/2002 to 09/02/2002   *Ron King and Circle Press*

09/01/2002 to Autumn 2002   *The Romantic Watercolor: The Hickman Bacin Collection*

09/26/2002 to 11/30/2002   *Late Turner: The Legacy of the Liber Studiorum*

Yale University Art Gallery
Affiliated Institution: Yale University
1111 Chapel St., New Haven, CT   06520

203-432-0600   www.yale.edu/artgallery
Open: 10-5 Tu-Sa, 1-6 Su; till 8 Th Sept 1-May 31   *Closed:* Mo, 1/1, 7/4, month of Aug, Thgv, 12/25
&: Entrance at 201 York St., wheelchairs available, barrier free
P: Metered street parking plus parking at Chapel York Garage, 201 York St.
Museum Shop   Group Tours: 203-432-8479 education dept.   *Drop-In Tours:* Noon We & other!
Sculpture Garden
Permanent Collection: Am: ptgs, sculp, dec/art; Eu: ptgs, sculp; Fr: Impr, Post/Impr; Om: drgs, gr; Cont: drgs, gr; It/Ren: ptgs; P/Col; Af: sculp; Ch; An/Grk; An/Egt

Founded in 1832 with an original bequest of 100 works from the John Trumbull Collection, the Yale University Gallery has the distinction of being the oldest museum in North America. Today over 100,000 works from virtually every major period of art history are represented in the outstanding collection of this highly regarded university museum.   ℂ "Night Cafe" by van Gogh

ON EXHIBIT 2002

10/26/2001 to 04/21/2002   *John Singer Sargent: The Painter as Sculptor*
In 1916–17 Sargent made 34 small bas-reliefs and one free standing sculpture in plaster.

11/20/2001 to 02/03/2002   *Dutch Print Culture of the 16th and 17th Centuries*
Mostly prints and drawings with a few paintings by Rembrandt van Rijn, Bloemart, Goudt Van de Velde, and others

Lyman Allyn Museum of Art at Connecticut College
625 Williams St., New London, CT   06320

860-443-2545   http://lymanallyn@concoll.edu
Open: 10-5 Tu-Sa, 1-5 Su   *Closed:* Mo, Leg/Hol!
Free Day: 1 Su of each month; Families 1st Su   *Adm:*   *Adult:* $4.00   *Children:* Free under 6
Students: $3.00   *Seniors:* $3.00
& P: Free   *Museum Shop*   ¶: Bookstore Cafe
Group Tours: 860-444-1715   *Drop-In Tours:* 2 weekly   *Sculpture Garden*
Permanent Collection: Am: ptgs, drgs, furn, Impr/ptgs, Cont Art; Hudson River School: ptgs; 19th c
landscape, Am/CT Dec/Art

Founded in 1926 by Harriet U. Allyn as a memorial to her whaling merchant father, Lyman Allyn, Lyman Allyn Art Museum was established for the community of southeastern Connecticut to use, enjoy, and learn about art and culture. The Museum is housed in a handsome Neo-Classical building designed by Charles A. Platt, architect of The Freer Gallery of Art in Washington DC, the Lyme Art Association Building, and several buildings on the campus of Connecticut College, with whom the Museum has recently affiliated. ¶ 19th century Deshon Allyn House open by appointment only, Toy and Doll Museum at 165 State Street, New London

Slater Memorial Museum
Affiliated Institution: The Norwich Free Academy
108 Crescent St., Norwich, CT   06360

860-887-2506
Open: Sept-June: 9-4 Tu-Fr & 1-4 Sa-Su; July-Aug: 1-4 Tu-Su   *Closed:* Mo, Leg/Hol! State/Hol!
Adm: *Adult:* $3.00   *Children:* Free under 12   *Seniors:* $2.00
P: Free along side museum. However parking is difficult between 1:30-2:30 during the week to allow for school buses to operate.   *Museum Shop*   *Group Tours:* ex 218
Historic Building: 1888 Romanesque building designed by architect Stephen Earle   *Theater*
Permanent Collection: Am: ptgs, sculp, gr; Dec/Art; Or; Af; Poly; An/Grk; Nat/Am

Dedicated in 1888, the original three-story Romanesque structure has expanded from its original core collection of antique sculpture castings to include a broad range of 17th- through 20th-century American art. This museum has the distinction of being one of only two fine arts museums in the U.S. located on the campus of a secondary school. ¶ Classical casts of Greek, Roman, and Renaissance sculpture

Florence Griswold Museum
96 Lyme St., Old Lyme, CT   06371

860-434-5542   www.flogris.org
Open: April thru Dec: 10-5 Tu-Sa, 1-5 Su; Feb through March: 1-5 We-Su   *Closed:* Mo, Leg/Hol!
Adm: *Adult:* $5.00   *Children:* Free under 12   *Students:* $4.00   *Seniors:* $4.00
&: Ground floors   P: Ample and free   *Museum Shop*
Group Tours   *Drop-In Tours:* daily upon request   *Historic Building*
Permanent Collection: Am: Impr/ptgs; Dec/Art

The beauty of the Old Lyme, Connecticut countryside in the early part of the 20th century attracted dozens of artists to the area. Many of the now famous American Impressionists worked here during the summer and lived in the Florence Griswold boarding house, which is now a museum that stands as a tribute to the art and artists of that era. The site includes eleven landscaped acres, gardens, river frontage, and the Hartman education center. ¶ The Chadwick Studio: restored early 20th-century artists' studio workplace of American Impressionist, William Chadwick. Free with adm, the Studio is open in the summer only.

Aldrich Museum of Contemporary Art
258 Main St., Ridgefield, CT   06877

203-438-4519
Open: 12-5 Tu-Su, Fr 12-8   *Closed:* Mo, Leg/Hol!
Free Day: Tu   *Adm:*   *Adult:* $5.00   *Children:* F, under 12   *Students:* $2.00   *Seniors:* $2.00
&. P: Free   *Museum Shop*   *Group Tours:* edu dept   *Drop-In Tours:* 2:00 Su   *Historic Building*
Sculpture Garden

The Aldrich Museum of Contemporary Art, one of the foremost contemporary art museums in the Northeast, offers a unique blend of modern art housed within the walls of a landmark building dating back to the American Revolution. One of the first museums in the country dedicated solely to contemporary art, it exhibits the best of the new art being produced. ℂ Outdoor Sculpture Garden

Whitney Museum of American Art at Champion
Atlantic St. & Tresser Blvd., Stamford, CT   06921

203-358-7630
Open: 11-5 Tu-Sa   *Closed:* Su, Mo, 1/1, Thgv, 7/4, 12/25
&.: No stairs; large elevator from parking garage
P: Free parking in the Champion garage on Tresser Blvd.   *Museum Shop*
Group Tours: 203-358-7641   *Drop-In Tours:* 12:30 Tu, Th, Sa

The Whitney Museum of American Art at Champion, the only branch of the renowned Whitney Museum outside of New York City, features changing exhibitions of American Art primarily of the 20th century. Many of the works are drawn from the Whitney's extensive permanent collection and exhibitions are supplemented by lectures, workshops, films, and concerts.

William Benton Museum of Art, Connecticut State Art Museum
Affiliated Institution: University of Connecticut
245 Glenbrook Rd. U-140, Storrs, CT   06269-2140

860-486-4520   www.benton.uconn.edu
Open: 10-4:30 Tu-Fr; 1-4:30 Sa, Su   *Closed:* Leg/Hol
&.: Entrance at rear of building; museum is fully accessible   P: Weekdays visitors may park in the campus parking garage or metered lot on Grenbrook Road; Weekends or evenings park in metered or unmetered spaces of in any campus lot. Handicapped spaces in visitor's lot behind the Museum.   *Museum Shop*
Group Tours: 860-486-1711   *Historic Building:* On National Register   *Theater*
Permanent Collection: Eu: 16-20; Am: 17-20; Kathe Kollwitz: gr; Reginald Marsh: gr

One of New England's finest small museums. Its Collegiate Gothic building, on the national register of Historic Places, is the setting for a wide variety of culturally diverse changing exhibitions. Call ahead for exhibition information and programs.   ℂ Newly discovered as a best kept secret in Connecticut

ON EXHIBIT 2002

01/22/2002 to 03/15/2002   *Sacred Objects of the Dalai Lama*

DELAWARE

DOVER

Sewell C. Biggs Museum of American Art
406 Federal Street P. O. Box 711, Dover, DE   19903

302-674-2111   www.biggsmuseum.org
Open: 10-4 We-Sa; 1:30-4:30 Su   *Closed:* Mo, Tu, Leg/Hol!
Vol/Contr.: Yes
&   P: Free   *Group Tours   Drop-In Tours:* by appt   *Historic Building*
Permanent Collection: Am; ptgs, sculp, Dec/Arts

A collection of about 500 objects assembled by one man. The focus is on the arts of Delaware and the Delaware Valley.

ON EXHIBIT 2002

11/07/2001 to 02/24/2002   *John McCoy: American Painter*

03/08/2002 to 05/26/2002   *Almost Forgotten: Delaware Women Artists*

09/02/2002 to Fall 2002   *Delaware Silver*

WILMINGTON

Broughton Masterpiece Presentations - First USA Riverfront Arts Center
800 South Madison Street, Wilmington, DE   19801

888-395-0005, 302-777-1600   www.broughtonmasterpiece.com
Open: 9-7 (last tour at 5pm)   *Closed:* Mo
&   P: Free   *Museum Shop*   ¶: Coffee shop   *Group Tours:* 888-395-0005, 302-777-1600

The Broughton Masterpiece Presentation international cultural exchange program features major, grand-scale international art exhibitions from the world's leading art, scientific, historic, and cultural institutions and private collections. Call for current exhibition information. Past internationally acclaimed exhibitions have included "Nicholas and Alexandra: The Last Imperial Family of Tsarist Russia" (1998/1999) and "Splendors of Meiji: Treasures of Imperial Japan" (1999).

Delaware Art Museum
2301 Kentmere Pkwy., Wilmington, DE   19806

302-571-9590   www.delart.org
Open: 9-4 Tu & Th-Sa, 10-4 Su, 9-9 We   *Closed:* Mo, 1/1, Thgv, 12/25
Free Day: 4-9 We; 9-12 Sa   *Adm: Adult:* $7.00   *Children:* Free 6 & under   *Students:* $2.50   *Seniors:* $5.00
&   P: Free behind museum   *Museum Shop*   ¶: The Museum Cafe
Group Tours: 302-571-9590   *Drop-In Tours:* 5:30 We; 12:15 Th; 10 & 11 Sa
Permanent Collection: Am: ptgs 19-20; Brit: P/Raph; Gr; Sculp; Phot; John Sloan and the Eight

Begun as a repository for the works of noted Brandywine Valley painter/illustrator Howard Pyle, the Delaware Art Museum has grown to include other collections of note especially in the areas of Pre-Raphaelite painting and 19th & 20th century American art.   ¶ "Summertime" by Edward Hopper; "Milking Time" by Winslow Homer; "Mermaid" by Howard Pyle

ON EXHIBIT 2002

02/15/2002 to 04/28/2000   *Impressionism Transformed: The Paintings of Edmund C. Tarbell*
Catalog   Will Travel

DISTRICT OF COLUMBIA

WASHINGTON

Art Museum of the Americas
201 18th St., N.W., Washington, DC   20006

202-458-6016
Open: 10-5 Tu-Su   *Closed:* Mo, Leg/Hol!
Vol/Contr.: Yes
P: Metered street parking   *Museum Shop   Group Tours:* 202-458-6301
Permanent Collection: 20th-century Lat/Am & Caribbean Art

Established in 1976, and housed in a Spanish colonial style building completed in 1912, this museum contains the most comprehensive collection of 20th century Latin American art in the country.   ❈ The loggia behind the museum opening onto the Aztec Gardens

Arthur M. Sackler Gallery
1050 Independence Ave., SW, Washington, DC   20560

202-357-2700   www.si.edu/asia
Open: 10-5:30 Daily   *Closed:* 12/25
&: All levels accessible by elevator
P: Free 3 hour parking on Jefferson Dr; some metered street parking
Museum Shop   Group Tours: 202-357-4880 ex 245   *Drop-In Tours:* 11:30 daily
Permanent Collection: Ch: jade sculp; Jap: cont/cer; Persian: ptgs; Near/E: an/silver

Opened in 1987 under the auspices of the Smithsonian Institution, the Sackler Gallery, named for its benefactor, houses some of the most magnificent objects of Asian art in America.

ON EXHIBIT 2002

10/21/2001 to 01/13/2002   *Cultural Dilemmas: Zu Bing and the Written Word (tentative title)*
Recognized as one of the most important artists to emerge in the last 15 years, taking the meaning of language and humankind's struggle as the theme of his work.

Corcoran Gallery of Art
17th St. & New York Ave., NW, Washington, DC   20006-4804

202-639-1700   www.corcoran.org
Open: 10-5 Mo & We-Su, till 9pm Th   *Closed:* 1/1, 12/25
Adm: Adult: $5.00, Family $8.00   *Children:* Free under 12   *Students:* $1.00   *Seniors:* $3.00
&   P: Limited metered parking on street; commercial parking lots nearby   *Museum Shop*
¶: Cafe 11-2 daily & till 8 Th; Gospel Brunch 10:30-2 Su (202-639-1786)
Group Tours: 202-786-2374   *Drop-In Tours:* Noon daily; 7:30 Th; 12 & 2:30 Sa, Su   *Theater*
Permanent Collection: Am & Eur: ptgs, sculp, works on paper 18-20

The beautiful Beaux Art building built to house the collection of its founder, William Corcoran, contains works that span the entire history of American art from the earliest limners to the cutting edge works of today's contemporary artists. In addition to being the oldest art museum in Washington, the Corcoran has the distinction of being one of the three oldest art museums in the country. Recently the Corcoran became the recipient of the Evans-Tibbs Collection of African-American art, one of the largest and most important groups of historic American art to come to the museum in nearly 50 years.   ❈ "Mt. Corcoran" by Bierstadt; "Niagra" by Church; Restored 18th-century French room Salon Dore

ON EXHIBIT 2002

10/06/2001 to 01/13/2002   *Joseph Goldyne Print Show*
Goldyne is part of the larger contemporary California print scene. Most of his prints are executed in intaglio techniques of etching, aquatint and drypoint. His images make use of the history of art and popular culture.   *Catalog*

11/03/2001 to 03/11/2002   *Antiquities to Impressionism: The Willaim Clark Collection*
Celebrating the 75th anniversary of the gift of painting and sculpture and the decorative arts, this exhibition showcases the depth and variety of this gift. Included among others are works by Chardin, Corot, Delacroix, and Gainsborough.

12/08/2001 to 02/04/2002   *Jim Dine and Roy Lichtenstein: Selected Prints*
A selective group of prints from the artists' most creative periods including works recently given to the Museum by the Lichtenstein Foundation

February 2002 to April 2002   *Wendy Ewald: A Retrospective*
Ewald's projects probe questions of identity and cultural differences. She explores the imagination of children and adults around the world.

03/16/2002 to 06/03/2002   *Jasper Johns to Jeff Koons: Four Decades of Art from the Broad Collection*
Twenty-one artists whose works exemplified important trends in the second half of the 20th century including American Neo-Dada, and Pop, German Neo-Expressionism, painting and conceptually based work from the 80s, and current art from Los Angeles. Included are Warhol, Twombly, and Ruscha.   *Catalog   Will Travel*

May 2002 to July 2002   *Larry Rivers Retrospective*
A Pop pioneer in the 50s, Rivers is an innovator in the figurative tradition. This is a first comprehensive treatment of his career.   *Catalog*

08/24/2002 to 11/2002   *Goya to Picasso: Spanish Painting from Romanticism to Impressionism from the Carmen Thyssen-Bornemisza Collection*
These artists were the Spanish forerunners of modernism. They are shown here with a range of 19th-century artists just being recognized.   *Catalog*

September 2002 to November 2002   *The Shape of Color: Joan Miro's Painted Sculpture*
The exhibit shows Miro at his most playful, produced in the 60s and 70s. Painted bronze, plaster, or polyester resin were used.

Dumbarton Oaks Research Library & Collection
1703 32nd St., NW, Washington, DC   20007-2961

202-339-6401   www.doaks.org
Open: 2-6 Tu-Su, Apr-Oct; 2-5 Nov-Mar Hearst   *Closed:* Mo, Leg/Hol
Adm: Adult: $4.00   *Children:* $3.00   *Seniors:* $3.00
&.; Partial access to collection   P: On-street parking only   *Museum Shop   Group Tours:* 202-339-6409
Historic Building: 19th-century mansion is site where plans for U.N. Charter were created.
Permanent Collection: Byz; P/Col; Am: ptgs, sculp, dec/art; Eur: ptgs, sculp, dec/art

This 19th-century mansion, site of the international conference of 1944 where discussions leading to the formation of the United Nations were held, is best known for its rare collection of Byzantine and Pre-Columbian art. Beautifully maintained and now owned by Harvard University, Dumbarton Oaks is also home to a magnificent French Music Room and to 16 manicured acres that contain formally planted perennial beds, fountains and a profusion of seasonal flower gardens. *1. Although there is no admission fee to the museum, a donation of $1.00 is appreciated. 2. With the exception of national holidays and inclement weather, the museum's gardens are open daily. Hours and admission from Apr to Oct are 2-6pm, $3.00 adults, $2.00 children & seniors. From Nov to Mar the gardens are open from 2-5pm with free admission.   ℭ Music Room; Gardens

Federal Reserve Board Art Gallery
2001 C St., Washington, DC   20551

202-452-3686
Open: 11-2 Mo-Fr or by reservation   *Closed:* Sa, Su, Leg/Hol! Weekends
&.; Off 20th St.   P: Street parking only   *Group Tours   Historic Building:* Designed in 1937 by Paul Cret
Permanent Collection: Ptgs, Gr, Drgs 19-20 (with emphasis on late 19th-century works by Am expatriots); Arch: drgs of Paul Cret; *The permanent collection may be seen by appointment only.

Founded in 1975, the collection, consisting of both gifts and loans of American and European works of art, acquaints visitors with American artistic and cultural values.   ❲ Exhibitions are open to the public in the atrium of this beautiful building which is considered one of the most magnificent public spaces in Washington, DC.

Freer Gallery of Art
Jefferson Dr. at 12th St., SW, Washington, DC   20560

202-357-2700   www.si.edu/asia
Open: 10-5:50 Daily   *Closed:* 12/25
&: Entry from Independence Ave.   P: Free 3 hour parking on the Mall   *Museum Shop*
Group Tours: 202-357-4880 ext. 245   *Drop-In Tours:* 11:30 Daily   *Historic Building:* Member NRHP
Permanent Collection: Or: sculp, ptgs, cer; Am/Art 20; (featuring works of James McNeill Whistler); Ptgs

One of the many museums in the nation's capitol that represent the results of a single collector, the Freer Gallery, renowned for its stellar collection of the arts of all of Asia, is also home to one of the world's most important collections of works by James McNeill Whistler.   ❲ "Harmony in Blue and Gold," The Peacock Room by James McNeill Whistler

Hillwood Museum
4155 Linnean Ave., NW, Washington, DC   20008

202-686-8500 or toll free @ 1-877-HILLWOOD   www.hillwoodmuseum.org
Open: By reservation only: 9-5 Tu-Sa   *Closed:* Feb & Leg/Hol except Veterans Day
Adm: *Adult:* $10.00   *Children:* $5.00   *Students:* $5.00   *Seniors:* $8.00 over 65
& P: Free   *Museum Shop*   ❙❙: Reservations recommended for cafe (202) 686-8505, ext 8811
Group Tours: 202-686-5807   *Drop-In Tours:* 9:30am, 11am, 1:30, 3   *Sculpture Garden*
Permanent Collection: Russ: ptgs, cer, dec/art; Fr: cer, dec/art, glass 18-19

The former home of Marjorie Merriweather Post, heir to the Post cereal fortune, is filled primarily with the art and decorative treasures of Imperial Russia which she collected in depth over a period of more than forty years. It also has an extensive collection of 18th century French furniture and porcelain.   ❲ Some 80 works by Carl Faberge including two Imperial Easter eggs, Russian and French porcelain; 25 acres of woods and glorious gardens surrounding the mansion.

Hirshhorn Museum and Sculpture Garden
Affiliated Institution: Smithsonian Institution
Independence Ave. at Seventh St., NW, Washington, DC   20560

202-357-2700   www.si.edu/hirshhorn
Open: Museum: 10-5:30 Daily; Plaza: 7:30am-5:30pm, S/G: 7:30am-dusk   *Closed:* 12/25
&; Through glass doors near fountain on plaza   P: metered parking nearby, commercial lots nearby
Museum Shop   ❙❙: Plaza Café Mem/Day to Lab/Day only
Group Tours: 202-357-3235   *Drop-In Tours:* 10:30-12 Mo-Fr; 12 -2 Sa, Su   *Sculpture Garden*
Permanent Collection: Cont: sculp, art; Am: early 20th; Eur: early 20th; Am: realism since Eakins

Endowed by the entire collection of its founder, Joseph Hirshhorn, this museum focuses primarily on modern and contemporary art of all kinds and cultures in addition to newly acquired works. One of its most outstanding features is its extensive sculpture garden. *No tours are given on holidays.   ❲ Rodin's "Burghers of Calais"; works by Henry Moore and Willem de Kooning, third floor

ON EXHIBIT 2002

10/18/2001 to 01/13/2002   *Juan Munoz*
Cast resin figure ensembles have invigorated contemporary figurative sculpture.

11/15/2001 to 02/18/2002   *Directions—Marina Abramovic*
A performance artist represented by "Hero," a video projection of the artist on a white horse.

01/01/2002 to 06/23/2003   *Directions—Ernesto Neto*
A site specific installation of organic form, cushiony surfaces, and exotic fragrances

02/14/2002 to 05/12/2002   *H. C. Westermann*
The first retrospective of sculptor Westermann presents many works never seen before including drawings, box works, and notebooks   *Catalog   Will Travel*

06/13/2002 to 09/08/2002   *"Open City": Street Photographs since 1950*
The start is the edgy look of the 50s and 60s and ends with contemporary views. Artists include Singh, Wall, Frank, and Winogrand.

07/18/2002 to 10/20/2002   *Directions: Artist to be Announced*

10/19/2002 to 01/12/2003   *"Zero to Infinity": Arte Povera, 1962–1972*
One hundred forty works by 14 artists who were part of the loosely knit group which propelled Italy with its process, materials, politics, and conceptual strategies.   *Will Travel*

Howard University Gallery of Art
2455 6th St., NW, Washington, DC   20059

202-806-7070
Open: 9:30-4:30 Mo-Fr; 1-4 Su (may be closed some Su in summer!)   *Closed:* Sa, Leg/Hol!
&   P: Metered parking; Free parking in the rear of the College of Fine Arts evenings and weekends   *Group Tours*
Permanent Collection: Af/Am: ptgs, sculp, gr; Eur: gr; It: ptgs, sculp (Kress Collection); Af

In addition to an encyclopedic collection of African and African-American art and artists there are 20 cases of African artifacts on permanent display in the east corridor of the College of Fine Arts. *It is advisable to call ahead in the summer as the gallery might be closed for inventory work. ☾ The Robert B. Mayer Collection of African Art

Kreeger Museum
2401 Foxhall Rd., NW, Washington, DC   20007

202-338-3552   www.kreegermuseum.com
Open: Tours only at 10:30 & 1:30 Tu-Sa   *Closed:* Su, Mo, Leg/Hol! & Aug; call for information on some additional closures
Vol/Contr.: Yes   *Sugg/Contr.:* $5.00/person
&: Limited to first floor only   P: Free parking   *Group Tours:* 202-338-3552   *Sculpture Garden   Theater*
Permanent Collection: Eur: ptgs, sculp 19, 20; Am: ptgs, sculp 19,20; Af; P/Col

Designed by noted American architect Philip Johnson as a stunning private residence for David Lloyd and Carmen Kreeger, this home has now become a museum that holds the remarkable art collection of its former owners. With a main floor filled with Impressionist and post-Impressionist paintings and sculpture, and fine collections of African, contemporary, and Washington Color School art on the bottom level, this museum is a "must see" for art lovers traveling to the D.C. area. *Only 35 people for each designated time slot are allowed on each 90 minute tour of this museum at the hours specified and only by reservation. Children under 12 are not permitted. ☾ nine Monet paintings

National Gallery of Art
4th & Constitution Ave., N.W., Washington, DC   20565

202-737-4215   www.nga.gov
Open: 10-5 Mo-Sa, 11-6 Su   *Closed:* 1/1, 12/25
&   P: Limited metered street parking; free 3 hour mall parking as available.   *Museum Shop*
¶: 3 restaurants plus Espresso bar   *Group Tours:* 202-842-6247   *Drop-In Tours:* daily!
Permanent Collection: Eur: ptgs, sculp, dec/art 12-20: OM: Am: ptgs, sculp, gr 18-20; Ren: sculp; Or: cer

The two buildings that make up the National Gallery, one classical and the other ultramodern, are as extraordinary and diverse and the collection itself. Considered one of the premier museums in the world, more people pass through the portals of the National Gallery annually than almost any other museum in the country. Self-guided family tour brochures of the permanent collection and walking tour brochures for adults are available for use in the museum. In addition, advance reservations may be made for tours given in a wide variety of foreign languages.   ☾ The only Leonardo Da Vinci oil painting in an American museum collection

ON EXHIBIT 2002

09/30/2001 to 01/06/2002   *Virtue and Beauty: Leonardo's Ginevra di Benci and Renaissance Portraits of Women*

10/07/2001 to 01/13/2002   *Aelbert Cuyp*

10/21/2001 to 01/27/2002   *Henry Moore*

11/18/2001 to 04/07/2002   *A Century of Drawing (working title)*

National Museum of African Art
Affiliated Institution: Smithsonian Institution
950 Independence Ave., S.W., Washington, DC   20560

202-357-4600   www.si.edu/nmafa
Open: 10-5:30 Daily   *Closed:* 12/25
& P: Free 3 hour parking along the Mall   *Museum Shop   Drop-In Tours:*
Permanent Collection: Af/Art

Opened in 1987, The National Museum of African Art is dedicated to the collection, exhibition, conservation, and study of the arts of Africa.

ON EXHIBIT 2002

06/09/2002 to 08/14/2002   *A Personal Journey: The Lawrence Gussman Collection of Central African Art*
From the Neuberger, the National Museum of African Art, Washington, and the Israel Museum outstanding Central African works will travel and then the Gussman gift will be integrated into the Neuberger collection.   *Catalog   Will Travel*

National Museum of Women in the Arts
1250 New York Ave., N.W., Washington, DC   20005

202-783-5000   www.nmna.org
Open: 10-5 Mo-Sa, 12-5 Su   *Closed:* 1/1, Thgv, 12/25
Adm: *Adult:* $3.00   *Children:* Free   *Students:* $2.00   *Seniors:* $2.00
& P: Paid parking lots nearby   *Museum Shop*   ¶: Cafe 11:30-2:30 Mo-Fr
Group Tours: 202-783-7370   *Drop-In Tours:* during open hours
Historic Building: 1907 Classical Revival building by Waddy Wood   *Theater*
Permanent Collection: Ptgs, Sculp, Gr, Drgs, 15-20; Phot

Unique is the word for this museum established in 1987 and located in a splendidly restored 1907 Classical Revival building. The approximately 2,600 works in the permanent collection are the result of the personal vision and passion of its founder, Wilhelmina Holladay, to elevate and validate the works of women artists throughout the history of art.   ℂ 18th-century botanical drawings by Maria Sybilla Merian; Lavinia Fontana "Portrait of a Noblewoman" c 1580; Frida Kahlo's "Self Portrait dedicated to Leon Trotsky" 1937

National Portrait Gallery
Affiliated Institution: Smithsonian Institution
F St. at 8th, N.W., Washington, DC   20560-0213

202-357-2700   www.npg.si.edu
Open: 10-5:30 Daily   *Closed:* Closed for major renovation January 2000 will reopen 2003
&: Through garage entrance corner 9th & G St.   P: Metered street parking; some commercial lots nearby   *Museum Shop*   ¶: 11-3:30
Group Tours: 202-357-2920 ex 1   *Drop-In Tours:* inquire at information desk
Historic Building: This 1836 Building served as a hospital during the Civil War   *Sculpture Garden*
Permanent Collection: Am: ptgs, sculp, drgs, photo

Housed in the Old Patent Office built in 1836, and used as a hospital during the Civil War, this museum allows the visitor to explore U.S. history as told through portraiture. Four traveling exhibitions during the museum's closure including "Portraits of the Presidents," "Notable Americans from the National Portait Gallery," "Modern American Portrait Drawings," and "Women of our Time: Photographs from the National Gallery." ℂ Gilbert Stuart's portraits of George and Martha Washington; Self Portrait by John Singleton Copley

Phillips Collection

1600 21st St., N.W., Washington, DC 20009-1090

202-387-2151 www.phillipscollection.org
Open: 10-5 Tu-Sa, 12-7 Su, 5-8:30 Th for "Artful Evenings," Summer: 12-5 Su *Closed:* Mo, 1/1, 7/4, Thgv, 12/25
Adm: *Adult:* $7.50 *Children:* Free 18 & under *Students:* $4.00 *Seniors:* $4.00
♿ P: Limited metered parking on street; commercial lots nearby *Museum Shop*
🍴: Cafe 10:45-4:30 Mo-Sa; 12-4:30 Su *Group Tours:* ext 247 *Drop-In Tours:* 2:00 We & Sa
Historic Building *Theater*
Permanent Collection: Am: ptgs, sculp 19-20; Eur: ptgs, sculp, 19-20

Housed in the 1897 former residence of the Duncan Phillips family, the core collection represents the successful culmination of one man's magnificent obsession with collecting the art of his time. *The museum fee applies to weekends only. Adm on weekdays is by contribution. Some special exhibitions may require a fee. ℂ Renoir's "Luncheon of the Boating Party"; Su afternoon concerts that are free with the price of museum admission and are held Sept.-May at 5pm; "Artful Evenings" ($5.00 pp) for art appreciation, entertainment, and refreshments.

ON EXHIBIT 2002

09/22/2001 to 01/13/2002 ***Impressionist and Post-Impressionist Still-Life Painting***

Renwick Gallery of the Smithsonian American Art Museum

Affiliated Institution: Smithsonian Institution
Pennsylvania Ave. at 17th St., N.W., Washington, DC 20560

202-357-2700 http://AmericanArt.si.edu
Open: 10-5:30 Daily *Closed:* 12/25
♿; Ramp that leads to elevator at corner 17th & Pa. Ave.
P: limited street parking, commercial lots and garages nearby *Museum Shop*
Group Tours: 202-357-2531 (no group tours June-Oct) *Drop-In Tours:* Available Nov-May only
Historic Building: French Second Empire style designed in 1859 by James Renwick, Jr.
Permanent Collection: Cont/Am: crafts; Am: ptgs

The Renwick Gallery of the Smithsonian American Art Museum, is dedicated to exhibiting American crafts of all historic periods and to collecting 20th century American crafts. The museum, which celebrated its 25th anniversary in 1997, rotates the display of objects from its permanent collection on a quarterly basis. It is housed in a charming French Second Empire style building across Pennsylvania Avenue from the White House that was designed in 1859 and named not for its founder, William Corcoran, but for its architect, James Renwick, Jr. ℂ Grand Salon furnished in styles of 1860s & 1870s

ON EXHIBIT 2002

09/14/2001 to 01/20/2002 ***The Furniture of Sam Maloof***
The first full scale retrospective of Maloof's 50 year career of sculptural furniture and as s leader in the American craft movement *Brochure*

03/15/2002 to 07/21/2002 ***Wood Turning since 1930***
The variety and beauty of turned wooden objects is shown here. *Brochure*

06/14/2002 to 10/14/2002 ***The Renwick Invitational: Five Discoveries in Craft***
A biennial series highlights five artists; Don Fogg, a bladesmith in Jasper, AL; James Koehler, a tapestry weaver in Santa Fe, NM; Gyongy Laky, a basket maker and fiber artist in San Francisco; Kristine Logan, a lampwork glass artist in Portsmouth, MH; Kim Rawdin, a jewelry maker in Scottsdale, AZ *Brochure*

09/13/2002 to 01/19/2003 *George Catlin and His Indian Gallery*
The first major Catlin exhibition in 20 years, he traveled from the Mississippi to North Dakota to Oklahoma. He assembled the basic paintings and artifacts for his Indian Gallery. *Book*

Sewall-Belmont House
144 Constitution Ave., NE, Washington, DC 20002

202-546-1210 www.natwomanpart.org
Open: 10-3 Tu-Fr; 12-4 Sa *Closed:* Mo, Su, 1/1, Thgv, 12/25
Vol/Contr.: Yes
P: Limited street parking only *Museum Shop Group Tours Drop-In Tours:* reg hours *Historic Building*
Permanent Collection: Sculp, Ptgs

Paintings and sculpture depicting heroines of the women's rights movement line the halls of the historic Sewall-Belmont House. One of the oldest houses on Capitol Hill, this unusual museum is a dedicated to the theme of women's suffrage.

Smithsonian American Art Museum *(Closed for major renovation all year)*
8th & G Sts., N.W., Washington, DC 20560

202-275-1500 http://AmericanArt.si.edu
Closed: All year for major renovation
& P: Metered street parking with commercial lot nearby *Museum Shop*
Group Tours: 202-357-3095 *Drop-In Tours:* weekdays at Noon & 2
Historic Building: Housed in Old Patent Office (Greek Revival architecture) mid 1800s
Permanent Collection: Am: ptgs, sculp, gr, cont/phot, drgs, folk, Impr; Af/Am

The Smithsonian American Art Museum, the first federal art collection, represents all regions, cultures, and traditions in the United States. Today the collection contains over 38,000 works in all media, spanning more than 300 years of artistic achievement. The Old Patent Office Building, which houses the Smithsonian American Art Museum and the National Portrait Gallery, and is considered one of the finest neoclassical structures in the world. ❡ Both on view in the Renwick Gallery: George Catlin's 19th-century American-Indian paintings; on view at Aldridge Folk Art Center in Williamsburg, VA: Thomas Moran's Western Landscape paintings; James Hampton's "The Throne of the Third Heaven of the Nation's Millennium General Assembly"

FLORIDA

BOCA RATON

Boca Raton Museum of Art
501 Plaza Real, Mitzner Park, Boca Raton, FL 33432

561-392-2500 infobocamuseum.org
Open: 10-5 Tu, Th, Sa; 10-9 We, Fr; 12-5 Su *Closed:* Mo, Leg/Hol!
Sugg/Contr.: Yes *Adm:* *Adult:* $8.00 Exclusive of special exhibitions *Children:* Free under 12
Students: $4.00 w/ ID *Seniors:* $6.00 over 65
& P: Free *Museum Shop Group Tours Drop-In Tours:* daily! *Sculpture Garden Theater*
Permanent Collection: Phot; Ptgs 20

The Museum's move to a 44,000-foot facility in Mitzner Park enables it to increase exhibition, education, and collection galleries. An assembly of modern masters Braque, Demuth, Glackens, Matisse, and Picasso, to name but a few. Recent donations include superb photography from the 19th century to present, African and Pre-Columbian art and a broad range of contemporary sculpture portraying a variety of styles and media.

International Museum of Cartoon Art
201 Plaza Real, Boca Raton, FL   33432

561-391-2200   www.cartoonart.org
Open: 10-6 Tu-Sa, 12-6 Su   *Closed:* Mo
Adm: Adult: $6.00   *Children:* 6-12 $3; Free under 5   *Students:* $4.00   *Seniors:* $5.00
&   P: Parking throughout Mitzner Park in which the museum is located.   *Museum Shop*   ¶: Café
Group Tours: ext 118   *Sculpture Garden*
Permanent Collection: Cart

Started by Mort Walker, creator of the "Beetle Bailey" cartoon comic, and relocated to Florida after 20 years of operation in metropolitan NY, this museum, with over 160,000 works on paper, 10,000 books, 1,000 hours of animated film, and numerous collectibles & memorabilia, is dedicated to the collection, preservation, exhibition, and interpretation of an international collection of original works of cartoon art. *On the many family weekends planned by the museum, event hours are 10-5 Sa, and 12-5 Su with admission at $4.00 per person. Call for information and schedule of programs.

CORAL GABLES

Lowe Art Museum
Affiliated Institution: University of Miami
1301 Stanford Dr., Coral Gables, FL   33124-6310

305-284-3535   www.lowemuseum.org
Open: 10-5 Tu, We, Fr, Sa; 12-7 Th; 12-5 Su   *Closed:* Mo, 1/1, Thgv, 12/25
Free Day: 1st Tu of the month   *Adm: Adult:* $5.00   *Children:* Free under 12   *Students:* $3.00
Seniors: $3.00
&   P   *Museum Shop   Group Tours:* 305-284-3621   *Drop-In Tours:* by appt   *Sculpture Garden*
Permanent Collection: Ren & Baroque: ptgs, sculp (Kress Collection); An/R; Sp/OM; P/Col; Eur: art; As: ptgs, sculp, gr, cer; Am: ptgs, gr; Lat/Am; Nat/Am; Af

Established in 1950, the Lowe recently underwent a multi-million dollar expansion and renovation. Its superb and diverse permanent collection is recognized as one of the major fine art resources in Florida. More than 11,000 works from a wide array of historical styles and periods including the Kress Collection of Italian Renaissance and Baroque Art, 17th-20th century European and American art, Greco-Roman antiquities, Asian, African, pre-Columbian, and Native American art.   ₵ Kress Collection of Italian Renaissance and Baroque art

DAYTONA BEACH

Museum of Arts and Sciences
1040 Museum Blvd., Daytona Beach, FL   32014

904-255-0285   www.moas.org
Open: 9-4 Tu-Fr, 12—5 Sa, Su   *Closed:* Mo, Leg/Hol!
Free Day: Tu afternoon for Volusia County residents   *Adm: Adult:* $5.00   *Children:* $2.00
Students: $1.00
&   P: Free   *Museum Shop*
Group Tours: 904-255-0285 ext.16   *Drop-In Tours:* daily 904-255-0285 ext. 22
Sculpture Garden
Permanent Collection: Reg: ptgs, gr, phot; Af; P/Col; Eur: 19; Am: 18-20; Folk; Cuban: ptgs 18-20; Or; Am: dec/art, ptgs, sculp 17-20

The Museum of Arts and Sciences recently added a wing designed to add thousands of square feet of new gallery space. A plus for visitors is the lovely nature drive through Tuscawillgo Park leading up to the museum.   ₵ The Dow Gallery of American Art, a collection of more than 200 paintings, sculptures, furniture, and decorative arts (1640–1910).

Southeast Museum of Photography
Affiliated Institution: Daytona Beach Community College
1200 West International Speedway Blvd., Daytona Beach, FL   32120-2811

904-254-4475   www.dbcc.cc.fl.us/dbcc/htm/smp/smphome.htm
Open: Mo, We-Fr 9:30-4:30, Tu 9:30-7, Sa & Su 12-4   *Closed:* Leg/Hol!
  P: On college campus   *Museum Shop   Group Tours:* 904-947-5469   *Drop-In Tours:* 20 minute

Thousands of photographs from the earliest daguerreotypes to the latest experiments in computer assisted manipulation are housed in this modern 2-floor gallery space opened in 1992. Examples of nearly every photographic process in the medium's 150 year old history are represented in this collection. Changing exhibitions of contemporary and historical photographs. (Kidspace, a Saturday afternoon program for children and parents where many aspects of the photographic process can be experienced.

DELAND

DeLand Museum of Art
600 N. Woodland Blvd., DeLand, FL   32720-3447

386-734-4371   www.delandmuseum.com
Open: 10-4 Tu-Sa, 1-4 Su   *Closed:* Mo, Leg/Hol!
Adm: Adult: $2.00   *Children:* under 12 free
  P: Free   *Museum Shop   Drop-In Tours   Theater*
Permanent Collection: Am: 19-20; Cont: reg; Dec/Art; Nat/Am

The DeLand, opened in the New Cultural Arts Center in 1991, is located between Daytona Beach and Orlando. It is a fast growing, vital institution that offers a wide range of art and art-related activities to the community and its visitors. *The permanent collection is not usually on display.

ON EXHIBIT 2002

01/04/2002 to 02/24/2002   *Florida Sculpture*
An invitational exhibition of sculpture by Florida artists

03/04/2002 to 04/14/2002   *Art of the Circus*
Original circus banners by Johnny Meah, the last of the great circus banner artists

03/04/2002 to 04/14/2002   *Gary Nofke and Friends*
Nofke is a highly regarded metalsmith and will exhibit with other craftsmen including Roger Bowersocks. Included are jewelry, large-scale hammered pieces, intricate vessels, and metal sculptures from copper, steel, tin, sterling silver, and pewter.

05/17/2002 to 06/30/2002   *Private Spaces: Photography by Les Slesnick*
Photography of private captivating Mexican scenes. They document the value of a culture represented in the home and other interior spaces.

05/17/2002 to 08/10/2002   *Natural Crafts*
An invitational exhibit of fine crafts

07/05/2002 to 08/03/2002   *Lon Keller: Illustrator*
Works by the designer of the official logo for the New York Yankees

07/05/2002 to 09/07/2002   *Award Winning Book Illustrations*
Curated by Dom Rodi, a founding member of the Royal Academy of Illustrators

Museum of Art, Fort Lauderdale
1 E. Las Olas Blvd., Ft. Lauderdale, FL   33301-1807

954-525-5500   www.MUSEUMOFART.org
Open: 10-5 Tu-Sa, 12-5 Su   *Closed:* Mo, Leg/Hol!
Adm: *Adult:* $10.00   *Children:* 10-18 $6.00, Free under 10   *Students:* $6.00
Seniors: $8.00 (also includes groups)
&.: Parking area & ramp near front door; wheelchairs available   P: Metered parking ($.75 per hour) at
the Municipal Parking facility on S.E. 1st Ave. bordering the museum on the East side.   *Museum Shop*
¶: Yes (Moa Café)   *Group Tours*   *Drop-In Tours:* 1:00 Tu, Th, Fr (Free)
Historic Building: Built by renowned architect Edward Larrabee Barnes   *Sculpture Garden*
Permanent Collection: Am: gr, ptgs, sculp 19-20; Eur: gr, ptgs, sculp 19-20; P/Col; Af; Oc; Nat/Am

Aside from an impressive permanent collection of 20th-century European and American art, this museum is home to the William Glackens collection, the most comprehensive collection of works by the artist and others of his contemporaries who, as a group, are best known as "The Eight" and/or the Ashcan School. It also is home to the largest collection of CoBrA art in the U.S.   ℂ The William Glackens Collection

ON EXHIBIT 2002

10/05/2001 to 01/06/2002   *Surrounding Interiors: View inside the Car*
Thirteen artists visions exploring the complex space of a car interior. Works include photography, sculpture, video, and painting.   *Will Travel*

10/28/2001 to 02/28/2002   *Fashion: The Greatest Show on Earth*
Fashion houses have completely transformed the runway show resulting in a new kind of performance art. The importance of this art will be looked at in leading couturiers and contemporary artists

11/16/2001 to 01/06/2002   *Birds in Art*
Sixty sculptures and paintings with humor and whimsy as well as harsh realities of nature.

01/20/2002 to 04/07/2002   *From Fauvism to Impressionism: Albert Marquet at the Pompidou*
Marquet was a famous painter and draughtman who, with Matisse, startled the critics at the Salon d'Automne in 1905. The show comes from the largest collection of his works.

Samuel P. Harn Museum of Art
Affiliated Institution: Univ. of Florida
SW 34th St. & Hull Rd., Gainesville, FL   32611-2700

352-392-9826   www.arts.ufl.edu/harn
Open: 11-5 Tu-Fr, 10-5 Sa, 1-5 Su   *Closed:* Mo, Leg/Hol
Vol/Contr.: Yes
& P   *Museum Shop*   *Group Tours*   *Drop-In Tours:* 2:00 Sa, Su; 12:30 We; Family tours 2nd S of month
Permanent Collection: Am: ptgs, gr, sculp; Eur: ptgs, gr, sculp; P/Col; Af; Oc; Ind: ptgs, sculp; Jap: gr; Cont

The Samuel P. Harn Museum of Art provides the most advanced facilities for the exhibition, study, and preservation of works of art. The Harn offers approximately 15 changing exhibitions per year. The museum's collection includes the arts of the Americas, Africa, Asia as well as contemporary international works of art. Exciting performance art, lectures, and films are also featured.   ℂ Approximately 15 changing exhibitions per year: the new art Bishop study center and library & related video & CD-ROM resource center of the permanent collection.

Cummer Museum of Art & Gardens
829 Riverside Ave., Jacksonville, FL   32204

904-356-6857   www.cummer.org
Open: 10-9 Tu & Th; 10-5 We, Fr, Sa; 12-5 Su   *Closed:* 1/1, Easter, 7/4, Thgv, 12/25
Free Day: Tu 4-9   *Adm: Adult:* $6.00   *Children:* $1.00 (5 & under)   *Students:* $3.00   *Seniors:* $4.00
&.; Ramps, restrooms, etc.   P: Opposite museum at 829 Riverside Ave.   *Museum Shop*
Group Tours: 904-356-6857   *Drop-In Tours:* 10-3 Tu-Fr (by appointment); 3 S (w/o appointment); 7 Th
Historic Building: Gardens founded in 1901 and 1931   *Sculpture Garden   Theater*
Permanent Collection: Am: ptgs; Eur: ptgs; Or; sculp; Cer; Dec/Art; An/Grk; An/R; P/Col; It/Ren

The Cummer Museum of Art & Gardens is located on the picturesque bank of the St. Johns
River. Adjacent to the river are 2.5 acres of formal gardens. The museum's permanent collection
ranges in date from 2,000 BC to the present, with particular strength in 18th- and 19th-century
American and European paintings. The Wark collection of 18th-century Meissen porcelain is
one of the two finest collections in the world. Art Connections, a nationally-acclaimed interactive education center, also schedules an impressive array of activities for children through
adults.   ℂ One of the earliest and rarest collections of Early Meissen Porcelain in the world

Hibel Museum of Art
5353 Parkside Drive, Jupiter, FL   33458

1-800-771-3362   www.hibel.org
Open: 10-6 Tu-Th; 10-9 Fr, Sa; 1-5 Su   *Closed:* Mo, 1/1, 7/4, Thgv, 12/25
Sugg/Contr.: $3.00
&   P: Free   *Museum Shop   Group Tours   Drop-In Tours:* Upon request if available
Permanent Collection: Edna Hibel: all media

The 25-year-old Hibel Museum is the world's only publicly owned non-profit museum
dedicated to the art of a living American woman. The Renaissance- and Impressionist-style
paintings, drawings, sculptures, original graphics, and porcelain have been exhibited over 60
years in 20 countries spanning four continents.   ℂ Life-sized portrait of Ginger Rogers

ON EXHIBIT 2002

November 2002 to December 2002   *The Eye of the Painter*

Polk Museum of Art
800 E. Palmetto St., Lakeland, FL   33801-5529

843-688-7743   www.polkmuseumofart.org
Open: 9-5 Tu-Fr, 10-5 Sa, 1-5 Su, 10-5 Mo   *Closed:* Leg/Hol!
Vol/Contr.: Yes   *Sugg/Contr.:* $3.00
&.: Hands-On for visually impaired   P   *Museum Shop   Group Tours   Drop-In Tours   Sculpture Garden*
Permanent Collection: P/Col; Reg; As: cer, gr; Eur: cer, glass, silver 15-19: Am: 20; Phot

Located in central Florida about 35 miles east of Tampa, the 37,000-square foot Polk Museum
of Art, built in 1988, offers a complete visual and educational experience to visitors and
residents alike. The Pre-Columbian Gallery, with its slide presentation and hands-on display
for the visually handicapped, is but one of the innovative aspects of this vital community
museum and cultural center.   ℂ "El Encuentro" by Gilberto Ruiz; Jaguar Effigy Vessel from
the Nicoya Region of Costa Rica (middle polychrome period, circa A.D. 800–1200)

ON EXHIBIT 2002

04/01/2002 to Summer 2002   *Impremature: Albert Paley; Sculpture, Drawings, Graphics, and Decorative
Arts   Will Travel*

Gulf Coast Museum of Art
12211 Walsingham Road, Largo, FL   33778

727-518-6833   www.gulfcoastmuseum.org
Open: 10-4 Tu, We, Fr, & Sa; 10-7 Th; 12-4 Su   *Closed:* Leg/Hol!
Adm: Adult: $3.00   *Children:* 12 and under free   *Students:* $2.00   *Seniors:* $2.00
  ♿ P: Free   *Museum Shop   Group Tours:* by res, ext. 204   *Drop-In Tours   Sculpture Garden*
Permanent Collection: Cont FL Art: 1960-present; Cont/Crafts

Founded in 1936, the Gulf Coast Museum of Art is a collecting, exhibiting, and teaching institution dedicated to the visual arts. Located in central Pinellas County in The Florida Botanical Gardens at Pinewood Cultural Park.

ON EXHIBIT 2002

12/01/2001 to 01/27/2002   *Andrew Morgan: Paintings of the 90s*
Morgan is a wonderful colorist who uses themes related to landscapes and still life.

12/01/2001 to 01/27/2002   *Outside the Box: Madi International Featuring Masters Carmello, Arden Quin, and Volf Roitman from the Masterson and Lehherr Collections*
An exploration of the Madi Movement originated in Argentina in the 40s. Using traditional construction methods and contemporary laser technology these two artists express the movement.   *Will Travel*

02/16/2002 to 04/14/2002 *Imprimature: Albert Paley; Sculpture, Drawings, Graphics, and Decorative Arts*
Fine and decorative art from jewelry through "Maquettes" for monumental sculptures and heroic scaled pieces as well   *Will Travel*

02/16/2002 to 04/14/2002   *William King: The Party*
Presented in a gallery party-like environment his whimsical figures in aluminum, burlap, balsa, polyester, mahogany, and stainless steel speak of our foibles, fashions, strengths, and hypocrisy.

05/04/2002 to 06/23/2002   *Selections from the Mennello Museum of Folk Art*
Folk art, or "Outsider Art" by untrained artists using non-traditional materials. Included are Samuels, Rowe, Finster, Young, Purvis, Tolson, Gerdes, and Morgan.

05/04/2002 to 06/23/2002   *Tomas Marais: Havana, Paris, Tampa Bay*
Marais was educated in Havana and later in Paris. Moved in the 80s to Tampa Bay and works in painting, drawings, printmaking, collage, and sculpture. The exhibition explores the evolution of an artist seeking artistic freedom.

07/14/2002 to 08/11/2002   *Studioworks*
Designed to demonstrate the strength of the Museum's teaching program

Maitland Art Center
231 W. Packwood Ave., Maitland, FL   32751-5596

407-539-2181   www.maitartcenter.org
Open: 9-4:30 Mo-Fr; 12-4:30 Sa, Su   *Closed:* Leg/Hol!
Vol/Contr.: Yes
  ♿ P: Across the street from the Art Center with additional parking just west of the Center
Museum Shop   Group Tours   Drop-In Tours: Upon request if available
Historic Building: State of Florida Historic Site
Permanent Collection: Reg: past & present

The stucco buildings of the Maitland Center are so highly decorated with murals, bas reliefs, and carvings done in the Aztec-Mayan motif, that they are a "must-see" work of art in themselves. One of the few surviving examples of "Fantastic" Architecture remaining in the southeastern U.S., the Center is listed in the NRHP. ❰ Works of Jules Andre Smith (1890–1959), artist and founder of the art center

MELBOURNE

Museum of Art and Science/Brevard
1463 Highland Ave., Melbourne, FL   32935

407-242-0737   www.artandscience.org
Open: 10-5 Tu-Sa, 1-5 Su   *Closed:* Mo, Leg/Hol!
Free Day: 1-5 Th   *Adm:*   *Adult:* $5.00   *Children:* $2.00   *Students:* $2.00   *Seniors:* $3.00
  ᕕ   P: Free in front of the museum   *Museum Shop*
Group Tours: 407-254-7782   *Drop-In Tours:* 2-4 Tu-Fr; 12:30-2:30 Sa; 1-5 Su; group tours scheduled
on request
Permanent Collection: Or; Reg: works on paper; Cont Woman's Art; Pre/Col; Reg Photo

Serving as an actively expanding artistic cultural center, the 20-year-old Brevard Museum of Art and Science is located in the historic Eau Gallie district of Melbourne southeast of Orlando. The Children's Science Center features more than 35 hands-on exhibits teaching concepts of physical science.

MIAMI

Lilia Fontana Miami-Dade Community College Kendall Campus Art Gallery
11011 Southwest 104th St., Miami, FL   33176-3393

305-237-2322   www.mdcc.edu
Open: 8-4 Mo, Th, Fr; 12-7:30 Tu, We   *Closed:* Sa, Su, Leg/Hol!, Acad!, first 3 weeks of Aug
  ᕕ   P: Free in student lots   ❙❙   *Drop-In Tours*
Permanent Collection: Cont: ptgs, gr, sculp, phot; Gr: 15-19

With over 750 works in its collection, the Kendall Campus Art Gallery is home to original prints by such renowned artists of the past as Whistler, Tissot, Ensor, Corot, Goya, in addition to those of a more contemporary ilk by Hockney, Dine, Lichtenstein, Warhol, and others. ❰ "The Four Angels Holding The Wings," woodcut by Albrecht Dürer, 1511

Miami Art Museum
101 W. Flagler St., Miami, FL   33130

305-375-3000
Open: 10-5 Tu-Fr; till 9 third Th; 12-5 Sa, Su   *Closed:* Mo, 1/1, Thgv, 12/25
Free Day: Su   *Adm:*   *Adult:* $5.00   *Children:* Free under 12   *Students:* $2.50   *Seniors:* $2.50
  ᕕ; Elevator on N.W. 1st St.   P: Discounted rate of $2.40 with validated ticket at Cultural Center Garage,
50 NW 2nd Ave.   *Museum Shop*   *Group Tours:* 305-375-4073   *Drop-In Tours:* by res
Historic Building: Designed by Philip Johnson in 1983   *Sculpture Garden*   *Theater*
Permanent Collection: Cont Art 40s to Present: Gr: Ptgs: Photo: Sculp; mixed media

MAM exhibits, and collects, preserves and interprets international art, with an emphasis on art of the western hemisphere. The focus is on works from the 1940s to the present complemented by art from other eras for historical perspective.

ON EXHIBIT 2002

10/26/2001 to 01/13/2002   *New Work Miami: Naomi Fisher and Glexus Novoa*

11/09/2001 to 07/07/2002   *Selections from the Collection*

12/14/2001 to 03/03/2002   *Vito Acconci*

02/01/2002 to 04/07/2002   *New Work*

03/22/2002 to 06/02/2002   *Matta in America: Paintings and Drawings of the 1940s*

04/26/2002 to 06/30/2002   *New Work*

06/21/2002 to 08/25/2002   *Ultrabaroque: Aspects of Post-Latin American Art*

MIAMI BEACH

Bass Museum of Art
2121 Park Ave., Miami Beach, FL   33139

305-673-7530   http://ci.miami-beach.fl.us/culture/bass/bass/html
Open: 10-5 Tu-Sa, 1-5 Su, 1-9 2nd & 4th We of the month   *Closed:* Mo, Leg/Hol!
Adm: *Adult:* $5.00   *Children:* Free under 6   *Students:* $3.00   *Seniors:* $3.00
&   P: On-site metered parking and street metered parking   *Museum Shop*   *Group Tours*
Sculpture Garden
Permanent Collection: Ptgs, Sculp, Gr 19-20; Ren: ptgs, sculp; Med; sculp, ptgs; Phot; Or: bronzes

Just one block from the beach in Miami, in the middle of a 9-acre park, is one of the great cultural treasures of Florida. Located in a stunning 1930 Art Deco building, the Museum is home to more than 6 centuries of artworks including a superb 500 piece collection of European art donated by the Bass family for whom the museum is named. Expansion and renovation plans are underway which will result in the addition of state-of-the-art gallery space, a cafe and new museum shop. *On occasion there are additional admission fees for some special exhibitions.   ❰ "Samson Fighting the Lion," woodcut by Albrecht Dürer

Wolfsonian-Florida International University
1001 Washington Ave., Miami Beach, FL   33139

305-531-1001   www.wolfsonian.org
Open: 10-6 Mo, Tu, Fr, Sa; 10-9 Th; 12-5 Su
Free Day: Th 6-9   *Adm:*   *Adult:* $5.00   *Children:* Free under 6   *Students:* $3.50   *Seniors:* $3.50
&   P: Metered street parking, valet parking at the Hotel Astor (opposite the museum at 956 Washington Ave), and 3 near-by Municipal lots   *Museum Shop*   *Group Tours*   *Theater*
Permanent Collection: Am & Eur: furn, glass, cer, metalwork, books, ptgs, sculp, works on paper, & industrial design 1885–1945

The Wolfsonian, showcases American and European decorative art and design dating from 1885–1945, and was established to demonstrate how art and design are used in cultural and social contexts. Shown from propaganda posters to World's Fair memorabilia, it has a unique array of objects. It is interesting to note that the museum is located in the heart of the lively newly redeveloped Art Deco District.

ON EXHIBIT 2002

12/14/2001 to 04/07/2002   *Aluminum by Design*
In 1827, Napoleon had tableware crafted from this lightweight malleable metal. Today its use in technology, architecture, and design are shown here as well as its impact on material culture through the years.   *Will Travel*

Fall 2002   *In Pursuit of Pleasure: The Hotel in America, 1875–1945*
Renderings and perspective drawings reveal how architects created opulent and fantastical environments as escapes from everyday life.

Naples Museum of Art
5833 Pelican Bay Blvd., Naples, FL   34108

941-597-1900   www.naplesphilcenter.org
Open: Oct-May: 10-4 Tu-Sa,; 12-4 Su   *Closed:* Leg/Hol!
Free Day: call for schedule   *Adm:*   *Adult:* $6.00   *Children:* 5 and under Free   *Students:* $3.00
& P: Free   ¶: Le Cafe at Naples Museum of Art, call for hours
Group Tours: ex 279   *Drop-In Tours:* Oct & May: 11am Tu & Sa   *Sculpture Garden*
Permanent Collection: Am Mod; Robert & Kay Gow Family Collection of Ancient Chinese Art

The Naples Museum is Southwest Florida's first full-scale art museum displaying international caliber art forms in a variety of mediums. Museum quality temporary exhibitions are presented from October through May of each year. *Free Family Days where gallery admissions and the 11am docent tour are offered free of charge are scheduled for the following Saturdays: 1/3, 2/7, 3/7, 4/4, 5/2, 5/16.   ¶ "Masters of Miniatures" an exceptional collection; The 9-room Pistner House, the Dennis Hillman Collection, and several Kupjack rooms

Joan Lehman Museum of Contemporary Art
770 NE 125th St., North Miami, FL   33161

305-893-6211   www.mocanomi.org
Open: 11-5 Tu-Sa; 12-5 Su; museum also 7-10pm last Fr of month during free Jazz at MOCA
Closed: 1/1, Thgv, 12/25
Free Day: Mem Day, Tu by donation   *Adm:*   *Adult:* $5.00   *Children:* Free under 12
Students: $3.00   *Seniors:* $3.00
& P: Free parking to the east, south, and west of the museum   *Museum Shop*
Group Tours: by appt   *Drop-In Tours:* 2pm Sa & Su   *Theater*
Permanent Collection: Cont

In operation since 1981, the museum was, until now, a small but vital center for the contemporary arts. In 1996, the museum opened a new state-of-the-art building renamed The Joan Lehman Museum of Contemporary Art in honor if its great benefactor. Part of a new civic complex for North Miami, the museum provides an exciting and innovative facility for exhibitions, lectures, films and performances. *Special language tours in Creole, French, German, Italian, Portuguese, and Spanish are available by advance reservation. Among the artists in the permanent collection are John Baldesarri, Dan Flavin, Dennis Oppenheim, Alex Katz, Uta Barth, Teresita Fernandez, Garry Simmons, and Jose Bedia.

Appleton Museum of Art
4333 NE Silver Springs Blvd., Ocala, FL   34470-5000

352-236-7100   www.AppletonMuseum.com
Open: 10-6pm Daily   *Closed:* 1/1, Easter Su; 12/25
Free Day: Mother's Day; Father's Day   *Adm:*   *Adult:* $6.00   *Children:* Free under 18
Students: $2.00   *Seniors:* $4.00
& P: Free   *Museum Shop*   ¶: Courtside Cafe 11-3 Mo-Sa; 12-4 Su
Group Tours: ext. 113   *Drop-In Tours:* 1:15 Mo-Fr, and by reservation
Permanent Collection: Eur; Pr/Col; Af; Or; Dec/Art; Islamic Ceramics; Antiquities

The Appleton Museum of Art in central Florida is home to one of the finest art collections in the Southeast. Situated among acres of tall pines and magnolias, the dramatic building sets the tone for the many treasures that await the visitor within its walls. With the addition of The Edith-Marie Appleton Wing in 1/97, the museum became one of the largest art institutions in Florida. "From antiquities to the art of our times... A World of Art at your Doorstep." ¶ Rodin's "Thinker," Bouguereau's "The Young Shepherdess" and "The Knitter"; 8th-century Chinese Tang Horse

ON EXHIBIT 2002

12/18/2001 to 01/27/2002   *Orientalist Art from the Dahesh Museum of Art, New York*

01/16/2002 to 04/21/2002   *20th-Century Masterpieces from the Art Gallery of Toronto*

02/02/2002 to March 2002   *Horseplay: Leslie Enders Lee*
Tour organized by the Higginbotham Museum

ORLANDO

Orlando Museum of Art
2416 North Mills Ave., Orlando, FL   32803-1483

407-896-4231   www.OMArt.org
Open: 10-5 Tu-Sa, 12-5 Su, 6-9 1st Th   *Closed:* Mo, Leg/Hol!
Free Day: Orange, Osceola and Seminole county residents are admitted free 1-5 Th   *Adm:*   *Adult:* $6.00
Children: $3.00 (4-11)   *Students:* $5.00   *Seniors:* $5.00
♿ P: Free on-site parking on campus in front of Museum. Overflow lot 1/8 mile away.   *Museum Shop*
Group Tours: ex 248   *Drop-In Tours:* 1:00, Th Sept-May
Permanent Collection: P/Col; Am; 19-20; Am gr 20; Af

Designated by the state of Florida as a "Major Cultural Institution" the Orlando Museum of Art, established in 1924, recently completed its major expansion and construction project making it the only museum in the nine county area of central Florida capable of providing residents and tourists with world class exhibits. ⓒ Permanent Collection of Art of the Ancient Americas (1200 BC to 1500 AD) complete with hands-on exhibit.

ON EXHIBIT 2002

06/09/2001 to 05/12/2002   *Of Power and Grace: The Art of Southern Africa, Selections and Gifts from the Norma Canelas and William D. Roth Collection*
The fourth in a series of exhibitions from these collections highlighting different traditions of the African continent. South Africa made extensive use of beads and feathers from the Ndebele, Xhosa, and Zulu in their powerful and elegant art.

12/07/2001 to 03/03/2002   *American Impressionists Abroad and at Home*
Thirty-nine works by 27 artists will describe the training that American Impressionists undertook abroad and at home; the complex attractions of Europe and America; the significance of the subjects they depicted and their responses to French Impressionism. *Catalog   Will Travel*

03/16/2002 to 05/26/2002   *An American Palette: Work from the Collection of John and Dolores Beck*
Fifty works from one of Florida's most important collections from mid-19th century to the 1950s. Traditional and modernist included are Bierstadt, Bellows, Inness, Henri, Benton, Dove, Marsh, Marin, Weber, Davis, and Sheeler.   *Catalog   Will Travel*

06/08/2002 to 07/28/2002   *Currents Series 8: Fabian Marcaccio*
A New York-based South American abstract artist who explores the very nature of abstraction *Brochure*

08/10/2002 to 11/03/2002   *Holocaust Project: From Darkness into Light*
A reference point for human condition—past, present, and future—this is a journey through a tapestry, two stained-glass pieces, and 13 large-scale tableaus combining painting and photography in an unprecedented manner. This was a vision of Judy Chicago and Donald Woodman.   *Book*

12/07/2002 to 02/09/2003   *An American Anthem: 300 Years of Painting from the Butler Institute of American Art*
A survey of American art history including the Colonial Period, Hudson River School, Luminism, American Impressionism, the American West, the Eight, Social Realism, and post-war to the present. Included are Cole, Church, Bierstadt, Eakins, Hopper, Henri, Chase, Bearden, and many others.   *Will Travel   Book*

Society of the Four Arts
Four Arts Plaza, Palm Beach, FL   33480

561-655-7226   www.fourarts.org
Open: 12/1-4/8: 10-5 Mo-Sa, 2-5 Su   *Closed:* Museum closed May-Nov.
Sugg/Contr.: Yes   *Adm:*   *Adult:* $5.00
  P: Free   *Group Tours*   *Historic Building*   *Sculpture Garden*   *Theater*
Permanent Collection: Sculp

Rain or shine, this museum provides welcome relief from the elements for all vacationing art fanciers by presenting monthly exhibitions of paintings or decorative arts. ℂ Philip Hulitar Sculpture Garden and the Botanical Garden

ON EXHIBIT 2002

12/05/2001 to 01/06/2002   *63rd Annual National Competition of American Paintings*

01/11/2002 to 02/10/2002   *Paul Signac: A Collection of Watercolors and Drawings from the Arkansas Art Center*

02/15/2002 to 04/14/2002   *An Impressionist Legacy: The Dixon Gallery and Gardens Collection*

02/15/2002 to 04/07/2002   *The Story of Harness Racing by Currier and Ives*

03/01/2002 to 04/14/2002   *Splendors of China: Selections from the Leon and Charlotte Amar Collection*

Pensacola Museum of Art
407 S. Jefferson St., Pensacola, FL   32501

850-432-6247   www.pensacolamuseumofart.org
Open: 10-5 Tu-Fr, 10-4 Sa   *Closed:* Su, Mo, Leg/Hol!
Free Day: Tu   *Adm:*   *Adult:* $2.00   *Students:* $1.00   *Seniors:* $2.00
  P: Free   *Museum Shop*   *Group Tours*   *Drop-In Tours:* check for availability   *Historic Building*
Permanent Collection: Cont/Am: ptgs, gr, works on paper; Glass:19, 20

Now renovated and occupied by the Pensacola Museum of Art, this building was in active use as the city jail from 1906–1954.

John and Mable Ringling Museum of Art
5401 Bay Shore Rd., Sarasota, FL   34243

941-359-5700 or 351-1660 (recording 24hr.)   www.ringling.org
Open: 10-5:30 Daily   *Closed:* 1/1, Thgv, 12/25
Free Day: Sa (Art Museum only)   *Adm:*   *Adult:* $9.00   *Children:* Free 12 & under   *Seniors:* $8.00
&.: All art & circus galleries; first floor only of mansion   P: Free
Museum Shop   ‖: Banyan Café 11-4 daily
Group Tours: 941-359-5725   *Drop-In Tours:* call 941-351-1660 (recorded message)
Historic Building: Ca'D'Zan was the winter mansion of John & Mable Ringling   *Sculpture Garden*
Permanent Collection: Am: ptgs, sculp; Eur: ptgs, sculp 15-20; Drgs; Gr; Dec/Art; Circus Memorabilia

Sharing the grounds of the museum is Ca'd'Zan, the winter mansion of circus impresario John Ringling and his wife Mable. Their personal collection of fine art in the museum features one of the country's premier collections of European, Old Master, and 17th century Italian Baroque paintings. Currently undergoing complete restoration to be completed in the fall of 2001. ℂ The Rubens Gallery—a splendid group of paintings by Peter Paul Rubens.

ON EXHIBIT 2002

10/11/2001 to 01/06/2002   *One Nation: Patriots and Pirates Portrayed by N. C. Wyeth and James Wyeth*
Audience is challenged to find the patriot and the pirate. All is not black and white.   *Catalog*

02/01/2002 to 04/14/2002   *Images from the World Between: The Circus in 20th Century American Art*
A multi-media exhibition including Arbus, Bitner, Calder, Curry, Demuth, Evans, Gremillion, Kuhn, Mark, Marsh, Segal, Schinn, and others, describing the Circus as more than a popular entertainment.   *Catalog   Will Travel*

ST.   PETERSBURG

Florida International Museum
100 Second St. North, St. Petersburg, FL   33701

727-822-3693   www.floridamuseum.org
Open: 10-5 Mo-Sa; 12-5 Su   *Closed:* 1/1, Thgv, 12/25
Adm: Adult: $13.95 (daypass) Individual exhibition tickets starting at $3.95 available in all categories
Children: $5.95 (daypass)   *Students:* College Stud $5.95 (daypass)   *Seniors:* $12.95 (daypass)
&; wheelchairs at no extra charge   P: An abundance of nearby garage, street parking. Museum parking garage at $5 for all day   *Museum Shop*
Group Tours: Call for reservations and information   *Drop-In Tours:* Mo-Su last tour at 4:30
Permanent Collection: Kennedy Galleries and Cuban Missile Crisis exhibition

The Florida International Museum is centered in the cultural heart of Tampa Bay-Downtown St. Petersburg BayWalk complex. It is Florida's premier museum for blockbuster exhibitions. The museum is a Smithsonian Institution affiliate.

Museum of Fine Arts
255 Beach Dr., N.E., St. Petersburg, FL   33701-3498

727-896-2667   www.fine-arts.org
Open: 10-5 Tu-Sa, 1-5 Su, till 9pm 3rd Th   *Closed:* Mo, Thgv, 12/25, 1/1
Free Day: Su   *Adm: Adult:* $6.00 ($4 for groups of 10 or more)   *Children:* Free 6 & under
Students: $2.00   *Seniors:* $5.00
&   P: Free parking also available on Beach Dr. & Bayshore Dr.   *Museum Shop*
Group Tours   Drop-In Tours: 10 (seasonal), 11, 1, 2, 3 (seasonal) Tu-Fr; 11 to 2 hourly Sa; 1 & 2 Su
Sculpture Garden
Permanent Collection: Am: ptgs, sculp, drgs, gr; Eur: ptgs, sculp, drgs, gr; P/Col; Dec/Art; Or; Steuben Glass; Nat/Am; As: art; Af/Art

The Museum of Fine Arts, considered one of the premier museums in the southeast, is truly an elegant showcase for its many treasures that run from Impressionist paintings to one of the finest collections of photography in the state. Spanish, Italian, German, Croatian, and French language tours are available by advance appointment.   ☾ Works by Rembrandt, Monet, Gauguin, Cézanne, Morisot, Renoir, Rodin, and O'Keeffe, Pre-Columbian Collection, Steuben Glass

ON EXHIBIT 2002

10/14/2001 to 01/05/2002   *Americanos; Portraits of the Latino Community in the United States*

Salvador Dali Museum
1000 Third St. South, St. Petersburg, FL   33701

727-823-3767   www.Salvadordalimuseum.com
Open: 9:30-5:30 Mo-Sa, 12-5:30 Su: 9:30-8:00 Th   *Closed:* Thgv, 12/25
Adm: Adult: $10.00   *Children:* Free 10 & under   *Students:* $5.00   *Seniors:* $7.00
&   P: Free   *Museum Shop   Group Tours:* tours 9:30-3:30 Mo-Sa   *Drop-In Tours:* Call for daily schedule
Permanent Collection: Salvador Dali: ptgs, sculp, drgs, gr

Unquestionably an extensive and comprehensive collection of Salvador Dali's works, the museum holdings amassed by Dali's friends A. Reynolds and Eleanor Morse include 95 original oils, 100 watercolors and drawings, 1,300 graphics, sculpture, and other objects d'art that span his entire career. ℂ Outstanding docent tours that are offered many times daily.

ON EXHIBIT 2002

11/03/2001 to 02/24/2002   *In Spite of Everything, Spring: Jacquiline Lamba (1910–1993)*
Lamba began working in New York as a surrealist in the 40s. After the war she returned to France.

05/11/2002 to 09/08/2002   *Forms of Cubism: Sculptures and the Avant-Garde, 1909–1918*
Sculptures and related drawings by early masters of Cubism including Lipschitz, Zadkine, Picasso, Braque, Gaudier-Brezca, Brancusi, Laurens, and Archipenko. It will demonstrate how drawing provided a bridge to the language of Cubism in three dimensions.   *Catalog*

10/19/2002 to 01/19/2003   *Dali in Focus: Gradiva*
Gravida, William Jensen's novel, fascinated Freud, Dali, and the surrealists.

TALLAHASSEE

Florida State University Museum of Fine Arts
Fine Arts Bldg., Copeland & W. Tenn. Sts., Tallahassee, FL   32306-1140

850-644-6836   www.fsu.edu/-svad/FSUMuseum/FSU-Museum.html
Open: 9-4 Mo-Fr; 1-4 Sa, Su (closed weekends during Summer Semester)   *Closed:* Leg/Hol! Acad!
& P: Metered parking in front of the building with weekend parking available in the lot next to the museum.   *Group Tours:* 850-644-1299   *Drop-In Tours:* Upon request if available
Permanent Collection: Eur; Or; Cont; Phot; Gr; P/Col: Peruvian artifacts; Jap: gr

With multiple gallery spaces, this is the largest art museum within 2-hours driving distance of Tallahassee. ℂ Works by Judy Chicago

ON EXHIBIT 2002

01/11/2002 to 02/10/2002   *Faculty Annual*

01/11/2002 to 02/10/2002   *Visiting Artists: Permanent Collection*

02/15/2002 to 03/30/2002   *Treasures of the Ringling and Appleton Museums*

05/10/2002 to 06/07/2002   *The Artists' League Summer Annual*

Lemoyne Art Foundation, Inc.
125 N. Gadsden, Tallahassee, FL   32301

850-222-8800   www.lemoyne.org
Open: 10-5 Tu-Sa, 1-5 Su   *Closed:* Mo, Major Holidays!
Free Day: Su   *Vol/Contr.:* $1.00   *Sugg/Contr.:* $1.00   *Adm:*   *Adult:* $1.00   *Children:* Free 12 & under
Students: $1.00   *Seniors:* $1.00
& P: parking lot adjacent to the Helen Lind Garden and Sculptures; also, large lot across street available weekends and evenings   *Museum Shop*
Group Tours: 850-222-8800   *Drop-In Tours:* daily when requested   *Historic Building*   *Sculpture Garden*
Permanent Collection: Cont; sculp

Located in an 1852 structure in the heart of Tallahassee's historic district, the Lemoyne is named for the first artist known to have visited North America. Aside from offering a wide range of changing exhibitions annually, the museum provides the visitor with a sculpture garden that serves as a setting for beauty and quiet contemplation. ℂ Three recently acquired copper sculptures by George Frederick Holschuh

Tampa Museum of Art
600 North Ashley Dr., Tampa, FL   33602

813-274-8130   www.tampamuseum.com
Open: 10-5 Tu-Sa, 10-8 Th, 1-5 Su   *Closed:* Mo, 1/1, 7/4, 12/25
Free Day: 5-8 Th, 10-12 Sa   *Adm:*   *Adult:* $5.00   *Children:* 6-18 $3.00; Free under 6
Students: $3.00 with I.D.   *Seniors:* $4.00
&.; Wheelchairs available, follow signs to handicapped entrance   P: Covered parking under the museum
for a nominal hourly fee. Enter the garage from Ashley Dr. & Twiggs St.   *Museum Shop*   ¶: nearby
Group Tours: 813-274-8698   *Sculpture Garden*
Permanent Collection: Ptgs: 19-20; Gr: 19-20; An/Grk; An/R; Phot

One of the Southeast's finest museums, there are changing exhibitions that range from contemporary to classic, and a renowned permanent collection of Greek and Roman antiquities. Complementing these exhibitions are a wide range of classes, lectures, lunchtime seminars, and walking tours. ℂ Joseph V. Noble Collection of Greek & Southern Italian antiquities on view in the Barbara & Costas Lemonopoulos Gallery.

ON EXHIBIT 2002

10/04/2001 to 01/13/2002   *Greek Vases from the Collection of William Suddaby and David Meier (working title)*
Pottery from the Greek Bronze age, ca 15 century B.C., to the classical period of Greek art, the fifth and fourth centuries B.C. Items include a rare form of perfume bottle, vessels for serving and drinking wine

01/13/2002 to 04/07/2002   *The River: A Multimedia Gallery Installation by Therman Statom*
Materials including painted plate glass, aluminum, and ceramics will be combined and constructed to create an experimental environment that explores the artist's African and Native-American ancestry.

01/20/2002 to 03/31/2002   *The Age of Anxiety*
After World War II the high Americans felt after the military victory turned to cynicism and bitterness. The so-called communist threat, the art world's shift from Paris to New York, and Abstract Expressionism the first movement to originate in America

04/21/2002 to 07/23/2002   *My Reality: Contemporary Art and the Culture of Japanese Animation*
Japanese animation has become almost a cult among young people globally during the past few decades. The effect of this on today's art in Japan and other Asian countries and in the West is examined. Much "anime" has a futuristic flavor because it affirms technology as a force in today's society.   *Will Travel*

07/07/2002 to 09/01/2002   *Undercurrent/Overview 6*
Florida's west coast artists are featured here.

USF Contemporary Art Museum
Affiliated Institution: College of Fine Arts
4202 E. Fowler Ave., Tampa, FL   33620

813-974-4133   www.usfeam.usf.edu
Open: 10-5 Mo-Fr, 1-4 Sa   *Closed:* Su, State & Leg/Hol!
&.   P: parking pass available for puchase from museum security guard $2.00 daily
Museum Shop   Group Tours
Permanent Collection: Cont: phot, gr

Located on the Tampa campus, the USF Contemporary Art Museum houses one of the largest selections of contemporary prints in the Southeast. *The museum is occasionally closed between exhibitions!

Center for the Arts, Inc.
3001 Riverside Park Dr., Vero Beach, FL   32963-1807

561-231-0707   www.verocfta.org
Open: 10-4:30 Mo-Sa; 10-8 Th; 1-4:30 Su   *Closed:* 12/25, 7/4, Thgv
Sugg/Contr.: Yes
&   P: Free   *Museum Shop*
Group Tours: ex 117   *Drop-In Tours:* 1:30-3:30 Sa, Su/ July-Oct; We-Su Nov-June   *Sculpture Garden*
Permanent Collection: Am/Art 20

Considered the premier visual arts facility on Florida's central coast, The Center, which offers national, international and regional art exhibitions throughout the year, maintains a leadership role in nurturing the cultural life of the region.   ⊄ "Transpassage T.L.S.," 20-ft. aluminum sculpture by Ralph F. Buckley, "American Eagle," Marshall M. Fredericks, 10-ft. bronze

ON EXHIBIT 2002

09/08/2001 to 01/05/2002   *Work from the Collection of the Center for the Arts*

01/19/2002 to 03/03/2002   *Florida Craftsmen Exhibition*

01/19/2002 to 03/03/2002   *Sculpture and Drawings from the Collection of the Center for the Arts*

01/26/2002 to 03/24/2002   *Japonisme: A Selection from the Zimmerli Art Museum*

03/09/2002 to 04/14/2002   *Robinson Murray*

04/06/2002 to 06/09/2002   *Will Barnett*

06/22/2002 to 08/25/2002   *Masterworks: Art from the Permanent Collection*

07/27/2002 to 09/15/2002   *Fran Hardy*

09/07/2002 to 11/10/2002   *Pere Daura: Master Painter*

09/21/2002 to 11/17/2002   *Vero Beach Art Club: Members Juried Exhibition*

11/23/2002 to 12/29/2002   *Rene Guerin*

11/23/2002 to 12/29/2002   *Vero Collects*

Norton Museum of Art
1451 S. Olive Ave., West Palm Beach, FL   33401

561-832-5196   www.norton.org
Open: 10-5 Tu-Sa, 1-5 Su   *Closed:* Mo, 1/1, Mem/Day, 7/4, Thgv, 12/25
Adm: *Adult:* $6.00   *Children:* Free 12 & under   *Students:* $2.00 (13-21)
&   P: Free   *Museum Shop*   ¶: Open Seasonally
Group Tours   *Drop-In Tours:* 12:30-1:30 weekdays, 2-3pm daily   *Sculpture Garden*
Permanent Collection: Am; Ch; Cont; Eur; Ren; Baroque; Phot

Started in 1940 with a core collection of French Impressionist and modern masterpieces, as well as fine works of American painting, the newly-renovated and expanded Norton's holdings also include major pieces of contemporary sculpture, and a noteworthy collection of Asian art. It is no onder that the Norton enjoys the reputation of being one of the finest small museums in the United States. *An admission fee may be charged for special exhibitions.   ⊄ Paul Manship's frieze across the main facade of the museum flanked by his sculptures of Diana and Actaeon

ON EXHIBIT 2002

11/17/2001 to 01/20/2002   *American Impressionism: Treasures from the Smithsonian American Art Museum*
A survey of a key moment in the history of art. Included are works by Cassatt, Whistler, Hassam, Robinson, and Chase.   *Catalog   Will Travel*

02/09/2002 to 04/21/2002   *Monks and Merchants: Silk Road Treasures from Northwest China, Gansu, and Ningxia, 4th–7th Century*
Recently excavated works, many never shown outside of China, demonstrating the international and multi-cultural aspects of China in this period   *Catalog   Will Travel*

02/16/2002 to 04/14/2002   *Milton Avery: The Late Paintings*
Avery pushed representation to the border of abstraction   *Catalog   Will Travel*

02/25/2002 to 07/08/2002   *A Thousand Hounds*
Man's relationship with dogs over 150 years of photography is studied here. Included are Nadar, Alget, Curtis, Muybridge, Riis, Hine, Steichen, Eakins, Stieglitz, Modotti, Lange, and Wegman.

WINTER PARK

Charles Hosmer Morse Museum of American Art
445 North Park Avenue, Winter Park, FL   32789

407-645-5311   www.morsemuseum.org
Open: 9:30-4 Tu-Sa, 1-4 Su   *Closed:* Mo, 1/1, Mem/Day, Lab/Day, Thgv, 12/25
Free Day: Open House Easter weekend, 7/4, Christmas Eve, 4-8pm Fr Sept.-May   *Adm: Adult:* $3.00
Children: Free under 12   *Students:* $1.00
& P   *Museum Shop   Group Tours   Drop-In Tours:* available during regular hours   *Theater*
Permanent Collection: Tiffany Glass; Am: ptgs (19 and early 20); Am: art pottery 19-20

Late 19th and early 20th century works of Louis Comfort Tiffany glass were rescued in 1957 from the ruins of Laurelton Hall, Tiffany's Long Island home, by Hugh and Jeannette McKean. These form the basis of the collection at this most unique little-known gem of a museum which has recently moved into new and larger quarters. Along with the Tiffany collection, the Museum houses a major collection of American art pottery, superb works by late 19th and early 20th century artists, including Martin Johnson Heade, Robert Henri, Maxfield Parrish, George Innis, and others.   ❡ Tiffany chapel for the 1893 Chicago World's Columbian Exposition, opened in April 1999; the "Electrolier," elaborate 10'-high chandelier, centerpiece of the Chapel; the Baptismal Font, also from the Chapel, which paved the way for Tiffany's leaded glass lamps; 2 marble, concrete, and Favrile glass columns designed 100 years ago by Tiffany for his Long Island Mansion.

Cornell Fine Arts Museum
Affiliated Institution: Rollins College
1000 Holt Ave., Winter Park, FL   32789-4499

407-646-2526   www.rollins.edu/cfam
Open: 10-5 Tu-Fr; 1-5 Sa, Su   *Closed:* Mo, 1/1, Thgv, 7/4, Lab/Day, 12/25
Vol/Contr.: Yes
& P: parking in adjacent lot
❘❘: Café Cornell nearby in Social Science Bldg   *Group Tours:* 407-646-1536
Historic Building: Case Bldg built in 1941 in continuous use as an art museum   *Theater*
Permanent Collection: Eur: ptgs, Ren-20; Sculp; Dec/Art; Am: ptgs, sculp 19-20; Phot; Sp: Ren/sculp, pr Eur & Am, dr; watch key coll

Considered one of the most outstanding museums in Florida, the Cornell, located on the campus of Rollins College, houses fine examples in many areas of art including American 19th-century landscape painting, French portraiture, works of Renaissance and Baroque masters, and contemporary prints.   ❡ Paintings from the Kress Collection; Cosimo Roselli, etc. "Christ with the Symbols of the Passion," by Lavinia Fontana, 1581

ON EXHIBIT 2002

01/04/2002 to 02/17/2002   *Paintings from the Permanent Collection by National Academicians*

01/04/2002 to 02/17/2002   *Photographs by Cindy Sherman*

03/01/2002 to 04/21/2002   *An American Collection: Paintings from the National Academy of Design*

June 2002 to September 2002   *American Art from the Collection*

September 2002 to October 2002   *Florida Artists*

November 2002 to January 2003   *Julia Margaret Cameron's Photographs*

GEORGIA

ALBANY

Albany Museum of Art
311 Meadowlark Dr., Albany, GA   31707

912-439-8400   www.albanymuseum.com
Open: 10-5 Tu-Fr, till 9pm Th; 12-5 Sa, Su   *Closed:* Mo, Leg/Hol!
Free Day: 5-9 Th, Su   *Sugg/Contr.:* Yes   *Adult:* $2.00   *Children:* $1.00
& P   *Museum Shop   Group Tours   Drop-In Tours*
Permanent Collection: Am: all media 19- 20; Eur: all media 19-20; Af: 19-20

The Albany Museum of Art is a landmark in the southwestern Georgia cultural landscape. The Museum houses one of the largest collections of Sub-Saharan African art in the southeast. The American and European Art collection include paintings by Edward Henry Potthast and Joseph Henry Sharp and 160 European drawings from the 18th and 17th centuries. A new children's wing houses AMAzing Space, a hands-on participatory gallery.   ❴ A 1,500-piece collection of African art that includes works from 18 different cultures, and a hands-on gallery for children

ON EXHIBIT 2002

01/14/2002 to 03/10/2002   *Upstream: Fly Fishing in the American West*

02/01/2002 to 03/07/2002   *The Peggy Slappey Day Collection: Contemporary Work from Africa*

03/22/2002 to 05/19/2002   *Beverly Buchanan*

08/09/2002 to 10/27/2002   *John Saurer*

ATHENS

Georgia Museum of Art
Affiliated Institution: The University of Georgia
90 Carlton St., Athens, GA   30602-1719

706-542-4662   www.uga.edu/gamuseum
Open: 10-5 Tu, Th, Fr, & Sa, 10-9 We, 1-5 Su   *Closed:* Mo, Leg/Hol!
Sugg/Contr.: $1.00
& P   *Museum Shop*   ❙❙: On Display Cafe open 10-2:30 Mo-Fr; Figgies Cafe 8:30-4, Mo-Fr
Group Tours: 706-542-1318   *Drop-In Tours:* by appt.
Permanent Collection: Am: sculp, gr; Eur: gr; Jap: gr; It/Ren: ptgs (Kress Collection); Am: ptgs 19-20

The Georgia Museum of Art, which moved to a new facility on Carlton St., on the east campus of the University of Georgia in September of '96, has grown from its modest beginnings, in 1948, of a 100 piece collection donated by Alfred Holbrook, to more than 7,000 works now included in its permanent holdings.   ❴ Paintings from the permanent collection on view continually in the C.L. Morehead Jr. Wing.

ON EXHIBIT 2002

12/18/2001 to 02/03/2002   *Maps and Arts of Historic Georgia*
Historical maps with a select grouping of decorative arts

01/16/2002 to 03/17/2002   *Muirhead Bone*
Glasgow printmaker as an etcher and drypoint engraver of architectural subjects

02/08/2002 to 03/17/2002   *The Arts and Crafts Movement in North Georgia*
The impact of the Arts and Crats movement on educational institutions in North Georgia in the beginning of the 20th century

02/16/2002 to 04/14/2002   *Landscapes of Retrospection: The Magoon Collection of British Drawings and Prints 1739–1854*
Landscapes from Oxford to London and the grandeur of Canterbury Cathedral to a dog kennel
Will Travel

04/28/2002 to 07/08/2002   *From Fauvism to Impressionism: Albert Marquet from the Pompidou*
Oil paintings, watercolors, and drawings from portraits to landscapes to figure studies
Catalog   Will Travel

05/25/2002 to 07/21/2002   *Lucy May Stanton*
Portaits, both miniature and full-scale, evoking character, expression, and mood especially in African Americans

07/20/2002 to 09/29/2002   *Romantics and Revolutionaries: Regency Portraits from the National Portrait Gallery, London*
Fifty remarkable paintings

mid-September 2002 to mid-December 2002   *Earl McCutchen*
Glass work by Earl McCutchen who created a technique to trap bubbles in glass for a surreal appearance

10/12/2002 to 01/05/2003   *Sacred Treasures: Early Italian Paintings from Southern Collections*
Paintings on panel from 1285–1510 illustrating religious themes in Tuscan art

10/12/2002 to 12/08/2002   *Sienese Drawings*
Works from the 1400s–1700s in public and private collections in Italy, many unpublished
Catalog

ATLANTA

Atlanta International Museum at Peachtree Center
285 Peachtree Center Avenue, Atlanta, GA   30303

404-688-2467
Open: 11-5 Tu-Sa   *Closed:* Su, Mo, Leg/Hol!
Free Day: 1-5 We   *Adm:*   *Adult:* $3.00   *Children:* $3.00   *Students:* $3.00   *Seniors:* $3.00
&   P: pay in Baker Street Garage   *Museum Shop*   ⅋: In Marriott Hotel   *Group Tours*
Permanent Collection: International Focus of Art and Design

The Atlanta International Museum celebrates cultural diversity and minority pride.

Hammonds House Galleries and Resource Center of African American Art
503 Peeples St., Atlanta, GA   31310-1815

404-752-8730   hammondshouse.org
Open: 10-6 Tu-Fr; 1-5 Sa, Su   *Closed:* Mo, Leg/Hol!
Adm: *Adult:* $2.00   *Children:* $1.00   *Students:* $1.00   *Seniors:* $1.00
&: wheelchair access from Oak St.   P: Free   *Museum Shop   Group Tours   Drop-In Tours:* Upon request
Historic Building: 1872 East Lake Victorian House restored in 1984 by Dr. Otis T. Hammonds
Permanent Collection: Af/Am: mid 19-20; Haitian: ptgs; Af: sculp

As the only fine art museum in the Southeast dedicated to the promotion of art by peoples of African descent, Hammonds House features changing exhibitions of nationally known African-American artists. Works by Romare Bearden, Sam Gilliam, Benny Andrews, James Van Der Zee, and others, are included in the 425-piece collection. ⊄ Romare Bearden Collection of post 60s serigraphs; Collection of Premier Contemporary Haitian Artists

High Museum of Art
1280 Peachtree St., N.E., Atlanta, GA   30309

404-733-HIGH   www.high.org
Open: 10-5 Tu-Fr, 10-5 Sa; 12-5 Su   *Closed:* Mo, 1/1, Thgv, 12/25, Mem/Day, Lab/Day
Adm: *Adult:* $8.00   *Children:* $4.00 6-17; Free under 6   *Students:* $6.00   *Seniors:* $6.00
&   P: Parking on deck of Woodruff Art Center Building on the side of the museum and neighborhood lots; some limited street parking   *Museum Shop*   ¶: Mo 9-3; Tu-Fr 9-5, weekends 10-5
Group Tours: 404-733-4550   *Drop-In Tours:* ! by appt
Historic Building: Building designed by Richard Meier, 1983
Permanent Collection: Am: dec/art 18-20; Eur: cer 18; Am: ptgs, sculp 19; Eur: ptgs, sculp, cer, gr, Ren 20; Phot 19-20; Am: cont (since 1970); self taught and folk

The beauty of the building, designed in 1985 by architect Richard Meier, is a perfect foil for the outstanding collection of art within the walls of the High Museum of Art itself. Part of the Robert W. Woodruff Art Center, this museum is a "must see" for every art lover who visits Atlanta. *Admission, hours and Cafe hours vary with timed and dated tickets. ⊄ The Virginia Carroll Crawford Collection of American Decorative Arts; The Frances and Emory Cocke Collection of English Ceramics: T. Marshall Hahn collection of Folk Art

ON EXHIBIT 2002

05/12/2001 to 01/06/2002   Downtown *New Treasures, Old Favorites: Self Taught Art at the High*
A companion exhibition to the "Let it Shine" featuring the growing folk art collection

09/22/2001 to 01/26/2002   Downtown *Pictures Tell the Story: Ernest C. Withers*
Withers could be called the original photographer of the Civil Rights Movement.   *Catalog*

02/09/2002 to 05/05/2002   *After the Scream: The Late Paintings of Edvard Munch*

02/16/2002 to 04/13/2002   *Contemporary Folk Art from the Smithsonian American Art Museum*

04/27/2002 to 08/03/2002   *ABCD: A Collection of Art Brut*

06/08/2002 to 09/01/2002   *American Impressionism: Treasures from the Smithsonian American Art Museum*   *Will Travel*

06/15/2002 to 09/08/2002   *Over the Line: The Art and Life of Jacob Lawrence*
For over 60 years Lawrence has depicted the social concerns of the 20th century in the lives and histories of African American.   *Will Travel*

High Museum of Folk Art & Photography Galleries at Georgia-Pacific Center
133 Peachtree Street, Atlanta, GA   30303

404-577-6940   www.high.org
Open: 10-5 Mo-Sa   *Closed:* Su, Leg/Hol!
&   P: Paid parking lot in the center itself with a bridge from the parking deck to the lobby; other paid parking lots nearby   *Museum Shop*
Group Tours: 404-733-4550   *Drop-In Tours:* call 404-733-4468   *Theater*
Permanent Collection: Occasional exhibits along with traveling exhibitions are drawn from permanent collection.

Folk art and photography are the main focus in the 4,500-square foot exhibition space of this Atlanta facility formally called The High Museum of Art at Georgia-Pacific Center.

Michael C. Carlos Museum
Affiliated Institution: Emory University
571 South Kilgo St., Atlanta, GA   30322

404-727-4282   www.cc.emory.edu/CARLOS
Open: 10-5 Mo-Sa, 12-5 Su   *Closed:* 1/1, Thgv, 12/25, Legal Hols
Sugg/Contr.: Yes   *Adm:*   *Adult:* $5.00
  P: Visitor parking for a small fee at the Boisfeuillet Jones Building; Fishburne Parking Deck; free parking on campus except in restricted areas. Handicapped parking Plaza level entrance on So. Kilgo St.
Museum Shop   ¶: Caffé Antico   *Group Tours:* 404-727-0519   *Drop-In Tours:* 2:30 Sa, Su   *Historic Building*
Permanent Collection: An/Egt; An/Grk; An/R; P/Col; As; Af; Oc; Work on Paper 14-20

Founded on the campus of Emory University in 1919 (making it the oldest art museum in Atlanta), this distinguished institution changed its name in 1991 to the Michael C. Carlos Museum in honor of its long time benefactor. Its dramatic 35,000-square foot building, opened in the spring of 1993, is a masterful addition to the original Beaux-Arts edifice. The museum recently acquired one of the largest (1,000 pieces) collections of Sub-Saharan African art in America.   ℭ Carlos Collection of Ancient Greek Art; Thibadeau Collection of Pre-Columbian Art; recent acquisition of rare 4th-century Volute-Krater by the Underworld painter of Apulia

ON EXHIBIT 2002

04/22/2001 to 01/06/2002   *The Collector's Eye: Masterpieces of Egyptian Art from the Thalassic Collection, Ltd*
This collection, one of the finest in the world is having it's first exhibition here. The 175 pieces include monumental statues of pharoahs and queens to exquisitely crafted amulets and jewels. From the Predynastic Period (about 3500 B.C.) to the time of Cleopatra are included.

10/06/2001 to 01/28/2002   *New Acquisitions of Old Masters: Dürer to Delacroix*
Recent additions including "Pilate Washing His Hands" from Dürer's "Engraved Passion," a view of the Colosseum in Rome by Piranese, and drawings by Boucher and Delacroix.

10/06/2001 to Ongoing   *Arts of India and the Himalayas: Recent Acquisitions*
Rotations focusing on Asia's vast geography. Works from Mathura, 11th C. high relief from Vishnu, 10th-century bronze Jain altar, a painted Tibetan tangka, and sculptures from Nepal and Tibet.

02/23/2002 to 06/16/2002   *Wrapped in Pride: Ghanian Kente and African American Identity*
Exhibition of Asante strip-woven cloth, or kente, the most popular and best known of all African textiles, linked to royalty in Africa and to black racial pride in the U.S. Focuses on the history and use of kente in Africa as well as contemporary kente and its manifestations.
Catalog   Will Travel

10/26/2002 to 01/19/2003   *Six Highlight Objects from 'Treasures from the Royal Tomb of Ur'*
More than 200 finely crafted objects in stone, metal, wood, characterize this exhibition from the excavation at Ur, a 3rd millenium Sumerium city in Mesopotamia.   *Catalog   Will Travel*

Oglethorpe University Museum
Affiliated Institution: Ogelthorpe University
4484 Peachtree Road, NE, Atlanta, GA   30319

404-364-8555   www.museum.oglethorpe.edu
Open: 12-5 Tu-Su   *Closed:* Mo, University Holidays
  P: Free   *Museum Shop*
Group Tours   Drop-In Tours: 2 pm Su during exhibitions and special appointments 2 weeks in advance
Historic Building
Permanent Collection: Realistic fig; historical, metaphysical, and international art

Established in 1993, this museum, dedicated to showing realistic art, has already instituted many "firsts" for this area including the opening of many exhibitions with a free public lecture, the creation of an artist-in-residence program, and a regular series of chamber music concerts. In addition, the museum is devoted to creating and sponsoring its own series of original and innovative special exhibitions instead of relying on traveling exhibitions from other sources. ℂ 14th-century Kamakura Buddha from Japan

ON EXHIBIT 2002

02/02/2002 to Spring 2002   *Work from the Permanent Collection*

04/07/2002 to 05/10/2002   *Changing Rhythms: Work by Leland Bell, 1950s–1991*   Catalog Will Travel

AUGUSTA

Morris Museum of Art
One 10th Street, Augusta, GA   30901-1134

706-724-7501   www.csra.net/mormuse
Open: 10-5:30 Tu-Sa, 12:30-5:30 Su   *Closed:* Mo, 1/1, Thgv, 12/25
Adm: Adult: $2.00   *Children:* Free under 12   *Students:* $1.00   *Seniors:* $1.00
& P: Free marked spaces in West Lot; paid parking in city lot at adjacent hotel.
Museum Shop   Group Tours
Permanent Collection: Reg: portraiture (antebellum to cont), st/lf, Impr, cont; Af/Am

Rich Southern architecture and decorative appointments installed in a contemporary office building present a delightful surprise to the first time visitor. Included in this setting are masterworks from antebellum portraiture to vivid contemporary creations that represent a broad-based survey of 250 years of panting in the South.   ℂ The Southern Landscape Gallery

COLUMBUS

Columbus Museum
1251 Wynnton Rd., Columbus, GA   31906

706-649-0713   www.columbusmuseum.com
Open: 10-5 Tu-Sa; 1-5 Su; 10-8 3rd Th   *Closed:* Mo, Leg/Hol!
Sugg/Contr.: Yes
& P   *Museum Shop* ||: The Place for Taste Café Tu-Fr 11:30am-2pm   *Group Tours   Drop-In Tours*
Permanent Collection: Ptgs; Sculp; Gr 19-20; Dec/Art; Reg; Folk

The Columbus Museum is unique in the Southeast for its dual presentation of American art and regional history. The Museum features changing art exhibitions and two permanent galleries, Chattahoochee Legacy (the history of the Chattahoochee Valley) and Transformations (a hands-on children's discovery gallery).   ℂ "Fergus, Boy in Blue" by Robert Henri; A hands-on discovery gallery for children.

ON EXHIBIT 2002

09/23/2001 to 01/06/2002   *An American Century of Photography: from Dry Plate to Digital—The Hallmark Photographic Collection*

02/03/2002   *Magnificent, Marvelous, Martele: American Art Nouveau Silver from the Collection of Robert and Julie Shelton*
A first comprehensive look at the silver produced by the Gorham Company at the beginning of the 20th century   Catalog   Will Travel

02/24/2002 to 05/19/2002   *Robert Bermelin (working title)*
Retrospective exhibition of the well-known figurative painter

05/19/2002 to 07/28/2002   *Work on Paper from the Permanent Collection*
Photographs, drawings, and prints from the fine works in the collection including Grossman, Vallerio, and Roszak

06/09/2002 to 08/04/2002   *Regional Invitational (working title)*
A showcase of regional art each summer

08/25/2002 to 10/20/2002   *Myth, Memory, and Imagination: Universal Themes in the Life and Culture of the South*
From the private collection of Julia Norell photography, painting, sculpture, and folk art illuminate the themes of small town and family life, ties to the land, religious rituals, and racial relationships.   *Catalog   Will Travel*

S A V A N N A H

Telfair Museum of Art
121 Barnard St., Savannah, GA   31401

912-232-1177
Open: 10-5 Tu-Sa, 1-5 Su   *Closed:* Mo, Leg/Hol!
Free Day: Su   *Adm: Adult:* $6.00   *Children:* $1.00 (6-12)   *Students:* $2.00   *Seniors:* $5.00
&.; Use President St. entrance   P: Metered street parking and 7 visitor spots   *Museum Shop*
Group Tours   Drop-In Tours: 2 daily
Historic Building: 1819 Regency Mansion designed by William Jay (National Historic Landmark)
Permanent Collection: Am: Impr & Ashcan ptgs; Am: dec/art; Brit: dec/art; Fr: dec/art

Named for its founding family, and housed in a Regency mansion designed in 1818 by architect William Jay, this museum features traveling exhibitions from all over the world. The Telfair, which is the oldest public art museum in the Southeast, also has major works by many of the artists who have contributed so brilliantly to the history of American art. The Telfair will break ground in late 1999 for a new building on Telfair Square.   ℂ American Impressionist collection Original Duncan Phyfe furniture; casts of the Elgin Marbles

HAWAII

H O N O L U L U

Contemporary Museum
2411 Makiki Heights Drive, Honolulu, HI   96822

808-526-1322 ; info 808-526-0232   www.tcmhi.org
Open: 10-4 Tu-Sa, Noon-4 Su   *Closed:* Mo, Leg/Hol!
Free Day: 3rd Th of month   *Adm: Adult:* $5.00   *Children:* Free under 12   *Students:* $3.00   *Seniors:* $3.00
&   P: Free but very limited parking   *Museum Shop*   ⑪: Cafe
Group Tours: 808-626-1322, ext 30   *Drop-In Tours:* 1:30 Tu-Su   *Historic Building:* The Spalding Estate
Sculpture Garden   Theater
Permanent Collection: Am: cont; Reg

Terraced gardens with stone benches overlooking exquisite vistas compliment this museum's structure which is situated in a perfect hillside setting. Inside are modernized galleries in which the permanent collection of art since 1940 is displayed. *The museum's other gallery location where exhibitions are presented is: The Contemporary Museum at First Hawaiian Center, 999 Bishop St., Honolulu, HI 96813 (open 8:30-3 Mo-Th, 8:30-6 Fr), which mainly features works by artists of Hawaii.   ℂ David Hockney's permanent environmental installation "L'Enfant et les Sortileges" built for a Ravel opera stage set.

ON EXHIBIT 2002

12/21/2001 to 04/03/2002   *Timothy Ojile, Ann Bush and Thomas Woodruff*
At the Contemporary Museum, First Hawaiian Center, 999 Bishop Street

03/29/2002 to 06/02/2002   *Tadashi Sato: A Retrospective Exhibition*

08/30/2002 to 11/03/2002   *Big Idea: The Maquettes of Robert Arneson*

11/15/2002 to 01/05/2003   *Jane Hammond: The John Ashbury Collaboration*

Honolulu Academy of Arts
900 S. Beretania St., Honolulu, HI   96814-1495

808-532-8700   www.honoluluacademy.org
Open: 10-4:30 Tu-Sa, 1-5 Su   *Closed:* Mo, Leg/Hol!
Free Day: 1st WeVol/Contr.: Yes   *Adm:*   Adult: $7.00   *Children:* Free under 12   *Students:* $4.00
Seniors: $4.00
&: Ward Ave. gate (call 532-8759 to reserve handicap)   P: Lot parking at the Academy Art Center for
$1.00 with validation; some metered street parking also available   *Museum Shop*
¶: 11:30-2:00 Tu-Sa (808-532-8734)   *Group Tours:* 808-532-3876   *Drop-In Tours:* 11:00 Tu-Sa; 1:15 Su
Historic Building: 1927 Building designed By Bertram G. Goodhue Assoc.   *Sculpture Garden*
Permanent Collection: Or: all media; Am: all media; Eur: all media; Hawaiiana Collection

Thirty-two galleries grouped around a series of garden courts form the basis of Hawaii's only general art museum. This internationally respected institution, 70 years old in '97, features extensive notable collections that span the history of art and come from nearly every corner of the world. *Exhibitions may be seen in the main museum and in the Museum's Academy Art Center, 1111 Victoria St. (808-532-8741).   ℂ Hawaiiana collection: James A. Michener collection of Japanese ukiyo-e; Korean celadons, Chinese furniture; ceramics and paintings; Kress Collection of Italian Renaissance Paintings

ON EXHIBIT 2002

11/16/2001 to 01/06/2002   *Charles Bartlets*

01/17/2002 to 03/17/2002   *American Watercolors and Drawings from the Academy's Collections*

01/31/2002 to 03/31/2002   *Taisho Chic: Japanese Romanticism and Art Deco (1900–1950)*
Images of old and new is a hallmark of the work created in the Taisho Period and of the changing role of women. Also illustrated is the influence of the West.

03/21/2002 to 05/19/2002   *Snowden Hodges: The Labors of Hercules*
Well-known for paintings of vegetables, fruit, and flowers, he has here done a series of oversize figure drawings depicting the twelve labors of Hercules. He renders him engaged in feats of great physical strength and epic nature.

04/08/2002 to ?   *75th Anniversary of the Opening of the Honolulu Academy of Arts*
A celebration of the place where people of Hawaii, especially children could learn about their cultural lagacy.   *Catalog*

07/18/2002 to 08/25/2002   *Ansel Adams in Hawaii*
Adams was a conservationist and nature lover. He created stunning, but little known photographs of Hawaii. Included are prints from the Museum's collection and private collections showing the urban environment, resources, diverse population at mid-20th century. *Catalog*

07/18/2002 to 08/25/2002   *Artists of Hawai'i 2002*
The oldest national juried exhibition in the state.

08/01/2002 to 09/15/2002   *Treasures of the Shingon Sect, 100th Anniversary Exhibition*
Objects from the Mt. Koya Temple Complex, headquarters of the Shingon Sect of esoteric Buddhism

09/05/2002 to 10/27/2002   *Gauguin's Zombie: An Installation by Debra Drexler*
An installation of seven large-scale paintings, a wood carving and fictional writing which relates to the paintings such as emails, faxes, press releases, journal entries, and artist statements. The work examines such issues as relationships between male artists and female models. Gauguin, the somnabulist, awakes to a world that is post-modern. Ms. Drexler finds Gauguin's treatment of women horrifying as is his depiction of people of Polynesia.

09/19/2002 to 11/10/2002   *Doris Duke's Jewelry and Islamic Art*
Spectacular jewelry and Islamic art from this private collection

12/01/2002 to 01/01/2003   *Kamama'aina Christmas*

12/05/2002 to 02/16/2003   *From Monet to Van Gogh: Impressionist and Post-Impressionist Masterpieces from Japan*
Masterpieces from Japanese Collections

IDAHO

BOISE

Boise Art Museum
670 S. Julia Davis Dr., Boise, ID   83702

208-345-8330   www.boiseartrmuseum.org
Open: 10-5 Tu-Sa; 12-5 Su; Open 10-5 Mo June thru Aug   *Closed:* Leg/Hol!
Free Day: 1st Th of month   *Adm:*   *Adult:* $4.00   *Children:* $1.00 (grades 1-12)   *Students:* $2.00
Seniors: $2.00
&   P: Free   *Museum Shop   Group Tours   Drop-In Tours:* 12:15 Tu; 3pm 1st Su
Historic Building: Original structure built by WPA in 1937   *Sculpture Garden*
Permanent Collection: Reg; Gr; Or; Am

The Boise Art Museum, in its parkland setting, is the only art museum in the state of Idaho. It's mission is to champion the visual azts through exhibitions, collections, and educational programs ❡ "Art in the Park," held every Sept, is one of the largest art and crafts festivals in the region.

ON EXHIBIT 2002

11/17/2001 to 02/16/2003   *MLN Asian Exhibit*
Museum Loan Network which facilitates the sharing of art and objects of cultural heritage presents important works of Chinese and Japanese art. The exhibition will focus on themes of ritual and lifestyle.

11/24/2001 to 02/24/2002   *NW Perspectives: Deborah Hardee*
Portraits that emulate the style and appearance of portraits from the turn of the century using tintype and daguerreotype

12/08/2001 to 03/03/2002   *NW Perspectives: Randy Hayes*
Photography and paintings are combined to produce provocative, multiple-layered images.

12/08/2001 to 05/05/2002   *Viola Frey*
Large-scale colorful bright expressionistic ceramic sculpture figures including 4 colossal works

12/14/2001 to 02/17/2002   *Jack Dollhausen*
Thirty electronic sculptures created from 1970 to the present. These convert electricity to ornate statements of musical and interactive complexity.   *Will Travel*

03/02/2002 to 05/09/2002   *True Grit: Seven Female Visionaries before Feminism*
Painting, sculpture, and drawing between 1951 and 1975 which has made an outstanding contribution to the history of art. Included are Lee Bontecou, Louise Bourgeois, Clair Falkenstein, Nancy Grossman, Louise Nevelson, and Nancy Spero.

06/01/2002 to 08/04/2002 *Hung Liu*
Large scale, historically based, photo-derived images exploring human rights and historical revisionism during the Cultural Revolution in China

07/01/2002 to 10/13/2002 *Patrick Dougherty*
Dougherty weaves sticks, branches, and twigs into mammoth environmental sculptures as do birds, beavers, and other nest builders. He uses small clippers as tools and twists sticks to support the final structure.

08/17/2002 to 10/13/2002 *Pop Art*
Artists radically redefined the subject matter for visual arts. Advertising, television, and mass media created "fine" art. Included are Dine, Indiana, Kienholz, Lichtenstein, Rosenquist, and Warhol.

ILLINOIS

CARBONDALE

University Museum

Affiliated Institution: Southern Illinois University at Carbondale
Carbondale, IL 62901-4508

618-453-5388 www.museum@siu.edu
Open: 9-3 Tu-Sa, 1:30-4:30 Su *Closed:* Mo, Acad; Leg/Hol!
♿ P: Metered lot just East of the Student Center (next to the football stadium) *Museum Shop*
Group Tours *Drop-In Tours:* Upon request if available *Sculpture Garden*
Permanent Collection: Am: ptgs, drgs, gr; Eur: ptgs, drgs, gr, 13-20; Phot 20; Sculp 20; Cer; Oc; Dec/Art

Continually rotating exhibitions feature the fine and decorative arts as well as those based on science related themes of anthropology, geology, natural history, and archaeology. Also history exhibits. ◖ In the sculpture garden, two works by Ernest Trova, "AV-A-7 and AV-YELLOW LOZENGER," and a sculpture entitled "Starwalk" by Richard Hunt. New: Formal Japanese Garden

ON EXHIBIT 2002

01/19/2002 to 03/08/2002 *Combined Faculty Exhibit in Art and Design, Cinema and Photography, Theater and Interior Design*

03/30/2002 to 07/21/2002 *Delyte Morris Furniture Collection: Modern Furniture Post 1950*

08/14/2002 to 10/11/2002 *Traditional African Art and Modern Quilts from the Edna and Reginald Petty Collection*

CHAMPAIGN

Krannert Art Museum

Affiliated Institution: University of Illinois
500 E. Peabody Dr., Champaign, IL 61820

217-333-1861 http://www.art.uiuc.edu/kam/
Open: 10-5 Tu-Fr, till 8pm We (Sept-May), 10-5 Sa, 2-5 Su *Closed:* Leg/Hol!
Vol/Contr.: Yes *Sugg/Contr.:* $3.00
♿: Ramps, elevators P: On-street metered parking *Museum Shop* ¥: Cafe/bookstore
Group Tours *Drop-In Tours:* !
Permanent Collection: P/Col; Am: ptgs; Dec/Art; Or; Gr; Phot; Eur: ptgs; As; Af; P/Col; Ant

Located on the campus of the University of Illinois, Krannert Art Museum is the second largest public art museum in the state. Among its 8,000 works ranging in date from the 4th millennium B.C. to the present are represented cultures of Europe, Asia, Africa and the Americas.

ON EXHIBIT 2002

09/21/2001 to 01/06/2002   *Lipchitz and the Avant-Garde: From Paris to New York*

11/27/2001 to 01/06/2002   *Featured Work VI, David Wojnarowicz: The Elements, Fire and Water,*
Earth and Wind

04/25/2002 to 08/04/2002   *Louise Bourgeois: The Early Work*

04/25/2002 to 08/04/2002   *1940 to 1950: The Breakthrough of American Painting*

08/30/2002 to 11/03/2002   *The Dream of the Audience: Theresa Hak Kyung Cha*

09/06/2002 to 11/03/2002   *Drawings of Choice from a New York Collection*

CHICAGO

Art Institute of Chicago
111 So. Michigan Ave., Chicago, IL   60603-6110

312-443-3600   www.artic.edu
Open: 10:30-4:30 Mo & We-Fr; 10:30-8 Tu; 10-5 Sa & Su   *Closed:* 12/25, Thgv
Free Day: Tu   *Sugg/Contr.:* Y   *Adm:*   *Adult:* $10.00   *Children:* $6.00   *Students:* $6.00   *Seniors:* $6.00
& P: Limited metered street parking; several paid parking lots nearby   *Museum Shop*
¶: Cafeteria & The Restaurant on the Park   *Group Tours:* 312-443-3933   *Drop-In Tours*
Historic Building   Sculpture Garden   Theater
Permanent Collection: Am: all media; Eur: all media; Ch; Korean; Jap; Ind; Eur: Med; Af; Phot;
architecture + textiles; South American

Spend "Sunday in the park with George" while standing before Seurat's "Sunday Afternoon on the Island of La Grande Jatte," or any of the other magnificent examples of the school of French Impressionism, just one of the many superb collections housed in this world-class museum. Renowned for its collection of post-World War II art, the museum also features the Galleries of Contemporary Art, featuring 50 of the strongest works of American and European art (1950s–1980). ¶ "American Gothic" by Grant Wood; "Paris Street; Rainy Day" by Gustave Caillebotte

ON EXHIBIT 2002

09/22/2001 to 01/13/2002   *Van Gogh and Gauguin: The Studio of the South*
The artists hoped to bring excitement to French art with their "Studio of the South." The Sunflower pictures will be examined for their role and significance   *Catalog   Book*

11/10/2001 to 04/21/2002   *Sight-Set-Sequence: Photographs from the Permanent Collection*
How artists and photographers execute individual photographs to be used in a single work

11/17/2001 to 04/28/2002   *The Sidewalk Never Ends: Street Photography*
Street photography is the essence of the medium. The development from the 19th century to the 1970s was explored in a previous exhibition called "Bystander: A History of Street Photography" in 1994. This now brings it up to date.

12/08/2001 to 07/28/2002   *Modern Trains and Splendid Stations: Architecture and Design for the 21st Century*
A comparison of designs around the world   *Catalog*

02/09/2002 to 06/01/2002   *Animals, Mortals, and Immortals in Indian Paintings*
In Indian art the rulers have been associated with animals to demonstrate their might and the extent of the empire.   *Catalog*

02/13/2002 to 05/27/2002   *The Nitty-Gritty of Weave Structure, Part 1*
The particular structures of weaves in textiles

02/23/2002 to 06/02/2002   *Ansel Adams at 100*
An appraisal of Adams as an artist and photographer   *Catalog   Will Travel   Book*

03/02/2002 to 05/12/2002 *Taken by Design: Photography from the Institute of Design, 1937–1971*
220 images by nationally and internationally known photographers and less known ones. A first look at the contributions the school has made.

06/15/2002 to 09/22/2002 *German Art and Its Revivals*
Mostly works on paper by Baselitz, Blechen, Runge, Polke, Kollwitz, and Meidner *Catalog*

06/22/2002 to 09/15/2002 *Gerhard Richter: 40 Years of Painting*
The first retrospective to introduce his works on canvas. It willl include subtly photo-based works, monochromatic abstractions, and heavily painted, highly colored works. *Catalog Will Travel*

07/03/2002 to 11/03/2002 *Fukasa and Furoshiki: A Gift of Splendid Japanese Gift Covers and Wrapping Cloths*
Beautiful textiles from the 18th century to the 20th

09/14/2002 to 12/08/2002 *Juan Munoz*
Figures in papier-mache, resin, and bronze situated in environments *Catalog Will Travel*

10/04/2002 to 02/15/2003 *African Artistry: Gifts from the Richard and Barbara Faletti Family Collection*
Yoruba from today's Nigeria and the Republic of Benin

11/09/2002 to 02/02/2003 *The Medici, Michelangelo, and the Art of the Late Renaissance Florence*
A detailed survey of porcelains, tapestries, costumes, paintings and sculpture. Many of the works have never traveled out of Florence.

11/23/2002 to 04/20/2003 *David Adler, Architect: The Elements of Style*
A first major retrospective of Adler's work designing urban areas

12/04/2002 to 04/06/2003 *Renaissance Velvets and Silks*
Patterns and designs as well as altar frontals and vestments

Arts Club of Chicago
201 East Ontario St., Chicago, IL   60611

312-787-3994
Open: 11-6 Mo-Fr; 11-4 Sa   *Closed:* Su
Theater

ON EXHIBIT 2002

01/24/2002 to 04/06/2002 *Alighiero Boetti*
Boetti was more involved in the social aspects of making art. He commissioned tapestries from Afganistan and Palistan weavers between 1971 and 1994. The pieces shown will give an idea of his multifaceted career. *Catalog*

04/25/2002 to 07/19/2002 *Richard Artschwager*
Incorporated in his art are painting and sculpture, abstraction and representation, as well as Pop, Minimalism, Photo Realism, and Conceptualism; yet his work remains unique. *Catalog*

Chicago Cultural Center
78 East Washington St., Chicago, IL   60602

312-744-6630   www.cityofchicago.org/tour/cultural/center
Open: 10-7 Mo-We, 10-9 Th, 10-6 Fr, 10-5 Sa, 11-5 Su   *Closed:* Leg/Hol
&: through the 77 E. Randolph St. entrance   P: Commercial facilities in area   *Museum Shop*
¶: Corner Bakery   *Group Tours:* 312-744-8032   *Drop-In Tours:* 1:15, We, Fr, Sa   *Historic Building*
Theater
Permanent Collection: Non-collecting institution

Located in the renovated 1897 historic landmark building originally built to serve as the city's central library, this vital cultural center, affectionately called the "People's Place," consists of eight exhibition spaces, two concert halls, two theaters, a cabaret performing arts space, and a dance studio. The facility, which serves as Chicago's architectural showplace for the lively and visual arts, features daily programs and exhibitions. There are architectural tours of the building at 1:15 We, Fr, Sa. ❡ The world's largest Tiffany stained-glass dome in Preston Bradley Hall on the third floor

ON EXHIBIT 2002

12/15/2001 to 02/10/2002   *Don't Forget the Lunches (Daily News): An Installation by Monica Bock*
Two rituals, packing children's lunches and reading the evening newspaper, consist of 418 lead-sheet bags embossed with school and day camp lunch menus.

01/12/2002 to 03/17/2002   *Ceramics National 2000*
An opportunity for emerging ceramacists and established clay artists from across the US including traditional vessels to abstract sculpture   *Catalog   Will Travel*

01/19/2002 to 03/31/2002   *Red Grooms: Graphic Work*
Forty years of printmaking including 110 wall pieces and 15 pedestal pieces from the private collection of Walter G. Knestich   *Catalog   Will Travel*

David and Alfred Smart Museum of Art
Affiliated Institution: The University of Chicago
5550 S. Greenwood Ave., Chicago, IL   60637

773-702-0200   http://smartmuseum.uchicago.edu
Open: 10-4 Tu-Fr; 12-6 Sa, Su; till 9pm Th   *Closed:* Mo, Leg/Hol!
& P: Free parking garage on the corner of 55th St. & Greenwood Ave. after 4:00 weekdays, and all day on weekends.   *Museum Shop*   ❙❙: Museum Café
Group Tours: 773-702-4540   *Drop-In Tours:* 1:30 Su during special exhibitions
Sculpture Garden   Theater
Permanent Collection: An/Grk: Vases (Tarbell Coll); Med/Sculp; O/M: ptgs, sculp (Kress Coll); OM: gr (Epstein Coll); Sculp:20

Among the holdings of the Smart Museum of Art are Medieval sculpture from the French Romanesque church of Cluny III, outstanding Old Master prints by Dürer, Rembrandt, and Delacroix from the Kress Collection, sculpture by such greats as Degas, Matisse, Moore, and Rodin, and furniture by Frank Lloyd Wright from the world famous Robie House.

ON EXHIBIT 2002

10/23/2001 to 04/28/2002   *A Well-Fashioned Image: Clothing and Costume in European Art, 1500–1800*
The exhibition investigates the symbolic role of dress and clothing as an image, an emblem, and a classification.   *Catalog*

01/24/2002 to 03/31/2002   *Mu Xin: A Tower within the Pagoda*
The work of Chinese contemporary artist Mu Xin revealing his responses to the changes within 20th century China. The exhibition features 33 landscape paintings and 66 pages of "Prison Notes" written while in solitary confinement from 1970–1973.   *Will Travel*

Martin D'Arcy Museum of Art
Affiliated Institution: The Loyola Univ. Museum of Medieval, Renaissance and Baroque Art
6525 N. Sheridan Rd., Chicago, IL   60626

773-508-2679   http://darcy.luc.edu
Open: 12-4 Tu-Sa during the school year; Summer hours 12-4 Tu-Th   *Closed:* Mo, Su, Acad!, Leg/Hol!
& P: $4.00 visitor parking on Loyola Campus
Group Tours: 773-508-2597   *Drop-In Tours:* by request only   *Theater*
Permanent Collection: Med & Ren & Baroque; ptgs, sculp, dec/art

Sometimes called the "Cloisters of the Midwest", The Martin D'Arcy Museum of Art is the only museum in the Chicago area focusing on Medieval, Renaissance, and Baroque art. Fine examples of Medieval, Renaissance, and Baroque ivories, liturgical vessels, textiles, sculpture, paintings, and secular decorative art of these periods are included in the collection. ❡ A pair of octagonal paintings on verona marble by Bassano; A German Renaissance Collectors Chest by Wenzel Jamitzer; A silver lapis lazuli & ebony tableau of the Flagellation of Christ that once belonged to Queen Christina of Sweden

Mexican Fine Arts Center Museum
1852 W. 19th St., Chicago, IL   60608-2706

312-738-1503   www.mfacmchicago.org
Open: 10-5 Tu-Su   *Closed:* Mo, Leg/Hol!
Free Day: Exhibitions free—Performance festivals are ticketed   *Vol/Contr.:* Yes
&   *Museum Shop   Group Tours:* ex 16
Permanent Collection: Mex: folk; Phot; Gr; Cont

Mexican art is the central focus of this museum, the first of its kind in the Midwest, and the largest in the nation. Founded in 1982, the center seeks to promote the works of local Mexican artists and acts as a cultural focus for the entire Mexican community residing in Chicago. A new expansion project is underway that will triple the size of the museum. ❡ Nation's largest Day of the Dead exhibit and 2 annual performing arts festivals.

ON EXHIBIT 2002

01/18/2002 to 05/26/2002   *Grand Maestro des Arte Popular*
The exhibition highlights the great masters of Mexican art to preserve their skills. It hopes to strengthen cultural identity.

09/28/2002 to 12/09/2002   *Dia de Muertos 2002 (working title)*
The Day of The Dead exhibit contains a wide range of expressions from Mexican communities for it's scope, size and uniqueness.

Museum of Contemporary Art
220 East Chicago Ave., Chicago, IL   60611-2604

312-280-2660   www.mcachicago.org
Open: We, Th, Fr, Sa, Su 10-5; Tu 10-8   *Closed:* Mo, 1/1, Thgv, 12/25
Free Day: Tu   *Adm: Adult:* $7.00   *Children:* Free 12 & under   *Students:* $4.50   *Seniors:* $4.50
&   P: On-street and pay lot parking available nearby   *Museum Shop*
¶: Puck's at the MCA: 11-8 Tu, Th, Fr; 11-5 We; 10-5 Sa, Su
Group Tours: 312-397-3898   *Drop In Tours:* several times daily!
Historic Building: Josef Paul Kleihues building opened July 1996   *Sculpture Garden*
Permanent Collection: Continually Changing Exhibitions of Cont Art

Some of the finest and most provocative cutting-edge art by both established and emerging talents may be seen in the building and sculpture garden, located on a prime 2-acre site with a view of Lake Michigan. Brilliantly designed, the building is the first American project for noted Berlin architect Josef Paul Kleihues. Among its many features is the restaurant on the second floor where visitors can enjoy a spectacular view of the sculpture garden and lakefront while dining on contemporary fusion cuisine. ❡ An entire room devoted to sculptures by Alexander Calder

ON EXHIBIT 2002

01/27/2001 to 09/2002   *Alexander Calder in Focus: Work from the Leonard and Ruth Horwich Family Loan*
Fifteen works from the 1920s to the 1960s spanning almost the entirety of Calder's career and demonstrating his extraordinary range.

10/20/2001 to 01/20/2002   *William Kentridge*
A survey of his animated films, drawings, and theater productions focusing on the complex and violent history of his native South Africa.

Museum of Contemporary Photography, Columbia College Chicago
600 South Michigan Ave., Chicago, IL   60605-1996

312-663-5554   www.mocp.org
Open: 10-5 Mo-We, Fr; 10-8 Th; 12-5 Sa   *Closed:* Su, Leg/Hol!
Vol/Contr.: Yes
&   P: Pay nearby   *Group Tours:* 312-344-7793   *Theater*
Permanent Collection: Cont/Phot

The basis of the permanent collection of this college museum facility is a stimulating and innovative forum for the collection, creation, and examination of photographically related images, objects, and ideas.

Oriental Institute Museum
Affiliated Institution: University of Chicago
1155 E. 58th St., Chicago, IL   60637-1569

773-702-8593   www-oi.uchicago.edu/01/MUS
Open: 10-4 Tu-Sa, 12-4 Su, till 8:30 We   *Closed:* Mo, 1/1, 7/4, Thgv, 12/25
Vol/Contr.: Yes
&.: Accessible by wheelchair from west side of building   P: On-street or coin-operated street level parking on Woodlawn Ave. between 58th & 59th Sts. (1/2 block east of the institute)   *Museum Shop*
Drop-In Tours: 1:30 Su   *Historic Building*
Permanent Collection: An: Mid/East

Hundreds of ancient objects are included in the impressive comprehensive collection of the Oriental Institute. Artifacts from the ancient Near East, dating from earliest times to the birth of Christ, provide the visitor with a detailed glimpse into the ritual ceremonies and daily lives of ancient civilized man.   (Ancient Assyrian 40-ton winged bull; 17'-tall statue of King Tut; Colossal Ancient Persian winged bulls

Polish Museum of America
984 North Milwaukee Ave., Chicago, IL   60622

773-384-3352   pncuofa.org/pmu
Open: 11-4 daily   *Closed:* Leg/Hol, Pulaski Day (last Mo in March), Good Friday, Easter, 12/24
Sugg/Contr.: Yes   *Adm:*   *Adult:* $3.00   *Children:* $1.00   *Students:* $2.00   *Seniors:* $2.00
&.: Wheelchairs available by reservation   P: Free parking with entrance from Augusta Blvd.
Museum Shop   Group Tours   Drop-In Tours   Theater
Permanent Collection: Eth: ptgs, sculp, drgs, gr

The promotion of Polish heritage is the primary goal of this museum founded in 1935. One of the oldest and largest ethnic museums in the U.S., their holdings range from the fine arts to costumes, jewelry, and a broad ranging scholarly library featuring resource information on all areas of Polish life and culture.   (Polonia stained glass by Mieczyslaw Jurgielewicz

Terra Museum of American Art
664 N. Michigan Ave., Chicago, IL   60611

312-664-3939   www.terramuseum.org
Open: 10-8 Tu, 10-6 We-Sa, 12-5 Su   *Closed:* 1/1, 7/4, Thgv, 12/25
Free Day: Tu & 1st Su   *Adm:*   *Adult:* $7.00   *Children:* Free under 14   *Students:* Free   *Seniors:* $3.50
&   *Museum Shop   Group Tours:* 312-654-2255   *Drop-In Tours:* 12 weekdays; 12 & 2 weekends
Historic Building

With over 800 plus examples of some of the finest American art ever created, the Terra, located in the heart of Chicago's "Magnificent Mile," reigns supreme as an important repository of a glorious artistic heritage.   ("Gallery at the Louvre" by Samuel Morse; Maurice Prendergast paintings and monotypes

ON EXHIBIT 2002

05/11/2002 to 07/20/2002   *Impressionism Transformed: Paintings of Edward C. Tarbell*

University Museum, Southern Illinois University
Affiliated Institution: So. Illinois Univ. at Edwardsville
Box 1150, Edwardsville, IL   62026-1150

618-650-2996
Open: 9-4:30 Mo-Fr, 1-4 Sa, Su   *Closed:* Leg/Hol
  P: Metered lot just East of the Student Center (next to the football stadium)   *Group Tours*
Sculpture Garden   Theater
Permanent Collection: Drgs; Folk; Cer; Nat/Am

Works in many media from old masters to young contemporary artists are included in the permanent collection and available on a rotating basis for public viewing. The museum is located in the western part of the state not far from St. Louis, Missouri.   ℭ Louis Sullivan Architectural Ornament Collection located in the Lovejoy Library

Mary and Leigh Block Museum
Affiliated Institution: Northwestern University
1967 South Campus Drive, Evanston, IL   60208-2410

847-491-4000   www.blockmuseum.northwestern.edu
Open: 12-5 Tu, We, 12-8pm Th-Su   *Closed:* Mo, Leg/Hol!
  Group Tours   Drop-In Tours   Sculpture Garden
Permanent Collection: Eur: gr, drgs 15-19; Cont: gr, phot; architectural drgs (Griffin Collection)

In addition to its collection of works on paper, this fine university museum features an outdoor sculpture garden (open free of charge year round) which includes outstanding examples of 20th-century works by such artistic luminaries as Joan Miro, Barbara Hepworth, Henry Moore, Jean Arp, and others.   ℭ The sculpture garden with works by Henry Moore, Jean Arp, Barbara Hepworth, and Jean Miro (to name but a few) is one of the major sculpture collections in the region.

ON EXHIBIT 2002

01/05/2002 to 02/28/2002   *Robert Lasmetter: The Preparatory Drawings*
The first examination of his drawings in relation to his larger paintings

01/12/2002 to 02/15/2002   *Self Portrait on World Map*
A projection, in cartographic terms of a three dimensional object, such as earth, onto a single plane such as a map.

01/12/2002 to 03/05/2002   *Adja Yunkers*
The most comprehensive retrospective to date including drawings, prints, paintings, and collaboration with poets

03/05/2002 to 04/20/2002   *Double Vision: Expanding Connections*
Indian artist Indira Johnsson is a founder of SHARE (Support for handicapped rehabilitation) comprised of women from the slums of Bombay. This installation is a culmination of their work in creating an object and personal artifacts and video's are included

04/06/2002 to 06/23/2002   *Curtis*
An evocative and poetic presentation of human desire for flight whether of imagination, physical dislocation, or transendence. As an installation, it combines contemporary video, sound, and digital prints.

04/30/2002 to 07/08/2002   *Fazal Sheikh: Work from Brazil*
Photographs of Grand Sertao National Park that are a testimonial to the people and how they have structured their lives there. It shows a country where the rift between wealth and poverty is vast.

Freeport Arts Center

121 No. Harlem Ave, Freeport, IL   61032

815-235-9755
Open: 10-6 Tu, 10-5 We-Su   *Closed:* Mo, 1/1, Easter. 7/4, Thgv, 12/25
Free Day: We   *Adm:*   *Adult:* $3.00   *Children:* $2.00   *Students:* $2.00   *Seniors:* $2.00
&.: Except for three small galleries   P: behind museum
Group Tours   Drop-In Tours: any time, if scheduled 2 weeks in advance   *Theater*
Permanent Collection: Eur: 15-20; Am: 19-20; Cont: ptgs, sculp; P/Col; An/R; Nat/Am; An/Egt; As; Af; Oc

The Freeport Arts Center, located in northwestern Illinois, has six permanent galleries of paintings, sculpture, prints, and ancient artifacts, as well as temporary exhibitions featuring the work of noted regional artists. It houses one of the largest Florentine mosaic collections in the world.   ❰ Especially popular with children of all ages are the museum's antiquities and the Native American galleries. FAC has one of the finest collections of pietre dure (Florentine mosaics) in the world.

ON EXHIBIT 2002

11/18/2001 to 01/06/2002   *Regional Juried Exhibition*

01/13/2002 to 03/03/2002   *Paintings by Tom Locker; Paper Sculpture by Roland Poska*

04/12/2002 to 05/10/2002   *American Watercolor Traveling Exhibit   Will Travel*

05/17/2002 to 07/07/2002   *The Vietnam Experience*

07/12/2002 to 09/08/2002   *Embroiderers Guild of America Traveling Exhibit*

09/13/2002 to 11/10/2002   *Painting Eden: Roger Goodspeed's Paintings and Artifacts*

11/17/2002 to 01/05/2003   *Holiday Gift Show*

Mitchell Museum

Richview Rd., Mount Vernon, IL   62864

618-242-1236   cedarhurst.org
Open: 10-5 Tu-Sa, 1-5 Su   *Closed:* Mo, Leg/Hol!
Vol/Contr.: Yes
& P   *Museum Shop   Group Tours   Sculpture Garden*
Permanent Collection: Am: ptgs, sculp (late 19-early 20)

Works from the "Ashcan School," with paintings by Davies, Glackens, Henri, Luks, and Maurice Prendergast, comprise one of the highlights of the Mitchell Museum, located in south central Illinois, which also features over 60 large-scale sculptures in Cedarhurst Sculpture Park. All are located on a 90-acre estate.   ❰ Sculpture park

ON EXHIBIT 2002

02/23/2002 to 05/05/2002   *St. Louis Art Quilters*
Artists' experimentation and techniques including pictorial applique, painted surfaces, hand-dyeing, beaded embellishment, and beaded applique

05/11/2002 to 08/25/2002   *Mary Sprague: High Tide in St. Louis*
A retrospective exhibition of a contemporary artist's 40-year career. She uses images of horses and animals, the sea, and domestic interiors as a metaphor for the human condition *Will Travel*

09/21/2002 to 11/10/2002   *Tom Sleet: Art, Architecture, Energy*
Nature, star patterns, and the universe inspire Sleet's paintings and sculptures. He uses a variety of materials including metal, cement, wood, plaster, glass oxides, natural and found materials, and industrial resins.

Lakeview Museum of Arts and Sciences
1125 West Lake Ave., Peoria, IL   61614

309-686-7000   www.lakeview-museum.org
Open: 10-5 Tu-Sa, 1-5 Su   *Closed:* Mo, Leg/Hol!
Free Day: Tu   *Adm:*   *Adult:* $2.50   *Children:* $1.50   *Students:* $1.50   *Seniors:* $1.50
&   P: Free   *Museum Shop   Group Tours   Sculpture Garden*
Permanent Collection: Dec/Art; Am: 19-20; Eur:19

A multi-faceted museum that combines the arts and sciences, the Lakeview offers approximately 6 changing exhibitions per year. *Prices of admission may change during special exhibitions! ℂ Discovery Center and Planetarium, a particular favorite with children.

Quincy Art Center
1515 Jersey St., Quincy, IL   62301

217-223-5900
Open: 1-4 Tu-Su   *Closed:* Mo, Leg/Hol!
Vol/Contr.: Yes   &   P: Free   *Museum Shop*
Group Tours: 217-223-6900   *Drop-In Tours:* Often available upon request
Historic Building: 1887 building known as the Lorenzo Bull Carriage House
Permanent Collection: Ptgs; Sculp; Gr

The center is housed in an 1887 carriage house designed by architect Joseph Silsbee, mentor and great inspiration to Frank Lloyd Wright. A modern wing added in 1990 features a gallery, studio, and gift shop. It is not far from the Missouri border. ℂ Located in an historic district that "Newsweek" magazine calls one of the most architecturally significant corners in the country, the center is composed of various buildings that runs from Greek Revival to Prairie Style.

Augustana College Museum of Art
7th Ave. & 38th St., Art & Art History Dept., Rock Island, IL   61201-2296

309-794-7469   www.augustana.edu
Open: 12-4 Tu-Sa (Sept-May)   *Closed:* Acad! & Summer
&: Call ahead for access assistance   P: Parking available next to Centennial Hall at the northwest corner of Seventh Ave. & 38th St.   *Group Tours:* 309-794-7231
Permanent Collection: Swedish Am: all media

Rockford Art Museum
711 N. Main St., Rockford, IL   61103

815-968-2787   www.rockfordartmuseum.org
Open: 11-5 Tu-Fr, 10-5 Sa, 12-5 Su   *Closed:* Mo, Leg/Hol!
Vol/Contr.: Yes
&   P: Free   *Museum Shop   Group Tours:* 815-972-2811   *Drop-In Tours:* by res   *Sculpture Garden*
Permanent Collection: Am: ptgs, sculp, gr, dec/art 19-20; Eur: ptgs, sculp, gr, dec/art 19-20; Am/Impr; Taos Art, Gilbert Coll: phot; Af/Am; self-taught; contemporary glass

With 17,000-square feet of exhibition space, this is one of the largest arts institutions in the state of Illinois. Up to 12 exhibitions are presented annually, as are works from the over 1,200-piece permanent collection of 20th century American and European art. ℂ "Her Daughter" by Walter Ufer, 1921; "Salt of the Earth" by Rudolph Ingorle, 1930; "End of Day" by John Koch, 1970; plaster casts by Lorado Taft, c. 1900

Rockford College Art Gallery / Clark Arts Center
5050 E. State, Rockford, IL   61108

815-226-4034
Open: 2-5 Daily   *Closed:* Acad!, Summer
&: Elevator at west side of Clark Art Center   P: Free; near Clark Arts Center
Permanent Collection: Ptgs, Gr, Phot, Cer 20; Eth; Reg

Located on a beautiful wooded site in a contemporary building, this museum presents a stimulating array of exhibitions that look at historic as well as contemporary artwork from around the country.

SPRINGFIELD

Springfield Art Association
700 North Fourth St., Springfield, IL   62702

937-325-4673   www.spfldmus-of-art.org
Open: 9-5 Tu-Th, Fr, 9-9 We, 9-3 Sa, 2-4 Su   *Closed:* Mo, Leg/Hol! (including Lincoln's birthday; 12/25-1/1)
&   P: Free   *Group Tours:* 937-324-3729   *Drop-In Tours:* by appt
Permanent Collection: Am: ptgs, gr, cer, dec/art; Eur: ptgs; Ch; Jap

Fanciful is the proper word to describe the architecture of the Italianate structure that houses the Springfield Art Association, a fine arts facility that has been important to the cultural life of the city for nearly a century.

INDIANA

ANDERSON

Anderson Fine Arts Center
32 West 10th Street, Anderson, IN   46016

765-649-1248   www.andersonart.org
Open: 10-5 Tu-Sa, 12-5 Su   *Closed:* Mo, Leg/Hol!
Free Day: Tu, 1st Su   *Adm:*   *Adult:* $2.00, fam $5.00   *Children:* $1.00   *Students:* $1.00   *Seniors:* $1.50
&   P   *Museum Shop*   *Group Tours*   *Historic Building*
Permanent Collection: Reg: all media; Am: all media 20

With an emphasis on education, this museum presents children's exhibitions annually; from May to the end of June.

BLOOMINGTON

Indiana University Art Museum
Affiliated Institution: Indiana University
Bloomington, IN   47405

812-855-IUAM   www.indiana.edu/~iuam
Open: 10-5 We-Sa, 12-5 Su   *Closed:* Mo Tu, Leg/Hol!
Vol/Contr.: Yes
&; north entrance   P: Indiana Memorial Union pay parking lot one block west of the museum
Museum Shop   ¶: Coffee Shop   *Group Tours:* 812-855-1045   *Drop-In Tours:* 2:00 Sa
Historic Building: Designed by I.M. Pei   *Sculpture Garden*
Permanent Collection: Af; An/Egt; An/R & Grk; Am: all media; Eur: all media 14-20; Oc; P/Col; Jap; Ch; Or

Masterpieces in every category of its collection, from ancient to modern, make this one of the finest university museums to be found anywhere. Among its many treasures is the best university collection of African art in the United States.   ℂ The stunning museum building itself designed in 1982 by noted architect I.M. Pei.

Indianapolis Museum of Art—Columbus Gallery
390 The Commons, Columbus, IN   47201-6764

812-376-2597
Open: 10-5 Tu-Th & Sa, 10-8 Fr, 12-4 Su   *Closed:* Mo, Leg/Hol!
Vol/Contr.: Yes
&   P: Free   *Group Tours*

In an unusual arrangement with its parent museum in Indianapolis, four exhibitions are presented annually in this satellite gallery, the oldest continuously operating satellite gallery inthe country. The Gallery is uniquely situated inside a shopping mall in an area designated by the city as an "indoor park."   ℂ Jean Tingley sculpture in mall.

Midwest Museum of American Art
429 S. Main St., Elkhart, IN   46516

219-293-6660
Open: 11-5 Tu-Fr 1-4 Sa, Su   *Closed:* Mo, Leg/Hol!
Free Day: Su   *Adm:*   *Adult:* $3.00   *Children:* Free under 5   *Students:* $1.00   *Seniors:* $2.00
&   P: Free city lot just north of the museum   *Museum Shop*
Group Tours   Drop-In Tours: 12:20-12:40 Th Noontime talks-free
Permanent Collection: Am/Impr; Cont; Reg; Sculp; Phot

Chronologically arranged, the permanent collection of 19th and 20th century paintings, sculptures, photographs, and works on paper, traces 150 years of American art history with outstanding examples ranging from American Primitives to contemporary works by Chicago Imagists. The museum is located in the heart of the mid-west Amish country.   ℂ Original paintings by Grandma Moses, Norman Rockwell, and Grant Wood; The Vault Gallery (gallery in the vault of this former bank building.)

ON EXHIBIT 2002

12/07/2001 to 02/24/2002   *The Roy Rogers and Dale Evans Memorabilia Collection from the Tom and Mary McClain Collection*

06/07/2002 to 07/14/2002   *Haitian Art from the Hunsberer Collection*

10/18/2002 to 12/01/2002   *24rd Elkhart Juried Regional*

Evansville Museum of Arts & Science
411 S.E Riverside Dr., Evansville, IN   47713

812-425-2406   www.emuseum.org
Open: 10-5 Tu-Sa, 12-5 Su   *Closed:* 1/1, Mem/Day, 7/4, Lab/Day, Thgv, 12/25
Vol/Contr.: Yes   *Sugg/Contr.:* $2.00 Adults/$1.00 Children
&.: Wheelchairs available   P: Free parking   *Museum Shop   Group Tours   Sculpture Garden*
Permanent Collection: Ptgs; Sculp; Gr; Drgs; Dec/Art

Broad-ranging in every aspect of its varied collections, the Evansville Museum is a general museum with collections in art, history, and science.   ℂ "Madonna and Child" by Murillo; Koch Planetarium; Transportation Hall (EMTRAC)—Evansville Museum Transportation Center.

ON EXHIBIT 2002

01/20/2002 to 03/10/2002   *After History: The Paintings of David Bierk*
Landscape, portraits, still life, and history paintings   *Will Travel*

03/17/2002 to 05/05/2002   *Will Rogers: A Reel Retrospective*
Original posters and lobby cards from his long movie career   *Will Travel*

05/12/2002 to 07/14/2002   *The 2002 Martha and Merritt DeJong Artist in Residence: Daniel Sprick*
A leading realist Colorado painter

07/21/2002 to 09/15/2002   *Hierophany: Tobi Kahn and the Manifestation of the Sacred*
Hierophany is defined as the juxtaposition of natural and supernatural elements. Here in a new series of work   *Will Travel*

09/22/2002 to 11/03/2002   *Egg Tempera Society*
Contemporary American and British artists utilizing this centuries old technique

11/10/2002 to 12/29/2002   *Rudy Pozzatti Exhibition*
A retrospective of the work of this distinguished professor   *Will Travel*

FORT   WAYNE

Fort Wayne Museum of Art
311 E. Main St., Fort Wayne, IN   46802-1997

219-422-6467   www.fwmoa.org
Open: 10-5 Tu-Sa, 12-5 Su; 2nd Th of month open to 9   *Closed:* Mo, 1/1, 7/4, Thgv, 12/25
Free Day: 1st Su and every We   *Adm:*   *Adult:* $3.00   *Children:* $2.00 (K-college)
Students: $2.00   *Seniors:* $3.00
&   P: Parking lot adjacent to building with entrance off Main St.   *Museum Shop*
Group Tours: 219-422-6467 x319   *Sculpture Garden*
Permanent Collection: Am: ptgs, sculp, gr 19-20; Eur: ptgs, sculp, gr 19-20; Cont

Since the dedication of the new state-of-the-art building in its downtown location in 1984, the Fort Wayne Museum, established more than 75 years ago, has enhanced its reputation as a major vital community and nationwide asset for the fine arts. Important masterworks from Dürer to de Kooning are included in this institution's 1,300 piece collection.   ℂ Outdoor sculptures, including "Helmholtz" by Mark diSuvero; bronze maquettes by Paul Manship, paintings by George Inness, Thomas Moran, Larry Rivers, and Janet Fish.

ON EXHIBIT 2002

11/17/2001 to 01/11/2002   *A Ceramic Continuum: Fifty Years of the Archie Bray Foundation*
The development of contemporary ceramics in the U.S. from utilitarian vessels to large-scale architectural sculpture

11/17/2001 to 01/11/2002   *Work by Sculptors in the Permanent Collection*
Drawings and prints by sculptors including Di Suvero, Serra, Catlett, and Stackhouse

01/26/2002 to 03/24/2002   *Dale Chihuly: The George R. Stroemple Collection*
More than 20 years of works by Chihuly   *Will Travel*

02/09/2002 to 04/28/2002   *Audrey Ushenko*
Exciting color, brushwork, and light and shadow

04/06/2002 to 05/26/2002   *The Human Factor: Figuration in American Art 1950–1995*
The wide range of focus on the figure in contemporary art. Among the artists are Bearden, Katz, Neel, Close, Pearlstein, Segal, Lomgo, and Fischl.   *Will Travel*   *Brochure*

04/06/2002 to 09/01/2002   *Selections from the Permanent Collection*

06/08/2002 to 08/18/2002   *2002 Biennial*
Visual artists from a 150-mile radius

09/07/2002 to 11/03/2002   *Contemporary Folk Art: Treasures from the Smithsonian American Art Museum*
Paintings and sculptures by self-taught artists of the past 40 years   *Will Travel   Book*

INDIANAPOLIS

Eiteljorg Museum of American Indians and Western Art
500 W. Washington St., White River State Park, Indianapolis, IN   46204

317-636-9378   www.eiteljorg.org
Open: 10-5 Tu-Sa, 12-5 Su; (Open 10-5 Mo June-Aug)   *Closed:* 1/1, Thgv, 12/25, Easter
Free Day: about 5 per year !   *Adm: Adult:* $6.00   *Children:* Free 4 & under   *Students:* $3.00
Seniors: $5.00
&   P: Free   *Museum Shop   Group Tours:* ext 150   *Drop-In Tours:* 1 daily
Historic Building: Landmark building featuring interior and exterior SW motif design
Permanent Collection: Nat/Am & Reg artifacts : ptgs, sculp, drgs, gr, dec/art

The Eiteljorg, one of only two museums east of the Mississippi to combine the fine arts of the American West with Native American artifacts, is housed in a Southwestern style building faced with 8,000 individually cut pieces of honey-colored Minnesota stone.   ❡ Works by members of the original Taos Artists Colony; 4 major outdoor sculptures including a 38' totem pole by 5th generation Haida carver Lee Wallace, and "Morning Prayer" a bronze by Alan Houser

ON EXHIBIT 2002

04/08/2000 to 01/07/2002   *From One Hand to Another: Native American Treasures from the Children's Museum*

03/02/2002 to 09/02/2002   *Unbroken Spirit: The Wild Horse in the American Landscape*
The wild horse has come to symbolize the spirit of the American West. A compelling picture of the animal is shown here.

06/22/2002 to Permanent   *Installation of the Native American Gallery*
First person narratives and videos, focus on the Woodland region, will bring a humanities approach to learning.

09/28/2002 to 01/05/2003   *New Art of the West 8*
A juried biennial exhibition by artists from the West or creating work about the West. Each of the 20 selected artists shows 3 works.

Indianapolis Museum of Art
1200 W. 38th St., Indianapolis, IN   46208-4196

317-923-1331   www.ima-art.org
Open: 10-5 Tu-Sa, till 8:30pm Th, 12-5 Su   *Closed:* Mo, Thgv, 12/25, 1/1
Vol/Contr.: Yes   *Sugg/Contr.:* Special Exhibitions only, $5.00
&   P: Outdoor parking lots and parking garage of Krannert Pavilion   *Museum Shop*
❡: 11am-1:45pm Tu-Sa; (Brunch Su by reservation 926-2628)
Group Tours   Drop-In Tours: 12 & 2 Tu-Su; 7pm Th   *Sculpture Garden*
Permanent Collection: Am: ptgs; Eur/OM; ptgs Eur/Ren:ptgs; Cont; Or; Af; Dec/Art; Textiles

Situated in a 152-acre park as part of a cultural complex, the Indianapolis Museum is home to many outstanding collections including a large group of works on paper by Turner, and world class collections of Post-Impressionist, Asian, and African art. *1. There is an admission fee for most special exhibitions. 2. The museum is open on 7/4. 3. Historic Lilly House closed for restoration will open summer 2002   ❡ Gardens of Oldfields Estate, Clowes Collection of Old Masters, Glick Contemporary Glass Collection, Josephowitz Collection of School of Art

ON EXHIBIT 2002

09/22/2001 to 01/13/2002   *The Art of Diplomacy: Gifts to the Tsars 1500–1700 Treasures from the Kremlin*
Magnificent and valuable works of art, most never before shown outside Russia.

LAFAYETTE

Art Museum of Greater Lafayette
102 South Tenth St., Lafayette, IN   47905

765-742-1128   www.glmart.org
Open: 10-4:45 Tu-Sa   *Closed:* Mo, Leg/Hol!
Sugg/Contr.: Yes   *Adult:* $2.00   *Seniors:* $1.00
♿ P: Free 10th St. entrance   *Museum Shop*
Group Tours: ask for paige@glmart.org   *Drop-In Tours:* 9-5 Tu-Fr
Permanent Collection: Am: ptgs, gr, drgs, art pottery 19-20; Reg: ptgs, works on paper; Lat/Am: gr

Art by regional Indiana artists, contemporary works by national artists of note, and a fine collection of art pottery.

ON EXHIBIT 2002

11/03/2001 to 01/25/2002   *Divine Bovines: Cows and Other Barnyard Animals in Indiana Art*

MUNCIE

Ball State University Museum of Art
2000 University Ave., Muncie, IN   47306

765-285-5242   www.bsu.edu/artmuseum
Open: 9-4:30 Mo-Fr; 1:30-4:30 Sa, Su   *Closed:* !, Leg/Hol
♿ P: Metered street parking and metered paid garages nearby   *Group Tours*
Permanent Collection: IT/Ren; Eur: ptgs 17-19; Am: ptgs, gr, drgs 19-20; Dec/Art; As; Af; Oc; P/Col

5,000 years of art history are represented in the 11,000-piece collection of the Ball State University Museum of Art. In addition to wonderful explanatory wall plaques, there is a fully cataloged Art Reference Terminal of the permanent collection.

NOTRE DAME

Snite Museum of Art
Affiliated Institution: University of Notre Dame
Notre Dame, IN   46556

219-631-5466   www.nd.edu/~sniteart
Open: 10-4 Tu, We, 10-5 Th-Sa, 1-5 Su   *Closed:* Mo, Leg/Hol!
Vol/Contr.: Yes
♿ P: Available southwest of the museum in the visitor lot   *Museum Shop   Group Tours:* 219-631-4435
Sculpture Garden   Theater
Permanent Collection: It/Ren; Fr: ptgs 19; Eur: phot 19; Am: ptgs, phot; P/Col: sculp; Du: ptgs 17-18

With 19,000 objects in its permanent collection spanning the history of art from antiquity to the present, this premier university museum is a "must see" for all serious art lovers.
❈ Af; P/Col and Nat/Am Collections

ON EXHIBIT 2002

01/01/2002 to February 2002   *Christiansen African Art*

01/01/2002 to mid March 2002   *Portraits of Money: Paintings by Djawid C. Borower*   Will Travel

09/10/2002 to Fall 2002   *Alan Riley Collection of British Drawings*

09/10/2002 to Fall 2002   *Janos Scholz 19th-Century Photography Collection*

RICHMOND

Richmond Art Museum
350 Hub Etchison Pkwy, Richmond, IN   47374

765-966-0256
Open: 10-4 Tu-Fr, 1-4 Sa, Su   *Closed:* Mo, Leg/Hol!
Sugg/Contr.: $5.00
&.: Northwest entrance wheelchair accessible   P: Free   *Group Tours   Drop-In Tours:* !
Permanent Collection: Reg; Am Art

Richmond Art Museum, in the north wing of Richmond High School across Whitewater Gorge, shows Bundy and Baker as well as Chase, Hassam, Reid, Steele, and Stark. ☾ Self portrait by William Merritt Chase, painted for the Museum, considered to be his most famous work; collection of Overbeck Pottery; Fountain by Janet Scudder

SOUTH BEND

South Bend Regional Museum of Art
120 S. St. Joseph St., South Bend, IN   46601

219-235-9102   www.sbt.infi.net/~nsbrma
Open: 11-5 Tu-Fr; 12-5 Sa, Su   *Closed:* Mo, Leg/Hol!
Sugg/Contr.: Yes   *Adult:* $3.00
&.   P: Free street parking. Also Century Center lot or other downtown parking garages.
Museum Shop   Group Tours
Permanent Collection: Am: ptgs 19-20; Eur: ptgs 19-20; Cont: reg

Since 1947, the South Bend Regional Museum of Art has been serving the artistic needs of its community by providing a wide variety of regional and national exhibitions year-round. This growing institution recently completed a reconstruction and expansion project adding, among other things, a Permanent Collections Gallery. ☾ Permanent site-specific sculptures are situated on the grounds of Century Center of which the museum is a part.

ON EXHIBIT 2002

01/01/2002 to February 2002   *79th Annual Scholastic Art Awards*
A recognition for creative young people all over the U.S. The visual compnent is shown here.

03/01/2002 to May 2002   *Pictures, Patents, Monkeys, and More ... On Collecting*
Three different types of collections: contemporary art; artifacts of popular culture; models used for patents. Also included will be toys from the South Bend Toy Company and Studebaker artifacts. In the context of collecting, we come to understand what is personally valuable to us.

06/01/2002 to July 2002   *Craft Work: A National Survey*
Crafts including pottery, weaving, metal smithing, glass blowing, and others

08/01/2002 to September 2002   *Bag, Box, and Bucket Show*
Artists use of these items in their work

10/01/2002 to November 2002   *Fire and Earth: Wood Fired Ceramics*
Eight to ten different artists from the Midwest and their kilns. Work will be fired at different locations since the process of firing is uncertain and never results in the same thing twice.

Swope Art Museum
25 S. 7th St., Terre Haute, IN 47807

812-238-1676 www.swope.org
Open: 10-5 Tu-Fr; 12-5 Sa, Su; 10-8pm Th   *Closed:* Mo, Leg/Hol
Vol/Contr.: Yes
  P: Pay lot on Ohio Blvd. (behind the museum)   *Museum Shop*
Group Tours: by appt   *Drop-In Tours:* 1st Sa of month 1pm
Historic Building: 1901 Italian Renaissance-style exterior; interior is 1942 Art Deco style.
Permanent Collection: Am: ptgs, sculp, drgs 19-20

The Swope Art Museum opened in 1942 as a museum devoted to contemporary American art and has expanded from the original core collection to include significant 19th- and 20th-century American works. The museum's historic 1901 exterior and Art Deco interior have been recently restored and renovated. ❮ Paintings by Grant Wood, Thomas Hart Benton, Edward Hopper; meticulously restored 1941–42 interior.

ON EXHIBIT 2002

12/07/2001 to 01/06/2002   *Wabash Currents: 3 Artists*
Current work of three regional artists

02/08/2002 to 03/24/2002   *American Abstract Artists: 50th Anniversary Print Portfolio*

06/21/2002 to 08/04/2002   *Modern Art: Work from the Swope's Collection*

09/21/2002 to 10/28/2002   *Annual Wabash Valley Juried Exhibition*
Artists living or working within 100 miles of Terre Haute

11/22/2002 to 01/05/2003   *Hierophany: Tobi Kahn and the Manifestation of the Sacred*
Hierophany is defined as the juxtaposition of natural and supernatural elements. Here in a new series of work   *Will Travel*

Brauer Museum of Art at Valparaiso University
Affiliated Institution: Valparaiso University
Valparaiso, IN 46383

219-464-5365

The museum is part of a Center for the Arts, which includes music and drama as well.

Purdue University Galleries
Affiliated Institution: Creative Arts Bldg., #1
West Lafayette, IN 47907

765-494-3061
Open: Stewart Center:10-5 & 7-9 Mo-Fr, 1-5 Su; Union Gallery:10-5 Mo-Fr   *Closed:* Acad
  P: Visitor parking in designated areas (a $3.00 daily parking permit for campus garages may be purchased at the Visitors Information Services Center); some metered street parking as well; Free parking on campus after 5 and on weekends.   *Group Tours*
Permanent Collection: Am: ptgs, drgs, gr; Eur: ptgs, gr, drgs; Am: cont/cer

In addition to a regular schedule of special exhibitions, this facility presents many student and faculty shows.

IOWA

CEDAR FALLS

James & Meryl Hearst Center for the Arts
304 W. Seerly Blvd., Cedar Falls, IA   50613

319-273-8641   www.hearstartscenter.com
Open: 8-9 Tu, Th; 8-5 We, Fr; 1-4 Sa, Su   *Closed:* 1/1, 7/4, Thgv, 12/25
&.   P: Free   *Museum Shop*   Group Tours: 319-268-5504   *Drop-In Tours*
Historic Building: Located in the former home of well-known farmer poet James Hearst
Sculpture Garden
Permanent Collection: Reg

Besides showcasing works by the region's best current artists, the Hearst Center's permanent holdings include examples of works by such well knowns as Grant Wood, Mauricio Lasansky, and Gary Kelly.   ⊂ "Man is a Shaper, a Maker," pastel by Gary Kelly; "Honorary Degree," lithograph by Grant Wood

ON EXHIBIT 2002

01/06/2002 to 03/24/2002   *Children's Book Illustrations: Contemporary Illustrators*
A look at the most prominent illustrators from around the world

05/12/2002 to 05/26/2002   *Bill Close: Twenty-two Years and Twenty-two Sculptures*
Close has orchestrated the construction of a mega-sculpture on the front lawn of the High School. A retrospective through photographs and sculpture

06/09/2002 to 07/28/2002   *Jim Kerns and Jim Russell: Form and Function*
Ceramicist Kerns and metalsmith Russell show us the art of material craft and design in modern home furnishings.

06/09/2002 to 07/28/2002   *Marjorie Nuhn: Conservation Show*
Conservation methods, perils of bad lighting, and how to "fix" a painting

07/01/2002 to 06/01/2003   *2002 Outdoor Sculpture Invitational : Gardens to Main*

08/11/2002 to 10/07/2002   *Society of Illustrators: Picturing a Story*

10/09/2002 to 11/22/2002   *Sleepy Hollow*

10/20/2002 to 01/17/2003   *Prairie Printmakers*

CEDAR RAPIDS

Cedar Rapids Museum of Art
410 Third Ave., S.E., Cedar Rapids, IA   52401

319-366-7503   www.crma.org
Open: 10-4 Tu-We & Fr-Sa, 10-7 Th, 12-4 Su   *Closed:* Mo, Leg/Hol!
Adm: Adult: $4.00   *Children:* Free under 7   *Students:* $3.00   *Seniors:* $3.00
&.; Entrance ramp 3rd Ave   P: Lot behind museum building; some metered parking on street
Museum Shop   Group Tours: education office   *Drop-In Tours:* !   *Historic Building:* Carnegie
Permanent Collection: Reg: ptgs 20; Ptgs, Sculp, Gr, Dec/Art, Phot 19-20

Spanning a city block, the Cedar Rapids Museum of Art houses 16 galleries in one wing and a museum shop, art library, and multi-media center in another. A regionally focused museum, it was observed that by The Other Museums that, "No museum of art in this country is more deeply rooted in its own community."   ⊂ Museum includes restored 1905 Beaux Art building, formerly the Carnegie Library (free to the public); collections of Grand Wood & Marvin Cone paintings, Malvina Hoffman sculptures, & Mauricio Lasansky prints and drawings

Davenport Museum of Art
1737 W. Twelfth St., Davenport, IA   52804

563-326-7804
Open: 10-4:30 Tu-Sa, 1-4:30 Su   *Closed:* Leg/Hol!
Adm: Adult: $3.00   *Seniors:* $3.00
 ♧ P: Free   *Museum Shop*   *Group Tours:* 563-888-2045   *Drop-In Tours*
Permanent Collection: Am/Reg; Am: 19-20; Eur: 16-18; OM; Mexican Colonial; Haitian Naive

Works by Grant Wood and other American Regionalists are on permanent display at the Davenport Museum, the first public art museum established in the state of Iowa (1925). ❰ Grant Wood's "Self Portrait"

ON EXHIBIT 2002

12/01/2001 to 01/27/2002   *The Photography of Alfred Stieglitz: Georgia O'Keeffe's Enduring Gift*
Until recently these images were never shown outside of the George Eastman House. The exhibition traces the career of one of the early 20th century's most important personalities and a proponent of photography as fine art.   *Catalog   Will Travel*

02/16/2002 to 03/31/2002   *Devotion and the Sacred: Work from the Collections*
Illuminated manuscript pages from the 15th century and religious prints and paintings from the 16th, 17th, and 18th centuries in Europe and Mexico

04/20/2002 to 06/30/2002   *Old West: New West*
Works from the collection and other public and private ones show the landscape and western myths as well. Shown are Leigh, Johnson, Couse, Sharp, Berninghaus, Russell, Remington, and Curtis with contemporary artists taking a fresh look at the "old" and "new" West.

08/10/2002 to 11/08/2002   *Defining Craft*
175 works by American and international artists showing craft over 50 years. Included are Voulkos, Larson, Frey, Tawney, and Arneson alongside young and emerging talent focusing on the middle of the 20th century to today

11/23/2002 to 01/04/2003   *American Art from the Collection*
American art is shown through 2 centuries in painting, photography, sculpture, prints, and decorative arts. Included are Chase, Wood, Benton. and Greenfield.

Des Moines Art Center
4700 Grand Ave., Des Moines, IA   50312-2099

515-277-4405   under construction
Open: 11-4 Tu-Sa, 12-4 Su, 11-9 Th & 1st Fr of the month   *Closed:* Mo, Leg/Hol!
♧; North door of north addition (notify info. desk prior to visit)   P: Free
Museum Shop   ☍: 11-2 lunch Tu-Sa; dinner 5:30-9 Th (by res.), 5-8 1st Fr (light dining)
Group Tours: 515-271-0317 ext. 15   *Sculpture Garden*
Permanent Collection: Am: ptgs, sculp, gr 19-20; Eur: ptgs, sculp, gr 19-20; Af

Its parklike setting is a perfect compliment to the magnificent structure of the Des Moines Art Center building, designed originally by Eliel Saarinen in 1948, with a south wing by the noted I.M. Pei & Partners added in 1968. Another spectacular wing, recognized as a masterpiece of contemporary architecture, was designed and built, in 1985, by Richard Meier & Partners. ❰ "Maiastra" by Constantin Brancusi; Frank Stella's "Interlagos"; "Ascension" by Bill Viola

ON EXHIBIT 2002

11/17/2001 to 01/20/2002   *Apocalypse: Visions and Prophecies*
Prints by Dürer, Sabatelli, and Redon spanning 5 centuries on the end of time theme

12/08/2001 to February 2002   *Anna Gaskell*
Large scale color photographs and video installation

05/04/2002 to 06/30/2002   *Modernism and Abstraction: Treasures from the Smithsonian American Art Museum*   Will Travel

07/01/2002 to October 2002   *Iowa Artists*

07/20/2002 to 10/13/2002   *Andy Goldsworthy: Three Cairns*
Photographs as well as ephemeral and permanent sculptures   Will Travel

11/02/2002 to February 2003   *Magic Markers: Contemporary Constructed Objects*
The objects refer to various belief systems. Artists included are Rauschenberg, Christenberry, Gober, Tuttle, Hammons, and contemporary Indian, Asian, African, and aboriginal artists.

Hoyt Sherman Place
1501 Woodland Ave., Des Moines, IA   50309

515-243-0913
Open: 8-4 Mo-Tu & Th-Fr; Closed on We from Oct1-end of May   *Closed:* Leg/Hol!
&.; Ramp, chairlift, elevator   P: Free   *Museum Shop*
Group Tours   Drop-In Tours: often available upon request
Historic Building: Complex of 1877 House, 1907 Art Museum, 1923 Theater
Permanent Collection: Ptgs; Sculp; Dec/Art 19; Eur; sculp; B.C. Artifacts

A jewel from the Victorian Era, the Hoyt Sherman Art Galleries offer an outstanding permanent collection of 19th-century American and European art, complimented by antique decorative arts objects that fill its surroundings. Listed NRHP   ⊄ Major works by 19th-century American masters including Church, Innes, Moran, Frieseke, and others

DUBUQUE

Dubuque Museum of Art
701 Locust St., Dubuque, IA   52001

563-557-1851   dbgartmuseum.com
Open: 10-5 Tu-Fr; 1-4 Sa, Su   *Closed:* 1/1, Easter, 7/4, Thgv, 12/25
Sugg/Contr.: Yes   *Adult:* $3.00   *Children:* Free under 12   *Students:* $2.00   *Seniors:* $2.00
&. P   *Museum Shop   Group Tours   Drop-In Tours:* daily upon request
Historic Building: Housed in 1857 Egyptian Revivalist Jail
Permanent Collection: Reg

ON EXHIBIT 2002

12/05/2001 to 02/17/2002   *Pat Edwards*
Oil paintings of landscapes in Midwest and France

01/05/2002 to 03/10/2002   *Contemporary Prints: 1900/2000*
Works by Warhol, Judd, and others

03/21/2002 to 05/12/2002   *Exotica: Plant Portraits from around the World*
Botanical prints from all over the world done from 1600–1850 before photography
Will Travel   Brochure

05/22/2002 to 08/02/2002   *Abstract Impressionists: Today*
A survey of 6 to 8 third-generation abstract artists

08/15/2002 to 09/29/2002   *Sandra Louise Dyas: The Lost Nation Photographs*
Photographs of rural life in Iowa

08/15/2002 to 10/28/2002   *Francesco Licciardi*
Bright intense figurative paintings

10/05/2002 to 12/01/2002   *Stephan Simons: New Work*
Still life paintings

FORT DODGE

Blanden Memorial Art Museum
920 Third Ave. South, Fort Dodge, IA   50501

515-573-2316   www.blanden.org
Open: 10-5 Tu-Fr, till 8:30 Th, 1-5 Sa & Su   *Closed:* Leg/Hols!
Vol/Contr.: Yes
&: Entrance on north side of building   P: Street parking and limited parking area behind the museum
Museum Shop   Group Tours   Historic Building
Permanent Collection: Am: ptgs, sculp, gr 19-20; Eur: ptgs, sculp, drgs, gr 15-20; Or: 16-20; P/Col

Established in 1930 as the first permanent art facility in the state, the Blanden's neo-classic building was based on the already existing design of the Butler Institute of American Art in Youngstown, Ohio. Listed NRHP. ℭ "Central Park" by Maurice Prendergast, 1901; "Self-Portrait in Cap & Scarf" by Rembrandt (etching, 1663)

ON EXHIBIT 2002

01/13/2002 to 03/04/2002   *American Fractal*
The new millennium is being called the era of complexity. Is fractal vision today a new form for art in the same way that Minimalism, Expressionism, Conceptualism were in the past?
Catalog   Will Travel

GRINNELL

Faulconer Gallery And Print and Drawing Study Room
Affiliated Institution: Grinnell College
1108 Park St., Grinnell, IA   50112

515-269-4660   www.grinell.edu/faulconergallery
Open: 12-5 Tu-Su, Th till 8   *Closed:* !
&   P: Available at 6th Ave. & Park St.   *Group Tours   Historic Building:* designed by Cesar Pelli
Permanent Collection: Work on Paper (available for study in the Print & Drawing Study Room)

1,400 works on paper, ranging from illuminated manuscripts to 16th-century European prints and drawings to 20th-century American lithographs, are all part of the study group of the Grinnell College Collection that started in 1908 with an original bequest of 28 etchings by J. M. W. Turner. A new gallery, designed by Cesar Pelli, exhibits historic and contemporary art in changing exhibitions. ℭ Temporary exhibitions of historic and contemporary art.

IOWA CITY

University of Iowa Museum of Art
150 North Riverside Dr., 112 Museum of Art, Iowa City, IA   52242-1789

319-335-1727   www.uiowa.edu.uima
Open: 10-5 We-Su, till 10 Th, Fr   *Closed:* 1/1, Thgv, 12/25
&   P: Metered lots directly across Riverside Drive & north of the museum   *Museum Shop*
Group Tours   Drop-In Tours   Sculpture Garden
Permanent Collection: Am: ptgs, sculp 19-20; Eur: ptgs, sculp 19-20; Af; Work on Paper

Over 11,000 objects form the basis of the collection at this 30 year old university museum that features, among its many strengths, 19th & 20th century American and European art, and the largest group of African art in any university museum collection. ℭ "Karneval" by Max Beckman; "Mural, 1943" by Jackson Pollock

11/16/2001 to 01/13/2002   *African Inspirations: Sculpted Headwear by Sonya Clark*

11/23/2001 to 02/03/2002   *From the Outside in: Buildings in Photography*

01/15/2002 to 04/28/2002   *Prints with a Conscience*

01/25/2002 to 04/14/2002   *William Wegman: Fashion Photographs*   Will Travel

MARSHALLTOWN

Central Iowa Art Association
Affiliated Institution: Fisher Community College
Marshalltown, IA   50158

515-753-9013
Open: 11-5 Mo-Fr; 1-5 Sa, Su (Apr 15-Oct 15)   *Closed:* Leg/Hol!
Vol/Contr.: Yes
&   P: Free parking in front of building   *Museum Shop   Group Tours   Sculpture Garden*
Permanent Collection: Fr/Impr: ptgs; Ptgs; Cer

You don't have to be a scholar to enjoy the ceramic study center of the Central Iowa Art Association, one of the highlights of this institution. 20th century paintings and sculpture at the associated Fisher Art Gallery round out the collection.   ℭ The Ceramic Study Collection

MASON CITY

Charles H. MacNider Museum
303 2nd St., S.E., Mason City, IA   50401-3988

641-421-3666   www.macniderart.org
Open: 9-9 Tu & Th; 9-5 We, Fr, & Sa; 1-5 Su   *Closed:* Leg/Hol!, pm 12/24, pm 12/31
&   P   *Museum Shop*
Group Tours   Drop-In Tours: available upon advance request during museum hours
Permanent Collection: Am: ptgs, gr, drgs, cer; Reg: ptgs, gr, drgs, cer; the "Bil Baird World of Puppets"

A lovely English Tudor mansion built in 1921, complete with modern additions, is the repository of an ever growing collection that documents American art and life. Though only a short two block walk from the heart of Mason City, the MacNider sits dramatically atop a limestone ravine surrounded by trees and other beauties of nature.   ℭ For young and old alike, a wonderful collection of Bil Baird Marionettes; "Gateways to the Sea," by Alfred T. Bricher; "Spring Tryout," by Thomas Hart Benton; "The Clay Wagon," by Arthur Dove

11/01/2001 to 01/06/2002   *Iowa Crafts*

MUSCATINE

Muscatine Art Center
1314 Mulberry Ave., Muscatine, IA   52761

563-263-8282   muscatineartcenter.org
Open: 10-5 Tu, We, Fr; 10-5 & 7-9 Th; 1-5 Sa, Su   *Closed:* Leg/Hol!
Vol/Contr.: Yes
&   P: Free   *Group Tours   Drop-In Tours:* self guided
Historic Building: 1908 Edwardian Musser Mansion
Permanent Collection: Am: ptgs, sculp, gr, drgs, dec/art 19-20; Nat/Am: ptgs

The original Musser Family Mansion built in Edwardian Style in 1908, has been joined since 1976 by the contemporary 3 level Stanley Gallery to form the Muscatine Art Center. In addition to its fine collection of regional and national American art, the center has received a bequest of 27 works by 19 important European artists including Boudin, Braque, Pissaro, Degas, Matisse, and others. ℂ The "Great River Collection" of artworks illustrating facets of the Mississippi River from its source in Lake Itasca to its southernmost point in New Orleans.

ON EXHIBIT 2002

05/12/2002 to 07/07/2002   *Of Samurai and Chrysanthemums: Edo Period Woodblock Prints and Meiji Bronze Sculptures*

05/12/2002 to 07/07/2002   *Truc Deegan Oriental Art in Watercolor and Ink*

08/04/2002 to 09/22/2002   *Out of the Woods: Turned Wood by American Craftsmen*   Will Travel

10/01/2002 to December 2002   *Giles Laroche: Bridges are to Cross*

SIOUX CITY

Sioux City Art Center
225 Nebraska St., Sioux City, IA   51101-1712

712-279-6272   www.sc-artcenter.com
Open: 10-5 Tu-We & Fr-Sa, 12-9 Th, 1-5 Su   *Closed:* Leg/Hol!
Adult: Admission for some special exhibitions
& P: Metered street parking & city lots within walking distance of the museum   *Museum Shop*
Group Tours: ext. 200   *Drop-In Tours:* By reservation
Permanent Collection: Nat/Am; 19-20; Cont/Reg; Ptgs, Work on Paper; Phot

Begun as a WPA project in 1938, the Center features an 800-piece permanent collection that includes regional art. A stunning 1997 $9 million Art Center building, designed by the renowned architectural firm of Skidmore, Owings and Merril, features a three-story glass atrium. ℂ New facility, a hands-on gallery for children featuring creative activity stations

ON EXHIBIT 2002

12/08/2001 to 03/10/2002   *Karen Chesterman: Layers of Discovery*
Chesterman's work requires returning again and again to the canvas . . . until lines, colors, textures, and shapes create . . . subtle relationships woven in layers.

12/15/2001 to 03/24/2002   *Robert Hillestad—The Texture of Textiles*
Fiber fashions by artist and designer Hillestad. Using conventional methods and materials, experimental construction, and non-traditional substances he creates wearable art, haute couture, and larger than life sculptural attire.

12/29/2001 to 03/31/2002   *Magical Absurdities: Gerald Guthrie*
Miniaturized environments in 15-inch cubes that contain realistic room interiors seen through a peephole. Lights and motors are activated by the viewer to animate them.

06/08/2002 to 08/04/2002   *Sunlight and Shadow: American Impressionism 1885–1945*
Americans took Impressionism with its sense of color and light to the American landscape in oil, watercolor, and pastels.

06/15/2002 to 08/11/2002   *Jan Zelfer-Redmond: Paintings*
Subtle undesipherable hieroglyphics are hidden beneath her layers of paints.

06/22/2002 to 08/04/2002   *Sheryl Ellinwood: Sculptured Glass*
Work that is whimsical, serious, and mysterious using the behavior of color in glass

09/28/2002 to 12/01/2002   *Bryan Holland: Connections*
Representational, non-traditional still lifes that fade or dissolve into their surroundings. He depicts chinese lanterns, vases, musical instruments, and fruits—all symbols of life

Waterloo Center for the Arts
225 Commercial St., Waterloo, IA   50701

319-291-4490   www.waterloo-ia.org/arts
Open: 10-5 Mo-Fr; 1-4 -Sa, Su   *Closed:* Leg/Hol!
Sugg/Contr.: $2.00
&   P: Free   *Museum Shop*   ¶: catered lunches available
Group Tours   Drop-In Tours: Mo-Fr 10-5   *Sculpture Garden*
Permanent Collection: Reg: ptgs, gr, sculp; Haitian: ptgs, sculp; Am: dec/art

This museum notes as its strengths its collection of Midwest art including works by Grant Wood and Marvin Cone; an outstanding collection of Haitian paintings, metal sculpture, and sequined banners; and an American decorative arts collection with particular emphasis on pottery. ⊄ Small collection of Grant Wood paintings, lithographs, and drawings. The largest public collection of Haitian art in US.

ON EXHIBIT 2002

11/30/2001 to 01/27/2002   *David Delafield Retrospective*

02/08/2002 to 04/07/2002   *Painting by Burton Chenet*
Haitian artist Chenet created this series based on the colorful pre-lenten Ra-Ra celebrations of Jacmel, Haiti.

KANSAS

Walker Art Collection of the Garnett Public Library
125 W. 4th Ave., Garnett, KS   66032

913-448-3388   www.kanza.net/garnett
Open: 10-8 Mo, Tu, Th; 10-5:30 We, Fr; 10-4 Sa   *Closed:* 1/1, Mem/Day, 7/4, Thgv, 12/25
Vol/Contr.: Yes
&   P: Free street parking   *Drop-In Tours:* Upon request if available   *Theater*
Permanent Collection: Am: ptgs: 20; Reg

Considered one of the most outstanding collections in the state, the Walker was started with a 110 piece bequest in 1951 by its namesake, Maynard Walker, a prominent art dealer in New York during the 1930s & 40s. Brilliantly conserved works by such early 20th-century American artists as John Stuart Curry, Robert Henri, and Luigi Lucioni are displayed alongside European and Midwest Regional paintings and sculpture. All works in the collection have undergone conservation in the past few years and are in pristine condition. ⊄ "Lake in the Forest (Sunrise)" by Corot; "Girl in Red Tights" by Walt Kuhn; "Tobacco Plant" by John Stuart Curry

Spencer Museum of Art
Affiliated Institution: University of Kansas
1301 Mississippi St., Lawrence, KS   66045

785-864-4710   www.ukans.edu/~sma
Open: 10-5 Tu-Sa, 12-5 Su, till 9pm Th   *Closed:* 1/1, 7/4, Thgv & following day, 12/24, 12/25
Sugg/Contr.: $3.00
&   P: Metered spaces in lot north of museum & parking anywhere when school not in session.
Museum Shop   Group Tours: 785-864-0125 School year only   *Drop-In Tours*
Permanent Collection: Eur: ptgs, sculp, gr 17-18; Am: phot; Jap: gr; Ch: ptgs; Med: sculp

The broad and diverse collection of the Spencer Museum of Art, located in the eastern part of the state not far from Kansas City, features particular strengths in the areas of European painting and sculpture of the 17th & 18th centuries, American photographs, Japanese and Chinese works of art, and Medieval sculpture. ❡ "La Pia de Tolommei" by Rosetti; "The Ballad of the Jealous Lover of Lone Green Valley" by Thomas Hart Benton

LINDSBORG

Birger Sandzen Memorial Gallery
401 N. 1st St., Lindsborg, KS   67456-0348

785-227-2220   www.sandzen.org
Open: 1-5 Tu-Su   *Closed:* Mo, Leg/Hol!
Vol/Contr.: Yes
& P: Free in front of gallery and in lot beside church across street   *Museum Shop   Group Tours*
Permanent Collection: Reg: ptgs, gr, cer, sculp; Jap: sculp

Opened since 1957 on the campus of a small college in central Kansas, about 20 miles south of Salina, this facility is an important cultural resource for the state. Named after Birger Sandzen, an artist who taught at the College for 52 years, the gallery is the repository of many of his paintings. ❡ "The Little Triton" fountain by sculptor Carl Milles of Sweden located in the courtyard.

ON EXHIBIT 2002

03/24/2002 to 04/21/2002   *Miserere Series: George Rouault Prints and Photographs*

03/24/2002 to 04/21/2002   *104th Annual Midwest Art Exhibition Featuring James Hamil and Rick Garnett: Swedish American Paintings*

05/07/2002 to 06/30/2002   *Aesthetics: A National Juried Exhibition of Two and Three Dimensional Arts*

07/02/2002 to 09/01/2002   *Kansas State University Faculty Show*

LOGAN

Dane G. Hansen Memorial Museum
110 W. Main, Logan, KS   67646

785-689-4846
Open: 9-12 & 1-4 Mo-Fr, 9-12 & 1-5 Sa, 1-5 Su & Holidays   *Closed:* 1/1, Thgv, 12/25
& P: Free   *Group Tours   Drop-In Tours*
Permanent Collection: Or; Reg

Part of a cultural complex completed in 1973 in the heart of downtown Logan, the Hansen Memorial Museum, a member of the Smithsonian Associates, also presents regional artists. Also, Annual Labor Day Celebration, Labor Day Sunday. Car show, live entertainment, fireworks at dark, volleyball tournament and much, much more. All Free. ❡ Annual Hansen Arts & Craft Fair (3rd Sa of Sept) where judges select 12 artists to exhibit in the Hansen's artist corner, one for each month of the year.

ON EXHIBIT 2002

01/05/2002 to 03/17/2002   *Plains Indians*

04/26/2002 to 06/02/2002   *American Indians of the Northwest Coast*

06/05/2002 to 08/01/2002   *Garden of the Heart*

08/04/2002 to 09/29/2002   *Samurai and Chrysanthemums*   Brochure

10/01/2002 to 10/10/2002   *Down Memory Lane: Hansen Exhibits of the Past and the Life of Barbie and Friends*

10/13/2002 to 12/08/2002   *Ceramic Continuum: 50 Years of the Archie Bray Influence and Artistic Landscapes by Betty Baird*

12/15/2002 to 02/23/2003   *Flash: The Associated Press Covers the World and Dolls: Part of Me*

OVERLAND PARK

Johnson County Community College Gallery of Art
Affiliated Institution: Johnson County Community College
12345 College Blvd., Overland Park, KS   66210

913-469-8500   jccc.net/gallery
Open: 10-5 Mo, Th, Fr; 10-7 Tu, We; 1-5 Sa, Su   *Closed:* Leg/Hol!
& P: Free   ¶ *Group Tours:* ext.3789   *Sculpture Garden*
Permanent Collection: Am/Cont: ptgs, cer, phot, works on paper

The geometric spareness of the buildings set among the gently rolling hills of the campus is a perfect foil for the rapidly growing permanent collection of contemporary American art. Sculptures by Jonathan Borofsky, Barry Flanagan, Judith Shea, Louise Bourgeois, and Magdalena Abakanowicz are joined by other contemporary works in the Oppenheimer-Stein Sculpture Collection sited over the 234-acre campus. (Oppenheimer-Stein Sculpture Collection

SALINA

Salina Art Center
242 S. Santa Fe, Salina, KS   67401

785-827-1431   www.salinaartcenter.org
Open: 12-5 Tu-Sa; 1-5 Su; till 7 Th   *Closed:* Mo, Leg/Hol!
& P: Free handicapped parking   *Group Tours*   *Drop-In Tours:* 9-5 Tu-Fr; call to schedule
Permanent Collection: Non-collecting institution

Recognized across the Midwest for bringing together art, artists, and audiences in innovative ways, the Salina Art Center specializes in exhibiting and interpreting contemporary art. Rotating high quality original multicultural exhibitions, traveling exhibitions (often featuring works by international artists), and a permanent Discovery Area hands-on laboratory for children are its main features. (A state of the art movie facility, Art Center Cinema, one block from the gallery, features the best contemporary international and American film. Open Th-Su weekly. Cinema phone: 785-452-9868

ON EXHIBIT 2002

11/18/2001 to 01/13/2002   *Annual Exhibition*
Works in all media selected by David Henry of Rhode Island School of Design

01/26/2002 to 03/31/2002   *(Un)mediated Vision*
New technologies have brought radical changes to the way we see ourselves and the world.

04/13/2002 to 06/30/2002   *Recent Work by Emerging Thai Artists*
A variety of media including video, installation, fiber, and process-oriented art

TOPEKA

Alice C. Sabatini Gallery-Topeka & Shawnee County Public Library
1515 W. 10th, Topeka, KS   66604-1374

785-580-4516
Open: 9-9 Mo-Fr, 9-6 Sa, 2-6 Su in summer   *Closed:* Leg/Hol!
&: Ground entry via automatic doors   P: Free   ¶: for 2002 new facility   *Group Tours*   *Drop-In Tours*
Historic Building: New Michael Graves building
Permanent Collection: Reg: ptgs, gr 20; W/Af; Am: cer, glass paperweights

Although the fine art permanent collection is usually not on view, this active institution presents rotating exhibitions that are mainly regional in nature. The museum will be closed until the year 2002 due to a major construction project that will double its exhibition space and allow for more of the permanent collection to be on display. ❡ Glass paperweights; Akan gold weights from Ghana and the Ivory Coast, West Africa

ON EXHIBIT 2002

01/01/2002 to February 2002 *Alice C. Sabitini & Selections of Huggins, Garzio/O'Brien and Steel Gifts & Dr. Cotter/Jeanne Hirshberg Collections*

04/01/2002 to May 2002 *Schoenhut Circus Toys & Permanent Collection*

06/01/2002 to August 2002 *William Howe (Butterfly Work), David Spitzer Photographs, Gary Martin Ceramic Sculpture & Snuff Bottles*

09/01/2002 to October 2002 *Recent Acquisitions & Small Clay Work*

11/01/2002 to December 2002 *Marjory Schick Retrospective, Installation, Jewelry Collection & Jewelry and Metalwork in Collection*

Mulvane Art Museum
Affiliated Institution: Washburn University
17th & Jewell, Topeka, KS 66621-1150

785-231-1124
Open: Sept-May: 10-7 Tu-We, 10-4 Th & Fr, 1-4 Sa, Su; Summer: 10-4 Tu-Fr & 1-4 Sa, Su *Closed:* Mo, Leg/Hol! & during exhibit installations
Vol/Contr.: Yes
& P: Free *Museum Shop*
Group Tours: 785-231-1010 x1322 *Drop-In Tours:* by appointment, 10-3 Tu-Fr
Historic Building: Oldest Art Museum in State of Kansas (1924) *Sculpture Garden*
Permanent Collection: Eur: dec/art 19-20; Am: dec/art 19-20; Jap: dec/art 19-20; Reg: cont ptgs; Gr; Sculp; Cer; Phot

Opened in 1924, the Mulvane is the oldest art museum in the state of Kansas, located on the campus of Washburn University. In addition to an ever growing collection of works by artists of Kansas and the Mountain-Plains region, the museum counts both an international and a Japanese print collection among its holdings.

ON EXHIBIT 2002

10/13/2001 to 12/23/2001 *Body Show*

WICHITA

Edwin A. Ulrich Museum of Art
Affiliated Institution: Wichita State University
1845 Fairmount St., Wichita, KS 67260-0046

316-978-3664 http://ulrich.wichita.edu
Open: 9-5 Mo-Fr, 12-5 Sa, Su *Closed:* Leg/Hols
& P: Visitor lot available. *Group Tours:* 316-978-6413 *Drop-In Tours:* by appt
Historic Building: Marble & glass mosaic mural by Spanish artist Joan Miro on museum facade
Sculpture Garden
Permanent Collection: Am: 19-20; Eur: 19-20; Prim; Am: gr; Eur: gr; Phot

The Edwin A. Ulrich Museum of Art at Wichita State University is recognized among university museums for its outdoor sculpture collection and for the quality of its exhibition program. 19th- and 20th-century European and American sculpture, prints, drawings, and paintings form the core of the 7,300 object collection. A major aspect of the collection is the 64-piece outdoor sculpture collection, named in honor of the founding director of the museum, placed around the 330-acre campus of Wichita State University. The collection contains a cross-section of 19th- and 20th-century sculptures by artists such as Auguste Rodin, Henry Moore, Louise Nevelson, George Rickey, Lynn Chadwick, and Luis Jimenez, among others. The museum is easily recognized by the centerpiece of this outdoor collection: the mosaic, Personnages Oiseaux, by Joan Miró, commissioned by the University in 1979. Consisting of nearly one million pieces of Venetian glass and marble, the mural depicts whimsical bird characters that inhabited the imagination of the artist. The Ulrich has an outstanding exhibition program and acts as a visual laboratory for the students of the University as well as the community. Exhibitions range from established art work—often from the museum's collection—to more contemporary exhibitions highlighting prominent artists working today. ❲ Sculpture collection on grounds of university; Collection of marine paintings by Frederick J. Waugh

ON EXHIBIT 2002

12/01/2001 to 01/27/2002   *Wichita State University Alumni Exhibition*
Works by University alumni in the first ever juried exhibition

02/08/2002 to 03/17/2002   *Contemporary Ceramics*
A survey of the nation's leading ceramic artists

02/21/2002 to 04/07/2002   *Sculpture by Christy Rupp*

04/25/2002 to 09/01/2002   *Travels in the Labyrinth: Mexican Art in the Pollak Collection*
Outstanding examples by 20th century Mexican artists and Mexican folk art   *Will Travel*

Indian Center Museum
650 N. Seneca, Wichita, KS   67203

316-262-5221   www.theiondiancenter.com
Open: 10-5 Tu-Sa, 1-5 Su   *Closed:* Mo, Jan-Mar; Leg/Hol!
Adm: *Adult:* $3.00 with Village $4.00   *Children:* Free 6 & under, $2.50   *Students:* $1.00   *Seniors:* $1.00
P: Free   *Museum Shop   Group Tours*
Permanent Collection: Nat/Am

The artworks and artifacts in this museum preserve Native American heritage and provide non-Indian people with insight into the culture and traditions of Native Americans. In addition to the art, Native American food is served on Tu from 11-4. ❲ Blackbear Bosin's 44-foot "Keeper of the Plains" located on the grounds at the confluence of the Arkansas & Little Arkansas Rivers.

Wichita Art Museum
619 Stackman Drive., Wichita, KS   67203-3296

316-268-4921   www.wichitaartmuseum.org
Open: 10-5 Tu-Sa, 12-5 Su   *Closed:* Mo, Leg/Hol
Vol/Contr.: Yes   *Sugg/Contr.:* $3.00
♿ P: Free   *Museum Shop   Group Tours:* 316-268-4907   *Drop-In Tours:* Su, 1:30pm
Historic Building: 1977 designed by Edward Larabee Barnes
Permanent Collection: Am: ptgs, ge, drgs; Eur: gr, drgs; P/Col; Charles Russell: ptgs, drgs, sculp; OM: gr

Outstanding in its collection of paintings that span nearly 3 centuries of American art, the Wichita is the largest museum in Kansas. A multi-million dollar expansion has begun adding 40 percent more exhibition space. *The museum will reopen early in 2003. ❲ The Roland P. Murdock Collection of American Art, including work by Mary Cassatt, Dove, Hartigan, Homer, and Hopper

Wichita Center for the Arts
9112 East Central, Wichita, KS   67206

316-634-2787   www.wcfta.com
Open: 1-5 Tu-Su   *Closed:* Mo, Leg/Hol!
& P: on-site free parking spaces   *Museum Shop   Group Tours   Theater*
Permanent Collection: Dec/Art: 20; Or; Ptgs; Sculp; Drgs; Cer; Gr

Midwest arts, both historical and contemporary, are the focus of this vital multi-disciplinary facility.   (3,500-piece Bruce Moore Collection

KENTUCKY

LEXINGTON

University of Kentucky Art Museum
Rose & Euclid Ave., Lexington, KY   40506-0241

859-257-5716   www.uky.edu/artmusueum
Open: 12-5 Tu-Su; 12-8 Fr   *Closed:* Mo, Acad!
Vol./Contr.: Yes
& P: Parking available in the circular drive in front of the Center and behind the Faculty Club on Columbia Ave.
Group Tours: 859-257-8164   *Drop-In Tours:* by appt
Permanent Collection: OM: ptgs, gr; Am: ptgs 19; Eur: ptgs 19; Cont/Gr; Ptgs 20; Af; Asian; WPA works

Considered to be one of Kentucky's key cultural resources, this museum houses over 3,500 art objects that span the past 2,000 years of artistic creation.

ON EXHIBIT 2002

10/14/2001 to 01/27/2002   *Spring-fed Pond: A Friendship with Five Kentucky Writers (Photographs by Kentucky Poet Laureate James Baker Hall)*

01/20/2002 to 03/10/2002   *Sunlight and Shadow: American Impressionism, 1885–1945*

02/17/2002 to 05/05/2002   *Ann Stewart Anderson: Mythic Women*

03/01/2002 to April 2002   *The Robert C. May Photography Endowment Lecture Series (Speakers and Dates to be Announced)*

03/31/2002 to 06/23/2002   *Robert James Foose: A Retrospective*

05/26/2002 to 08/18/2002   *Cole Carothers*

LOUISVILLE

Photographic Archives
Affiliate Institution: University of Louisville Libraries
Ekstrom Library, University of Louisville, Louisville, KY   40292

502-852-6752   http://www.louisville.edu/library/ekstrom/special/pa-info.html
Open: 10-4 Mo-Fr, 10-8 Th   *Closed:* Sa, Su, Leg/Hol!
& P: Limited (for information call 502-852-6505)
Permanent Collection: Phot; Gr

With 33 individual collections, and over one million items, the Photographic Archives is one of the finest photography and research facilities in the country.   (2,000 vintage Farm Security Administration photos; more than 1,500 fine prints "from Ansel Adams to Edward Weston."

Speed Art Museum
2035 S. Third St. Louisville, KY   40208

502-634-2700   www.speedmuseum.org
Open: 10:30-4 Tu-We, Fr, Sa 10:30-5, 12-5 Su, till 8pm Th   *Closed:* Mo 1/1, Kentucky Derby Day, 7/4, Thgv
Sugg./Contr.: $4.00
& P: Adjacent to the museum; $3.00 fee for non-members
Museum Shop ¶: Bristol Cafe,11:30-2 Tu-Sa
Group Tours: 502-634-2725   *Drop-In Tours:* 2pm Sa, 1 & 3pm Su, 7pm Th   *Sculpture Garden   Theater*
Permanent Collection: Am: dec/art; Ptgs; Sculp: Gr; Prim; Or; Du: 17; Fl: 17; Fptgs 18; Cont

Founded in 1927, and located on the main campus of the University of Louisville, the newly renovated Speed Art Museum is the largest (over 8,000 works) and the most comprehensive (spanning 6,000 years of art history) public art collection in Kentucky. Free "Especially for Children" tours are offered at 1:00 pm each Sa. *A fee is charged for selected exhibitions.
€ "Two Apples on a Table" by Cézanne 1895–1900; "Nydia, The Blind Girl of Pompeii" by Randolph Rogers, after 1854; Stained Glass Windows by Jacob Lawrence

ON EXHIBIT 2002

11/16/2001 to 01/27/2002   *A Brush with History: Paintings from the Collection of the National Portrait Gallery*
Including 75 portraits by the most important portrait artists in the past 200 years.   *Will Travel*

02/19/2002 to 04/14/2002   *A Bountiful Plenty from the Shelburne Museum: Folk Art Traditions in America*
Drawn fromone of America's most outstanding folk art collections including trade signs, cigar store figures, carousel figures, weather vanes, scrimshaw, decoys, quilts, furniture and "primitive" paintings of the 18th and 19th centuries. Folk art's role in the development of American art is studied.

03/16/2002 to 05/12/2002   *Masterworks from the Albertina*
Drawings and prints from Vienna, one of the world's most important and oldest collections of Old Masters

11/05/2002 to 02/02/2002   *Millet to Matisse: Nineteenth and Twentieth Century French Paintings from Kelvingrove Art Gallery, Glasgow*
Impressionist, Post-Impressionist and Modern periods including Monet, Renoir, Cassatt, Cézanne, van Gogh, and Picasso

OWENSBORO

Owensboro Museum of Fine Art
901 Frederica St., Owensboro, KY   42301

502-685-3181
Open: 10-4 Tu-Fr; 1-4 Sa, Su   *Closed:* Mo, Leg/Hol!
Vol./Contr.:   Adm: Adult: $2.00   Children: $1.00
& P: Free   *Museum Shop   Group Tours   Sculpture Garden*
Permanent Collection: Am: ptgs, drgs, gr, sculp 19-20; Brit: ptgs, drgs, gr, sculp 19-20; Fptgs, sculp, drgs, gr 19-20; Cont/Am; Dec/Art 14-18

The collection of the Owensboro Museum, the only fine art institution in Western Kentucky, features works by important 18-20th century American, English, and French masters. Paintings by regional artists stress the strong tradition of Kentucky landscape painting. There is a restored Civil War era mansion, the John Hampdem Smith House, serves as a decorative arts wing for objects dating from the 15th to 19th century. € 16 turn-of-the-century stained glass windows by Emil Frei (1867–1941) permanently installed in the new wing of the museum; revolving exhibitions of the museum's collection of Appalachian folk art; 20th-century painting and sculpture

ON EXHIBIT 2002

01/20/2002 to 03/17/2002   *Kentucky's Women Artists: 1850–2000: Part Two*
A historical documentary designed to provide a permanent record of the contribution of women to cultural history of Kentucky over 150 years. Part Two will show artists from 1850–1970.

03/24/2002 to 05/12/2002   *Hats and Headdresses: Adornments of the Head from Around the World*
Lifestyles of people from 60 countries in Africa, Asia, Europe, Middle East, North and South America

05/19/2002 to 07/07/2002   *Two Centuries of American Printmaking*
Printmaking in America from Currier and Ives to Andy Warhol from the corporate collection of A.G. Edwards & Sons, St. Louis, Mo

07/16/2002 to 08/25/2002   *Happy Birthday OMFA*
Major acquisitions, 1977–2002

PADUCAH

Yeiser Art Center
200 Broadway, Paducah, KY   42001-0732

270-442-2453   www.yeiser.org
Open: 10-4 Tu-Sa, 1-4 Su   *Closed:* Mo, Leg/Hol! & Jan
Adm: Adult: $1.00
& P: Free   *Museum Shop   Drop-In Tours:* Usually available upon request
Historic Building: Located in the historic Market House (1905)
Permanent Collection: Am, Eur, As & Af: 19-20

The restored 1905 Market House (listed NRHP), home to the Art Center and many other community related activities, features changing exhibitions that are regional, national, and international in content.   ☾ Annual national fiber exhibition mid Mar thru Apr (call for exact dates)

LOUISIANA

ALEXANDRIA

Alexandria Museum of Art
933 Main St., Alexandria, LA   71301-1028

318-443-3458   www.themuseum.org
Open: 10-5 Tu-Fr, 1-5 Sa   *Closed:* Mo, Leg/Hol!
Adm: Adult: $4.00   *Children:* $2.00   *Students:* $3.00   *Seniors:* $3.00
& P: Free General, Handicap and Bus parking in front of building.   *Museum Shop*
¶: Catered lunch can be pre-arranged in atrium café.
Group Tours: 318-443-3458 ext. 18   *Drop-In Tours:* often available upon request!
Historic Building: 1900 Bank Building   *Sculpture Garden*
Permanent Collection: Cont: sculp, ptgs; Reg; Folk

The grand foyer of the new wing of the Alexandria Museum of Art, was constructed and opened to the public in March of 1998. The Museum was founded in 1977 and originally occupied the Historic Rapides Bank Building, circa 1898, listed on the National Historic Register. The expanded AMoA is the centerpiece of Alexandria's riverfront, situated on the entire 900 block of Main Street.   ☾ Native expression exhibit of Louisiana art and children's gallery.

BATON ROUGE

Louisiana Arts and Science Center
100 S. River Rd., Baton Rouge, LA   70802

225-344-5272   www.lascmuseum.org
Open: 10-3 Tu-Fr, 10-4 Sa, 1-4 Su   *Closed:* Mo, Leg/Hol!
Free Day: 1st Su of month   *Adm:*   *Adult:* $4.00   *Children:* $2.00 (2-12)
Students: university $2.00   *Seniors:* $2.00
&   P: Limited free parking in front of building and behind train; other parking areas available
within walking distance   *Museum Shop*   *Group Tours:* 225-344-9478
Historic Building: Housed in reconstructed Illinois Central Railroad Station   *Sculpture Garden*
Permanent Collection: Sculp; Eth; Gr; Drgs; Phot; Egt; Am: ptgs 18-20; Eur: ptgs 18-20

LASC, housed in a reconstructed Illinois Central Railroad Station, offers changing fine art exhibitions, Egyptian tomb with mummies, and a five-car train (undergoing restoration). Hands-on areas for children include Discovery Depot—an "edutainment" area—and Science Station, an interactive science gallery. The Challenger Learning Center is a simulated space station and mission control center (reservations required). LASC will open its stae-of-the-art planetarium space theater in early 2002. This advanced facility will feature planetarium shows as well as large format films.   ℂ Works by John Marin, Charles Burchfield, Asher B. Durand; Baroque, Neo-Classic, and Impressionist Works; Native American totem pole; 2nd largest collection in the U.S. of sculpture by Ivan Mestrovic.

JENNINGS

Zigler Museum
411 Clara St., Jennings, LA   70546

318-824-0114   www.JettDavis.org
Open: 9-5 Tu-Sa, 1-5 Su   *Closed:* Mo, Leg/Hol!
Sugg/Contr.: Yes   *Adm:*   *Adult:* $2.00   *Children:* $1.00
&   P: Free   *Museum Shop*   *Group Tours*   *Drop-In Tours:* Usually available upon request   *Theater*
Permanent Collection: Reg; Am; Eur

The gracious colonial style structure that had served as the Zigler family home since 1908, was formerly opened as a museum in 1970. Two wings added to the original building feature many works by Louisiana landscape artists in addition to those by other American and European artists. *The museum is open every day for the Christmas festival from the first weekend in December to December 22.   ℂ Largest collection of works by African-American artist, William Tolliver

ON EXHIBIT 2002

04/29/2001 to 06/07/2002   *Produce for Victory: Poster on the American Home Front, 1941–1945*
The exhibition shows posters displayed in factories, libraries, and shops to rally a nation to take steps to support the soldiers in the field. It shows how the movement affected factory workers and pushed laborers to become more productive.   *Will Travel*

LAFAYETTE

University Art Museum
Joel L. Fletcher Hall, 2nd Floor, East Lewis & Girard Park Dr., Lafayette, LA   70504

318-482-5326   www.lousiana..edu/vam/
Open: 9-4 Tu-Fr, 2-5 Su   *Closed:* Mo, Sa, 1/1, Mardi Gras, Easter, Thgv, 12/25, Leg/Hol!
&   P: Free with validation in paylot   *Group Tours:* 337-482-5326   *Drop-In Tours:* reservation only
Permanent Collection: Am/Reg: ptgs, sculp, drgs, phot 19-20; Jap: gr; *Selections from the permanent collection are on display approximately once a year (call for specifics)

The University Art Museum is situated on the beautiful campus of The University of Louisiana Lafayette, home of Cypress Lake. The UAM offers visitors art exhibitions of regional, national, and international acclaim. The Permanent Collection is housed in an 18th-century style plantation home on the corner of Girard Park Drive and St. Mary Boulevard. Permanent holdings include works by Henri Le Sidaner, Franz Marc, Sir Godfrey Kneller, G.P.A. Healy, Henry Pember Smith, and Adolph Rinck to name only a few. Overlooking Girard Park, touring exhibits can be seen in the more modern Fletcher Hall Gallery located in the Art & Architecture Building on the U.L. Lafayette campus.

MONROE

Masur Museum of Art
1400 S. Grand, Monroe, LA   71202

318-329-2237   www.ci.monroe.la.us/mma
Open: 9-5 Tu-Th, 2-5 Fr-Su   *Closed:* Mo, Leg/Hol!
&: Access to first floor only   P: Free   *Group Tours   Drop-In Tours:* call for hours
Historic Building   Sculpture Garden
Permanent Collection: Am: gr 20; Reg/Cont

Twentieth-century prints by American artists, and works by contemporary regional artists, form the basis of the permanent collection of this museum which is housed in a stately modified English Tudor estate situated on the tree-lined banks of the Ouachita River.

NEW ORLEANS

Historic New Orleans Collection
533 Royal St., New Orleans, LA   70130

504-523-4662   www.hnoc.org
Open: 10-4:30 Tu-Sa   *Closed:* Su, Mo, Leg/Hol!
Free Day: Main Exhibition Hall Tu-Sa   *Adm: Adult:* $4.00
& *Museum Shop   Group Tours   Drop-In Tours:* 10, 11, 2 & 3 daily
Historic Building: 1792 Jean Francois Merieult House located in French Quarter   *Theater*
Permanent Collection: Reg: ptgs, drgs, phot; Maps; Rare Books, Manuscripts

Located within a complex of historic French Quarter buildings, the Historic New Orleans Collection serves the public as a museum and research center for state and local history. Merieult House, one of the most historic buildings of this complex, was built in 1792 during Louisiana's Spanish Colonial period. It is one of the few structures in the French Quarter that escaped the fire of 1794. The Williams Research Center, 410 Chartres St., part of this institution, contains curatorial, manuscript, and library material relating to the history and culture of Louisiana.   ❰ Tours of the LA. History Galleries and Founders Residence

Louisiana State Museum
751 Chartres St., Jackson Square, New Orleans, LA   70116

800-568-6968   http://lsm.crt.state.la.us
Open: 9-5 Tu-Su   *Closed:* Mo, Leg/Hol!
Adm: Adult: $5.00   *Children:* Free 12 & under   *Students:* $4.00   *Seniors:* $4.00
&: Presbytere, Old U.S. Mint, and Cabildo are accessible   *Museum Shop*
Group Tours   Drop-In Tours: Gallery talks on weekends - call for specifics   *Historic Building*
Permanent Collection: Dec/Art; Folk; Phot; Ptgs; Textiles

Several historic buildings, located in the famous New Orleans French Quarter are included in the Louisiana State Museum complex, provide the visitor with a wide array of viewing experiences that run the gamut from fine art to decorative art, textiles, Mardi Gras memorabilia, and even jazz music. The Cabildo, Presbytere, and 1850 House (all located on Jackson Square) and the Old U.S. Mint are currently open to the public. *(1) Although the entry fee of $5.00 is charged per building visited, a discounted rate is offered for a visit to two or more sites. (2) 1850 House features special interpretive materials for handicapped visitors. ℂ Considered the State Museum's crown jewel, the recently reopened Cabildo features a walk through Louisiana history from Colonial times through Reconstruction. Admission to the Arsenal, featuring changing exhibits, is included in the entry fee to the Cabildo.

New Orleans Museum of Art
1 Collins Diboll Circle, City Park, P.O. Box 19123, New Orleans, LA   70119-0123

504-488-2631   www.noma.org
Open: 10-5 Tu-Su   *Closed:* Mo, Leg/Hol!
Free Day: 10-12 Th for Louisiana residents only except for some special exh   *Adm:*   *Adult:* $6.00
Children: $3.00 (3-17)   *Students:* $5.00   *Seniors:* $5.00
& P: Free   *Museum Shop*   ¶: Courtyard Cafe 10:30-4:30 Tu-Su (children's menu available)
Group Tours   *Drop-In Tours:* 11:00 & 2:00 Tu-Su and by appointment for groups of 10 or more
Sculpture Garden
Permanent Collection: Am; OM: ptgs; It/Ren: ptgs (Kress Collection); Fr; P/Col: Mex; Af; Jap: gr; Af; Oc; Nat/Am; Lat/Am; As; Dec/Art: 1st century AD-20; Reg; Phot; Glass

Located in the 1,500 acre City Park, this 90-year-old New Orleans Museum recently completed a $23 million dollar expansion and renovation program that doubled its size. Serving the entire Gulf South as an invaluable artistic resource, the museum houses over one dozen major collections that cover a broad range of fine and decorative art. ℂ Treasures by Faberge; Chinese Jades; French Art; contemporary art; New 3rd floor showcase for Non-Western Art; The Starting Point, a new hands-on gallery area with interactive exhibits and 2 computer stations designed to help children and adults understand the source of artists' inspiration.

ON EXHIBIT 2002

11/10/2001 to 01/13/2002   *Magnificent, Marvelous, Martele: American Art Nouveau Silver from the Collection of Robert and Julie Shelton*
A first comprehensive look at the silver produced by the Gorham Company at the beginning of the 20th century   *Catalog   Will Travel*

02/16/2002 to 04/28/2002   *Life, Death, and Sport: The Mesoamerican Ballgame*
The first team sport in history. The religious, ceremonial, and political aspects of the game are on view

05/31/2002 to 08/11/2002   *A Brush with History: Paintings from the Collection of the National Portrait Gallery*
Including 75 portraits by the most important portrait artists in the past 200 years   *Will Travel*

08/31/2002 to 10/26/2002   *An Enduring Visison: Japanese Paintings from the 17th–20th Century*
An in depth view of the Edo (1615–1868) periods and Meiji (1868–1912) periods from the collection of Dr. Kurt A. Gitter and Alice Rae Yelen who assembled this premier collection
Will Travel

09/01/2002 to Autumn 2002   *The Sydney and Walda Besthoff Sculpture Garden*
A five-acre garden adjacent to the museum with spaces for 60 sculptures by major twentieth century European, American, Israeli, and Japanese artists

11/08/2002 to 01/12/2003   *Working on a Building: New Orleans Building Arts through the Generations*
The role of New Orleans craftsmen in the built environment

Meadows Museum of Art of Centenary College
2911 Centenary Blvd., Shreveport, LA   71104-1188

318-869-5169   centenary.edu
Open: 12-4 Tu, We, Fr, 12-5 Th, 1-4 Sa, Su   *Closed:* Mo, Leg/Hol!
&;   P: Free behind the building   *Museum Shop*
Group Tours: 318-869-5169   *Drop-In Tours:* Upon request if available
Permanent Collection: Ptgs, Sculp, Gr, 18-20; Indo-Chinese: ptgs, gr

This museum, opened in 1976, serves mainly as a repository for the unique collection of works in a variety of media by French artist Jean Despujols and the Centenary College collection. The Museum's galleries also boast a series of temporary exhibitions throughout the year.   ❰ The permanent collection itself which offers a rare glimpse into the people & culture of French Indochina in 1938. Also includes American and European paintings and works on paper from the college collection.

R. W. Norton Art Gallery
4747 Creswell Ave., Shreveport, LA   71106

318-865-4201   www.softdisk.com/comp/norton
Open: 10-5 Tu-Fr; 1-5 Sa, Su   *Closed:* Mo, Leg/Hol!
&   P: Free   *Museum Shop   Group Tours   Drop-In Tours:* Tu-Fr by appt   *Theater*
Permanent Collection: Am: ptgs, sculp (late 17-20); Eur: ptgs, sculp 16-19; Brit: cer

With its incomparable collections of American and European art, the Norton, situated in a 46-acre wooded park, has become one of the major cultural attractions in the region since its opening in 1966. Among its many attractions are the Bierstadt Gallery, the Bonheur Gallery, and the Corridor which features "The Prisons," a 16-part series of fantasy etchings by Piranesi. Those who visit the museum from early to mid April will experience the added treat of seeing 13,000 azalea plants that surround the building in full bloom.   ❰ Outstanding collections of works by Frederic Remington & Charles M. Russell; The Wedgewood Gallery (one of the finest collections of its kind in the southern U.S.)

ON EXHIBIT 2002

04/07/2002 to 06/02/2002   *West by Southwest*
Approximately 62 paintings, watercolors, and bronze sculptures from the Museum of the Southwest in Midland, Texas

06/30/2002 to 08/18/2002   *Norman Rockwell Lithographs*
Signed original lithographs from the Powers Collection

09/01/2002 to 10/13/2002   *Painted Essays: William Keith's Landscapes of the West*
Oils, watercolors, and drawings from the Hearst Art Gallery Collection

MAINE

Bowdoin College Museum of Art
9400 College Station, Brunswick, ME   04011-8494

207-725-3275   www.bowdoin.edu/artmuseum
Open: 10-5 Tu-Sa, 2-5 Su   *Closed:* Leg/Hol!; also closed week between 12/25 & 1/1
Vol/Contr.: Yes
&.: Call for assistance (207) 725-3275   P: All along Upper Park Row
Museum Shop   Group Tours: 207-725-3276
Historic Building: 1894 Walker Art Building designed by Charles Follen McKim
Permanent Collection: An/Grk; An/R; An/Egt; Am: ptgs, sculp, drgs, gr, dec/art; Eur: ptgs, sculp, gr, drgs, dec/art; Af: sculp; Interior Murals by LaFarge, Thayer, Vedder, Cox

From the original bequest of artworks given in 1811 by James Bowdoin III, who served as Thomas Jefferson's minister to France and Spain, the collection has grown to include important works from a broad range of nations and periods. ℭ The American collections including Gilbert Stuart's presidential portraits of Jefferson and Madison and object by significant artists working in every period of U.S. history.

L E W I S T O N

Bates College Museum of Art
Affiliated Institution: Bates College
Olin Arts Center, Bates College, Lewiston, ME   04240

207-786-6158   www.bates.edu/acad/museum
Open: 10-5 Mo-Sa, 1-5 Su   *Closed:* Leg/Hol!
& P: Free on-street campus parking   *Group Tours:* by appt   *Theater*
Permanent Collection: Am: ptgs, sculp; Gr 19-20; Eur: ptgs, sculp, gr; drgs

The Bates College Museum of Art houses a major collection of works by American artist Marsden Hartley. It also specializes in 20th-century American and European prints, drawings, and photographs, and has a small collection of 20th century American paintings. ℭ Collection of Marsden Hartley drawings and memorabilia

O G U N Q U I T

Ogunquit Museum of American Art
543 Shore Rd., Ogunquit, ME   03907-0815

207-646-4909   www.maineartmueums.org
Open: (open 7/1 through 10/15 only) 10:30-5 Mo-Sa, 2-5 Su   *Closed:* Lab/Day
Adm: Adult: $4.00   *Children:* Free under 12   *Students:* $3.00   *Seniors:* $3.00
&: Enter lower level at seaside end of bldg; wheelchairs available   P: Free on museum grounds
Museum Shop   Group Tours   Drop-In Tours: Upon request if available   *Sculpture Garden*
Permanent Collection: Am: ptgs, sculp 20

Situated on a rocky promontory overlooking the sea, this museum has been described as the most beautiful small museum in the world! Built in 1952, the Museum houses over 1,400 pieces of important 20th-century American paintings and works of sculpture in addition to site-specific sculptures spread throughout its three acres of land. ℭ "Mt. Katadhin, Winter" by Marsden Hartley; "The Bowerey Drunks" by Reginald Marsh; "Pool With Four Markers" by Dozier Bell; "Sleeping Girl" by Walt Kuhn

O R O N O

University of Maine Museum of Art
5712 Carnegie Hall, Orono, ME   04469-5712

207-581-3255   umaine.edu/artmuseum
Open: 9-4:30 Mo-Sa; (summer hours 9-4)   *Closed:* Su, State & Leg/Hol!
P: Free with visitor permits available in director's office.   *Group Tours:* by appt
Historic Building: 1904 Library of Palladian Design
Permanent Collection: Am: gr, ptgs 18-20; Eur: gr, ptgs 18-20; Cont; Reg

Housed in a beautiful 1904 structure of classic Palladian design, this university art museum, located just to the northeast of Bangor, Maine, features American and European art of the 18th-20th centuries, and works by Maine-based artists of the past and present. The permanent collection is displayed throughout the whole university and in the Maine Center-for-the-Arts building.

Portland Museum of Art
Seven Congress Square, Portland, ME   04101

207-775-6148   www.portlandmuseum.org
Open: 10-5 Tu, We, Sa, Su; 10-9 Th, Fr; (open 10-5 Mo, Mem/Day to Columbus Day)   *Closed:* Leg/Hol!,
12/25, 1/1, Thgv
Free Day: 5-9 Fr   *Adm:*   *Adult:* $6.00   *Children:* $1.00 (6-12)   *Students:* $5.00   *Seniors:* $5.00
&   P: Nearby garages   *Museum Shop* ||: Museum Cafe
Group Tours: 207-775-6148   *Drop-In Tours:* 2pm
Permanent Collection: Am; ptgs, sculp 19-20; Reg; Dec/Art; gr

The Portland Museum of Art is the oldest and largest art museum in the state of Maine.
Established in 1882, the outstanding museum features European and American masterworks
housed in an award-winning building designed by renowned architect I.M. Pei & Partners.
*Also, there is a toll-free number (1-800-639-4067) for museum recorded information.

ON EXHIBIT 2002

10/06/2001 to 01/27/2002   *Dahlov Ipcar (working title)*

11/08/2001 to 01/06/2002   *Harmonica and Contrasts: The Art of Marguerite and William Zorach*

01/05/2002 to 02/24/2002   *Open House: Tanja Alexis Hollander*

01/24/2002 to 03/24/2002   *Robert Doisneau's Paris*

02/09/2002 to 05/27/2002   *William Thon (working title)*

03/09/2002 to 05/19/2002   *Archives: Monotypes by Alan Magee*

04/11/2002 to 06/09/2002   *Bernard Langlais (working title)*

06/07/2002 to 09/08/2002   *Paul Caponigro's New England*

06/27/2002 to 10/20/2002   *Neo-Impressionism: Artists on the Edge*

09/21/2002 to 12/01/2002   *Leonard Baskin: Monumental Woodcuts*

11/07/2002 to 01/05/2003   *Charles Codman (working title)*

Farnsworth Art Museum and Wyeth Center
16 Museum Street, Rockland, ME   04841-9975

207-596-6457   www.farnsworthmuseum.org
Open: Summer: 9-5 daily; Winter: 10-5 Tu-Sa, 1-5 Su   *Closed:* Thgv, 12/25, 1/1
Adm: *Adult:* $9.00   *Children:* Free under 17   *Students:* $5.00   *Seniors:* $8.00
&   P: Free   *Museum Shop*   *Group Tours:* ex t. 104   *Drop-In Tours*
Historic Building: 1850 Victorian Homestead and Olson House open Mem/Day to Columbus Day.
Permanent Collection: Am: 18-20; Reg; Phot; Gr

Nationally acclaimed for its collection of American Art, the Farnsworth, located in the
mid-coastal city of Rockland, counts among its important holdings the largest public collection
of works by sculptor Louise Nevelson. The museum's 12 galleries offer a comprehensive survey
of American art. Recently, the museum opened the Wyeth center, a new gallery building and
study center, to house the works of Andrew, N. C., and Jamie Wyeth. The Jamison Morehouse
wing offers 4 new galleries and another entrance on Main St.   ❲ Major works by N.C.,
Andrew, and Jamie Wyeth, Fitz Hugh Lane, John Marin, Edward Hopper, Neil Welliver, Louise
Nevelson; The Olson House, depicted by Andrew Wyeth in many of his most famous works

ON EXHIBIT 2002

10/14/2001 to 05/19/2002   *Andrew Wyeth Selections*
Tempera paintings, watercolors, and drawings

10/21/2001 to 02/24/2002   *Samuel Gelber: The Seasons Suite*
Large scale paintings of the landscape outside his Maine farmhouse   *Brochure*

10/28/2001 to 02/24/2002   *Characters in Hand: Puppets by Maine Puppeteers*

03/03/2002 to 06/02/2002   *Recent Work by Celeste Roberge and John Von Bergen*
Contemporary artists with mixed media paintings by Allison Hildreth

04/28/2002 to 09/09/2002   *An Artistic Friendship: Beauford Delaney and Lawrence Calgano*

06/30/2002 to 10/13/2002   *Kenneth Noland: Themes and Variations*
Major phases of the artist's career emphasizing his most recent series "Mysteries"

07/02/2002 to October 2002   *Capturing Nureyev: Jamie Wyeth Paints the Dancer*

WATERVILLE

Colby College Museum of Art
Mayflower Hill, Waterville, ME   04901

207-872-3228   www.colby.edu/museum
Open: 10-4:30 Mo-Sa, 2-4:30 Su   *Closed:* Leg/Hol!
&   P: Free   *Museum Shop   Group Tours*
Permanent Collection: Am: Impr/ptgs, folk, gr; Winslow Homer: watercolors; Or: cer

Located in a modernist building on a campus dominated by neo-Georgian architecture, the museum at Colby College houses a distinctive collection of several centuries of American Art. Included among its many fine holdings is a 36-piece collection of sculpture donated to the school by Maine native, Louise Nevelson.   ℭ 25 watercolors by John Marin; "La Reina Mora" by Robert Henri (recent acquisition)

ON EXHIBIT 2002

01/03/2002 to March 2002   *Lawrence Hayden Drawing*

02/01/2002 to Mid-June 2002   *The Joan Whitney Payson Collection*

03/01/2002 to April 2002   *Maine Decoys*

03/15/2002 to mid April 2002   *Old Master Prints from the Permanent Collection*

04/15/2002 to mid June 2002   *Andrew Forge*

07/17/2002 to 10/12/2002   *Aerial Muse: The Art of Yvonne Jacquet*

08/01/2002 to October 2002   *Work by Rudy Burckhardt*

MARYLAND

ANNAPOLIS

Mitchell Gallery
Affiliated Institution: St. John's College
60 College Ave., Annapolis, MD   21401-1655

410-626-2556 www.sjca.edu/gallery/gallery.html
Open: 12-5 Tu-Su; 7-8 Fr; closed for the summer   *Closed:* Mo, Leg/Hol!
&   P: 2-hour metered street parking near museum; parking at the U.S. Naval & Marine Corps Stadium
on Rowe Blvd. with free shuttle bus service; Parking available in campus lots on weekends. Call ahead to
arrange for handicap parking.   ¶: College Coffee Shop open 8:15-4
Group Tours   Drop-In Tours: by appt   *Historic Building   Theater*
Permanent Collection: non-collecting institution

Established in 1989 primarily as a center of learning for the visual arts, this institution,
though young in years, presents a rotating schedule of educational programs and high quality
exhibitions containing original works by many of the greatest artists of yesterday and today.

ON EXHIBIT 2002

January 2002 to March 2002   *The Lithographs of James McNeill Whistler*
Whistler was inspired by the prints of Toulouse-Lautrec and Bonnard late in his career.
Includes his rare colored lithographs, which are regarded as his most personal expression in art.

March 2002 to April 2002   *The New York School and Beyond: Paintings from the Art Enterprises,
Limited Collection*
Artists working in the New York School in the 40s and 50s shifted the center of visual art with
their highly innovative style known as Abstract Expressionism. Artists included Motherwell,
Kline, Pollock, Hofmann, Olitski, Louis, Mitchell, and Francis.   *Will Travel   Brochure*

August 2002 to October 2002   *The Sweet Uses of Adversity: Images of the Biblical Job*

11/17/2002 to 01/12/2003   *The Human Factor: Figuration in American Art 1950–1995*
The wide range of focus on the figure in contemporary art. Among the artists are Bearden,
Katz, Neel, Close, Pearlstein, Segal, Lomgo, and Fischl.   *Will Travel   Brochure*

BALTIMORE

American Visionary Art Museum
800 Key Highway & Covington in the Baltimore Inner Harbor, Baltimore, MD   21202-3940

410-244-1900 avam.org
Open: 10-6 Tu-Su   *Closed:* Thgv, 12/25
Free Day: $1 7/4   *Adm:* *Adult:* $6.00   *Children:* Free under 4   *Students:* $4.00   *Seniors:* $4.00
&.: Fully accessible with street drop-off lane   P: $3.00 parking in large lot across the street from the
Museum; many 24-hour metered spaces on Covington.   *Museum Shop*
¶: Joy America Cafe open 11:30am-10pm Tu-Sa, Brunch Su 11-4:30 (call 410-244-6500 to reserve)
Historic Building: 1913 elliptical brick building   *Sculpture Garden*
Permanent Collection: Visionary art

Dedicated to intuition, this museum, designated by Congress, is the nation's official repository
for original self-taught (a.k.a. "outsider") visionary art. Among the many highlights of the
4,000-piece permanent collection are Gerlad Hawkes' one-of-a-kind matchstick sculptures, 400
original pen and ink works by postman/visionary Ted Gordon, and the entire life archive of the
late Otto Billig, M.D., an expert in transcultural psychiatric art who was the last psychiatrist to
Zelda Fitzgerald.   ¶ Towering whirligig by Vollis Simpson in the central plaza, which is like a
giant playwheel during the day and a colorful firefly-like sculpture when illuminated at night;
Joy America Cafe featuring ultra-organic gourmet food created by four-star chef Peter Zimmer,
formerly of The Inn of the Anasazi in Santa Fe, NM; Wildflower sculpture garden complete
with woven wood wedding chapel by visionary artist Ben Wilson.

Baltimore Museum of Art
Art Museum Drive, Baltimore, MD   21218-3898

410-396-7100   www.artbma.org
Open: 10-5 We-Fr, 11-6 Sa, Su; 5-9 1st Th of month   *Closed:* Mo, 1/1, 7/4, Thgv, 12/25
Adm: Adult: $7.00   Children: Free 18 & under   Students: $5.00 w/ ID   Seniors: $5.00 over 65
&   P: Metered & limited on-site; or parking on weekends at The Johns Hopkins University adjacent
to Museum   *Museum Shop*   ¶: Gertrudes at the BMA 410-889-3399
Group Tours: 410-396-6320   *Drop-In Tours Historic Building:* 1929 bldg designed by John
Russell Pope   *Sculpture Garden*   *Theater*
Permanent Collection: Ptgs, Ren-20; OM/drgs 15-20; Cont; Sculp 15-20; dec/art; Or; p/col

One of the undisputed jewels of this important artistic collection is the Cone Collection, the
largest collection of the works of Matisse in the Western hemisphere housed in the new
17-gallery wing for contemporary art.   ℂ The new installation of the Cone Collection,
American dec/arts; Antioch mosaics; Sculp Garden; Am Paintings 19; OM paintings

ON EXHIBIT 2002

11/14/2001 to 02/03/2002   *Installations from the Collection: Picasso's Classicism*

02/06/2002 to 05/05/2002   *Looking Forward/Looking Black*
A contemporary reexamination of racial and gender stereotypes in 20th-century America.
Artists include Weeden, McIver, Walker, Michael Charles, Weems, Harris, Colescott, Ligon,
Golub, Williams, and Alison Saar.

02/17/2002 to 05/26/2002   *Reflections of the Sea and Light: Paintings and Drawings by J. M. W.
Turner from the Tate*
The first major exhibit of Turner's work in 2 decades. The 100 watercolors, paintings, and
prints, many never seen before.   *Only Venue*

10/02/2002 to 01/05/2003   *Northern Renaissance Painter Prints (working title)*
Large numbers of painted prints were created from the 15th century to the 17th. The exhibit
includes a 16th-century print colorist's studio, recipes for the manufacture of pigments, and a
chart documenting the names, composition, and date of the paints.   *Will Travel*

Contemporary
100 West Centre St., Baltimore, MD   21201

410-783-5720   www.contemporary.org
Open: Tu-Fr 10-5; Sa-Su 11-5   *Closed:* please call!
Sugg/Contr.: Yes
Group Tours: 410-783-5720, x102   *Theater*

The Contemporary presents the art of our time in unusual sites. The museum's innovative
approach to exhibitions and education brings art directly to diverse and underserved
communities, promotes creative interaction between artists and the public, and connects
new art to everyday experience. Founded in 1989, the Museum has gained international acclaim
for its thought provoking exhibitions and for its innovative use of spaces not typically
associated with contemporary art.

Evergreen House
Affiliated Institution: The Johns Hopkins University
4545 N. Charles St., Baltimore, MD   21210-2693

410-516-0341   www.jhu.edu.historichouses
Open: 10-4 Mo-Fr, 1-4 Sa, Su   *Closed:* Leg/Hol!
Adm: Adult: $6.00   Children: Free under 5   Students: $3.00   Seniors: $5.00
&   P: Free   *Museum Shop*   ¶: Call ahead for box lunches, high tea & continental breakfast for groups
Group Tours: 410-516-0341 (Groups more than 20 $5 pp)   *Drop-In Tours:* call for specifics
Historic Building: 1850–1860 Evergreen House
Permanent Collection: Fr: Impr, Post/Impr; Eur: cer; Or: cer; Jap

Restored to its former beauty and reopened to the public in 1990, the 48 rooms of the magnificent Italianate Evergreen House (c 1878), with classical revival additions, contain outstanding collections of French and Post-Impressionist works of art collected by its founders, the Garrett family of Baltimore. *All visitors to Evergreen House are obliged to go on a 1-hour tour of the house with a docent. It is recommended that large groups call ahead to reserve. It should be noted that the last tour of the day begins at 3:00. ℂ Japanese netsuke and inro; the only gold bathroom in Baltimore; private theatre designed by Leon Bakst.

ON EXHIBIT 2002

10/12/2001 to 01/13/2002   *The Collectors' Series: Rare Books and Related Contemporary Artist's Books*
T. Harrison Garrett and his son collected the 30,000 books that are part of the Rare Book Library of Johns Hopkins University. Five evening presentations are planned with 20 artists from all over Maryland, Northern Virginia, Delaware, New York, Philadelphia, and Boston.

04/05/2002 to 06/30/2002   *Camelot at Dawn: Jacqueline and John Kennedy in Georgetown, May 1954*
An exceptional collection of photographs

05/05/2002 to 09/29/2002   *Sculpture at Evergreen*
Ten artists will again be selected to create artworks for sites around the estate. Each artist will be paid $3000 for their new work and up to $1000 for installation.   *Catalog*

10/2002 to 01/2003   *Early Paintings of Joseph Sheppard*
With the Walters Art Museum, Evergreen will celebrate 50 years of Mr. Sheppard's work and his early paintings during Alice Warner Garrett's lifetime.

Walters Art Gallery
600 N. Charles St., Baltimore, MD   21201

410-547-9000   www.thewalters.org
Open: 10-4 Tu-Fr; 11-5 Sa, Su; till 8pm 1st Th of each month   *Closed:* 12/25
Free Day: Sa from 11am to 1pm, first Th of each month   *Adm: Adult:* $5.00
Children: Free 6 & under; 7-17 $1.00   *Students:* Young Adults (18-25) $3.00   *Seniors:* $3.00
&: Wheelchair ramps at entrances, elevators to all levels   P: Ample parking on the street and nearby lots   *Museum Shop*   ‖: Classic café 9:30-3:30 Tu-Fr; 10:30-4:30 Sa, Su
Group Tours: ex 337   *Drop-In Tours:* 12 We, 1:30 Su year round
Historic Building: 1904 building modeled after Ital. Ren. & Baroque palace designs   *Theater*
Permanent Collection: An/Egt; An/Grk; An/R; Med; Dec/Art 19; OM: ptgs; Eur: ptgs & sculp; Dec/Art

The Walters, considered one of America's most distinguished art museums, features a broad-ranging collection that spans more than 5,000 years of artistic achievement from Ancient Egypt to Art Nouveau. Remarkable collections of ancient, medieval, Islamic & Byzantine art, 19th-century paintings and sculpture, and Old Master paintings are housed within the walls of the magnificently restored original building and in a large modern wing as well. *1. For the time being there will be a reduction in the Museum's hours of operation. Please call for updates. 2. The 1974 building will be closed until Fall 2001 for renovation and repair.   ℂ Hackerman House, a restored mansion adjacent to the main museum building, filled with oriental decorative arts treasures.

ON EXHIBIT 2002

01/01/2002 to Permanent Installation   *Wondrous Journeys: The Walters Collection from Egyptian Tombs to Medieval Castles*
Tracing the artistic acheive,ment from pre-dynastic Egypt to the early Renaissance throuch nearly 2000 works of art.

01/20/2001 to 06/01/2002   *Facing Museums*
A site specific installation by Dennis Adams in a collaboration with Baltimore's Contemporary Art Museum

10/20/2001 to 01/13/2002   *Impressionism Transformed: The Paintings of Edmund C. Tarbell*
Catalog   Will Travel   Admission Fee

10/20/2001 to 01/20/2002   *Expanding World Views: A Millennium of Maps*
Rare maps and manuscripts from the Museum's collection

10/20/2001 to 04/01/2002   *The American Artist as Painter and Draftsman*
19th-century drawings and paintings from the Walters permanent collection

EASTON

Academy Art Museum
106 South Sts., Easton, MD   21601

410-822-ARTS   www.art-academy.org
Open: 10-4 Mo-Sa, till 9 We   *Closed:* Su, Leg/Hol! month of Aug
&   P: Free with 2 hour limit during business hours; handicapped parking available in the rear of the
Academy   *Group Tours:* 410-822-5997   *Drop-In Tours   Historic Building:* Housed in Old Schoolhouse
Permanent Collection: Ptgs; Sculp; Gr: 19-20; Phot

Housed in two 18th-century buildings, one of which was an old school house, the Academy's permanent collection contains an important group of original 19th- & 20th-century prints. This museum serves the artistic needs of the community with a broad range of activities including concerts, exhibitions, and educational workshops.   ☾ "Oysterman" by Kenneth Herlihy, AM located in the Academy Courtyard; Works by James McNeill Whistler, Grant Wood, Bernard Buffet, Leonard Baskin, James Rosenquist, and others.

ON EXHIBIT 2002

12/07/2001 to 01/31/2002   *Art for Everyday: Designed to be Different*

HAGERSTOWN

Washington County Museum of Fine Arts
91 Key St., City Park, Box 423, Hagerstown, MD   21741

301-739-5727   www.washcomuseum.org
Open: 10-5 Tu-Sa, 1-5 Su   *Closed:* Leg/Hol!
Vol/Contr.: Yes
&   P: Free and ample.   *Museum Shop   Group Tours   Drop-In Tours:* 2 weeks notice   *Sculpture Garden*
Permanent Collection: Am: 19-20; Reg; OM; 16-18; Eur: ptgs 18-19; Ch

In addition to the permanent collection of 19th- and 20th-century American art, including works donated by the founders of the museum, Mr. & Mrs. William H. Singer, Jr., the Museum has a fine collection of Oriental Art, African Art, American pressed glass, and European paintings, sculpture, and decorative arts. Hudson River landscapes, Peale family paintings, and works by "The Eight," all from the permanent collection, are displayed throughout the year on an alternating basis with special temporary exhibitions. The museum is located in the northwest corner of the state just below the Pennsylvania border.   ☾ "Sunset Hudson River" by Frederic Church

ON EXHIBIT 2002

01/04/2002 to 02/17/2002   *69th Annual Cumberland Valley Photographic Salon*

01/27/2002 to 04/28/2002   *19th-Century Highlights from the Permanent Collection*
Portrait, still life, and genre works with furniture and decorative arts

02/01/2002 to 03/03/2002   *Valley Art Association Juried Exhibition*

02/22/2002 to April 2002   *American Society of Marine Artists*

03/08/2002 to 05/12/2002   *Women Artists from the Permanent Collection*

04/26/2002 to 06/09/2002   *Sculpture of Irene Gennaro*

06/07/2002 to 07/28/2002   *70th Annual Juried Cumberland Valley Artist Exhibition*

06/28/2002 to 08/25/2002   *French Prints from the Perry Collection*

10/18/2002 to 12/15/2002   *Sculpture of Leonard Cave*

11/08/2002 to 01/05/2003   *Charms of Childhood*

MASSACHUSETTS

AMHERST

Mead Art Museum
Affiliated Institution: Amherst College
Amherst, MA   01002-5000

413-542-2335   www.amherst.edu/~mead
Open: Sept-May: 10-4:30 Weekdays, 1-5 Weekends; Summer: 1-4 Tu-Su   *Closed:* Leg/Hol!; Acad!;
Mem/Day; Lab/Day
Vol/Contr.: Yes
  ♿ P   *Group Tours:* by Appt, 413-542-2335   *Drop-In Tours*   *Sculpture Garden*
Permanent Collection: Am: all media; Eur: all media; Du: ptgs 17; Phot; Dec/Art; An/Grk: cer; Fr: gr 19

Surrounded by the Pelham Hills in a picture perfect New England setting, the Mead Art Museum at Amherst College houses a rich collection of 14,000 art objects dating from antiquity to the present. *Summer hours are 1-4 Tu-Su. Closed until Feb 2001 for renovations ❨ American paintings and watercolors including Eakins "The Cowboy" & Homer's "The Fisher Girl"

University Gallery, University of Massachusetts
Affiliated Institution: Fine Arts Center
University of Massachusetts, Amherst, MA   01003

413-545-3670
Open: 11-4:30 Tu-Fr; 2-5 Sa, Su   *Closed:* Jan
 ♿   *Group Tours*
Permanent Collection: Am: ptgs, drgs, phot 20

With a focus on the works of contemporary artists, this museum is best known as a showcase for the visual arts. It is but one of a five college-complex of museums, making a trip to this area of New England a worthwhile venture for all art lovers.

ON EXHIBIT 2002

02/02/2002 to 03/15/2002   *The Culture of Violence*

02/02/2002 to 03/15/2002   *Under Pressure: Prints from the Two Palms Press*

03/29/2002 to 05/17/2002   *The Culture of Violence*

03/29/2002 to 05/17/2002   *Selections from the Permanent Collection*

Addison Gallery of American Art
Affiliated Institution: Phillips Academy
Andover, MA   01810-4166

978-749-4015   www.andover.edu/addison
Open: 10-5 Tu-Sa, 1-5 Su   *Closed:* Mo, Leg/Hol!; 12/24
&   P: Limited on street parking   *Group Tours   Drop-In Tours:* Upon request   *Sculpture Garden*
Permanent Collection: Am: ptgs, sculp, phot, works on paper 17-20

Since its inception in 1930, the Addison Gallery has been devoted exclusively to American art. The original benefactor, Thomas Cochran, donated both the core collection and the neo-classic building designed by noted architect Charles Platt. With a mature collection of more than 12,000 works, featuring major holdings from nearly every period of American art history, a visit to this museum should be high on every art lover's list.   ☾ Marble fountain in Gallery rotunda by Paul Manship; "The West Wind" by Winslow Homer; R. Crosby Kemper Sculpture Courtyard

BOSTON

Boston Athenaeum
10 1/2 Beacon St., Boston, MA   02108

617-227-0270   www.botonathenaeum.org
Open: June-Aug: 9-5:30 Mo-Fr; Sept-May: 9-5:30 Mo-Fr, 9-4 Sa   *Closed:* Leg/Hol!
&   *Museum Shop   Group Tours:* ex 221   *Historic Building:* National Historic Landmark Building
Permanent Collection: Am: ptgs, sculp, gr 19

The Boston Athenaeum is closed for renovation until at least September 2001. Consult the website for updates. The Athenaeum, one of the oldest independent libraries in America, features an art gallery established in 1827. Most of the Athenaeum building is closed to the public except for the 1st & 2nd floors of the building (including the Gallery). In order to gain access to many of the most interesting parts of the building, including those items in the "do not miss" column, free tours are available on Tu & Th at 3pm. Reservations must be made at least 24 hours in advance by calling The Circulation Desk, 617-227-0270 ex 221.   ☾ George Washington's private library; 2 Gilbert Stuart portraits; Houdon's busts of Benjamin Franklin, George Washington, and Lafayette from the Montecello home of Thomas Jefferson.

Boston Museum of Fine Arts
465 Huntington Ave., Boston, MA   02115

617-267-9300   www.mfa.org
Open: 10-4:45 Mo & Tu; 10-9:45 We-Fr; 10-5:45 Sa, Su: The Gund Gallery closes 15 min before the rest of the Museum   *Closed:* Thgv, 12/24, 12/25
Free Day: after 4 We, vol cont: after 5 Th & Fr adm reduced $2.00
Adm: *Adult:* $14.00: all admissions are 30-day, 2-visit tickets
Children: $5.00 before 3 school days, 7-17 & under   *Students:* $12.00   *Seniors:* $12.00
&: Completely wheelchair accessible   P: $3.50 first hour, $1.50 every half hour following in garage on Museum Rd. across from West Wing entrance.   *Museum Shop   ¶:* Cafe, Restaurant & Cafeteria
Group Tours: ex 368   *Drop-In Tours:* on the half hour from 10:30-2:30 Mo-Fr
Permanent Collection: An/Grk; An/R; An/Egt; Eur: om/ptgs; Fr: Impr, post/Impr; Am: ptgs 18-20; Or: cer

A world class collection of fine art with masterpieces from every continent is yours to enjoy at this great Boston museum. Divided between two buildings the collection is housed both in the original (1918) Evans Wing, with its John Singer Sargeant mural decorations above the Rotunda, and the dramatic West Wing (1981), designed by I.M. Pei. *1. There is a "pay as you wish" policy from 4pm-9:45pm on We and a $2.00 admission fee on Th & Fr evenings. 2. The West Wing only is open after 5pm on Th & Fr.   ☾ Egyptian Pectoral believed to have decorated a royal sarcophagus of the Second Intermediate Period (1784–1570 B.C.), part of the museum's renowned permanent collection of Egyptian art.

ON EXHIBIT 2002

01/23/2002 to 04/29/2002   *From Paris to Provincetown: Blanche Lazzell and the Color Woodcut*
Inspired by Japanese ukiyo-e prints, a group of artists in 1916 formed Provincetown Printers.
Included are 140 prints createds over 40 years.

02/17/2002 to 06/09/2002   *Impressionist Still Life*
A list of artists reflects the breadth of approaches to still life painting in the 2nd half of the 19th
century. Included are Basil, Caillebotte, Cassatt, Cézanne, Courbet, Degas, Fantin-Latour,
Gauguin, van Gogh, Gonzales, Manet, Monet, Morisot, Pissaro, Renoir, and Sisley.
Catalog   Will Travel

03/13/2002 to 07/21/2002   *Draped in Dragons: Chinese Court Costumes (working title)*
Exceptional and glamorous costumes shown in a setting that evokes the opulence of the Qing
Court

04/17/2002 to 10/01/2002   *RSVP: Sarah Sze*
Unconventional sculpture from such things as electric fans and plastic plants will create a site
specific installation.

04/24/2002 to 10/27/2002   *Recent Acquisitions from the Department of Contemporary Art*
Works including Beuys, Riley, Naumann, and Mangold

06/12/2002 to 09/22/2002   *The Poetry of Everyday Life: Dutch Paintings in Boston Collections*
Landscapes, portraits, still lifes, and history paintings from 15 Boston collections illustrating
the skill and craftsmanship of the Dutch School

07/21/2002 to 09/20/2002   *Jasper Johns to Jeff Koons: Four Decades of Art from the Broad Collection*
The Los Angeles based collection includes pieces by the most prominent artists of the 20th century including Warhol, Twombly, Ruscha, and Lichtenstein.   *Catalog   Will Travel   Admission Fee*

10/23/2002 to 01/02/2003   *The Photography of Charles Sheeler*
A founder of American modernism and a master photographer. Included are photographs done
from 1915–1950. Included also will be Manhattan, the short film done with Paul Strand in
1920.   *Catalog   Will Travel*

12/15/2002 to 04/27/2003   *From Corot to van Gogh: The French Landscape*   *Admission Fee*

Boston Public Library
Copley Square, Boston, MA   02117-3194

617-536-5400
Open: Oct 1-May 22!: 5-9 Mo-Th, 9-5 Fr-Sa, 1-5 Su   *Closed:* Leg/Hol! & 5/28
&: General library only (Boylston St.); Also elevators, restrooms
Group Tours: ex 216   *Drop-In Tours:* 2:30 Mo; 6:00 Tu, Th; 11am Fr, Sa, 2:00 Su Oct-May
Historic Building: Renaissance "Palace" designed in 1895 by Charles Follen McKim
Permanent Collection: Am: ptgs, sculp; Fr: gr 18-19; Brit: gr 18-19; OM: gr, dr; Am: phot 19, gr 19-20; Ger:
gr; arch/drgs

Architecturally a blend of the old and the new, the building that houses the Boston Public
Library, designed by Charles Follon McKim, has a facade that includes noted sculptor Augustus
Saint-Gauden's head of Minerva which serves as the keystone of the central arch. A wing
designed by Philip Johnson was added in 1973. *While restoration of the McKim Building is in
progress, some points of interest may temporarily be inaccessible.   ℭ 1500 lb. bronze entrance
doors by Daniel Chester French; staircase mural painting series by Puvis de Chavannes;
Dioramas of "Alice in Wonderland," "Arabian Nights" & "Dickens' London" by Louise Stimson.

Boston University Art Gallery
855 Commonwealth Ave., Boston, MA   02215

617-353-3329
Open: mid Sept-mid Dec; mid Jan-mid May: 10-5 Tu-Fr; 1-5 Sa, Su   *Closed:* Mo, 12/25
&: Limited (no wheelchair ramp and some stairs)   P: On-street metered parking; pay parking
lot nearby   *Historic Building*

Several shows in addition to student exhibitions are mounted annually in this 41-year-old university gallery which seeks to promote under-recognized sectors of the art world by including the cultural and historical context and regional developments. Additional emphasis is placed on the promotion of 20th-century figurative art.

ON EXHIBIT 2002

01/18/2002 to 02/24/2002   *Looking East: Contemporary Painters' Engagement with Chinese Art*

03/01/2002 to 04/07/2002   *SFA Faculty Exhibition 2002*

Institute of Contemporary Art
955 Boylston St., Boston, MA   02115-3194

617-266-5152   www.icaboston.idu
Open: 12-5 We, Fr-Su, 12-9 Th   *Closed:* Mo, Tu; Leg/Hol
Free Day: Th after 5   *Adm:* *Adult:* $6.00   *Children:* Free under 12   *Students:* $4.00   *Seniors:* $4.00
&   P: pay lots nearby   *Museum Shop*   *Group Tours:* 617-927-6602   *Historic Building*   *Theater*
Permanent Collection: No permanent collection

Originally affiliated with the Modern Museum in New York, the ICA, founded in 1936, has the distinction of being the oldest non-collecting contemporary art institution in the country. By presenting contemporary art in a stimulating context, the ICA has, since its inception, been a leader in introducing such "unknown" artists as Braque, Kokoschka, Munch, and others who have changed the course of art history.   (Video Collection. Video viewing during open hours.

Isabella Stewart Gardner Museum
280 The Fenway, Boston, MA   02115

617-566-1401   www.gardnermuseum.org
Open: 11-5 Tu-Su (galleries begin closing at 4:45)   *Closed:* Leg/Hol, Thgv, 1/1, 12/25
Adm: *Adult:* $10.00, weekdays: $11.00 weekends   *Children:* Free under 18   *Students:* $5.00
Seniors: $7.00
&   P: Street parking plus garage two blocks away on Museum Road   *Museum Shop*
||: Cafe 11:30-4 Tu-Fr, 11-4 Sa, Su   *Group Tours:* 617-278-5147   *Drop-In Tours:* 2:30 Fr Gallery tour
Historic Building   *Sculpture Garden*
Permanent Collection: Ptgs; Sculp; Dec/Art; Gr; OM

Designed in the style of a 15th-century Venetian palace, the museum has three floors of galleries that open onto a central courtyard filled with flowering plants and trees.   (Rembrandt's "Self Portrait"; Italian Renaissance works of art; Titian's "Europa"

ON EXHIBIT 2002

01/30/2002 to 05/12/2002   *Cosme Tura and Ferrara: A Forgotten Renaissance*
A first exhibition devoted to Tura's work (1430–1495) exploring his style at the court of Ferrara. Also included are tapestries, medals, drawings, and manuscript illuminations. A public symposium will take place 3/2/02.

05/01/2002 to September 2002   *Manfred Bischoff*
One of the foremost contemporary European jewelry artists. He makes miniature sculptures of gold, silver, coral, and some jade and diamonds.

09/01/2002 to January 2003   *Contemporary Exhibition*

Museum of the National Center of Afro-American Artists
300 Walnut Ave., Boston, MA   02119

617-442-8614
Open: 1-5 Tu-Su
Adm: Adult: $4.00   *Children:* Free under 5   *Students:* $3.00   *Seniors:* $3.00
Group Tours   Historic Building: 19th C
Permanent Collection: Af/Am: ptgs; sculp; Gr

Art by African-American artists is highlighted along with art from the African continent itself.

Nichols House Museum
55 Mount Vernon St., Boston, MA   02108

617-227-6993
Adm: Adult: $5.00   *Children:* Free under 12
Group Tours   Drop-In Tours: guided individualized tours Tu-Sa 12-4:15

The Nichols House Museum offers a rare glimpse into 19th- and early 20th-century life on Boston's Beacon Hill. The house contains furniture, decorative objects, European and Asian art accumulated over several generations.

BROCKTON

Fuller Museum of Art
455 Oak St., Brockton, MA   02301-1399

508-588-6000   www.fullermuseum.org
Open: Noon-5 Tu-Su   *Closed:* Mo, 1/1, 7/4, Lab/Day, Thgv, 12/25
Adm: Adult: $5.00   *Children:* Free under 18   *Students:* $3.00   *Seniors:* $3.00
&   P: Free   *Museum Shop   Group Tours:* ext 124   *Drop-In Tours   Sculpture Garden*
Permanent Collection: Am: 19-20; Cont: reg

A park-like setting surrounded by the beauty of nature is the ideal site for this charming museum that features works by artists of New England with particular emphasis on contemporary arts and cultural diversity.

ON EXHIBIT 2002

12/08/2001 to 02/24/2002   *Dwellings (Domesticity)*
Works dealing with how we view and relate to the home as a dwelling and structure we encounter everyday.

CAMBRIDGE

Arthur M. Sackler Museum
Affiliated Institution: Harvard University
485 Broadway, Cambridge, MA   02138

617-495-9400   www.artmuseums.harvard.edu
Open: 10-5 Mo-Sa, 1-5 Su   *Closed:* Leg/Hol!
Free Day: We & Sa 10-12   *Adm: Adult:* $5.00   *Children:* Free under 18   *Students:* $3.00   *Seniors:* $4.00
&: Ramp at front and elevators to all floors   P: Subway accessibility, Red line to Harvard stop
Museum Shop   Group Tours: 617-496-8576   *Drop-In Tours:* 2:00 Mo-Fr
Permanent Collection: An/Islamic; An/Or; Nat/Am

Opened in 1985, the building and its superb collection of ancient, Asian, and Islamic art were all the generous gift of the late Dr. Arthur M. Sackler, noted research physician, medical publisher, and art collector. Recent gifts from variuos alumni highlight Harvard's Sackler Museum as an institution dedicated to research and scholarship.   (World's finest collections of ancient Chinese jades; Korean ceramics; Japanese woodblock prints; Persian miniatures

Busch-Reisinger Museum
Affiliated Institution: Harvard University
32 Quincy St., Cambridge, MA   02138

617-495-2317   www.artmuseums.harvard.edu
Open: 10-5 Mo-Sa, 1-5 Su   *Closed:* Leg/Hol!
Free Day: All day We; Sa 10-12   *Adm:*   Adult: $5.00   *Children:* Free under 18   *Students:* $3.00
Seniors: $4.00
&.; Ramp at Library entrance (rear) and elevators to all floors   P: Subway accessible. Red line to
Harvard Square stop   *Museum Shop*   *Group Tours:* 617-496-8576   *Drop-In Tours:* 1:00 Mo-Fr
Permanent Collection: Ger: ptgs, sculp 20; Gr; Ptgs; Dec/Art; Cer 18; Med/Sculp; Ren/Sculp

Founded in 1901 with a collection of plaster casts of Germanic sculpture and architectural monuments, the Busch-Reisinger later acquired a group of modern "degenerate" artworks purged by the Nazi's from major German museums. All of this has been enriched over the years with gifts from artists and designers associated with the famous Bauhaus School, including the archives of artist Lyonel Feininger and architect Walter Gropius.   ℂ Outstanding collection of German Expressionist Art

Fogg Art Museum
Affiliated Institution: Harvard University
32 Quincy St., Cambridge, MA   02138

617-495-9400   www.artmuseums.harvard.edu
Open: 10-5 Mo-Sa, 1-5 Su   *Closed:* Leg/Hol!
Free Day: All day We, Sa 10-noon   *Adm:*   Adult: $5.00   *Children:* Free under 18   *Students:* $3.00
Seniors: $4.00
&.: Ramp at library entrance (rear) and elevators to all floors   P: Subway accessibility. Red line to
Harvard Square stop   *Museum Shop*   *Group Tours:* 617-496-8576   *Drop-In Tours:* 11:00 Mo-Fr
Permanent Collection: Eur: ptgs, sculp, dec/art; Am: ptgs, sculp, dec/art; Gr; Phot, Drgs

The Fogg, the largest university museum in America, with one of the world's greatest collections, contains both European and American masterpieces from the Middle Ages to the present. Access to the galleries is off of a two story recreation of a 16th-century Italian Renaissance courtyard.   ℂ The Maurice Wertheim Collection containing many of the finest Impressionist and Post-Impressionist paintings, sculptures, and drawings in the world.

ON EXHIBIT 2002

12/08/2001 to 04/07/2002   *Extreme Connoisseurship*
Connoisseurship with its implications of authenticity, authorship, and market value has been discredited by art historians. Connoisseurship of contemporary art in which the value of an object is contested seems to be a contradiction of terms. This contradiction is the starting point for this exhibition feeaturing woorks by Hammons, Orozco, Judd, Horn, Broodthaers, Rainer, and Ader. The exhibition asks "What is it that we are looking at when we see a contemporary work of art, and what are we looking for." It suggests that another art history might be found, neither thematic or stylistic.

12/22/2001 to 03/17/2002   *Calming the Tempest with Peter Paul Rubens*
An oil sketch by Rubens: "Neptune Calming The Tempest" is examined from two points of view: What would an uninformed viewer see; and what social and traditional circumstances Rubens was working in to produce this in Antwerp in the 1630s. The exhibition shows Greek coins to a Belgian work of contemporary conceptual art to place the sketch in a visual matrix.

MIT-List Visual Arts Center
20 Ames St., Wiesner Bldg., Cambridge, MA   02142

617-253-4680   web.mit.edu/lvac/www
Open: 12-6 Tu-Th, Sa, Su; till 8 Fr   *Closed:* Mo, Leg/Hol
Sugg/Contr.: Yes   *Adm:*   Adult: $5.00
&.   P: Corner of Main & Ames Sts.   *Museum Shop*   *Group Tours:* 617-253-4400
Historic Building: 1985 I.M. Pei building   *Sculpture Garden*
Permanent Collection: Sculp; Ptgs; Phot; Drgs; Work on Paper

Approximately 10 temporary exhibitions of contemporary art are mounted annually in MIT's List Visual Arts Center with an interior mural by Kenneth Noland and seating by Scott Burton. Artists featured have included Issac Julien, Paul Pfeiffer, Johan Grimonpriz, Elmgreen e Drayset, Monica Bonvicini, and Kiki Smith. ☾ Alexander Calder, "The Big Sail" (1965), MIT's first commissioned public outdoor sculpture.

CHESTNUT HILL

McMullen Museum of Art Boston College
Affiliated Institution: Boston College
Devlin Hall, 140 Commonwealth Ave., Chestnut Hill, MA   02167-3809

617-552-8587 or 8100   www.bc.edu:80/bc_org/avp/cas/artmuseum/
Open: Feb-May Mo-Fr; 12-5 Sa, Su June-Aug: 11-3 Mo-Fr   *Closed:* Leg/Hol!
  P: 1 hour parking on Commonwealth Ave.; in lower campus garage on weekends & as available on weekdays (call 617-552-8587 for availability)   ¶: On campus   *Group Tours   Historic Building*
Permanent Collection: It: ptgs 16 & 17; Am: ptgs; Jap: gr; Med & Baroque Tapestries 15-17

Devlin Hall, the Neo-Gothic building that houses the museum, consists of two galleries featuring a display of permanent collection works on one floor, and special exhibitions on the other. ☾ "Madonna with Christ Child & John the Baptist" by Ghirlandaio, 1503–1577

CONCORD

Concord Art Association
37 Lexington Rd., Concord, MA   01742

978-369-2578
Open: 10-4:30 Tu-Sa, 1-4 Su   *Closed:* Mo, Leg/Hol!
  P: Free street parking   *Museum Shop   Group Tours*
Historic Building: Housed in building dated 1720   *Sculpture Garden*
Permanent Collection: Am: ptgs, sculp, gr, dec/art

Historic fine art is appropriately featured within the walls of this historic (1720) building. The beautiful gardens are perfect for a bag lunch picnic during the warm weather months. ☾ Ask to see the secret room within the building which was formerly part of the underground railway.

COTUIT

Cahoon Museum of American Art
4676 Falmouth Rd., Cotuit, MA   02635

508-428-7581   www.cahoonmuseum.org
Open: 10-4 Tu-Sa   *Closed:* Su, Mo, Leg/Hol!; Also closed Jan
Vol/Contr.: Yes
 : Limited to first floor only   P: Free   *Museum Shop*
Drop-In Tours: Talks at various times for each special exhibits
Historic Building: 1775 Former Cape Cod Colonial Tavern
Permanent Collection: Am: ptgs 19-20; Cont/Prim

Named in honor of the contemporary primitive painters, R & M Cahoon, their work is shown with works by prominent American marine, landscape and still life painters. The Museum is approximately 9 miles west of Hyannis. ☾ Mermaid paintings of Ralph Cahoon

Cape Museum of Fine Arts
Rte. 6A, Dennis, MA   02638-5034

508-385-4477   www.cmfa.rg
Open: 10-5 Tu-Sa, 1-5 Su, till 7:30 Th, open Mo May-Sept   *Closed:* Leg/Hol!
Adm: Adult: $7.00   *Children:* Free 18 and under
  P: Free   *Museum Shop*   *Group Tours:* ext.16   *Drop-In Tours:* 11am Sa; 1:30 Su
Sculpture Garden   Theater
Permanent Collection: Reg

Art by outstanding Cape Cod artists, from 1900 to the present, is the focus of this rapidly growing permanent collection which is housed in the restored former summer home of the family of Davenport West, one of the original benefactors of this institution. New galleries provide wonderful new space for permanent collections and special exhibitions. On the grounds of the Cape Playhouse and Center for the Arts.

ON EXHIBIT 2002

01/26/2002 to 02/24/2002   *Beauty and the Beast; Howard Dunn Photography*

03/02/2002 to 03/31/2002   *Women Creating; Heather Blume Sculpture*

04/06/2002 to 05/12/2002   *Harry Holl Retrospective; Carol Ginandes Photography*

05/18/2002 to 07/07/2002   *R. H. Ives Gammell; Grand Gesture: Abstract and Figurative Expressionism; Linda Ohlsen Graham*

07/13/2002 to 09/22/2002   *Grand Gesture Continues; Jan CollinsSelmann Retrospective; Kenneth Stubbs*

09/28/2002 to 12/01/2002   *Botanica; Making Faces; Romunus Rizk*

12/07/2002 to 01/19/2003   *Fine Craft Triennial; Making Faces Continues; Paul Schulenburg*

Art Complex Museum
189 Alden St. Box 2814, Duxbury, MA   02331

781-934-6634   www.artcomplex.org
Open: 1-4 We-Su   *Closed:* Mo, Tu, Leg/Hol!
Vol/Contr.: Yes
  P: Free   *Group Tours   Sculpture Garden   Theater*
Permanent Collection: Or: ptgs; Eur: ptgs; Am: ptgs; gr

In a magnificent sylvan setting that compliments the naturalistic wooden structure of the building, The Art Complex houses a remarkable core collection of works on paper that includes Rembrandt's "The Descent from the Cross by Torchlight." An authentic Japanese Tea House, complete with tea presentations in the summer months, is another unique feature of this fine institution. The museum is located on the eastern coast of Massachusetts just above Cape Cod.   ☾ Shaker furniture; Tiffany stained glass window

ON EXHIBIT 2002

09/30/2001 to 01/20/2002   *Imagination Highway*
The Caldecott Awards artists demonstrate the imagination and diversity in children's book.

09/30/2001 to 01/28/2002   *Children's Book Illustrations*

02/02/2002 to 04/27/2002 *Winter Juried Show; On Their Own; Pamela Hoss; A. E. Ryan;*
Leah Deprizio

05/12/2002 to 09/08/2002 *Small Worlds/Art of India; & Contemporary Artists Exhibition;*
Retroformations

09/22/2002 to 01/19/2003 *Gadgets, Gizmos, and Games; Pinhole Photography*

FITCHBURG

Fitchburg Art Museum
185 Elm St., Fitchburg, MA   01420

978-345-4207
Open: 11-9:00 Tu-Su   *Closed:* Mo, Leg/Hol!
Adm: *Adult:* $5.00   *Children:* Free under 18   *Seniors:* $3.00
&: 90% handicapped accessible   P: Free on-site parking   *Museum Shop*
Group Tours   Drop-In Tours   Sculpture Garden
Permanent Collection: AM: ptgs 18-20 Eur: ptgs 18-20; Prts & Drgs: 15-20; Phot 20; An/Grk; An/R; As;
Ant; Illustrated Books & Manuscripts 14-20

Eleanor Norcross, a Fitchburg artist who lived and painted in Paris for 40 years, became
impressed with the number and quality of small museums that she visited in the rural areas of
northern France. This led to the bequest of her collection and personal papers, in 1925, to
her native city of Fitchburg, and marked the beginning of what is now a 40,000-square foot,
block-long museum complex. The museum is located in north central Massachusetts near the
New Hampshire border.   ❈ "Sarah Clayton" by Joseph Wright of Derby, 1770

FRAMINGHAM

Danforth Museum of Art
123 Union Ave., Framingham, MA   01702

508-620-0050
Open: 12-5 We-Su   *Closed:* Mo, Tu, Leg/Hol!
Adm: *Adult:* $3.00   *Children:* Free 12 & under   *Students:* $2.00   *Seniors:* $2.00
&   P: Free   *Museum Shop   Group Tours   Drop-In Tours:* !
Permanent Collection: Ptgs; Sculp; Drgs; Phot; Gr

The Danforth, a museum that prides itself on being known as a community museum with a
national reputation, offers 19th- & 20th-century American and European art as the main
feature of its permanent collection.   ❈ 19th & 20th c American works with a special focus on
the works of New England artists

ON EXHIBIT 2002

01/14/2002 to 03/31/2002   *Brazilian Carnevale*

04/04/2002 to 06/09/2002   *Bill Brauer and New England Currents*

06/13/2002 to 08/18/2002   *Summer Show, Members Show, and Recent Acquisitions*

10/31/2002 to 01/15/2003   *Provinetown Artists*

GLOUCESTER

Cape Ann Historical Association
27 Pleasant St., Gloucester, MA   01930

978 283-0455
Open: 10-5 Tu-Sa   *Closed:* Su, Mo, Leg/Hol!; Feb
Free Day: month of Jan   *Adm:* *Adult:* $5.00   *Children:* Free under 6   *Students:* $3.50   *Seniors:* $4.50
&.   P: In the lot adjacent to the museum and in the metered public lot across Pleasant St. from
the museum   *Museum Shop*   *Group Tours*
Historic Building: 1804 Federal period home of Captain Elias Davis is part of museum   *Sculpture Garden*
Permanent Collection: Fitz Hugh Lane: ptgs; Am: ptgs, sculp, Dec/Art 19-20; Maritime Coll

Within the walls of this most charming New England treasure of a museum is the largest
collection of paintings (40), drawings (100), and lithographs by the great American artist, Fitz
Hugh Lane. A walking tour of the town takes the visitor past many charming small art studios
& galleries that have a wonderful view of the harbor as does the 1849 Fitz Hugh Lane House
itself. Be sure to see the famous Fisherman's Monument overlooking Gloucester Harbor.
℄ The watercolor by Fitz Hugh Lane which is his earliest known work

LINCOLN

DeCordova Museum and Sculpture Park
51 Sandy Pond Rd., Lincoln, MA   01773-2600

781-259-8355   www.decordova.org
Open: 11-5 Tu-Su   *Closed:* Leg/Hol!
Adm: *Adult:* $6.00   *Children:* Free 5 & under   *Students:* $4.00   *Seniors:* $4.00
&.   P: Free   *Museum Shop*   ¶: Cafe open 11-4 We-Sa
Group Tours: 781-259-0505   *Drop-In Tours:* We & Su 2:00   *Sculpture Garden*
Permanent Collection: Am: ptgs, sculp, gr, phot 20; Reg

In addition to its significant collection of modern and contemporary art, the DeCordova
features the only permanent sculpture park of its kind in New England. While there is an
admission charge for the museum, the sculpture park is always free and open to the public from
8am to 10pm daily. The 35-acre park features nearly 80 site-specific sculptures. *The museum is
open on selected Mo holidays!   ℄ Annual open air arts festival first Sunday in June; plus other
special events throughout the year, visit the web site for details.

ON EXHIBIT 2002

09/15/2001 to 01/06/2002   *Creature Feature: Monsters in Contemporary Art*
Monsters have a presence in art from cave paintings to the present. In addition to good versus
evil, they reflect popular culture in horror, humor, satire, and Hollywood.

LOWELL

Whistler House Museum of Art and Parker Gallery
243 Worthen St., Lowell, MA   01852-1822

978-452-7641   www.valley.uml.edu/lowell/historic/museums/whistler.html
Open: May-Oct 11-4 We-Sa, 1-4 Su; Nov, Dec, Mar, Apr 11-4 We-Sa   *Closed:* Mo, Tu, Leg/Hol! Jan & Feb
Adm: *Adult:* $3.00   *Children:* Free under 5   *Students:* $2.00   *Seniors:* $2.00
&.: Limited to first floor of museum and Parker Gallery   P: On street; commercial lots nearby
Group Tours: 978-452-7641   *Drop-In Tours:* Upon request   *Historic Building*   *Sculpture Garden*   *Theater*
Permanent Collection: Am: ptgs

Works by prominent New England artists are the highlight of this collection housed in the
1823 former home of the artist.   ℄ Collection of prints by James A. M. Whistler

MEDFORD

Tufts University Art Gallery
Affiliated Institution: Tufts University
Aidekman Arts Center, Medford, MA   02115

617-627-3518   www.tufts.edu/as/gallery
Open: Sept to mid Dec & mid Jan to May: 12-8 We-Sa, 12-5 Su   *Closed:* Leg/Hol!; Acad!; Summer
& *Group Tours   Sculpture Garden*
Permanent Collection: Ptgs, Gr, Drgs, 19-20; Phot 20; An/R; An/Grk; P/Col

Located just outside of Boston, Tufts University Art Gallery features art ranging from historical
to contemporary as well as works by students.

NORTH ADAMS

Massachusetts Museum of Contemporary Art
87 Marshall St., North Adams, MA   01247

413-664-4481   www.massmoca.org
Open: 6/1-10/31 10-6 daily; 11/1-5/31 11-5 We-Mo   *Closed:* 1/1, Thgv, 12/25
Adm: Adult: $8.00   *Children:* Free under 6, $3.00
& P   *Museum Shop*   ¶: Mass Moca Café   *Group Tours   Drop-In Tours*
Historic Building: Museum is located in a late 19th-century industrial site.
Permanent Collection: The Museum has two permanent works of sound art in its collection; the majority of
work shown here will be long-term loans of oversized or sited works from major museum collections.

Created from a 27-building historic mill complex on 13 acres in the Berkshires of Western
Massachusetts, MASS MoCA promises to be an exciting multi-disciplinary center for visual
and performing arts. International in scope, MASS MoCA offers exhibitions of evocative,
provocative art being made today.

ON EXHIBIT 2002

05/27/2001 to April 2002   *Game Show*
Contemporary artist's exploration of games. Included are Sophie Calle, Perry Hoberman,
Natalie Bookchin, Christian Janowski, Uri Tzaig, Christoph Draeger, and Chris Finley as well
as a site-specific word game by Kay Rosen called "The Sound of Music"   *Catalog*

NORTHAMPTON

Smith College Museum of Art
Elm St. at Bedford Terrace, Northampton, MA   01063

413-585-2760   www.smith.edu/artmuseum
Open: Sept-June: 9:30-4 Tu, Fr, Sa; 12-8 Th, Noon-4 We, Su; Jul & Aug: Noon-4 Tu-Su   *Closed:* Mo, 1/1,
7/4, Thgv, 12/25
&: Wheelchair accessible; wheelchairs provided upon request   P: Nearby street parking with campus
parking available on evenings and weekends only; Handicapped parking behind Hillyer art
building.   *Museum Shop*
Permanent Collection: Am: ptgs, sculp, gr, drgs, dec/art 17-20; Eur: ptgs, gr, sculp, drgs, dec/art 17-20; Phot;
Du: 17; An Art

With in-depth emphasis on American and French 19th- & 20th-century art, and literally
thousands of superb artworks in its permanent collection, Smith College remains one of the
most highly regarded college or university repositories for fine art in the nation. *Print Room
hours are 1-4 Tu-Fr & 1-5 Th from Sept to May—other hours by appointment only. ℭ "Mrs.
Edith Mahon" by Thomas Eakins; "Walking Man" by Rodin

Words & Pictures Museum
136 West Main St., Northampton, MA   01060

413-586-8545   www.wordsandpictures.org
Permanent Collection: Original cont sequential/comic book art & fantasy illustration, 1970s-present

Museum has closed the facility. All exhibits and programming are solely on the web.

PITTSFIELD

Berkshire Museum
39 South St., Pittsfield, MA   01201

413-443-7171   www.berkshiremuseum.org
Open: 10-5 Mo-Sa, 1-5 Su   *Closed:* 1/1, Mem/Day, 7/4, Lab/Day, Thgv, 12/25
Free Day: on one's birthday   *Adm:*   *Adult:* $6.00   *Children:* $4.00 (4-18), Free under 3   *Seniors:* $5.00
&: Wheelchair lift south side of building; elevator to all floors   P: Metered street parking; inexpensive rates at the nearby Crowne Plaza Hotel and municipal parking garage.
Museum Shop   ¶: Snacks at the Vendo-Mat Snack Room
Group Tours: 413-443-7171 x11   *Drop-In Tours:* 10 am Sa in Jul, Aug
Historic Building: 1903 Italian Renaissance Revival   *Theater*
Permanent Collection: Am: 19-20; Eur: 15-19; An/Grk; An/R; Dec/Art; Phot; Natural Science; Aquarium

Three Museums in one—art, natural science, and history—set the stage for a varied and exciting visit to this complex in the heart of the beautiful Berkshires. In addition to its rich holdings of American art of the 19th and 20th centuries, the museum has an interactive aquarium and exciting changing exhibitions.   ¶ "Hudson River School Collection;" Special family exhibitions Feb thru May; newly renovated Science Galleries; Jonas Studio Dinosaur Exhibition

PROVINCETOWN

Provincetown Art Association and Museum
460 Commercial St., Provincetown, MA   02657

508-487-1750   www.CapeCodAccess.com/Gallery/PAAM.html
Open: Summer, 8-10 &12-5 daily; Spring/Fall: 12-5 Fr, Sa, Su; Winter: 12-4 Sa, Su   *Closed:* Open most holidays!
Free Day: Fr evening openings   *Sugg/Contr.:* Yes   *Adm:*   *Adult:* $5.00   *Students:* $1.00   *Seniors:* $1.00
&   *Museum Shop*   *Group Tours:* by appt   *Historic Building:* 1731 Adams family house   *Sculpture Garden*
Permanent Collection: Ptgs; Sculp; Gr; Dec/Art; Reg

Works by regional artists are an important focus of the collection.   ¶ Inexpensive works of art by young artists that are for sale in the galleries

SOUTH HADLEY

Mount Holyoke College Art Museum
South Hadley, MA   01075-1499

413-538-2245   www.mtholyoke.edu/go/artmuseum
Open: 11-5 Tu-Fr, 1-5 Sa-Su   *Closed:* Leg/Hol!, Acad!; Museum will be closed for renovation from 6/28/00 to February 2002
&   P: Free   *Museum Shop*
Group Tours: 413-538-2085   *Drop-In Tours:* by appointment at least 3 weeks prior   *Sculpture Garden*
Permanent Collection: As; P/Col; An/Egt; It: med/sculp; Eur: ptgs; An/Grk; Am: ptgs, dec/art, gr, phot; Eur: ptgs, dec/art, gr, phot

A stop at this leading college art museum is a must for any art lover traveling in this area. Founded in 1876, it is one of the oldest college museums in the country. *The Museum will be closed for renovation from 6/28/00 to 01/01/02   ¶ Albert Bierstadt's "Hetch Hetchy Canyon"; A Pinnacle from Duccio's "Maesta" Altarpiece; Head of Faustina the Elder, 2nd century AD, Roman

George Walter Vincent Smith Art Museum
At the Quadrangle, Corner State & Chestnut Sts., Springfield, MA   01103

413-263-6800   www.quadrangle.org
Open: 12-5 We-Fr; 11-4, Sa, Su (Tu-Su July & Aug)   *Closed:* Mo, Leg/Hol
Adm: *Adult:* $6.00 provides admission to all 4 Museums in Quadrangle   *Children:* $2.00 (6-18)
Students: $3.00   *Seniors:* $3.00
& P: Free parking in Springfield Library & Museum lots on State St. & Edwards St.
¶: year-round café   *Group Tours:* ext. 472   *Drop-In Tours:* by reservation   *Historic Building:* Built in 1896
Permanent Collection: 19th-C Am Art; Or; Mid/E Rugs; Dec/Art 17-19; Ch: jade; Jap: bronzes, ivories,
armor, tsuba 17-19; Dec/Art: cer; Am: ptgs 19

With the largest collection of Chinese cloisonné in the western world, the G. W. V. Smith Art
Museum, built in 1895 in the style of an Italian villa, is part of a four museum complex that also
includes the Museum of the Fine Arts. The museum reflects its founder's special passion for
collecting the arts of 17th- to 19th-century Japan and American art by his contemporaries.
❑ Early 19th-century carved 9'-high wooden Shinto wheel shrine

ON EXHIBIT 2002

03/02/2002 to 06/09/2002   *From Mickey to the Grinch: Art of the Animated Film*
The art, history, and process of American animated film in animation cels, model sheets,
drawings, and samples of scripts and assignment sheets. Featured will be an animation station
where visitors can create their own animations.   *Will Travel*

Museum of Fine Arts
At the Quadrangle, Corner of State & Chestnut Sts., Springfield, MA   01103

413-263-6800   www.quadrangle.org
Open: We-Fr 12-5; 11-4 Sa, Su; Tu-Su July & Aug   *Closed:* Mo, Leg/Hol
Adm: *Adult:* $6.00 single adm provides entry to all four museums   *Children:* $2.00 (6-18)
Students: $3.00   *Seniors:* $3.00
& P: Free in Springfield Library & Museum's lots on State St. and Edwards St.   *Museum Shop*   ¶
Group Tours: ex 472   *Drop-In Tours:* by reservation
Permanent Collection: Am: 19-20; Fr: 19-20; It Baroque; Dutch + Flemish

Part of a four-museum complex located on The Quadrangle in Springfield, the Museum of Fine
Arts, built in the 1930s Art Deco Style, offers an overview of European and American art. Single
admission fee provides entry to all four museums on the Quadrangle.   ❑ "The Historical
Monument of the American Republic," 1867–1888 by Erastus S. Field, a monumental painting
in the court of the museum

ON EXHIBIT 2002

09/26/2001 to 01/06/2002   *Brother Thomas Ceramics*
A self taught potter whose work relies on simple forms and unique color and depth of the glazes

01/16/2002 to 03/10/2002   *The Photographs of Richard Swiatlowski*
Digitally painted photographs with brilliant colors and bold brush strokes

02/17/2002 to 04/14/2002   *American Impressionism: Treasures from the Smithsonian American
Art Museum*
A survey of a key moment in the history of art. Included are works by Cassatt, Whistler,
Hassam, Robinson, and Chase.   *Catalog   Will Travel*

10/05/2002 to 12/01/2002   *Out of Time: 20th Century Design*
Futuristic visions of architecture, transportation, urban communities (under sea and on land),
space exploration, and robotics in watercolors, oil paintings, pen and ink drawings
Will Travel

Chesterwood
Off Rte. 183, Glendale Section, Stockbridge, MA   01262-0827

413-298-3579   www.chesterwood.org
Open: 10-5 Daily (May 1-Oct 31)   *Closed:* None during open season
Adm: *Adult:* $8.50   *Children:* $5.00 (13-18), $3.00 (6-12)   *Students:* $2.50 (10 or more)
Seniors: $7.50 over 65
&: Limited   P   *Museum Shop   Group Tours:* ex 211   *Drop-In Tours:* hourly throughout the day
Historic Building: Two Buildings (1898 studio & 1901 house) of Daniel Chester French   *Sculpture Garden*
Permanent Collection: Sculp; Ptgs; Work of Daniel Chester French; Phot

Located on 120 wooded acres is the original studio Colonial Revival house and garden of Daniel Chester French, leading sculptor of the American Renaissance. Working models for the Lincoln Memorial and the Minute Man, his most famous works, are on view along with many other of his sculptures and preliminary models. PLEASE NOTE: There are reduced admission rates to see the grounds only, and a special family admission rate of $16.50 for the museum buildings, grounds, and tour. ☾ Original casts and models of the seated Abraham Lincoln for the Memorial.

Norman Rockwell Museum at Stockbridge
Stockbridge, MA   01262

413-298 4100   www.nrm.org
Open: May-Oct 10-5 daily; Nov-Apr 10-4 Mo-Fr 10-5 Sa, Su & Hols   *Closed:* 1/1, Thgv, 12/25
Adm: *Adult:* $12.00   *Children:* 18 & under free when accompanied by adult, 4 per adult
Students: $7.00   *Seniors:* $4.50 (We, Nov-Apr)
&: main building, not studio   P: Free   *Museum Shop*
Group Tours: ex 220   *Drop-In Tours:* tours daily on the hour
Historic Building: Museum building designed by architect Robert A. M. Stern
Sculpture Garden   Theater
Permanent Collection: Am; ptgs

The Norman Rockwell Museum at Stockbridge preserves and exhibits the world's largest collection of original art by America's favorite illustrator, as well as changing exhibitions of notable illustrators past and present. Founded in 1969 with the assistance of Molly and Norman Rockwell. Rockwell's Stockbridge studio, filled with his furnishings, library and travel mementos is open May to October.

ON EXHIBIT 2002

11/03/2001 to 05/05/2002   *Speak Softly and Carry a Beagle: The Art of Charles Schultz*
Peanuts and its development   *Will Travel*

Rose Art Museum
Affiliated Institution: Brandeis University
415 South St., Waltham, MA   02254-9110

781-736-3434   www.brandeis.edu/rose
Open: 12-5 Tu-Su, 12-9 Th   *Closed:* Mo, Leg/Hol!
&: Entrance & galleries accessible by elevator   P: Visitor parking on campus
Group Tours   Drop-In Tours: by advance reservation
Permanent Collection: Am: ptgs, sculp 19-20; Eur: ptgs, sculp 19-20; Cont; ptgs, drgs, sculp, phot. *The permanent collection is not always on view!

The Rose Art Museum, founded in 1961, and located on the campus of Brandeis University just outside of Boston, features one of the largest collections of contemporary art in New England. Selections from the permanent collection and an exhibition of the works of Boston area artists are presented annually. *Tours are given by advance reservation only.

Davis Museum and Cultural Center

Affiliated Institution: Wellesley College
106 Central St., Wellesley, MA   02181-8257

781-283-2051   www.wellesley.edu/DavisMuseum/davismenu.html
Open: 11-5 Tu & Fr, Sa, 11-8 We, Th; 11-5 during summer, 1-5 Su   *Closed:* 1/1, 12/25
&: Museum and Cafe   P: Free   ¶: Cafe Collins open Mo-Fr (call 781-283-3379 for hours and info.)
Group Tours: 617-283-2081   *Sculpture Garden*
Permanent Collection: Am: ptgs, sculp, drgs, phot; Eur: ptgs, sculp, drgs, phot; AN; Af; Med; Ren

Established over 100 years ago, the Davis Museum and Cultural Center, formerly the Wellesley College Museum, is located in a stunning 61,000 square foot state-of-the-art museum building. One of the first encyclopedic college art collections ever assembled in the United States, the museum is home to more than 5,000 works of art. *The museum closes at 5pm on We & Th during the month of Jan. and from 6/15 to 8/15).   ⊄ "A Jesuit Missionary in Chinese Costume," a chalk on paper work by Peter Paul Rubens (recent acquisition)

ON EXHIBIT 2002

02/21/2002 to 06/09/2002   *Surrounding Interiors: Views inside the Car*
The focus is the inside of a car. 15 artists in all media explore the nature of this moveable space. A sculpture by Carl Scholz—a hermetically sealed Jaguar—will be displayed.

Sterling and Francine Clark Art Institute

225 South St., Williamstown, MA   01267

413-458-2303   www.clarkart.edu
Open: 10-5 Tu-Su; also Mo during Jul & Aug; open President Day, Mem/Day, Lab/Day, Columbus Day
Closed: 1/1, Thgv, 12/25
Free Day: Tu, 07/02-Oct 31   *Adm:*   Adult: $5.00   *Seniors:* $5.00
&: Wheelchairs available   P   *Museum Shop*   ¶
Group Tours: ext 363   *Drop-In Tours:* 3:00 daily during Jul & Aug
Permanent Collection: It: ptgs 14-18; Fl: ptgs 14-18; Du: ptgs 14-18; OM: ptgs, gr, drgs; Fr: Impr/ptgs;
Am: ptgs 19

More than 30 paintings by Renoir and other French Impressionist masters as well as a collection of old master paintings and a significant group of American works account for the high reputation of this recently expanded, outstanding 45-year-old institution. *Recorded tours of the permanent collection are available for a small fee.   ⊄ Impr/ptgs; works by Homer, Sargent, Remington, Cassatt; Silver coll.; Ugolino Da Siena Altarpiece; Alma Tadema piano

ON EXHIBIT 2002

10/07/2001 to 01/06/2002   *Goltzius and the Third Dimension*
A esteemed Netherlandish engraver of the late 16th century who made engraving a rival art to painting and sculpture

10/07/2001 to 01/06/2002   *Stockbridge Portfolio: Photographs by George Henry Seeley*
Seeley created this 32 print portfolio in mid 1910, and it is now being shown for the first time.

02/17/2002 to 05/05/2002   *Artic Diary: Paintings and Photographs by William Bradford*
Photographs from his "The Artic Regions Illustrated with photographs Taken on an Art Expedition to Greenland" (London 1873) and also expeditionary photographs of the late 19th century

06/30/2002 to 10/13/2002   *Gustav Klimt Landscapes*
Colorful and poetic landscapes are not usually associated witrh Klimt. These, created in the latter years of his life, present a new part of his work.

Williams College Museum of Art
15 Lawrence Hall Drive, Ste 2, Williamstown, MA   01267-2566

413-458-2429   www.williams.edu/WCMA
Open: 10-5 Tu-Sa, 1-5 Su (open Mo on Mem/Day, Lab/Day, Columbus Day)   *Closed:* 1/1, Thgv, 12/25
&   P: Limited in front of and behind the museum, and behind the Chapel. A public lot is available at the foot of Spring St.   *Museum Shop*
Group Tours: 413-597-2038   *Drop-In Tours:* 2:00 We & Su Jul & Aug only
Historic Building: 1846 Brick Octagon by Thomas Tefft; 1983–86 additions by Chas. Moore
Permanent Collection: Am: cont & 18-19; As & other non-Werstern civilizations; Brit: ptgs 17-19; Sp: ptgs 15-18; It/Ren: ptgs ; Phot; Gr/Arts; An/Grk; An/R

Considered one of the finest college art museums in the U.S., the museum's collection of 12,000 works that span the history of art, features particular strengths in the areas of contemporary & modern art, American art from the late 18th century to the present, and non-Western art. The original museum building of 1846, a two-story brick octagon with a neoclassical rotunda, was joined, in 1986, by a dramatic addition designed by noted architect Charles Moore.   ❬ Edward Hopper"Morning in the City," and Sol LeWitt wall drawing in the atrium

ON EXHIBIT 2002

06/30/2001 to 06/12/2002   *Celebrating 75 Years—American Dreams: American Art in the Williams College Museum of Art*
A unique vision of American works which takes the hopes, dreams, and ideas of the artists. Included are women, native Americans, African-Americans, and the anonymous artists and craftsmen who produced works worthy of national pride.   *Book*

WORCESTER

Iris & B. Gerald Cantor Art Gallery
Affiliated Institution: College of Holy Cross
1 College St., Worcester, MA   01610

508-793-3356   www.holycross.edu/visitor/cantor/cantor/html
Open: 9-Noon & 1-4 Mo & Tu, Th & Fr, and by appointment   *Closed:* Acad!, Su, Leg/Hol!
& P: Free   *Group Tours:* 205-932-8327   *Drop-In Tours:* daily during Museum hours   *Historic Building*
Permanent Collection: Am: ptgs 20; folk

Housed in a 1930s former schoolhouse, this collection consists of more than 3,500 works of 20th-century American art.   ❬ One of the largest collections of folk art in the Southeast.

Worcester Art Museum
55 Salisbury St., Worcester, MA   01609-3123

508-799-4406   www.woresterart.org
Open: 11-5 We-Fr, 10-5 Sa, 11-5 Su; Closed Su Jul & Aug   *Closed:* 7/4, Thgv, 12/25
Adm: *Adult:* $6.00   *Children:* Free under 12   *Students:* $4.00   *Seniors:* $4.00
&: Restrooms & some galleries; wheelchairs available on request   P: Free parking in front of museum and along side streets; handicapped parking at the Hiatt Wing entrance off Tuckerman Street.
Museum Shop ❙❙: Cafe 11:30-2 We-Sa (ex. 3068)
Group Tours: ex 3061   *Drop-In Tours:* 2:00 most Su Sept-May; 2:00 Sa   *Sculpture Garden*
Permanent Collection: Am: 17-19; Jap: gr; Brit: 18-19; Fl: 16-17; Ger: 16-17; Du: 17; P/Col; An/Egt; Ori sculp; Med: sculp; Am: dec/art

Opened to the public in 1898, the Worcester Art Museum is the second largest art museum in New England. Its exceptional 35,000-piece collection of paintings, sculpture, decorative arts, photography, prints, and drawings is displayed in 36 galleries and spans 5,000 years of art and culture, ranging from Egyptian antiquities and Roman mosaics to Impressionist paintings and contemporary art. Throughout its first century, the museum has proven itself a pioneer. Among its many "firsts," the museum was the first American museum to purchase work by Claude Monet (1910) and Paul Gauguin (1921); the first museum to bring a medieval building to America; a sponsor of the first major excavation at Antioch, one of the four great cities of ancient Rome (1932); the first museum to organize a Members' Council (1949); and the first museum to create an Art All-State program for high school artists. ◖ Antiochan Mosaics; American portrait miniatures; New Roman Art Gallery; New Contemporary Art Gallery

ON EXHIBIT 2002

10/07/2001 to 01/06/2002 *Modernism and Abstraction: Treasures from the Smithsonian's American Art Museum*

MICHIGAN

ANN ARBOR

University of Michigan Museum of Art
525 S. State St. at S. Univ., Ann Arbor, MI 48109

734-764-0395 www.umich.edu/~umma/
Open: 10-5 Tu-Sa, till 9 Th, 12-5 Su *Closed:* Mo, 1/1, 7/4, Thgv, 12/25
Sugg/Contr.: $5.00
&: North museum entrance & all galleries; limited access to restrooms P: Limited on-street parking with commercial lots nearby *Museum Shop*
Group Tours Drop-In Tours: 12:10-12:30 Th; 2 Su *Theater*
Permanent Collection: Cont; gr, phot; OM; drgs 6-20; Or; Af; Oc; Is

This museum, which houses the second largest art collection in the state of Michigan, also features a changing series of special exhibitions, family programs, and chamber music concerts. With over 12,000 works of art ranging from Italian Renaissance panel paintings to Han dynasty tomb figures, this 50-year-old university museum ranks among the finest in the country. ◖ Works on paper by J. M. W. Whistler

ON EXHIBIT 2002

10/13/2001 to 01/06/2002 *Pattern and Purpose: Japanese Fishermen's Coats from Awaji Island*

02/17/2002 to 05/05/2002 *Women Who Ruled: Queens, Goddesses, Amazons 1500–1650*

BATTLE CREEK

Art Center of Battle Creek
265 E. Emmett St., Battle Creek, MI 49017-4601

616-962-9511 www.artcenterofbc.org
Open: 10-5 Mo-Sa; to 7pm Th *Closed:* Mo, Leg/Hol
Sugg/Contr.: Yes
& P: 70 spaces with handicapped access at building *Museum Shop Group Tours*
Historic Building: core of bldg is an old church
Permanent Collection: Reg

The mission of the Art Center is to present quality exhibitions and programming in the visual arts for the education, enrichment, and enjoyment of the southwestern Michigan region. ◖ KIDSPACE, a hands-on activity gallery for children.

Cranbrook Art Museum

39221 North Woodward Ave., Bloomfield Hills, MI   48303-0801

248-645-3323   www.cranbrook.edu/museum
Open: 11-5 Tu-Su, till 8pm Th (Sept-May) June-August 11-5 Th-Su, Fr till 9   *Closed:* Mo, Leg/Hol!
Adm: Adult: $5.00   *Children:* Free 5 and under   *Students:* $3.00   *Seniors:* $3.00
&. P   *Museum Shop   Group Tours:* ext. 3323   *Drop-In Tours:* ! varies
Historic Building: Designed by noted Finnish-Amer. architect, Eliel Saarinen   *Sculpture Garden*
Permanent Collection: Arch/Drgs; Cer; Ptgs; Sculp; Gr 19-20; Dec/Art 20

The newly restored Saarinen House, a building designed by noted Finnish-American architect Eliel Saarinen, is part of Cranbrook Academy, the only institution in the country solely devoted to graduate education in the arts. In addition to outdoor sculpture on the grounds surrounding the museum, the permanent collection includes important works of art that are influential on the contemporary trends of today. *Please call ahead (248-645-3323) for specific information on tours and admission fees, Cranbrook Art Museum, and Saarinen House, as well as outdoor sculpture/architecture tours.   ❢ Works by Eliel Saarinen; carpets by Loja Saarinen

Detroit Institute of Arts

5200 Woodward Ave., Detroit, MI   48202

313-833-7900   www.dia.org
Open: 11-4 We-Fr; 11-5 Sa, Su   *Closed:* Some Holidays !
Sugg/Contr.: Y   *Adm: Adult:* $4.00   *Children:* $1.00
&.: Wheelchairs available at barrier free Farnsworth Entrance! 833-9754   P: Underground parking adjacent to museum; metered street parking
Museum Shop   ❢: Kresge Court Cafe (833-1932), Gallery Grille (833-1857)
Group Tours: 313-833-7981   *Drop-In Tours:* 1:00 We-Sa; 1 & 2:30 Su   *Theater*
Permanent Collection: Fr: Impr; Ger: Exp; Fl; ptgs; As; Fgt; Eur: 20; Af; Cont; P/Col; Nat/Am; Eur: ptgs, sculp, dec/art; Am: ptgs, sculp, dec/art

With holdings that survey the art of world cultures from ancient to modern times, The Detroit Institute of Arts, founded in 1885, ranks fifth largest among the nation's fine art museums. ❢ "Detroit Industry" by Diego Rivera, a 27-panel fresco located in the Rivera court.

ON EXHIBIT 2002

09/15/2001 to 02/03/2002   *Small Wonder: Worlds in a Box*
David Levinthal photographs toy soldiers, circus performers, and miniature charioteers.

10/21/2001 to 01/06/2002   *Artists Take on Detroit: Projects for the Tricentennial*
Projects from sculpture installation to video projection to community activities. The catalog will be the first electronic-based product by a museum.   *Catalog*

02/24/2002 to 05/19/2002   *Over the Line: The Art and Life of Jacob Lawrence*
For over 60 years Lawrence has depicted the social concerns of the 20th century in the lives and histories of African American.   *Will Travel*

Kresge Art Museum
Affiliated Institution: Michigan State University
East Lansing, MI   48824-1119

517-355-7631   www.msu.edu/unit/kamuseum
Open: 10-5 Mo-Fr; 10-8 Th, 12-5 Sa, Su; Summer 11-5 Tu-Fr; 12-5 Sa, Su   *Closed:* Leg/Hol! Acad!;
closed August
Vol/Contr.: Yes
& P: Small fee at designated museum visitor spaces in front of the art center.   *Museum Shop*
Group Tours: 517-353-9834   *Drop-In Tours   Sculpture Garden*
Permanent Collection: Gr 19-20; Am: cont/ab (1960s), Phot

Founded in 1959, the Kresge, an active teaching museum with over 6,500 works ranging from
prehistoric to contemporary, is the only fine arts museum in central Michigan. ❡ "St.
Anthony" by Francisco Zurbaran; "Remorse" by Salvador Dali; Contemporary collection

Flint Institute of Arts
1120 E. Kearsley St., Flint, MI   48503-1991

810-234-1695   www.flintarts org
Open: 10-5 Tu-Sa, 1-5 Su   *Closed:* Mo, Leg/Hol!
Vol/Contr.: Yes
& P: Free   *Museum Shop   Group Tours:* 810-234-1695   *Drop-In Tours:* 10-5 Tu-Sa   *Sculpture Garden*
Permanent Collection: Am: ptgs, sculp, gr 19-20; Eur: ptgs, sculp, gr 19-20; Fr/Ren: It/Ren: dec/art; Ch; cer,
sculp

The Flint Institute of Arts, founded in 1928, has grown to become the largest private museum
collection of fine art in the state. In addition to the permanent collection with artworks from
ancient China to modern America, visitors to this museum can enjoy the renovated building
itself, a stunning combination of classic interior gallery space housed within the walls of a
modern exterior. ❡ Bray Gallery of French & Italian Renaissance decorative art.

Calvin College Center Art Gallery
Affiliated Institution: Calvin College
Grand Rapids, MI   49546

616-957-6271   www.calvin.edu
Open: 9-9 Mo-Th, 9-5 Fr, 12-4 Sa   *Closed:* Su, Acad!
& P   *Group Tours*
Permanent Collection: Du: ptgs, drgs 17-19; Gr, Ptgs, Sculp, Drgs 20

17th- & 19th-century Dutch paintings are one of the highlights of the permanent collection.

Grand Rapids Art Museum
155 N. Division, Grand Rapids, MI   49503

616-831-1000   www.gramonline.org
Open: 11-6 Tu-Su; Fr 11-9   *Closed:* Mo, Leg/Hol!
Free Day: Fr 5-9   *Adm: Adult:* $5.00   *Children:* Free under 5 w/ adult, $1.00 6-17
Students: $2.00   *Seniors:* $2.00
& P: Less than 1 block from the museum   *Museum Shop*
Group Tours: 616-831-2928   *Drop-In Tours:* by appt   *Historic Building:* Beaux Arts Federal Building
Permanent Collection: Ren: ptgs; Fr: ptgs 19; Am: ptgs 19-20; Gr; Exp/Ptgs; Phot; Dec/Art

Located in a former Federal Building, the Grand Rapids Art Museum, founded in 1911, exhibits paintings and prints by established and emerging artists, as well as photographs, sculpture, and a collection of furniture & decorative arts from the Grand Rapids area and beyond. ℭ Picasso ceramics, "Ingleside" by Richard Diebenkorn, and other works. Free Fr eve, Rhythm and Blues. Cash Bar. There are admission fees for some special exhibitions.

ON EXHIBIT 2002

10/12/2001 to 01/06/2002   *Light Screens: The Leaded Glass of Frank Lloyd Wright*
Windows designed from 1890–1923 which Wright saw as simmilar to Japanese shoji screens. The installation is lit from behind to reflect that quality.   *Catalog   Will Travel*

02/15/2002 to 06/09/2002   *Landmarks of Modernism: 20th-Century Painting from the Detroit Institute of Arts*
Paintings which span 100 years of striking change in 20th-century works   *Only Venue*

06/01/2002 to mid June 2002   *Festival 2002*
A juried exhibition of regional artists featuring several hundred works

06/01/2002 to Summer 2002   *Kilim Weaving: Past and Present, New Work by Dell Michel*
Carpets of the Middle East and the tradition of weaving   *Brochure*

10/01/2002 to Fall 2002   *Eye of the Beholder: The Photography of Ellsworth Kelly*
Kelly has always been inspired by nature. Both his black-and-white and colored prints and maquettes will be featured.   *Catalog   Will Travel*

KALAMAZOO

Kalamazoo Institute of Arts
314 South Park St., Kalamazoo, MI   49007

616-349-7775 www.kiarts.org
Open: 10-5 Tu, We, Fr, Sa, 10-8 Th, 12-5 Su   *Closed:* Mo, Leg/Hol
Vol/Contr.: Yes
& P   *Museum Shop   Group Tours:* ext 3162   *Drop-In Tours*
Historic Building: architecturally significant   *Sculpture Garden*
Permanent Collection: sculp, ptgs, drgs, cer, gr, photo

The Kalamazoo Institute, established in 1924, is known for its collection of 20th-century American art and European graphics, as well as for its outstanding art school. More than 3,000 objects are housed in a building that in 1979 was voted one of the most significant structures in the state and in 1998 underwent a significant expansion. ℭ The state of the art interactive gallery and permanent collection installations, including "La Clownesse Aussi (Mlle. Cha-U-Ka-O)" by Henri de Toulouse Lautrec; "Sleeping Woman" by Richard Diebenkorn; "Simone in a White Bonnet" by Mary Cassatt; "Untitled" by Cindy Sherman

ON EXHIBIT 2002

09/09/2001 to 01/13/2002   *A Bountiful Plenty from the Shelburne Museum: Folk Art Traditions in America*
The collection of Electra Havemeyer Webb (1888–1960) and reflects here keen eye for collecting highly significant paintings, sculpture, and furniture. "The best of the best" includes trade signs, carousel figures, quilts, tobacconist figures, decoys, weather vanes, and ship figureheads.

Muskegon Museum of Art
296 W. Webster, Muskegon, MI   49440

231-720-2570   www.muskegon.k12.m.us//mma
Open: 10-5 Tu-Fr; 12-5 Sa, Su   *Closed:* Mo, Leg/Hol!
Vol/Contr.: Yes
&   P: Limited street and adjacent mall lots; handicapped parking at rear of museum
Museum Shop   Group Tours   Drop-In Tours: by appt
Permanent Collection: Am: ptgs, gr 19-early 20; Eur: ptgs; Phot; Sculp; OM: gr; Cont: gr

The award-winning Muskegon Museum, which opened in 1912, and has recently undergone major renovation, is home to a permanent collection that includes many fine examples of American and French Impressionistic paintings, Old Master through contemporary prints, photography, sculpture, and glass. The museum features a diverse schedule of changing exhibitions. Call for possible date changes!   ℂ American Art Collection

ON EXHIBIT 2002

01/20/2002 to 03/17/2002   *West by Southwest: From the Collection of the Museum of the Southwest*
Paintings, prints, and bronze sculpture from the Taos Society of Artists and historic and contemporary Santa Fe artists including Berninghaus, Bierstadt, Couse, Hennings, Hurd, and Sharp   *Will Travel*

02/03/2002 to 03/24/2002   *Grant Wood and Marvin Cohn: The Origins of Regionalism*
Paintings that highlight the work of Grant Wood and a lesser known fellow artist. It reveals the origins of Regionalism in the 1930s

10/14/2002 to 11/25/2002   *Oxymorons: Absurdly Logical Quilts*
Quilts that feature word play.

Crooked Tree Arts Council
461 E. Mitchell St., Petoskey, MI   49770

616-347-4337   www.crockedtreecrg
Open: 10-5 Mo-Fr, 11-4 Sa   *Closed:* Su, Leg/Hol!
&   P: 60 parking spaces on city lot next door to museum   *Museum Shop   Group Tours*
Historic Building: 1890 Methodist Church
Permanent Collection: Regional & Fine Art

This fine arts collection makes its home on the coast of Lake Michigan in a former Methodist church built in 1890.

Meadow Brook Art Gallery
Affiliated Institution: Oakland University
208 Wilson Hall, Rochester, MI   48309-4401

248-370-3005
Open: 12-5 Tu-Fr; 1-5:30 Sa, Su (open evenings during theater performances)
Vol/Contr.: Yes
&   P: Free   *Group Tours   Sculpture Garden   Theater*
Permanent Collection: Af; Oc; P/Col; Cont/Am: ptgs, sculp, gr; Cont/Eur: ptgs, gr, sculp

Located 30 miles north of Detroit on the campus of Oakland University, the Meadow Brook Art Gallery offers four major exhibitions annually.   ℂ Informative lectures in conjunction with exhibitions.

ON EXHIBIT 2002

01/11/2002 to 02/17/2002   *Native American Art from the Archives of the Cranbrook Museum*

03/01/2002 to 04/10/2002   *Innocents and Amateurs: Folk Painting of American People and Their Places, from the Collection of the Detroit Institute of Arts*

SAGINAW

Saginaw Art Museum
1126 N. Michigan Ave., Saginaw, MI   48602

989-754-2491
Open: Tu-Sa 10-5; Su 1-5   *Closed:* Mo, Leg/Hol!
Sugg/Contr.: $3.00
& P: Free   *Museum Shop*   *Group Tours:* (ask for Kara or Elizabeth)   *Drop-In Tours:* by appt
Historic Building: former 1904 Clark Lombard Ring Family Home
Permanent Collection: Eur: ptgs, sculp 14-20; Am: ptgs sculp; Or: ptgs, gr, dec/art; Jap: Gr; John Rogers Sculp; Charles Adams Platt: gr

The interesting and varied permanent collections of this museum, including an important group of John Rogers sculptures, are housed in a gracious 1904 Georgian-revival building designed by Charles Adams Platt. The former Clark Lombard Ring Family home is listed on the state & federal registers for historic homes.   ℂ T'ang Dynasty Marble Buddha

ON EXHIBIT 2002

11/30/2001 to 01/27/2002   *Mike Volker & Matt Lewis: Inside & Out*
Interior paintings and exterior monographs

11/30/2001 to 02/17/2002   *Piranesi*
Piranesi's series "The Views of Rome" has several works in this exhibition of the first classical Roman ruins

12/20/2001 to 02/17/2002   *Sugden and Elchert: Images of Tibet*
A artistic and socio-political view of Tibetan culture

02/01/2002 to 03/17/2002   *African Sculptures*
Masks and sculptures from the Ben Cox Collection

02/01/2002 to 04/28/2002   *Linda McCartney: Roadworks*
Lively candid photographs

02/22/2002 to 04/21/2002   *Duane Miller: Saginaw Scenes*
Etchings of the Old Town and Court Street districts

03/22/2002 to 04/28/2002   *Jan Upp*
Regional watercolor scenes

04/26/2002 to 12/31/2002   *American Impressionist*
From the permanent collection featuring Dougherty, Hassam, and others

05/03/2002 to 06/09/2002   *Andrea Lozano*
A winner of the statewide Latino Artists juried exhibition

05/10/2002 to 06/09/2002   *Gilda Snowden: Abstract Expressionism*

06/14/2002 to 08/04/2002   *All Area One Person Show*
Best of show from All Statewide Juried exhibition

09/06/2002 to 10/27/2002   *Marshall M. Fredericks*
Newly acquired pieces by the sculptor

09/06/2002 to 11/03/2002   *South African Aesthetic*
Social and political issues are melded.

ST. JOSEPH

Krasl Art Center
707 Lake Blvd., St. Joseph, MI 49085

616-983-0271 www.krasl.org
Open: 10-4 Mo-Th & Sa, 10-1 Fr, 1-4 Su *Closed:* Major Holidays & Sa of Blossomtime Parade
in early May
& P: Free *Museum Shop Group Tours:* 616-983-0271 *Drop-In Tours:* by appt
Permanent Collection: ptgs, sculp

Located on the shores of Lake Michigan, site-specific sculptures are palced in and around the
area of the center. Maps showing location and best positions for viewing are provided for the
convenience of the visitor. The center is also noted for hosting one of the finest art fairs each
July. ❛ Blown glass chandelier by Dale Chihuly. "The Heavyweight (nicknamed lotus)" by Dr.
Burt Brent, "Three Lines Diagonal Jointed-Wall" by George Rickey, "Allegheny Drift" by
Michael Dunbar.

TRAVERSE CITY

Dennos Museum Center
Affiliated Institution: Northwestern Michigan College
1701 East Front St., Traverse City, MI 49686

616-922-1055 dmc.nmc.edu
Open: 10-5 Mo-Sa, 1-5 Su *Closed:* Leg/Hol!
Adm: *Adult:* $2.00; Subject to change for special exhibitions *Children:* $1.00 *Students:* $1.00
Seniors: $2.00
& P: Reserved area for museum visitors adjacent to the museum. *Museum Shop*
Group Tours: 231-922-1029 *Drop-In Tours:* by appointment *Sculpture Garden*
Permanent Collection: Inuit art; Cont: Canadian Indian graphics; Am; Eur; Nat/Am

With a collection of more than 1,600 works, the Dennos Museum Center houses one of the
largest and most historically complete collections of Inuit art from the peoples of the Canadian
Arctic. The museum also features a "hands-on" Discovery Gallery. ❛ The Power Family Inuit
Gallery with over 880 Inuit sculptures and prints; The Thomas A. Rutkowski interactive
"Discovery Gallery"

MINNESOTA

DULUTH

Tweed Museum of Art
Affiliated Institution: University of Minnesota
10 University Dr., Duluth, MN 55812

218-726-8222 www.d.umn.edu/tma
Open: 9-8 Tu, 9-4:30 We-Fr, 1-5 Sa-Su *Closed:* Mo, Acad!
Sugg/Contr.: Yes
& P *Museum Shop Group Tours:* 218-726-8527 *Drop-In Tours*
Historic Building: on campus of University of Minnesota Duluth *Sculpture Garden*
Permanent Collection: OM: ptgs; Eur: ptgs 17-19; F: Barbizon ptgs 19; Am: all media 19-20; Cont; Af; Jap:
cer; Cont/Reg

Endowed with gifts of American and European paintings by industrialist George Tweed,
this fine institution also has an important growing permanent collection of contemporary art.
One-person exhibitions by living American artists are often presented to promote national
recognition of their work. ❛ "The Scourging of St. Blaise," a 16th-century Italian painting by a
follower of Caravaggio

ON EXHIBIT 2002

10/23/2001 to 01/13/2002   *Fritz Scholder: Last Portraits, Skulls, and Related Images*
Known for his unsentimental depictions of Native Americans Scholder felt that traditional subject matter merged with contemporary idiom will give a truer picture of the Indian.

11/06/2001 to 01/13/2002   *Neil Welliver: Prints*
Large scale woodcuts by a most respected landscape artist

01/22/2002 to 03/30/2002   *Here by Design (Made in Minnesota)*
Unique products from designers including beadwork, architecture, and graphics. How the design project becomes a finished product

05/14/2002 to 10/06/2002   *Selections from the Collection: Glenn C. Nelson Ceramics and Sculpture*

06/13/2002 to 10/13/2002   *Reconstructions: Photographs by Jane Calvin*
Photographs that relate to memories, impulses, and fantasies

07/23/2002 to 10/06/2002   *Gilbert Munger: Search for Distinction*
Little known today Munger was well known in the late 1800s for his landscape painting. *Catalog   Will Travel*

10/22/2002 to 12/21/2002   *Joel Philip Myers: New Work, 1996–2000, and Studio Glass from the Collection of Don and Carol Wiiken*
Myers is a glassmaker who comments on social conditions and relationships between individuals. The Wiiken collection is by American artisans.

MINNEAPOLIS

Frederick R. Weisman Art Museum at the University of Minnesota
Affiliated Institution: University of Minnesota
333 East River Road, Minneapolis, MN   55455

612-625-9494   hudson.acad.umn.edu
Open: 10-5 Tu, We, Fr; 10-8 Th; 11-5 Sa, Su   *Closed:* Mo, Acad!, Leg/Hol!
&   P: Paid parking in the Museum Garage is $1.60 per hour with a weekend flat rate of $3.50 per day.
Museum Shop   Group Tours: 612-625-9656   *Drop-In Tours:* 1pm Sa, Su
Historic Building: Terracotta brick & stainless steel bldg. (1993) by Frank O. Gehry
Permanent Collection: Am: ptgs, sculp, gr 20; Korean: furniture 18-19; Worlds largest coll of works by Marsden Hartley & Alfred Maurer (plus major works by their contemporaries such as Feninger & O'Keeffe)

Housed since 1993 in a striking, sculptural stainless steel and brick building designed by architect Frank Gehry, the Weisman Art Museum offers a convenient and friendly museum experience. The museum's collection features early 20th-century American artists, such as Georgia O'Keeffe and Marsden Hartley, as well as a selection of contemporary art. A teaching museum for the University and the community, the Weisman provides a multidisciplinary approach to the arts through an array of programs and a changing schedule of exhibitions. ℭ "Oriental Poppies," by Georgia O'Keeffe

Minneapolis Institute of Arts
2400 Third Ave. So., Minneapolis, MN   55404

612-870-3000   www.artsmia.org
Open: 10-5 Tu-Sa, 10-9 Th, Fr, 12-5 Su   *Closed:* 7/4, Thgv, 12/25
Vol/Contr.: Yes
&   P: Free and ample   *Museum Shop*   ¶: Restaurant 11:30-2:30 Tu-Sa; 12-3 Su
Group Tours: 612-870-3140   *Drop-In Tours:* 2:00 Tu-Su, 1:00 Sa & Su, 7pm Th
Historic Building: 1915 Neo-Classical building by McKim Mead & White   *Sculpture Garden   Theater*
Permanent Collection: Am: ptgs, sculp; Eur: ptgs, sculp; Dec/Art; Or; P/Col; Af; Oc; Islamic; Phot; Gr; Drgs; Jap: gr; textiles, arch, asian

The Minneapolis Institute of Arts is a familiar landmark located just south of downtown Minneapolis. Its architecture combines the original 1915 neo-classical structure designed by McKim, Mead & White with additions in 1974 by Kenzo Tange and in 1998 by RSP Architects. The museum is home to more than 100,000 works of art spanning 5,000 years of cultural history; approximately 4,000 objects are on view at any one time. Masterpieces by Rembrandt, Goya, Poussin, van Gogh, Degas and Bonnard, as well as leading contemporary artists, are some of highlights of the painting collection. The sculpture collection ranges from Egyptian, Greek, and Roman examples to modern works by Calder, Picasso, and Moore. Twenty-two new Asian galleries feature Chinese and Japanese screens, ceramics, bronzes, jades, paintings and woodblock prints, as well as Buudhist, Himalayan, Indian, Islamic, and Southeast Asian art. Two original Chinese period rooms date from the 17th and 18th centuries, and traditional Chinese gardens are visitors favorites. In addition to 11 fascinating period rooms, the museum has extensive holdings in the decorative arts and architecture. The prints and drawing collection features work by Dürer, Rembrandt, Toulouse-Lautrec, Lichtenstein, Johns and others and the photography collection documents the history of the medium from 1836 to the present. Among the more than 10,000 photographs are works by Stieglitz, Steichen, Evans, Adams, and others. The museum also has respected collections of textiles, ceramics, and Judaica, as well as African, Oceanic, Pre-Columbian, and Native American art. ❰ Rembrandt's "Lucretia"

ON EXHIBIT 2002

12/01/2001 to 03/10/2002   *Jack Lenor Larsen: The Company and the Cloth*

12/15/2001 to 04/21/2002   *Recent Accessions*

12/20/2001 to 02/10/2002   *Evans/Rinklin/Holmberg (working title)*

02/03/2002 to 04/14/2002   *An Artistic Dynasty: The Yoshida Family of Japanese Artists*
Oil paintings, watercolors, and woodblock prints from nine artists in this family over four generations and over 100 years   *Admission Fee*

04/01/2002 to Spring 2002   *Jim Dine Prints: 1985–2000*
100 lithographs, intaglios, woodcuts and illustrated books   *Admission Fee*

06/15/2002 to Summer 2002   *Bruce Dayton: 60 Years a Trustee (working title)*

09/15/2002 to Fall 2002   *The American Sublime*
American landscape painters of the mid-19th century especially the Hudson River School picture the magnificent, dramatic, and subtle. Included are works by Bierstadt, Church, Colke, and Cropsey. *Admission Fee*

12/22/2002 to 03/16/2003   *Eternal Egypt: Masterworks of Ancient Art from the British Museum*
The objects in this exhibition, many never shown outside the British Museum were created as gifts to the gods to accompany the dead. Ancient Egypt, the lives and beliefs including Tutankhamun, Sety, and Rameses are explored   *Catalog   Will Travel   Admission Fee*

Walker Art Center
Vineland Place, Minneapolis, MN   55403

612-375-7622   www.walkerart.org
Open: Gallery: 10-5 Tu-Sa, 11-5 Su, till 9pm Th   *Closed:* Leg/Hol!
Adm: Adult: $6.00   *Children:* Free under 12   *Students:* $4.00   *Seniors:* $4.00
&   P: Hourly metered on-street parking & pay parking at nearby Parade Stadium lot
Museum Shop   ❙❙: *Sculpture Garden*   11:30-3 Tu-Su; Gallery 8 Restaurant 11:30-3, till 8 We
Group Tours: 612-375-7609   *Drop-In Tours:* 2 Sa, Su; 2 & 6 Th (Free with adm.)   *Sculpture Garden*
Permanent Collection: Am & Eur Cont: ptgs, sculp; Gr; Drgs

Housed in a beautifully designed building by noted architect Edward Larabee Barnes, the Walker Art Center, with its superb 7,000 piece permanent collection, is particularly well known for its major exhibitions of 20th-century art. *1. The sculpture garden is open free to all from 6am to midnight daily. There is a self-guided audio tour of the Garden available for rent at the Walker lobby desk. 2. For information on a wide variety of special needs tours or accommodations call 612-375-7609. ◖ Minneapolis Sculpture Garden at Walker Art Center (open 6-midnight daily; Adm Free); "Standing Glass Fish" by F. Gehry at Cowles Conservatory (open 10-8 Tu-Sa, 10-5 Su; Adm Free)

S T .   P A U L

Minnesota Museum of American Art
505 Landmark Center-75 West Fifth St., St. Paul, MN   55102-1486

651-292-4355   www.mtn.org/mmaa/
Open: 11-4 Tu-Sa, 11-7:30 Th, 1-5 Su   *Closed:* Mo, Leg/Hol!
&: Elevator; restroom; special entrance   P: Street parking and nearby parking facilities
⫪: 11:30-1:30 Tu-Fr; 11-1 Sa
Group Tours: 651-292-4395   *Drop-In Tours:* Group tours scheduled daily, regular Museum hours
Historic Building
Permanent Collection: Am

The Minnesota Museum of American Art, located in the Historic Landmark Center in downtown Saint Paul, is an accessible, intimate museum experience. The MMAA exhibits a diverse collection of American artists in the Permanent Collection Galleries and an exciting mix of national touring exhibitions in the Exhibition Galleries. Come enjoy installations of recently acquired sculpture, collages, and photographs by artists Louise Nevelson, George Morrison, and Gordon Parks. The MMAA is within easy walking distance of the new Science Museum of Minnesota and downtown hotels.

ON EXHIBIT 2002

12/15/2001 to 02/10/2002   *The Sculpture of Harriet Frishmuth*
Bronze sculptures, primarily of young women   *Will Travel*

03/02/2002 to 04/21/2002   *I Want You! World War I Posters, 1916–1919*

05/11/2002 to 08/11/2002   *Minnesota Biennial: 3D 2002*

08/31/2002 to 10/06/2002   *In Response to Place: Photographs from the Nature Conservancy's Last Great Places*
America's great photographers focus on natural wonders

10/27/2002 to 12/29/2002   *Robert Henri and His Influence*
Twelve artists of the late 19th century and early 20th influenced by Henri

MISSISSIPPI

B I L O X I

George E. Ohr Arts and Cultural Center
136 George E. Ohr St., Biloxi, MS   39530

228-374-5547   www.georgeohr.org
Open: 9-5 Mo-Sa   *Closed:* Su, 1/1, 7/4, Thgv, 12/25
Adm: Adult: $3.00   Seniors: $2.00
&.   P: Free parking in the lot across the street from the museum.   *Museum Shop*
Group Tours   Drop-In Tours
Permanent Collection: George Ohr pottery

In addition to a 300-piece collection of pottery by George Ohr, a man often referred to as the mad potter of Biloxi, this museum features a gallery dedicated to the promotion of local talent and another for rotating and traveling exhibitions.

JACKSON

Mississippi Museum of Art

201 E. Pascagoula St., Jackson, MS   39201

601-960-1515   www.msmuseumart.org
Open: Please call for hours   *Closed:* Leg/Hol
Adm: *Adult:* Call for Admission rates
& P: Pay lot behind museum   *Museum Shop*
¶: Palette Restaurant (open for lunch 11:00-2:00 Mo-Fr)
Group Tours: 601-960-1515   *Drop-In Tours:* Upon request if available   *Sculpture Garden*
Permanent Collection: Am: 19-20; Reg: 19-20; Brit: ptgs, dec/art mid 18-early 19; P/Col: cer; Jap: gr

Begun as an art association in 1911, the Mississippi Museum now has more than 3,400 works of art in a collection that spans more than 30 centuries.

LAUREL

Lauren Rogers Museum of Art

5th Ave. at 7th St., Laurel, MS   39441-1108

601-649-6374
Open: 10-4:45 Tu-Sa, 1-4 Su   *Closed:* Mo, Leg/Hol!
&: Wheelchair accessible, elevator, restrooms   P: Lot at rear of museum and along side of the museum on 7th Street   *Museum Shop   Group Tours   Drop-In Tours:* 10-12 & 1-3 Tu-Fr
Permanent Collection: Am:19-20; Eur: 19-20; Nat/Am; Jap: gr 18-19; Nat/Am: baskets; Eng: silver

Located among the trees in Laurel's Historic District, the Lauren Rogers Museum was the first art museum to be established in the state, has grown rapidly since its inception in 1922. While the original Georgian Revival building still stands, the new adjoining galleries are perfect for the display of the fine art collection of American and European masterworks.   ⊄ One of the largest collections of Native American Indian baskets in the U.S.; Gibbons English Georgian Silver Collection

MERIDIAN

Meridian Museum of Art

25th Ave. & 7th St., Meridian, MS   39301

601-693-1501
Open: 1-5 Tu-Su
P: Free but limited   *Group Tours   Drop-In Tours:* Upon request if available
Permanent Collection: Am: phot, sculp, dec/art; Reg; Works on Paper 20; Eur: portraits 19-20

Housed in the landmark Old Carnegie Library Building, built in 1912–13, the Meridian Museum, begun in 1933 as an art association, serves the cultural needs of the people of East Mississippi and Western Alabama.   ⊄ 18th-century collection of European portraits

Walter Anderson Museum of Art

510 Washington Ave. P.O. Box 328, Ocean Springs, MS   39564

228-872-3164   www.walterandersonmuseum.org
Open: October -April 9:30-4:30 Mo-Sa, 12.30-5 Su   *Closed:* 1/1, Easter, Thgv, 12/25
Free Day: 1st Mo of the month   *Adm:*   *Adult:* $5.00   *Children:* $2.00 (6-18), Free under 6
Students: $3.00   *Seniors:* $3.00
&; Wheelchair accessible (& available at museum)   P: Limited free parking at the adjacent Community
Center and on the street.   *Museum Shop*
Group Tours: Education Director   *Drop-In Tours:* Education Director   *Sculpture Garden*
Permanent Collection: Works by Walter Inglis Anderson (1903–1965), in a variety of media and from
all periods.

This museum celebrates the works of Walter Inglis Anderson, whose vibrant and energetic images of plants and animals of Florida's Gulf Coast have placed him among the forefront of American painters of the 20th century. ❲ "The Little Room," a room with private murals seen only by Anderson until after his death when it was moved in its entirety to the museum.

ON EXHIBIT 2002

09/28/2001 to 01/13/2002   *The Sellars Collection: Art by American Women*
Paintings from 1850 to 1930, a neglected period in history

01/25/2002 to 04/28/2002   *Visions of Nature: The World of Walter Anderson*
Watercolors, drawings, and block prints highlighting the flora and fauna of Mississippi

05/10/2002 to 09/15/2002   *Shearwater Pottery: The Anderson Brothers in Context*
Walter Anderson as a decorator and ceramic sculptor whose company still produces fine art pottery

09/27/2002 to 01/15/2003   *Shaped by Ancient Voices: Walter Anderson in Context*
The influences of ancient American, Egyptian, Greek, and Paleolithic cave art on Anderson

09/29/2002 to 01/30/2003   *Centennial Exhibition: Walter Inglis Anderson: Everything I See Is So Strange and New (tentative opening venue)*
Anderson's captured the essence of the natural world.   *Catalog   Will Travel*

Tupelo Artist Guild Gallery

211 W. Main St., Tupelo, MS   38801

662-844-Arts   tupeloartgallery.com
Open: 10-4 Tu-Th, 1-4 Fr   *Closed:* Mo, 1/1, 7/4, Thgv, 12/25
& P   *Museum Shop   Group Tours   Drop-In Tours:* Upon request if available
Historic Building: Built 1905

Housed in the former original People's Bank Building (1904–5) this small but effective non-collecting institution is dedicated to bringing traveling exhibitions from all areas of the country to the people of the community and its visitors.

MISSOURI

COLUMBIA

Museum of Art and Archaeology
Affiliated Institution: MU campus, University Of Missouri
1 Pickard Hall, Columbia, MO   65211

573-882-3591   www.research.missouri.edu/museum
Open: 9-5 Tu, We, Fr; 12-5 Sa, Su; 9-5 & 6-9 Th   *Closed:* Mo, Leg/Hol!; 12/25-1/1
Vol/Contr.: Yes
&   P: Parking is available at the university visitors' garage on University Avenue; metered parking spaces
on Ninth St.   *Museum Shop   Group Tours:* 2 wks notice   *Historic Building*
Permanent Collection: An/Egt; An/Grk; An/R; An/Persian; Byz; Drgs 15-20; Gr 15-20; Af; Oc; P/Col; Or

Ancient art and archaeology from Egypt, Palestine, Iran, Cyprus, Greece, Etruria, and Rome as
well as early Christian and Byzantine art, the Kress study collection, and 15th-20th century
European and American artworks are among the treasures from 6 continents and five millennia
that are housed in this museum.   ℂ "Portrait of a Musician," 1949, Thomas Hart Benton

KANSAS CITY

Kemper Museum of Contemporary Art
4420 Warwick Blvd., Kansas City, MO   64111-1821

816-753-5784   www.kemperart.org
Open: 10-4 Tu-Th, 10-9 Fr, Sa, 11-5 Su   *Closed:* Mo, 1/1, 7/4, Thgv, 12/25
Vol/Contr.: Yes   &   P: Free   *Museum Shop*   ¶: Café Sebastienne 11-2:30 Tu-Su, 6-9pm Fr, Sa
Group Tours   Drop-In Tours   Sculpture Garden
Permanent Collection: Am, Eur Modern, Cont, Emerging and Established Artists

Designed by architect Gunnar Birkerts, the stunning Kemper Museum of Contemporary Art
(a work of art in itself) houses a rapidly growing permanent collection of modern and
contemporary works, and hosts temporary exhibitions and creative programs designed to both
entertain and challenge. A Museum Shop and the lively Café Sebastienne round out the
Museum's amenities.   ℂ Louise Bourgeois's bronze "Spider" sculptures; a Waterford crystal
chandelier by Dale Chihuly; Ursula Von Rydingsvaard's "Bowl with Sacks"; "Ahulani" bronze
sculpture by Deborah Butterfield; Frank Stella's "The Prophet"; "The History of Art" in Café
Sebastienne, a 110-painting cycle by Frederick James Brown.

Nelson-Atkins Museum of Art
4525 Oak St., Kansas City, MO   64111-1873

816-751-1ART   www.nelson-atkins.org and www.kansascity.com
Open: 10-4 Tu-Th, 10-9 Fr, 10-5 Sa, 12-5 Su   *Closed:* Mo, 1/1, 7/4, Thgv, 12/25
&: wheelchairs available   P: Free lot on 45th St; parking lot for visitors with disabilities at Oak St.
Business Entrance on west side of the Museum   *Museum Shop*
¶: Rozzelle Court Restaurant 11-3 Tu-Th, 11-8 Fr (closed 3-5), 11-3 Sa,12-3 Su
Group Tours: 816-751-1238   *Drop-In Tours:* 10:30, 11, 1, & 2 Tu-Sa; 1:30, 2, 2:30, 3 Su
Sculpture Garden   Theater
Permanent Collection: Am: all media; Eur: all media; Per/Rms; Nat/Am; Oc; P/Col; Or

Among the many fine art treasures in this outstanding 65-year-old museum is their world
famous collection of Oriental art and artifacts that includes the Chinese Temple Room with its
furnishings, a gallery displaying delicate scroll paintings, and a sculpture gallery with glazed
T'ang dynasty tomb figures.   ℂ Largest collection of works by Thomas Hart Benton; Kansas
City Sculpture Park; "Shuttlecocks," a four-part sculptural installation by Claes Oldenburg and
Coosje van Bruggen located on the grounds of the museum

ON EXHIBIT 2002

04/12/2002 to 07/07/2002   *Eternal Egypt: Masterworks of Ancient Art from the British Museum*
The objects in this exhibition, many never shown outside the British Museum were created as gifts to the gods to accompany the dead. Ancient Egypt, the lives and beliefs including Tutankhamun, Sety, and Rameses are explained   *Catalog   Will Travel*

10/06/2002 to 05/04/2003   *Art of the Lega*
Masterpiece quality African art

POPLAR BLUFF

Margaret Harwell Art Museum
421 N. Main St., Poplar Bluff, MO   63901

573-686-8002   www.mham.org
Open: 12-4 Tu-Fr; 1-4 Sa, Su   *Closed:* Mo, Leg/Hol!
Vol/Contr.: Yes
& P   *Museum Shop   Group Tours   Historic Building:* Located in 1883 mansion
Permanent Collection: Dec/Art; Reg; Cont

The 1880s mansion in which this museum is housed is a perfect foil for the museum's permanent collection of contemporary art. Located in the southeastern part of the state, just above the Arkansas border, the museum features monthly exhibitions showcasing the works of both regional and nationally known artists.

ON EXHIBIT 2002

06/16/2001 to 01/20/2002   *Birmingham Totem (working title)*
This exhibition is the last in a four-part series exploring the changing definitions of freedom throughout the history of African-Americans.

01/05/2002 to 01/27/2002   *Papermaking by Tom Lang*
Hand papermaking and the inherent techniques

02/02/2002 to 03/02/2002   *Celebrating African American Month at MHAM with the Art of George Young Jr.*

03/03/2002 to 04/07/2002   *Speak*
A traveling exhibit of original book illustrations of artists favorite dogs   *Will Travel*

06/01/2002 to 06/30/2002   *Alternative Photography by Gwen Walstrand*
Personal experiences of life, work, and motherhood

SAINT JOSEPH

Albrecht-Kemper Museum of Art
2818 Frederick Avenue, Saint Joseph, MO   64506

816-233-7003   www.albrecht-kemper.org
Open: 10-4 Tu-Sa, till 8pm Th, 1-4 Su   *Closed:* Mo, 1/1, Easter, 7/4, Thgv, 12/25, Mem/Day, Lab/Day
Adm: Adult: $3.00 (18 & over)   *Children:* Free under 6   *Students:* $1.00   *Seniors:* $2.00
&; Fully wheelchair accessible (doors, lifts, restrooms, theater)   P: Free on-site parking   *Museum Shop*
¶: Special Events Only; Lunch We 11:30-1:30   *Group Tours:* 816-233-7003   *Sculpture Garden   Theater*
Permanent Collection: Am: ldscp ptgs, Impr ptgs, gr, drgs 18-20

Considered to have the region's finest collection of 18th- through 20th-century American art, the Albrecht-Kemper Museum of Art is housed in the expanded and transformed 1935 Georgian-style mansion of William Albrecht.   ℂ North American Indian Portfolio by Catlin; illustrated books by Audubon; Thomas Hart Benton collection

Springfield Art Museum
1111 E. Brookside Dr., Springfield, MO   65807-1899

417-837-5700
Open: 9-5 Tu, We, Fr, Sa; 1-5 Su; till 8pm Th   *Closed:* Mo, Local & Leg/Hol!
Vol/Contr.: Yes
&   P: West parking lot with handicapped spaces; limited on-street parking north of the museum
Museum Shop   Group Tours   Drop-In Tours
Permanent Collection: Am: ptgs, sculp, drgs, gr, phot 18-20; Eur: ptgs, sculp, gr, drgs, phot 18-20; Dec/Art;
Nat/Am; Oc; P/Col

Watercolor U.S.A., an annual national competition is but one of the features of the Springfield Museum, the oldest cultural institution in the city.   ⊄ New Jeannette L. Musgrave Wing for the permanent collection; John Henry's "Sun Target," 1974, a painted steel sculpture situated on the grounds directly east of the museum; paintings and prints by Thomas Hart Benton

ON EXHIBIT 2002

01/01/2002 to Winter 2002   *African Art from Missouri Southern State College Spiva Art Collection*

02/14/2002 to 11/12/2002   *"Jimmy Ernst"*

03/16/2002 to 06/02/2002   *The Lutheran Brotherhood Print Collection*

11/16/2002 to 01/05/2003   *MOAK 4-State Regional Juried Exhibition*

Forum for Contemporary Art
3540 Washington Avenue, St. Louis, MO   63103

314-535-4660   www. forumart.org
Open: 10-5 Tu-Sa   *Closed:* Su, Mo, Leg/Hol! & Installations
Vol/Contr.: $2.00
&: First floor accessible; elevator to third floor gallery   P: Metered on street or commercial lot.
Group Tours   Drop-In Tours: regular museum hours
Permanent Collection: No permanent collection. Please call for current exhibition information not listed below.

The Forum for Contemporary Art enriches and educates visitors by presenting a broad range of media and topics representing today's artists. Its goal is to engage people of all ages in the appreciation and interpretation of contemporary art and ideas. A new building at the corner of Spring and Washington designed by Brad Cloepfil, Allied Works Architecture, is to open Fall 2002

ON EXHIBIT 2002

11/16/2001 to 01/05/2002   *Michael Byron: The Amitin Notebook Project*
A series of drawings from an old notebook and working with what was there began to draw, paint and collage images in layers on the pages. Some had photographic information, etc

11/16/2001 to 01/05/2002   *Warren Rosser: New Paintings (working title)*
Large scale abstract acrylic paintings on canvas and smaller mixed media works on paper which address color, space, and opticality

01/18/2002 to 03/09/2002   *Mapping: Byte by Bit*
Maps can diagram specific or imaginary location. For the exhibition a broad view of mapping will be taken with 6 to 8 local, regional, and international artists represented including Denes, Kosloff, Ott, Rees, Ritchie, and Wilson.

03/22/2002 to 05/11/2002   *Staging: Janieta Eyre, Julie Moos, & Zwelethu Mthethwa*
Young photographers have an interest in purposefully staging their subjects in real and imaginary environments. The artistic motivation behind these latest staged devices is examined here.

Laumeier Sculpture Park Museum
12580 Rott Rd., St. Louis, MO   63127

314-821-1209
Open: Park: 8am-1/2 hour after sunset; Museum: 10-5 Tu-Sa & 12-5 Su   *Closed:* For Sculpture
Park & Museum: 1/1, Thgv, 12/25
&: Paved trails; ramps to museum & restrooms   P: Free   *Museum Shop*   ¶: Picnic Area
Group Tours: 314-821-1298; 2 weeks advance reservation required   *Drop-In Tours:* 1st & 3rd Su of month
at 2pm (May-Oct), free   *Sculpture Garden*
Permanent Collection: Cont/Am; sculp: Native Sculp & Art; Site Specific Sculp

More than 75 internationally acclaimed site-specific sculptures that complement their natural
surroundings are the focus of this institution whose goal is to promote greater public
involvement and understanding of contemporary sculpture. There are, for the visually
impaired, 12 scale models of featured works, accompanied by descriptive braille labels, that are
placed near their full sized outdoor counterparts.   ☾ Works by Alexander Liberman, Beverly
Pepper, Dan Graham, Jackie Ferrara Mark di Suvero, Jonathan Borofsky

Saint Louis Art Museum
1 Fine Arts Park, Forest Park, St. Louis, MO   63110-1380

314-721-0072   www.slam.org
Open: 1:30-8:30 Tu, 10-5 We-Su   *Closed:* Mo, 1/1, Thgv, 12/25
Free Day: special exh is free Tu
& P: Free parking in small lot on south side of building; also street parking available.
Museum Shop   ¶: Cafe 11-3:30 & 5-8 Tu; 11-3:30 We-Sa; 10-2 Su (brunch); Snack Bar also
Group Tours: ex 484   *Drop-In Tours:* 1:30 We-Fr (30 min.); 1:30 Sa, Su (60 min.)
Historic Building: Located in a 1904 World's Fair Exhibition Building designed by Cass Gilbert
Sculpture Garden   Theater
Permanent Collection: AN/Egt; AN/Ch; Jap; Ind; Oc; Af; P/Col; Nat/Am; Ren; Ptgs:18-Cont;
Sculp: 18-Cont

Just 10 minutes from the heart of downtown St. Louis, this museum is home to one of the most
important permanent collections of art in the country. A global museum featuring
pre-Columbian and German Expressionist works that are ranked among the best in the world,
this institution is also known for its Renaissance, Impressionist, American, African, Oceanic,
Asian, and ancient through contemporary art.   ☾ The Sculpture Terrace with works by
Anthony Caro, Pierre Auguste Renoir, Henry Moore, Alexander Calder, and Aristide Maillol;
Egyptian mummy and Cartonnage on display with a full-size x-ray of the mummy.

ON EXHIBIT 2002

02/09/2002 to 05/12/2002   *John Singer Sargent: Beyond the Portrait Studio, Paintings and Drawings
from the Metropolitan Museum of Art*
Sargent's diverse interests of travel, figure, and mural studies are featured. Also included are
sketches as an official war artist during WWI as well as late watercolors of Florida's beaches and
palmettos.   *Catalog   Will Travel   Admission Fee*

06/15/2002 to 09/15/2002   *The Gentileschi: Father and Daughter*
Important baroque painters of the 17th century showing the most representative works of all
stages of their careers. Orazio arrived at a form of elegant classicism. Artemisia settled for a time
in Naples as it was emerging as an important art center.   *Catalog   Will Travel   Admission Fee*

Washington University Gallery of Art, Steinberg Hall (*Museum Closed to 2004*)
One Brookings Drive, St. Louis, MO   63130-4899

314-935-4523   www.wustl.edu/galleryofart
Open: Currently closed: to open in new facility in 2004
& P: meters north side of the building   *Museum Shop*
Group Tours: 314-935-7918   *Drop-In Tours:* advance notice preferred
Permanent Collection: Eur: ptgs, sculp 16-20; OM: 16-20; Cont/Gr; Am: ptgs, sculp 19-20; Dec/Art; Fr:
academic; Ab/Exp; Cubists

With a well-deserved reputation for being one of the premier university art museums in the nation, the more than 100 year old Gallery of Art at Washington University features outstanding examples of works by Picasso (25 in all) and a myriad of history's artistic greats, including Dupre, Daumier, Church, Gifford, Picasso, Ernst, deKooning and Pollock, among a host of other artists. ❡ Hudson River School Collection

MONTANA

BILLINGS

Yellowstone Art Museum
410 N. 27th St., Billings, MT 59101

406-256-6804   yellowstone.artmuseum.org
Open: 10-5 Tu-Sa, Th till 8pm; 12-5 Su   *Closed:* Mo, Leg/Hol!
Adm: *Adult:* $5.00   *Children:* $2.00 6-18; Free under 6   *Students:* $3.00   *Seniors:* $5.00
♿   P: Pay lot next to building is free to museum patrons.   *Museum Shop*
Group Tours   Drop-In Tours: 12 Th   *Historic Building:* Original building built in 1884. Completed expansion and remodel in Feb 28, 1998. 30,000 sq. ft. added to orig. structure.
Permanent Collection: Cont/Historical: ptgs, sculp, cer, phot, drgs, gr

Situated in the heart of downtown Billings, the focus of the museum is on displaying the works of contemporary regional artists and on showcasing artists who have achieved significant regional or national acclaim. With nearly 2,000 objects in its permanent collection, the museum is well-known for its "Montana Collection" dedicated to the preservation of art of the West. The museum collection includes work by notable artists such as Rudy Autio, John Buck, Deborah Butterfield, Clarice Dreyer, Peter Voulkos, and Theodore Waddell. Additionally, the museum houses a collection of 90 abstract expressionist paintings from the George Poindexter family of New York and the largest private collection of work by cowboy author and illustrator Will James. The museum re-opened its doors February 28, 1998 after closing for two years to complete a 6.2 million dollar expansion and renovation project. The expansion added 30,000 square feet to the original structure. In addition to tripling the exhibition space, other visitor amenities were added including: an education classroom/studio, public meeting room, courtyard, and enhanced museum store. Wheel chairs are also available.

ON EXHIBIT 2002

08/01/2001 to 01/06/2002   *In the Spirit of Sharing: Ceramic Work from Billings Area Collections*
Eclectic art honoring the Archie Bray Foundation

10/09/2001 to 05/05/2002   *Lone Cowboy: Paintings and Drawings by Will James*
Montana's favorite cowboy remains vibrant and alive.

03/23/2002 to 06/30/2002   *An American Anthem: 300 Years of Painting from the Butler Institute of American Art*
A survey of American art history including the Colonial Period, Hudson River School, Luminism, American Impressionism, the American West, the Eight, Social Realism, and post-war to the present. Included are Cole, Church, Bierstadt, Eakins, Hopper, Henri, Chase, Bearden, and many others.   *Will Travel   Book*

03/23/2002 to 06/30/2002   *The Most Difficult Journey: The Poindexter Collections of Abstract Art*
Works including DeNiro Sr, Pollock, and deKooning   *Catalog   Will Travel*

03/23/2002 to 06/18/2002   *The Romance Paintings: Lanny Frances DeVuono*
Beautiful landscape paintings

04/13/2002 to 07/14/2002   *Crow Country and Other Documents: Ken Blackbird*
Powerful photographs of Montana culture

GREAT FALLS

C. M. Russell Museum

400 13th St. North, Great Falls, MT 59401-1498

406-727-8787 www.cmrussell.org
Open: May 1-Sept 30: 9-6 Mo-Sa; 12-5 Su; Winter: 10-5 Tu-Sa & 1-5 Su *Closed:* 1/1, Easter, Thgv, 12/25
Free Day: Dec-Feb Su 12-5 *Adm:* *Adult:* $6.00 *Children:* Free under 6 *Students:* $3.00 *Seniors:* $4.00
♿ P: Free *Museum Shop*
Group Tours *Drop-In Tours:* 9:15 & 1:30 Mo-Fr June; 9:15, 1:30, 2;30 Jul-Aug *Historic Building*
Sculpture Garden
Permanent Collection: Reg; Cont; Cer

Constructed of telephone poles in 1903, the log cabin studio of the great cowboy artist C. M. Russell still contains the original cowboy gear and Indian artifacts that were used as the artist's models. Adjoining the cabin, and in contrast to it, is the fine art museum with its modern facade. It houses more than 12,000 works of art that capture the flavor of the old west and its bygone way of life. The Russell Home is on the museum grounds (built 1900). ☾ Collection of Western art by Charles M. Russell and many of the American greats

ON EXHIBIT 2002

09/20/2001 to 02/08/2002 ***Portraits of Native America: Faces of the American West***
The tradition of portrait-making face-to-face with Native Americans. All the works are part of the permanent collection.

Paris Gibson Square Museum of Art

1400 1st Ave., North, Great Falls, MT 59401-3299

406-727-8255
Open: Winter Hours Lab/Day to Mem/Day 10-5 Mo-Fr; 12-5 Sa, 7-9 Tu; Summer; Tu-Fr 10-5, Tu 7-9; 12-5 Sa, Su *Closed:* Leg/Hol!
♿; Wheelchair accessible; elevators P: Free *Museum Shop*
🍴: Lunch Tu-Fr, Res suggested *Group Tours*
Historic Building: 19th C Romanesque structure built in 1895 as a high school *Sculpture Garden*
Permanent Collection: Reg: ptgs, sculp, drgs, gr

Contemporary arts are featured within the walls of this 19th century Romanesque building which was originally used as a high school.

ON EXHIBIT 2002

11/01/2001 to 01/30/2002 ***Contemporary Baskets***

02/15/2002 to 05/01/2002 ***Bently Spang: Recent Work/Patrick Zentz***

05/15/2002 to 08/01/2002 ***Contemporary Design /Our Vehicles, Our Lives***
Furniture

08/15/2002 to 10/25/2002 ***Paper Pieces/Stone Poems***

11/01/2002 to 01/30/2003 ***Woman Photographers***

KALISPELL

Hockaday Center for the Arts

Second Ave E. & Third St, Kalispell, MT 59901

406-755-5268
Open: 10-6 Tu-Sa, 10-8 We *Closed:* Mo, Leg/Hol!
Free Day: We *Adm:* *Adult:* $2.00 *Children:* Free *Students:* $1.00 *Seniors:* $1.00
♿ P *Museum Shop* *Group Tours:* 406-755-5268 *Drop-In Tours:* Upon request if available
Historic Building *Sculpture Garden*
Permanent Collection: Cont/Northwest: ptgs, sculp, gr, port, cer

The Hockaday Center for the Arts which places strong emphasis on contemporary art is housed in the renovated Carnegie Library built in 1903. A program of rotating regional, national, or international exhibitions is presented approximately every 6 weeks. ❡ The Hockaday permanent collection of works by NW Montana artists and our museum shop featuring fine arts and crafts.

MILES CITY

Custer County Art Center
Water Plant Rd., Miles City, MT   59301

406-232-0635
Open: 1-5 Tu-Su   *Closed:* 1/1, Easter, Thgv, 12/25
Vol/Contr.: Yes
ᜒ P   *Museum Shop   Group Tours*
Historic Building: Located in the old holding tanks of the water plant (member NRHP)
Permanent Collection: Cont/Reg; 126 Edward S. Curtis Photogravures; 81 William Henry Jackson Photochromes, 200 Regional Artist's Work on Display

The old holding tanks of the water plant (c. 1914) provide an unusual location for the Custer County Art Center. Situated in the southeastern part of the state in a parkland setting overlooking the Yellowstone River, this facility features 20th century Western and contemporary art. The gift shop is worthy of mention due to the emphasis placed on available works for sale by regional artists. ❡ Annual Western Art Roundup & Quick Draw Art Auction 3rd weekend in May

MISSOULA

Art Museum of Missoula
335 North Pattee, Missoula, MT   59802

406-728-0447   artmissoula.org
Open: 12-8 Tu; 12-6 We-Sa & 12-5 Mo-Fr   *Closed:* most Leg/Hol!
Sugg/Contr.: $2.00   *Adm:*   *Children:* under 18 free
ᜒ: first floor galleries   P: Limited metered on-street parking   *Museum Shop*
Group Tours   Drop-In Tours: by appt   *Historic Building*
Permanent Collection: Am West; Reg: Cont Am Ind

International exhibitions and regional art of Montana and other Western states is featured in this lively community-based museum which is housed in the 1903 Carnegie Library building in downtown Missoula.

Museum of Fine Arts
Affiliated Institution: School of Fine Arts, University of Montana
Missoula, MT   59812

406-243-4970
Open: 9-12 & 1-4 Mo-Fr   *Closed:* State/Hol & Leg/Hol!
ᜒ P: Free on-street parking and in Springfield Library & Museum lots on State St. and Edwards St.
Permanent Collection: Reg

Great American artists are well represented in this University museum with special emphasis on Western painters and prints by such contemporary artists as Motherwell and Krasner. The permanent collection rotates with exhibitions of a temporary nature.

NEBRASKA

Museum of Nebraska Art
Affiliated Institution: University of Nebraska at Kearney
24th & Central, Kearney, NE   68848

308-865-8559
Open: 11-5 Tu-Sa,1-5 Su   *Closed:* Mo, Leg/Hol!
&   P   *Museum Shop   Group Tours   Historic Building   Sculpture Garden*
Permanent Collection: Reg: Nebraskan 19-present

The museum building, listed in the National Register of Historic Places, has been remodeled and expanded with new gallery spaces and a sculpture garden. Featured is the Nebraska Art Collection—artwork by Nebraskans from the Artist-Explorers to the contemporary scene.   ❲ "The Bride," by Robert Henri

LINCOLN

Great Plains Art Collection
Affiliated Institution: University of Nebraska
215 Love Library, 1155 9th Street, Lincoln, NE   68588-0250

402-472-6220   www.unl.edu/plains/gallery/gallery.html/
Open: 10-5 Tu-Sa, 1:30-5 Su   *Closed:* Mo, closed holiday weekends, between exhibits and Acad
Vol/Contr.: Yes
&   P: Limited metered parking   *Museum Shop   Group Tours*
Permanent Collection: Western: ptgs, sculp 19, 20; Nat/Am

This collection of western art which emphasizes the Great Plains features sculptures by such outstanding artists as Charles Russell & Frederic Remington, and paintings by Albert Bierstadt, John Clymer, Olaf Wieghorst, Mel Gerhold and others.   ❲ William de la Montagne Cary (1840–1922), "Buffalo Throwing the Hunter," bronze

Sheldon Memorial Art Gallery and Sculpture Garden
Affiliated Institution: University of Nebraska
12th and R Sts., Lincoln, NE   68588-0300

402-472-2461   www. Sheldon.unl.edu
Open: 10-5 Tu-Sa, 7-9 Th & Sa, 2-9 Su   *Closed:* Mo, Leg/Hol!
Vol/Contr.: Yes
&   P   *Museum Shop   Group Tours   Drop-In Tours:* during public hours   *Historic Building*
Sculpture Garden
Permanent Collection: Am: ptgs 19, 20, sculp, phot, w/col, drgs, gr

This highly regarded collection is housed in a beautiful Italian marble building designed by internationally acclaimed architect Philip Johnson. It is located on the University of Nebraska Lincoln campus and surrounded by a campus-wide sculpture garden consisting of more than 30 key examples by artists of renown including di Suvero, Lachaise, David Smith, Heizer, Shea, Serra, and Oldenburg.   ❲ "Torn Notebook," a new 22-foot monumental sculpture by Claes Oldenburg and Coosje van Bruggen, 3 pieces.

OMAHA

Joslyn Art Museum
2200 Dodge St., Omaha, NE   68102-1292

402-342-3300   www.joslyn.org
Open: 10-4 Tu-Sa, 12-4 Su   *Closed:* Mo, Leg/Hol!
Free Day: 10-12 Sa   *Adm:*   *Adult:* $6.00   *Children:* 5-17 $3.50, under 5 Free   *Students:* $4.00
Seniors: $4.00
&: At atrium entrance   P: Free   *Museum Shop*   ¶: Tu-Sa 11-3:30, Su 12-3:30
Group Tours: ext 206   *Drop-In Tours:* We 1pm; Sa 11am   *Historic Building*
Permanent Collection: Am: ptgs 19, 20; Western Art; Eur: 19, 20

Nebraska's only art museum with an encyclopedic collection, featuring works from antiquity to the present with emphasis on 19th- and 20th-century American and European art   (World-renowned collection of watercolors and prints by Swiss artist Karl Bodmer that document his journey to the American West 1832–34; Noted collection of American Western art including works by Catlin, Remington, and Leigh.

ON EXHIBIT 2002

06/08/2002 to 09/01/2002   *The Sport of Life and Death: The Mesoamerican Ballgame*
A team sport played with a rubber ball in elaborate masonry courts. Originating with the Olmecs from the central coast of Mexico from 1500 BC to 600 BC trhrough the Aztecs. Most of the works have never been shown in this country   *Will Travel*

05/04/2002 to 07/28/2002   *Midlands Invitational 2002: Painting and Sculpture*
The fifth in a series of media-based exhibitions from Nebraska and six contiguous states

08/10/2002 to 09/29/2002   *Exotica: Plant Portraits from around the World*
Plant art only happened once in history, between 1650 and 1850 prior to the camera. Artists include Audubon, Redoute, Seligmann, and Thornton.

09/28/2002 to 12/29/2002   *"A Faithful and Vivid Picture": Karl Bodmer's North American Prints*
Original watercolors and drawings made between 1832–34 and their evolution to book illustration

NEVADA

RENO

Nevada Museum of Art/E. L. Weigand Gallery
160 W. Liberty Street, Reno, NV   89501

775-329-3333   nevadaart.org
Open: 10-4 Tu, We, Fr, 10-7 Th, 12-4 Sa, Su   *Closed:* Mo, Leg/Hol!
Adm: *Adult:* $5.00   *Children:* $1.00 (6-12)   *Students:* $3.00   *Seniors:* $3.00
& P   *Museum Shop*   *Group Tours*   *Drop-In Tours:* 2pm Sa
Permanent Collection: Am: ptgs 19, 20, Nat/Am; Reg

Visit Nevada's premiere art museum and enjoy world-class exhhibitions ranging from contemporary to historic perspectives. Recipient of the 1999 National Award for Museum service awarded by the Institute of Museum and Library Services in Washington, DC.

NEW HAMPSHIRE

CORNISH

Saint-Gaudens National Historic Site
St. Gaudens Rd RR 3 Box 73, Cornish, NH   03745-9704

603-675-2175   www.sgnhs.org./www.nps.gov/saga
Open: 9:00-4:30 Daily, last weekend May-Oct 31
Free Day: Aug 25th   *Adm:*   *Adult:* $4.00   *Children:* Free under 17
P   *Museum Shop   Group Tours:* ext. 115   *Drop-In Tours:* adv res req   *Historic Building   Sculpture Garden*
Permanent Collection: Augustus Saint-Gaudens: sculp

The house, the studios, and gardens of Augustus Saint-Gaudens (1848–1907), one of America's greatest sculptors.

DURHAM

Art Gallery, University of New Hampshire
Paul Creative Arts Center, 30 College Road, Durham, NH   03824-3538

603-862-3712
Open: 10-4 Mo-We, 10-8 Th, 1-5 Sa-Su (Sept-May)   *Closed:* Fr, Acad!
&.; Limited   P: Metered or at Visitors Center   *Group Tours:* 603-862-3713   *Theater*
Permanent Collection: Jap: gr 19; Eur & Am: drgs 17-20; Phot; Eur: works on paper 19, 20

Each academic year The Art Gallery of the University of New Hampshire presents exhibitions of historical to contemporary art in a variety of media. Exhibitions also include work by the University art faculty, alumni, senior art students, and selections from the permanent collection.

HANOVER

Hood Museum of Art
Affiliated Institution: Dartmouth College
Hanover, NH   03755

603-646-2808   www.dartmouth.edu/~hood
Open: 10-5 Tu, Th-Sa, 10-9 We, 12-5 Su   *Closed:* Mo, Leg/Hol!
Vol/Contr.: Yes
&   P   *Museum Shop*   ¶   *Group Tours:* 603-646-1469   *Drop-In Tours*
Permanent Collection: Am: ptgs 19, 20; Gr; Picasso; Eur: ptgs

The Museum houses one of the oldest and finest college collections in the country in an award-winning post-modern building designed by Charles Moore and Chad Floyd.   ¶ Set of 9th-century BC Assyrian reliefs from the Palace of Ashurnasirpal II

ON EXHIBIT 2002

01/12/2002 to 03/10/2002   *Mel Kendrick: Core Samples*
Wood sculptures that respond to the form of the trees from which they originate

01/12/2002 to 03/10/2002   *Reflections in Black: Smithsonian African American Photography, Art and Activism*
The role of African American photographers in motivating cultural change

03/26/2002 to 05/19/2002   *High Societies: Psychedelic Rock Posters of Haight-Ashbury*
An examination of American culture and consciousness   *Catalog   Will Travel*

06/08/2002 to 12/15/2002   *Jose Clemente Orozco in the United States 1927–1934*
A crucial period in Orozco's work during the era of the American depression
Catalog   Will Travel

09/14/2002 to 12/01/2002   *Carrie Mae Weems: The Hampton Project*
Photographs by Weems and Frances Benjamin Johnson showing the Hampton Normal and
Agricultural School   *Catalog   Will Travel*

KEENE

Thorne-Sagendorph Art Gallery
Affiliated Institution: Keene State College
Wyman Way, Keene, NH   03435-3501

603-358-2720   www.keene.edu/TSAG
Open: 12-4 Mo, We, 12-7 Tu-Fr, 12-4 Sa, Su   *Closed:* Acad!
Vol/Contr.: Yes
&   P: Free   *Group Tours   Drop-In Tours:* by appt
Permanent Collection: Reg: 19; Am & Eur: cont, gr

Changing exhibitions as well as selections from the permanent collection are featured in the
contemporary space of this art gallery.

ON EXHIBIT 2002

01/26/2002 to 03/03/2002   *The Biennial KSC Art Faculty*
Works in a variety of media

MANCHESTER

Currier Gallery of Art
201 Myrtle Way, Manchester, NH   03104

603-669-6144   www.currier.org
Open: 11-5 Mo, We, Th, Su, 11-8 Fr, 10-5 Sa   *Closed:* Tu, Leg/Hol!
Free Day: 10-1 Sa   *Adm: Adult:* $5.00   *Children:* Free under 18   *Students:* $4.00   *Seniors:* $4.00
&   P: Adjacent on-street parking, lot across street   *Museum Shop*   ¶
Group Tours: 603-626-6144, ext 113   *Drop-In Tours*
Historic Building: Registered in National Landmark of historic places (circa 1929)   *Theater*
Permanent Collection: Am & Eur: ptgs, sculp 13-20; Am: furniture, dec/art, Am photo

Set on beautifully landscaped grounds, The Gallery is housed in an elegant 1929 Beaux
Arts building reminiscent of an Italian Renaissance villa.   ¶ Zimmerman House (separate
admission: Adults $9, Seniors and Students $6) designed in 1950 by Frank Lloyd Wright. It is
one of five Wright houses in the Northeast and the only Wright designed residence in New
England that is open to the public.

ON EXHIBIT 2002

10/13/2001 to 01/06/2002   *Impressionism Transformed: The Paintings of Edmund C. Tarbell*
The 45 paintings in this exhibition demonstrate the range of Tarbell's work in portraits, family
scenes, interiors, riding pictures, and still lifes.   *Will Travel*

04/06/2002 to 05/30/2002   *A Print in the North—The Age of Albrecht Dürer and Lucas Van Leyden:
Selections from the Metropolitan Museum of Art*
A survey of major developments in printmaking in Northern Europe from 1440–1550

NEW JERSEY

CAMDEN

Stedman Art Gallery
Affiliated Institution: The State University of New Jersey
Rutgers Fine Arts Center, Camden, NJ   08102

609-225-6245
Open: 10-4 Mo-Sa   *Closed:* Su, Mem/Day, 7/4, Lab/Day, Thgv, 12/24-1/2
& P
Permanent Collection: Am & Eur: Cont works on paper

Located in southern New Jersey, the gallery brings visual arts into focus as an integral part of the human story.

JERSEY CITY

Jersey City Museum
472 Jersey Ave, Jersey City, NJ   07302

201-547-4514
Open: 10:30-5 Tu, Th-Sa, 10:30-8 We   *Closed:* Su, Mo, Leg/Hol!, 12/24, 12/31, closed Sa in summer
&: 5 steps into building, small elevator   P: Street   *Group Tours:* 201-547-4380   *Historic Building*
Permanent Collection: August Will Collection: views of Jersey City, 19; Am: ptgs, drgs, gr, phot; Hist: dec/art; Jersey City Industrial Design

Established in 1901, the museum is located in the historic Van Vorst Park neighborhood of Jersey City in the 100-year-old public library building. In addition to showcasing the works of established and emerging contemporary regional artists, the museum presents exhibitions from the permanent collection documenting regional history.

LINCROFT

Monmouth Museum
Newman Springs Road, Lincroft, NJ   07738

432-747-2266   monmouthmuseum.org
Open: Tu-Sa 10-4:30; Su 1-5   *Closed:* Mo, Leg/Hol
Adm: *Adult:* $4.00   *Children:* $4.00   *Students:* $4.00   *Seniors:* $4.00
& P   *Group Tours*   *Drop-In Tours:* on request
Permanent Collection: Non-collecting institution

A Museum of Ideas. Changing exhibitions in fields of art, culture, history, and nature. Two areas for hands on activities for children

MILLVILLE

Museum of American Glass at Wheaton Village
1501 Glasstown Road, Millville, NJ   08332-1566

856-825-6800 or 800-998-4552   www.wheatonvillage.org
Open: 10-5 daily (Apr-Dec), 10-5 We-Su (Jan-Mar)   *Closed:* 1/1, Easter, Thgv, 12/25
Adm: *Adult:* $8.00   *Children:* Free under 5   *Students:* $5.00   *Seniors:* $7.00
& P: Free   *Museum Shop*   ¶: 7am-9pm, PaperWaiter Restaurant and Pub, adjacent to Village
Group Tours: 800-998-4552, ext. 2730   *Drop-In Tours:* by appt   *Historic Building*   *Sculpture Garden*
Permanent Collection: Am/Glass

The finest collection of American glass in the country. Over 6,500 objects on display ranging from Mason jars to Tiffany masterpieces, paperweights, and fiber optics, to the world's largest bottle. ❰ In addition to the Museum, Wheaton Village offers: A fully operational glass factory with daily demonstrations; Crafts and Trades Row with ongoing demonstrations in pottery, woodworking, flameworking, and tin; Stained Glass Studio; Down Jersey Folklife Center; unique museum stores, train ride, picnic area, and restaurant.

ON EXHIBIT 2002

04/06/2002 to 10/20/2002   *Carnival Glass*

11/30/2002 to 01/05/2003   *Holiday Exhibition*

MONTCLAIR

Montclair Art Museum
3 South Mountain Ave, Montclair, NJ   07042-1747

973-746-5555   www.montclairartmuseum.org
Open: 11-5 Tu, We, Fr, Sa; 11-9 Th; 11-5 Su   *Closed:* Mo, Leg/Hol!
Free Day: Sa, 11-2   *Adm:* *Adult:* $5.00   *Children:* Free under 12   *Students:* $4.00   *Seniors:* $4.00
&: Main floor and restroom   P: Free on site parking   *Museum Shop*   ¶: nearby restaurants
Group Tours: ext. 221   *Drop-In Tours:* most Su, 2pm !   *Theater*
Permanent Collection: Nat/Am: art 18-20; Am: ldscp, portraits 19; Am; Hudson River School: Am Impr

Located just 12 miles west of midtown Manhattan and housed in a Greek Revival style building, this museum, founded in 1914, features an impressive American art collection of a quality not usually expected in a small suburb.

ON EXHIBIT 2002

11/18/2001 to 02/03/2002   *Primal Visions: Albert Bierstadt "Discovers" America*
Fifty works by Bierstadt, Thomas and Edward Moran, Church, and Muybridge showing European explorers impression of the New World

02/24/2002 to May 2002   *Art in 2 Worlds: The Native American Fine Art Invitational 1983–1997*
Contemporary Native Americans including Kay Walkingstick, Jaune Quick-to-Smith, Nora Navajo-More, Lomaheftewa, and Whitehorse whose work challenge traditional perceptions

05/01/2002 to August 2002   *New Jersey Crafts Annual*

05/02/2002 to August 2002   *Strokes of Genius 11*
Artist-designed miniature golf course opened in 1998. This will feature 6–8 holes designed by New Jersey artists

09/02/2002 to 01/2003   *On the Edge of Your Seat: Popular Theater and Film in Early 20th-Century Art*
Combining art history, theater, and film history from 1890–1930 by major American modernists including Hopper, Demuth, Sloan, Henri

NEW BRUNSWICK

Jane Voorhees Zimmerli Art Museum
Affiliated Institution: Rutgers, The State University of New Jersey
71 Hamilton Street, New Brunswick, NJ   08901

732-932-7237   www.zimmerlimuseum.rutgers.edu
Open: 10-4:30 Tu-Fr, Noon-5 Sa, Su   *Closed:* Leg/Hol!; Month of August; Mo, Tu in July
Free Day: 1st Su each month   *Adm:* *Adult:* $3.00   *Children:* Free   *Students:* $3.00   *Seniors:* $3.00
&   P: Nearby or metered   *Museum Shop*
Group Tours: 732-932-7237, x636   *Drop-In Tours:* res req   *Historic Building*
Permanent Collection: Fr: gr 19; Am: 20; Eur: 15-20; P/Col: cer; Cont/Am: gr; The Norton and Nancy Dodge Collection of Nonconformist Art from The Soviet Union

Housing the Rutgers University Collection of more than 50,000 works, this museum also incorporates the International Center for Japonisme which features related art in the Kusakabe-Griffis Japonisme Gallery. ℭ The George Riabov Collection of Russian Art; The Norton and Nancy Dodge Collection of Nonconformist Russian Art from the Soviet Union.

ON EXHIBIT 2002

11/12/2000 to Ongoing   *Opening Up: A Half-Century of Artistic Dialogue between Japan and the West*

NEWARK

Newark Museum
49 Washington Street,, Newark, NJ   07101-0540

973-596-6550   www.newarkmuseum.org
Open: 12-5 We-Su, 12-8:30 Th   *Closed:* Mo, Tu, 1/1, 7/4, Thgv, 12/25
&.: Ramp entrance, elevators, wheelchair accessible, restrooms   *P:* $6.00 in the museum's adjacent parking lot   *Museum Shop*   ‖: Cafe in Engelhard Court 12-3:30 We-Su (wheelchair accessible)
Group Tours: 973-596-6615   *Drop-In Tours:* 12:30-3:30 We-Su
Historic Building: Ballantine House, schoolhouse   *Sculpture Garden*   *Theater*
Permanent Collection: Am: ptgs 17-20; Am: folk; Af/Am; Dec/Arts; Glass; Jap; Cont; Am: Hudson River School ptgs; Af; An/Grk; An/R; Egt

Established in 1909 as a museum of art and science, the Newark Museum features one of the finest collection of Tibetan art in the world. The museum encompasses 80 galleries and includes the historic 1885 Ballantine House, a landmark Victorian mansion; New Jersey's first planetarium; a Mini Zoo; and an 18th-century one-room schoolhouse. ℭ Joseph Stella's 5-panel mural "The Voice of the City of New York Interpreted," 1920–22; the Tibetan Altar, consecrated in 1990 by His Holiness the 14th Dalai Lama.

ON EXHIBIT 2002

09/02/2000 to Continuing   *The Eugene Schaefer Collection of Ancient Glass*
Glass from 1500 B.C. through Greece, Rome, and the Islamic cultures to 1200 A.D. Glass in jewelry and vanity items is included.

08/15/2001 to January 2002   *Fire and Light: 3000 Years of Glass Artistry*
The beauty of ancient glass is shown.

09/25/2001 to 01/20/2002   *Dutch Influence on 19th-Century American Art*

09/26/2001 to 01/20/2002   *Art and Home: Dutch Interiors in the Age of Rembrandt*
Fifty paintings and furniture, silver, porcelain, and other decorative arts   *Will Travel*

11/02/2001 to January 2002   *Santos from the Newark Museum Collection*

11/21/2001 to 01/02/2002   *Christmas in the Ballantine House: Feasting with Family and Friends*

Newark Public Library
5 Washington Street, Newark, NJ   07101

973-733-7745
Open: 9-5:30 Mo, Fr, Sa, 9-8:30 Tu, We, Th   *Closed:* Leg/Hol!
&.; Ramp   *Historic Building*   *Theater*
Permanent Collection: Am & Eur: gr

Since 1903 the library can be counted on for exhibitions which are of rare quality and well documented.

Noyes Museum of Art
Lily Lake Rd, Oceanville, NJ   08231

609-652-8848   www.noyesmuseum.org
Open: 10-4:30 Tu-Sa; 12-5 Su   *Closed:* Mo, 1/1, 12/25
Free Day: Fr   *Adm: Adult:* $3.00   *Children:* Free under 18   *Students:* $2.00   *Seniors:* $2.00
& P: Free   *Museum Shop   Group Tours:* ext. 10   *Drop-In Tours:* by appt   *Theater*
Permanent Collection: Am: 19th, 20th C., craft, folk; NJ: reg; Vintage Bird Decoys

Nestled in a peaceful lakeside setting, the Museum displays rotating exhibitions of American art and craft. Southern New Jersey's only fine art museum, it is a hidden treasure worth discovering and is located only 15 minutes from Atlantic City.   ℭ Purple Martin Palace, view of Lily Lake

ON EXHIBIT 2002

10/05/2001 to 01/06/2002   *Work by the Philadelphia/Tri-State Artists Equity*
Juried exhibition of works in various media

11/24/2001 to 01/20/2002   *Treasures and Trinkets: A Holiday Sampler*
Favorite folk art from the collection including the VanFleet circus

01/19/2002 to 04/21/2002   *Recreation: The Fine Art of the Tin Can*

01/19/2002 to 04/21/2002   *Stories and Dreams: Marcia S. Wilson and Susanna Bergtold*
Friends from different backgrounds share artistic dialogue through wood carvings and prints.

05/04/2002 to 09/15/2002   *Lynn Clibanoff: Mid-Career Retrospective*
Interior constructions, puzzles, and prints

05/04/2002 to 09/15/2002   *Roswell Widener*
Pastel images of Southern New Jersey Pine Barrens

10/25/2002 to 01/10/2003   *Philadelphia Watercolor Society*

Hiram Blauvelt Art Museum
705 Kinderkamack Road, Oradell, NJ   07649

201-261-0012
Open: 10-4 We-Fr, 2-5 Sa, Su   *Closed:* Mo, Tu, Leg/Hol
Vol/Contr.: Yes
& P: Free   *Museum Shop   Group Tours   Drop-In Tours:* by appt   *Historic Building*
Sculpture Garden   Theater
Permanent Collection: Wildlife Art; Audubon Folio; Ivory Gallery; Big Game Animals, Extinct Birds, Reptiles

Founded in 1957 the museum is dedicated to bringing awareness to issues facing the natural world and to showcasing the artists who are inspired by it. It is located in an 1893 shingle and turret style carriage house. The 1679 Demarest House in River Edge, NJ is also owned by the Blauvelt-Demarest Foundation.   ℭ Carl Rungius oil

ON EXHIBIT 2002

02/01/2002 to 06/2002   *Lynn Bogue Hunt*

09/02/2002 to 12/2002   *John Banovich*

Art Museum, Princeton University
Affiliated Institution: Princeton University
Nassau Street, Princeton, NJ   08544-1018

609-258-3788   www.princeton.edu/ARTMUSEUM
Open: 10-5 Tu-Sa, 1-5 Su   *Closed:* Mo, Leg/Hol!
&   P: On-street or nearby garages; special parking arrangements for the handicapped are available
(call ahead for information)   *Museum Shop   Group Tours:* 609-258-3043   *Drop-In Tours:* 2:00 Sa
Historic Building: original 1890 Romanesque revival building designed by A. Page Brown   *Theater*
Permanent Collection: An/Grk; An/R+Mosaics; Eur: sculp, ptgs 15-20; Ch: sculp, ptgs; Gr; P/Col; OM:
ptgs, drgs; Af

An outstanding collection of Greek and Roman antiquities. Roman mosaics from Princeton
University's excavations in Antioch are but one of the features of this highly regarded eclectic
collection housed in a modern building on the lovely Princeton University campus.   ℭ Picasso
sculpture, "Head of a Woman"

ON EXHIBIT 2002

10/06/2001 to 01/06/2002   *Camera Women*

10/13/2001 to 01/20/2002   *Pliny's Cup: Roman Silver in the Age of Augustus*
Rare 1st-century silver gilt wine cups

10/13/2001 to 02/20/2002   *Empire of Stone: Roman Sculpture from the Art Museum, Princeton
University*
Among the works exhibited are some of the finest in America shown in a dramatically
illuminated gallery   *Catalog*

11/20/2001 to 01/06/2002   *Contemporary Photographs*

New Jersey Center for Visual Arts
68 Elm Street, Summit, NJ   07901

908-273-9121   www.njmuseums.com/njcva/index.htm
Open: 12-4 Mo-Fr, 7-9 Th, 2-4 Sa, Su   *Closed:* Leg/Hol! & last 2 weeks in August
Sugg/Contr.: yAdult: $1.00   *Children:* Free under 12   *Students:* $1.00
&   P: Free   *Museum Shop   Group Tours   Drop-In Tours:* !   *Sculpture Garden*
Permanent Collection: non-collecting institution

The Center presents exhibitions of contemporary art by artists of national and international
reputation as well as classes for people of all ages and levels of ability.   ℭ "Melvin Edwards—
Sculpture" in the NJCVA Sculpture Park

African Art Museum of the S. M. A. Fathers
23 Bliss Ave, Tenafly, NJ   07670

201-894-8611   www.smafathers.org
Open: 10-5 Daily   *Closed:* Leg/Hol!
&   P: Free   *Group Tours   Drop-In Tours:* by appt   *Theater*
Permanent Collection: Af; sculp, dec/art

Located in a cloistered monastery with beautiful gardens in the gracious old town of Tenafly,
this museum features changing collection and loan exhibitions.

ON EXHIBIT 2002

09/09/2001 to 03/15/2002   *Legends, Sorcerers, and Enchanted Lizards: Door Locks of the Bamana of Mali from the Collection of Dr. Pascal James and Eleanor M. Imperato*

10/20/2001 to 03/31/2002   *Asanti Goldweights from the Collections of Afrikacentrum*

01/2002 to 06/2002   *The Arts of Personal Adornment Wing Collection*

05/04/2002 to 12/31/2002   *Beauty and the Beasts: Kifwebe Masks of the Songe, Luba, and Related Peoples from the Collection of Stewart J. Warkow*

TRENTON

New Jersey State Museum
205 West State Street, P.O. Box 530, Trenton, NJ   08625-0530

609-292-6464   www.njstatemuseum.org
Open: 9-4:45 Tu-Sa, 12-5 Su   *Closed:* Mo, State Holidays
Adult: Planetarium $3.00   *Children:* Planetarium $2.00
&   P: Free parking available in garage near museum   *Museum Shop*   ¶: Museum Café, 9am-3pm
Group Tours: 609-292-6347   *Drop-In Tours*
Permanent Collection: Am: cont, gr; Af/Am

The museum is located in the Capitol Complex in downtown Trenton. The fine art collections cover broad areas of interest with a special focus on New Jersey and culturally diverse artists.   ℭ Stieglitz Circle

NEW MEXICO

ABIQUIU

Georgia O'Keeffe Home and Studio
Affiliated Institution: The Georgia O'Keeffe Foundation
Abiquiu, NM   87510

505-685-4539
Open: open by reservation only! 1 hr Tours seasonally on Tu, Th, Fr   *Closed:* Leg/Hol
Adm: *Adult:* $22   *Students:* $15.00   *Seniors:* $15.00
&: exterior only   P: no buses   *Group Tours*   *Historic Building*   *Theater*
Permanent Collection: Home and studio of artist Georgia O'Keeffe

ALBUQUERQUE

University of New Mexico
Affiliated Institution: The University of New Mexico
Fine Arts Center, Albuquerque, NM   87131-1416

505-277-4001
Open: 9-4 Tu-Fr, 5-8 Tu, 1-4 Su, Jonson Gallery closed on weekends   *Closed:* Mo, Sa, Leg/Hol!
&   P: Limited free parking   *Museum Shop*   *Group Tours*   *Sculpture Garden*   *Theater*
Permanent Collection: Cont; 19, 20; Gr; Phot; Sp/Col; OM

In addition to changing exhibitions of work drawn from the permanent collection the Museum features significant New Mexico and regional artists working in all media.

10/09/2001 to 01/20/2002   *Antonella Russo/Linea de Confine*

10/09/2001 to 01/20/2002   *Ignatovich Photos*

LOS ALAMOS

Art Center at Fuller Lodge
2132 Central Avenue, Los Alamos, NM   87544

505-662-9331   http://artful@losalamos.com
Open: 10-4 Mo-Sa   *Closed:* Su, Leg/Hols
&   P   *Museum Shop   Group Tours:* 505-662-9331   *Drop-In Tours   Historic Building   Sculpture Garden*

Located in historic Fuller Lodge, this art center presents changing exhibitions of local and regional fine arts and crafts.   ℂ Gallery Shop offers fine arts and crafts by 70-plus Southwestern artists.

ROSWELL

Roswell Museum and Art Center
100 West 11th, Roswell, NM   88201

505-624-6744   www.roswellmuseum.org
Open: 9-5 Mo-Sa, 1-5 Su & Hol   *Closed:* 1/1, Thgv, 12/25
Vol/Contr.: Yes   *Sugg/Contr.:* $2.00 pp
&   P   *Museum Shop   Group Tours:* x 22, 1 week advance notice   *Drop-In Tours:* self-guided
Historic Building: original WPA arts center 1937   *Sculpture Garden*
Permanent Collection: SW/Art; History; Science; NM/Art; Nat/Am

Sixteen galleries featuring works by Santa Fe and Taos masters and a wide range of historic and contemporary art in its impressive permanent collection make this museum one of the premier cultural attractions of the Southwest. Temporary exhibitions of Native American, Hispanic, and Anglo art are often featured.   ℂ Rogers Aston Collection of Native American and Western Art

ON EXHIBIT 2002

01/01/2002 to 05/05/2002   *Peter Moran's Southwest*

01/01/2002 to 12/01/2002   *Curator's Choice: Revisiting the Aston Collection*

02/22/2002 to 06/09/2002   *Flora, Not Fauna*

05/24/2002 to 05/04/2003   *Howard Cook: New York Paintings*

09/27/2002 to 02/23/2003   *2002 Invitational Exhibition*

SANTA FE

Institute of American Indian Arts Museum
108 Cathedral Place, Santa Fe, NM   87501

505-988-6281   www.iaiancad.org
Open: 9-5 daily June-Sept;10-5 daily Oct-May   *Closed:* 1/1, 4/4, 12/25: Easter: Thgv
Adm: Adult: $4.00; Free Nat/Am   *Children:* Free under 16   *Students:* $2.00   *Seniors:* $2.00
&   P: Local garages available   *Museum Shop   Group Tours   Sculpture Garden*
Permanent Collection: the National Collection of Contemporary Indian Art

The Museum cares for and presents the National Collection of Contemporary Indian Art which chronicles the development 1960–present. Contemporary Native American arts and crafts and Alaskan native arts are featured.   ℂ Admission to Allan Houser Art Park with Museum admission

Museums of New Mexico
113 Lincoln Ave., Santa Fe, NM   87501

505-827-6463   www.museumofnewmexico.org
Open: All Museums 10-5 Tu-Su!, Monuments, 8:30-5 daily   *Closed:* Mo, Leg/Hol
Adm: Adult: $5 1 museum, 1 day; $10, 4 day pass all   *Children:* Free under 17   *Seniors:* Free We
&.: In most buildings   P   *Museum Shop*   Group Tours: 505-476-5008   *Drop-In Tours:* ! each Museum
Historic Building
Permanent Collection: (5 Museums with varied collections): Taos & Santa Fe Masters; Phot; SW/Reg;
Nat/Am; Folk; 5 State Monuments

In 1917 when it opened, the Museum of Fine Arts set the Santa Fe standard in Pueblo-Revival
architecture. The Palace of the Governors, built by Spanish Colonial and Mexican governors in
1610, has the distinction of being the oldest public building in the US. Its period rooms and
exhibitions of life in New Mexico during the Colonial Period are unique. Also included in the
Museum are the Museum of Indian Arts and Culture and the Museum of International Folk
Art.   ℂ The entire complex

Wheelwright Museum of the American Indian
704 Camino Lejo, Santa Fe, NM   87502

505-982-4636   www.wheelwright.org
Open: 10-5 Mo-Sa, 1-5 Su   *Closed:* 1/1, 12/25, Thgv
&.   P: in front of building   *Museum Shop*   Group Tours   *Drop-In Tours:* 2pm Mo, Tu, Fr; 11 Sa
Historic Building   *Sculpture Garden*
Permanent Collection: Nat/Am, Navajo; SW Ind (not always on view)

Inside this eight-sided building, shaped like a Navajo "hooghan" or home, on a hillside with vast
views, you will find breathtaking American Indian art.   ℂCase Trading Post museum shop.

T A O S

Harwood Museum of the University of New Mexico
Affiliated Institution: University of New Mexico
238 Ledoux St, Taos, NM   87571

505-758-9826   www.nmculture.org
Open: 10-5 Tu-Sa, 12-5 Su   *Closed:* Mo, Leg/Hol!
Free Day: Su free for New Mexico residents   *Adm:*   Adult: $5.00   *Children:* under 12 free
&.   P   *Museum Shop*   Group Tours: *Drop-In Tours*   Historic Building   Theater
Permanent Collection: Hispanic and 19th-C Retablos; Bultos, American Mod.

Many of the finest artists who have worked in Taos are represented in this collection. Seven
galleries include the Taos Society of Artists, American Modernists, Taos Moderns, Hispanic
traditional arts, mid & late 20th-century art, and a permanent installation of seven paintings by
Agnes Martin. The landmark building is an early example of Pueblo Revivial Architecture
Expansion and renovation completed in 1997. Call for changing exhibitions schedule.
ℂ "Winter Funeral" by Victor Higgins, Agnes Martin Gallery; Hispanic Traditions Gallery

Millicent Rogers Museum
Museum Road, 4 miles N of Taos, 1504 Millicent Rogers Road, Taos, NM   87571

505-758-2462   http:millicentrogers,org
Open: 10-5 Daily Apr-Oct, closed Mo Nov-Mar   *Closed:* 1/1, Easter, San Geronimo Day 9/30,
Thgv, 12/25
Free Day: Su for Taos County residents   *Adm:*   Adult: $6.00   *Children:* 6-16 $1.00
Students: $5.00   *Seniors:* $5.00
&.: 95%   P   *Museum Shop*   Group Tours   *Drop-In Tours:* !   Historic Building   Sculpture Garden
Permanent Collection: Nat/Am & Hisp: textiles, basketry, pottery, jewelry; Reg

Dedicated to the display and interpretation of the art and material of the Southwest,
the Millicent Rogers Museum places particular focus on New Mexican cultures.   ℂ Extensive
collection of pottery by Maria Martinez

NEW YORK

Albany Institute of History and Art
125 Washington Ave, Albany, NY   12210

518-463-4478   www.albanyinstitute.org
Open: 12-5 We-Su   *Closed:* Mo, Tu, Leg/Hol!
Free Day: We   *Adm:*   *Adult:* $3.00   *Children:* Free under 12
&   P: Nearby pay garage   *Museum Shop*   *Group Tours*   *Historic Building*
Permanent Collection: Ptgs: Hudson River School & Limner; Am: portraits 19; Cast Iron Stoves;
Dec/Arts: 19

Founded in 1791, this museum, one of the oldest in the nation, presents permanent displays and changing exhibitions throughout the year. There are over 20,000 objects in the permanent collection. The Museum will be under construction and renovation beginning in April 1999 and reopening in 2001. Please call ahead for exhibition information. ℭ Hudson River School paintings by Cole, Durand, Church, Kensett, Casilear, and the Hart Brothers

University Art Museum
Affiliated Institution: University at Albany, State University of NY
1400 Washington Ave, Albany, NY   12222

518-442-4035   www.albany.edu/museum
Open: 10-5 Tu-Fr, 12-4 Sa, Su   *Closed:* Mo, Leg/Hol!
&   P: Free   ¶: In Campus Center
Permanent Collection: Am: gr, ptg, dr 20

This museum, the largest of its kind among the State University campuses and one of the major galleries of the Capitol District, features work from student and mid-career to established artists of national reputation. ℭ Richard Diebenkorn, "Seated Woman," 1966, (drawing)

Schein-Joseph International Museum of Ceramic Art
New York State College of Ceramics at Alfred University, Alfred, NY   14802

607-871-2421   www.ceramicsmuseums.alfred.edu
Open: 10am-5 pm Tu-Su   *Closed:* Mo, Some holidays!
Group Tours: 607-871-2421   *Theater*

Center for Curatorial Studies Museum
Bard College, Annandale on Hudson, NY   12504

845-758-7598   www.bard.edu/ccs
Open: 1-5 We-Su   *Closed:* 12/31, 1/1, Mem/Day, 7/4, Thgv, 12/25
&   P   *Group Tours*   *Theater*
Permanent Collection: Cont: Ptgs; Sculp; Phot; gr; video: installation 1960-present

Housed in a facility which opened in 1992, the CCS Museum features changing exhibitions of contemporary art curated by director Amada Cruz, internationally renowned guest curators, and graduate thesis candidates.

ASTORIA

American Museum of the Moving Image
35th Ave at 36th St, Astoria, NY   11106

718-784-0077   www.ammi.org
Open: 12-5 Tu-Fr, 11-6 Sa-Su   *Closed:* 12/25
Adm: *Adult:* $8.50   *Children:* $4.50 (5-18) under 4 Free   *Students:* $5.50   *Seniors:* $5.50
   P: street parking available   ‖: cafe
Group Tours: 718-784-4520   *Drop-In Tours:* 2-3pm insider's Tour   *Historic Building*
Permanent Collection: Behind the Screen, combination of artifacts, interactive experiences, live
demonstrations and video screenings to tell the story of the making, marketing, and exhibiting of
film, television, and digital media. Especially popular are Automated Dialogue Replacement where
visitors can dub their own voices into a scene from a movie and Video Flipbook where visitors can
create a flipbook of themselves that they can pick up at the gift shop as a memento.

The only Museum in the US devoted exclusively to film, TV, video and interactive media and
theirimpact on 20th-century American life. ℂ "Tut's Fever Movie Palace," Red Grooms and
Lysiane Luongs interpretation of a 1920s neo-Egyptian movie palace showing screenings of
classic movie serials daily.

AUBURN

Schweinfurth Memorial Art Center
205 Genesee St, Auburn, NY   13021

315-255-1553
Open: 10-5 Tu-Sa, 1-5 Su   *Closed:* Mo, Leg/Hol!
Sugg/Contr.: $3.00   P   *Museum Shop   Group Tours*
Permanent Collection: Non-collecting institution

Regional fine art, folk art, and crafts are featured in changing exhibitions at this cultural center
located in central New York State.   ℂ Made in New York gift shop featuring regional fine arts
and crafts. Annual juried Quilt Show, Nov 3, 2001–Jan 6, 2002

BAYSIDE

QCC Art Gallery
Affiliated Institution: Queensborough Community College
222-05 56th Ave., Bayside, NY   11364-1497

718-631-6396
Open: 9-5 Mo-Fr and by appt.   *Closed:* Sa, Su, Acad!
  Museum Shop   ‖: 9am-2pm   *Group Tours   Historic Building*
Permanent Collection: Am: after 1950; Women Artists

The Gallery which reflects the ethnic diversity of Queensborough Community College and its
regional residents also highlights the role art plays in the cultural history of people.

BINGHAMTON

Roberson Museum Science Center
30 Front St., Binghamton, NY   13905-4779

607-772-0660   www.roberson.org
Open: 10-5 Mo-Sa, 12-5 Su   *Closed:* Leg/Hol!
Adm: *Adult:* $6.00   *Children:* Free under 4   *Students:* $4.00   *Seniors:* $4.00
  P   *Museum Shop   Group Tours   Historic Building*
Permanent Collection: Reg Textiles; Phot; Ptgs; Dec/Art: late 19,20, agricultural tools and archeological
materials

A regional museum featuring 19th and 20th c art, history, folklife, natural history, and technology. It includes a 1907 mansion, a museum, a Planetarium, and the off-site Kopernik Observatory. ❧ "Blue Box" trainer circa 1942 by Edwin Link; mammoth tusk and mammoth tooth c.9000 B.C.

BLUE MOUNTAIN LAKE

Adirondack Museum
Blue Mountain Lake, NY   12812

518-352-7653   www.adkmuseum.org
Open: Mem/Day-mid-Oct 9:30-5:30 daily
Adm: *Adult:* $10.00   *Children:* 7-17 $5.00; under 7 free   *Seniors:* $9.00
&   P   *Museum Shop*   ⑪   *Historic Building*
Permanent Collection: Am: Ptgs, Gr, Drgs, 1850-present

The Museum tells the stories of how people lived, moved, worked, and played in the Adirondacks. There are 20 indoor and outdoor exhibit areas featuring special events and programs. Just an hour from Lake Placid and Lake George, the museum has a cafeteria overlooking Blue Mountain Lake.

ON EXHIBIT 2002

2002 Season   *In Search of the National Landscape: William Trost Richards in the Adirondacks*
Richards in the first half of his career from 1853–1870 he was a prominent landscape painter. He produced drawings and paintings that are among the most important and beautiful records of the region produced at mid-century. He later, a year before his death did a series of plein air oil studies in 1904.   *Catalog*   *Will Travel*

BRONX

Bronx Museum of the Arts
1040 Grand Concourse, Bronx, NY   10456

718-681-6000
Open: 12-9 We; 12-6 Th-Su   *Closed:* Mo, Tu, Thgv, 12/25
Free Day: WeSugg/Contr.: Yes   *Adm:*   *Adult:* $3.00   *Children:* Free under 12   *Students:* $2.00
Seniors: $2.00
&   P: nearby garage   *Museum Shop*   *Group Tours:* Ext.132   *Theater*
Permanent Collection: Af: Lat/Am: SE/As: works on paper 20; Cont/Am: eth

Noted for its reflection of the ethnically diverse NYC metro area, it is the only fine arts museum in the Bronx. The collection and exhibitions are a fresh perspective on the urban experience. And it has a commitment to stimulating audience participation in the visual arts.

Hall of Fame for Great Americans
Affiliated Institution: Bronx Community College
University Ave and W. 181 St, Bronx, NY   10453

718-289-5161   www.bcc.cuny.edu
Open: 10-5 Daily
&: Ground level entrance to Colonnade   P   ⑪   *Group Tours*   *Drop-In Tours:* by appt   *Historic Building*
Sculpture Garden   *Theater*
Permanent Collection: Colonnade of 98 bronze busts of Americans elected to the Hall of Fame since 1900 (includes works by Daniel Chester French, James Earle Fraser, Frederick MacMonnies, August Saint-Gaudens

Overlooking the Bronx & Harlem Rivers, this beautiful Beaux Arts style architectural complex, once a Revolutionary War fort, contains a Stanford White designed library modeled after the Pantheon in Rome. Ninety-eight recently restored bronze portrait busts of famous Americans elected to the Hall of Fame since 1900 and placed within the niches of the Men of Renown classical colonnade allow the visitor to come face-to-face with history through art.

Brooklyn Museum of Art

200 Eastern Parkway, Brooklyn, NY   11238

718-638-5000   www.brooklynart.org
Open: 10-5 We-Fr, 11-6 Sa, open 11-11 first Sa of month, 11-6 Su   *Closed:* Thgv, 12/25, 1/1
Sugg/Contr.: Yes   *Adm:*   *Adult:* $6.00   *Children:* Free under 12   *Students:* $3.00   *Seniors:* $3.00
&   P: Pay parking on site   *Museum Shop*
¶: open until 4 weekdays, till 5 Weekends & holidays, coffee/wine bar Sa eve
Group Tours: ext 234   *Drop-In Tours:* ! various times   *Historic Building   Sculpture Garden   Theater*
Permanent Collection: Egt; Am-Eur ptgs, sculp, dec/art 18-20; As; Af; Oc; NW/Am; W/Col

The Brooklyn Museum of Art is one of the nation's premier art institutions. Housed in a Beaux-Arts structure designed in 1893 by McKim, Mead & White, its collections represent virtually the entire history of art from Egyptian artifacts to modern American paintings.

ON EXHIBIT 2002

10/12/2001 to 01/06/2002   *Vital Forms: American Art in the Atomic Age, 1940–1960*
The most innovative works of the 40s and 50s which embraced a vocabulary of vital, or organic, forms. Through architecture, decorative and industrial arts, graphic design, painting, photography, and sculpture, Vital Forms will examine the collective use of such forms derived from nature during the post war era.   *Catalog   Will Travel*

11/23/2001 to 02/24/2002   *The Eternal Egypt: Egyptian Antiquities from the British Museum*
The exhibition will span the entire pharonic period from 3000 B.C. to 4th century A.D. with many large scale works represented.   *Catalog   Will Travel*

12/07/2001 to 01/27/2002   *Grandma Moses in the 21st Century*
A re-examination of her most important paintings   *Catalog   Will Travel*

04/05/2002 to 07/07/2002   *Star Wars: The Magic of Myth*
Artworks, props, character models, and costumes used to create the Star Wars trilogy. A 26-minute video playing continuously will trace the making of the films.   *Catalog   Will Travel*

05/03/2002 to 07/26/2002   *Jewish Life in Ancient Egypt*
Drawn from the Museum's collection of ancient Aramaic papyri that reveal details about Egyptian and Jewish life in Dynasty 27 (525–402 B.C.). The exhibition will also present related works of ancient Egyptian and Persian art from the Museum's collections.

09/02/2002 to 01/05/2003   *Exposed: The Victorian Nude*
A first exhibition to survey the full range of representations of the nude in Victorian art. Although primarily dealing with painting and sculpture, photographs, illustrations, advertising, and caricature are included.   *Catalog   Only Venue*

11/01/2002 to 01/26/2003   *The Adventures of Hamza*
A fantastic adventure story of Hamza, uncle of the Prophet Muhammad who traveled throughout the world spreading the doctrines of Islam. Of the 1,400 illustrations only a tenth remain. 70 have been brought together from collections all over the world   *Catalog Will Travel*

Rotunda Gallery

33 Clinton Street, Brooklyn, NY   11201

718-875-4047
Open: 12-5 Tu-Fr, 11-4 Sa   *Closed:* Mo, Leg/Hol!
&   P: Metered street parking; nearby pay garage   *Group Tours*
Permanent Collection: non-collecting institution

The Gallery's facility is an architecturally distinguished space designed for exhibition of all forms of contemporary art. It is located in Brooklyn Heights which is well known for its shops, restaurants, and historic brownstones.

ON EXHIBIT 2002

01/17/2002 to 02/23/2002   *Curatorial Initiative*
Selected from proposals submitted, it seeks to feature new curators and their vision.

03/28/2002 to 04/18/2002   *Untitled: Interactive Exhibition*
Artwork that requires participation and active interaction of the viewer to be fully realized. The exhibition explores what art asks of the viewer.

Rubelle & Norman Schafler Gallery
Affiliated Institution: Pratt Institute
200 Willoughby Ave, Brooklyn, NY   11205

718-636-3517   www.pratt.edu/exhibitions
Open: 9-5 Mo-Fr   *Closed:* Leg/Hol!
P: on street parking only   *Theater*
Permanent Collection: Currently building a collection of Art and Design Works by Pratt Alumni, Faculty, & Students

Varied programs of thematic, solo, and group exhibitions of contemporary art, design, and architecture are presented in this gallery.

ON EXHIBIT 2002

12/07/2001 to 01/30/2002   *Half a Century of Book Arts at Pratt*
Artist books and related works by alumni and students

BUFFALO

Albright Knox Art Gallery
1285 Elmwood Ave, Buffalo, NY   14222

716-882-8700   www.albrightknox.org
Open: 11-5 Tu-Sa, 12-5 Su   *Closed:* Thgv, 12/25, 1/1
Free Day: 11-1 Sa   *Adm:*   *Adult:* $5.00   *Children:* Free under 12   *Students:* $4.00   *Seniors:* $4.00
& P   *Museum Shop*   *Group Tours*   *Drop-In Tours:* 12:15 We-Th, 1:30 Sa-Su   *Historic Building*
Sculpture Garden
Permanent Collection: Ab/Exp; Cont: 70s & 80s; Post/Impr; Pop; Op; Cubist; Am & Eur: 18-19

With one of the world's top international surveys of twentieth-century painting and sculpture, the Albright-Knox is especially rich in American and European art of the past fifty years. The permanent collection which also offers a panorama of art through the centuries dating from 3000 BC, is housed in a 1905 Greek Revival style building designed by Edward B. Green with a 1962 addition by Gordon Bunshaft of Skidmore, Owings and Merrill.

ON EXHIBIT 2002

11/02/2001 to 01/06/2002   *The Triumph of French Painting*
Masterpieces of 19th-century and early 20th-century painting from the Baltimore Museum and the Walters Art Gallery. Artists include Ingres, Corot, Manet, Monet, Renoir, Cézanne, van Gogh, Picasso, and Matisse.

12/15/2001 to 03/10/2002   *Following a Line: Part Two*
Seldom seen works on paper and drawings from 1940–2001

01/26/2002 to 04/07/2002   *The Tumultuous Fifties: A View from the New York Times Archives*
Photographs focusing on the 50s including McCarthyism, Cold War, Sputnik and Bebop, Abstract Expressionism and Beat poetry   *Will Travel*

04/27/2002 to 07/14/2002   *Edwin Dickinson: Dreams and Realities*
The first retrospective in 20 years includes paintings and works on paper, nudes, landscapes, self-portraits, still lifes, and large-scale multifigured compositions.

05/11/2002 to 07/28/2002   *Romare Bearden: Upstate New York Collections*
Lesser known works in oil and watercolor as well as loans from area institutions

10/19/2002 to 01/12/2003   *Modigliani and the Artists of Montparnasse*
The first major Modigliani exhibition in 40 years, it also shows Picasso, Brancusi, Mondrian, and Soutine.   *Will Travel*

Burchfield-Penney Art Center
Affiliated Institution: Buffalo State College
1300 Elmwood Ave, Buffalo, NY   14222-1095

716-878-6011   www.burchfield-penney.org
Open: 10-5 Tu-Sa, 1-5 Su; open most We until 7:30pm   *Closed:* Leg/Hol!
Vol/Contr.: Yes   *Sugg/Contr.:* $3
&.: special tours   P: Some on campus and metered parking; lot across street often available
Museum Shop   ⫙: on college grounds
Group Tours: 716-878-6020   *Drop-In Tours:* by appt   *Historic Building*
Permanent Collection: Am; West/NY: 19, 20: Charles E. Burchfield; Charles Cary Ramsey, Roycroft, Photo

The Burchfield-Penney Art Center is the only museum dedicated to the art and artists of western New York. Particular emphasis is given to the works of renowned American watercolorist Charles E. Burchfield. The museum holds the largest archives and collection in the world of his works. ⫙ World's largest collection of work by Charles E. Burchfield; "Oncoming Spring,""Fireflies and Lightening" hand crafted objects by Roycroft Arts and Crafts community artists, sculpture by Charles Cary Rumsey.

ON EXHIBIT 2002

10/13/2001 to 01/06/2002   *The Pan-American Exposition Centennial: Images of the American Indian*
A historical perspective of how Indians were represented in art during the past century

10/27/2001 to 01/20/2002   *Neil Tetkowski and the Common Ground World Project*
The mandala is recognized as a symbol of unity and the cosmos. Tetkowski has used clay and sand from 188 countries.

10/27/2001 to 01/20/2002   *Tenth Anniversary Selections from the Charles Rand Penney Collection of Western New York Art*

12/01/2001 to 02/24/2002   *Nancy Belfer: Master of Textiles*

12/09/2001 to 03/24/2002   *Country Life and the Hunt: Burchfield and Wallpaper Design*

01/19/2002 to 03/30/2002   *New Media Arts*
A survey of artists influencing museums to represent non-traditional art forms

04/13/2002 to 06/30/2002   *American Twentieth-Century Watercolors at the Munson-Williams-Proctor Arts Institute*
Works by Demuth, Hopper, Luks, Marin, Marsh, and Zorach will be exhibited. Paper conservation issues will also be covered.

07/13/2002 to 09/01/2002   *Emerging Artists*

09/14/2002 to 01/19/2003   *Craft Art in Western New York 2002*

Canajoharie Library and Art Gallery
2 Erie Blvd, Canajoharie, NY   13317

518-673-2314   www.clag.org
Open: 10-4:45 Mo-We, Fr, 10-8:30 Th, 10-1:30 Sa   *Closed:* Su, Leg/Hol!
& P   *Museum Shop   Group Tours   Sculpture Garden*
Permanent Collection: Winslow Homer; American Impressionists; The Eight

Located in downtown Canajoharie, the gallery's collection includes 21 Winslow Homers.

Emerson Gallery
Affiliated Institution: Hamilton College
198 College Hill Road, Clinton, NY   13323

315-859-4396
Open: 12-5 Mo-Fr, 1-5 Sa, Su, closed weekends June, July & Aug   *Closed:* Leg/Hol! & Acad/Hol
& P
Permanent Collection: Nat/Am; Am & Eur: ptgs, gr 19, 20; West Indies Art

While its ultimate purpose is to increase the educational scope and opportunity for appreciation of the fine arts by Hamilton students, the gallery also seeks to enrich campus cultural life in general, as well as to contribute to the cultural enrichment of the surrounding community.   (Outstanding collection of works by Graham Sutherland

Corning Museum of Glass
One Corning Glass Center, Corning, NY   14830-2253

800-732-6845, 607-937-5371   www.cmog.org
Open: 9-5 daily, 9-8 July & Aug   *Closed:* 1/1, Thgv, 12/24, 12/25!
Adm: *Adult:* $7.00, family $16   *Children:* $5 (6-17)   *Students:* $6.00   *Seniors:* $6.00
& P   *Museum Shop*   ¶   *Group Tours:* 607-974-2000   *Drop-In Tours:* by reservation
Historic Building   Theater
Permanent Collection: Glass: worldwide 1500 BC-present

The museum houses the world's premier glass collection—more than 30,000 objects representing 3,500 years of achievement in glass design and craftsmanship. New hot-glass studio presents workshops, classes, and demonstrations. In June 1999, the New Glass Innovation Center and the Sculpture Gallery open.   (The Hot Glass show where visitors can watch artisans make glass objects; the new Glass Innovation Center

Rockwell Museum
111 Cedar St., Corning, NY   14830

607-937-5386   www.rockwellmuseum.org
Open: 9-5 Mo-Sa, 11-5 Su; July-Lab/Day 9-8 Mo-Sa, 11-5 Su   *Closed:* 1/1, Thgv, 12/24, 12/25
Free Day: 12-5 Su (Dec- Apr)   *Adm:*   *Adult:* $6.50, family $20.00   *Children:* $4.50, 6-17, Free under 6
Students: $4.50   *Seniors:* $5.50
& P: Municipal lot across Cedar St.   *Museum Shop   Group Tours:* 607-974-4830   *Drop-In Tours*
Historic Building: 1893 City Hall, Corning, NY   *Theater*
Permanent Collection: Ptgs & Sculp: by Western Artists including Bierstadt, Remington and Russell 1830-1920; Native Am Art

Located in the 1893 City Hall of Corning, NY, and nestled in the lovely Finger Lakes Region of New York State is the finest collection of American Western Art in the Eastern U.S. The museum building is in a Romanesque revival style and served as a City Hall, firehouse and jail until the 1970s.   (Model of Cyrus E. Dallin's famous image, "Appeal to the Great Spirit"

Dowd Fine Arts Gallery
Affiliated Institution: State University of New York College at Cortland
SUNY Cortland, Cortland, NY   13045

607-753-4216   www.cortland.edu/art/dowd.html
Open: 11-4 Tu-Sa   *Closed:* Acad!
Vol/Contr.: Yes
& P: Adjacent to building   *Group Tours*   *Drop-In Tours:* scheduled by request
Permanent Collection: Am & Eur: gr,drgs 20; Cont: art books

Temporary exhibitions of contemporary and historic art which are treated thematically are presented in this university gallery.

Guild Hall Museum
158 Main Street, East Hampton, NY   11937

631-324-0806   guild-hall.org
Open: 11-5 daily (Summer), 11-5 We-Sa, 12-5 Su (Winter)   *Closed:* Thgv, 12/25, 1/1, Leg/Hol!
Sugg/Contr.: $3.00; Summer Exhibitions $5
& P   *Museum Shop*   *Group Tours:* 631-324-0806   *Historic Building*   *Sculpture Garden*
Permanent Collection: Am: 19, 20: reg

Located in one of America's foremost art colonies, this cultural center combines a fine art museum and a 400-seat professional theater.

Islip Art Museum
50 Irish Lane, East Islip, NY   11730

631-224-5402   islipartmuseum.org
Open: 10-4 We-Sa, 12-4 Su   *Closed:* Leg/Hol!
Vol/Contr.: Yes
& P   *Museum Shop*   *Group Tours:* 631-224-5402   *Drop-In Tours:* by request   *Historic Building*
Sculpture Garden
Permanent Collection: Am/Reg: ptgs, sculp, cont

The Islip Museum is the leading exhibition space for contemporary and Avant Garde Art on LI. The Carriage House Project Space, open in the summer and fall, features cutting-edge installations and site-specific work. A satellite gallery called the Anthony Giordano Gallery is at Dowling College in Oakdale, LI.

Arnot Art Museum
235 Lake St, Elmira, NY   14901-3191

607-734-3697
Open: 10-5 Tu-Sa, 1-5 Su   *Closed:* Thgv, 12/25, 1/1
Adm: Adult: $2.00   Children: $.50 (6-12)   Students: $1.00   Seniors: $1.00
& P: Free   *Museum Shop*   *Group Tours*   *Drop-In Tours*   *Historic Building*
Permanent Collection: Am: salon ptgs 19, 20; Am: sculp 19

The original building is a neo-classical mansion built in 1833 in downtown Elmira. The museum modern addition was designed by Graham Gund. ℭ Matthias Arnot Collection; one of last extant private collections housed intact in its original showcase

Godwin-Ternbach Museum
Affiliated Institution: Queens College
65-30 Kissena Blvd, Flushing, NY   11367

718-997-4734
Open: 11-7 Mo-Th Call!   *Closed:* Acad!
&: Not at present   P: On campus   *Theater*
Permanent Collection: Gr: 20; Ant: glass; An/Egt; An/Grk; Ptgs; Sculp

This is the only museum in Queens with a broad and comprehensive permanent collection which includes a large collection of WPA/FAP prints.

Hyde Collection
161 Warren St., Glens Falls, NY   12801

518-792-1761   www.hydeartmuseum.org
Open: 10-5 Tu-Sa; 10-7 Th, 12-5 Su   *Closed:* Mo, Leg/Hol!
Vol/Contr.: Yes
&   P   *Museum Shop   Group Tours:* ext 15   *Drop-In Tours:* 1-4   *Historic Building*
Sculpture Garden   Theater
Permanent Collection: O/M: ptgs; Am: ptgs; Ant; Ir/Ren; Fr: 18

The central focus of this museum complex is an Italianate Renaissance style villa built in 1912 which houses an exceptional collection of noted European Old Master and significant modern European and American works of art from 4th C. through 20th C. They are displayed among an important collection of Italian Renaissance and French 18th century furniture. The collection spans western art from the 4th c B.C. –20th c. Since 1985 temporary exhibitions and year round programming are offered in the Edward Larabee Barnes Education Wing.   ❡ "Portrait of a Young Man" by Raphael; "Portrait of Christ" by Rembrandt; "Coco" by Renoir; "Boy Holding a Blue Vase" by Picasso; "Geraniums" by Childe Hassam

Picker Art Gallery
Affiliated Institution: Colgate University
Charles A. Dana Center for the Creative Arts, Hamilton, NY   13346-1398

315-228-7634   www.picker.colgate.edu
Open: 10-5 Daily   *Closed:* Acad!; (also open by request!)
&   P: 2 large lots nearby   *Group Tours   Drop-In Tours   Sculpture Garden   Theater*
Permanent Collection: Ant; Ptgs & Sculp 20; As; Af

Located on Colgate University campus, the setting of the Charles A. Dana Art Center is one of expansive lawns and tranquility. Exhibition information: 315-228-7749

Hofstra Museum
Affiliated Institution: Hofstra University
112 Hofstra University, Hempstead, NY   11549

516-463-4743   www.hofstra.edu/museum
Open: 10-5 Tu-Fr, 1-5 Sa, Su; varying hours in galleries   *Closed:* Easter weekend; Thgv weekend; Leg/Hol
Vol/Contr.: Yes
&   P   *Museum Shop*   ❙❙   *Historic Building   Sculpture Garden*
Permanent Collection: Sculp: Henry Moore, H. J. Seward Johnson, Jr, Tony Rosenthal; Paul Manship, Greg Wyatt, Mihail Chemiakin

Hofstra University is a living museum. Five exhibition areas are located throughout the 240-acre campus, which is also a national arboretum. ❑ Sondra Rudin Mack Garden designed by Oehme, Van Sweden and Assoc. Henry Moore's "Upright Motive No. 9," and Tony Rosenthal's "T"s; Paul Manship's "Brisei, Group of Bears," "Atalanta"; Gregg Wyatt's "Hippomenes,'"The Hofstra Victory Eagle"; Mihail Chemiakin's "Plato Having a Dialogue with Socrates," and a permanently installed Bluestone II circuit labyrinth

HUDSON

Olana State Historic Site
5720 Route 9G, Hudson, NY   12534

518-828-0135
Open: 10-4 We-Su 4/1-11/1   *Closed:* open Mem/Day, 7/4, Lab/Day, Columbus Day (open Mo Hols), closed Nov-Mar
Free Day: Special Holiday program 1st two weekends in Dec   *Adm:*   *Adult:* $3.00
Children: $1.00 (5-12)   *Seniors:* $2.00
& P: Limited   *Museum Shop   Group Tours:* e xt.301   *Historic Building*
Permanent Collection: Frederic Church: ptgs, drgs; Phot Coll; Correspondence

Olana, the magnificent home of Hudson River School artist Frederic Edwin Church, was designed by him in the Persian style, and furnished in the Aesthetic style. He also designed the picturesque landscaped grounds. Many of Church's paintings are on view throughout the house. The house is only open by guided tour. Visitor's Center and grounds are open 7 days a week.

HUNTINGTON

Heckscher Museum of Art
2 Prime Ave, Huntington, NY   11743

631-351-3250   www.heckscher.org
Open: 10-5 Tu-Fr, 1-5 Sa, Su, 1st Fr till 8:30   *Closed:* Thgv; 12/25
Vol/Contr.:   Adult: $5.00   *Children:* $1.00 6-12 years   *Students:* $3.00   *Seniors:* $3.00
&: Steps to restrooms   P   *Museum Shop   ¶:* picnic tables & chairs available
Group Tours   Drop-In Tours: 1:30, 2:30 & 3:30 Sa; 2:30, 3:30 Su; 1-3 We & Th   *Historic Building*
Permanent Collection: Am: ptg & Sculp 16-present; Am: Modernist ptgs, drgs, works on paper; Eur Ptgs & Sculp 16-present

Located in a 18.5 acre park, the museum, whose collection numbers more than 1,800 works, was presented as a gift to the people of Huntington by philanthropist August Heckscher. ❑ "Eclipse of the Sun," by George Grosz (not always on view!)

ITHACA

Herbert F. Johnson Museum of Art
Affiliated Institution: Cornell University
Cornell University, Ithaca, NY   14853-4001

607-255-6464   www.museum.cornell.edu
Open: 10-5 Tu-Su   *Closed:* Mem/Day, 7/4, Thgv + next day
& P: Metered   *Group Tours   Drop-In Tours:* 12 noon every other Th
Historic Building: IM Pei, 1973   *Sculpture Garden*
Permanent Collection: As; Am: gr 19, 20

The Gallery, in an IM Pei building, with a view of Cayuga Lake, is located on the Cornell Campus in Ithaca, NY. ❑ "Fields in the Month of June," by Daubigny; "Walking Man" by Giacometti

ON EXHIBIT 2002

to 01/13/2002   *Carlos Ulloa*
Contemporary surreal collage works by a Latino artist

to 01/13/2002   *No Ordinary Land: Encounters in a Changing Environment*
Two photographers, Anne Mcphee and Virginia Beehan capture nature's beauty and the less than beautiful impact of humans on the environment.

to 01/17/2002   *Red Grooms: Bus*
A New York City bus roars into the gallery with an assortment of eccentric passengers.

01/27/2002 to 03/24/2002   *Shaped with a Passion: The Carl A. Weyerhausern Collection of Japanese Ceramics from the 1970s*
120 ceramics by established potters who became "Living National Treasures"

03/30/2002 to 08/11/2002   *Photography since 1950*
A look at major trends and ideas of photography during the last 50 years

04/06/2002 to 07/14/2002   *Oh Mona*
A look at the enduring fascination of Western art's most famous painting and what has been done to her, including work by contemporary artists

04/13/2002 to 06/16/2002   *Redoute Prints and Watercolors*
Works from a private collection

K A T O N A H

Caramoor Center for Music and the Arts
149 Girdle Ridge Road, Katonah, NY   10536

914-232-5035   www.caramoor.com
Open: May-Oct 11-4 We-Su, last tour at 3; Nov-Apr, by appt Mo-Fr only   *Closed:* Leg/Hol!
Adm: *Adult:* $7.00   *Children:* Free under 16   *Students:* $6.00   *Seniors:* $7.00
&   P: Free   *Museum Shop*   ¶: Picnic facilities and snack bar
Group Tours: ext. 221   *Drop-In Tours:* art tour at 2 We-Su May-Oct, & by request   *Historic Building   Sculpture Garden*
Permanent Collection: Furniture; Ptgs; Sculp; Dec/Art; Ren; Or: all media

Built in the 1930s by Walter Rosen as a country home, this 54-room Italianate mansion is a treasure trove of splendid collections spanning 2,000 years. There are six unusual gardens including the Marjorie Carr Sense Circle (for sight-impaired individuals). Tours of the gardens are by appt spring and fall and every weekend during the festival at 2:30pm. Caramoor also presents a festival of outstanding concerts each summer and many other programs throughout the year. At 11 We Apr-Nov a short recital in the music room is followed by a tour of the house.   ℭ Extraordinary house-museum with entire rooms from European villas and palaces

Katonah Museum of Art
Route 22 at Jay Street, Katonah, NY   10536

914-232-9555   www.katonah-museum.org
Open: 1-5 Tu-Fr, Su, 10-5, Sa; summer 12-5 Tu-Fr,   *Closed:* 1/1, Mem/Day; Presidents/Day, 7/4, Thgv, 12/25
Adm: *Adult:* $3.00
&   P: Free   *Museum Shop   Group Tours   Drop-In Tours:* 2:30pm, Tu-Su   *Sculpture Garden   Theater*
Permanent Collection: Non-collecting institution

Moved to a building designed by Edward Larabee Barnes in 1990, the museum has a commitment to outstanding special exhibitions which bring to the community art of all periods, cultures, and media.

ON EXHIBIT 2002

01/13/2002 to 03/31/2002   *Divine Mirrors: The Madonna Unveiled*
The exhibition looks at the theme of women not from a religious point of view, but as secular identity   *Catalog   Will Travel*

01/13/2002 to 06/09/2002   *Robert Lobe*
The interplay of surface, shapes textures, and light are created by pounding large sheets of aluminum over natural objects so it conforms to their shapes.

05/05/2002 to 06/09/2002   *Print/Photography Exhibition/Sale*

06/23/2002 to 09/15/2002   *American Spectrum: Paintings and Sculpture from the Smith College Museum of Art*

09/29/2002 to 01/05/2003   *American Folk Art from the Abby Aldrich Rockefeller Folk Art Center   Will Travel*

LONG ISLAND CITY

Isamu Noguchi Garden Museum
32-37 Vernon Blvd, Long Island City, NY   11106

718-721-1932 www.noguchi.org
Open: 10-5, We-Fr, 11-6 Sa, Su (Apr-Oct only)
Adm: *Adult:* $4.00   *Children:* $2.00   *Students:* $2.00   *Seniors:* $2.00
&: 1/3 of the collection is accessible   P: Street parking   *Museum Shop*   ¶: Café
Group Tours: 718-721-1932 x203   *Drop-In Tours:* 2 pm daily, not for groups   *Historic Building Sculpture Garden*
Permanent Collection: Work of Isamu Noguchi

Designed by Isamu Noguchi (1904–1988), this museum offers visitors the opportunity to explore the work of the artist on the site of his Long Island City studio. The centerpiece of the collection is a tranquil outdoor sculpture garden. The Museum is in 13 galleries of a converted warehouse and surrounding gardens. *A shuttle bus runs to the museum on Sa & Su every hour on the half-hour starting at 11:30am from midtown Manhattan. Please call the Museum at 718-721-1932 for information. The round trip fare is $5.00 and does not include the price of museum admission.   ℂ Permanent exhibition of over 250 sculptures as well as models, drawings, and photo-documentation of works of Noguchi; stage sets designed for Martha Graham; paper light sculptures called Akari

P.S.1 Contemporary Arts Center
2225 Jackson Avenue, Long Island City, NY   11101

718-784-2084
Open: 12-6 We-Su   *Closed:* Mem/Day, 7/4, Lab/Day, Thgv, 12/25
Adm: *Adult:* $4.00   *Children:* $2.00   *Students:* $2.00   *Seniors:* $2.00
& P: on street and near-by garages   ¶: coffee shop   *Historic Building   Sculpture Garden*
Permanent Collection: Cont, Am

P.S.1 recognizes and introduces the work of emerging and lesser known artists.   ℂ "Meeting" by James Turrell, 1986

MOUNTAINVILLE

Storm King Art Center
Old Pleasant Hill Rd, Mountainville, NY   10953

845-534-3115 www.stormking.org
Open: 11-5:30 daily (Apr-Nov 15), Special eve hours Sa May 26-Sept 1   *Closed:* closed 11/16-3/31
Adm: *Adult:* $9.00   *Children:* Free under 5   *Students:* $5.00   *Seniors:* $7.00
&.; Partial, 1st floor of building and portions of 500 acres   P   *Museum Shop*
Group Tours: 845-534-3115 x110   *Drop-In Tours:* 2pm daily   Historic Building   *Sculpture Garden*
Permanent Collection: Sculp: Alice Aycock, Alexander Calder, Mark di Suvero, Andy Goldsworthy, Louise
Nevelson, Isamu Noguchi, Richard Serra, David Smith, Kenneth Snelson

America's leading sculpture park and museum has a large collection of outdoor sculpture on
view amid 500 acres of lawns, fields, and woodlands. Works are also on view in a 1935
Normandy style building that has been converted to museum galleries.   ℂ "Momo Taro" by
Isamu Noguchi; Pyramidian, Mother Peace by Mark di Suvero; The Arch; Alexander Calder;
XI Books and Apples, Personage of May, Becca, The Sitting Printer by David Smith.

MUMFORD

Genesee Country Village & Museum
410 Flint Hill Road, P.O. box 310, Mumford, NY   14511

716-538-6822   www.gcv.org
Open: 10-5 Tu-Su Jul, Aug; 10-4 Tu-Fr, 10-5 Sa, Su; May, June; Sept-Oct
Adm: *Adult:* $12   *Children:* 4-16 $7.00, under 3 Free   *Students:* $9.50   *Seniors:* $9.50
&.: partial   P: Free   *Museum Shop*   ❙❙   *Group Tours:* ext 242   *Sculpture Garden*
Permanent Collection: Am, ptgs, sculp; Am\SW; late 19; Nat/Am; sculp; Wildlife art; Eur & Am sport
art 17-20

The outstanding J. L. Wehle collection of sporting art is housed in the only museum in New
York specializing in sport, hunting, and wildlife subjects. The collection and carriage museum
are part of an assembled village of 19th-century shops, homes, and farm buildings.

NEW PALTZ

Samuel Dorsky Museum of Art
Affiliated Institution: State University of New York at New Paltz
New Paltz, NY   12561

914-257-3844   www.newpaltz.edu/museum
Open: 11:30-4 We, Th, Fr; 1-4, Sa, Su   *Closed:* Leg/Hol, Acad/Hol!, Closed 3 weeks Jan, 2 weeks June !
&. P   *Museum Shop*   *Group Tours*   *Drop-In Tours*
Permanent Collection: Am; gr, ptgs 19, 20; Jap: gr; Ch: gr; P/Col; Cont: phot

The Samuel Dorsky Museum of Art is the second largest museum in the State University
system. Not only does the museum enhance the educational mission of the college, it promotes
cross disciplinary research and collaboration. It serves as a cultural resource for the Hudson
Valley.   ℂ The opening of the gallery and installation of the permanent collection which spans
over 4,000 years

Alternative Museum
594 Broadway, New York, NY   10012

212-966-4444   www.alternativemuseum.org

This contemporary arts institution is devoted to the exploration and dissemination of new avenues of thought on contemporary art and culture and operates solely as an internet museum.

ON EXHIBIT 2002

2002   *On the Line/Online: The Pursuit of Justice*
Exhibitions of photography as well as text and panel discussions, the complex issues related to civil and human rights, political freedom, issues of race, ethnicity, class, religion and sexual orientation, environmental, technology, the media, youth at risk, education, freedom to travel, and freedom of the press. It will present the story of people who have endured conditions of historical and social extremity and the celebration of those who have acheived human rights.

June 2002   *On the Line/Online*
One hundred fifty award winning photographic images from more than 20 international photographers. Each will focus on a particular area with human and civil rights issues. Included will be Afganhistan, Bosnia, Burma, Chechnya, China, Columbia, India, Indonesia, Northern Ireland, Kosovo, Kuwait, Pakistan, Russia, Sierra Leone, Serbia, USA, and Zimbabwe with a downloadable catalog.   *Catalog*

June 2002 to December 2002   *Digital Media 2002*
Through the Digital Media Commisions program the museum is reaching out to meet the needs of emerging artists who are on the cutting edge of this new art form. The six commissioned works will be shown for 6 months.

Americas Society
680 Park Avenue, New York, NY   10021

212-249-8950   www.americas-society.org
Open: 12-6 Tu-Su   *Closed:* 7/4, Thgv, 12/24, 12/25
Adm: *Adult:* $3.00   *Children:* $2.00   *Students:* $2.00   *Seniors:* $2,00
& P: Nearby pay garage   *Museum Shop*
Group Tours: ext. 364   *Drop-In Tours:* by appointment   *Historic Building*
Permanent Collection: No permanent collection

Located in a historic neo-federal townhouse built in 1909, the goal of the Americas Society is to increase public awareness of the rich cultural heritage of our western hemisphere neighbors.

ON EXHIBIT 2002

01/2002 to 03/2002   *Jennifer Allora and Guillermo Cazadilla*
A site-specific installation

04/2002 to 07/2002   *Literally Lateral: Willys de Castro and Cesar Paternosto*

09/2002 to 12/2002   *Colonial and Popular Art of Paraguay*

Asia Society
725 Park Ave, New York, NY   10021

212-288-6400   www.asiasociety.org
Open: 11-6 Tu-Su, 11-9 Fr   *Closed:* Leg/Hol!
Free Day: Fr, 6-9pm   *Adm:*   *Adult:* $7.00   *Children:* Free under 16   *Students:* $4.00   *Seniors:* $4.00
& P: Nearby pay garages   *Museum Shop*
Group Tours   *Drop-In Tours:* 12:30 Tu-Sa, 6:30 Th, 2:30 Su   *Theater*
Permanent Collection: The Mr. and Mrs. John D. Rockefeller III Collection of Asian Art

The Asia Society is America's leading institution dedicated to fostering understanding of Asia and communication between Americans and the peoples of Asia and the Pacific.

ON EXHIBIT 2002

10/13/2001 to 01/06/2002 *Monks and Merchants: Silk Road Treasures from Northwest China, 4th–7th Century*
Artifacts including Buddhist images, metalwork, textiles, glass, funerary furniture, and ceramics many recently excavated and never seen in the West. *Catalog*

10/13/2001 to 02/17/2002 *Conversations with Traditions: Nilima Sheikh and Shazia Sikander*
These two artists draw upon tradional techniques of Indian miniature painting in their work. The 50 objects include works the artists love and find particularly inspiring. *Catalog*

10/13/2001 to 04/13/2002 *A New Look at the Rockefeller Collection*
In a gallery specially designed to house it, The Creative Eye asks artists to select pieces they find particularly intriguing or inspiring from the collection. Visual artissts include Chu, Clemente, Dono, Senju, Lin, Shapiro, Sikander, Viola, Wilson, and Bing. Also ceramacists Forer, Thomas, Anderson, Dun, Glaser, MacFadden, Jones, Amelan, Chandrelekha, Sarukkai, Hwang, and others. They will celebrate the collection and provide a fresh perspective.

AXA Gallery
787 Seventh Avenue, New York, NY   10019

212-554-4818   www.axa-equitable.com/gallery.html
Open: 11-6 Mo-Fr, 12-5 Sa   *Closed:* Leg/Hol
&   P: pay   ¶: 3 fine restaurants located in the space overlooking the Galleria   *Theater*
Permanent Collection: Public Art in Lobby of Equitable Tower: Roy Lichtenstein's Mural with Blue Brushstroke

The gallery presents works from all fields of the visual arts that would not otherwise have a presence in New York City.

Chaim Gross Studio Museum
526 LaGuardia Place, New York, NY   10012

212-529-4906
Open: 12-6 Tu-Fr   *Closed:* Sa, Su, Mo, Leg/Hol
&   P: Nearby pay parking   *Museum Shop*   *Group Tours:* fee req, off-site lectures 212-529-4906
Historic Building: 1880 cast-iron façade   *Theater*
Permanent Collection: Sculp, wood, stone, bronze; sketches, w/c, prints

A seventy year sculpture collection of several hundred Chaim Gross (1904–1991) works housed on three floors of the Greenwich Village building which was the artist's home and studio for thrity-five years. The studio is left intact and is also open to the public. ¶ "Roosevelt and Hoover in a Fistfight" 1932, Mahogany 72 x 20 x 1.5. The 1932 cubist inspired wood sculptures were done in the only year when Gross submitted to modernist influences. The Charles A. Lindburgh Family, 1932, golden streak epilwood.

China Institute Gallery, China Institute in America
125 East 65th Street, New York, NY   10021-7088

212-744-8181   www.chinainstitute.org
Open: 10-5 Mo & We-Sa, 1-5 Su, 10-8 Tu & Th   *Closed:* Leg/Hol!, Chinese New Year, between exhibitions
Adm: *Adult:* $3.00   *Children:* Free   *Students:* $2.00   *Seniors:* $2.00
P: Pay garage nearby, limited street parking   *Museum Shop*
Group Tours: ext. 146, 147   *Drop-In Tours:* Varies   *Historic Building*
Permanent Collection: Non-collecting institution

China Institute Gallery presents original and and traveling exhibitions ranging from traditional Chinese paintings, calligraphy, and objects to to Chinese folk arts, textiles, and architecture. Exhibitions are accompanied by catalogs and art education programs, such a gallery tours, lectures, and symposia.

Cloisters
Affiliated Institution: The Metropolitan Museum of Art
Fort Tryon Park, New York, NY   10040

212-923-3700   www.metmuseum.org
Open: 9:30-5:15 Tu-Su (3/1-10/30), 9:30-4:45 Tu-Su (11/1-2/28)   *Closed:* 1/1, Thgv, 12/25
Adm: *Adult:* $10 includes Met Museum on the same day   *Children:* Free under 12   *Students:*
$5.00   *Seniors:* $5.00
&.: Limited, several half-floors are not accessible to wheelchairs   P: Free limited street parking in Fort
Tryon Park   *Museum Shop*   *Group Tours:* 212-650-2280   *Drop-In Tours:* 3pm Tu-Fr, 12 & 2pm Sa; 12 Su
Historic Building: 1938 bldg resembling medieval monastery, incorporates actual medieval architectural
elements   *Theater*
Permanent Collection: Arch: Med/Eur; Tapestries; Illuminated Manuscripts; Stained Glass; Sculp;
Liturgical Objects

This unique 1938 building set on a high bluff in a tranquil park overlooking the Hudson
River re-creates a medieval monastery in both architecture and atmosphere. Actual 12th–15th
century medieval architectural elements are incorporated within various elements of the
structure which is filled with impressive art and artifacts of the era. ℂ "The Unicorn
Tapestries"; "The Campin Room"; Gardens; Treasury

Cooper-Hewitt, National Design Museum, Smithsonian Institution
2 East 91st Street, New York, NY   10128

212-849-8300   www.si.edu/ndm
Open: 10-9 Tu, 10-5 We- Sa, 12-5 Su   *Closed:* Mo, Leg/Hol!
Free Day: Tu 5-9   *Adm:*   *Adult:* $8.00   *Children:* Free under 12   *Students:* $4.00   *Seniors:* $4.00
&   P: Nearby pay garages   *Museum Shop*
Group Tours: 212-849-8380   *Drop-In Tours:* times vary; call 212-849-8389   *Historic Building*
Sculpture Garden
Permanent Collection: Drgs; Textiles; Dec/Art; Cer

Cooper Hewitt, housed in the landmark Andrew Carnegie Mansion, has more than 250,000
objects which represent 3,000 years of design history from cultures around the world. It is the
only museum on Museum Mile with an outdoor planted garden and lawn open during regular
museum hours—weather permitting.

ON EXHIBIT 2002

08/21/2001 to 01/06/2002   *Glass of the Avant-Garde: from Vienna Secession to Bauhaus: The Torsten
Brohan Collection from the Museo Nacional de Artes Decorativas, Madrid*
One-of-a-kind art glass by Lotz and other objects by Secessionist and Weiner Werkstatt
designers Hoffman, Moser, and Peche.   *Will Travel*

11/20/2001 to 03/10/2002   *Russel Wright: Creating American Lifestyle*
Wright marketed a gracious, informal, contemporary approach to the middle class, mid-
century American home. He championed an ideal of high quality, modern design for all.

02/12/2002 to 07/28/2002   *Skin: Surface and Structure in Contemporary Design*
Skin as outer surface and structural form. Products of fashion, furniture, architecture, and
digital media to explore this role of "skin"

Dahesh Museum of Art
601 Fifth Avenue, New York, NY   10017

212-759-0606   www.daheshmuseum.org
Open: 11-6 Tu-Sa   *Closed:* Su, Mo, Leg/Hol!
Vol/Contr.: Yes
&   P: pay parking nearby   *Museum Shop*   *Group Tours*   *Drop-In Tours*
Permanent Collection: Acad ptg;19, 20

More than 2,000 works collected by writer, philosopher Dr. Dahesh (born Salim Moussa Achi)
form the collection of this relatively new museum housed on the second floor of a commercial
building built in 1911. Collections include works by Rosa and Auguste Bonheur, Jean-Leon
Gerome, Alexandre Cabanel, Lord Leighton, Edwin Long, and Paul Delaroche.

ON EXHIBIT 2002

09/25/2001 to 01/05/2002 *Telling Tales II: Religious Images in Nineteenth Century Academic Art*
The images later in the 19th century became less didactic and more anecdotal or naturalistic. This trend from the serious and literal Prix de Rome to the generalized images of Lhermitte and Gale. *Catalog*

January 2002 to April 2002 *Charles Bargue*
A "little master" artist whose works are miniaturized costume pieces functioning as theatrical vignettes. The study of these drawing manuals was considered a first step in the training of an artist. *Brochure*

02/19/2002 to 05/18/2002 *French Master Drawings from the Collection of Muriel Butkin*
Eighteenth- and nineteenth-century drawings by Boucher, Saint-Aubin, Gericault, Millet, and Degas *Catalog* *Will Travel*

06/04/2002 to 08/24/2002 *Fire and Ice: Treasures from Photographic Collection of Frederic Church at Olana*
These photographs were taken to document Church's travels particularly to the Middle East. This has never been cataloged or exhibited. *Catalog*

09/10/2002 to 12/07/2002 *Against the Modern: Jean Dagnan-Bouveret and the Rebirth of the Academic Tradition*
Dagnan-Bouveret was the most important of Gerome's French students. He recreated academic studies, naturalistic genre scenes, photo-realist compositions, portraits, and religous compositions. *Catalog* *Will Travel*

Dia Center for the Arts
548 West 22nd Street, New York, NY 10011

212-989-5566 www.diacenter.org
Open: 12-6 Th-Su Sept-Jun *Closed:* Leg/Hol!
Adm: *Adult:* $6.00 *Children:* Free under 10 *Students:* $3.00 *Seniors:* $3.00
♿ *Museum Shop* 🍴: Rooftop café and video lounge *Group Tours:* 212-989-5566
Permanent Collection: not permanently on view

With several facilities and collaborations Dia has committed itself to working with artists to determine optimum environments for their most ambitious and uncompromising works which are usually on view for extended exhibition periods. ℂ Two Walter De Maria extended exhibitions, "The New York Earth Room" at the gallery at 141 Wooster Street and "The Broken Kilometer" at 393 Broadway. Both are open 12-6 We-Sa, closed July and August, adm Free

Drawing Center
35 Wooster Street, New York, NY 10013

212-219-2166
Open: 10-6 Tu-Fr; 11-6 Sa *Closed:* Su, Mo, 12/25, 1/1, all of Aug, Thgv
Vol/Contr.: Yes
♿ P: On street and nearby pay garages *Museum Shop* *Group Tours* *Historic Building* *Theater*
Permanent Collection: non-collecting institution

Featured at The Drawing Center are contemporary and historical drawings and works on paper both by internationally known and emerging artists.

Frick Collection
1 East 70th Street, New York, NY 10021

212-288-0700 www.frick.org
Open: 10-6 Tu-Sa, 1-6 Su, also short hours Pres. Day, Election Day, Veteran's Day *Closed:* 1/1, 7/4, Thgv, 12/24, 12/25
Adm: *Adult:* $10.00 *Children:* under 10 not adm *Students:* $5.00 *Seniors:* $5.00
♿ P: Pay garages nearby *Museum Shop* *Group Tours:* group vst. sched but no lecture in gall.
Historic Building *Sculpture Garden* *Theater*
Permanent Collection: Ptgs; Sculp; Furniture; Dec/Art; Eur, Or, Porcelains

The beautiful Henry Clay Frick mansion built in 1913–14, houses this exceptional collection while preserving the ambiance of the original house. In addition to the many treasures to be found here, the interior of the house offers the visitor a tranquil respite from the busy pace of city life outside of its doors. *Children under 10 are not permitted in the museum and those from 11-16 must be accompanied by an adult. (Boucher Room; Fragonard Room; Paintings by Rembrandt, El Greco, Holbein, Vermeer, and Van Dyck

ON EXHIBIT 2002

09/01/2000 to 08/01/2003   *Mantegna's "Descent into Limbo," from the Barbara PiaseckaJohnson Collection*
Because the painting was so highly regarded, several small versions were also made, including this one.

11/14/2001 to 02/17/2002   *The Art of the Timekeeper: Masterpieces from the Winthrop Edey Bequest*
Thirteen clocks and eight watches dating from the 16th–19th centuries. Many have not been shown publically in decades. They will show the technical developments and the impact on civilization.

05/14/2002 to 08/04/2002   *Greuze: The Draftsman*
Sixty works on paper from many institutions and 20 from St. Petersburg which have rarely left there. The exhibition will show viewers what a unique and thoroughly modern artist Greuze was.   *Catalog   Will Travel*

George Gustav Heye Center of the National Museum of the American Indian
Affiliated Institution: Smithsonian Institution
One Bowling Green, New York, NY   10004

212-514-3800   www.si.edu/nmai
Open: 10-5 daily, 10-8 Th   *Closed:* 12/25
Vol/Contr.: Yes
& P: Nearby pay   *Museum Shop   Group Tours:* 212-514-3705   *Drop-In Tours:* daily!   *Historic Building*
Permanent Collection: Nat/Am; Iroq silver, jewelry, NW Coast masks

The Heye Foundation collection contains more than 1,000,000 works which span the entire Western Hemisphere and present a new look at Native American peoples and cultures. Newly opened in the historic Alexander Hamilton Customs House it presents masterworks from the collection and contemporary Indian art.

ON EXHIBIT 2002

06/26/1999 to Indefinite   *Spirit Capture: Native Americans and the Photographic Image*
Photographs which will reveal new and deeper images in the development of cultural stereotypes

Grey Art Gallery
Affiliated Institution: New York University Art Collection
100 Washington Square East, New York, NY   10003-6619

212-998-6780   www.nyu.edu/greyart
Open: 11-6 Tu, Th, Fr, 11-8 We, 11-5 Sa   *Closed:* Su, Mo, Leg/Hol!
Adm: Adult: $2.50   Children: $2.50   Students: $2.50   Seniors: $2.50
& P: Nearby pay garages   *Group Tours   Drop-In Tours   Theater*
Permanent Collection: Am: ptgs 1940-present; Cont; As; Middle East

Located at Washington Square Park and adjacent to Soho, the Grey Art Gallery occupies the site of the first academic fine arts department in America established by Samuel F. B. Morse in 1835.

ON EXHIBIT 2002

11/13/2001 to 01/26/2002   *Pastoral to Postindustrial: British Work on Paper from the Whitworth Art Gallery*
Late 18th- through 20th-century drawings and watercolors showing the changes in landscape in England. A major highlight are 6 watercolors by J.M.W. Turner, Constable, Cotman, Cox, Cozens, Girten, Jones, and others. Included also are works showing the carnage of the landscape in WWI, and finally, recent additions in photographic media by Hirst, Goldsworthy, Long, and Whiteread.

02/12/2002 to 04/20/2002   *Seeing and Believing: the Art of Nancy Burson*
Burson's territory has been the human face. She delves into the beautiful, the normal, the exceptional—the imprint of genetics, the traces of time, and illness. She was among the first to link computers with photography and is licensed by the FBI to locate missing children, and adults, sometimes years after they have disappeared.   *Catalog   Will Travel*

05/07/2002 to 07/03/2002   *Priceless Children: Lewis Hine and the Photo-Secession (1890–1925)*
Two strikingly different views of the American child at the turn of the 20th century: one working class toiling in factories, the other softly romanticized playing in idyllic setting or interiors   *Will Travel*

09/10/2002 to 12/07/2002   *Between Word and Image: Modern Iranian Visual Culture*
The first major exhibition to focus on Iranian culture of the 60s and 70s. It will show the rich artistic heritage and the complex political situation.

Guggenheim Museum Soho
575 Broadway at Prince St, New York, NY   10012

212-423 3500   www.guggenheim.org
Open: 11-6 Th-Mo   *Closed:* 1/1, 12/25
&   P: Nearby pay garages   *Museum Shop*   ¶   *Group Tours   Historic Building*
Permanent Collection: International Cont Art

As a branch of the main museum uptown, this facility, located in a historic building in Soho, was designed as a museum by Arata Isozaki.

Hispanic Society of America
155th Street and Broadway, New York, NY   10032

212-926-2234   www.hispanicsociety.org
Open: 10-4:30 Tu-Sa, 1-4 Su   *Closed:* Leg/Hol! Library Closed Holy Sa, Mo of August
Vol/Contr.: Yes
&.: Limited, exterior and interior stairs   P: Nearby pay garage   *Museum Shop   Group Tours: ext. 254*
Historic Building   Sculpture Garden   Theater
Permanent Collection: Sp: ptgs, sculp; arch; Hispanic

Representing the culture of Hispanic peoples from prehistory to the present, this facility is one of several diverse museums located within the same complex on Audubon Terrace in NYC.
€ Paintings by El Greco, Goya, Velazquez, Sorsolla

International Center of Photography
1133 Avenue of the Americas, New York, NY   10036

212-860-1777   www.icp.org
Open: 10-5 Tu-Th, 10-8 Fr, 10-6 Sa, Su   *Closed:* 1/1, 7/4, Thgv, 12/25
Free Day: 5-8 Fr, Vol. Contribution   *Adm: Adult:* $8.00   *Students:* $6.00   *Seniors:* $6.00
&   P: Nearby pay garages   *Museum Shop*   ¶: Nearby   *Group Tours:* 212-860-1777 x154   *Drop-In Tours*
Historic Building
Permanent Collection: Primarily Documentary Phot: 20

ICP was established in 1974 to present exhibitions of photography, to promote photographic education at all levels, and to study 20th-century images, primarily documentary.

Japan Society Gallery
333 E. 47th Street, New York, NY   10017

212-832-1155   www.jpn.org
Open: 11-6 Tu-Fr, 11-5 Sa, Su   *Closed:* Mo, Leg/Hol!
Sugg/Contr.: Yes   *Adm:*   *Adult:* $5.00   *Students:* $3.00   *Seniors:* $3.00
&   P: Nearby pay garages   *Group Tours:* 212-715-1253   *Historic Building   Sculpture Garden*
Permanent Collection: Japanese Art

Exhibitions of the fine arts of Japan are presented along with performing and film arts at the Japan Society Gallery which attempts to promote better understanding and cultural enlightenment between the peoples of the U.S. and Japan.

ON EXHIBIT 2002

09/26/2001 to 01/06/2002   *Traditional Japanese Design: Five Tastes*
Utilitarian objects developed between the 16th and 19th centuries in lacquer, ceramics, metalwork, basketry, and textiles. Included are Artless Simplicity (*Sobuku*); Zen Minimalism (*Wabi*); Gorgeous Splendor (*Karie*); Edo Chic (*Iki*); Ancient Times (*Kodai no bi*).   Catalog
Only Venue

The Jewish Museum
1109 5th Ave., New York, NY   10128

212-423-3200   www.thejewishmuseum.org
Open: 11-5:45 Su, Mo, We & Th, 11-3 Fr, 11-8 Tu   *Closed:* Jewish/Hol, Martin Luther King Day, Thgv
Free Day: Tu after 5 pay what you wish   *Adm:*   *Adult:* $8.00   *Children:* Free under 12   *Students:* $5.50
Seniors: $5.50
&   P: Nearby pay garages   *Museum Shop*   ¶: Cafe Weissman, kosher cuisine!
Group Tours: 212-423-3225   *Drop-In Tours:* 12:15, 2:15, 4:15 Mo-Th, 6:15 Tu   *Historic Building   Theater*
Permanent Collection: Judaica: fine arts; ceremonial objects; mixed media installations; Arch; Artifacts; broadcast media materials

28,000 works of art and artifacts covering 4,000 years of Jewish history or illuminating the Jewish experience are displayed in the original building (the 1908 Felix Warburg Mansion), and in the new addition added in 1993. The collection is the largest of its kind outside of Israel. Culture and Continuity: The Jewish Journey, the centerpiece of the museum, is a core exhibition on the Jewish experience that conveys the essence of Jewish identity—the basic ideas, values and culture developed over 4,000 years.   ❰ "The Holocaust" by George Segal

ON EXHIBIT 2002

09/09/2001 to 02/10/2002   *Arnold Dreyblatt: Re-Collection Mechanism*
A museum visitor is guided through a multimedia environment of projected and recited text taken from "Who's Who in Central and East Europe 1933–" a biographical almanac of contemporary writers, artists, scientists, politicians and philanthropists

09/09/2001 to 02/10/2002   *Ben Katchor: Picture-Stories*
Creator of the character Julius Knipl, Real Estate Photographer and comic strip novel "The Jew of New York" Katchor has found the irreverent and insightful mirror into the poetry and futility of everyday life

09/09/2001 to 02/10/2002   *Doug and Mike Starn: Rampart's Cafe*
A multimedia installation in the artist's words, is "archeology over archeology over archeology of written accounts of the fighting over and occupations of Jerusalem."

09/09/2001 to June 2003   *Camels and Caravans: Daily Life in Ancient Israel*
A childrens exhibition taking them through a Jeruselem home and marketplace 2,000 years ago

Metropolitan Museum of Art
5th Ave at 82nd Street, New York, NY   10028

212-879-5500   www.metmuseum.org
Open: 9:30-5:30 Tu-Th, Su; 9:30-9pm Fr, Sa   *Closed:* Thgv,12/25, 1/1
Sugg/Contr.: Yes   *Adm:*   *Adult:* $10.00 including same day adm to Cloisters   *Children:* Free under 12
Students: $5.00   *Seniors:* $5.00
&   P: Pay garage   *Museum Shop*   ¶   *Group Tours:* 212-570-3711   *Historic Building*
Sculpture Garden   *Theater*
Permanent Collection: Eur: all media; Gr & Drgs: Ren-20; Med; Gr; Phot; Am: all media; Dec/Art: all
media; As: all media; Af; Islamic; Cont; An/Egt; An/R; An/Gr; An/Assyrian

The Metropolitan is the largest world class museum of art in the western hemisphere. Its comprehensive collections includes more than 2 million works from the earliest historical artworks thru those of modern times and from all areas of the world. Just recently, the museum opened the Florence & Herbert Irving Galleries for the Arts of South & Southeast Asia, one of the best and largest collections of its kind in the world. New and Recently Opened Installations: Sculpture and Decorative Arts of the Quattrocento New Chinese Galleries The New Amarna Galleries: Egyptian Art 1353–1295 B.C. Phase 1 of the New Greek and Roman Art Galleries: The Robert and Renee Belfer Court Studiolo from the Palace of Duke Federico de Montefeltro at Gubbio the African Gallery Antonio Ratti Textile Center   ¶   Temple of Dendur; The 19th-century European paintings & sculpture galleries (21 in all), designed to present the permanent collection in chronological order and to accommodate the promised Walter Annenberg collection now on view approximately 6 months annually.

ON EXHIBIT 2002

06/26/2001 to 01/06/2002   *A Century of Design, Part IV: 1975–2000*
The last in a series of 20th-century design in a presentation of significant objects in all media drawn from the museum's collection

Sept 2001 to Spring 2002   *Courtly Radiance: Metalwork from Islamic India*
The objects dating from the 16th to the 19th century reveal varied technical and decorative effects. Select paintings that complement their use are shown.

10/02/2001 to 01/13/2002   *Glass of the Sultans*
One hundred fifty objects from the Islamic world ranging from 7th century to late 19th century, including Persian and Indian glass.   *Catalog   Will Travel*

10/05/2001 to 01/13/2002   *Klee Figures*
Figures in oil, watercolor, gouache, and pen and ink

10/10/2001 to 01/06/2002   *Candace Wheeler: The Art and Enterprise of American Design, 1875–1900*
The highlights of the career of America's first important woman textile and interior designer. Also shown will be work of Tiffany and deForest.   *Catalog*

10/18/2001 to 01/13/2002   *Treasury of the World: Jeweled Arts of India in the Days of the Mughals*
Two hundred objects from the al-Sabah collection including personal adornment, jeweled and jade objects and weapons   *Catalog   Will Travel*

11/06/2001 to 05/06/2002   *Bill Viola: The Quintet of Remembrance*
The first piece of video art to enter the collection, it connects the art of early Renaissance Europe and 21st-century America

11/24/2001 to 01/06/2002   *Annual Christmas Tree and Neapolitan Baroque Creche*
A holiday tradition! Lighting ceremony Friday and Saurday at 7:00. Recorded music adds to the display.

12/06/2001 to April 2002   *Extreme Beauty: The Body Transformed*
A unique opportunity to see fashion adapting to shifting adjustments of physical figures. From a 16th-century iron corset to Mugler's notorious "Motorcycle" bustier with paintings, prints, drawings, and caricatures by Cruikshank, Gilray, Daumier, and Vernet.   *Catalog*

12/12/2001 to 08/04/2002 *Splendid Isolation: Art of Easter Island*
The first American exhibition devoted to Easter Island's distinctive art forms as expressions of supernatural and secular power. Dating from te 13th to the late 19th century included are stone images, wooden sculpture, rare barkcloth figures, and examples of rongorongo, the island's unique and undeciphered script. *Catalog*

mid-January 2002 to April 2002 *Earthly Bodies: Irving Penn's Nudes 1949–50*
Penn's fashion photographs were unlike the voluptuous, faceless, sculptural forms depicted here. *Catalog*

01/23/2002 to 04/21/2002 *Benjamin Brecknell Turner: Rural England through a Victorian Lens*
These large-format richly toned albumen silver prints are very rare. The exhibition is from an album assembled by Turner. *Catalog*

02/01/2002 to 05/05/2002 *Surrealism: Desire Unbound*
This exhibition will present the richness and diversity of this human and constant theme in 400 paintings, sculpture, prints, photographs, films, poetry, and texts. Included are de Chirico, Dali, Duchamp, Ernst, Giacometti, Magritte, Masson, Miro, Picabia, Picasso, and Man Ray. The achievement of women will also be shown in Kahlo and Tanning.

02/14/2002 to 05/12/2002 *Orazio and Artemisia Gentileschi: Father and Daughter Painters in the Age of Caravaggio*
The first full scale exhibition devoted to Caravaggio's most gifted followers. Artemesia was the first woman to live exclusively by her brush, unbound by conventions. *Catalog* *Will Travel*

03/14/2002 to 06/19/2002 *Tapestry in the Renaissance: Art and Magnificence*
The first major tapestry exhibition in the US in 25 years. Preparatory drawings and cartoon fragments will explore the stylistic and technical development in the Low Countries, France, and Italy from 1460–1560 and highlight the contributions made to art, liturgy, and propaganda of the day. *Catalog* *Will Travel*

Miriam and Ira D. Wallach Art Gallery

Affiliated Institution: Columbia University
Schermerhorn Hall, 8th Fl., 116th St. and Broadway, New York, NY 10027

212-854-7288
Open: 1-5 We-Sa; The gallery is open only when there is an exhibition! *Closed:* Mo, Tu, Su, 1/1, week of Thgv, 12/25, 6/3-10/10, Mem/Day weekend
♿: Enter on Amsterdam Avenue P: Nearby pay garages *Group Tours* *Drop-In Tours* *Historic Building*
Permanent Collection: non-collecting institution

Operated under the auspices of Columbia University and situated on its wonderful campus, the gallery functions to complement the educational goals of the university.

Morgan Library

29 East 36th Street, New York, NY 10016-3490

212-685-0610 www.morganlibrary.org
Open: 10:30-5 Tu-Th, 10:30-8 Fr, 10:30-6 Sa, noon-6 Su *Closed:* Leg/Hol!
Sugg/Contr.: Yes *Adm:* *Adult:* $8.00 *Children:* Free under 12 *Students:* $6.00 *Seniors:* $6.00
♿: except original Library P: Nearby pay garage *Museum Shop*
🍴: Cafe open daily for luncheon and afternoon tea 212-685-0008, ext 511
Group Tours: 212-590-0332 *Drop-In Tours:* daily ! *Historic Building*
Permanent Collection: Med: drgs, books, ptgs, manuscripts, obj d'art

Both a museum and a center for scholarly research, the Morgan Library is a perfect Renaissance style gem both inside and out. Set in the heart of prosaic NY, this monument comes to the city as a carefully thought out contribution to the domain for the intellect and of the spirit. Wonderful views, beverage and sandwich service as weather permits. Wonderful views, beverage and sandwich service as weather permits. ℂ Stavelot Triptych, a jeweled 12th-century reliquary regarded as one of the finest medieval objects in America; Pierpont Morgan's private study and Library

ON EXHIBIT 2002

09/04/2001 to 01/20/2002   *Views of Yellowstone: William Henry Jackson Photographs from the Gilder Lehrman Collection*
Albumen prints from the summer of 1871 with several stereo cards. Historical documents of the period provide a context

09/14/2001 to 01/13/2002   *Oscar Wilde: A Life in Six Acts*
With works from the British Library, this celebrates his life with his Irish childhood, the three trials, imprisonment, and his physical and spiritual decline

10/11/2001 to 01/27/2002   *Cottontails and Corgis: The Children's Books of Beatriz Potter and Tasha Tudor*
Watercolors, original manuscripts, and artwork as well as Potter's drawings

El Museo del Barrio
1230 Fifth Ave, New York, NY   10029-4496

212-831-7272   www.elmuseo.org
Open: 11-5 We-Su, 11-6 Th Summer 6/6-9/26   *Closed:* Leg/Hol!
Adm: *Adult:* $5.00   *Children:* Free under 12   *Students:* $3.00   *Seniors:* $3.00
&   P: Discount at Merit Parking Corp 12-14 E 107 St.
Permanent Collection: Lat/Am: P/Col; Cont: drgs, phot, sculp

One of the foremost Latin American cultural institutions in the United States, this museum is also the only one in the country that specializes in the arts and culture of Puerto Rico. ℂ Santos: Sculptures between Heaven and Earth

ON EXHIBIT 2002

10/12/2001 to 01/27/2002   *O Flo Da Trauma/The Thread Unraveled: Contemporary Brazilian Art*
Works created in the 90s using fabric, thread, embroidery, and knitting with drawing, sculpture, photography, and multi-media installation.

February 2002 to May 2002   *Frida Kahlo, Diego Rivera, and Twentieth-Century Mexican Art: The Jacques and Natasha Gelman Collection*
A showcase of the broad range of Mexican art in paintings, drawings, sculpture, and photographs dating from 1910 to the 90s   *Catalog   Will Travel*

June 2002 to September 2002   *The S-Files/The Selected Files and Festival*
A biennial showcase of emerging, innovative Latino and Latin American artists in the greater New York area. The Festival extends beyond the museum to alternative spaces and the street.

Museum for African Art
593 Broadway, New York, NY   10012

212-966-1313   www.africanart.org
Open: 10:30-5:30 Tu-Fr; 12-6 Sa, Su   *Closed:* Leg/Hol!
Free Day: Su, 5:30-7:30 third Th of month   *Adm:*   *Adult:* $5.00   *Children:* $2.50
Students: $2.50   *Seniors:* $2.50
&   P: Nearby pay garages   *Museum Shop   Group Tours:* x, 118   *Drop In Tours:* !   *Historic Building*
Permanent Collection: Af: all media

This facility is in a historic building with a cast iron facade designed by Maya Lin, architect of the Vietnam Memorial in Washington, D.C. Her conception of the space is "less institutional, more personal and idiosyncratic." She is using "color in ways that other museums do not, there will be no white walls here."

ON EXHIBIT 2002

February 2002 to August 2002   *Material Differences in African Art*
An examination of the range of materials used in the creation of African art and the artistic techniques, media employed, and the makers of art in African societies. Photographic and video footage will show religious, social, economic, geographic, and traditional factors involved.

Fall 2002   *Unmasking Masks*
Masks provide windows to gain an understanding of the cultures from which they come. The masquerade practices for which masks were worn will be revealed

Museum of American Folk Art
Two Lincoln Square, New York, NY   10023-6214

212-595-9533   www.folkartmus.org
Open: 11:30-7:30 Tu-Su   *Closed:* Leg/Hol!
& P: pay garage nearby   *Museum Shop   Group Tours*
Permanent Collection: Folk: ptgs, sculp, quilts, textiles, dec/art

The museum is known both nationally and internationally for its leading role in bringing quilts and other folk art to a broad public audience.   ❧ "Girl in Red with Cat and Dog," by Ammi Phillips; major works in all areas of folk art

Museum of Modern Art
11 West 53rd Street (after summer 2002 at 45-20 33 Street, Long Island City),
New York, NY   10019-5498

212-708-9400   www.moma.org
Open: 10:30-5:45 Th-Tu; 10:30-8:15 Fr   *Closed:* Thgv,12/25
Free Day: Fr 4:30-8:15 vol cont   *Adm:*   *Adult:* $10.00   *Children:* Free under 16 with adult
Students: $6.50   *Seniors:* $6.50
& P: Pay nearby   *Museum Shop*   ‖: Sette Moma (open for dinner exc We & Su)
Group Tours: 212-708-0400   *Drop-In Tours:* !Weekdays, Sa, Su 1 & 3
Historic Building: 1939 Bldg by Goodwin & Stone considered one of first examples of Int. Style
Sculpture Garden   Theater
Permanent Collection: Work by Picasso, Matisse, Van Gogh, Warhol and Monet, Design 20

The MoMA offers the world's most comprehensive survey of 20th-century art in all media as well as an exceptional film library. MoMA Bookstore hours: 10-6:30 Sa-Tu, Th, 10-9 Fr; MoMA Design Store: 10-6:00 Sa-Tu, Th, 10-8 Fr Garden Cafe: 11-5 Sa-Tu, Th, 11-7:45 Fr; Sette MoMA: 12-3, 5-10:30 daily exc. See www.ticketweb.com for advance adm. tickets (service fee on ticketweb)   ❧ Outstanding collection of 20th-century photography, film, and design

ON EXHIBIT 2002

10/11/2001 to 01/08/2002   *Alberto Giacometti*
The exhibition contains 90 sculptures, 40 paintings, and 60 drawings and works in plaster not usually seen outside of Zurich. Both the works of his early (surrealistic) years and later (classic) Giacometti will be shown to demonstrate their shared properties and contrasts.
Catalog   Only Venue

Winter 2001 to 02/19/2002   *Collection Highlights*
Fifty masterworks of modern art from the permanent collection

02/21/2002 to 05/21/2002   *Gerhard Richter: 40 Years of Painting*
The first retrospective to introduce his works on canvas. It will include subtly photo-based works, monochromatic abstractions, and heavily painted, highly colored works.   *Catalog Will Travel*

03/21/2002 to 06/11/2002   *The Russian Avant-Garde Book, 1910–1934*
Included in the 300 books on display are pre-revolutionary and post-revolutionary works. Russian Modernism, and children's literature, Judaica, periodicals, exhibition catalogs, and sheet music will be included.

Late June 2002 to Ongoing *MoMA Queens Collection Highlights*
Masterworks from the permanent collection and key examples of mid-century and contemporary art

10/17/2002 to 01/07/2003 *MoMA Queens Contemporary Drawings: Eight Propositions*
A presentation of current drawings by about 40 international artists organized in eight groupings as a framework for works today.

Museum of the City of New York
Fifth Ave. at 103rd Street, New York, NY 10029

212-534-1672 www.mcny.org
Open: 10-5 We-Sa, 12-5 Su; 10-2 Tu for pre-registered groups only *Closed:* Leg/Hol!
Adm: *Adult:* $7.00: family $12.00 *Children:* $4.00 *Students:* $4.00 *Seniors:* $4.00
♿: 104th St Entrance P: Nearby pay garages *Museum Shop* *Group Tours:* ext 206 *Drop-In Tours:* !
Historic Building
Permanent Collection: New York:Interiors: 17-20; Broadway: History of American Theater; Peoples Hall of Fame/City Lore: The New York Center for Urban Folk Culture

Founded in 1933 this was the first American museum dedicated to the history of a major city. The Museum's collections encompass the City's heritage, from its exploration and settlement to the NY of today ☾ Period Rooms

National Academy of Design Museum and School of Fine Arts
1083 Fifth Avenue, New York, NY 10128

212-369-4880 www.nationalacademy.org
Open: 12-5 We, Th; 10-6 Fr; 10-5 Sa, Su *Closed:* Leg/Hol!
Adm: *Adult:* $8.00 *Students:* $4.50 *Seniors:* $4.50
♿ P: Nearby pay garage *Museum Shop* *Group Tours:* ext. 245 *Theater*
Permanent Collection: Am: all media 19-20

With outstanding special exhibitions as well as rotating exhibits of the permanent collection, this facility is a school as well as a resource for American Art. ☾ The oldest juried annual art exhibition in the nation is held in spring or summer with National Academy members only exhibiting in the odd-numbered years and works by all U.S. artists considered for inclusion in even-numbered years.

National Arts Club
15 Gramercy Park South, New York, NY 10024

212-475-3424
Open: 1-6 daily *Closed:* Leg/Hol!
P: Nearby pay garage, some metered street parking *Museum Shop* 🍴: For members *Historic Building*
Permanent Collection: Am: ptgs, sculp, works on paper, dec/art 19, 20; Ch: dec/art

The building which houses this private club and collection was the 1840s mansion of former Governor Samuel Tilden. The personal library of Robert Henri which is housed here is available for study on request.

New Museum of Contemporary Art
583 Broadway, New York, NY 10012

212-431-5328 www.newmuseum.org
Open: 12-6 Tu-Su, 12-8 Th *Closed:* Mo, 1/1, 12/25
Adm: *Adult:* $6.00 *Children:* Free under 18 *Students:* $3.00 *Seniors:* $3.00
♿ P: Nearby pay garages *Museum Shop* *Group Tours:* ext 216
Historic Building: Astor Building *Theater*
Permanent Collection: Semi-permanent collection

The New Museum is the premiere contemporary art museum in New York and among the most important internationally. Located in the heart of Soho, the New Museum offers three floors of the most innovative contemporary art from around the world as well as the New Museum Bookstore featuring the best selection of art books and unique and desgner created gifts.

ON EXHIBIT 2002

10/05/2001 to 01/13/2002   *Jacqueline Fraser: Portrait of Lost Boys/A Work in Progress: Selections from the New Museum Collection*

10/05/2001 to 02/03/2002   *Jason Middlebrook: Dig*

10/12/2001 to 02/03/2002   *Tom Friedman*

01/25/2002 to 04/14/2002   *Wim Delvoye: Cloaca*

02/14/2002 to 04/21/2002   *Francesco Vezzoli: The Films of Francesco Vezzoli*

02/22/2002 to 06/02/2002   *Marlene Dumas: Name No Names*

05/02/2002 to 07/14/2002   *Leah Gilman: Agenda for a Landscape*

05/17/2002 to 08/11/2002   *Jose Antonio Hernandez-Doaz*

New-York Historical Society
170 Central Park West, New York, NY   10024

212-873-3400   www.nyhistory.org
Open: 11-5 Tu-Su, Library 11-5 Tu-Sa   *Closed:* Leg/Hol!
Adm: *Adult:* $5.00   *Students:* $3.00   *Seniors:* $3.00
&.   P: Pay garages nearby   *Museum Shop   Group Tours:* ext. 264   *Drop-In Tours:* 1pm & 3pm
Historic Building   Theater
Permanent Collection: Am: Ptgs 17-20; Hudson River School; Am: gr, phot 18-20; Tiffany Glass; Circus & Theater: post early 20; Colonial: portraits (includes Governor of NY dressed as a woman)

Housed in an elegant turn of the century neoclassical building is a collection of all but 2 of the 435 "Birds of America" watercolors by John James Audubon. In addition there are 150 works from Tiffany Studios.   ℂ 435 original watercolors by John James Audubon; The Henry Luce center for the Study of American Culture on the museum's 4th Floor puts tens of thousands of treasures on permanent exhibition

ON EXHIBIT 2002

November 2000 onward   *The Henry Luce Center for the Study of American Culture*
The abundance of significant objects in the Luce Center, its availability to evoke the America which once was, promises a meaningful experience. There are many levels of interpretive guidance.

Pratt Manhattan Gallery
142 W 14th St, New York, NY   10011

718-636-3785   www.pratt.edu/exhibitions
Open: 10-9 Mo-Th; 10-4 Fr-Su
&.: Possible but difficult   P: Nearby pay garage   *Historic Building:* Puck Building
Permanent Collection: Not continuously on view

Pratt Manhattan and Schafler Galleries in Brooklyn present a program of exhibitions of contemporary art, design, and architecture in thematic exhibitions as well as solo and group shows of work by faculty, students, and alumni.

Salmagundi Museum of American Art
47 Fifth Avenue, New York, NY   10003

212-255-7740   Salmagundi.org
Open: 1-5 daily   *Closed:* Leg/Hol!
P: Nearby pay garage   ¶: Members Only   *Group Tours   Drop-In Tours:* by appt   *Historic Building*
Permanent Collection: Am: Realist ptgs 19, 20

An organization of artists and art lovers in a splendid landmark building on lower 5th Avenue.

Sidney Mishkin Gallery of Baruch College
135 East 22nd Street, New York, NY   10010

212-802-2690   www.baruch.cuny.edu/mishkin
Open: 12-5 Mo-We, Fr, 12-7 Th   *Closed:* Sa, Su, Acad!
  P: Nearby pay garages   *Historic Building*
Permanent Collection: Gr; Phot 20

The building housing this gallery was a 1939 Federal Courthouse erected under the auspices of the WPA.   ❰ Marsden Hartley's "Mount Katadin, Snowstorm," 1942

Society of Illustrators Museum of American Illustration
128 East 63rd St, New York, NY   10021

212-838-2560   www.stet
Open: 10-5 We-Fr, 10-8 Tu, 12-4 Sa   *Closed:* Leg/Hol!
  P: Nearby pay garages   *Museum Shop*   ¶: by membership @ $175/Yr   *Group Tours*   *Historic Building*
Permanent Collection: Norman Rockwell

A very specialized collection of illustrations familiar to everyone.

ON EXHIBIT 2002

01/09/2002 to 02/02/2002	*Tom Lovell*
02/09/2002 to 03/09/2002	*44th Annual Exhibition Book and Editorial*
03/16/2002 to 04/13/2002	*44th Annual Exhibition Adv. & Inst*
04/24/2002 to 05/25/2002	*Jim Spanfeller*
05/01/2002 to 05/25/2002	*Scholarship 2002*
05/29/2002 to 06/29/2002	*Chris Spollen*
05/29/2002 to 06/29/2002	*Jack Davis*
07/03/2002 to 08/03/2002	*New Acquisitions: Permanent Collection*
07/03/2002 to 08/03/2002	*Spots*
09/04/2002 to 09/28/2002	*Arnold Roth*
09/04/2002 to 09/28/2002	*U.S. Air Force*
10/02/2002 to 10/26/2002	*Our Own Show*
10/30/2002 to 02/27/2002	*The Original Art*
12/11/2002 to 01/04/2003	*Dimension Ill. Group*

Solomon R. Guggenheim Museum
1071 Fifth Ave, New York, NY   10128

212-423-3500   www.guggenheim.org
Open: 9-6 Su-We, 9-8 Fr, Sa   *Closed:* 12/25
Sugg/Contr.: Fr, 6-8 pm   *Adm:*   *Adult:* $12.00   *Children:* Free under 12 w/adult   *Students:* $8.00
Seniors: $8.00
  P: Nearby pay garages   *Museum Shop*   ¶   *Group Tours:* 212-423-3774   *Drop-In Tours*
Historic Building   *Sculpture Garden*   *Theater*
Permanent Collection: Am & Eur: ptgs, sculp; History based on 6 private collections: Justin K. and Hilde Thannhauser's impressionist, post impressionist, and early Modern masterpieces; Karl Nierendorf's coll. German expressionism; Peggy Guggenheim coll. of surrealist, & abstract artworks; Panza diBiumo Coll: minimalist art 1960s -70s

Designed by Frank Lloyd Wright in 1950, and designated a landmark building by New York City, the museum was recently restored and expanded in '92. Originally called the Museum of Non-Objective Painting, the Guggenheim houses one of the world's largest collections of paintings by Kandinsky as well as prime examples of works by such modern masters as Picasso, Giacometti, Mondrian and others. ¶ Kandinsky's "Blue Mountain"

ON EXHIBIT 2002

10/12/2001 to 01/27/2002   *Brazil: Body and Soul*
Focusing on two distict periods of Brazilian art, the Baroque and the Modern. It will trace European and African influence in both periods

11/16/2001 to 03/03/2002   *Norman Rockwell: Pictures for the American People*
The most comprehensive ever assembled of the artist's caree including his complex working method, rough sketches, photographs of models and studies in pencil and oil   *Will Travel*

02/15/2002 to 05/05/2002   *Matthew Barney: The Cremaster Cycle*
An epic five part film accompanied by related sculptures, photographs and drawings

05/30/2002 to 09/04/2002   *Art and the Holy Image: The Rise of Russian Icon Painting, 14th–16th Century*
Over 100 icons produced in Novgorod, Pskov and Moscow adorned with gold and using sensual, jewel like colors

05/30/2002 to 09/04/2002   *Kazimir Malevich: Suprematism*
Between 1915 and 1932 Malevitch developed a system of abstract painting meant to be universally comprehensible regardless of ethnic or cultural origin. A first exhibit to focus on this moment in his career including works never shown in the west before

09/27/2002 to 01/19/2003   *James Rosenquist: A Retrospective*
A player in the Pop movement and his own "new realist" style in which fragmented images from advertising are combined and juxtaposed to create narratives and abstractions

Studio Museum in Harlem
144 West 125th Street, New York, NY   10027

212-864-4500   www.studiomuseuminharlem.org
Open: 12-6 We -Th, 12-8 Fr, 10-6 Sa-Su   *Closed:* Leg/Hol!
Adm: *Adult:* $5.00   *Children:* $1.00 (under 12)   *Students:* $3.00   *Seniors:* $3.00
&   P: pay garages nearby   *Museum Shop*   *Group Tours:* ext. 258   *Drop-In Tours:* ! varies
Sculpture Garden   *Theater*
Permanent Collection: Af/Am; Carribean; Latino

This is the premier center for the collection, interpretation and exhibition of the art of Black America and the African Diaspora. The five-story building is located on 125th Street, Harlem's busiest thoroughfare and hub of it's commercial rebirth and redevelopment.

ON EXHIBIT 2002

Fall to Winter 2002   *Whitfield Lovell: Whispers from the Walls*
Mixed media installation centering on memory and history evoking a harrowing tale of post-reconstruction life

Whitney Museum of American Art
945 Madison Ave, New York, NY   10021

212-570-3676   www.echony.com/nwhitney
Open: 11-6 Tu-Th, Fr,1-9, 11-6 Sa, Su   *Closed:* 1/1, Thgv, 12/25
Free Day: Pay as you wish Fr 6-9   *Adm:*   *Adult:* $10.00   *Children:* Free under 12
Students: $8.00 with ID   *Seniors:* $8.00 over 62
&   P: Nearby pay parking lots   *Museum Shop*   ¶
Group Tours: 212-570-7720   *Drop-In Tours:* We-Su, & Th eve 212-570-3676   *Historic Building*
Sculpture Garden
Permanent Collection: Am: all media, 20

Founded by leading American art patron Gertrude Vanderbilt Whitney in 1930, the Whitney is housed in an award winning building designed by Marcel Breuer. The museum's mandate, to devote itself solely to the art of the US, is reflected in its significant holdings of the works of Edward Hopper (2,500 in all), Georgia O'Keeffe, and more than 850 works by Reginald Marsh. New directions and developments in American art are featured every 2 years in the often cutting edge and controversial Whitney Biennial. Satellite Galleries: Whitney Museum of American Art at Philip Morris,120 Park Ave, NYC Whitney Museum of American Art at Champion, Stamford, CT ℂ Alexander Calder's "Circus"

ON EXHIBIT 2002

09/22/2001 to 01/07/2007   *First Exposure—Sharon Harper: Photographs from the Floating World*
Rural landscapes taken from a high speed train

10/05/2001 to 01/04/2002   *Alex Katz: Small Paintings*
A look at Katz's style which merges abstraction and representation   *Will Travel*

10/06/2001 to 02/10/2002   *Charles Burchfield: Work on Paper*
Works from the collection including an unknown lithograph and a master set of engravings

10/18/2001 to 01/27/2002   *Into the Light: The Projected Image in American Art*
A first look at visual art of salides, film and video

11/08/2001 to 01/27/2002   *Burt Barr: Projections*
A look at the artifice of the cinematic image

11/08/2001 to 02/03/2002   *Over the Line: The Art and Life of Jacob Lawrence*
His importance in the history of 20th century art is recognized here

12/13/2001 to 02/24/2002   *Pail Pfeiffer*
Digitally produced videos and sculpture

01/12/2002 to 05/12/2002   *Dancer: Photographs by Irving Penn*
Penn and a modern dancer collaborated to create 27 photographs of a woman posing and dancing nude   *Will Travel*

03/07/2002 to May 2002   *2002 Biennial*
A panorama of American contemporary art

06/02/2002 to September 2002   *Claes Oldenburg & Coosje Van Bruggen: Drawings, 1958–98*
The largest exhibition of Oldenburg's drawings to date

06/02/2002 to October 2002   *The Paintings of Joan Mitchell*
A first full scale retrospective since her death

07/01/2002 to September 2002   *Michal Rovner*
A Israeli born photographer and video artist

Yeshiva University Museum
15 West 16th Street, New York, NY   10011

212-294-8330   www.yu.edu.museum
Open: 11-5 Tu-We, Th 11-8, 11-5 Su   *Closed:* Leg/Hol!, Jewish/Hol!
Adm: *Adult:* $6.00   *Children:* $4.00, 4-16   *Students:* $4.00   *Seniors:* $4.00
&   P: neighboring streets and pay lots   ‖: Cafe   *Group Tours   Drop-In Tours*
Permanent Collection: Jewish: ptgs, gr, textiles, ritual objects, cer

Major historical and contemporary exhibitions of Jewish life and ceremony are featured in this museum.   ℂ Architectural models of historic synagogues

ON EXHIBIT 2002

09/01/2001 to February 2002   *Jewish Artists: On the Edge*
Fifty artists who explore Jewish identity through the visual arts

09/01/2001 to May 2002   *Jewish Traders to Tartary*
Travels from the Middle Ages to the Industrial Revolution

09/01/2001 to May 2002   *One Chair, Many Tables*

11/25/2001 to May 2002   *Continuity and Change: 92 Years of Judaica at Bezalel*
At Israel's National art school this traces the development of art since 1906

NIAGARA FALLS

Castellani Art Museum-Niagara University
Niagara Falls, NY   14109

716-286-8200   www.niagara.edu/~cam
Open: 11-5 We-Sa, 1-5 Su   *Closed:* Acad!
&   P   *Group Tours*
Permanent Collection: Am: ldscp 19; Cont: all media; Work on Paper: 19-20; Phot: 20

Minutes away from Niagara Falls, Artpark, and the New York State Power Vista, the Castellani Art Museum features an exciting collection of contemporary art and a permanent folk arts program in a beautiful grey marble facility.   ❡ "Begonia," 1982, by Joan Mitchell

NORTH SALEM

Hammond Museum
Deveau Rd. Off Route 124, North Salem, NY   10560

914-669-5033   www.hammondmuseum.org.com
Open: 12-4 We-Sa   *Closed:* 12/25, 1/1
Adm: *Adult:* $4.00   *Children:* Free under 12   *Students:* $3.00   *Seniors:* $3.00
&   P   *Museum Shop*   ❙❙: Apr through Oct   *Group Tours*   *Drop-In Tours:* Res
Permanent Collection: Changing exhibitions

The Hammond Museum and Japanese Stroll Garden provide a place of natural beauty and tranquility to delight the senses and refresh the spirit.

OGDENSBURG

Frederic Remington Art Museum
303/311 Washington Street, Ogdensburg, NY   13669

315-393-2425   wwwfredericremington.org
Open: 9-5 Mo, Sa,1-5 Su (5/1-10/31), 11-5 We-Sa (11/1-4/30) 1-5 Su   *Closed:* 1/1, Easter, Thgv, 12/25
Adm: *Adult:* $4.00   *Children:* Free under 5   *Students:* $3.00   *Seniors:* $3.00
&   P   *Museum Shop*   *Group Tours*   *Historic Building*
Permanent Collection: Remington: ptgs, w/col, sculp, works on paper

The library, memorabilia, and finest single collections of Frederic Remington originals are housed in a 1809–10 mansion with a modern gallery addition.   ❡ "Charge of the Rough Riders"

Yager Museum
Oneonta, NY   13820

607-431-4480   www.hartwick.edu/museum
Open: 11-5 Tu-Sa, 1-4 Su   *Closed:* Leg/Hol!
Sugg/Contr.: Yes
& P   *Museum Shop   Group Tours   Theater*
Permanent Collection: Nat/Am: artifacts; P/Col: pottery; Van Ess Collection of Ren, Baroque & Am (ptgs 19); masks; shells; botanical specimens; ethno coll

An excellent college museum with community involvement and travelling exhibitions which reflects its unique collections ranging from fine art of the Renaissance, 19th- and 20th-century American paintings, upper Susquehanna area/archeology, ethnologic coll, Mesoamerican and North American.

Plattsburgh State Art Museum
Affiliated Institution: State University Of New York
State University of New York, Plattsburgh, NY   12901

518-564-2474   www.plattsburgh.edu/museum
Open: 12-4 daily   *Closed:* Leg/Hol!
& P: Free   *Museum Shop*   ‖: on campus across from museum
Group Tours: 518-564-2813   *Drop-In Tours:* by appt   *Sculpture Garden*
Permanent Collection: Rockwell Kent: ptgs, gr, cer; Largest Collection of Nina Winkel Sculpture

This University Museum features a "museum without walls" with late 19th- and 20th-century sculptures, paintings, and graphics displayed throughout its campus and in four secure galleries.   (Largest collection of Rockwell Kent works

Roland Gibson Gallery
Affiliated Institution: State University of New York College at Potsdam
Potsdam, NY   13676-2294

315-267-3290   www.potsdam.edu/gibson
Open: 12-5 Mo-Fr, 12-4 Sa, Su, 7-9:00 Mo-Th eve and by appt   *Closed:* Leg/Hol!
& P   *Group Tours:* 315-267-3290   *Sculpture Garden*
Permanent Collection: Cont: all Media; Work on Paper; Jap: ptgs; It: ptgs, sculp

Based on the New York State University campus in Potsdam, this is the only museum in northern New York that presents a regular schedule of exhibitions of contemporary art.
(Hollis Sigler "Expect the Unexpected"

Frances Lehman Loeb Art Center at Vassar College
Affiliated Institution: Vassar College
124 Raymond Ave., Poughkeepsie, NY   12601

914-437-5235   vassun.vassar.edu/~orfuac/
Open: 10-5 Tu-Sa, 1-5 Su   *Closed:* Easter, Thgv, 12/25-1/1
& P   *Museum Shop   Group Tours:* 914-437-5237   *Drop-In Tours   Sculpture Garden   Theater*
Permanent Collection: Am, Eur: ptgs, sculp; An/Gr & An/R: sculp; Gr: old Master to modern

Housed in a newly built facility, this is the only museum between Westchester County and Albany exhibiting art of all periods.   (Magoon Collection of Hudson River Paintings

PURCHASE

Donald M. Kendall Sculpture Gardens at Pepsico
700 Anderson Hill Road, Purchase, NY   10577

914-253-2082
Open: 9 am to dusk daily   *Closed:* Leg/Hol!
& P: Free   *Sculpture Garden   Theater*
Permanent Collection: 45 site-specific sculp by 20th-century artists

Forty-five site-specific sculptures are located throughout the 168 magnificently planted acres that house the headquarters of PepsiCo, corporate sculpture gardens designed in 1970 by noted architect Edward Durell Stone. A large man-made lake and wandering ribbons of pathway invite the visitor to enjoy the sculptures within the ever-changing seasonal nature of the landscape. The garden, located at a corporate headquarters in Westchester County about 30 miles outside of NYC, is an art lover's delight.

Neuberger Museum of Art
Affiliated Institution: Purchase College, SUNY
735 Anderson Hill Rd, Purchase, NY   10577-1400

914-251-6100   www.neuberger.org
Open: 10-4 Tu-Fr 11-5 Sa, Su   *Closed:* Leg/Hol
Free Day: 1st Sa of each month   *Adm:*   *Adult:* $4.00   *Children:* Free under 12
Students: free w/ ID   *Seniors:* $2.00
& P: Free   *Museum Shop*   ¶: Museum Cafe 11:30-2:30 Tu-Fr, 12-4 Sa, Su
Group Tours: 914-251-6110   *Drop-In Tours:* 1pm Tu-Fr; 2 and 3pm Su   *Theater*
Permanent Collection: Ptgs, Sculp, Drgs 20; Roy R. Neuberger Collection; Edith and George Rickey Collection of Constructivist Art; Aimee Hirshberg Collection of African Art; Hans Richter Bequest of Dada and Surrealist Objects; An/Grk, Etr Vases gift of Nelson A. Rockefeller

On the campus of Purchase College, SUNY, the Neuberger Museum of Art houses a prestigious collection of 20th-century American, European and African art. ℂ Selections from the Roy R. Neuberger Collection of 20th-century American art

ON EXHIBIT 2002

09/09/2001 to 01/13/2002   *A Personal Journey: The Lawrence Gussman Collection of Central African Art*
From the Neuberger, the National Museum of African Art, Washington, and the Israel Museum outstanding Central African works will travel and then the Gussman gift will be integrated into the Neuberger collection.   *Catalog   Will Travel*

09/23/2001 to 01/06/2002   *Howard Ben Tre*
The only East Coast venue of this retrospective of the glass sculptures and drawings of Ben Tre. He is well known for pioneering the use of cast glass as a sculptural medium   *Catalog Will Travel   Book*

09/30/2001 to 01/06/2002   *Grace Hartigan*
Eighteen large scale paintings in a survey from the early 1950's to the present showing her abstract expressionist improvisation and her interest in figuration.   *Catalog*

02/03/2002 to 05/19/2002   *Nature Takes a Turn*
Celebrating fine craftsmanship, innovation and personal expression in Wood Turning this juried exhibition by the American Association of Woodturners organizes this exhibition

02/03/2002 to 05/19/2002   *Renewing Tradition: The Revitalization of Bogolan in Mali and Abroad*
Bogolan, known as "mudcloth" in the U.S. is unique in technique and style. Its geometric patterns created by applying mud around the motifs so the designs appear white on a black background. The exhibition explains how and why it has become an easily recognized and heavily marketed product in fashion and design

02/03/2002 to 05/26/2002 *Beyond the Pale: Material Possibilities*
Works by 17 artists whose work presents a visual dialogue about forms in contemporary art using paint as a material whichgoes beyond traditional boundaries

05/26/2002 to 08/18/2002 *Grace Knowlton*
Abstact works by an artist who works with spherical and commonly found shapes

05/29/2002 to 09/08/2002 *Michel Gerard: The American Decade: 1989–1999*
A conceptual sculptor including floor and hanging sculpture, wall installations, collages and photographs

06/16/2002 to 09/08/2002 *The Art of Nathan Oliveira*
Retrospective of the paintings, monotypes, drawings, watercolors and sculpture by this key figure in American art in the 2nd half of the century *Will Travel Booklet*

09/29/2002 to 12/29/2002 *Jean Dubuffet*
The artist's work in New York from 1943 to 1950. Included are genre scenes, people in the Paris subway, walking past buildings, cyclists in the French countryside aand urban graffiti including messages on decrepit walls, pavements and newspapers *Catalog*

09/29/2002 to 01/05/2003 *Threnody*
Clive Grey's original work for the opening of the Neuberger Museum in 1974

QUEENS

Queens Museum of Art
New York City Building, Flushing Meadows Corona Park, Queens, NY 11368-3393

718-592-9700 www.queensmuse.org
Open: 10-5 Tu-Fr, 12-5 Sa, Su, *Closed:* 1/1, Thgv, 12/25
Adm: Adult: $5.00 *Children:* Free under 5 *Students:* $2.50 *Seniors:* $2.50
& P: Free *Museum Shop Group Tours Drop-In Tours:* Tours of Panorama 3pm Sa
Historic Building Theater
Permanent Collection: Changing Exhibitions of 20th-Century Art and Contemporary Art

The Panorama is where all of NYC fits inside one city block. You will feel like Gulliver when you experience it for the first time. The building was built for the 1939 World's Fair and was later used for United Nations meetings. Satellite Gallery at Bulova Corporate Center, Jackson Heights, Queens. ☾ "The Panorama of NYC," largest architectural scale model of an Urban Area. "Tiffany in Queens: Selections from the Neustadt Museum Collection" lamps, desk objects, and a window on long term loan.

ROCHESTER

George Eastman House, International Museum of Photography and Film
900 East Ave, Rochester, NY 14607

716-271-3361 www.eastman.org
Open: 10-4:30 Tu-Sa, 1-4:30 Su *Closed:* Mo, Leg/Hol!
Adm: Adult: $6.50 *Children:* $2.50 (5-12) *Students:* $5.00 *Seniors:* $5.00
& P *Museum Shop* ¶ *Group Tours:* 716-271-3361, ext 238 *Drop-In Tours:* 10:30 & 2 Tu-Sa, 2 Su
Historic Building Permanent Collection: Phot: prints; Motion Pictures; Motion Picture Stills; Cameras; Books

The historic home of George Eastman, founder of Eastman Kodak Co. includes a museum that contains an enormous and comprehensive collection of over 400,000 photographic prints, 21,000 motion pictures, 25,000 cameras, 41,000 books and 5,000,000 motion picture stills. Semi-Permanent Exhibitions: Through the Lens: Selections from the Permanent Collection A Picture Perfect Restoration: George Eastman's House and Gardens Enhancing the Illusion: The Origins and Progress of Photography George Eastman in Focus An Historical Timeline of Photoimaging ☾ Discovery room for children

Memorial Art Gallery
Affiliated Institution: University of Rochester
500 University Ave, Rochester, NY   14607

716-473-7720   http://mag.rochester.edu
Open: 12-9 Tu, 10-4 We-Fr, 10-5 Sa, 12-5 Su   Closed: Leg/Hol!
Adm: Adult: $7.00, $2 Tu 5-9   Children: 6-18 $2.00, Free 5 and under   Students: $5.00   Seniors: $5.00
& P   Museum Shop   ¶ Group Tours   Drop-In Tours: 2pm, Fr, Sa; 7:30 pm Tu   Historic Building
Sculpture Garden   Permanent Collection: Med; Du: 17; Fr: 19; Am: ptgs, sculp 19,20; Folk

The Gallery's permanent collection of 10,000 works spans 50 centuries of world art and includes masterworks by artists such as Monet, Cézanne, Matisse, Homer, and Cassatt. An interactive learning center focuses on Learning to Look. Also included is an interactive CD-ROM "tour" of the Gallery.   ℂ "Waterloo Bridge, Veiled Sun" 1903, by Monet; Inner Coffin of Pa-debehu-Assese; Homer, Artists Studio in an Afternoon Fog

ON EXHIBIT 2002

10/28/2001 to 01/13/2002   American Spectrum: Painting and Sculpture from the Smith College Museum of Art   Will Travel

02/17/2002 to 04/01/2002   Sandy Skoglund: Breathing Glass
An installation artist who creates mosaic encrusted mannequins floating upside down in a backdrop of deep blue and thousands of hand made glass dragonflies.

02/17/2002 to 04/21/2002   Ken Aptekar: Eye Contact
Ken Aptekar asks what people see when they look at art. He makes paiontings inspired by those in museum collections, superimposes text- ina variety of voices—to help viewers make their own collections.

06/16/2002 to 09/15/2002   Circa 1900: From the Genteel Tradition to the Glass Age
Six upstate New York museums celebrate art and culture 1880–1920 with and eclectic mix of painting, sculpture, photography and decorative arts. Included are Homer, Cézanne and MacMonnies.

10/13/2002 to 01/05/2003   Degas in Bronze
Seventy-four sculptures from the Museu de Arte de Sao Paulo, Brazil also including some paintings and works on paper by the artist.

ROSLYN HARBOR

Nassau County Museum of Art
One Museum Drive, Roslyn Harbor, NY   11576

516-484-9338   www.nassaumuseum.org
Open: 11-5 Tu-Su   Closed: Leg/Hol!
Adm: Adult: $4.00   Children: $2.00   Students: $2.00   Seniors: $3.00
& P: Free   Museum Shop   ¶ Group Tours: ext-11   Drop-In Tours: 2pm Tu-Sa
Historic Building   Sculpture Garden
Permanent Collection: Am: gr, sculp

Situated on 145 acres of formal gardens, rolling lawns and meadows, the museum presents four major exhibitions annually and is home to one of the east coasts' largest publicly accessible outdoor sculpture gardens.

ON EXHIBIT 2002

11/18/2001 to 02/03/2002   *Twentieth Century Exiles in America*
How European emigres altered the course of artistic development. Included are Beckmann, Chagall, Duchamp, Pascin, Leger, Feininger, Grosz, Hofmann, Mondrian, Ernst, Dali, Masson, Matta, Gorky, de Kooning and many others.

02/17/2002 to 04/28/2002   *How the West Was Won*
The West lured artists including Bierstadt and Thomas Moran as well as Catlin and Remington who depicted cowboys, Native Americans, pioneers and others. Post-Civil war era thru the turn of the century will be the focus

SARATOGA SPRINGS

Schick Art Gallery
Affiliated Institution: Skidmore College
Skidmore Campus North Broadway, Saratoga Springs, NY   12866-1632

518-580-5000   dom.skidmore.edu/academics/art/mosaic/schick
Open: 9-5 Mo-Fr ; 9-4 Mo-Fr, (summer) 1-3:30 Sa   *Closed:* Leg/Hol!, Acad!
&   P: On campus   ¶ *Group Tours:* 518-580-5049   *Theater*

Theme oriented or one person exhibitions that are often historically significant are featured in this gallery located on the beautiful Skidmore Campus.

SOUTHAMPTON

Parrish Art Museum
25 Job's Lane, Southampton, NY   11968

631-283-2118
Open: 11-5 Mo, Th, Fr, Sa, 1-5 Su; Open Daily Jun 1-Sep 15   *Closed:* 1/1, Easter, 7/4, Thgv, 12/25
Sugg/Contr.: Yes   *Adm:*   *Adult:* $2.00   *Students:* Free (with valid ID)   *Seniors:* $1.00
&   P   *Museum Shop*   *Group Tours:* ext.30   *Drop-In Tours:* !   *Historic Building*
Sculpture Garden   *Theater*
Permanent Collection: Am: ptgs, gr 19, 20; William Merritt Chase; Fairfield Porter

This Museum is a "don't miss" when one is near the Eastern tip of Long Island. It is located in an 1898 building designed by Grosvenor Atterbury. It features temporary exhibitions and exhibitions by renowned and emerging artists

STATEN ISLAND

Jacques Marchais Museum of Tibetan Art
338 Lighthouse Ave., Staten Island, NY   10306

718-987-3500   www.tibetanmusem.com
Open: 1-5 We-Su (Apr-mid Nov or by appt. Dec-Mar)1-5 We-Fr   *Closed:* Easter, 7/4, Lab/Day,
Thgv & day after, 12/25, 1/1
Adm: *Adult:* $5.00   *Children:* $2.00 (under 12)   *Students:* $3.00   *Seniors:* $3.00
P: limited street parking in front of Museum   *Museum Shop*   *Group Tours*   *Drop-In Tours:* on the hour
Historic Building: N, there are only 2 Tibetan style buildings in the Western world, the other other on is in St. Petersburg, Russia   *Sculpture Garden*
Permanent Collection: Tibet; Or: arch; Garden, Buddhist, Himalayan: As

This unique museum of Himalayan art within a Tibetan setting consists of two stone buildings resembling a Buddhist temple. A quiet garden and a goldfish pond help to create an atmosphere of serenity and beauty. It is the only museum in this country devoted primarily to Tibetan art.

Noble Maritime Collection
1000 Richmond Terrace, Staten Island, NY   10301

718-447-6490   www.johnanoble.com
Open: by appoint until Fall, 2000   *Closed:* Mo, Tu, We, Leg/Hol
Adm: *Adult:* $2.00   *Children:* under 12   *Seniors:* $1.00
& P   *Group Tours   Historic Building   Theater*
Permanent Collection: Ptgs; Lithographs; Documents and Artifacts

John Noble wrote "My life's work is to make a rounded picture of American Maritime endeavor of modern times." He is widely regarded as America's premier marine lithographer. The Collection, in a new site at historic Snug Harbor Cultural Center, features exhibitions, a library, printmaking studios, and prorgams for children & seniors in art and maritime history. The Collections have recently undergone a rehabilitation, converting a former mariner's dormitory into an elegant museum.

Snug Harbor Cultural Center
Affiliated Institution: Newhouse Center for Contemporary Art
1000 Richmond Terrace, Staten Island, NY   10301

718-448-2500
Open: 12-5 We-Su   *Closed:* Mo, Leg/Hol!
Adm: *Adult:* $2.00
P: Free   ¶   *Group Tours   Historic Building   Sculpture Garden*
Permanent Collection: Non-collecting institution

Once a 19th-century home for retired sailors Snug Harbor is a landmarked 83-acre, 28-building complex being preserved and adapted for the visual and performing arts. The Newhouse Center for Contemporary art provides a forum for regional and international art.   ℂ The award winning newly restored 1884 fresco ceiling in the Main Hall.

Staten Island Institute of Arts and Sciences
75 Stuyvesant Place, Staten Island, NY   10301

718-727-1135
Open: 9-5 Mo-Sa, 1-5 Su   *Closed:* Leg/Hol!
Sugg/Contr.: Yes   *Adult:* $2.50   *Students:* $1.50   *Seniors:* $1.50
&   P: Pay lot across the street   *Museum Shop   Group Tours:* 718-727-1135, x24
Permanent Collection: Ptgs; Dec/Art; Sculp; Staten Island: arch

One of Staten Island's oldest and most diverse cultural institutions, this facility explores and interprets the art, natural resources and cultural history of Staten Island.   ℂ Ferry Collection on permanent exhibition. This exhibition on the history of the world-famous ferry service is located in the Staten Island Ferry terminal.

STONY BROOK

The Long Island Museum of American Art, History and Carriages
12008 Rte. 25A, Stony Brook, NY   11790-1992

631-751-0066   www.longislandmuseum.org
Open: 10-5 We-Sa, 12-5 Su, July, Aug 10-5 Mo-Sa, 12-5 Su   *Closed:* 1/1, Thgv, 12/24, 12/25
Free Day: We, for Students   *Adm:*   *Adult:* $4.00   *Children:* $2.00, 6-17, under 6 Free
Students: $2.00   *Seniors:* $3.00
& P   *Museum Shop   Group Tours:* Ext.248   *Drop-In Tours:* !   *Theater*
Permanent Collection: Am: ptgs; Horse Drawn Carriages; Miniature Rooms; Ant: decoys; early Am art

A museum complex on a nine acre site with art, history, and carriage museums, blacksmith shop, 19th-century one room schoolhouse, carriage shed and 1794 barn.   ℂ Paintings by William Sidney Mount (1807–1868), 100 horse drawn carriages.

ON EXHIBIT 2002

09/29/2001 to 01/13/2002   *Lions and Eagles and Bull: A Roadside Gallery of Early American Art*
Twenty-five works from the largest collection of 18th- and 19th-century inn and tavern signs.

01/26/2002 to 05/05/2002   *Norman Rockwell: Drawing the American Dream*
A chronicle of the idealized image of the American dream. Drawings produced in the 50s and 60s in national magazines.

02/23/2002 to 06/02/2002   *Quilts: A Window to the Past*
From the early 19th century to the present, these frame traditional patterns.

05/18/2002 to 07/14/2002   *The Gilded Age: Treasures from the Smithsonian*
Artists who brought new elegance and sophistication to art from the 1870s to the 1920s. These included John Singer Sargent, Irving Wiles, Cecilia Beauxwith La Farge and Saint-Gaudens as well as Tiffany, Brigman, Thayer and Homer.

06/15/2002 to 11/03/2002   *More Than a Game: Spectator Sports on Long Island*
The history of popular sports is examined in the context of social change.

SYRACUSE

Everson Museum of Art
401 Harrison Street, Syracuse, NY   13202

315-474-6064   www.everson.org
Open: 12-5 Tu-Fr; 10-5 Sa; 12-5 Su   *Closed:* Mo, Leg/Hol
Sugg/Contr.: Yes   *Adm:*   *Adult:* $2.00
& P: Nearby pay garages, limited metered on street   *Museum Shop*   ¶   *Group Tours*   *Drop-In Tours:* I
Historic Building   *Sculpture Garden*
Permanent Collection: Am: cer; Am: ptgs 19, 20; Am sculp 20; Am: Arts/Crafts Movement Objects collection of early video works

When it was built, the first museum building designed by I.M. Pei was called "a work of art for works of art." The Everson's Syracuse China Center for the Study of Ceramics is one of the nation's most comprehensive, collections of American ceramics housed in an open-storage gallery. The installation is arranged chronologically by culture and includes samples from, the Americas, Asia and Europe.   ℂ One of the largest, most comprehensive permanent exhibitions of American and world ceramics

TARRYTOWN

Kykuit, The Rockefeller Estate
Affiliated Institution: Historic Hudson Valley
150 White Plains Road, Tarrytown, NY   10591

914-631-9491   www.hudsonvalley.org
Open: Mo, We-Fr 10am-3pm; Sa/Su 10 am-4 pm   *Closed:* Open May through October
Adm: *Adult:* $20.00   *Children:* not rec under 12   *Students:* under $18 $17.00   *Seniors:* $19.00
& P: Free at Visitor's Center   *Museum Shop*   ¶: Café at Visitor's Center
Group Tours: by reservation   *Drop-In Tours:* Indiviual reservation no longer required. All tours begin at Visitor's Center, Phillipsburg Manor, Route 9, Sleepy Holllow, NY   *Historic Building*   *Sculpture Garden*

The six-story stone house which was the Rockefeller home for four generations is filled with English and American furnishings, portraits and extraordinary collections of Asian ceramics. In the art galleries are paintings and sculpture by Andy Warhol, George Segal, Alexander Calder, Henry Moore, Picasso, David Smith, Robert Motherwell, Louis Nevelson, and many others. Visitors also view the enclosed gardens and terraces with their collections of classical and 20th-century sculpture and stunning river views. The Coach Barn contains horse-drawn carriages and classic automobiles. The Beaux-Arts gardens were designed by William Welles Bosworth and are filled with an extraordinary collection of modern sculpture.

Munson-Williams Proctor Institute Museum of Art
310 Genesee Street, Utica, NY   13502

315-797-0000   www.mwpi.edu
Open: 10-5 Tu-Sa, 1-5 Su   *Closed:* Leg/Hol!
Sugg/Contr.: Yes
  P   *Museum Shop*   ¶: Mo-Fr 11:30-3   *Group Tours:* ext 2170   *Drop-In Tours:* by appt
Historic Building   Sculpture Garden
Permanent Collection: Am: ptgs, dec/art; Eur: manuscripts, gr, drgs

The Museum is a combination of the first art museum designed by renowned architect Philip Johnson (1960) and Fountain Elms, an 1850 historic house museum which was the home of the museum's founders.

Hudson River Museum
511 Warburton Ave, Yonkers, NY   10701-1899

914-963-4550   www.hrm.org
Open: 12-5 We-Su, (Oct-Apr), 12-5 We, Th, Sa, Su, 12-9 Fr (May-Sept)   *Closed:* Mo, Tu, Leg/Hol!
Adm: *Adult:* $3.00   *Children:* $1.50 under 12   *Seniors:* $1.50
 : a "Touch Gallery" for visually-impaired   P: Free   *Museum Shop*
¶: The Hudson River Cafe overlooking the Hudson River
Group Tours: 914-963-4550 ext 40   *Drop-In Tours:* by appt   *Historic Building   Sculpture Garden   Theater*
Permanent Collection: Am: ldscp/ptgs 19,20; Dec/Art; Gr: 19,20; Costumes; Phot: 19,20.

The Hudson River Museum overlooking the Palisades, provides a dramatic setting for changing exhibitions of art, architecture, design, history and science—many designed for families. Discover the Hudson River's special place in American life as you enjoy the art. The Museum Shop was designed by Pop artist Red Grooms. There are Planetarium Star Shows in the Andrus Planetarium at 1:30, 2:30, 3:30 Sa, Su.   ℂ Hiram Powers's "Eve Disconsolate," marble statue, 1871,(gift of Berol family in memory of Mrs. Gella Berolzheimer, 1951). Also, woodwork and stencils in the decorated period rooms of the 1876 Glenview Mansion.

NORTH CAROLINA

Asheville Art Museum
2 S. Pack Square, Asheville, NC   28801

828-253-3227   www.ashvilleart.org
Open: 10-5 Tu-Sa also 1-5 Su, and until 8 Fr   *Closed:* Mo, 1/1, Mem/Day, 7/4, Lab/Day, Thgv,12/25
Free Day: 1st We 3-5pm   *Adm:*   *Adult:* $6.00   *Children:* $5.00   *Students:* $5.00   *Seniors:* $5.00
  P: on street   *Museum Shop*   *Group Tours:* 800-935-0204   *Drop-In Tours   Historic Building*
Permanent Collection: Am/Reg:ptgs, sculp, crafts 20

The Museum is housed in the splendidly restored Old Pack Memorial Library, a 1920 Beaux Arts Building.   ℂ "Art IS . . .": the museum's collection of 20th-century art asks this question and there are historical and contemporary responses by noted artists.

Ackland Art Museum
Columbia & Franklin Sts-University of North Carolina, Chapel Hill, NC   27599

919-966-5736   www.ackland.org
Open: 10-5 We-Sa, 1-5 Su   *Closed:* Mo, Tu, 12/25, 12/31, 1/1, 7/4
Sugg/Contr.: $3.00
& P: in nearby municipal lots   *Group Tours:* 919-962-3342   *Theater*
Permanent Collection: Eur & Am: ptgs, gr 15-20; Phot; Reg, Asian Cont, African

The Ackland, with a collection of more than 15,000 works of art ranging from ancient times to the present, includes a wide variety of categories conveying the breadth of mankind's achievements.   ℂ Large Asian collection, only one of its kind in North Carolina

ON EXHIBIT 2002

12/20/2001 to 02/17/2002   *Young America: Treasures from the Smithsonian American Art Museum*
Fifty-four major paintings and sculptures by Copley, Peale, and Stuart as well as landscapes and scenes of early America   *Will Travel*

02/25/2002 to 02/2003   *Buddhist Art in Ritual from Tibet and Nepal*
A rare opportunity to see sculpture and religious objects from Nepal and Tibet.

Mint Museum of Art
2730 Randolph Road, Charlotte, NC   28207-2031

704-337-2000   www.mintmuseum.org
Open: 10-10 Tu, 10-5 We-Sa, 12-5 Su   *Closed:* Mo, Leg/Hol
Free Day: Tu 5-10, 2nd Su of month   *Adm:*   *Adult:* $6.00   *Children:* Free under 12
Students: $4.00   *Seniors:* $4.00
& P: Free   *Museum Shop   Group Tours:* 704-337-2032   *Drop-In Tours:* 2pm daily   *Historic Building*
Permanent Collection: Eur & Am ptgs, Ren, Cont, Ch; Dec/Art; Am pottery, glass; Brit cer

The building, erected in 1836 as the first branch of the US Mint, produced 5 million dollars in gold coins before the Civil War. In 1936 it opened as the first art museum in North Carolina. When the museum was moved to its present parkland setting the facade of the original building was integrated into the design of the new building.   ℂ Extensive Delhom collection of English pottery, beautifully displayed

Gaston County Museum of Art and History
131 W. Main Street, Dallas, NC   28034

704-922-7681
Open: 10-5 Tu-Fr, 1-5 Sa, 2-5 4th Su of month   *Closed:* Mo, Su, other than 4th of month, Leg/Hol!
& P *Museum Shop   Group Tours:* 704-923-8103   *Drop-In Tours:* Th, Sa at 3pm   *Historic Building*
Permanent Collection: Cont; Artifacts relating to the U.S., NC, & the Southeast

The museum, housed in the 1852 Hoffman Hotel located in historic Court Square, features period rooms and contemporary galleries and furnishings. Regional history from the 1840s to the present.   ℂ Carriage exhibit, the largest public collection of horse-drawn vehicles in the Southeast

DAVIDSON

William H. Van Every Gallery and Edward M. Smith Gallery
Davidson College, Visual Arts Center, 315 N. Main Street, Davidson, NC   28036

704-894-2519
Open: 10-5 Mo-Fr, 12-4 Sa, Su (Sept-May)   *Closed:* Leg/Hol! Acad
Vol/Contr.: Yes
& P   *Group Tours   Historic Building:* designed by Graham Gund 1993
Permanent Collection: Work on Paper, Ptgs, Hist, Cont

In the fall of 1993 the Gallery moved to a new building designed by Graham Gund where selections from the 2,500-piece permanent collection are displayed at least once during the year. The Gallery also presents a varied roster of contemporary and historical exhibitions. ❏ Auguste Rodin's "Jean d'Aire," bronze

ON EXHIBIT 2002

01/22/2002 to 03/01/2002   *Rev. McKendree Long (1888–1976)*   Catalog

03/11/2002 to 04/21/2002   *Kimberley Richards*
A multimedia installation based on ongoing research into genetic manipulations of animals

DURHAM

Duke University Museum of Art
Affiliated Institution: Duke University
Buchanan Blvd at Trinity, Durham, NC   27701

919-684-5135   www.duke.edu/duma
Open: 10-5 Tu-Fr, 11-2 Sa, 2-5 Su   *Closed:* Mo, Leg/Hol!
Sugg/Contr.: $3.00
& P   *Museum Shop   Group Tours:* aderas@duke.edu   *Drop-In Tours*
Permanent Collection: Med: sculp; Dec/Art; Af: sculp; Am & Eur: all media

Duke University Art Museum, with its impressive collection ranging from ancient to modern works includes the Brumner collection of Medieval art, widely regarded as a one of a kind in the US, and a large pre-Columbian collection from Central and South America as well as a collection of contemporary Russian art.

FAYETTEVILLE

Fayetteville Museum of Art
839 Stamper Road, Fayetteville, NC   28303

910-485-5121   www.fayetteville.comefmaster
Open: 10-5 Mo-Fr, 1-5 Sa, Su   *Closed:* Mo, 1/1, Easter, 7/4, Thgv, 12/23-12/31
& P   *Museum Shop   Group Tours:* 910-485-0548   *Drop-In Tours   Sculpture Garden*
Permanent Collection: Cont: North Carolina art; Ptgs, Sculp, Cer, Af artifacts

The museum, whose building was the first in the state designed and built as an art museum, also features an impressive collection of outdoor sculpture on its landscaped grounds.   ❏ "Celestial Star Chart," by Tom Guibb

Weatherspoon Art Gallery
Affiliated Institution: The University of North Carolina
Spring Garden & Tate Street, Greensboro, NC   27402-6170

336-334-5770   www.uncg.edu/wag
Open: 10-5 Tu, Th, Fr, 1-5 Sa-Su, 10-8 We   *Closed:* Mo, Acad! and vacations
& P *Museum Shop* ¶: Many restaurants nearby *Group Tours* *Drop-In Tours:* 1st Su 2pm !
Historic Building *Sculpture Garden*
Permanent Collection: Am: 20; Matisse prints & bronze Sculp; Or

Designed by renowned architect, Romaldo Giurgola, the Weatherspoon Art Gallery features six galleries showcasing special exhibitions and a predominantly 20th-century collection of American art with works by Willem de Kooning, Alex Katz, Louise Nevelson, David Smith, and Robert Rauschenberg.   ℂ The Cone Collection of Matisse prints and bronzes

ON EXHIBIT 2002

Fall 2002   *Childhood Deployed: Pictorialism and Social Documentary in the US (1890–1925)*
Images by photographers including Riis, Stieglitz, Hine, Steichlin Day, Broughton, Kasebier, and others. The working class and middle class child will be presented.

Greenville Museum of Art Inc
802 Evans Street, Greenville, NC   27834

252-758-1946   gma.greenvillene.com
Open: 10-4:30 Th, Fr, 1-4 Su   *Closed:* Mo-We, Leg/Hol!
& P *Group Tours*
Permanent Collection: Am: all media 20

Founded in 1939 as a WPA Gallery, the Greenville Museum of Art focuses primarily on the achievements of 20th-century American art. Many North Carolina artists are represented in its collection which also includes works by George Bellows, Thomas Hart Benton, Robert Henri, Louise Nevelson, and George Segal, to name but a few.   ℂ Major collection of Jugtown pottery

Wellington B. Gray Gallery
Affiliated Institution: East Carolina University
Jenkins Fine Arts Center, Greenville, NC   27858

252-328-6336   www.ecu.edu/art/home.html
Open: 10-5 Mo-We, Fr & Sa, 10-8 Th   *Closed:* Leg/Hol!, Acad/Hol
& P *Sculpture Garden*
Permanent Collection: Cont; Af

One of the largest contemporary art galleries in North Carolina.   ℂ Print portfolio, Larry Rivers "The Boston Massacre"; African Art Collection; Baltics ceramics collection

Hickory Museum of Art
243 Third Ave. NE, Hickory, NC   28601

704-327-8576
Open: 10-5 Tu-Fr, 10-4 Sa, 1-4 Su   *Closed:* Mo, Leg/Hol!
& P *Museum Shop* *Group Tours* *Historic Building* *Theater*
Permanent Collection: Am: all media 19, 20; Art Pottery; Am: Impr

The second oldest art museum in North Carolina and the first in the southeast US to collect American art, the museum is located in one of Hickory's finest examples of neo-classic revival architecture.   ℂ William Merritt Chase painting (untitled)

Wilkes Art Gallery
800 Elizabeth Street, North Wilkesboro, NC   28659

336-667-2841   www.northwilkesboro.com/community
Open: 10-5 Tu-Fr, 12-4 Sa   *Closed:* Su, Mo, 1/1, Easter, Easter Mo, 7/4, 12/25
& P *Museum Shop*
Permanent Collection: Reg & Cont: all media

This 80-year-old neighborhood facility which was formerly the Black Cat Restaurant presents monthly changing exhibitions often featuring minority artists.

RALEIGH

North Carolina Museum of Art
2110 Blue Ridge Road, Raleigh, NC   27607-6494

919-839-6262   www.ncartmuseum.org
Open: 9-5 Tu-Th, Sa, 9-9 Fr, 11-6 Su   *Closed:* Mo, Leg/Hol!
Vol/Contr.: Yes
& P *Museum Shop* ¶: Cafe serves lunch daily & dinner Fr 5:30-8:45
Group Tours: ext. 2145   *Drop-In Tours:* 1:30 daily   *Sculpture Garden*
Permanent Collection: Eur/OM: ptgs; Am: ptgs 19; Ancient Art; Af; Reg; Jewish Ceremonial Art

The Kress Foundation, in 1960, added to the museum's existing permanent collection of 139 prime examples of American and European artworks, a donation of 71 masterworks. This gift was second in scope and importance only to the Kress bequest to the National Gallery in Washington, D.C.   ℂ Kress Collection

ON EXHIBIT 2002

11/11/2001 to 03/10/2002   *Speed of Light: Video Now*

11/21/2001 to 01/06/2002   *Indivisible: Stories of American Community*
Photographers and interviewers explored grassroots democracy in the U.S. from volunteer police to fly-fishing in Alaska   *Will Travel   Book*

01/03/2002 to Through 2002   *Bill Viola; Quilter of Remembrance*

04/01/2002 to 08/25/2002   *The Reverend McKendree Long: Picture Painter of the Apocalypse*

05/18/2002 to 07/28/2002   *Empire of the Sultans: Ottoman Art from the Khalili Collection*
Catalog   Will Travel

09/15/2002 to 01/05/2003   *Cranach Exhibition*   *Will Travel*

11/13/2002 to 01/05/2003   *Jan Mience Molenaer: Painter of the Dutch Golden Age*
Catalog   Will Travel

11/27/2002 to 03/03/2003   *Contemporary African Art*   *Will Travel*

North Carolina State University Gallery of Art & Design
Cates Ave., University Student Center, Raleigh, NC   27695-7306

919-515-3503   www2.acs.ncsu.edu/visualart
Open: 12-8 We-Fr, 2-8 Sa, Su   *Closed:* Mo, Tu, Acad!
& P ¶ *Group Tours*
Permanent Collection: Am: cont, dec/art, phot, outsider art, textiles, ceramics, paintings

The Center hosts exhibitions of contemporary arts and design of regional and national significance and houses research collections of photography, historical and contemporary ceramics, textiles, glass, and furniture.

ON EXHIBIT 2002

01/03/2002 to March 2002   *Early American Moderns: Highlights from the Weatherspoon Art Gallery Permanent Collections*
American artists had ambitions for the future. Included are Dove, Marin, Bolotowsky, Storrs and Kramer in a unique period of experimentation   *Catalog   Will Travel*

01/03/2002 to March 2002   *North Carolina Pottery Center Juried Exhibition*
A survey of ceramic art being done in the state   *Will Travel   Brochure*

04/01/2002 to June 2002   *Folk and Outsider Art from the Permanent Collection*

08/01/2002 to October 2002   *The Cutting Edge: Artist and Textile Technologies*
Six nationally recognized artists who use digital printing or weaving equipment to construct their work   *Catalog   Only Venue*

08/01/2002 to December 2002   *Cherokee Baskets*
Shown is the vitality, quality, and significance of the baskets from the last half of the 20th century   *Catalog   Will Travel*

10/01/2002 to December 2002   *The Form of Pattern*
Pattern in both 2 and 3 dimensions including ceramics, quilts, and paintings   *Catalog*

TARBORO

Blount Bridgers House/Hobson Pittman Memorial Gallery
130 Bridgers Street, Tarboro, NC   27886

252-823-4159   www2.coastalnet.com/ng3f3w5rm
Open: 10-4 Mo-Fr, 2-4 Sa, Su   *Closed:* Leg/Hol!, good Fr, Easter
Adm: *Adult:* $2.00
&   P: Street   *Group Tours   Drop-In Tours:* Mo-Fr 10-4, Sa, Su, 2-4   *Historic Building*
Permanent Collection: Am: 20; Dec/Art

In a beautiful North Carolina town, the 1808 Plantation House and former home of Thomas Blount houses decorative arts of the 19th Century and the Hobson Pittman (American, 1899–1972) Collections of paintings and memorabilia.   ❆ "The Roses," oil, by Hobson Pittman

WILMINGTON

St. John's Museum of Art/ Louise Wells Cameron Art Museum
(Name Change April 2002)
114 Orange Street—Address change April 2002: 3201 17th Street , 28412, Wilmington, NC   28401

910-763-0281   www.stjohnsmuseum.com
Open: 10-5 Tu-Sa, 12-4 Su   *Closed:* Mo, Leg/Hol!
Free Day: 1st Su of month   *Vol/Contr.:* Yes   *Adm*   *Adult:* $3.00   *Children:* $1.00 under 18
&: ground floor   P   *Museum Shop   Group Tours   Drop-In Tours   Historic Building   Sculpture Garden*
Permanent Collection: Am: ptgs, sculp

Housed in a new architecturally significant building designed by Charles Gwathmey, the Cameron Art Museum is the primary visual arts center in southeastern North Carolina. The Museum highlights 4 centuries of North Carolina and American masters.   ❆ Mary Cassatt color prints

WINSTON-SALEM

Reynolda House, Museum of American Art
Reynolda Road, PO Box 11765, Winston-Salem, NC   27116

336-725-5325, 888-663-1149   www.reynoldahouse.org
Open: 9:30-4:30 Tu-Sa, 1:30-4:30 Su   *Closed:* Mo, 1/1, Thgv, 12/25
Adm: *Adult:* $6.00   *Children:* $3.00   *Students:* $3.00   *Seniors:* $5.00
&   P   *Group Tours   Drop-In Tours   Historic Building*
Permanent Collection: Am: ptgs 18-present; Hudson River School

Reynolda House, an historic home designed by Charles Barton Keen, was built between 1912 and 1917 by Katharine Smith Reynolds, and her husband Richard Joshua Reynolds. the founder of R.J.R. Tobacco Co.   ℂ Costume Collection

ON EXHIBIT 2002

02/28/2002 to 06/02/2002   *Passions. Politics. Prohibition: Benton's "Bootleggers"*

Southeastern Center for Contemporary Art
750 Marguerite Drive, Winston-Salem, NC   27106

336-725-1904   www.secca.org
Open: 10-5 Tu-Sa, 2-5 Su   *Closed:* Mo, Leg/Hol!
Adm: *Adult:* $3.00   *Children:* Free under 12   *Students:* $2.00   *Seniors:* $2.00
&: Main floor in the galleries only. Not accessible to 2nd floor   P: Free   *Museum Shop*
Group Tours: Ext 14   *Historic Building   Sculpture Garden   Theater*
Permanent Collection: Non-collecting institution

Outstanding contemporary art being produced throughout the nation is showcased at the Southeastern Center for Contemporary Art, a cultural resource for the community and its visitors.

ON EXHIBIT 2002

10/20/2001 to 01/13/2002   *Half Past Autumn: The Art of Gordon Parks*
A retrospective of a 50-year career as a photographer, filmmaker, author, and composer balancing between social issues, memory and his feelings

NORTH DAKOTA

FARGO

Plains Art Museum
704 First Avenue North, Fargo, ND   58102-2338

702-232-3821   www.plainsart.org
Open: 10-5 Mo, 10-8 Tu, Th, 10-6 We-Fr, Sa, 12-6 Su   *Closed:* Leg/Hol!
Free Day: 2nd & 4th Tu of month   *Adm:*   *Adult:* $3.00   *Children:* $2.00   *Students:* $2.50   *Seniors:* $2.50
&   P   *Museum Shop*   ¶   *Group Tours:* ext 101   *Drop-In Tours*
Historic Building: Renovated turn of century warehouse
Permanent Collection: Am/Reg; Nat/Am; Af; Phot 20

The historically significant warehouse which has been turned into a state-of-the-art facility. It blends the old with the new with a result that is both stunning and functional. Large permanent collection. 9,000 feet of exhibit space.

North Dakota Museum of Art

Affiliated Institution: University of North Dakota
Centennial Drive, Grand Forks, ND   58202

701-777-4195   www.ndmoa.com
Open: 9-5 Mo-Fr, 1-5 Sa, Su   *Closed:* 7/4, Thgv, 12/25
&   P: Metered on street   *Museum Shop*   ¶: Coffee bar   *Group Tours   Historic Building
Sculpture Garden*
Permanent Collection: Cont: Nat/Am; Cont: reg ptgs, sculp; Reg Hist (not always on display)

In *Artpaper* 1991 Patrice Clark Koelsch said of this museum "In the sparsely populated state that was the very last of all the US to build an art museum, . . . (The North Dakota Museum of Art) is a jewel of a museum that presents serious contemporary art, produces shows that travel internationally, and succeeds in engaging the people of North Dakota." Building for the 21st Century: The Museum in cooperation with 2 local architectural firms, will sponsor a year-long series of lectures and seminars addressing the building or re-building of urban spaces from a global perspective.

OHIO

AKRON

Akron Art Museum

70 East Market Street, Akron, OH   44308-2084

330-376-9185   www.akronartmuseum.org
Open: 11-5 daily   *Closed:* Leg/Hol!
&   P: $2.00; free for members   *Group Tours:* ext 229   *Drop-In Tours:* Museum hours
Historic Building: 1899 Italian Renaissance Revival structure, listed NRHP   *Sculpture Garden*
Permanent Collection: Edwin C. Shaw Collection; Am: ptgs, sculp, phot

Conveniently located in the heart of downtown Akron, the Museum offers three floors of galleries exhibiting art from collections across the country and abroad. The museum's own collection presents a distinctive look at some of the finest regional, national, and international art from 1850 to the present, with special focus on contemporary art and photography. ¶ Claus Oldenberg "Soft Inverted Q," 1976; The Myers Sculpture Courtyard

ON EXHIBIT 2002

11/17/2001 to 02/24/2002   *Picture, Patents, Monkeys and More . . . On Collecting*
An investigation of the collecting impulse from 3 collections: contemporary art from the Robert J. Shiffler Foundation; 19th-century Patent models from the U.S. Patent Office; 100 "sock monkey" toys from a large collection

03/16/2002 to 06/02/2002   *Ohio Perspectives: Contemporary African American Artists*
The rich body of work being produced by African Americans living in the state today

06/15/2002 to 09/01/2002   *Milk and Eggs: The American Revival of Tempera Painting, 1930–1950*
Why three unconnected artists shared the revival of tempera painting   *Will Travel*

06/15/2002 to 09/01/2002   *N. C. Wyeth: Work from the Collection of the Brandywine River Museum*
Images of romance and adventure from a great illustrator

09/21/2002 to 01/05/2003   *My Reality: Contemporary Art and the Culture of Japanese Animation*
Japanese animation has become almost a cult among young people globally during the past few decades. The effect of this on today's art in Japan and other Asian countries and in the West is examined. Much "anime" has a futuristic flavor because it affirms technology as a force in today's society.   *Will Travel*

Kennedy Museum of Art
Affiliated Institution: Ohio University
Lin Hall, Athens, OH   45701-2979

740-593-1304   www.ohiou.edu/museum
Open: 12-5 Tu, We, Fr; 12-8 Th; Sa, Su, 1-5   *Closed:* Mo, Leg/Hol!
Vol/Contr.: Yes
& P   *Group Tours:* 740-593-0955   *Drop-In Tours:* by appt   *Historic Building*
Permanent Collection: Nat/Am; Am art

Housed in the recently renovated 19th-century Lin Hall, the Museum collections include the
Edwin L. and Ruth E. Kennedy Southwest Native American, American textiles and jewelry, and
the Martha and Foster Harmon Collection which is on long-term loan.

Canton Museum of Art
1001 Market Ave. N., Canton, OH   44702

330-453-1034   www.cantonart.org
Open: 10-5 & 7-9 Tu-Th, 10-5 Fr, Sa, 1-5 Su   *Closed:* 1/1, Thgv, 12/25
Vol/Contr.: Yes   *Adm:*   Adult: Admission for special exhibitions only $4.00   *Children:* $2.50
Seniors: $2.50
& P   *Museum Shop*   *Group Tours:* 330-453-7666   *Drop-In Tours*   *Sculpture Garden*   *Theater*
Permanent Collection: Work on Paper; Am & Eur: ptgs 19-20; Cer: after 1950

Located in the Cultural Center for the Arts, the Canton Museum of Art is the only visual arts
museum in Stark County. A mix of permanent with traveling exhibitions creates a showcase for
a spectrum of visual art. (Painting by Winslow Homer "Girl Picking Clover"

ON EXHIBIT 2002

11/22/2001 to 02/24/2002   *Summertime and the Living Is Easy: Permanent Collection*

11/24/2001 to 02/24/2002   *Paul Soldner: The Last Ten Years*

11/24/2001 to 02/24/2002   *Viola Frey: Clay Figures and Drawings*

04/26/2002 to 07/21/2002   *Bart Walter: Soul of Africa*

11/29/2002 to 01/21/2003   *Art & the Animal*

Cincinnati Art Museum
935 Eden Park Drive, Cincinnati, OH   45202-1596

513-639-2995   www.cincinarttiartmuseum.org
Open: 11-5 Tu, Th, Fr; 11-9 We; 10-5 Sa; 12-6 Su   *Closed:* 1/1, Thgv, 12/25
Free Day: Sa   *Adm:*   Adult: $5.00   *Children:* Free under 17   *Students:* $4.00   *Seniors:* $4.00
& P: Free   *Museum Shop*   ¶
Group Tours: 513-639-2975   *Drop-In Tours:* 1pm weekdays, 1 & 2pm weekends   *Historic Building:* Yes
Sculpture Garden
Permanent Collection: As; Af; Nat/Am: costumes, textiles; Am & Eur: ptgs, dec/art, gr, drgs, phot

The oldest museum west of the Alleghenies, the Cincinnati Art Museum's collection includes
the visual arts of the past 6,000 years from almost every major civilization in the world.
("Undergrowth with Two Figures," Vincent van Gogh, 1890

ON EXHIBIT 2002

10/07/2001 to 01/06/2002   *The Photographic Impulse: Selections from the Joseph and Elaine Monsen Collection*
Two hundred photos spanning the history of the medium. Included are Baldus, Cameron, Stieglitz, Talbot, Weston and Fuss, Polke, Sherman, and Struth.

10/14/2001 to 01/06/2002   *Posters of the Belle Epoque: Toulouse-Lautrec to Mucha*
Large, brightly colored lithographs which decorated Paris in the 1890s

02/03/2002 to 04/28/2002   *American Watercolors: Whistler to Wyeth*
American artists from the Museum's collection including Sargent and Marin

02/03/2002 to 04/28/2002   *Positively Alive: The Photographs of Maureen France*
A 20-year career of shooting real people at street fairs, circuses, carnivals, rodeos, fairs, senior citizen homes, slauterhouses, and boys reform school

03/17/2002 to 06/09/2002   *Egypt in the Age of the Pyramids*
An exceptional collection from the Museum of Fine Arts, Boston, dealing with this rarely shown period in Egypt's history   *Will Travel*

05/18/2002 to 08/18/2002   *New Acquisitions from the Prints and Drawings Collection*
Works by Twachtman, Moore, Jiro, Morrison, and Mars

07/14/2002 to 09/15/2002   *Weegee's World: Life, Death, and Human Drama*
The "underside" of life in New York during the first half of the 20th century tracing his career
Catalog   Will Travel

Contemporary Arts Center
115 E. 5th St., Cincinnati, OH   45202-3998

513-345-8400   www.spiral.org
Open: 10-6 Mo-Sa, 12-5 Su   *Closed:* Leg/Hol!
Free Day: Mo   *Adm: Adult:* $3.50   *Children:* Free under 12   *Students:* $2.00   *Seniors:* $2.00
&   P: Pay garage 1 block away under Fountain Square   *Museum Shop*
Group Tours: 513-345-8400   *Theater*
Permanent Collection: Non-collecting institution

This is one of the first contemporary art museums in the United States, founded in 1939. Art of today in all media including video is presented.

Taft Museum of Art (*Closed 11/01-04/03*)
316 Pike Street, Cincinnati, OH   45202-4293

513-241-0343   www.taftmuseum.org
Open: 10-5 Mo-Sa, 1-5 Su & Hol!   *Closed:* 1/1, Thgv, 12/25
Free Day: We & Su   *Adm: Adult:* $4.00   *Children:* Free 18 and under   *Students:* $2.00   *Seniors:* $2.00
&   P: Limited free parking   *Museum Shop   Group Tours:* ext. 17   *Drop-In Tours:* by appt, 10 to 4
Historic Building   Theater
Permanent Collection: Ptgs; Ch: Kangzi-period cer; Fr/Ren: Limoges enamels; Eur & Am: furniture 19

Collections include masterpieces by Rembrandt, Hals, Gainsborough, Turner, and Corot. ℭ Highlights from the Taft collection will be shown at the Metropolitan Museum (New York), the Minneapolis Museum, and the Seattle Art Museum.

Cleveland Museum of Art
11150 East Blvd, Cleveland, OH   44106

216-421-7350 or 1-888-262-0033   www.clevelandart.org
Open: 10-5 Tu, Th, Sa, Su, 10-9 We, Fr   *Closed:* Mo, 1/1, 7/4, Thgv, 12/25
&   P: Pay and street   *Museum Shop*   ¶ *Group Tours:* 216-707-2380   *Drop-In Tours:* by appt
Historic Building   Sculpture Garden   Theater
Permanent Collection: An: Med, Egt, Gr, R; Eur; Am; Af; P/Col; Or; phot, gr, text, drgs

One of the world's major art museums, the Cleveland Museum of Art is known for the exceptional quality of its collections with exquisite examples of art spanning 5,000 years. Especially noteworthy are the collections of Asian and Medieval European art and the renovated 18th-20th c galleries. A portion of the museum includes a wing designed in 1970 by Marcel Breuer. Some special exhibitions have admission fees. ¶ Guelph Treasure, especially the Portable Altar of Countess Gertrude (Germany, Lower Saxony, Brunswick, c 1040; gold, red porphyry, cloisonné, enamel, niello, gems, glass, pearls; "La Vie" by Picasso; "Burning of the Houses of Parliament" by J. M. W. Turner; Frans Hals's "Tideman Roostermin"; works by Faberge.

ON EXHIBIT 2002

10/13/2001 to 02/27/2002   *Artists Photographing Artists*
From the Museum's collection the ways in which photographers in the past 144 years have portrayed their fellow artists

10/21/2001 to 01/06/2002   *Picasso: The Artist's Studio*
Sixty paintings and a limited number of works on paper represent the styles, periods, and genre of his work.

11/18/2001 to 01/27/2002   *The Stamp of Impulse: Abstract Impressionist Prints*
Prints from 1942 to 1975 surveying the diverse approach and stylistic and technical experimentation. Included are Pollock, de Kooning, Gottlieb, Diebenkorn, and Oliveira.

12/22/2001 to 02/27/2002   *Gordon Parks: Photojournalism*
These vintage black-and-white photo essays portray: life in Harlem in the 1940s; the Black Muslim and civil rights movements of the 60s; portraits of Malcolm X and Muhammad Ali.

02/17/2002 to 04/28/2002   *Photographs from the Metropolitan Bank and Trust Collection (working title)*
An important corporate collection showing the striking changes in contemporary photography in the last 25 years

02/24/2002 to 05/19/2002   *Treasury of the World; Jeweled Arts of India in the Days of the Mughals*
Two hundred objects from the al-Sabah collection including personal adornment, jeweled and jade objects, and weapons   *Catalog   Will Travel*

05/19/2002 to 07/28/2002   *From Paris to Provinetown: Blanche Lazzell and the Color Woodcut*
Among the earliest non-representational prints created in the U.S.

06/23/2002 to 09/01/2002   *Into the Light: The Projected Image in American Art, 1964–1978*
Early work of pioneers of film and video-installation including Nauman, Oppenheim, Graham, Warhol, Sharits, Acconci, Lucier, Ono, and others

08/25/2002 to 10/27/2002   *A Print in Focus: Antonio Pollaiuolo's Battle of the Nudes*
A first impression of this monumental engraving

08/25/2002 to 10/27/2002   *Raphael and His Age: Drawings from Lille*
Twenty drawings by Raphael and othere by Botticelli, Lippi, and Bartolomeo

09/15/2002 to 01/05/2003   *Elizabeth Catlett: Work on Paper, 1944–1996*
Catlett says that her purpose is to"present black people in their beauty and dignity for ourselves
and others to understand and enjoy and to exhibit my work where black people can visit and
find art to which they can relate."   *Will Travel*

COLUMBUS

Columbus Museum of Art
480 East Broad Street, Columbus, OH   43215

614-221-6801   www.columbusart.mus.oh.us
Open: 10-5:30 Tu, We, Fr-Su, 10-8:30 Th   *Closed:* Mo, Leg/Hol!
Free Day: Th 5:30-8:30   *Sugg/Contr.:* Yes   *Adm:*   *Adult:* $4.00
Children: 5 and under free; 6 and older $2.00   *Students:* $2.00   *Seniors:* $2.00
&   P: $2.00; free for members   *Museum Shop*   ¶: Palette Café
Group Tours: 614-629-0359   *Drop-In Tours:* Fr noon, Su 2   *Historic Building*   *Sculpture Garden*   *Theater*
Permanent Collection: Eur & Am: ptgs 20; Reg

Located in downtown Columbus in a Renaissance-revival building, the Museum is an
educational and cultural center for the people of central Ohio, dedicated to the pursuit of
excellence in art through education, collections, and exhibitions. Features in-depth collections
connected to this region including wood carvings by Columbus folk artist Elijah Pierce and
paintings by Columbus native George Bellows.   ℂ Eye Spy: Adventures in Art, an interactive
exhibition for children and families. On view through 2001

ON EXHIBIT 2002

09/08/2001 to 01/06/2002   *Andrew Boroweic: Ohio River Valley Photographs*

09/15/2001 to 02/01/2002   *From Ancient Fires: Pre-Columbian Art From Columbus Collections*

10/06/2001 to 01/13/2002   *Laura Ziegler: A Columbus Sculptor Comes Home*

01/01/2002 to 03/20/2002   *An American in Europe*

02/07/2002 to 04/28/2002   *Edward Middleton Manigault: A Willful Modernist*

02/16/2002 to 05/05/2002   *Gilda Edwards Memorial Exhibition*

02/28/2002 to 05/12/2002   *Primal Visions: Albert Bierstadt "Discovers" America, 1859–1893*

03/23/2002 to June 2002   *Short Distances, Definite Places: The Photographs and Notebooks of
William Gedney*

05/11/2002 to 07/28/2002   *Grandma Moses in the 21st Century*
A re-examination of her most important   *Catalog*   *Will Travel*

05/11/2002 to 08/11/2002   *Ohio Art League*

09/01/2002 to January 2003   *Georgia O'Keeffe*

09/30/2002 to 11/24/2002   *Museums for a New Millennium: Concepts, Projects, Buildings*

12/13/2002 to April 2003   *Aminah Robinson*

Schumacher Gallery

Affiliated Institution: Capital University
2199 East Main Street, Columbus, OH   43209-2394

614-236-6319
Open: 1-5 Mo-Fr, 2-5 Sa   *Closed:* Leg/Hol!; Acad!; Closed May through August & University holidays
&   P   *Group Tours   Theater*
Permanent Collection: Eth; As; Reg; Cont; Ptgs, Sculp, Gr 16-19

In addition to its diverse 2,000-object collection, the gallery, located on the 4th floor of the University's library building, hosts exhibitions which bring to the area artworks of historical and contemporary significance.

Wexner Center for the Arts

Affiliated Institution: The Ohio State University
1871 N. High Street, Columbus, OH   43210-1393

614-292-3535   www.wexarts.org
Open: 10-6 Tu, We, Fr-Sa, 10-9 Th, 12-6 Su   *Closed:* Mo, Leg/Hol!
Free Day: 5-9 Th   *Adm: Adult:* $3.00   *Children:* Free under 12   *Students:* $2.00   *Seniors:* $2.00
&   P: pay garage nearby   *Museum Shop*   ‖: Café 8am-4pm Mo-Fr; limited service during exhibitions
4pm-8pm Thurs; 11am-3pm Sa; Noon-4pm Su   *Group Tours:* 614-292-6982   *Drop-In Tours:* 1:00 Su

Located on the campus of Ohio State University, Wexner Center is a multidisciplinary contemporary arts center dedicated to the visual, performing, and media arts with a strong commitment to new work. Its home, designed by Peter Eisenmann and the late Richard Trott, is a landmark of postmodern architecture.   ❰ Maya Lin's "Groundswell," a permanent outdoor sculpture made of shattered glass.

ON EXHIBIT 2002

07/20/2001 to Spring 2002   *Notations/Franz West: 2topia*
Using 150 chairs in patterned fabrics based on West African prints, he will change the look of the cafe, an adjoining social space

02/03/2002 to Spring 2002   *Mood River*
Thousands of objects of everyday life to create moods in design. Moods include Bliss, Ecstasy, Rage, and Trauma. Objects include toothbrushes and electronic gadgets.   *Catalog*

DAYTON

Dayton Art Institute

456 Belmonte Park North, Dayton, OH   45405

937-223-5277   www.daytonartinstitute.org
Open: 10-5 daily, 10-9 Th
&   P   *Museum Shop*   ‖: Café Monet 11-4 daily, 5-8:30 Th
Group Tours: ext 337   *Drop-In Tours:* Tu-Su 1:30, 3:30; Th 7   *Historic Building*
Sculpture Garden   Theater
Permanent Collection: Am; Eur; As; Oceanic; Af; Cont; P/Col

The Dayton Art Institute is located at the corner of Riverview Avenue and Belmonte Park North in an Edward B. Green designed Italian Renaissance style building built in 1930. ❰ "Water Lilies," by Monet; "Two Study Heads of an Old Man" by Rubens; "St. Catherine of Alexandria in Prison," by Preti; "High Noon," by Hopper

ON EXHIBIT 2002

01/12/2002 to 03/24/2002   *Scenes of American Life: Treasures From the Smithsonian American Art Museum*
The excitement of the Roaring Twenties, the drama of the Great Depression, The War Years, and WWII and beyond. The diversity of the artists is shown in Cadmus, Hopper, Kent, Marsh, Wood, the Soyers, Sloan, and Manship.   *Will Travel*

01/12/2002 to 06/23/2002   *The Shaw Collection*
From the highlands of ancient Peru to Teotihuacan, a picture of the civilizations that flourished

04/20/2002 to 06/23/2002   *Linda McCartney's Sixties: Portrait of an Era*
Some of the most memorable images of the Rock and Roll era   *Will Travel*

07/09/2002 to 09/08/2002   *Looking Forward, Looking Black*
Race, representation and identity among contemporary Black American artists including Weems, Colescott, Saar, Traylor, Walker, Cox, Amos, and others   *Will Travel*

Wright State University Galleries
Affiliated Institution: Wright State University
A 128 CAC Colonel Glenn Highway, Dayton, OH   45435

937-775-2978   www.wright.edu/artgalleries
Open: 10-4 Tu-Fr, 12-5 Sa, Su   *Closed:* Mo, Acad!
& P
Permanent Collection: Ptgs, Work on Paper, Sculp 20

The Museum is located on the Wright State University campus.

GRANVILLE

Denison University Gallery
Burke Hall of Music & Art, Granville, OH   43023

740-587-6255
Open: 1:00-4 daily   *Closed:* Acad!
&: Includes parking on ground level   P   *Group Tours:* on request
Permanent Collection: Burmese & SE/As; Eur & Am: 19; Nat/Am

Located on the Denison University Campus

KENT

Kent State University Art Galleries
Affiliated Institution: Kent State University
Kent State University, School of Art, Kent, OH   44242

330-672-7853
Open: 10-4 Mo-Fr; 2-5 Su   *Closed:* Acad!
&   *Museum Shop   Group Tours*
Permanent Collection: Gr & Ptgs: Michener coll; Ige Coll: Olson photographs; Gropper Prints: (political prints)

Operated by the School of Art Gallery at Kent State University since its establishment in 1972, the gallery consists of two exhibition spaces both exhibiting Western and non-Western 20th-century art and craft.

Cleveland Artists Foundation at the Beck Center for the Arts
17801 Detroit Ave, Lakewood, OH   44107

216-227-9507   www.clevelandartist.org
Open: 1-6 Tu, Th, Fr, Sa   *Closed:* Su, Mo, We, Leg/Hol!
&   P: Free   *Group Tours:* by appt.
Permanent Collection: Reg. Ptgs, sculp, gr

The Cleveland Artists Foundation is a non-profit arts organization located at the Beck Center for the Arts. The Cleveland Artists Foundation shows five exhibits a year on art of the Northeast Ohio region.

Allen Memorial Art Museum
Affiliated Institution: Oberlin College
87 North Main Street, Oberlin, OH   44074

440-775-8665   www.oberlin.edu/allenart
Open: 10-5 Tu-Sa,1-5 Su   *Closed:* Mo, Leg/Hol!
Vol/Contr.: Yes
&.: Through courtyard entrance   P: Free   *Museum Shop   Group Tours:* 440-775-8671
Historic Building   Sculpture Garden
Permanent Collection: Du & Fl: ptgs; Cont/Am: gr; Jap: gr; Islamic: carpets

Long ranked as one of the finest college or university art collections in the nation, the Allen continues to grow in size and distinction. The museum's landmark building designed by Cass Gilbert was opened in 1917. *The Weitzheimer/Johnson House, one of Frank Lloyd Wright's Usonian designs is open on the first Su 1-5pm. Admission is $5.00 pp with tickets available at the house.   ℂ Hendrick Terbrugghen's "St. Sebastian Attended by Irene," 1625; Modigliani "Nude With Coral Necklace"

Miami University Art Museum
Affiliated Institution: Miami University
Patterson Ave, Oxford, OH   45056

513-529-2232   www.muohio.edu/artmuseum/
Open: 11-5 Tu-Su   *Closed:* Mo, Leg/Hol! Acad!
&   P   *Group Tours   Sculpture Garden*
Permanent Collection: Am: ptgs, sculp; Fr: 16-20; Nat/Am; Ghandharan, sculp

Designed by Walter A. Netsch, the museum building is located in an outstanding natural setting featuring outdoor sculpture.

Southern Ohio Museum and Cultural Center
825 Gallia Street, Portsmouth, OH   45662

740-354-5629
Open: 10-5 Tu-Fr, 1-5 Sa, Su   *Closed:* Mo, Leg/Hol!
Free Day: Fr   *Adm: Adult:* $1.00   *Children:* $0.75   *Students:* $0.75   *Seniors:* $1.00
&   P: Free on street and municipal lot   *Museum Shop*
Group Tours: 740-354-5629   *Drop-In Tours:* by arrangement   *Historic Building*
Permanent Collection: Portsmouth Native Artist Clarence Carter; Ant: doll heads

Constructed in 1918, this beaux art design building is located in the heart of Portsmouth.

Springfield Museum of Art
107 Cliff Park Road, Springfield, OH   45501

937-325-4673   www.spfld-museum-of-art.org
Open: 9-5 Tu, Th, Fr, 9-9 We, 9-3 Sa, 2-4 Su   *Closed:* Mo, Mem/Day, 7/4, Lab/Day, Thgv weekend, 12/24-1/1
& P   *Museum Shop   Group Tours:* 937-324-3729   *Drop-In Tours:* by appt
Permanent Collection: Am & Eur:18, 19, 20; Rookwood Pottery; Reg: ptgs, works on paper

Located in Cliff Park along Buck Creek in downtown Springfield, this 54-year-old institution is a major and growing arts resource for the people or Southwest Ohio. Its 1,400-piece permanent collection attempts to provide a comprehensive survey of American art enhanced by works that represent all of the key movements in the development of Western art during the past two centuries. ❑ Gilbert Stuart's "Portrait of William Miller," 1795

ON EXHIBIT 2002

03/02/2002 to 04/14/2002   *Robert Knipschild: Paintings*
A retrospective

04/20/2002 to 05/26/2002   *Main Street, Springfield, Ohio: Photographs by Terence Byrnes and Berenice Abbott: Portraits of Maine*

08/03/2002 to 09/22/2002   *Tim Rietenback: Recent Work*
A three-dimensional site specific installation involving light and motion

10/05/2002 to 11/24/2002   *Christine Heindl: Paintings*
Large scale abstract works

12/07/2002 to 01/05/2002   *Western Ohio Watercolor Society Winter Exhibition*

Toledo Museum of Art
2445 Monroe Street, Toledo, OH   43697

419-255-8000   www.toledomuseum.org
Open: 10-4 Tu-Th, Sa, 10-10 Fr, 11-5 Su   *Closed:* Mo, 1/1, 7/4, Thgv, 12/25
& P: $2.00 in lot on Grove St.   *Museum Shop* ¶ *Group Tours:* 419-254-5772   *Drop-In Tours:* by appt
Historic Building   Sculpture Garden   Theater
Permanent Collection: Eur: glass, ptgs, sculp, dec/art; Am: ptgs; Af;Ind;Or

Founded in 1901 by Edward Drummond Libbey of Libbey Glass, the Museum is internationally known for the quality and depth of its collections. Housed in a perfectly proportioned neo-classical marble building designed by Edward Green, the Museum features American, European, African, Chinese, and Indian art, along with glass and decorative arts. Award winning architect Frank Gehry designed the adjacent Center for the Visual Arts which opened in 1993. ❑ "The Crowning of St. Catherine" Peter Paul Rubens, 1633; "The Architect's Dream" Thomas Cole, 1840

ON EXHIBIT 2002

08/05/2001 to 01/05/2002   *Star Wars: The Magic of Myth*
Original artwork, props, models, costumes, characters, and other artifacts used to create the original Star Wars trilogy.

11/18/2001 to 01/06/2002   *Lithographs by James McNeill Whistler from the Collection of Steven Block*
Whistler elevated lithographs from a commercial to a fine art and conveyed the luminous qualities of the Impressionists in his images.

01/18/2002 to 02/17/2002   *In Focus: Olivia Parker*

03/24/2002 to 06/16/2002   *The Alliance of Art and Industry: Toledo Designs for Modern America*

05/24/2002 to 08/25/2002   *Transparent Color: Watercolors at the Toledo Museum of Art*

10/18/2002 to 01/04/2003   *Hendrick Goltzius (title tentative)*

YOUNGSTOWN

Butler Institute of American Art
524 Wick Ave, Youngstown, OH   44502

330-743-1711   www.butlerart.com
Open: 11-4 Tu-Sa, 11-8 We, 12-4 Su   *Closed:* Mo, 1/1, Easter, 7/4, Thgv, 12/25
& P: Adjacent   *Museum Shop*   ¶: adjacent   *Group Tours:* ext 114   *Drop-In Tours:* by appt
Historic Building   Sculpture Garden   Theater
Permanent Collection: Am: ptgs 19, 20; Early/Am: Marine coll; Am/Impr; Western Art; Am: sports art

Dedicated exclusively to American Art, this exceptional museum, containing numerous national artistic treasures is often referred to as "America's Museum." It is housed in a McKim, Mead and White building that was the first structure erected in the United States to house a collection of American art.   ℭ Winslow Homer's "Snap the Whip," 1872, oil on canvas

ON EXHIBIT 2002

01/02/2002 to February 2002   *More Than One: Prints and Portfolios from the Center Street Studio, Boston*
This studio has been used by the most respected artists in printmaking. One hundred fifty images by 20 artists from landscape to still lifes, and expressive to whimsical subjects

02/02/2002 to April 2002   *Don Gummer; Sculpture*
A 30-year retrospective of Gummer's work with a site specific monumental work "Primary Compass," 22 feet combining stained glass and steel. Maquettes, preliminary studies, and a video tape will be shown.   *Will Travel*

ZANESVILLE

Zanesville Art Center
620 Military Road, Zanesville, OH   43701

740-452-0741
Open: 10-5 Tu, We, Fr, 10-8:30 Th, 1-5 Sa, Su   *Closed:* Mo, Leg/Hol
& P   *Museum Shop   Group Tours   Drop-In Tours*
Permanent Collection: Zanesville: cer; hand blown Early Glass; Cont; Eur

In addition to the largest public display of Zanesville art pottery (Weller, Roseville & J. B. Owens), the Art Center also has a generally eclectic collection including Old and Modern Masters, African, Oriental and European, Indian, Pre-Columbian, Mexican, and regional art.   ℭ Rare areas (unique) hand blown glass & art pottery; 300-year-old panel room from Charron Garden, London

OKLAHOMA

ARDMORE

Charles B. Goddard Center for Visual and Performing Arts
First Ave & D Street SW, Ardmore, OK   73401

405-226-0909
Open: 9-4 Mo-Fr, 1-4 Sa, Su   *Closed:* Leg/Hol!
&: North parking and entrance   P   *Group Tours*
Permanent Collection: Ptgs, Sculp, Gr, Cont 20; Am: West/art; Nat/Am

Works of art by Oklahoma artists as well as those from across the United States & Europe are featured in this multicultural center.

BARTLESVILLE

Woolaroc Museum
Affiliated Institution: The Frank Phillips Foundation, Inc
State Highway, 123, Rt 3, Box 2100, Bartlesville, OK   74003

918-336-0307   www.woolaroc.org
Open: 10-5 Tu-Su, Mem day-Lab day 10-5 daily   *Closed:* Mo, Thgv, 12/25
Adm: Adult: $5.00   *Children:* Free under 12   *Students:* $4.00   *Seniors:* $4.00
& P   *Museum Shop*   ‖: Snack bar w/sandwiches, etc.
Group Tours: school 6th grade & under free, grades 7-12 $2   *Historic Building   Sculpture Garden*
Permanent Collection: West: ptgs; sculp, firearms

Brilliant mosaics surround the doors of this museum situated in a wildlife preserve. The large Western art collection includes Remington, Russell, Leigh, and others. On the upper level is the Woolaroc monoplane, winner of the 1927 race across the Pacific to Hawaii.   ❈ The Lodge is a separate building. The original country home of oilman Frank Phillips called his Lodge (built in 1926–27) is completely restored.

MUSKOGEE

Five Civilized Tribes Museum
Agency Hill, Honor Heights Drive, Muskogee, OK   74401

918-683-1701   thefivecivilizedtribesmseum.org
Open: 10-5 Mo-Sa, 1-5 Su   *Closed:* 1/1, Thgv, 12/25
Adm: Adult: $2.00   *Children:* Free under 6   *Students:* $1.00   *Seniors:* $1.75
& P   *Museum Shop   Group Tours   Drop-In Tours   Historic Building   Theater*
Permanent Collection: Nat/Am

Built in 1875 by the US Government as the Union Indian Agency, this museum was the first structure ever erected to house the Superintendency of the Cherokee, Chickasaw, Choctaw, Creek, and Seminole Tribes.

NORMAN

Fred Jones Jr. Museum of Art
Affiliated Institution: University of Oklahoma
410 West Boyd Street, Norman, OK   73019-0525

405-325-3272   www.ou.edu/fjjma
Open: 10-4:30 Tu, We, Fr, 10-9 Th, 12-4:30 Sa, Su, Summer 12-4:30 Tu-Su   *Closed:* Mo, Leg/Hol!;
Acad!; Home Football Games 10-4:30
& P: Free passes available at admission desk   *Museum Shop*
Group Tours   Drop-In Tours: 10 days advance notice required   *Theater*
Permanent Collection: Am: ptgs Fr Imp; 20; Nat/Am; Photo; con; Gr 16-present

Considered one of the finest university museums in the country with a diverse permanent collection of nearly 6,000 objects, it also hosts the states most challenging exhibitions of contemporary art. ℂ Van Gogh "Portrait of Alexander Reid"; Monet "Riverbank at Lavacount"; Pisarro "Sheperdess Bringing in Sheep"

OKLAHOMA CITY

National Cowboy Hall of Fame and Western Heritage Museum
1700 N.E. 63rd Street, Oklahoma City, OK   73111

405-478-2250   www.nationalcowboymuseum.com
Open: 9-5 daily   *Closed:* 2/25, Thgv, 1/1
Adm: *Adult:* $8.50   *Children:* 6-12 $4.00   *Seniors:* $7.00 (over 62)
& P   *Museum Shop*   ¶ *Group Tours:* ext. 277   *Drop-In Tours   Sculpture Garden*
Permanent Collection: West/Art

Housing the largest collection of contemporary Western art available for public view, this unusual and unique museum features work by Frederic Remington, Charles M. Russell, Charles Schreyvogel, Nicolai Fechin, and examples from the Taos School. Cowboy and Native historical exhibits from the Museum's impressive holdings are on display. Western Town, Prosperity Junction; American Cowboy Gallery, American Rodeo Gallery now open, Joe Grandee Museum of th Frontier West   ℂ Gerald Balciar's 18' Colorado yule marble "Canyon Princess"; Wilson Hurley's 5 majestic landscape paintings; 7-ft bronze of former President Ronald Reagan; The Native American Gallery

Oklahoma City Art Museum
3113 Pershing Blvd, Oklahoma City, OK   73107

405-946-4477   www.oakhartmuseum.com
Open: 10-5 Tu-Sa, 10-9 Tu, 1-5 Su, Fairgrounds 10-8 Th   *Closed:* Mo, Leg/Hol!
Adm: *Adult:* $3.50   *Children:* Free under 12   *Students:* $2.50   *Seniors:* $2.50
& P   *Museum Shop*   ¶: Lobby Bistro   *Group Tours   Drop-In Tours   Sculpture Garden*
Permanent Collection: Am: ptgs, gr 19, 20; Ashcan School Collection

The Museum complex includes the Oklahoma City Art Museum at the Fairgrounds built in 1958 (where the design of the building is a perfect circle with the sculpture court in the middle).   ℂ Works by Washington color school painters and area figurative artists are included in the collection of modern art from the former Washington Gallery.

OMNIPLEX
2100 NE 52nd, Oklahoma City, OK   73111

405-602-6664 or 1-800-532-7652   www.omniplex.org
Open: 9-6 Tu-Sa, 11-6 Su (Mem/Day-Lab/Day); 9:00-5 Tu-Fr, 9-6 Sa,11-6 Su (Winter months)
Closed: Thgv, 12/25, Mo (except Mo hols)
Adm: *Adult:* $7.50 + tax   *Children:* 3-5, $5.00 + tax; 6-12 $6.00 + tax   *Students:* $7.50   *Seniors:* $6.00
& P: Free   *Museum Shop*   ¶: Limited   *Group Tours:* 405-602-3732   *Theater*
Permanent Collection: Varied; Reg; Af; As

Omniplex includes the Kirkpatrick Science and Air Space Museum; the International Photography Hall of Fame and Museum; Red Earth Indian Center as well as the Kirkpatrick Planetarium; Conservatory and Botanical Garden, Omnidome Theater and numerous galleries.   ℂ Sections of the Berlin Wall; traveling exhibits

Mabee-Gerer Museum of Art
1900 West MacArthur Drive, Shawnee, OK   74801

405-878-5300
Open: 10-4 Tu-Sa, 1-5 Su   *Closed:* 1/1, Good Fr, Holy Sa, Easter, Thgv, 12/25
Sugg/Contr.: Yes   *Adm:*   *Adult:* $3.00   *Children:* $1.00   *Students:* $3.00   *Seniors:* $3.00
&; Ground level ramp access from parking   P: Free   *Museum Shop*   *Group Tours*   *Sculpture Garden*
Permanent Collection: Eur: ptgs (Med-20); An/Egt; Nat/Am; Greco/Roman; Am: ptgs

The oldest museum collection in Oklahoma.   ☾ Egyptian mummy 32nd Dynasty and associated funerary and utilitarian objects.

Gilcrease Museum
1400 Gilcrease Museum Road, Tulsa, OK   74127-2100

918-596-2700   www.gilcrease.org
Open: 9-5 Tu-Sa, 1-5 Su and Holidays, Mem Day-Lab Day open Mo   *Closed:* 12/25
Adm: *Adult:* $3.00 (Family $5)   *Children:* Free under 18
& P: Free   *Museum Shop*   ¶: Rendezvous Restaurant open 11-2 Tu-Su, Reservations 918-596-2720
Group Tours: 918-596-2712   *Drop-In Tours:* 2pm daily   *Sculpture Garden*
Permanent Collection: Thomas Moran, Frederic Remington, C. M. Russell, Albert Bierstadt, Alfred Jacob Miller, George Catlin, Thomas Eakins

Virtually every item in the Gilcrease Collection relates to the discovery, expansion, and settlement of North America, with special emphasis on the Old West and the American Indian. The Museum's 460-acre grounds include historic theme gardens.   ☾ "Shoshone Falls on the Snake River, Idaho," by Thomas Moran

ON EXHIBIT 2002

12/15/2001 to 02/11/2002   *The Poetry of Place: Work on Paper by Thomas Moran from the Gilcrease Museum*
Drawings, watercolors, and prints used as source material in his studio and some of his most sensitive works

02/11/2002 to 04/14/2002   *The Hewitt Collection of African American Art*
Collected over a 40-year period this represents the most diverse African American art of the 20th century.

02/27/2002 to 04/14/2002   *Grandma Moses in the 21st Century*
A re-examination of her most important paintings   *Catalog*   *Will Travel*

Philbrook Museum of Art Inc
2727 South Rockford Road, Tulsa, OK   74114

918-749-7941 or 800-324-7941   www.philbrook.org
Open: 10-5 Tu-Sa, 10-8 Th, 11-5 Su   *Closed:* Mo, Leg/Hol
Free Day: Twice each year in May & Oct!   *Adm:*   *Adult:* $5.00 plus tax   *Children:* Free 12 & under
Students: $3.00 plus tax   *Seniors:* $3.00 plus tax
& P: Free   *Museum Shop*   ¶: 11-2 Tu-Su, Su Brunch, Cocktails 5-7 Th
Group Tours: 918-749-5309   *Drop-In Tours:* Upon request   *Historic Building*   *Sculpture Garden*   *Theater*
Permanent Collection: Nat/Am; It/Ren: ptgs, sculp; Eur & Am: ptgs 19-20

An Italian Renaissance style villa built in 1927 on 23 acres of formal and informal gardens and grounds. The collections, more than 6,000 works, are from around the world, more than half of which are by Native Americans. Visitors enter a 75,000-square foot addition via a striking rotunda which was completed in 1990 and is used for special exhibitions, a shop, a restaurant.

ON EXHIBIT 2002

02/10/2002 to 04/07/2002   *A Personal Journey: The Lawrence Gussman Collection of Central African Art*
From the Neuberger, the National Museum of African Art, Washington, and the Israel Museum outstanding Central African works will travel and then the Gussman gift will be integrated into the Neuberger collection.   *Catalog   Will Travel*

08/23/2002 to 11/17/2002   *American Modern, 1925–1940: Design for a New Age*
Design pioneers including Bel Geddes, Lescaze, Noguchi, Saarinen, Sheeler, and Wright in furniture, glass, ceramics, appliances, and graphics from the collection of the Metropolitan Museum of Art   *Catalog   Will Travel*

OREGON

COOS BAY

Coos Art Museum
235 Anderson, Coos Bay, OR   97420

541-267-3901
Open: 10-4 Tu-Fr, 1-4 Sa   *Closed:* Leg/Hol!; Mo, Su
&: Complete facilities   P: Free   *Museum Shop   Historic Building*
Permanent Collection: Cont: ptgs, sculp, gr; Am; Reg

This cultural center of southwestern Oregon is the only art museum on the Oregon coast. Its collection includes work by Robert Rauschenberg, Red Grooms, Larry Rivers, Frank Boyden, Henk Pander, and Manuel Izquierdo. Newly added is the Prefontaine Room, a special memorial to the late Olympic track star who was a native of Coos Bay.   ℂ "Mango, Mango," by Red Grooms

EUGENE

University of Oregon Museum of Art
Affiliated Institution: University of Oregon
1430 Johnson Lane, Eugene, OR   97403

541-346-3027   www.uoma.uoregon.edu
Open: 12-5 Th-Su, 12-8 We   *Closed:* Mo, Tu, 1/1, 7/4, Thgv, 12/25, Acad
Free Day: We 5-8   *Adm: Adult:* $3.00
&   *Museum Shop   Group Tours:* 541-346-0968   *Drop-In Tours:* 2pm Su   *Historic Building*
Permanent Collection: Cont: ptgs, phot, gr, cer; Nat/Am

Enjoy one of the premier visual art experiences in the Pacific Northwest. The second largest museum of in the state, the collection features more than 12,500 objects from throughout the world as well as contemporary Northwest art and photography.   ℂ Museum Fountain Courtyard

KLAMATH FALLS

Favell Museum of Western Art and Indian Artifacts
125 West Main Street, Klamath Falls, OR   97601

541-882-9996   www.favellmuseum.com
Open: 9:30-5:30 Mo-Sa   *Closed:* Su, Leg/Hol!
Adm: Adult: $4.00   *Children:* $2.00 (6-16)   *Seniors:* $3.00
&   P   *Museum Shop   Drop-In Tours*
Permanent Collection: Cont/West: art; Nat/Am; Artifacts; Mini Firearms

The museum is built on an historic campsite of the Klamath Indians. There are numerous artifacts—some of which have been incorporated into the stone walls of the museum building itself.

PORTLAND

Douglas F. Cooley Memorial Art Gallery
Affiliated Institution: Reed College
3203 S.E. Woodstock Blvd., Portland, OR   97202-8199

503-777-7790   www.reed.edu/resources/gallery
Open: 12-5 Tu-Su   *Closed:* Mo, Leg/Hol   &   *P:* Adjacent   *Theater*
Permanent Collection: Am: 20; Eur: 19

The gallery is committed to a program that fosters a spirit of inquiry and questions the status quo.

ON EXHIBIT 2002

02/01/2002 to March 2002   *Stephanie Snyder 91: Performing Judaism*
Ken Aptekar, Miriam Shapiro, Paul Brach, Anita Meyer, Nancy Goldberg, Nikos Stavroulakis, Gila Gevurtz, Stephanie Snyder, and Susan Sebeloff

04/01/2002 to June 2002   *Exhibition of Roman Antiquities; What is Man? Changing Images of Antiquity in Late Antique Art*

08/02/2002 to September 2002   *The WPA in Oregon*

Portland Art Museum
1219 S.W. Park Ave., Portland, OR   97205

503-226-2811   www.pam.org/pam/
Open: 10-5 Tu-Sa, 12-5 Su, 10-8 We & 1st Th   *Closed:* Mo, 12/25, Easter
Adm: *Adult:* $7.50   *Children:* Free under 5; $4 through 18   *Students:* $4.00   *Seniors:* $6.00
&: Ramp to main lobby, elevator to all floors   *Museum Shop*   *Group Tours:* 506-276-4289
Historic Building   *Sculpture Garden*
Permanent Collection: Nat/Am, As, Cameroon, Eur, English Silver, Am; Sculp, Print; Cont; Northwest Reg

Don't miss the world-famous collections of the oldest art museum in the Pacific Northwest, with treasures spanning 35 centuries of European, American, Asian and contemporary art.

ON EXHIBIT 2002

09/08/2001 to 01/06/2002   *En Suite: Contemporary Prints from the Collection of Jordan D. Schnitzer and the Jordan and Mina Schnitzer Foundation*
Post World War II prints: international but with emphasis on American and Northwest artists including Johns, Lichtenstein, and Warhol

10/06/2001 to 01/06/2002   *European Masterpieces: Six Centuries of Painting from the National Gallery of Victoria, Australia*
Old master and modern paintings from the 14th to the 20th century will be shown including El Greco, Rembrandt, Van Dyck, Gainsborough, Pissaro, Monet, Picasso, Hockney, and others.
Catalog   *Will Travel*

01/12/2002 to 03/24/2002   *Equivalents: Faces of the Oregon Art Scene Drawings by George Johanson*
Johanson refers to his portraits as "Equivalents." Larger than life-size drawings of 80 artists done in one hour sessions with some additions from memory later   *Catalog*   *Will Travel*

02/02/2002 to 04/28/2002   *Matieres de Reves: Stuff of Dreams, Highlights from the Paris Musee des Arts Decoratifs*
One hundred exceptional works of French art and beauty created between the Middle Ages and the present   *Catalog*   *Will Travel*

06/01/2002 to 09/22/2002 *Meiji Arts of Imperial Japan: Masterwork from the Khalili Collection*
Exceptional works of art in metal, enamel, lacquer, ceramic, and porcelain without parallel in any other culture *Catalog Will Travel*

08/17/2002 to 12/01/2002 *Beyond Beads and Feathers: Recent Work by Six Contemporary Native American Artists*
The inspiration for the subject matter ranges from Lakota cosmology to environmental and Native land rights and Native American culture. The artists are all at the height of their careers and have received international acclaim. *Catalog Will Travel*

08/17/2002 to 12/01/2002 *Grandma Moses in the 21st Century*
A re-examination of her most important paintings *Catalog Will Travel*

10/12/2002 to 01/05/2003 *Contemporary Art from the UBS Paine Webber Collection*
A private collection in all media never before shown or published including works by Baselitz, Basquiat, de Kooning, Freud, Guston, Hirst, Kiefer, Lichtenstein, Polke, Schnabel, Ruscha, Salle, Sherman, Smith, Twombly, and Warhol *Catalog*

WARM SPRINGS

The Museum at Warm Springs, Oregon
Affiliated Institution: Confederated Tribes of the Warm Springs Reservation
2189 Hwy 26, Warm Springs, OR 97761

541-553-3331
Open: 9am Open, Winter 5pm close; Summer 6pm close *Closed:* 12/25, 1/1, Thgv
Adm: Adult: $6.00 *Children:* $3.00 5-12; Free under 5 *Students:* With ID $4.50 *Seniors:* $5.00
&: wheelchair accessible; wheelchairs available P *Museum Shop Group Tours Theater*
Permanent Collection: Nat/Am: art, phot, artifacts

The Museum at Warm Springs draws from a rich collection of native artwork, photographs, and stories that tell the long history of the three tribes (Wasco, Warm Springs, and Paiute) that comprise the Confederated Tribes of Warm Springs. It is architecturally designed to evoke a creekside encampment among a stand of cottonwoods. ❲ A trio of traditional buildings built by tribal members; the tule mat wickiup, or house of the Paiutes, the Warm Springs summer teepee, and the Wasco wooden plank house

PENNSYLVANIA

ALLENTOWN

Allentown Art Museum
Fifth & Court Street, P.O.Box 388, Allentown, PA 18105-0388

610-432-4333 www.allentownartmuseum.org
Open: 11-5 Tu-Sa, 12-5 Su *Closed:* Leg/Hol!
Free Day: Su *Adm:* Adult: $4.00 *Children:* Free under 12 *Students:* $2.00 *Seniors:* $3.00
& P: On street meters and several pay garages, free Sunday *Museum Shop* ❙❙: small cafe
Group Tours: ext. 32 *Drop-In Tours:* by appt
Permanent Collection: Eur: Kress Coll; Am: Frank Lloyd Wright: library; OM: gr; gem collection

Discover the intricate and visual riches of one of the finest small art museums in the country. ❲ "Piazetti in Venice," by Canaletto

ON EXHIBIT 2002

11/25/2001 to 02/03/2002 *Ten Contemporary Artists 5 x 2*
An exhibition in two parts highlighting the work of 6 painters, 3 sculptors, and a fiber artist. The museum uses this as an opportunity to show gifted artists. Included are Francine LeClerq, Seann McCollum, Kevin Kautenburger, Marilyn Holsing, and Sarah McEneaney

11/25/2001 to 02/03/2002   *The Modern and Contemporary Print: Selections from the Museum's Collection*
The Renaissance and Baroque Print will be seen in 2001. The wide range of the collection will be shown.

02/13/2002 to 06/30/2002   *Traditional Indian Art: Sculptures and Temple Hangings*
The aesthetic and technical diversity of Indian art is shown here.

02/21/2002 to 04/28/2002   *Light Screens: The Leaded Glass of Frank Lloyd Wright*
The leaded glass windows designed 1886–1923 are abstract geometric shapes and clear glass for his "light screens" as he called his windows. The exhibition is divided into three sections: Pre-Prairie section (1886–1900), Prairie Period (1900–1911), and Post Prairie Period (1911–1923).   *Catalog   Will Travel*

03/24/2002 to 06/02/2002   *Frank Lloyd Wright and the Japanese Print (working title)*
Wright was an avid collector of Japanese prints and greatly influenced by them.

05/12/2002 to 07/07/2002   *28th Juried Exhibition*

05/19/2002 to 07/28/2002   *Poetry in a Steel Mill: Canvas Embroideries by Mildred Johnstone*
Eight remarkable canvas embroideries made in the late 1940s and early 1950s

AUDUBON

Mill Grove The Audubon Wildlife Sanctuary
Pawlings and Audubon Roads, Audubon, PA   19407-7125

610-666-5593   www.montcopa/org
Open: 10-4 Tu-Sa, 1-4 Su grounds open dawn to dusk Tu-Su   *Closed:* 1/1, Easter, 7/4, Thgv, 12/24, 12/25, 12/31
Vol/Contr.: Yes   &.: first floor only   P   *Museum Shop   Group Tours:* by appt   *Historic Building*
Permanent Collection: John James Audubon: all major published artwork (complete 19th C editions) and related items; original ptgs by John Woodhouse Audubon

Housed in the 1762 National Historic Landmark building which was the first American home of John James Audubon, artist/naturalist. This site is also a wildlife sanctuary complete with nature trails and feeding stations. Grounds self-guide map Free.   (Exceptionally large oil painting by Audubon called "Eagle and the Lamb"

BETHLEHEM

Lehigh University Art Galleries
Affiliated Institution: Zoellner Arts Center
420 East Packer Ave, Bethlehem, PA   18015-3007

610-758-3615   www.lehigh.edu/zoellner
Open: 11-5 We-Sa; 1-5 Su; Some galleries are open late, others closed weekends !   *Closed:* Leg/Hol!
&   P: Limited - on street; attached parking garage $1.00 fee   *Museum Shop*
¶: In Iacocca Bldg. open until 2pm   *Group Tours   Sculpture Garden*
Permanent Collection: Eur & Am: ptgs; Jap: gr; Phot

The Galleries do not permanently exhibit all the important works in its collections. Call to inquire.   (Outdoor sculpture throughout 3 campuses, including work by Henry Moore, David Cerulli, and Menash Kadishman

ON EXHIBIT 2002

01/12/2002 to 04/06/2002   *Arlene Gottfried: Eternal Light, Photographs*

01/18/2002 to 03/30/2002   *PA Photographers*

02/20/2002 to 04/28/2002   *Kathy Vargas: Photographs*

05/15/2002 to 07/14/2002   *International Video Exhibit*

05/24/2002 to 07/27/2002   *Selections from 20th Century Prints and Drawings (Brandywine Diversity Prints)*

07/31/2002 to 10/06/2002   *3-D Fiber Show*

08/01/2002 to October 2002   *Afro/American Presence in Printmaking (Brandywine)*

10/23/2002 to 01/05/2003   *Ha Sigg, Recent Work: Paintings, Sculpture, Collage*

BRYN ATHYN

Glencairn Museum: Academy of the New Church
1001 Cathedral Road, Bryn Athyn, PA   19009

215-938-2600   www.glencairnmuseum.org
Open: 9-5 Mo-Fr by appt, 2-5 selected second Su each month (Sept-Nov; Feb-May)   *Closed:* Leg/Hol!
Adm: Adult: $5.00   *Children:* under 5 free   *Students:* $2.00   *Seniors:* $4.00
P   *Group Tours:* 215-914-2993
Permanent Collection: Med, Gothic & Romansque: sculp; Stained Glass; Egt, Grk & Roman: cer, sculp; Nat/Am

Glencairn is a unique structure built in the Romanesque style using building processes unknown since the middle ages. It is the former home of Raymond and Mildred Pitcairn. ℂ French Medieval stained glass and sculpture

CARLISLE

The Trout Gallery, Dickinson College, Weiss Center for the Arts
Affiliated Institution: Dickinson College
High Street, PO Box 1773, Carlisle, PA   17013

717-245-1344   www.dickinson.edu/departments/trout
Open: 10-4 Tu-Sa; Summer 10-4 We   *Closed:* Leg/Hol!; Acad!
& P   *Group Tours:* 717-245-1492
Permanent Collection: Gr; 19, 20; Af

The exhibitions and collections here emphasize all periods of art history. ℂ Gerofsky Collection of African Art and the Carnegie Collection of prints. Rodin's "St. John the Baptist" and other gifts from Meyer P. and Vivian Potamkin.

ON EXHIBIT 2002

11/10/2001 to 01/12/2002   *Out of the Shadow: Artists of the Warhol Circle, Then and Now*

01/25/2002 to 03/02/2002   *Art Historical Methods Exhibition*

03/08/2002 to 04/13/2002   *Jim Dine/Roy Lichtenstein*

08/09/2002 to 09/14/2002   *Shoebox Sculpture Exhibition*

CHADDS FORD

Brandywine River Museum
U.S. Route 1, Chadds Ford, PA   19317

610-388-2700   www.brandywinemuseum.org
Open: 9:30-4:30 Daily   *Closed:* 12/25
Adm: Adult: $5.00   *Children:* Free under 6   *Students:* $2.50   *Seniors:* $2.50
& P   *Museum Shop*   ¶: 10-3 (Closed Mo and Tu, Jan through Mar)   *Group Tours:* 610-388-8366   *Historic Building*
Permanent Collection: Am: ptgs by three generations of the Wyeth Family

Situated in a pastoral setting in a charming converted 19th century grist mill, this museum is devoted to displaying the works of three generations of the Wyeth family and other Brandywine River School artists. Particular focus is also placed on 19th c American still-life & landscape paintings and on works of American illustration.

ON EXHIBIT 2002

11/23/2001 to 01/06/2002   *The Spirit of Dickens: "A Christmas Carol" in Pictures*

01/19/2002 to 03/03/2002   *Highlights from the Collection*
The Museum now has 3,000 works by members of the Wyeth family, American illustration, still life, and landscape painting

03/09/2002 to 05/19/2002   *Milk and Eggs: The American Revival of Tempera Painting, 1930–1950*
Why three unconnected artists shared the revival of tempera painting   *Will Travel*

06/01/2002 to 09/02/2002   *A Summer Idyll: Landscapes of the Brandywine Valley*
Ons, Lewis, and Doughty were first attracted, then came Shaw, Cope, Pyle, and members of the Wyeth family. 70 original landscapes of southeastern Pennsylvania and Northern Delaware during the summer months

09/13/2002 to 11/24/2002   *N. C. Wyeth Arrives in Wilmington*
The business and technology of illustration at the turn of the century featuring the most popular illustrators of the time

11/29/2002 to 01/12/2003   *A Brandywine Christmas*
Fabulous holiday displays

CHESTER

Widener University Art Collection and Gallery
Affiliated Institution: Widener University
14th and Chestnut Street, Chester, PA   19013

610-499-1189   www.widener.edu
Open: 10-4:30 We-Sa, 10-7 Tu (call for summer hours)   *Closed:* Mo, Leg/Hol
&   *P:* on street parking in addition to various university parking lots
Permanent Collection: Am & Eur: ptgs 19, 20

The Gallery is located in the new University Center on 14th St on the main campus. It includes in its holdings the Widener University Collection of American Impressionist paintings, the Alfred O. Deshong Collection of 19th and 20th c European and American painting, 19th c Asian art, and pre-Columbian, and African pottery. In addition contemporary exhibitions are hosted throughout the year. *Children under 16 must be accompanied by an adult.

COLLEGEVILLE

Philip and Muriel Berman Museum of Art at Ursinus College
601 E. Main Street, Collegeville, PA   19426-1000

610-409-3500   www.ursinus.edu
Open: 10-4 Tu-Fr, 12-4:30 Sa, Su   *Closed:* Mo, Leg/Hol!
Vol/Contr.: Yes   &   *P:* On campus adjacent to Museum
Group Tours: 609-409-3500   *Drop-In Tours:* by appt   *Historic Building   Sculpture Garden*
Permanent Collection: Am: ptgs 19, 20; Eur: ptgs 18; Jap: ptgs; Pennsylvania German Art: cont outdoor sculp

With 145 works from 1956–1986, the Berman Museum of Art holds the largest private collection of sculpture by Lynn Chadwick in a U.S. museum, housed in the original Georgian Style stone facade college library built in 1921.   ☾ "Seated Couple on a Bench" (1986 bronze), by Lynn Chadwick (English b. 1914)

ON EXHIBIT 2002

11/01/2001 to February 2002   *Judy Chicago's*
Works created by needleworkers from previous projects reinterpreting old adages in the hope for a better future   *Will Travel*

01/01/2002 to April 2002   *Mel Stark: A Retrospective*

02/20/2002 to 04/10/2002   *Hans Moller: A Retrospective*   *Catalog*

04/10/2002 to July 2002   *Rembrandt Etchings*   *Catalog   Will Travel*

05/18/2002 to 07/21/2002   *National Watercolor Society/Philadelphia Watercolor Society Collaborative Exhibition*

08/04/2002 to 09/22/2002   *African American Work on Paper : The Wes and Missy Cochran Collection*
Seventy-five works by 64 artists creating since the 30s. Included are Lawrence, Ringgold, Gilliam, Catlett, Pindell, and Bearden   *Will Travel   Brochure*

09/02/2002 to October 2002   *Donald Myer: The Exton Triptych*

10/13/2002 to 12/08/2002   *Of Samurai and Chrysanthemums: Edo Period Woodblock Prints and Meiji Bronze Sculptures*
The 55 prints include images of actors, Kabuki Theater, historical prints, daily life, and landscapes. The bronze sculptures show the influence of western sculpture in a Japanese context.   *Will Travel   Brochure*

11/01/2002 to December 2002   *Cliff Lamoree: Paintings and Sculpture*

DOYLESTOWN

James A. Michener Art Museum
138 South Pine Street, Doylestown, PA   18901

215-340-9800   www.michenerartmuseum.org
Open: 10-4:30 Tu-Fr, till 9pm We, 10-5 Sa, Su   *Closed:* Mo, Leg/Hol!
Adm: Adult: $6.00   *Children:* Free under 12   *Students:* $2.50   *Seniors:* $5.50
&   P: Free   *Museum Shop*   ¶: Blu's Café   *Group Tours:* ext 131   *Drop-In Tours:* 2pm, Sa, Su, & by appt
Historic Building   Sculpture Garden
Permanent Collection: Am: Impr/ptgs 19-20; Bucks Co.: 18-20; Am: Exp 20; Sculp 20; Nakashima Reading Room; Creative Bucks County

Situated in the handsomely reconstructed buildings of the antiquated Bucks County prison, the Museum features the finest collection of Pennsylvanian Impressionist in public or private hands and a wonderful collection of 19th and 20th century American art.   ◖ Spectacular 22-foot mural, "A Wooded Watershed" by Daniel Garber

ON EXHIBIT 2002

09/29/2001 to 01/06/2002   *Artists of the Commonwealth: Realism in Pennsylvania Painting, 1950–2000*
Nationally acclaimed Realist artists including Burko, Goodman, Neel, Pearlstein, Shanks, Warhol, Welliver, and Wyeth

10/20/2001 to 01/27/2002   *Taking Liberties: Photographs by David Graham*
Graham has been described as a photo-anthropologist recording the ways in which we mark our territory.   *Book*

01/18/2002 to 04/14/2002   *Stylish Hats: 200 Years of Sartorial Sculpture*
Beginning with a rare calash (1780) the exhibit tours the history of 19th century hats including Virot, Felix, Schiaparelli, and Fredericks.

02/09/2002 to 05/05/2002   *Roy C. Nuse: Figures and Farms*
Nuce's portraits and figure paintings as well as landscapes of farms and countryside influenced many Bucks county artists.

04/27/2002 to 07/07/2002   *Bucks County Invitational V*
Four distinguished living artists: Vincent Ceglia, painter; Karl Karhumaa, sculptor; Lisa Mannheim painter and Claus Mroczynski, photographer are featured

EASTON

Lafayette College Art Gallery, Williams Center for the Arts
Hamilton and High Streets, Easton, PA   18042-1768

610-330-5361   www.lafayette.edu
Open: 10-5 Tu, Th, Fr; 10-8 We; 12-5 Mo, 2-5 Sa Sept-May   *Closed:* Acad!
&   P: On-street   *Group Tours*
Permanent Collection: Am: ptgs, portraits, gr

Located in Easton, Pennsylvania, on the Delaware River, the collection is spread throughout the campus.   ❡ 19th c American history paintings and portraits

ERIE

Erie Art Museum
411 State Street, Erie, PA   16501

814-459-5477   www.erieartmuseum.org
Open: 11-5 Tu-Sa, 1-5 Su   *Closed:* Mo, Leg/Hol!
Free Day: We   *Adm:*   *Adult:* $2.00   *Children:* $.50 (under 12)   *Students:* $1.00   *Seniors:* $1.00
&   P: Street parking   *Museum Shop*   *Group Tours:* 814-459-5477   *Drop-In Tours:* 11-5   *Historic Building*
Permanent Collection: Ind: sculp; Or; Am & Eur: ptgs, drgs, sculp gr; Phot

The museum is located in the 1839 Greek Revival Old Customs House built as the U.S. Bank of PA. Building plans are underway to provide more gallery space in order to exhibit works from the 4,000 piece permanent collection.   ❡ Soft Sculpture installation "The Avalon Restaurant"

GREENSBURG

Westmoreland Museum of American Art
221 North Main Street, Greensburg, PA   15601-1898

724-837-1500   www.wmuseumaa.org
Open: 11-5 We-Su, 11-9 Th   *Closed:* Mo, Tu, Leg/Hol!
Sugg/Contr: $3.00   Children Free under 13
&   P: Free   *Museum Shop*   ❙❙: coffee bar   *Group Tours*   *Drop-In Tours:* by appt
Permanent Collection: Am: ptgs (18-20), sculp, drgs, gr, furniture, dec/art

This important collection of American art is located in a beautiful Georgian style building situated on a hill overlooking the city.   ❡ Portraits by William Merritt Chase and Cecilia Beaux; Largest known collection of paintings by 19th century southwestern Pennsylvania artists.

ON EXHIBIT 2002

02/14/2002 to 05/05/2002   *Patterns in Time: American Quilts: 1800–2000*
Historical and contemporary quilts. Another exhibition "Blending the Old and the New: Quilts by Paul Pilgrim" will also be shown.

05/26/2002 to 07/21/2002   *Cory Rockwood: Paintings*
Large scale paintings from the winner of the Associated Artists of Pittsburgh Exhibition

05/26/2002 to 07/21/2002   *Robert Henri and His Influence*
The scope of his influence on The Eight and the Ashcan School is shown in this look into modernism in the twentieth century. Artists include Bellows, Chase, Davies, Glackens, Davies, Kuhn, Prendergast, and Shinn.   *Will Travel   Brochure*

08/04/2002 to 10/13/2002   *Colorado Gold: The Landscape Photographs of Joseph Valvo*

08/04/2002 to 10/13/2002   *Scenes of American Life: Treasures from the Smithsonian American Art Museum*
The excitement of the Roaring Twenties, the drama of the Great Depression, The War Years and WWII and beyond. The diversity of the artists is shown in Cadmus, Hopper, Kent, Marsh, Wood, the Soyers, Sloan, and Manship.   *Will Travel*

11/17/2002 to 01/12/2003   *Holiday Toy and Train Exhibition*
Antique and modern toys

HARRISBURG

State Museum of Pennsylvania
3rd and North Streets, Harrisburg, PA   17108-1026

717-787-7789   www.statemuseumpa.org
Open: 9-5 Tu-Sa, 12-5 Su   *Closed:* Mo, Leg/Hol
&: 717-787-6997   *Museum Shop   Group Tours:* 717-772-6997   *Drop-In Tours:* !   *Theater*
Permanent Collection: Violet Oakley Coll; Peter Rothermel Military Series; PA: cont

A newly renovated Art Gallery collecting, preserving, and interpreting contemporary art and historical works relating to Pennsylvania's history, culture, and natural heritage is the main focus of this museum whose collection includes 4,000 works of art from 1650 to the present produced by residents/natives of Pennsylvania.   ℂ The 16' x 32'"Battle of Gettysburg: Pickett's Charge," by P. F. Rothermel (the largest battle scene on canvas in North America)

INDIANA

University Museum
Affiliated Institution: Indiana University
John Sutton Hall, Indiana University of Penn, Indiana, PA   15705-1087

724-357-6495   www.iup.edu/fa/museum
Open: 11-4 Tu-Fr, 7-9 Th, 1-4 Sa, Su   *Closed:* Mo, Acad!
Free Day: everyday
&   P: Metered lot just East of the Student Center (next to the football stadium)
Group Tours: 724-357-6495   *Historic Building:* yes   *Theater*
Permanent Collection: Am: 19, 20; Nat/Am; Milton Bancroft: ptgs & drgs; Inuit: sculp

The University Museum at Indiana University of Pennsylvania, one of just three university museums in Pennsylvania, offers a diverse program of changing exhibits, related cultural events, and educational activities to the university community and residents of the four-county area. Each year, the museum stages more than ten exhibitions, designed to appeal to a variety of interests. Local, regional, and international artists display contemporary works in a wide range of media. Special interdisciplinary exhibits explore the cultural heritage of the region and other themes from an aesthetic viewpoint. Rotating displays drawn from the museum's permanent collection round out the exhibit schedule. The museum's permanent collection, started in 1946 and refined during the early 1990s, consists of more than 5,000 works. An active program of new acquisitions focuses on American fine and folk art and native arts of North and Central America.

LEWISBURG

Edward and Marthann Samek Art Gallery, Elaine Langone Center
Affiliated Institution: Bucknell University
Seventh Street and Moore Ave, Lewisburg, PA   17837

570-577-3792
Open: 11-5 Mo-Fr, 1-4 Sa, Su   *Closed:* Leg/Hol!
& P: Free   *Museum Shop   Drop-In Tours*
Permanent Collection: It/Ren: ptgs; Am: ptgs 19,20; Jap

The permanent collection, which numbers approximately 8,000 objects has been established primarily through large bequests and gifts. Most impressive are the 24 items from the Samuel H. Kress Foundation, including the earliest documented painting by Pontormo, "Cupid and Apollo," a very early Rosso Fiorentino, "Madonna and Child," and works by Tintoretto, Veronese, Francesco Cossa, Agostino Tassi, and Andrea Sansovino; the Andrew J. Sordoni Collection of Japanese art which includes 500 objects, mostly 19th-century netsuke, okimono, and inro boxes of extremely high quality; and the Cook Collection of 156 musical instruments from all over the world and dating back as far as the 18th century. ❨ "Cupid and Apollo," by Pontormo

ON EXHIBIT 2002

02/21/2002 to 03/08/2002   *Spirit of Community: Photographs by Charles Harris*
Harris was a student of Gordon Parks, but photographed the Hill District of Pittsburgh, PA.

03/18/2002 to 04/14/2002   *Issues of Identity*

LORETTO

Southern Alleghenies Museum of Art
Affiliated Institution: Saint Francis College
Saint Francis University Mall, P. O. Box 9, Loretto, PA   15940

814-472-3920   www.sama-sfc.org
Open: 10-5 Tu-Fr, 1:00-5:00 Sa, Su   *Closed:* Leg/Hol
& P   *Museum Shop*   ❙❙: Nearby and on college campus   *Group Tours:* by appt   *Drop-In Tours:* by appt
Sculpture Garden
Permanent Collection: Am: ptgs 19, 20; sculp; drwg; gr

The museum was founded in 1976 to bring museum services to a geographically isolated rural region and to provide the audience with an opportunity to view important trends in American Art. Also: Southern Alleghenies Museum of Art, Brett Bldg, 1210 11th Ave, Altoona, PA 16602, 814-946-4464; at Johnstown, Pasquerilla Performing Arts Center, University of Pittsburgh at Johnstown, PA 15904, 814-946-4464; at Ligonier Valley, One Boucher Lane, Route 711S, Ligonier, PA 15658, 724-238-6015   ❨ John Sloan's "Bright Rocks"

MERION STATION

Barnes Foundation
300 North Latch's Lane, Merion Station, PA   19066

610-667-0290   www.barnesfoundation.org
Open: 9:30-5 Fr, Sa; 9:30-5 Su (Sept to June); 9:30-5 We-Fr Jul & Aug, adv reservation only   *Closed:* 12/25
Adm: Adult: $5.00, $7.00 for audio   *Children:* $5.00 per person
& P   *Museum Shop   Group Tours   Drop-In Tours*
Permanent Collection: Fr: Impr, post/Impr; Early Fr Modern; Af; Am

The core of the collection includes a great many works by Renoir, Cézanne, and Matisse, but also contains works by Picasso, van Gogh, Seurat, Braque, Modigliani, Soutine, Monet, and Manet. Various traditions are displayed in works by El Greco, Titian, Corbet, Corot, Delacroix, and others. Works also include American antique furniture, ironwork, ceramics and crafts. The building has just undergone a 3-year, $12 million renovation. ❡ This outstanding collection should not be missed.

MILL RUN

Fallingwater
Rt. 381, Mill Run, PA   15464

724-329-8501   www.paconserve.org
Open: 11/21-12/20, 2/27-3/14, weekends only, Xmas week 10-4 Tu-Su, Closed Jan/Feb
Closed: some Leg/Hol!
Free Day: Fayette Country Day   *Adm:*   *Adult:* $10.00 Tu-Fr; $15 wknds
&.   P: Free   *Museum Shop*   ❙❙: Open 5/1-11/1   *Group Tours*
Historic Building: National Historic Landmark   *Sculpture Garden*
Permanent Collection: Arch; Ptgs; Jap: gr; Sculp; Nat/Am

Magnificent is the word for this structure, one of Frank Lloyd Wright's most widely acclaimed works. The key to the setting of the house is the waterfall over which it is built. Fallingwater is undergoing some renovation. Special restoration tours are planned ! ❡ View of the House from the Overlook

PHILADELPHIA

Pennsylvania Academy of the Fine Arts
Broad Street and Cherry Street, Philadelphia, PA   19102

215-972-7600   www.pafa.org
Open: 10-5 Tu-Sa, 11-5 Su   *Closed:* Leg/Hol!
Free Day: 3-5 Su   *Adm:*   *Adult:* $5.00   *Children:* $3.00 Free under 5   *Students:* $4.00 w/ ID
Seniors: $4.00
&.   P: Public parking lots nearby (discount at Parkway Corp. lots at Broad & Cherry and 15th & Cherry); some street parking   *Museum Shop*   ❙❙
Group Tours: 215-972-1667   *Drop-In Tours:* Tu-Fr 11:30-1:15; Sa & Su 12, 1:45   *Historic Building*
Permanent Collection: Am: ptgs, sculp 18-20

The Pennsylvania Academy of Fine Arts is housed in a Victorian Gothic masterpiece designed by Frank Furness and George Hewitt located in the heart of downtown Philadelphia. Its roster of past students includes some of the most renowned artists of the 19th & 20th centuries and its holdings of 2 centuries of American paintings, sculpture, and works on paper is one of the world's most acclaimed

ON EXHIBIT 2002

10/06/2001 to 01/13/2002   *Process on Paper: Eakins Paintings from the Bregler Collection*
The first its kind, the exhbition examines the importance of drawing in Eakin's artistic and teaching practices.   *Brochure*

11/30/2001 to 02/03/2002   *Basekamp*
This installation by the collaborative team of Dempewolf, Matherly, Rigby, and Stevens who contribute on a project by project basis   *Brochure*

01/12/2002 to 04/07/2002   *American Modern, 1925–1940: Design for a New Age*
Design pioneers including Bel Geddes, Lescaze, Noguchi, Saarinen, Sheeler, and Wright in furniture, glass, ceramics and appliances, and graphics from the collection of the Metropolitan Museum of Art   *Catalog   Will Travel*

02/03/2002 to 04/14/2002   *Francis Criss, American Modernist: Paintings from the 1930s*
Cityscapes and portraits blending Precisionism and School Surrealism   *Will Travel*

African-American Museum in Philadelphia
701 Arch Street, Philadelphia, PA   19106

215-574-0380   www.aampmuseum.org
Open: 10-5 Tu-Sa, 12-5 Su   *Closed:* Mo, Leg/Hol
Free Day: Discounted charge on Martin Luther King Jr. day   *Adm:*   *Adult:* $6.00   *Children:* $4.00
Students: $4.00   *Seniors:* $4.00
  P: Pay parking nearby   *Museum Shop   Group Tours:* ext. 228   *Drop-In Tours   Theater*
Permanent Collection: Jack Frank Coll: phot; Pearl Jones Coll: phot drgs, dec/art: Joseph C. Coleman
personal papers, photos and awards

A diverse and unique showplace, this is the first museum built by a major city to house and interpret collections of African-American art, history, and culture primarily in, but not limited, to the Commonwealth of Pennsylvania. The museum contains over 500,000 objects.

Institute of Contemporary Art
Affiliated Institution: University of Pennsylvania
118 South 36th Street at Sansom, Philadelphia, PA   19104-3289

215-898-7108   www.upenn.edu/ica
Open: 10-5 We, Fr-Su, 10-7 Th   *Closed:* Mo, Tu, 1/1, 12/25
Free Day: Su 10-12   *Adm:*   *Adult:* $3.00   *Children:* $2.00, Free under 12   *Students:* $2.00   *Seniors:* $2.00
  P: lots nearby   *Group Tours:* 215-898-7108   *Drop-In Tours:* Th, 5:15
Historic Building: Contemporary Building designed by Adele Naude Santos

The museum, founded in 1963, is one of the premier institutions solely dedicated to the art of our time.

La Salle University Art Museum
Affiliated Institution: LaSalle University
20th and Olney Ave, Philadelphia, PA   19141

215-951-1221
Open: 11-4 Tu-Fr, 2-4 Su, Sep-May   *Closed:* Acad!
  P: Campus lot
Permanent Collection: Eur: ptgs, sculp, gr 15-20; Am: ptgs

Many of the major themes and styles of Western art since the Middle ages are documented in the comprehensive collection of paintings, prints, drawings, and sculpture at this museum.

Philadelphia Museum of Art
26th Street & Benjamin Franklin Parkway, Philadelphia, PA   19130

215-763-8100   www.philamuseum.org
Open: 10-5 Tu-Su, 10-8:45 We   *Closed:* Leg/Hol!
Free Day: Su, 10-1; after 1, pay what you wish   *Adm:*   *Adult:* $10.00   *Children:* Free 12 and under
Students: $7.00
  P: Free   *Museum Shop*   ¶: Tu-Sa 11:30-2:30, We 5-7:30, Su 11-3:30
Group Tours   Drop-In Tours: on the hour 10-3   *Historic Building   Sculpture Garden*
Permanent Collection: Eur: ptgs 19-20; Cont; Dec/Art; Gr; Am: ptgs, sculp 17-20

With more than 400,000 works in the permanent collection the Philadelphia Art Museum is the 3rd largest art museum in the country. Housed within its more than 200 galleries are a myriad of artistic treasures from many continents and cultures.   ⟨ Van Gogh's "Sunflowers"; A Ceremonial Japanese Teahouse; Medieval & Early Renaissance Galleries (25 in all) which include a Romanesque cloister, a Gothic chapel, and a world-class collection of early Italian & Northern paintings.

ON EXHIBIT 2002

10/07/2001 to 01/06/2002   *Thomas Eakins*
A major retrospective of his work including 60 major paintings, watercolors, drawings, and many photographs   *Will Travel   Book*

10/27/2001 to 01/20/2002   *Dox Thrash: An African American Master Printmaker Rediscovered*
A first major retrospective of Thrash's work beginning in 1930s   *Catalog   Will Travel*

12/08/2001 to April 2002   *Italian Renaissance Ceramics, 1500–1560: The Howard and Janet Stein Collection*
This Maiolica (tin glazed earthenware) is the finest in the US. It is noted for its shapes, ornamentation, and colors which survive with undiminished brilliance.   *Catalog   Will Travel*

03/24/2002 to 07/07/2002   *Barnett Newman*
A pioneer abstract and influential painter of the 20th century. The exhibition will show works which have not been shown together in over 30 years. He was at the center of the New York Scene and a friend of Gottlieb, Rothko, Still, and Pollock.

Rodin Museum
Benjamin Franklin Parkway at 22nd Street, Philadelphia, PA   19130

215-763-8100   www.rodinmuseum.org
Open: 10-5 Tu-Su   *Closed:* Mo, Leg/Hol!
Sugg/Contr.: Yes
&   P: Free on-street   *Museum Shop   Group Tours   Drop-In Tours   Historic Building Sculpture Garden   Theater*
Permanent Collection: Rodin: sculp, drgs

The largest collection of Rodin's sculptures and drawings outside of Paris is located in a charming and intimate building designed by architect Paul Cret.   ❨ "The Thinker," by Rodin

Rosenbach Museum & Library
2010 DeLancey Place, Philadelphia, PA   19103

215-732-1600   www.rosenbach.org
Open: 11-4 Tu-Su   *Closed:* Mo, Leg/Hol!
Free Day: Bloomsday, June 16th   *Adm:*   *Adult:* $5.00 incl guide   *Children:* $3.00   *Students:* $3.00   *Seniors:* $3.00
Museum Shop   Group Tours   Drop-In Tours   Historic Building   Theater
Permanent Collection: Brit & Am: ptgs; Mini Scale Dec/Arts; Book Illustrations; Rare books and Manuscripts

In the warm and intimate setting of a 19th-century townhouse, the Rosenbach Museum & Library retains an atmosphere of an age when great collectors lived among their treasures. It is the only collection of its kind open to the public in Philadelphia.   ❨ Maurice Sendak drawings

Rosenwald-Wolf Gallery, The University of the Arts
Broad and Pine Streets, Philadelphia, PA   19102

215-717-6480   www.uarts.edu
Open: 10-5 Mo, Tu & Th, Fr, 10-8 We, 12-5 Sa, Su (10-5 weekdays Jun & Jul)   *Closed:* Acad!
&   P: Pay garages and metered parking nearby   *Group Tours:* 215-717-6480
Permanent Collection: non-collecting institution

This is the only university in the nation devoted exclusively to education and professional training in the visual and performing arts. The gallery presents temporary exhibitions of contemporary art.

University of Pennsylvania Museum of Archaeology and Anthropology
Affiliated Institution: University of Pennsylvania
33rd and Spruce Streets, Philadelphia, PA   19104

215-898-4000   www.upenn.edu/museum
Open: 10-4:30 Tu-Sa, 1-5 Su, closed Su Mem day-Lab day   *Closed:* Leg/Hol
Adm: *Adult:* $5.00   *Children:* Free under 6   *Students:* $2.50   *Seniors:* $2.50
&   P   *Museum Shop*   ❙❙   *Group Tours:* 215-898-4015   *Drop-In Tours:* 1:30 Sa, Su (mid Sep-mid May)!
Sculpture Garden   Theater
Permanent Collection: Greco/Roman; Af; An/Egt; As; Mesopotmia; Mesoamerican; Polynesian; Americas

Dedicated to the understanding of the history and cultural heritage of humankind, the museum's galleries include objects from China, Ancient Egypt, Mesoamerica, South America, North America (Plains Indians), Polynesia, Africa, and the Greco-Roman world. ℭ Monumental architectural pieces from the Palace of Merenptah

ON EXHIBIT 2002

07/24/2001 to 03/24/2002   *Six Highlight Objects from 'Treasures from the Royal Tomb of Ur'*
More than 200 finely crafted objects in stone, metal, wood, characterize this exhibition from the excavation at Ur, a 3rd millenium Sumerian city in Mesopotamia.   *Catalog   Will Travel*

10/20/2001 to July 2002   *Modern Mongolia: Reclaiming Genghis Khan*
Our view of Genghis Khan is challenged in this exhibition. Mongolian life from the beginning of the 20th century to today discovering his lasting legacy.   *Book*

Woodmere Art Museum
9201 Germantown Ave, Philadelphia, PA   19118

215-247-0476   www.woodmereartmuseum.org
Open: 10-5 Tu-Sa, 1-5 Su   *Closed:* Mo, 1/1, Easter, 7/4, Thgv, 12/25
Adm: Adult: $5.00   *Children:* Free under 12   *Students:* $3.00   *Seniors:* $3.00
&   P: Free   *Museum Shop   Group Tours:* 215-247-0948   *Theater*
Permanent Collection: Am: ptgs 19, 20, prints, gr, drgs; Eur (not always on view); Art & Artists from the Philadelphia region

The Woodmere Art Museum, located in a mid 1850s Victorian eclectic house, includes a large rotunda gallery. The collection of local, Philadelphia area, and Pennsylvania Impressionist art is outstanding.   ℭ Benjamin West's "The Death of Sir Phillip Sydney"

ON EXHIBIT 2002

12/02/2001 to 01/13/2002   *Art is Everywhere: Twenty Years of 'Art Matters'*
A celebration of the arts in the Greater Philadelphia region. Museums, galleries, organizations, and universities have chosen works which represent their place in the Philadelphia art world.

01/01/2002 to 07/07/2002   *Central High School*
Artists who are graduates of the school include Glackens, Richards Eakins, Knight, Beale, Richards, Kahn, Mednick, and Carles. Works from private and public collections will be shown.

01/27/2002 to 03/31/2002   *62nd Annual Juried Exhibition*
Multimedia in style and variety, hundreds of artists submit work

07/22/2002 to 09/02/2002   *62nd Members Exhibition*
Members submit work in all media

PITTSBURGH

Andy Warhol Museum
117 Sandusky Street, Pittsburgh, PA   15212-5890

412-237-8300   www.warhol.org and www.warholstore.com
Open: 10-5 We-Su; until 10pm Fr
Adm: Adult: $7.00   *Children:* $4.00   *Students:* $4.00   *Seniors:* $6.00
&: Ramp, elevators, restrooms   P: Museum lot, Sandusky St. $3.00   *Museum Shop*   ¶: Cafe
Group Tours: 412-237-8347
Historic Building: Former Vokwein building renovated by Richard Gluckman Architects   *Theater*
Permanent Collection: Andy Warhol

The most comprehensive single-artist museum in the world, this 7-story museum with over 40,000 square feet of exhibition space permanently highlights artworks spanning every aspect of Warhol's career. A unique feature of this museum is a photo booth where visitors can take cheap multiple pictures of themselves in keeping with the Warhol tradition.   ℭ Rain Machine, a "daisy waterfall" measuring 132' by 240'; "Last Supper" paintings; 10' tall "Big Sculls" series

Carnegie Museum Of Art
4400 Forbes Ave, Pittsburgh, PA   15213

412-622-3131   www.clpgh.org
Open: 10-5 Tu-Sa, 1-5 Su, 10-5 Mo, 10-9 Fr July/Aug only   *Closed:* Leg/Hol!
Adm: Adult: $6.00   *Children:* $4.00   *Students:* $4.00   *Seniors:* $5.00
&   P: Pay garage   *Museum Shop*   ¶: cafe open weekdays; coffee bar daily
Group Tours: 412-622-3289   *Drop-In Tours:* 1:30 Tu-Sa, 3 Su   *Historic Building*
Sculpture Garden   Theater
Permanent Collection: Fr/Impr: ptgs; Post/Impr: ptgs; Am: ptgs 19,20; Ab/Impr; Video Art

The original 1895 Carnegie Institute, created in the spirit of opulence by architects Longfellow, Alden and Harlowe, was designed to house a library with art galleries, the museum itself, and a concert hall. A stunning light filled modern addition offers a spare purity that enhances the enjoyment of the art on the walls. ☾ Claude Monet's "Nympheas" (Water Lilies)

Hunt Institute for Botanical Documentation
Affiliated Institution: Carnegie Mellon University
Pittsburgh, PA   15213-3890

412-268-2440   http://huntbot.andrew.cmu.edu/
Open: 9-12 & 1-5 Mo-Fr; 1-4 Su during exhibition   *Closed:* Leg/Hol!,12/24-1/1
&   P: Pay parking nearby   *Museum Shop   Group Tours*
Permanent Collection: Botaical w/Col 15-20; Drgs; Gr

Thirty thousand botanical watercolors, drawings, and prints from the Renaissance onward represented in this collection.

ON EXHIBIT 2002

10/28/2001 to 02/28/2002   *10th International Exhibition of Botanical Art & Illustration*

03/15/2002 to Spring 2002   *Linnaeus*
Books, artworks and portraits from the Museum's collections which will explain the importance of Linneaus classification scheme

09/15/2002 to Fall 2002   *Anne Ophelia Todd Dowden*
A celebration of the artist's 95th birthday. She is known as America's leading botanical artist.

Mattress Factory Ltd
500 Sampsonia Way, satellite bldg at 1414 Monterey, Pittsburgh, PA   15212

412-231-3169   www.mattress.org
Open: 10-5 Tu-Sa, 1-5 Su   *Closed:* 1/1, Easter, Leg/Hol; Aug
Free Day: ThSugg/Contr.: Yes   *Adm: Adult:* $6.00   *Children:* under 12 Free   *Students:* $4.00
Seniors: $4.00
&   P   *Museum Shop   Group Tours   Historic Building   Sculpture Garden*
Permanent Collection: Site-specific art installations completed in residency

A museum of contemporary art that commissions, collects, and exhibits site-specific art installations. Founded in 1977 in a six-story warehouse in the historic Mexican War Streets of Pittsburgh's North Side. ☾ Yayoi Kusama, "Repetitive Vision" 1997 and James Turrell: permanent installations

ON EXHIBIT 2002

06/02/2002 to 04/30/2003   *Into the Light: James Turrell*
New site-specific works will be the center of activities celebrating the Museum's 25th anniversary   *Catalog*

The Frick Art and Historical Center
7227 Reynolds Street, Pittsburgh, PA   15208

412-371-0600
Open: 10-6 Tu-Sa, 12-6 Su   *Closed:* Leg/Hol!
& P: Free   *Museum Shop*   ¶: Cafe: 11-2 Tu-Sa : Tea 3-5 Su
Group Tours: ext. 158   *Drop-In Tours:* We, Sa, Su 2pm   *Theater*
Permanent Collection: Early It/Ren: ptgs; Fr & Fl: 17; Brit: ptgs; Dec/Art

The Frick Art Museum features a permanent collection of European paintings, sculptures, and decorative objects and temporary exhibitions from around the world. Clayton House: Admission, Adults $6.00, Seniors $5.00, Students $4.00; Car and Carriage Museum: Adults $4.00, Seniors $3.00, Students $2.00; Combination admission: Adults $7.00, Seniors $6.00, Students $5.00

ON EXHIBIT 2002

01/05/2002 to 03/03/2002   *Masterworks from the Albertina*
Drawings and prints from Vienna, one of the world's most important and oldest collections of Old Masters.   *Catalog   Will Travel*

04/05/2002 to 06/02/2002   *Rubens, Jordaens, Van Dyke and Their Circle: Flemish Master Drawings from the Museum Boijmans Van Bueningen*
Focusing on the 3 17th-century masters, it will also feature artists who worked in their shadows and the preparatory drawings for paintings and prints.   *Catalog   Will Travel*

06/28/2002 to 09/22/2002   *Artist-in-Residence: Christian Milovanoff*
A photographer fascinated with the invention of place   *Catalog*

10/19/2002 to 01/02/2003   *Nineteenth- and Twentieth-Century French Drawings from the Danish National Gallery*
Drawings from Barbizon School to Abstraction including Ingres, Millet, Rousseau, Moreau, Toulouse Lautrec, Manet, Degas, Pissarro, Gauguin, and Picasso   *Catalog   Will Travel*

READING

Freedman Gallery
Affiliated Institution: Albright College
Center for the Arts, 13th and Bern Streets, Reading, PA   19604

610-921-7715   www.albright.edu
Open: 12-8 Tu; 12-6 We-Fr, 12-4 Sa, Su   *Closed:* Leg/Hol!, Acad!
& P   *Group Tours:* 610-921-7541   *Sculpture Garden*
Permanent Collection: Cont: gr, ptgs

An exhibition and educational program of the latest issues and provocative work by today's leading artists and emerging figures   ¶ Mary Miss Sculpture creates an outdoor plaza which is part of the building

ON EXHIBIT 2002

09/15/2002 to Winter 2002   *Mexico Illuminado (Lluminado)*
Mexican contemporary art as a consortium for five institutions: The Freedman Gallery; The Freyberger Gallery; The Sharadin Gallery; The Reading Public Library, and The Hispanic Center. The Freedman will focus on painting and sculpture. The purpose of the exhibitions is to promote understanding of other cultures and community pride.   *Catalog Will Travel   Bilingual*

SCRANTON

Everhart Museum
1901 Mulberry Street, Nay Aug Park, Scranton, PA   18510

570-346-7186   www.everhart-museum.org
Open: 12-5 We-Su; Th until 8pm   *Closed:* Thgv, 12/25
Sugg/Contr.: Yes   *Adm:*   *Adult:* $5.00   *Children:* $2.00, Free under 6   *Students:* $3.00   *Seniors:* $3.00
  P   *Museum Shop   Group Tours*
Permanent Collection: Am: early 19, 20; Am: folk, gr; Af; Glass; Nat/Hist

This art, science, and natural history museum is the only wide-ranging museum of its type in Northeastern Pennsylvania.

UNIVERSITY PARK

Palmer Museum of Art
Affiliated Institution: The Pennsylvania State University
Curtin Road, University Park, PA   16802-2507

814-865-7672   www.psu.edu/dept/palmermuseum
Open: 10-4:30 Tu-Sa, 12-4 Su   *Closed:* Mo, Leg/Hol!, 12/25-1/1
Vol/Contr.: Yes
  P: Limited meter, nearby pay   *Museum Shop*   ¶: Java Market next door
Group Tours   Drop-In Tours   Sculpture Garden
Permanent Collection: Am; Eur; As; S/Am: ptgs, sculp, works on paper, ceramics

A dramatic and exciting facility for this collection of 35 centuries of artworks.   ℂ The building by Charles Moore, a fine example of post-modern architecture

ON EXHIBIT 2002

11/27/2001 to 02/10/2002   *The Geldzahler Portfolio*
A champion of young artists at the Metropolitan Museum, Visual Arts at National Endowmment and Cultural Affairs, New York City. Worked in his honor by Bourgeois, Hockney, Johns, Kelly, Lichtenstein, Salle, and Stella, also included is Warhol's 1964 video "Henry Geldzahler"

02/26/2002 to 06/02/2002   *John Paul Caponigro*
Works which unite drawing, painting, calligraphy, and photography

03/12/2002 to 06/09/2002   *Carrie Mae Weems: Jefferson Suite*
A multimedia installation by an artist thinking about DNA. Large scale digitally produced photographs on semi-transparent fabric hung ceiling to floor

06/02/2002 to August 2002   *Tools as Art: The Hechinger Collection*
Elegant and witty sculptures of tools, constructions of found objects and building materials, paintings, prints, and photographs of tools

VALLEY FORGE

Wharton Esherick Museum
Horseshoe Trail (Mail Address Box 595), Paoli, PA 19301, Valley Forge, PA   19301

610-644-5822
Open: 10-4 Mo-Fr, 10-5 Sa, 1-5 Su (Mar-Dec)   *Closed:* Leg/Hol!
Adm: *Adult:* $9.00   *Children:* $4.00 under 12   *Seniors:* $9.00
  P   *Museum Shop   Group Tours   Drop-In Tours:* Hourly, (reservations required)   *Historic Building Theater*
Permanent Collection: Wood Sculp; Furniture; Woodcuts; Ptgs

Over 200 works in all media, produced between 1920–1970 which display the progression of Esherick's work are housed in his historic studio and residence.   ℂ Oak spiral stairs

Sordoni Art Gallery

Affiliated Institution: Wilkes University
150 S. River Street, Wilkes-Barre, PA   18766-0001

570-408-4325
Open: 12-4:30 daily   *Closed:* Leg/Hol!
& P
Permanent Collection: Am: ptgs 19,20; Work on Paper

Located on the grounds of Wilkes University, in the historic district of downtown Wilkes-Barre, this facility is best known for mounting both historical and contemporary exhibitions.

RHODE ISLAND

KINGSTON

Fine Arts Center Galleries, University of Rhode Island

105 Upper College Road, Suite 1, Kingston, RI   02881-0820

401-874-2775 or 2627   www.uri.edu/artsci/art/gallery
Open: Main Gallery 12-4 & 7:30-9:30 Tu-Fr, 1-4 Sa, Su, Phot Gallery 12-4 Tu-Fr, 1-4 Sa, Su
Closed: Leg/Hol!; Acad!
& P   *Group Tours   Drop-In Tours:* !
Permanent Collection: non-collecting institution

A university affiliated "kunsthalle" distinguished for the activity of their programming (20–25 exhibitions annually) and in generating that programming internally. Contemporary exhibitions in all media are shown as well as film and video showings. The Corridor Gallery is open from 9-9 daily.

NEWPORT

Newport Art Museum

76 Bellevue Avenue, Newport, RI   02840

401-848-8200   newportartmuseum.com
Open: Winter:10-4 Mo-Sa, 12-4 Su (Mem Day-Col Day Mo-Sa, 12-5)   *Closed:* Thgv, 12/25, 1/1, 7/4
Free Day: Sa 10-12   *Adm: Adult:* $6.00   *Children:* Free under 5   *Students:* $4.00   *Seniors:* $5.00
& P   *Museum Shop   Group Tours:* by appt 401-848-2787   *Drop-In Tours:* Sa, Su afternoon !
Historic Building
Permanent Collection: Am: Hist; Reg

Historic J. N. A. Griswold House and Cushing Gallery museum is located was designed by Richard Morris Hunt in 1864.   ℂ Howard Gardner Cushing's portraits of his wife and family

Redwood Library and Athenaeum

50 Bellevue Avenue, Newport, RI   02840

401-847-0292   www.redwood1747.org
Open: 9:30-5:30 Mo, Fr, Sa, Tu, Th, 9:30-8, 1-5 Su   *Closed:* Leg/Hol!
Sugg/Contr.: $3 per person
&: all except restroom   P   *Group Tours   Drop-In Tours:* 10:30 Mo-Fr   *Historic Building*
Permanent Collection: Am: gr, drgs, phot, portraits, furniture, dec/art 18,19

Established in 1747, this facility serves as the oldest circulating library in the country. Designed by Peter Harrison, considered America's first architect, it is the most significant surviving public building from the Colonial period.   ℂ Paintings by Gilbert Stuart and Charles Bird King

David Winton Bell Gallery
Affiliated Institution: Brown University
List Art Center, 64 College Street, Providence, RI   02912

401-863-2932   www.brown.edu/facilities/david-winton-bell-gallery
Open: 11-4 Mo-Fr, 1-4 Sa-Su   *Closed:* 1/1, Thgv, 12/25
& P: On-street
Permanent Collection: Gr & Phot 20; Work on Paper 16-20; Cont: ptgs

Located in the List Art Center, an imposing modern structure designed by Philip Johnson, the Gallery presents exhibitions which focus on the arts and issues of our time.

ON EXHIBIT 2002

01/26/2002 to 03/10/2002   *Mark Dion: The New England Digs*

Museum of Art
Affiliated Institution: Rhode Island School of Design
224 Benefit Street, Providence, RI   02903

401-454-6500   www.risd.edu/museum.cfy
Open: 10-5 Tu-Su; 10-9 third Th monthly (free 5-9)   *Closed:* Leg/Hol!
Free Day: 5-9 3rd Th monthly; last Sa of month   *Adm:*   *Adult:* $5.00   *Children:* $1.00 (5-18)
Students: $2.00   *Seniors:* $4.00
& P: Nearby pay, 1/2 price with museum adm   *Museum Shop*
Group Tours: 401-454-6534   *Drop-In Tours   Sculpture Garden   Theater*
Permanent Collection: Am & Eur: ptgs, dec/art; Jap: gr, cer; Lat/Am

The museum's outstanding collections are housed on three levels: in a Georgian style building completed in 1926; in Pendleton House, completed in 1906; and in The Daphne Farago Wing, a center dedicated to the display and interpretation of contemporary art in all media.   ℂ Manet "Portrait of Berthe Morisot"

ON EXHIBIT 2002

02/01/2001 to ongoing   *Roman Sculpture from the Permanent Collection*
A reassessment of the small exceptional holdings in the light of new findings.

10/05/2001 to 01/06/2002   *Adrian Piper: Food for the Spirit*
Featured is the 1971 series of self portrait photographs

10/12/2001 to February 2002   *In the High Himalayas: Textiles from the Kingdom of Bhutan*
Beautiful handmade textiles from southeast Asia

11/09/2001 to 01/20/2002   *Ann Hamilton: Malediction and Other Work*
A large scale installation with a voice reciting Walt Whitman's poetry

11/09/2001 to 01/27/2002   *Jonathan Bonner: Front Pockets*
Eleven pairs of objects all made to fit in the two front trouser pockets. He plays with the traditional relationship of function to design

11/15/2001 to January 2002   *Art Con Text: David McGee*
McGee looks for ways to bring images of the Museum into library branches and images of communities into the Museum

11/16/2001 to 01/27/2002   *William Congdon*
He uses densely pigmented canvases in the language of Abstract Expressionism doing piazzas, skyscrapers, and Venetian palaces, as well as landscapes.

11/16/2001 to 02/17/2002   *New York School Painting (working title)*
Changes in the style of painting after WWII provides important reference for Congdon's work

12/07/2001 to 03/03/2002   *Fan Prints (working title)*
An outstanding collection of fan prints (uchiwa-e) from 19th century Japan from the Abby Aldrich Rockefeller Museum

01/01/2002 to 04/14/2002   *Richard Neutra's Windshield House*
Architectural models, drawings, models, and photographs of the house designed by Neutra on Fishers Island in 1938

01/02/2002 to 11/31/2002   *Community Voices: A Celebration of RISD's 125th Anniversary*
For the year the Museum has invited artists, students, designers, etc., to share reminiscences of the Museum.

01/11/2002 to 04/07/2002   *Roy DeCarava*
Celebrating the 100th birthday of Langston Hughes, works used in a book with text by Hughes will be shown.

02/01/2002 to April 2002   *Art Con Text: Edgar Heap of Birds*
The collaboration of the artist with the Narragansett Tribe. Pulse of forms in action

02/28/2002 to 08/18/2002   *Secret Games: Wendy Ewald, Collaborative Work with Children 1969–1999*
Ewald used the imagination of children to challenge the traditional notions of documentary photography. She encourages her subjects to use cameras and create their own portraits.
Catalog   Will Travel

02/28/2002 to October 2002   *Art Con Text: Wendy Ewald*

March-June; June-October; to October-December 2002   *A Tribute to Miss Lucy: Asian Textiles from the Permanent Collection; I, II, III*
The eldest daughter of State Senator Nelson Aldrich collected Japanese prints, Asian textiles, and European porcelains and gave them to the Museum.

03/08/2002 to 06/02/2002   *Meiji and Taisho-Period Prints*

06/07/2002 to Early September 2002   *Nature Studies in Japanese Prints*

07/01/2002 to September 2002   *Contemporary British Prints*
One of the strengths of the Museum is the 18th and 19th century watercolor collection. Recent acquisitions include Hamilton, Long, Rego, and others.

09/20/2002 to 11/17/2002   *Print, Power, and Persuasion: Graphic Design in Germany, 1890–1945*
Posters, books, menus, brochures, drawings, prints, and other printed materials from the turn of the century

Rhode Island Black Heritage Society
202 Washington Street, Providence, RI   02903

401-751-3490
Open: 10-5 Mo-Fr, 10-2 Sa & by appt   *Closed:* Leg/Hol!
&   P: on street and nearby pay garages   *Museum Shop*
Permanent Collection: Phot; Af: historical collection

The Society collects, documents, and preserves the history of African-Americans in the state of Rhode Island with an archival collection which includes photos, rare books, and records dating back to the 18th century. Ongoing: Permanent Exhibition—Creative Survival   ☾ Polychrome relief wood carvings by Elizabeth N. Prophet

SOUTH CAROLINA

CHARLESTON

City Hall Council Chamber Gallery
Broad & Meeting Streets, Charleston, SC   29401

803-724-3799
Open: 9-5 Mo-Fr, closed 12-1   *Closed:* Leg/Hol!
Vol/Contr.: Yes
&   *Group Tours   Drop-In Tours:* 9-5 (closed 12-1)   *Historic Building*
Permanent Collection: Am: ptgs 18,19

What is today Charleston's City Hall was erected in 1801 in Adamsesque style to be the Charleston branch of the First Bank of the United States. ❰ "George Washington," by John Trumbull is unlike any other and is considered one of the best portraits ever done of him.

Gibbes Museum of Art
135 Meeting Street, Charleston, SC   29401

843-722-2706   www.gibbes.com
Open: 10-5 Tu-Sa, 1-5 Su   *Closed:* Mo, Leg/Hol!
Adm: Adult: $7.00   *Children:* $4.00   *Students:* $6.00   *Seniors:* $6.00
&: Right side of museum   P: Municipal on Queen Street and on Cumberland   *Museum Shop*
Group Tours: ext. 25   *Drop-In Tours:* Tu & Sa 2:30pm, and by appt   *Historic Building:* Y, built in 1905
Sculpture Garden
Permanent Collection: Am: reg portraits, miniature portraits; Jap: gr; miniature rooms; Eur Sc

Charleston's only fine arts museum offers a nationally significant collection of American art from the 1700 to the present, a miniature portrait collection (the oldest and finest in the country), Japanese prints, and a variety of traveling exhibitions. ❰ "John Moultie and Family" ca 1782 by John, Francis Rigaud

ON EXHIBIT 2002

01/03/2002 to 04/07/2002   *Masks and Theater*

01/03/2002 to 04/14/2002   *Walter O. Evans Collection of African American Art*
In a variety of media, a comprehensive survey of African American artists in the last 150 years

02/01/2002 to 10/20/2002   *African-American Images in Charleston*
From the collection of Reba and Dave Williams

04/12/2002 to 08/04/2002   *Thomas Moran Prints of the American West—The Rick Throckmorton Collection*

05/11/2002 to 08/04/2002   *Ansel Adams, A Legacy: Masterworks From the Friends of Photography Collection*
A survey of Adams wide ranging career including portraits, close-ups, and architectural views

05/17/2002 to 12/31/2002   *Ballard Print Collection*
European prints from the permanent collection including Piranesi, Carracci, and Dürer

05/31/2002 to October 2002   *Landscapes from the Gibbes Museum of Art Japanese Print Collection*

06/28/2002 to 09/29/2002   *Charleston in My Time: The Paintings of West Fraser*
A plein air painter with a response to the natural landscape   *Will Travel*

09/15/2002 to 11/17/2002   *A Portrait of the People*
Three hundred years of Jewish culture in paintings, miniatures, photographs, and unique cultural objects

11/03/2002 to 02/17/2003   *Twentieth Century in Review*
From impressionism to modernism, regionalism, and post-modernism, American art will be seen through Harrison, Biddle, Henri, Hassam, Halsey, Bearden, Lawrence, Johns, Fraser, and Green to name a few

COLUMBIA

Columbia Museum of Art
Main at Hampton, Columbia, SC   29202

803-799-2810   www.columbiamuseum.org
Open: 10-5 Tu-Sa, 1-5 Su   *Closed:* 1/1, Thgv, 12/24 open 1/2 day, 12/25
Free Day: 1st Sa each month   *Adm:*   *Adult:* $5.00   *Children:* Free under 6   *Students:* $2.00   *Seniors:* $4.00
& P   *Museum Shop*
Group Tours: 803-343-2208   *Drop-In Tours:* regular public tours, Sa 1; Th 12:15, Fr 1 & 2, Su 1:30
Historic Building
Permanent Collection: Kress Coll of Med, Baroque & Ren; As; Reg

The museum emphasizes a broad spectrum of European and American fine arts dating from the 14th c to the present. It also has one of the Southeast's most important collections of Italian Renaissance and Baroque paintings, sculpture, and decorative art by the Old Masters.

ON EXHIBIT 2002

01/19/2002 to 03/10/2002   *Testimony: African-American Vernacular Art of the South*
Self-taught black artists rarely seen by the public. Works range from large scale by known masters like Thornton Dial, Sr, to assemblages of metal, wood, and fiber.   *Catalog   Will Travel*

FLORENCE

Florence Museum of Art, Science & History
558 Spruce Street, Florence, SC   29501

843-662-3351
Open: 10-5 Tu-Sa, 2-5 Su   *Closed:* Mo, Leg/Hol
&: Limited, not all areas accessible   P   *Museum Shop   Group Tours   Drop-In Tours   Historic Building*
Permanent Collection: Am/Reg: ptgs; SW Nat/Am; pottery; Cer

Founded to promote the arts and sciences, this museum, located in a 1939 art deco style building originally constructed as a private home, is surrounded by the grounds of Timrod Park.   ("Francis Marion Crossing to Pee Dee," by Edward Arnold

ON EXHIBIT 2002

Spring 2002   *Special Exhibit of Computer Art*

GREENVILLE

Bob Jones University Museum & Gallery, Inc
Jones University, Greenville, SC   29614

864-242-1050   www.bju.edu/artgallery/
Open: 2-5 Tu-Su   *Closed:* 1/1, 7/4, 12/20 thru 12/25, Commencement Day (early May)
Free Day: Su   *Adm:*   *Adult:* $5.00   *Children:* Free 6-12, under 6 not admitted   *Students:* $3.00
Seniors: $4.00
& P: Nearby   *Museum Shop   Group Tours:* ext 1053   *Drop-In Tours:* 1
Permanent Collection: Eur: ptgs including Rembrandt, Tintoretto, Titian, Veronese, Sebastiano del Piombo

One of the finest collections of religious art in America.

ON EXHIBIT 2002

12/01/2001 to 01/02/2002   *A Christmas Story in Art: Each Work Will Illustrate Some Aspect of the Events Surrounding the Birth of Christ*

Greenville County Museum of Art
420 College Street, Greenville, SC   29601

864-271-7570   www.greenvillemuseum.org
Open: 10-5 Tu-Sa, 1-5 Su   *Closed:* Mo, Leg/Hol!
Vol/Contr.: Yes
&   P   *Museum Shop   Group Tours:* ext.17
Permanent Collection: Am: ptgs, sculp, gr; Reg

The Southern Collection is nationally recognized as one of the countries best regional collections. It provides a survey of American art history from 1726 to the present through works of art that relate to the South. The Museum recently acquired 24 watercolors by Andrew Wyeth which the artist described as one of the best collections of his watercolors in any public museum in this country. They present under-represented artists such as women and minorities.

ON EXHIBIT 2002

10/03/2001 to 01/06/2002   *Father and Son: Jerry and Brian Pinkney*
Illustrators who explore African American folklore, biographies, and legend

10/06/2001 to 01/06/2002   *Mary Cassatt: Color Prints from the Collection of St. John's Museum of Art*

11/07/2001 to 01/06/2002   *Jack Leigh: The Land I'm Bound To*
Precise photographs of the spirit of the southeastern coast   *Will Travel*

01/23/2002 to Ongoing   *Hubert Shuptrine*
Realist watercolor painter

01/23/2002 to 03/24/2002   *Upstate Artists Invitational*
Twenty-five Greenville artists in a great range of disciplines

04/17/2002 to 06/09/2002   *Charleston in My Time: The Paintings of West Fraser*
A landscape painter who has captured the soul and vision of Charleston   *Booklet*

07/01/2002 to September 2002   *An American Palette: Work from the Collection of John and Delores Beck*
Works by important American artists including Bierstadt, Inness, Benton, Burchfield, Henri, Davis, Weber, and Sheeler

MURRELLS INLET

Brookgreen Gardens
1931 Brookgreen Gardens Drive, Murrells Inlet, SC   29576

843-235-6000 or 800-849-1931   www.brookgreen.org
Open: 9:30-4:45 daily, call for summer hours   *Closed:* 12/25
Adm: Adult: $8.50   *Children:* $4.00 5-12   *Students:* $8.50   *Seniors:* $8.50
&   P   *Museum Shop   ¶:* Terrace Cafe open year round
Group Tours: 800-849-1931, ext 6016   *Drop-In Tours:* call for group tours
Historic Building   Sculpture Garden

The first public sculpture garden created in America is located on the grounds of a 200-year-old rice plantation. It is the largest permanent outdoor collection of American Figurative Sculpture in the world with 542 works by 240 American sculptors on permanent display.   ℭ "Fountain of the Muses," by Carl Milles

Spartanburg County Museum of Art
385 South Spring Street, Spartanburg, SC   29306

864-582-7616   www.spartanarts.org
Open: 9-5 Mo-Fr, 10-2 Sa, 2-5 Su   *Closed:* Leg/Hol!, Easter, 12/24
& P: Adjacent to the building   *Museum Shop   Group Tours:* 864-583-2776   *Drop-In Tours*
Historic Building: 1930's Elementary School Building   *Theater*
Permanent Collection: Am/Reg: ptgs, gr, dec/art

A multi-cultural Arts Center that presents 20 exhibits of regional art each year.   ❆ "Girl With
The Red Hair," by Robert Henri

SOUTH DAKOTA

South Dakota Art Museum
Medary Ave at Harvey Dunn Street, Brookings, SD   57007-0899

605-688-5423   http://sdartmuseum.sdstate.edu
Open: 8-5 Mo-Fr, 10-5 Sa, 1-5 Su, Holidays   *Closed:* 1/1, Thgv, 12/25
Vol/Contr.: Yes
&: Elevator service to all 3 levels from west entrance   P   *Museum Shop*
Group Tours: 605-688-5423   *Drop-In Tours:* 605-688-5423   *Sculpture Garden*
Permanent Collection: Harvey Dunn: ptgs; Oscar Howe: ptgs; Nat/Am; Reg 19, 20, marghab Linens

Many of the state's art treasures including the paintings by Harvey Dunn of pioneer life on the
prairie, a complete set of Marghab embroidery from Madeira, outstanding paintings by regional
artist Oscar Howe, and masterpieces from Sioux tribes are displayed in the 6 galleries of this
museum established in 1970.

Middle Border Museum of American Indian and Pioneer Life
1311 S. Duff St., PO Box 1071, Mitchell, SD   57301

605-996-2122
Open: 8-6 Mo-Sa & 10-6 Su (Jun-Aug), 9-5 Mo-Fr & 1-5 Sa, Su (May-Sep), by appt (Oct-Apr)
Closed: 1/1, Thgv, 12/25
Adm: *Adult:* $3.00   *Children:* Free under 12   *Students:* $.50   *Seniors:* $2.00
&: Partially, the art gallery is not wheelchair accessible (new building will be accessible)   P
Museum Shop   Group Tours   Historic Building   Sculpture Garden
Permanent Collection: Am: ptgs 19, 20; Nat/Am

The Middle Border Museum depicts regional history from 1600-1939: An eclectic art collection
in the Case Art Gallery, the oldest regional art gallery, including works by Harvey Dunn, James
Earle Fraser, Gutzon Borglum, Oscar Howe, Charles Hargens, Anna Hyatt Huntington, and
many others; Charles Hargens Gallery; Oscar Howe Art Gallery; and changing exhibitions
Gallery.   ❆ Fraser's "End of the Trail" and Lewis and Clark Statues, Harvey Dunn's "Dakota
Woman"

Oscar Howe Art Center
119 W. Third, Mitchell, SD   57301

605-996-4111
Open: 9-5 Mo-Sa   *Closed:* Su, Leg/Hol!
Vol/Contr.: Yes   *Adm:*   *Adult:* $2.50   *Children:* $1.00   *Seniors:* $2.00
P   *Museum Shop   Group Tours:* 605-996-4111   *Drop-In Tours:* Upon request   *Historic Building*
Permanent Collection: Oscar Howe: ptgs, gr

Housed in a beautifully restored 1902 Carnegie Library, the Oscar Howe Art Center displays both a collection of work by Yanktonai Sioux artist Oscar Howe and rotating exhibits of work by regional artists. ❨ "Sun and Rain Clouds Over Hills," dome mural painted by Oscar Howe in 1940 as a WPA project (Works Progress Administration)

PINE RIDGE

Heritage Center Inc
Affiliated Institution: Red Cloud Indian School
Pine Ridge, SD   57770

605-867-5491   www.basic.net/rcheritaqe
Open: 9-5 Mo-Fr   *Closed:* Sa, Su, Easter, Thgv, 12/25
  P   *Museum Shop   Group Tours   Historic Building   Theater*
Permanent Collection: Cont Nat/Am; Gr; NW Coast; Eskimo: 19, 20

The Center is located on the Red Cloud Indian school campus in an historic 1888 building built by the Sioux and operated by them with the Franciscan and Jesuit sisters. The Holy Rosary Mission church built in 1998 has stained glass windows designed by the students.

RAPID CITY

Dahl Arts Center
713 Seventh Street, Rapid City, SD   57701

605-394-4101
Open: 9-5 Mo-Sa, 1-5 Su   *Closed:* Leg/Hol!
  P: Metered   *Museum Shop   Group Tours*
Permanent Collection: Cont; Reg: ptgs; gr 20

The Dahl presents a forum for all types of fine arts: visual, theater, and music, that serve the Black Hills region, eastern Wyoming, Montana, and Western Nebraska. ❨ 200-foot cyclorama depicting the history of the US.

ON EXHIBIT 2002

02/17/2002 to 04/14/2002   *A Ceramic Continuum: Fifty Years of the Archie Bray Influence*
The contribution of the Archie Bray Foundation for Ceramic Art to its residency program and ceramic art showing 85 works

The Journey Museum
Affiliated Institution: SD School of Mines & Technology's Museum of Geology
222 New York Street, Rapid City, SD   57701

605-394-6923
Adm: Adult: $6.00   *Children:* 11-17 $4.00   *Seniors:* $5.00

Sioux Indian Museum
222 New York Street, Rapid City, SD   57701

605-394-2381   www.journeymuseum.org
Open: 9-5 daily summer; 10-5 Mo-Sa, 1-4 Su winter   *Closed:* 1/1, Thgv, 12/25
Vol/Contr.: Yes see web site!   *Adm: Adult:* $6.00   *Children:* free under 10   *Students:* $4.00 11-17
Seniors: $5.00 over 62
  P   *Museum Shop   Group Tours:* 605-394-6923
Permanent Collection: Sioux Arts

The rich diversity of historic and contemporary Sioux art may be enjoyed in the Journey Museum, location of the Sioux Indian Museum. This museum with rotating exhibitions, and interactive displays dramatically reveal the geography, people, and historical events that shaped the history and heritage of the Black Hills area. ❨ The Journey, Black Hills History through sight, sound, and touch

Washington Pavilion of Arts and Sciences
Affiliated Institution: Visual Arts Center
301 S. Main Ave., Sioux Falls, SD   57104

605-367-7397 or toll free 1-877-WASHPAV   www.washingtonpavilion.org
Open: call for hours; Summer open 7 days   *Closed:* Thgv, 12/25
Free Day: 1st Fr 5-8pm   *Sugg/Contr.:* Yes   *Adult:* Admission charge for special exh
& P   *Museum Shop*   ¶   *Group Tours:* ext 2319   *Drop-In Tours   Historic Building   Sculpture Garden*
Permanent Collection: Reg/Art: all media

Opened in June 1999 the 250,000 square foot Washington Pavilion of the Arts and Science features the Visual Arts Center, Kirby Science Discovery Center, Wells Fargo Cinedome and the Husby Performing Arts Center.   ¶ The Washington Pavilion of Arts and Sciences is the region's newest and largest cultural and educational center. The Washington Pavilion includes the Husby Performing Arts Center, the Kirby Science Discovery Center, Wells Fargo Cinedome Theater, and the Visual Arts Center. The facility also houses Leonardo's Café and the Discovery Store gift shop. For more information, call 605-367-7397 or 1-877-WASHPAV (Toll free in SD, ND, NE, IA, and MN) Visit our website at www.washingtonpavilion.org.

University Art Galleries
Affiliated Institution: University of South Dakota
Warren M. Lee Center, 414 E. Clark Street, Vermillion, SD   57069-2390

605-677-5481   www.usd.edu/cfa/art/gallery
Open: 10-4 Mo-Fr, 1 5 Sa, Su   *Closed:* Acad!
& P   *Group Tours:* 605-677-5481
Permanent Collection: Sioux artist Oscar Howe; Hist Reg/Art

The University Art Galleries, established in 1976, exists in recognition of a commitment to the visual arts which may be traced to the founding of the University in 1862. The University Art Galleries' major purpose is to support the formal educational process of the University, but its impact extends beyond the academic community to serve artists and audiences in South Dakota and the region. The University Art Galleries is responsible for the operation of the Main Gallery, Gallery 110, several on-campus exhibition spaces, the University Permanent Collection, the Campus Beautification Project, and a touring exhibition program.

TENNESSEE

Hunter Museum of American Art
10 Bluff View, Chattanooga, TN   37403-1197

423-267-0968   www.huntermuseum.org
Open: 10-4:30 Tu-Sa, 1-4:30 Su; 10-8 1st Fr of month   *Closed:* Mo, Leg/Hol!
Free Day: 1st Fr of month   *Adm: Adult:* $5.00   *Children:* $2.50, 3-12   *Students:* $3.00   *Seniors:* $4.00
& P   *Museum Shop   Group Tours   Drop-In Tours   Historic Building   Sculpture Garden*
Permanent Collection: Am: ptgs, gr, sculp, 18-20

Blending the old and the new, the Hunter Museum consists of a recently restored 1904 mansion with a 1975 contemporary addition.

ON EXHIBIT 2002

12/15/2001 to 02/24/2002   *An American Anthem: 300 Years of Painting from the Butler Institute of American Art*
A survey of American art history including the Colonial Period, Hudson River School, Luminism, American Impressionism, the American West, the Eight, Social Realism, and post-war to the present. Included are Cole, Church, Bierstadt, Eakins, Hopper, Henri, Chase, Bearden, and many others.   *Will Travel   Book*

01/12/2002 to 03/10/2002   *Jacob Lawrence: The Frederick Douglass and Harriet Tubman Series of 1938–40*

03/30/2002 to 04/28/2002   *New Hudson Valley Painters*

05/04/2002 to 06/16/2002   *Chasing Napoleon: Paintings by Tony Scherman*

06/28/2002 to 08/18/2002   *Edward Weston: Life Work / Louis Hine: Photographs of Norris Dam*

09/14/2002 to 11/24/2002   *Hubert Shuptrine*

12/07/2002 to 03/02/2003   *A Stitch in Time/Breathing Glass*

KNOXVILLE

Knoxville Museum of Art
1050 World's Fair Park Drive, Knoxville, TN   37916-1653

615-525-6101   www.knoxart.org
Open: 10-5 Tu-Th, Sa, 10-9 Fr, 12-5 Su   *Closed:* Mo, Leg/Hol!
Adm: Adult: $4.00   *Children:* $1; under12; $2,13-17   *Students:* $3.00   *Seniors:* $3.00
&   P: Free parking across the street   *Museum Shop*   ¶
Group Tours   Drop-In Tours: 3pm Su for focus exh.
Permanent Collection: Cont; Gr; Am: 19

Begun in 1961 as the Dulin Gallery of art located in a antebellum mansion, the Museum because of its rapidly expanding collection of contemporary American art then moved to the historic Candy Factory. It now occupies a building designed in 1990 by Edward Larabee Barnes. *Some exhibitions have admission charge.   ℭ Historic Candy Factory next door; the nearby Sunsphere, trademark building of the Knoxville Worlds Fair

MEMPHIS

Dixon Gallery & Gardens
4339 Park Ave, Memphis, TN   38117

901-761-5250   www.dixon.org
Open: 10-5 Tu-Sa, 1-5 Su, Gardens only Mo 1/2 price   *Closed:* Mo, Leg/Hol!
Adm: Adult: $5.00   *Children:* $1.00 under 12   *Students:* free with ID   *Seniors:* $4.00
&   P: Free   *Museum Shop   Group Tours   Drop-In Tours:* ! by appt   *Historic Building*
Sculpture Garden   Theater
Permanent Collection: Fr: Impr, 19; Ger: cer

Located on 17 acres of woodlands and formal gardens, the Dixon was formerly the home of Hugo and Margaret Dixon, collectors and philanthropists.

Memphis Brooks Museum of Art
Overton Park, 1934 Poplar Ave., Memphis, TN   38104-2765

901-544-6200   www.brooksmuseum.org
Open: 10-4 Tu-Fr, 10-8 first We each month; 10-5 Sa, 11:30-5 Su   *Closed:* Mo, 1/1, 7/4, Thgv, 12/25
Free Day: We   *Adm: Adult:* $5.00   *Children:* $2.00 (7-17)   *Students:* $2.00   *Seniors:* $4.00
&   P: Free   *Museum Shop*   ¶: Brushmark Restaurant; Lunch 11:30-2:30
Group Tours: 901-544-6122   *Drop-In Tours:* 10:30, 1:30 Sa; 1:30 Su   *Historic Building*
Permanent Collection: It/Ren, N/Ren & Bar: ptgs; Brit & Am: portraits 18,19; Fr/Impr; Am: modernist

Founded in 1916, this is the mid-south's largest and most encyclopedic fine arts museum. Works in the collection range from those of antiquity to present day creations. ℂ Global Survey Galleries

ON EXHIBIT 2002

11/03/2001 to 01/20/2002 *English and American Silver: The Enlightened Years*
The development of silver from 1700 to 1910 featuring de Lamier and Storr to Tiffany and Gorham

11/18/2001 to 01/13/2002 *The Art of Warner Bros. Cartoons*
Drawings, paintings, cels, and related artwork from 1930–1960 giving a step by step breakdown of how animated films are made

02/23/2002 to 05/19/2002 *Presidential Portraits from the National Portrait Gallery, Smithsonian Institution*
Outstanding works by Peale, Bingham, and Rockwell with a discussion of the origin and significance of the portrait

05/12/2002 to 07/21/2002 *Myth, Memory, and Imagination*
Painting, photography, sculpture, and folk art from the Julia C. Norrell Collection including works by Evans, Green, Weems, Christenberry, Dunlap, Finster, Tolliver, and Bagley

06/02/2002 to 07/28/2002 *Almost Warm and Fuzzy*
Interesting to both gallery goers and children and teens, installation art including Skoglund's environment of thousands of jellybeans

08/18/2002 to 10/13/2002 *Art of the South Seas: Melanesia, Polynesia, Micronesia, and the Islands of Southeast Asia from the Collection of the Barbier-Mueller Museum*
This collection from Geneva is superb and varied particularly in its works from the South Seas.

09/01/2002 to 10/27/2002 *Worlds of Transformations: Tibetan Art of Wisdom and Compassion*
Sacred paintings from a premier collection of art

11/15/2002 to 02/02/2003 *Speak Softly and Carry a Beagle: The Art of Charles Schultz*
Peanuts and its development *Will Travel*

MURFREESBORO

Baldwin Photographic Gallery
Affiliated Institution: Middle Tennessee State University
Learning Resources Center, Murfreesboro, TN 37132

615-898-5628
Open: 8-4:30 Mo-Fr, 8-noon Sa, 6-10pm Su *Closed:* Easter, Thgv, 12/25
♿: 1st floor complete with special electric door P: Free parking 50 yards from gallery
Permanent Collection: Cont: phot

A college museum with major rotating photographic exhibitions.

NASHVILLE

Cheekwood — Tennessee Botanical Garden and Museum of Art
1200 Forrest Park Drive, Nashville, TN 37205-4242

615-356-8000 www.cheekwood.org
Open: 9:30-4:30 Tu-Sa, 11-4:30 Su (Grounds open 11-5 Su), Open Mo for Federal Holidays *Closed:* 1/1, Thgv, 12/25
Adm: *Adult:* $10.00 *Children:* $5.00 (6-17) *Students:* $5.00 w/ID *Seniors:* $8.00
♿ P 🍴: 11-2 *Group Tours:* 615-353-2155 *Historic Building*
Permanent Collection: Am: ptgs, sculp, dec/art 19-20

One of the leading cultural centers in the South, the Museum of Art is a former mansion built in the 1930s. Located in a luxuriant botanical garden, it retains a charming homelike quality. ℭ Contemporary Art Galleries and Sculpture Garden trail

ON EXHIBIT 2002

02/01/2002 to 04/28/2002   *Photography's Multiple Roles: Art, Document, Market, Science*
Among the artists represented here are Adams, Arbus, Dahl-Wolfew, Evans, Frank, Goldin, Hurrell, Lange, Leibovitz, Mann, Newhall, Penn, Weems, and Wegman. The importance of photography in interrelated areas of cultural interpretation   *Catalog*

07/13/2002 to 10/13/2002   *A Century of Progress; Twentieth Century Paintings in Tennessee*
Museums and private collections will tell the story of painting in the state. The Tennesee Historical Quarterly will be the the catalog. Included are Douglas, Delaney, Ryman, and Grooms   *Catalog*

11/01/2002 to 12/31/2002   *The Sight of Music: From the Collection of Reba and Dave Williams*
The exhibit focuses on subjects that use musical themes. Artists included are Bearden, Benton, Cage, Close, Grooms, Hirshfeld, Johns, Johnson, Lichtenstein, and Warhol.
Catalog   Bilingual

Fisk University Galleries
1000 17th Avenue North, Nashville, TN   37208-3051

615-329-8720   www.fisk.edu
Open: 10-5 Tu-Fr; 1-5 Sa-Su, Summer closed Su   *Closed:* Mo, Acad!
Vol/Contr.: Yes
&   P   *Museum Shop   Group Tours:* 615-329-8593   *Historic Building   Theater*
Permanent Collection: Eur; Am; Af/Am: Af

The Galleries are located on the campus of Fisk University and housed in a historical (1888) building and in the University Library   ℭ The Alfred Stieglitz Collection of Modern Art; The Aaron Douglas Galleries

Parthenon
Centennial Park, Nashville, TN   37201

615-862-8431   www.parthenon.org
Open: 9-4:30 Tu-Sa, 12:30-4:30 Su; (April-Sept Su 12:30-8)   *Closed:* Mo, Leg/Hol!
Adm: Adult: $3.50   *Children:* $2.00, 4-17   *Students:* $2.00   *Seniors:* $2.00
&   P: Free   *Museum Shop   Group Tours   Drop-In Tours:* !   *Historic Building   Theater*
Permanent Collection: Am: 19, 20; The Cowan Collection

First constructed as the Art Pavilion for the Tennessee Centennial Exposition in 1897, The Parthenon is the world's only full size reproduction of the 5th-century B.C. Greek original complete with the 42-foot statue of Athena Parthenos.   ℭ "Mt. Tamalpais," by Albert Bierstadt; "Autumn in the Catskills" by Sanford Gifford

ON EXHIBIT 2002

02/02/2002 to 03/23/2002   *A Passion for Paint: The Art of Willie Bette Newman (1863–1935)*
She studied at the Academie Julian in Paris but returned to Nashville in 1902. This is her first posthumous show.

04/06/2002 to 06/08/2002   *Installation*
Adrienne Outlaw, Richard Mitchell, Terry Thacker, Meg Walborn, Greg Pond

04/13/2002 to 06/15/2002   *Candie Ferrell*
Still life painting

06/15/2002 to 08/17/2002   *Irish Textiles from the Ulster Folk Museum*

06/22/2002 to 08/25/2002   *Tennessee Textile Exhibit*
A companion to the Ulster show featuring local and regional work

08/24/2002 to 10/26/2002   *Modern Hudson River School*
Paintings by contemporary artists in the style of the 19th-century Hudson River School and the Luminists

11/02/2002 to 01/04/2003   *Lost Nashville*
Charles Waterfield photographs

11/09/2002 to 01/11/2003   *Felix Maxwell*
Grey to white shades of pastels in current scenes and portraits

Tennessee State Museum-Polk Culture Center
5th and Deaderick, Nashville, TN   37243-1120

615-741-2692   www.tnmuseum.org
Open: 10-5 Tu-Sa; 1-5 Su   *Closed:* Mo, 1/1, Easter, Thgv, 12/25
Vol/Contr.: Yes
& P: parking meters and paid lots   *Museum Shop*
Group Tours: Mo-Fr for school groups 615-741-0830   *Theater*
Permanent Collection: Artifacts and art relating to Tennessee's history, beginning with prehistoric peoples and going through the early 1900s.

General history museum with collections of decorative arts   ℭ Outstanding collections of quilts and silver

Vanderbilt University Fine Arts Gallery
23rd at West End Ave, Nashville, TN   37203

615-322-0605   www.vanderbilt.edu/AnS/finearts/gallery.html
Open: 12-4 Mo-Fr, 1-5 Sa, Su; Summer 12-4 Tu-Fr; 1-5 Sa   *Closed:* Note summer hours, Acad!
P *Group Tours   Historic Building*
Permanent Collection: Or: Harold P. Stern Coll; OM & Modern: gr (Anna C. Hoyt Coll); Contini-Volterra Phot Archive; Eur: oth/ptgs (Kress Study Coll)

The history of world art may be seen in the more than 5,000 works from over 40 countries and cultures housed in this university gallery. Rich in contemporary prints and Oriental art, this historical collection is the only one of its kind in the immediate region.   ℭ "St. Sebastian," 15th century Central Italian tempera on wood

ON EXHIBIT 2002

01/10/2002 to 01/31/2002   *The 2000 Margaret Stonewall Woolridge Hamblet Award Winner*
A juried exhibition of works in ceramic by Jennie Gill

02/07/2002 to 03/21/2002   *An Artistic Friendship: Beauford Delaney and Lawrence Calcogno*
Expatriate abstract artists who worked in Paris   *Catalog   Will Travel*

06/18/2002 to 08/17/2002   *Summer Reading: Artist's Books from the Collections of Vanderbilt University and the Cheekwood Museum of Art*
Important works of literature and works of art

08/29/2002 to 10/12/2002   *The George and Helen Spelvin Folk Art Collection*
Outstanding "outsider" art

10/17/2002 to 12/05/2002   *Sculpture by Salvatore Dali from the Isidro Clot Collection*
Modeled in wax betweeen 1969 and 1976 they were then cast in bronze. Includes portrayal of characters from religious and secular literature

OAK RIDGE

Oak Ridge Arts Center
201 Badger Avenue, Oak Ridge, TN   37830

423-482-1441   korrnet.org.art
Open: 9-5 Tu-Fr, 1-4 Sa-Mo   *Closed:* Leg/Hol!
Vol/Contr.: Yes
& P   *Group Tours   Drop-In Tours*
Permanent Collection: Ab/Exp: Post WWII

Two galleries with monthly changing exhibitions, educational programming and art lectures. Call for schedule.

TEXAS

ABILENE

Grace Museum, Inc
102 Cypress, Abilene, TX   79601

915-673-4587
Open: 10-5 Tu, We, Fr, Sa, 10:30 Th   *Closed:* Leg/Hol!
Free Day: Th 5-8:30   *Adm:*   Adult: $3.00   *Children:* $1.00 (4-12)   *Students:* $2.00   *Seniors:* $2.00
& P   *Group Tours   Historic Building   Theater*
Permanent Collection: TX/Reg; Am: gr, Cont: gr; Abeline, TX, & Pacific Railway: 18-20

The museums are housed in the 1909 Mission Revival style Railroad Hotel.   ℂ Children's Museum

ALBANY

Old Jail Art Center
201 South 2nd, Albany, TX   76430

915-762-2269   www.albanytexas.com
Open: 10-5 Tu-Sa, 2-5 Su   *Closed:* Mo, Leg/Hol!
&: Except 2-story original jail building   P   *Museum Shop   Group Tours   Historic Building*
Sculpture Garden   Theater
Permanent Collection: As, Eur, Brit cont, Mod, P/Col

The Old Jail Art Center is housed partly in a restored 1878 historic jail building with a small annex which opened in 1980 and new wings added in 1984 and 1998 featuring a courtyard, sculpture garden and educational center. ℂ "Young Girl With Braids," by Modigliani; 37 Chinese terracotta tomb figures

ON EXHIBIT 2002

11/03/2001 to 02/10/2002   *The French Connection: Murray Bewley and James Blake*

AMARILLO

Amarillo Museum of Art
2200 S. Van Buren, Amarillo, TX   79109

806-371-5050   www.amarilloart.org
Open: 10-5 Tu-Fr, 1-5 Sa, Su   *Closed:* Mo, Leg/Hol!
& P   *Drop-In Tours:* by appt *Sculpture Garden*
Permanent Collection: Cont Am; ptgs, gr, phot, sculp; Jap gr; SE/As sculp, textiles

Opened in 1972, the Amarillo Museum of Art is a visual arts museum featuring exhibitions, art classes, tours, and educational programs. The building was designed by Edward Durell Stone.

ARLINGTON

Arlington Museum of Art
201 West Main St., Arlington, TX   76010

817-275-4600   www.arlingtonmuseum.org
Open: 10-5 We-Sa   *Closed:* Su, Mo, Tu, Leg/Hol, 12/25-1/2!
Sugg/Contr.: $1.00
&: Partial   *Museum Shop   Group Tours   Drop-In Tours:* Occasional
Permanent Collection: Non-collecting institution

Texas contemporary art by both emerging and mature talents is featured in this North Texas museum located between the art-rich cities of Fort Worth and Dallas. It has gained a solid reputation for showcasing contemporary art in the six exhibitions it presents annually.

Center for Research in Contemporary Arts
Fine Arts Bldg, Cooper Street, Arlington, TX   76019

817-273-2790
Open: 10-3 Mo-Th, 1-4 Sa-Su   *Closed:* Acad!
P   *Theater*
Permanent Collection: Non-collecting institution

A University gallery with varied special exhibitions.

AUSTIN

Austin Museum of Art-Downtown
823 Congress Avenue, Austin, TX   78701

512-495-9224   www.amoa.org
Open: 10-6 Tu-Sa, 10-8 Th, 12-5 Su   *Closed:* Mo, Leg/Hol
Adm: Adult: $3.00, $1 day Th   *Children:* Free under 12   *Students:* $2.00   *Seniors:* $2.00
&   P: 923 Parking Garage at 9th and Congress Streets   *Museum Shop*
Group Tours: ext. 224   *Drop-In Tours:* 2pm Sa during exhibitions
Permanent Collection: Works on Paper, photo

Aproximately 300 items focusing on American visual art significant to our time and the region inclusive of Mexico and the Caribbean

ON EXHIBIT 2002

01/19/2002 to 03/24/2002   *Visualizing the Blues: Images of the American South*
Photographs by 19th- and 20th-century masters presenting the same traditions encountered in blues music, a soulful, often searing, evocation of the Southern experience   *Will Travel*

04/06/2002 to 05/26/2002   *Twenty to Watch: Austin Area Art Update*
A survey of the most exciting art in all media, being created in Austin since 2000   *Catalog*

06/08/2002 to 08/18/2002   *Images from the World Between: The Circus in Twentieth Century American Art*
A multi-media exhibition including Arbus, Bitner, Calder, Curry, Demuth, Evans, Gremillion, Kuhn, Mark, Marsh, Segal, Schinn, and others, describing the Circus as more than a popular entertainment.   *Catalog   Will Travel*

Austin Museum of Art-Laguna Gloria
3809 W. 35th Street, Austin, TX   78703

512-458-8191   www.amo2.org
Open: 10-5 Tu-Sa, 10-8 Th, 1-5 Su   *Closed:* Mo, Leg/Hol!
Adm: Adult: $2.00, $1.00 Th; No charge during restoration   *Children:* Free under 16   *Students:* $1.00
Seniors: $1.00
&   P: Free   *Museum Shop*   *Group Tours:* ext 224   *Historic Building*   *Sculpture Garden*
Permanent Collection: Work on Paper, photo

The Museum is Located on the 1916 Driscoll Estate which is listed in the National Register of Historic Places located in Mediterranean style villa on the banks of Lake Austin. *The galleries at the museum at Laguna Gloria will undergo restoration beginning in June 2000.   ℂ The beautiful setting.

Jack S. Blanton Museum of Art
Affiliated Institution: University of Texas at Austin
Art Bldg 23rd & San Jacinto, Austin, TX   78712

512-471-7324   www.blantonmuseum.org
Open: 9-5 Mo, Tu, We, Fr, 9-9 Th, 1-5 Sa, Su   *Closed:* Mem/Day, Lab/Day, Thgv, Christmas week
&   P   *Museum Shop*   *Group Tours:* 512-471-5025   *Drop-In Tours:* !
Permanent Collection: Lat/Am; Cont; Gr; Drgs, OM, Gr

The encyclopedic collection of this university gallery, one of the finest and most balanced in the southern US, features an artistic, cultural, and historical record of Western European and American Art dating from antiquity to the present. Including 16,000 works spanning the history of Western civilization. The Blanton is currently in the design phase of a new Museum facility to open in 2005.   ℂ The Mari and James A. Michener Collection of 20th c. American Art; Contemporary Latin American Collection; European paintings featuring the Suida-Manning collection; and the encyclopedic collection of prints and drawings

BEAUMONT

Art Museum of Southeast Texas
500 Main Street, Beaumont, TX   77701

409-832-3432   www.amset.org
Open: 9-5 Mo-Sa, 12-5 Su   *Closed:* Leg/Hol!
&   P: Free   *Museum Shop*   ¶   *Group Tours*   *Drop-In Tours:* We, noon   *Sculpture Garden*   *Theater*
Permanent Collection: Am: ptgs, sculp, dec/art, Folk: 19, 20

This new spacious art museum with 4 major galleries and 2 sculpture courtyards is located in downtown Beaumont.

COLLEGE STATION

MSC Forsyth Center Galleries
Affiliated Institution: Texas A&M University
1237 TAMU, Memorial Student Center, College Station, TX   77843-1237

979-845-9251   www.forsyth.tamu.edu
Open: 9-8 Mo-Fr, 12-6 Sa-Su; 10-4:30 Mo-Fr, 12-4:30 Sa, Su May-Aug   *Closed:* 7/4, Thgv, 12/25-1/2
&   P: garage   *Group Tours*   *Drop-In Tours:* by appt
Permanent Collection: Eur, Brit, & Am; glass; Am: western ptgs

The Gallery is particularly rich in its collection of American Art glass, and has one of the finest collections of English cameo glass in the world.   ℂ Works by Grandma Moses, Mary Cassatt, Frederic Remington

Texas A&M University/J. Wayne Stark University Center Galleries
Mem Student Ctr. Joe Routt Blvd, College Station, TX   77844-9083

409-845-6081   www.starktamued
Open: 9-8 Tu-Fr, 12-6 Sa-Su   *Closed:* Mo, Acad
&   P   *Group Tours*
Permanent Collection: Reg; Ger 19

A University gallery featuring works by 20th-century Texas artists

CORPUS CHRISTI

Art Museum of South Texas
1902 N. Shoreline, Corpus Christi, TX   78401

512-884-3844
Open: 10-5 Tu-Sa, 1-5 Su   *Closed:* Mo, 1/1, 7/4, Thgv, 12/25
Free Day: Th   *Adm:*   *Adult:* $3.00   *Children:* $1.00 (2-12)   *Students:* $2.00   *Seniors:* $2.00
&   P: Free   *Museum Shop*   ¶   *Sculpture Garden*
Permanent Collection: Am; Reg

The award winning building designed by Philip Johnson, has vast expanses of glass which provide natural light for objects of art and breathtaking views of Corpus Christi Bay.

Asian Cultures Museum and Educational Center
1809 North Chaparral, Corpus Christi, TX   78412

512-882-2641
Open: 12-5 Tu-Sa   *Closed:* Mo, Leg/Hol!, Easter
Vol/Contr.: Yes   *Adm:*   *Adult:* $4.00   *Children:* $2.50, 6-15   *Students:* $3.50   *Seniors:* $3.50
&   P: Street   *Museum Shop*   *Group Tours*   *Drop-In Tours:* by request
Permanent Collection: Jap, Ch, Ind, As Culture

An oasis of peace and tranquility as well as a resource of Asian history and information for the Corpus Christi Community.   ₵ Cast bronze Buddha weighing over 1,500 lb.

DALLAS

African American Museum
3536 Grand Avenue, Dallas, TX   75210

214-565-9026
Open: 12-5 Th-Fr, 10-5 Sa, 1-5 Su   *Closed:* Mo, Tu, We, Leg/Hol!
&   P   *Museum Shop*   ¶   *Group Tours:* 214-565-9026, ext 328   *Drop-In Tours:* by appt   *Historic Building*
Sculpture Garden
Permanent Collection: Af/Am: folk

The African American Museum collects, preserves, exhibits, and researches artistic expressions and historic documents which represent the African-American heritage. Its mission is to educate and give a truer understanding of African-American culture to all.

Biblical Arts Center
7500 Park Lane, Dallas, TX   75225

214-691-4661   www.biblicalarts.org
Open: 10-5 Tu-Sa, 10-9 Th, 1-5 Su   *Closed:* Mo, 1/1, Thgv, 12/24, 12/25
Adm: *Adult:* $4.00   *Children:* $2.50 (6-12)   *Students:* $3.00 (13-18)   *Seniors:* $3.50
&   P   *Museum Shop*   *Group Tours*   *Historic Building*
Permanent Collection: Biblical Art

The sole purpose of this museum is to utilize the arts as a means of helping people of all faiths to more clearly envision the places, events, and people of the Bible. The building, in Romanesque style, features early Christian era architectural details.   ₵ "Miracle at Pentecost," painting with light and sound presentation

Dallas Museum of Art
1717 N. Harwood, Dallas, TX   75201

214-922-1200   www.dma-art.org
Open: 11-5 Tu, We, Fr, 11-9 Th, 11-5 Sa, Su   *Closed:* 1/1, Thgv, 12/25
Free Day: Th after 5, 1st Tu of month;   *Adm:*   *Adult:* $6.00   *Children:* Free under 12
Students: $4.00   *Seniors:* $4.00
  P: Large underground parking facility   *Museum Shop*   ¶: 2 restaurants
Group Tours: 214-922-1331   *Drop-In Tours:* Tu, Fr 1pm, Sa, Su 2pm, Th 7pm   *Sculpture Garden*
Permanent Collection: P/Col; Af; Am: furniture; Eur: ptgs, sculp, Post War Am; Af; As; Cont; South Asia
Sculp; Indo Sculp and Textiles

Designed by Edward Larabee Barnes, the 370,000-square foot limestone building houses a broad and eclectic permanent collection. The art of the Americas from the pre-contact period (which includes a spectacular pre-Columbian gold Treasury of more than 1,000 works) through the mid-20th century is outstanding. ❡ "The Icebergs" by Frederick Church; Claes Oldenburg's pop art "Stake Hitch in the Barrel Vault"; Colonial and post-Colonial decorative arts; early and late paintings by Piet Mondrian; The Reves Collection of Impressionist Paintings and sculpture in a setting reminiscent of the donor's villa on the Riviera

ON EXHIBIT 2002

10/07/2001 to 01/01/2002   *Great Masters of Mexican Folk Art*
One thousand objects from every corner of Mexico including clay, guitars, and textiles

10/21/2001 to 02/17/2002   *Art Deco and Streamlined Modern: Design, 1920–1940*
The second in a series focusing on 20th century design. Appliances and furniture show the differences between classic French Art Deco of the 20s and American design of the 30s.

05/12/2002 to 08/18/2002   *Thomas Struth*
A retrospective view of the beautiful work of this photographer from black-and-white of cities to "Museum Pictures" to portraiture   *Catalog   Will Travel*

10/13/2002 to 01/05/2003   *Anne Vallayer-Coster: Still Life Painting in the Age of Marie Antoinette*
A first retrospective of this foremost still life painter and her contemporaries including Chardin and Delaporte   *Catalog   Will Travel*

Meadows Museum
Affiliated Institution: SMU School of the Arts
Bishop Blvd. at Binkley Ave., Dallas, TX   75275-0356

214-768-2516   www.smu.edu/meadows/museum
Open: 10-5 Mo, Tu, Fr, Sa, 10-8 Th, 1-5 Su   *Closed:* We, 1/1, Easter, 7/4, Thgv, 12/25
Vol/Contr.: Yes
  P   *Museum Shop   Group Tours:* 214-823-7644   *Drop-In Tours:* 2pm Su, Sept-May
Sculpture Garden   Theater
Permanent Collection: Sp; ptgs, sculp, gr, drgs; Am: sculp 20

The collection of Spanish Art is the most comprehensive in the US with works from the last years of the 10th century through the 20th century. ❡ "Sibyl With Tabula Rasa" by Diego Rodriquez de Silva y Velazquez, Spanish, 1599–1660

El Paso Museum of Art
One Arts Festival Plaza, El Paso, TX   79901

915-532-1717   www.elpasoartmuseum.org
Open: 9-5 Tu-Sa, 1-5 Su   *Closed:* Mo, Leg/Hol!
Adm: *Adult:* $1.00   *Children:* $.50   *Students:* $.50
  P: metered parking and lots in area   *Museum Shop*
Group Tours: ext 16, by appt   *Drop-In Tours:* by appt
Permanent Collection: Eur: Kress Coll 13-18; Am; Mex: 18,19; Mex Santos: 20; Reg

The museum houses the renowned permanent Kress collection of works by European masters; one of the most important concentrations of Mexican Colonial art; American painting (1800 to the present); and over 2000 works on paper by Dürer, Degas, Miro, Benton, Rivera, and Orozco. Two changing galleries display work by recognized contemporary regional artists.

ON EXHIBIT 2002

11/03/2001 to 01/27/2002   *Members Choice*
Members vote to purchase one of exhibited works

12/01/2001 to 02/24/2002   *Framing the Border: Photographs from the Permanent Collection*

01/12/2002 to 03/31/2002   *Burning Desires: Acquisitions at the El Paso Museum of Art 1997–2001*
Included are Adams, Corpron, Curtis, Drake Jimenez, Jidd, Lea, and Rauschenberg

FORT WORTH

Amon Carter Museum
3501 Camp Bowie Blvd, Fort Worth, TX   76107-2695

817-738-1933   www.cartermuseum.org
Open: 10-5 Tu-Sa, 12-5 Su, 10-8 Th!   *Closed:* Mo, 1/1, 7/4, Thgv,12/25
&: Lancaster Ave main entrance   P: Free   *Museum Shop   Group Tours*
Permanent Collection: Am: ptgs, sculp, gr, phot 19, 20

One of the foremost museums of American Art, the Amon Carter is located in Fort Worth's cultural district. It represents the Western experience and embraces the history of 19th- and 20th-century American Art.   ❆ "Swimming," by Thomas Eakins

ON EXHIBIT 2002

10/21/2001 to 02/10/2002   *Revealed Treasures: Drawings from the Permanent Collection*
Important works on paper dating from 1791–1965. Artists include Moran, Demuth, Homer, Dove, O'Keeffe, and Marin.   *Booklet*

10/21/2001 to 03/03/2002   *Masterworks of American Photography*
The role photography has played in the American art tradition.

10/21/2001 to 03/31/2002   *Avedon's American West*
Fashion photographer who spent 1979–1985 photographing working-class people in the American West.

10/21/2001 to 03/31/2002   *Common Ground: Settling Colorado*
Historic photographs of Colorado's settlement after the 1958 "Pikes Peak Gold Rush"

10/21/2001 to 03/31/2002   *Laura Gilpin and Eliot Porter in New Mexico*
A sampling of the work of these two masters of photography

10/21/2001 to 05/26/2002   *The Artist and the American West: A Century of Western Art*
Ninety paintings, sculptures, watercolors, drawings, and rare books beginning with an 1826 view of Hudson Bay by Rindisbacher to California clouds by Edward Weston

03/02/2002 to 05/12/2002   *Stomp of Impulse: Abstract Expressionist Prints*
A survey of the era's diverse approaches to printmaking which revolutionized American graphic arts   *Will Travel*

05/25/2002 to 08/25/2002 *Eye Contact: Modern American Portrait Drawings from the National Portrait Gallery*
Famous Americans in all walks of life. Outstanding effects achieved in graphic media

09/14/2002 to 11/17/2002 *Celebrating America: Masterworks from Texas Collections*
Major works of American art

12/07/2002 to 03/23/2003 *Eliot Porter: The Color of Wildness*
Revealed are Porter's roots and working methods and his central role in the acceptance of color photography. *Catalog*

Kimbell Art Museum
3333 Camp Bowie Blvd, Fort Worth, TX   76107-2792

817-332-8451   www.kimbellart.org
Open: 10-5 Tu-Th, Sa, 12-8 Fr, 12-5 Su   *Closed:* Mo, 1/1, 7/4, Thgv, 12/25
Free Day: Perm Coll. Free daily, Adm for Special exhibitions   *Adm:*   Adult: $10.00
Children: 6-12 $6.00   *Students:* $8.00   *Seniors:* $8.00
& P   *Museum Shop* ¶ *Group Tours:* ext. 229   *Drop-In Tours:* 2pm Tu-Fr, Su, exh tours 2 & 3pm Su
Sculpture Garden
Permanent Collection: Eur: ptgs, sculp 14-20; As; Af; Med/Ant

Designed by Louis I. Kahn, this classic museum building is perhaps his finest creation and a work of art in its own right. It was the last building completed under his personal supervision. It is often called "America's best small museum." The permanent collection of the Museum is free. Admission is for special exhibitions. € "The Cardsharps" by Caravaggio

ON EXHIBIT 2002

03/10/2002 to 06/02/2002 *Bartolome Estaban Murillo (1617–1682): Paintings from American Collections*
Murillo was a most important painter of the 17th century. This exhibition fills a gap as a retrospective of his work. *Catalog   Will Travel*

Modern Art Museum of Fort Worth
1309 Montgomery Street, Fort Worth, TX   76107

817-738-9215   www.mamfw.org
Open: 10-5 Tu-Fr, 11-5 Sa, 12-5 Su   *Closed:* Mo, Leg/Hol!
& P   *Museum Shop*   *Group Tours*   *Drop-In Tours:* Sa 2pm   *Sculpture Garden*
Permanent Collection: Am; Eur; Cont; ptgs, sculp, works on paper, photo, 14 new works by Modern and Contemporary photographers and artists

Chartered in 1892 (making it one of the oldest museums in the western U.S.), this museum has evolved into a celebrated and vital showcase for works of modern and contemporary art. Great emphasis at the Modern is placed on the presentation of exceptional traveling exhibitions, making a trip to this facility and others in this "museum rich" city a rewarding experience for art lovers. € Important collections of works by Robert Motherwell, Jackson Pollock, Morris Louis, and Milton Avery as well as contemporary photography

ON EXHIBIT 2002

10/21/2001 to 01/20/2002 *Trenton Hancock: The Life and Death of #1*

02/10/2002 to 04/14/2002 *Museums for a New Millennium: Concepts, Projects, Buildings*

11/01/2002 to 01/2003 *110 Years: The Permanent Collection of the Modern Art Museum of Fort Worth*
Inaugural exhibition in new building designed by Tadao Ando

Sid Richardson Collection of Western Art

309 Main Street, Fort Worth, TX 76102

817-332-6554 (888-332-6554) www.sidrmuseum.org
Open: 10-5 Tu, We, 10-8 Th, Fr, 11-8 Sa, 1-5 Su *Closed:* Mo, Leg/Hol!
♿ P: 2 1/2 hours free at Chisholm Trail Lot-4th and Main with ticket validation. *Museum Shop*
Group Tours *Drop-In Tours* *Historic Building*
Permanent Collection: Am/West: ptgs

Dedicated to Western art, the museum is located in historic Sundance Square in a reconstructed 1890s building. The area, in downtown Fort Worth, features restored turn-of-the-century buildings housing shops, restaurant, theater, and museum. ℂ 56 Remington and Russell paintings on permanent display

The Modern at Sundance Square

Affiliated Institution: The Modern Art Museum
410 Houston Street, Fort Worth, TX 76102

817-335-9215 www.mamfw.org
Open: 11-6 Mo-Th, 11-10 Fr & Sa, 1-5 Su *Closed:* Leg/Hol
♿ *Museum Shop* *Group Tours* *Historic Building* *Theater*
Permanent Collection: Am, Eur: Cont ptg, sculp, works on paper, Cont photo

Opened in 1995 in the historic Sanger Building in downtown Fort Worth as an annex for both the permanent collections and temporary exhibitions of the Modern Art Museum.

HOUSTON

Contemporary Arts Museum

5216 Montrose Boulevard, Houston, TX 77006-6598

713-284-8250 www.camh.org
Open: 10-5 Tu-Sa, 10-9 Th 12-5 Su *Closed:* Mo, 1/1, Thgv, 12/25
♿ P: On-street parking *Museum Shop* 🍴: Starbucks cafe *Group Tours* *Sculpture Garden*
Permanent Collection: Non-collecting institution

Located in a metal building in the shape of a parallelogram, this museum is dedicated to presenting the art of our time to the public.

Menil Collection

1515 Sul Ross Street, Houston, TX 77006

713-525-9400 www.menil.org
Open: 11-7 We-Su *Closed:* Mo, Tu, Leg/Hol!
♿ P *Museum Shop* *Group Tours* *Historic Building* *Sculpture Garden* *Theater*
Permanent Collection: Ptgs, Drgs, & Sculp 20; Ant; Tribal Cultures; Med; Byz

The Menil Collection was founded to house the art collection of John and Dominique de Menil. Considered one of the most important privately assembled collections of the 20th c. it spans human creative efforts from antiquity to the modern era. The Renzo Piano designed Museum building is renowned for its innovative architecture and naturally-illuminated galleries. ℂ In collaboration with the Dia Center for the Arts, NY, the Cy Twombly Gallery designed by Renzo Piano is a satellite space featuring works in all media created by Cy Twombly. Dan Flavin installation at Flavin Pavilion

ON EXHIBIT 2002

09/25/2001 to 02/03/2002 *Mineko Grimmer*
Light, shadow, water, and music in this new installation

10/12/2001 to 01/06/2002 *Victor Brauner: Surrealist Eccentric*
A comprehensive view of this Romanian born artist. He integrates his roots in mysticism and folklore with Western modernism.

02/01/2002 to 05/26/2002   *Agnes Martin*
Minimalist canvases in the artist's 90th year

02/20/2002 to 06/02/2002   *Vik Muniz*
Muniz started as a sculptor and then turned to photography. He is influenced by optical illusions, photorealist paintings, abstractions, and real-life absurdities.

10/04/2002 to 01/05/2003   *H. C. Westermann*
The first retrospective of sculptor Westermann presents many works never seen before including drawings, box works, and notebooks.   *Catalog   Will Travel*

Museum of Fine Arts, Houston
1001 Bissonnet, Houston, TX   77005

713-639-7300   www.mfahorg
Open: 10-5 Tu-Sa, 5-9pm Th, 12:15-6 Su   *Closed:* Mo, 1/1, 7/4, Lab/Day, Thgv, 12/25
Free Day: Th   *Adm:*   *Adult:* $5.00   *Children:* Free under 5, 6-18 $2.50   *Students:* $2.50   *Seniors:* $2.50
&   P: Free   *Museum Shop*   ❚   *Group Tours:* 713-639-7324   *Drop-In Tours:* 12 and by appt
Sculpture Garden   Theater
Permanent Collection: Straus Coll of Ren & 18th C Work; Beck Coll: Impr; Glassell Coll: Af gold

Over 31,000 works are housed in the largest and most outstanding museum in the southwest. Ongoing: African Gold: Selections from the Glassell Collection Impressionist and Modern Painting: The John and Audrey Jones Beck Collection   ❲ Audrey Jone Beck building opened March 2000, designed by Raphael Moneo housing European art from antiquity to 1920, American art to 1945. Bayou Bend Collection and Gardens is a 28-room house with 2800 works of fine and decorative American arts from colonial to mid-19th c. Separate admission and hours. 733-639-7750. Rienzi, a newly opened house museum showcasing an important collection of 18th and 19th c. European art and antiques and English porcelain. Separate admission and hours. 713-639-7800

ON EXHIBIT 2002

10/27/2001 to 01/21/2002   *Space: Sculptors Drawings, Drawings about Sculpture*
Drawings by Maillol, Smith, Hesse, Heizer ,Moscowitz, and Giacometti

10/28/2001 to 02/03/2002   *Earth and Fire: Italian Terracotta Sculpture from Donatello to Canova*
The exhibition will juxtapose models with finished works. A full range of sculptures from reliefs by Donatello and Luca Della Robbia to sculptures in the round by Algardi and Bernini. Drawings by Leonardo and decorative objects by Soldani will show the evolution of a project. *Catalog*

10/28/2001 to 02/17/2002   *American Traditions: Quilts and Coverlets*
Bedcoverings, in wholecloth, pieced, surface-appliqued, and album quilts. Production techniques and historical significance will be shown.

12/02/2001 to 02/14/2002   *Color Myth and Music: Stanton MacDonald-Wright and Synchromism*
A pioneer of modernism he went on to become an influential teacher, write a treatise on color theory, explore film and promote "Synchromist Theatre" returning at the end of his career to abstraction.   *Catalog   Will Travel*

01/13/2002 to 04/28/2002   *Texas Flags: 1836–1945*

01/17/2002 to 03/10/2002   *Peter Sarkisian*
Digital technology and film create video installations that are between sculpture and cinema. Walking into his installations one shares space with with a moving, changing element with which an audio track is also played.   *Catalog*

01/20/2002 to 03/31/2002   *Richard Pousette-Dart: Timeless Perspective Works on Paper 1930–1992*
A first retrospective of the works on paper of the youngest member of the Abstract Expressionist group

01/20/2002 to 04/14/2002   *Japanese Prints by Goyo*

01/20/2002 to 04/14/2002   *Louis Faurer Retrospective*
Faurer photographed cities, primarily New York and masters empty streets, overlapping signs, and illogical spaces creeated by reflections

02/02/2002 to 04/28/2002   *Post-War Italian Photography*
The Carlo and Lorenzo Borlenghi Collection of photographs in the three decades before World War II

03/17/2002 to 06/16/2002   *Dancer: Photographs by Irving Penn*
Penn and a modern dancer collaborated to create 27 photographs of a woman posing and dancing nude.   *Will Travel*

03/31/2002 to 08/04/2002   *Splendors of Vice Regal Mexico: Three Centuries of Treasures from the Museo Franz Mayer*
The artistic heritage from the Conquest in 1521 to the Revolution in 1821. The exhibition at the museum in Mexico City in a late 16th-century building contains paintings, sculpture, furniture, lacquer, silver, and ceramics.   *Catalog   Will Travel   Bilingual*

05/12/2002 to 08/04/2002   *Americanos: Latino Life in the United States*
Photographs by 32 of the top Latino photographers documenting the diversity of the subjects: Gloria Estafan, Oscar de la Renta, Rita Moreno, to a flag seamstress in Texas. These capture the contributions and quiet family moments.

06/30/2002 to 10/27/2002   *Treasury of the World; Jeweled Arts of India in the Days of the Mughals*
Two hundred objects from the al-Sabah collection including personal adornment, jeweled and jade objects, and weapons   *Catalog   Will Travel*

09/08/2002 to 11/17/2002   *The Quilts of Gees Bend*
A body of quilts from African American women quilters from this small community in Alabama

10/06/2002 to 01/05/2003   *Over the Line: The Art and Life of Jacob Lawrence*
A first black artist whose work comprised historical and contemporary subjects. He was responsive for 60 years to the ruptures and shifts in American society.

12/08/2002 to 02/17/2003   *Leonardo da Vinci and the Splendor of Poland*
A feature is Leonardo's "Portrait of the Lady with the Ermine." Paintings reflect the history of collecting in Poland. Also included are works by Bellotto and David.

12/15/2002 to 03/09/2003   *Masterworks of French Painting from the State Pushkin Museum of Fine Arts*
A survey of French painting of three centuries with Poussin and Lorrain, Boucher, David, Ingres, Corot, Courbet, as well as classic impressionist works. Many unknown in the U.S.
Catalog   Will Travel

Rice University Art Gallery
6100 Main Street, MS-21, Houston, TX   77005

713-527-6069   www.rice.edu-ruag
Open: 11-5 Tu-Sa, 11-8 Th, 12-5 Su   *Closed:* Mo, Acad, Summer
&   P   ¶: Cafeteria on campus   *Group Tours*
Permanent Collection: Rotating Exhibitions

The Gallery features changing exhibitions of contemporary art with an emphasis on site-specific installations.

Cowboy Artists of America Museum
1550 Bandera Hwy, Kerrville, TX   78028

210-896-2553   www.caamuseum.com
Open: 9-5 Mo-Sa, 1-5 Su   *Closed:* 1/1, Easter, Thgv, 12/25
Adm: *Adult:* $3.00   *Children:* $1.00 (6-18)   *Seniors:* $2.50
&   P: Free   *Museum Shop*   *Group Tours*   *Drop-In Tours:* daily !   *Historic Building*   *Sculpture Garden*
Permanent Collection: Am/Western: ptgs, sculp

Located on a hilltop site just west of the Guadalupe River, the museum is dedicated to perpetuating America's western heritage. Exhibitions change quarterly.

Longview Museum of Fine Arts
215 E. Tyler St, Longview, TX   75601

903-753-8103   www.lmfa.org
Open: 10-4 Tu-Fr, 12-4 Sa   *Closed:* Su, Mo, 12/25, 1/1
Free Day: no charge for permanent exhibitions   *Sugg/Contr.:*   *Adult:* $3.00; *Student:* $1.00
&   P: Adjacent to the building   *Museum Shop*   *Group Tours:* 903-753-8103   *Historic Building*
Permanent Collection: Cont Texas Art (1958-1999)

Located in downtown Longview, this renovated building was used by many businesses in the city's history.   ☾ Millennium celebration highlighting LMFA's fine art permanent collection since 1959

Museum of East Texas
503 N. Second Street, Lufkin, TX   75901

409-639-4434
Open: 10-5 Tu-Fr, 1-5 Sa-Su   *Closed:* Mo, Leg/Hol!
&   P   *Museum Shop*   *Group Tours*   *Drop-In Tours*   *Historic Building*   *Theater*
Permanent Collection: Am, Eur, & Reg: ptgs

The Museum is housed in St. Cyprians Church, whose original Chapel was built in 1906. An award-winning wing was completed in 1990.   ☾ Historic photographic collection covering a period of over 90 years of Lufkin's history

Michelson Museum of Art
216 N. Bolivar, Marshall, TX   75670

903-935-9480
Open: 12-5 Tu-Fr, 1-4 Sa-Su   *Closed:* Mo, Easter, Mem/Day, 7/4, Thgv, 12/25
Vol/Contr.: Yes
&   P   *Museum Shop*   *Group Tours*   *Drop-In Tours:* 12-5 daily
Historic Building: Y, Southwestern Bell Telephone Building
Permanent Collection: Work of Russian American Artist Leo Michelson, 1887–1978; Kronenberg Collection of American Artists including Avery, Burliuk, Matisse, Rouault, Walkowitz; Jay Ward Collection of African Masks and Artifacts

ON EXHIBIT 2002

11/07/2001 to 01/26/2002   *Cambodian People and Landscape*

01/22/2002 to 03/17/2002   *Ramona and Jay Ward Collection African Masks and Artifacts*

02/05/2002 to 03/10/2002   *Texas Watercolor Society*   *Will Travel*

04/02/2002 to 05/31/2002   *Isabel Chapman*

M C A L L E N

McAllen International Museum
1900 Nolana, McAllen, TX   78504

956-682-1564   www.hiline.net/mim
Open: 9-5 Mo-We, Sa; Th 12-8; Su 1-5   *Closed:* Thgv, 12/25
Free Day: 9-1 Sa   *Adm:*   *Adult:* $2.00   *Children:* $1.00 under 13   *Students:* $1.00   *Seniors:* $1.00
&   P   *Museum Shop*   ¶: small café
Group Tours: 956-682-1564, ext. 116   *Drop-In Tours:* 8:30-11, 12-2:30
Permanent Collection: Lat/Am: folk; Am; Eur: gr 20

The museum caters to art & science on an equal level. See the hands-on mobile exhibits.

M I D L A N D

Museum of the Southwest
1705 W. Missouri Ave, Midland, TX   79701-6516

915-683-2882
Open: 10-5 Tu-Sa, 2-5 Su   *Closed:* Mo, Leg/Hol
&   P   *Group Tours*   *Drop-In Tours:* on request   *Sculpture Garden*
Permanent Collection: Reg; Gr; SW

The Museum of the Southwest is an educational resource in art including a Planetarium and Children's Museum. It focuses on the Southwest. Housed in a 1934 mansion and stables, the collection also features the Hogan Collection of works by founder members of the Taos Society of Artists.   ⟨ "The Sacred Pipe," by Alan Houser, bronze

O R A N G E

Stark Museum of Art
712 Green Ave, Orange, TX   77630

409-883-6661
Open: 10-5 Tu-Sa   *Closed:* Su, Mo, 1/1, Easter, 7/4, Thgv, 12/25
&   P   *Museum Shop*   *Group Tours*   *Drop-In Tours:* by appt   *Sculpture Garden*
Permanent Collection: Am: 1830-1950; Steuben Glass; Nat/Am; Birds by Dorothy Doughty & E. M. Boehm

In addition to Great Plains and SW Indian crafts the Stark houses one of the finest collections of Western American art in the country. The museum also features the only complete Steuben Glass collection of "The US in Crystal."   ⟨ Bronze sculptures by Frederic Remington

S A N   A N G E L O

San Angelo Museum of Fine Arts
704 Burgess, San Angelo, TX   76903

915-658-4084   http://web2.airmail/net
Open: 10-4 Tu-Sa, 1-4 Su   *Closed:* Mo, Leg/Hol
Adm: *Adult:* $2.00   *Children:* Free under 6   *Seniors:* $1.00
&   P: On-site   *Museum Shop*   *Group Tours*   *Historic Building*   *Sculpture Garden*
Permanent Collection: Am: cont cer; Reg; Mex: 1945-present

The completely renovated museum building was originally the 1868 quartermaster's storehouse on the grounds of Fort Concho, a National Historic Landmark. It is currently undergoing a major Capitol Building Campaign to construct a new museum to be started in the spring of 1997.   ⟨ "Figuora Accoccolata," by Emilio Greco

McNay Art Museum
6000 N. New Braunfels Ave, San Antonio, TX   78209-4618

210-824-5368   www.mcnayart.org
Open: 10-5 Tu-Sa, 12-5 Su   *Closed:* Mo, 1/1, 7/4, Thgv, 12/25
& P   *Museum Shop   Group Tours   Drop-In Tours   Historic Building   Sculpture Garden*
Permanent Collection: Fr & Am: sculp 19, 20; SW: folk ; Gr & Drgs: 19, 20; Theater Arts

The McNay Art Museum also has an outstanding 19th- and 20th-century collection of European and American art. The print and drawings collection is one of the best in the southwest. The Tobin theatre arts collection containing over 20,000 books and drawings as well as models of stage sets. It is located on beautifully landscaped grounds of the late Marion Koogler McNay's home in a classic Mediterranean style mansion.

San Antonio Museum of Art
200 West Jones Street, San Antonio, TX   78215

210-978-8100   www.samuseum.org
Open: 10-5,We, Fr, Sa, 10-9 Tu, 12-5 Su   *Closed:* Mo, Thgv, 12/25
Free Day: Tu 3-9   *Adm:*   *Adult:* $5.00   *Children:* $1.75 (4-11)   *Students:* $4.00   *Seniors:* $4.00
& P: Free   *Museum Shop* ¶   *Group Tours:* 210-978-8138   *Drop-In Tours:* most Su at 2pm !
Historic Building   Sculpture Garden
Permanent Collection: An/Grk; An/R; Egt; Cont: ptgs, sculp

The San Antonio Museum of Art is located in the restored turn-of-the-century former Lone Star Brewery. In addition to its other varied and rich holdings it features the most comprehensive collection of ancient art in the south.   ℂ The spectacular Ewing Halsell Wing for Ancient Art.

Tyler Museum of Art
1300 S. Mahon Ave, Tyler, TX   75701

903-595-1001
Open: 10-5 Tu-Sa, 1-5 Su   *Closed:* Mo, Leg/Hol!
& P   *Museum Shop*   ¶: Cafe open Tu-Fr 11-2   *Group Tours   Historic Building*
Permanent Collection: Phot; Reg 20

Art Center of Waco
1300 College Drive, Waco, TX   76708

254-752-4371
Open: 10-5 Tu-Sa; 1-5 Su   *Closed:* Mo, Leg/Hol!
Sugg/Contr.: Yes   *Adm:*   *Adult:* $2.00   *Children:* $1.00   *Students:* $1.00   *Seniors:* $1.50
&: 1st floor   P   *Museum Shop   Group Tours   Historic Building   Sculpture Garden   Theater*
Permanent Collection: Cont; Reg

Housed in the Cameron Home, The Art Center is located on the McLennan Community College campus. It features an exhibit of sculpture on the grounds.   ℂ"Square in Black," by Gio Pomodoro;"The Waco Door" 6 1/2-ton steel sculpture by Robert Wilson

Wichita Falls Museum and Art Center
Two Eureka Circle, Wichita Falls, TX   76308

817-692-0923
Open: 10-5 Tu-Sa, 1-5 Su   *Closed:* Mo, Leg/Hol!
Adm: *Adult:* $3.00   *Children:* Free under 3, $2.00   *Students:* $2.00   *Seniors:* $2.00
&   P   *Museum Shop*   *Group Tours*
Permanent Collection: Am: gr; Cont

The art collection has the singular focus of representing the history of American art through the medium of printmaking.   ❉ The "Magic Touch Gallery" featuring hands-on science and the Discovery Gallery emphasizing family programming. Also high energy, high tech laser programs and planet shows in the planetarium.

UTAH

Nora Eccles Harrison Museum of Art
Affiliated Institution: Utah State University
650 N. 1100 E., Logan, UT   84322-4020

435-797-0163   www.hass.usu.edu/2museum
Open: 10:30-4:30 Tu, Th, Fr, 10:30-8 We, 2-5 Sa-Su   *Closed:* Mo, Leg/Hol!
&   P: Within one block   *Group Tours:* 435-797-0165   *Drop-In Tours*   *Sculpture Garden*
Permanent Collection: Nat/Am; Am: cont art, cer 20

The Nora Eccles Harrison Museum of Art is the major center for the exhibition of the visual arts in Northern Utah. Emphasizing the breadth of artistic expression and the history of art in the western United States, the Museum's permanent collections include 20th century American sculpture, ceramics, paintings, graphic arts, photographs, and American Indian arts. Selections from the collection are always on view and are rotated periodically to reflect the continuing growth and refinement of the collection. In addition to installations of its permanent holdings, the Museum organizes temporary and traveling exhibitions and serves as a venue for exhibitions of national and international stature. Artist talks, films, docent tours, and educational activities are additional dimensions of the Museum's programs which are designed to interpret, present, and foster the development of the visual arts.   ❉ "Untitled" (Standing Woman), 1959, by Manuel Neri

Salt Lake Art Center
20 S.W. Temple, Salt Lake City, UT   84101

801-328-4201
Open: 10-5 Tu-Th, 10-9 Fr, 10-5 Sa, 1-5 Su   *Closed:* Mo, Leg/Hol!
Sugg/Contr.: Yes   *Adm:*   *Adult:* $2.00pp
&   P: Paid on street parking   *Museum Shop*   ❙❙   *Group Tours*   *Drop-In Tours*
Permanent Collection: Reg: all media

The 60-year-old art center is located in the Bicentennial complex in the heart of downtown Salt Lake City.

Utah Museum of Fine Arts
101 AAC, University of Utah, Salt Lake City, UT   84112

801-581-7332
Open: 10-5 Mo-Fr, 2-5 Sa, Su   *Closed:* Leg/Hol!
  ♿ P: Free on campus parking Sa & Su; metered parking on weekdays   *Museum Shop*
Group Tours   Sculpture Garden
Permanent Collection: Eur & Am: ptgs 17-19; Af; As; Egt

With a permanent collection of over 10,000 works spanning a broad spectrum of the world's art history, this major Utah cultural institution is a virtual artistic treasure house containing the only comprehensive collection of art in the state or the surrounding region.   ℂ "Dance Around The Maypole" by Pieter Breughel, The Younger

SPRINGVILLE

Springville Museum of Art
126 E. 400 S., Springville, UT   84663

801-489-2727
Open: 10-5 Tu-Sa, 3-6:30 Su, 10-9 We   *Closed:* 1/1, 12/25, 7/4
Vol/Contr.: Yes
♿ P   *Museum Shop   Group Tours   Drop-In Tours   Sculpture Garden*
Permanent Collection: UT: ptgs, sculp

The museum, housed in a Spanish colonial revival style building, features a collection noted for the art of Utah dating from pioneer days to the present.

VERMONT

BENNINGTON

Bennington Museum
W. Main Street, Bennington, VT   05201

802-447-1571
Open: 9-5 daily, Weekends 9-7, Mem/Day-Lab/Day   *Closed:* Thgv
Adm: *Adult:* $5.00, family $ *Children:* Free under 12   *Students:* $3.50   *Seniors:* $4.50
♿.: Partial first floor only   P   *Museum Shop   Group Tours   Historic Building   Theater*
Permanent Collection: Am: dec/art; Military Hist; Am: ptgs

Visitors can imagine days gone by while gazing at a favorite Grandma Moses painting at The Bennington, one of the finest regional art and history museums in New England. The original museum building is the 1855 St. Francis de Sales church.

BURLINGTON

Robert Hull Fleming Museum
Affiliated Institution: University of Vermont
61 Colchester Ave., Burlington, VT   05405

802-656-0750   www.uvm.edu/~fleming, www.fleming museum.org
Open: 9-4 Tu-Fr, 1-5 Sa, Su (summer May 1st-Labor/Day 12-4 Th, Fr, 12-5 Sa, Su)   *Closed:* Leg/Hol!, Acad!
Adm: *Adult:* $3.00, Fam $5.00   *Children:* $2.00   *Students:* $2.00   *Seniors:* $2.00
♿   P   *Museum Shop   Group Tours   Historic Building*
Permanent Collection: An/Egt; Cont; Eu & Am; Mid/East; As; Af

Vermont's primary art and anthropology museum is located in a 1931 McKim, Mead and White building.   ℂ Assyrian Relief

Southern Vermont Art Center
West Road, Manchester, VT   05254

802-362-1405   www.svac.org
Open: Winter 10-5 Mo-Sa; Summer 10-5 Tu-Sa; 12-5 Su   *Closed:* Su in winter, Mo in summer 1/1,
Columbus Day, 12/25
Free Day: Sa, 10-1   *Adm:*   *Adult:* $6.00   *Children:* Free under 13   *Students:* $3.00
&.: partial   P   *Group Tours   Historic Building   Sculpture Garden*
Permanent Collection: Ptgs, Sculp, Phot, Gr; Cont: 20

Built in 1917, by Mr. & Mrs. W. M. Ritter of Washington D.C., the Art Center is housed in a
Georgian Colonial Mansion located on 450 acres on the eastern slope of Mt. Equinox. Included
in the facility is a theater with dance, music and film programs.   ☾ Works by Winslow Homer
and Ogden Pleissner

ON EXHIBIT 2002

12/06/2001 to 01/09/2002   *10th Annual Little Picture Show*
Small and affordable works of art. Included are Jane Pincus, John Costa Rosis, Clarence King,
John Leavey, Teru Simon, Michael McCovern, The Vermont Watercolor Society

01/12/2002 to 02/06/2002   *10th Annual Winter Members Exhibition*
Juried artists from the New England region

02/09/2002 to 03/06/2002   *February Solo and Group Exhibition*
Included are Richard Weis, Robvert Carsten, Eric Slayton Nick Loscalzo, Lisa Palumbo, David
Utiger, Thomas Vieth

02/16/2002 to 03/30/2002   *Granite and Cedar: Photographs of Rural Vermont by John C. Miller*
Black-and-white documentary photographs

03/09/2002 to 04/01/2002   *March Solo and Group Exhibitions*
Eugene Colin, Adelaide Werger, Joy Huckins-Noss

Middlebury College Museum of Art
Middlebury College, Middlebury, VT   05753

802-443-5007   www.middlebury.edu/~museum
Open: 10-5 Tu-Fr, 12-5 Sa, Su   *Closed:* Acad!, 12/18-1/1
&.   P: Free   *Museum Shop*   ‖   *Group Tours* 802-443-5007   *Theater*
Permanent Collection: Anc/R/Grk; cer, sculp; As; Eur, Am: sculp, drg, ptgs, phoios, and Cont all media

Designed by the New York firm of Hardy Holzman Pfeiffer Associates, the new (1992) Center
for the Arts also includes a theater, concert hall, music library, and dance studios. It is located
midway between Rutland and Burlington.   ☾ "Bimbo Malato (Sick Child)," 1893 by Medardo
Rosso (wax over plaster)

ON EXHIBIT 2002

01/02/2002 to April 2002   *Tennie Harris: A Legacy in Black and White, 1939–1975*

01/02/2002 to May 2002   *Stories in Art*

05/01/2002 to August 2002   *David Bumbeck Prints and Sculpture*

05/01/2002 to August 2002   *Sabra Field*

Sheldon Art Museum, Archeological and Historical Society
1 Park Street, Middlebury, VT   05753

802-388-2117   www.middlebury.edu/~shel-mus
Open: 10-5 Mo-Sa; Research Center Tu-Fr 1-5   *Closed:* Leg/Hol!, 1/1, Mem/Day, 7/4, Lab/Day, Thgv
Adm: Adult: $4.00, $10.00 fam   *Children:* $2.00 6-18   *Students:* $3.50   *Seniors:* $3.50
&   P: Public parking nearby   *Museum Shop   Group Tours   Drop-In Tours   Historic Building   Theater*
Permanent Collection: Dec/Art; Per/Rms; Artifacts

Regional Vermont's exciting and interesting history is interpreted in this century old museum located in the 1829 Judd Harris house and Fletcher History Center.   ℂ Portraits by itinerant artist Benjamin Franklin Mason.

MONTPELIER

T. W. Wood Gallery and Arts Center
Affiliated Institution: Vermont College
College Hall, Montpelier, VT   05602

802-828-8743
Open: 12-4 Tu-Su   *Closed:* Mo, Leg/Hol!
Free Day: Su   *Adm:*   Adult: $2.00   *Children:* Free under 12   *Seniors:* $2.00
&   P: on street   *Museum Shop   Group Tours   Historic Building*
Permanent Collection: Thomas Waterman Wood: ptgs; Portraits; WPA Work

Included in the more than 200 oils and watercolors in this collection are the works of Thomas W. Wood and his American contemporaries of the 1920s and 30s including A. H. Wyant and Asher B. Durand.   ℂ Exhibits of Vermont's artists and craftspeople

SHELBURNE

Shelburne Museum
U.S. Route 7, Shelburne, VT   05482

802-985-3346   www.shelburnemuseum.org
Open: Seasonal Hours !   *Closed:* 1/1, Easter, Thgv, 12/25
Adm: Adult: $17.50/ $10   *Children:* $7.00 (6-14)/$3.50   *Students:* $10.50/$5.00
&: Limited (certain buildings are handicap accessible)   P: Free   *Museum Shop*   ‖
Group Tours: 802-985-3348, ext. 3389   *Drop-In Tours:* 1pm late Oct-late May   *Historic Building*
Permanent Collection: Folk; Dec/Art; Havermeyer Coll

Thirty-seven historic and exhibition buildings on 45 scenic acres combine to form this nationally celebrated collection of American folk art, artifacts, and architecture.   ℂ Steamboat Ticonderoga, "Louise Havemeyer and her Daughter Electra" by Mary Cassatt, 1895

ST. JOHNSBURY

St. Johnsbury Athenaeum
30 Main Street, St. Johnsbury, VT   05819

802-748-8291   www.stjothenaeum.org
Open: 10:00-8:00 Mo, We, 10:00-5:30 Tu, Fr, 9:30-4 Sa   *Closed:* Leg/Hol!
Adm: Adult: $2.00pp
&   P: Limited   *Museum Shop   Group Tours   Drop-In Tours   Historic Building*
Permanent Collection: Am: ptgs 19; Hudson River School

The Athenaeum was built as a public library and presented to the townspeople of St. Johnsbury by Horace Fairbanks in 1871. In 1873 an art gallery, which today is an authentic Victorian period piece, was added to the main building. The collection of American landscapes and genre paintings is shown as it was in 1890 in the oldest unaltered art gallery in the US.   ℂ "Domes of The Yosemite," by Albert Bierstadt

VIRGINIA

CHARLOTTESVILLE

Bayly Art Museum of the University of Virginia
Rugby Road, Thomas H. Bayly Memorial Bldg, Charlottesville, VA   22903-2427

804-924-3592   www.virginia.edu/~bayly/bayly.html
Open: 1-5 Tu-Su   *Closed:* Mo, 12/24-1/2
Sugg/Contr.: Yes   *Adm:*   *Adult:* $3.00   *Seniors:* $3.00
&   P: Limited parking behind the museum   *Museum Shop*   *Group Tours:* 804-924-7458   *Drop-In Tours*
Permanent Collection: Nat/Am; Meso/Am; Af; Dec/Art 18; OM: gr; Am: ptgs, sculp, works on paper, phot 20; P/Col

This handsome Palladian-inspired building is located on the grounds of Jefferson's University of Virginia. With its wide ranging collections and special exhibitions, it serves as a museum for all ages and interests, for art lovers and scholars alike.

ON EXHIBIT 2002

01/26/2002 to 04/07/2002   *"See America First" The Complete Graphic Work by H. C. Westermann*   *Will Travel*

01/26/2002 to 04/07/2002   *William Blake from the Ross Collection*   *Will Travel*

03/31/2002 to 06/09/2002   *Selections from the Collection: Native American Art*

04/19/2002 to 06/30/2002   *Re-Imagining Ireland: Contemporary Irish Art*

Second Street Gallery
201 2nd Street, NW, Charlottesville, VA   22902

804-977-7284
Open: 10-5 Tu-Sa, 1-5 Su   *Closed:* Mo, Leg/Hol!
&   P: On-street parking   *Historic Building*
Permanent Collection: Non-collecting Cont art space

Nationally known for its innovative programming, Second Street Gallery presents work of talented, regional and national artists working in a variety of media from painting and photography to sculpture and site-specific installations. The McGuffey Art Center which houses the Gallery is a historic former primary school building and is now an artist cooperative with open studios.

CLIFTON FORGE

Allegheny Highlands Arts and Craft Center
439 East Ridgeway Street, Clifton Forge, VA   24422

703-862-4447
Open: 10:30-4:30 Mo-Sa May-Dec, 10:30-4:30 Tu-Sa Jan-Apr   *Closed:* Su, Thgv, 12/24-01/12
&   P   *Museum Shop*   *Group Tours:* on request
Permanent Collection: Non-collecting institution

Housed in an early 1900s building, the galleries' changing exhibits feature works produced by Highlands and other artists.

Danville Museum of Fine Arts & History
975 Main Street, Danville, VA   24541

804-793-5644   www.danvillemuseum.org
Open: 10-5 Tu-Fr, 2-5 Sa, Su   *Closed:* Mo, Leg/Hol!
Vol/Contr.: Yes
&   P   *Museum Shop   Group Tours   Drop-In Tours:* by appt   *Historic Building*
Permanent Collection: Reg: portraits, works on paper, dec/art, furniture, textiles

The Museum, located in Sutherlin Mansion built about 1857, was the residence of Confederate President Jefferson Davis for one week in April 1865.   ℂ Restored Victorian Parlor; Between the Lines Civil War Historical Exhibition

ON EXHIBIT 2002

02/03/2002 to 03/17/2002   *Georgia O'Keeffe: The Artist's Landscape, Photographs by Todd Webb*

02/03/2002 to 03/17/2002   *Visions in Wood-Work by Charles Farrar, Woodturnings*

03/24/2002 to 05/05/2002   *Emotional Validity: Work by Bridget Dobson*

11/16/2002 to 12/20/2002   *Danville Art League Juried Show*

Belmont, The Gari Melchers Estate and Memorial Gallery
224 Washington St., Fredericksburg, VA   22405

540-654-1015
Open: 10-5 Mo-Sa, 1-5 Su; Dec 1-Feb 28 10-4 Mo-Sa, 1-4 Su   *Closed:* 1/1, Thgv, 12/24, 12/25, 12/31
Adm: Adult: $4.00   *Children:* Free under 6   *Students:* $1.00   *Seniors:* $3.00
&: Very limited (with prior notice assistance will be provided)   P   *Museum Shop*
Group Tours: 540-654-1841   *Drop-In Tours:* on the hour and half hour   *Historic Building*
Permanent Collection: Eur & Am: ptgs (mostly by Gari Melchers)

This 18th-century estate features many paintings by Gari Melchers (its former resident). Also on view are works by his American and European contemporaries as well as some old masters.

Hampton University Museum
Hampton University, Hampton, VA   23668

757-727-5308   www.hamptonu.edu
Open: 8-5 Mo-Fr, 12-4 Sa   *Closed:* Leg/Hol!, Acad!
&   P   *Museum Shop   Group Tours:* 757-727-5508   *Historic Building*
Permanent Collection: Af; Nat/Am: Am: ptgs 20

The Museum is housed in the spectacular, newly renovated Huntington Building, formerly the University Library. It is the oldest African American museum in the US and one of the oldest museums in Virginia. The collections include over 9,000 objects including traditional African, Native American, Asian, and Pacific Island art as well as a fine art collection.   ℂ "The Banjo Lesson," by Henry O. Tanner

Maier Museum of Art
Affiliated Institution: Randolph-Macon Woman's College
2500 Rivermont Avenue, Lynchburg, VA   24503

804-947-8136   www.rmwc.edu/maier
Open: 1-5 Tu-Su Sept-May, 1-4 We-Su, June-Aug   Closed: Acad/Hol!
&: Limited (no handicap bathroom)   P: Limited   Museum Shop   Group Tours: ext 3   Drop-In Tours
Permanent Collection: Am: ptgs 19, 20

19th- and 20th-century American paintings, including works by Gilbert Stuart, Winslow Homer, Thomas Eakins, Thomas Cole, George Bellows, Mary Cassatt, Georgia O'Keeffe, and Andrew Wyeth, are among the many highlights of the Maier Museum of Art. ◖ George Bellows'"Men of the Docks"

ON EXHIBIT 2002

01/13/2002 to 03/03/2002   James Abbe: Photographer

NEWPORT NEWS

Peninsula Fine Arts Center
101 Museum Drive, Newport News, VA   23606

757-596-8175   www.pfac-vol.org
Open: 10-5 Mo-Sa, 1-5 Su; 10-9 Th   Closed: 1/1, Thgv, 12/24pm, 12/25
Vol/Contr.: Yes
&: Limited, 1st fl only incl all galleries and one classroom   P   Museum Shop
Group Tours   Drop-In Tours: by appt   Sculpture Garden
Permanent Collection: Non-collecting institution

Changing exhibitions of primarily contemporary art by emerging artists that often contrast with exhibitions of historical significance are featured at this fine arts center which also has a Hands On For Kids gallery. The Center is located within the Mariner's Museum Park with the Noland Trail.

NORFOLK

Chrysler Museum of Art
245 West Olney Road, Norfolk, VA   23510-1587

757-664-6200   www.chrysler.org
Open: 10-9 We, 10-5 Th, Fr, Sa, 1-5 Su   Closed: Mo, Tu, 1/1, 7/4, Thgv, 12/25
Free Day: We   Adm: Adult: $7.00   Children: under 12 Free   Students: $5.00   Seniors: $5.00
&   P: Free   Museum Shop   ¶: Phantoms   Group Tours: 757-333-6283   Drop-In Tours
Historic Building   Theater
Permanent Collection: Glass; It/Baroque: ptgs; Fr: 19; An/Egt; Am: sculp, ptgs

Home to one of America's premier art collections spanning 5,000 years of art history in an Italianate-Style building on the picturesque Hague of the Elizabeth River. There are three historic houses.   ◖ Gianlorenzo Bernini's "Bust of the Savior"; Degas "Dancer with Bouquet"

Hermitage Foundation Museum
7637 North Shore Road, Norfolk, VA   23505

757-423-2052
Open: 10-5 Mo-Sa, 1-5 Su   Closed: 1/1, Thgv, 12/25
Adm: Adult: $4.00   Children: $1.00   Seniors: $4.00
&   P   Historic Building
Permanent Collection: Or; Eur; As; 16, 17

Nestled in a lush setting along the Lafayette River is the 12-acre estate of the Hermitage Foundation Museum whose turn-of-the-century English Tudor home appears to have been frozen in time. It is, however, alive with treasures from the past. ⊄ 1,400-year-old Buddha

RADFORD

Radford University Galleries
200 Powell Hall, Radford, VA   24142

540-831-5754   www.runet,edu/~rumuseum
Open: Sept-Apr 10-5 Mo-Fr, 1-4 Su (5/1-7/30 Mo-Fr 10-4)   *Closed:* Mo, Aug, Acad
& P   *Group Tours   Drop-In Tours:* by appt   *Sculpture Garden*
Permanent Collection: Cont works in all media

Located in the New River Valley, the gallery is noted for the diversity of its special exhibitions.

RICHMOND

Anderson Gallery, School of the Arts
Affiliated Institution: Virginia Commonwealth University
907 1/2 W. Franklin Street, Richmond, VA   23284-2514

804-828-1522   www.vcu.edu/artweb/gallery/index.html
Open: 10-5 Tu-Fr, 1-5 Sa, Su   *Closed:* Mo, Leg/Hol! Acad!
Vol/Contr.: Yes
&: no elevator; museum has 3 floors   P: Metered on-street parking   *Group Tours*
Permanent Collection: Cont: gr, phot, ptgs, sculp

The gallery is well known in the US and Europe for exhibiting work of nationally and internationally renowned artists.

ON EXHIBIT 2002

01/18/2002 to 03/10/2002   *Imagescape*
Video and digital media by Jennifer Steinkamp, Jeremy Blake, Stephen Murphy, and Kiki Seror

01/18/2002 to 03/10/2002   *The George and Helen Spelvin Collection*
Folk art collection   *Will Travel*

Marsh Art Gallery, University of Richmond Museums
George M. Modlin Center for the Arts, Richmond, VA   23173

804-289-8276   www.richmond.edu/cultural/museums
Open: 1-5 Tu-Su   *Closed:* Mo, Acad !
& P: Free   *Museum Shop*   ¶: College Cafeteria
Permanent Collection: Am: As: Eur: cer, drgs, gr, photo, ptg, sculp

The new galleries feature outstanding exhibitions of contemporary and historical art.   ⊄ The new Cram-inspired building designed by the architectural firm of Marcellus, Wright, Cox, and Smith.

ON EXHIBIT 2002

01/08/2002 to 07/27/2002   *Thomas Weaver: Punchlist*

01/11/2002 to 02/24/2002   *Power of Thought: The Prints of Jessie Oomark*

01/18/2002 to 02/24/2002   *Silent History: The Still Lifes of G. Daniel Massad*

03/15/2002 to 06/29/2002   *Fifth American Print Biennial*

03/20/2002 to 07/28/2002   *Buds, Blooms, and Blossoms: Boehm Porcelains from the Permanent Collection*

04/03/2002 to 06/29/2002   *Machines of the Mind: Sculpture by Lawrence Fane*

Virginia Museum of Fine Arts
2800 Grove Ave, Richmond, VA   23221-2466

804-340-1400   www.vmfa.state.va.us
Open: 11-5 Tu-Su, 11-8 Th   *Closed:* Mo, 1/1, 7/4, Thgv, 12/25
Sugg/Contr.: $5.00 pp
& P: Free   *Museum Shop*   ¶
Group Tours: 804-340-1437   *Drop-In Tours:* 2:30 Tu-Su, 6pm Th except summer   *Sculpture Garden*
Permanent Collection: Am: ptgs, sculp; Lillain Thomas Pratt Coll of Jewels by Peter Carl Faberge; Eur: all media (Ren to cont)

Diverse collections and outstanding special exhibits abound in the internationally prominent Virginia Museum which houses one of the largest collections in the world of Indian, Nepalese, and Tibetan art. It also holds the Mellon Collection of British sporting art and the Sydney and Francis Lewis Collection of late 19th- and early 20th-century decorative arts, contemporary American paintings and sculpture.   ¶ "Caligula," Roman, AD 38-40 marble 80'-high. Also the largest public collection of Faberge Imperial Easter eggs in the West; one of the world's finest collections of Art Nouveau and Art Deco decorative arts

ON EXHIBIT 2002

10/15/2001 to 01/06/2002   *Print Matters: New Work and Modern Treasures*
Modern and contemporary prints including Serra, Close, Saar, Lawrence, and Kentridge. A broad range of approaches to printmaking

11/21/2001 to 02/24/2002   *Worlds of Wonder and Desire: Indian Paintings from the Virginia Museum of Fine Arts*
Evolution of painting from the 12th to the 20th century in South Asian *Catalog*

01/19/2002 to 03/17/2002   *Outer and Inner Space: A Video Exhibition in Three Parts, I Pipilotti Rist, Sip My Ocean*
Themes of love, loss, and body politics in double screen projection. Works by Wegman, Acconci Antin, Birnbaum, Jonas, McCarthy, and Rosler

04/06/2002 to 06/02/2002   *Outer and Inner Space: II Shirin Neshat*
Projections on opposite walls showing the division between men and women in Islamic countries

06/22/2002 to 08/18/2002   *Outer and Inner Space: III Jane and Louise Wilson, "Stasi City"*
Abandoned headquarters of the East German Police   *Catalog*

Art Museum of Western Virginia
One Market Square, Roanoke, VA   24011

540-342-5760   www.artmuseumroanoke.org
Open: 10-5 Tu-Sa, 1-5 Su (10-2 12/24, 12/31)   *Closed:* Mo, 1/1, 12/25
& P: Pay   *Museum Shop   Group Tours   Sculpture Garden   Theater*
Permanent Collection: Am & Eur: ptgs 20; Am: folk, gr, phot

The collection reflects all cultures formerly and presently found there. By collecting, exhibiting, preserving, and interpreting works of art, the Museum plays a significant role in the cultural history of the region. Exhibitions are of both national and regional significance   ¶ Sidewalk Art Show, June 3-4, 2000

Sweet Briar College Art Gallery
Sweet Briar College, Sweet Briar, VA   24595

804-381-6248   www.artgallery.sbc.edu
Open: Pannell: 12-9:30 Mo-Th, 12-5 Fr-Su, Babcock: 9-9 daily   *Closed:* Acad!
& P   *Museum Shop*   ¶: On campus   *Group Tours   Historic Building   Sculpture Garden*
Permanent Collection: Jap: woodblock prints; Eur: gr, drgs 19; Am: ptgs 20

Th exterior design of the 1901 building is a rare collegiate example of Ralph Adams Cram
Georgian Revival Style architecture.

ON EXHIBIT 2002

01/11/2002 to 03/25/2002   *Jian Xu: Painting*
Traditional Chinese landscape painting for which he won many awards in China and those
influenced by Western art and culture

03/29/2002 to 05/13/2002   *Pam Fox: Photographs*
Exploring still life, machines, the human figure, and momento mori imagery, Fox links the
mechanical with the poetic.

Contemporary Art Center of Virginia
2200 Parks Avenue, Virginia Beach, VA   23451

757-425-0000   www.cacv.org
Open: 10-5 Tu-Fr, 10-4 Sa   *Closed:* Su, Leg/Hol!
Adm: Adult: $3.00   Children: under 4 free   Students: $2.00   Seniors: $2.00
& P   *Museum Shop   Group Tours   Drop-In Tours   Sculpture Garden*
Permanent Collection: Non-collecting institution

This non-profit center exists to foster awareness and understanding of the significant art of our
time.

Abby Aldrich Rockefeller Folk Art Museum
307 S. England Street, Williamsburg, VA   23185

757-220-7698   www.colonialwilliamsburg.org
Open: 11-5 daily Jan-mid Mar; 10-5 mid Mar-Dec
Adm: Adult: $8.00   Children: $4.00
& P: Free   *Museum Shop   Group Tours:* 757-220-7667   *Historic Building*
Permanent Collection: Am: folk

Colonial Williamsburg is the site of the country's premier showcase for American folk art. The
museum, originally built in 1957 and expanded in 1992, demonstrates folk art's remarkable
range and inventiveness in textiles, paintings, and decorative arts.

ON EXHIBIT 2002

11/22/2001 to 03/03/2002   *The Hennage Collection of Antique Toys*
A private collection of American and German tin toys from the late 19th century to the first half
of the 20th

11/22/2001 to 03/03/2002   *Holiday Favorites*
Doll houses and paper dolls

11/22/2001 to 03/03/2002   *Tasha Tudor's Pictures for the Holidays*
Original artwork by the book illustrator

11/22/2001 to mid-February 2003   *Life in Perspective: The Woodcarvings of Rupert Kreider*
Large carvings by an itinerent Arkansas artist in the 3rd quarter of the 20th century

05/24/2002 to 09/01/2002   *Made in America: Coverlets from the Collection of Foster and Muriel McCarl*
A look at the technology and the weavers who made these bedcovers

Muscarelle Museum of Art
College of William and Mary, PO Box 8795, Williamsburg, VA   23187-8795

757-221-2700   www.wm.edu/muscarelle
Open: 10-4:45 Mo-Fr, 12-4 Sa-Su   *Closed:* Leg/Hol!
Vol/Contr.: Yes
&   P   *Museum Shop*   *Group Tours:* 757-221-2703   *Drop-In Tours:* by appt   *Historic Building*
Permanent Collection: Brit & Am: portraits 17-19; O/M: drgs; Cont: gr; Ab; Eur & Am: ptgs

The mission of the Museum is to pursue an active role in the cultural life of the region through education and presentation of works of art. ❑ "Portrait of William Short" by Rembrandt Peale; "Teacup and Bread on Ledge" by John Frederick Peto; "Moonlit Landscape" by Henry Ossawa Tanner; "White Flower" by Georgia O'Keeffe

ON EXHIBIT 2002

10/21/2001 to 01/13/2002   *Exploring Ancient Egypt*

10/21/2001 to 01/13/2002   *Huda Lufti: Contemporary Egyptian Art on Paper*

03/30/2002 to 05/12/2002   *Sculpture by Lawrence Fane*

06/01/2002 to Summer 2002   *American Drawing Biennial*

08/24/2002 to 10/06/2002   *Ken Aptekar: Painting Between the Lines, Work from 1990–2000*

10/19/2002 to 01/12/2003   *Window on the West: The Phelan Collection*

WASHINGTON

BELLEVUE

Bellevue Art Museum
301 Bellevue Way NE, Bellevue, WA   98004

425-519-0770   www.bellevueart.org
Open: 10-5 Tu, We, Fr, Sa, 10-8 Th, 12-5 Su   *Closed:* Mo, 1/1, Easter, 7/4, Mem/Day, Lab/Day, Thgv, 12/25
Free Day: 3rd Th of month   *Adm:*   *Adult:* $6.00   *Children:* Free under 12   *Students:* $4.00   *Seniors:* $4.00
&   P: Free   *Museum Shop*
Group Tours: 425-519-0745   *Drop-In Tours:* 2:00 daily docent tour; 1:00 building tour
Permanent Collection: Non-collecting institution

Located across Lake Washington about 10 minutes drive from Seattle, the museum is a place to see, explore, and make art.

ON EXHIBIT 2002

10/13/2001 to 01/06/2002   *2001 Pacific Northwest Annual*
Juried annual exhibition

12/08/2001 to 03/24/2002   *Telling Tales: Roger Shimomura: An American Diary*
Fifty years of his grandmother's memories as a Japanese picture bride and internment camp survivor

12/08/2001 to 03/10/2002   *Telling Tales: Shaping Stories*
Innovative tales and narrative stories by visual artists

01/18/2002 to 03/10/2002   *John Stamets: BAM as Built*
Photographs of the construction of the Museum

03/23/2002 to 06/24/2002   *Alfredo Arreguin: Patterns of Dreams and Nature*
Arreguin was commissioned to do a mural which would be finished by the visiting public
according to his design, as well as a site-specific work.   *Will Travel   Bilingual   Book*

04/06/2002 to 07/14/2002   *Locurto/Outcault: Self Portrait.map*
Large prints of images to manipulate scans of their bodies using cartographic tools and
technique

BELLINGHAM

Whatcom Museum of History & Art
121 Prospect Street, Bellingham, WA   98225

360-676-6981   www.cob.org.museum
Open: 12-5 Tu-Su   *Closed:* Mo, Leg/Hol!
&.   *Museum Shop   Group Tours   Historic Building*
Permanent Collection: Kinsey: phot coll; Hanson: Naval arch drgs; NW/Coast: ethnography; Victoriana

An architectural and historic landmark, this museum building is situated in a 1892 former City
Hall on a bluff with a commanding view of Bellingham Bay.

CLARKSTON

Valley Art Center, Inc
842 6th Street, Clarkston, WA   99403

509-758-8331
Open: 9-4 Mo-Fr, by appt other times   *Closed:* 7/4, Thgv, 12/25-1/1
&.: Building accessible except for restrooms   P   *Museum Shop   Group Tours   Historic Building*
Permanent Collection: Reg; Nat/Am

Valley Art Center is located in southeast Washington at the Snake and Clearwater Rivers in the
heart of the city's historic district made famous by Lewis and Clarke.   ℭ Beadwork, Piute
Cradle Board Tatouche

GOLDENDALE

Maryhill Museum of Art
35 Maryhill Museum Drive, Goldendale, WA   98620

509-773-3733   www.maryhillmuseum.org
Open: 9-5 daily, Mar 15-Nov 15   *Closed:* Open Hol
Adm: Adult: $7.00   Children: Free under 6   Students: $2.00   Seniors: $6.00
&.   P: Free   *Museum Shop*   ⅼⅼ: cafe, picnic grounds   *Group Tours   Historic Building   Sculpture Garden*
Permanent Collection: August Rodin Sculp; Orthodox Icons: 18; ptgs; Nat/Am: baskets, dec/art;
Furnishings of Queen Marie of Romania; International Chess Sets

Serving the Pacific Northwest, the Maryhill Museum is a major cultural resource on the Lewis
and Clark Trail in the Columbia River Gorge region.   ℭ Theatre de la Mode: 1946 French
Fashion collection

Art Gallery, Lower Columbia College Fine Arts Gallery
1600 Maple Street, Longview, WA   98632

360-577-2300
Open: 10-4 Mo, Tu, 10-8 We, Th Sept-June   *Closed:* Leg/Hol, Acad/Hol
  P ❦: cafeteria in student center   *Group Tours:* 360-577-2314   *Theater*
Permanent Collection: Various locations on campus

A College Gallery that features temporary exhibitions by local, regional, and national artists.

ON EXHIBIT 2002

02/07/2002 to 03/07/2002   *Dale Horghner*
Oregon photographer

03/28/2002 to 04/25/2002   *Cultural Edge: Contemporary Views of Native Artists*
Contemporary Northwest native art

Washington State Capitol Museum
211 West 21st Avenue, Olympia, WA   98501

360-753-2580   www.wshs.org
Open: 10-4 Tu-Fr, 12-4 Sa   *Closed:* Leg/Hol!
Adm: Adult: $2.00, $5.00 Families   *Students:* $1.00   *Seniors:* $1.75
  P   *Museum Shop   Group Tours   Drop-In Tours:* by appt   *Historic Building*
Permanent Collection: Reg: Nat/Am: 18, 19

The Museum is housed in the Lord Mansion, a 1924 Italian Renaissance Revival Style building. It also features a permanent exhibit on the history of Washington State government and cultural history.   ❦ Southern Puget Sound American Indian exhibit welcome healing totem pole figure.

Museum of Art
Washington State University, Pullman, WA   99164

509-335-1910   www.wsu.ed/artmuse
Open: 10-4 Mo-Fr, 10-9 Th, 1-5 Sa-Su   *Closed:* Acad!
  P: Parking permits may be purchased at Parking Services, adjacent to the Fine Arts Center
Group Tours   Drop-In Tours
Permanent Collection: NW: art; Cont/Am & Cont/Eur: gr 19

The WSU Museum of Art, in the university community of Pullman, presents a diverse program of changing exhibitions, including paintings, prints, photography, and crafts.

Frye Art Museum
704 Terry Avenue, Seattle, WA   98104

206-622-9250   www.fryeart.org
Open: 10-5 Tu-Sa, 10-9 Th, 12-5 Su   *Closed:* Mo, 1/1, Thgv, 12/25
  P: Free across from Museum   *Museum Shop*   ❦: 11-4 Tu-Sa, 11-7:30 Th, 12-4 Su
Group Tours: 2 weeks adv res   *Sculpture Garden   Theater*
Permanent Collection: Am Realist 19-20; Eur Realist ptgs, Munich School

A mid-sized museum with representational art from Colonial times to the present. Hailed by the press as a "little gem of a museum" it presents European and American art. Charles and Emma Frye bequeathed their collection to create a free public art museum.

Henry Art Gallery

Affiliated Institution: University of Washington
15th Ave. NE & NE 41st Street, Seattle, WA   98195-3070

206-543-2280   www.henryart.org
Open: 11-5 Tu, We, Fr-Su, 11-8 Th   *Closed:* 1/1, 7/4, Thgv, 12/25
Free Day: 5-8pm Th pay what you wish   *Adm:*   *Adult:* $6.00   *Children:* Free under 12   *Seniors:* $4.50
& P: Pay   *Museum Shop* ¶ *Group Tours:* 206-221-4980   *Drop-In Tours:* 2nd Sa, 3rd Th: 12-2 Tu-Th
Historic Building   Sculpture Garden
Permanent Collection: Ptgs: 19, 20; Phot; Cer; Eth: textiles & W/Coast

The major renovation designed by Charles Gwathmey of Carl F. Gould's 1927 building re-opened in April 1997. The expansion adds 10,000 square feet of galleries and additional visitor amenities and educational facilities.

ON EXHIBIT 2002

09/14/2001 to 01/01/2002   *Jeffry Mitchell*
The gallery is divided between Heaven and Earth with personal visions of both places.

11/10/2001 to 02/03/2002   *Superflat*
The tendency in Japanese art, animation, and graphic design to two dimensionality. Included are some of the most exciting artists working in Japan.

03/07/2002 to 05/26/2002   *Gene(sis): Contemporary Art Explores Human Genomics*
A look at human genomics featuring four works developed by artists in collaboration with scientists commissioned for the exhibition   *Will Travel*

Nordic Heritage Museum

3014 N.W. 67th Street, Seattle, WA   98117

206-789-5707   www.nordicmuseum.com
Open: 10-4 Tu-Sa, 12-4 Su   *Closed:* 12/24, 12/25, 1/1
Free Day: 1st Tu each month   *Adm:*   *Adult:* $4.00   *Children:* $2.00 (6-16)   *Students:* $3.00   *Seniors:* $3.00
& P: Free   *Museum Shop   Group Tours   Drop-In Tours:* on request
Permanent Collection: Scandinavian/Am: folk; Phot: fine art

Follow the immigrants journey across America in this museum located in Ballard north of the Ballard Locks.   ¶ "Dancing Angels" original bronze sculpture by Carl Milles

ON EXHIBIT 2002

01/18/2002 to 04/28/2002   *They Left for America/De Drogo Till Amerika*
Monumental tapestries illustrating Swedish immigration history

05/10/2002 to 07/14/2002   *Four Nordic Artists*
Asdia Frimannadottir, jewelry; Steffan Herrik, sculpture; Astrid Larsen, fire artist; Erik Reime, tatoo artist. An interpretation of Nordic heritage in various media including prehistoric images

07/23/2002 to 09/08/2002   *Eva Isaksen, Sonia Blomdahl, and Greta Bodegaard*

09/19/2002 to 11/10/2002   *Anders Zorn: Etchings and Jerry Wingren*
Zorn is a famous Swedish artist from Dalama, and Wingren, a sculptor.

11/25/2002 to mid-February 2003   *Karl Erik Harr*
Norwegian landscape painter

Seattle Art Museum

100 University Street, Seattle, WA   98101-2902

206-625-8900   www.seattleartmuseum.org
Open: 10-5 Tu-Su, 10-9 Th, open Mo on Holidays   *Closed:* Thgv, 12/25, 1/1
Free Day: 1st Th; Sr. 1st Fr over 62   *Adm:*   *Adult:* $7.00   *Children:* Free under 12
Students: $5.00 with ID   *Seniors:* $5.00
&   P: Limited pay parking   *Museum Shop*   ¶
Group Tours: 206-654-3123   *Drop-In Tours:* Group tours 2 weeks advance appt   *Sculpture Garden*
Permanent Collection: As; Af; NW Nat/Am; Cont; Phot; Eur: dec/art; NW/Cont

Designed by Robert Venturi, architect of the new wing of the National Gallery in London, this stunning new five story building is but one of the reasons for visiting the outstanding Seattle Art Museum. The new downtown location is conveniently located within walking distance of many of Seattle's most interesting landmarks including Pike Place Market, and Historic Pioneer Square. The Museum features 2 complete educational resource centers with interactive computer systems. ℂ NW Coast Native American Houseposts; 48' kinetic painted steel sculpture "Hammering Man" by Jonathan Borofsky

ON EXHIBIT 2002

09/20/2001 to 01/06/2002   *Women at SAM: Annie Leibovitz: Women*
Celebrity photos. There is an admission charge of $10 adults; $7 seniors, children 6-12. Tickets at door only   *Will Travel   Book   Admission Fee*

09/20/2001 to 02/17/2002   *Documents Northwest: The Poncho Series Anna Skibska's Con.*

10/13/2001 to January 2002   *Kilengi: African Art from the Bareiss Family Collection*
Works from Tanzania, Malawi, Zambia, Angola, and the Democratic Republic of the Congo

Seattle Asian Art Museum

Volunteer Park, 1400 East Prospect Street, Seattle, WA

206-625-8900   www.seattleartmuseum.org
Open: 10-5 Tu-Su, 10-9 Th   *Closed:* Leg/Hol
Free Day: 1st Th, Sr 1st Fr, 1st Sa   *Adm:*   *Adult:* $3.00   *Children:* Free under 12
&   P: Free   *Museum Shop   Group Tours:* 206-654-3123   *Drop-In Tours:* !   *Historic Building*
Permanent Collection: Wonders of Clay and Fire: Chinese Ceramics through the Ages (with partial rotation): A comprehensive survey of chinese ceramic history from the fifth millennium BC through the 15th c AD

The historical preservation of the Carl Gould designed 1932 building (the first Art-Deco style art museum in the world) involved uniting all areas of the structure including additions of 1947, 1954, and 1955. Now a "jewel box" with plush but tasteful interiors perfectly complementing the art of each nation. 900 of the 7,000 objects in the collection are on view.

ON EXHIBIT 2002

04/20/2000 to Ongoing   *Himalayan Art*

Northwest Museum of Arts and Culture (*The New Museum will Open 12/05/01*)

2316 W. First Avenue, Spokane, WA   99204

509-456-3931   www.northwestmuseum.org
Open: 11-5 Tu, Th, Sa, Su; 10-8 We, Fr   *Closed:* Leg/Hol! open Martin Lurther King and Presidents Day
Free Day: 1st Fr pay as you wish   *Adm:*   *Adult:* $7.00   *Children:* under 5 free
Students: $5.00 ID over 18   *Seniors:* $5.00 over 62
&   P   *Museum Shop*   ¶: cafe   *Group Tours   Historic Building*
Permanent Collection: NW Nat/Am; Reg; Dec/Art

The mission of the Cheney Cowles Museum is to actively engage the people of the Inland Northwest in life-long learning about regional history, visual arts, and American Indian and other cultures especially those specific to the region.

ON EXHIBIT 2002

07/18/2001 to 09/22/2002   *Edward Kleinholz*
The seven television sculptures are assembled in a living room setting with viewers asked to contemplate their feelings about television

12/05/2001 to 03/31/2002   *Social Landscapes—James Lavadour: Landscapes*
Lavadour is a Walla Walla Indian who operates a school for Native Americans to develop through artistic exposure. He paints on oil on board and recalls Turner and Moran.

12/05/2001 to 06/30/2004   *Hometowns: Heart of the Inland Northwest*
An introduction to the culture and built environment of the region. 3 generations of dreams, memories, reflections, and keepsakes are shown.

12/05/2001 to 06/30/2002   *The Davenport Hotel Revisited (working title)*
This famous hostelry entertained many celebrities and was world famous.

12/05/2001 to 12/31/2003   *People of the Rivers: Lifeways on the Northern Plateau*
The sights, sounds, and smells of the Inland Northwest's waterways

04/18/2002 to 07/14/2002   *Social Landscapes—Robert Adams: Sunlight to Civilization*
Adams feels that photography is where culture, personal history, and nature intersect.

08/01/2002 to 11/03/2002   *Social Landscapes—Jim Hodges: Subway Music Box*
A portrait of New York City consisting of multiple video projection of 24 musicians playing different songs, all at once

10/10/2002 to 12/29/2002   *Kristen Capp—Hutterite: A World of Grace*
A photographer often compared to Dorothea Lange, Capp photographed the Hutterite community early in her career. She creates an atmosphere of time standing still.

11/21/2002 to 03/02/2003   *Waves of Creativity: Artists of the Palouse (tentative)*
Artists from the permanent collection from this region of southeastern Washington. The unique landscape has encouraged each artist to have an individual technique and interpretation.

TACOMA

Tacoma Art Museum
12th & Pacific (downtown Tacoma), Tacoma, WA   98402

206-272-4258
Open: 10-5 Tu-Sa, 10-7 Th, 12-5 Su   *Closed:* 1/1, Thgv, 12/25
Free Day: Tu   *Adm:*   *Adult:* $3.00   *Children:* Free under 12   *Students:* $2.00   *Seniors:* $2.00
&   P: Street parking   *Museum Shop   Group Tours*
Permanent Collection: Cont/NW; Am: ptgs

The only comprehensive collection of the stained glass of Dale Chihuly in a public institution.
℃ Chihuly Retrospective Glass Collection

Tacoma Public Library/Thomas Handforth Gallery
1102 Tacoma Avenue South, Tacoma, WA   98402

206-591-5666   www.tpl.lib.wa.us
Open: 9-9 Mo-Th, 9-6 Fr-Sa   *Closed:* Su, Leg/Hol!
&   P   *Historic Building*
Permanent Collection: Historical; Phot; Artifacts

Built in 1903 as an original Andrew Carnegie Library, the Gallery has been serving the public since then with rotating exhibits by Pacific Northwest artists and touring educational exhibits. ℃ Rare book room containing 750 prints including "North American Indian," by Edward S. Curtice

Sheehan Gallery
Affiliated Institution: Whitman College
900 Isaacs-Olin Hall, Walla Walla, WA   99362

509-527-5249
Open: 10-5 Tu-Fr, 1-4 Sa-Su   *Closed:* Mo, Acad!
&: Enter from parking lot   P: On campus   *Group Tours*
Permanent Collection: Scrolls; Screens; Bunraku Puppets; Cer

The Sheehan Gallery administrates the Davis Collection of Oriental Art which is not on permanent display. !

WEST VIRGINIA

Sunrise Museum
746 Myrtle Road, Charleston, WV   25314

304-344-8035   (under construction) sunrisemuseum.org
Open: 11-5 We-Sa, 12-5 Su   *Closed:* Leg/Hol!
Adm: *Adult:* $3.50   *Students:* $2.50   *Seniors:* $2.50
& P   *Museum Shop   Group Tours   Historic Building   Sculpture Garden*
Permanent Collection: Am: ptgs, sculp, gr; Sci Coll

This multimedia center occupies two historic mansions overlooking downtown Charleston. Featured are a Science Hall, Planetarium, and an art museum.

Huntington Museum of Art, Inc
2033 McCoy Road, Huntington, WV   25701-4999

304-529-2701   www.hmoa.org
Open: 10-9 Tu, 10-5 We-Sa, 12-5 Sa   *Closed:* Mo, 1/1, 7/4, Thgv, 12/25
& P   *Museum Shop*   ¶: Cafe Bauhaus open during Museum hours
Group Tours   Drop-In Tours: 10:30, 11:30 Sa, 2, 3 Su   *Historic Building   Sculpture Garden*
Permanent Collection: Am: ptgs, dec/art 18-20; Glass; Silver

The serene beauty of the museum complex on a lovely hilltop surrounded by nature trails, herb gardens, an outdoor amphitheater, and a sculpture courtyard is enhanced by an extensive addition designed by the great architect Walter Gropius. The Museum is home to the state's only plant conservatory.

WISCONSIN

Wright Museum of Art
Affiliated Institution: Beloit College
Prospect at Bushnell, Beloit, WI   53511

608-363-2677   www.beloit.edu/~museum/index/index.html
Open: 9-5 Mo-Fr, 11-4 Sa, Su   *Closed:* Acad!
& P   *Museum Shop   Group Tours*
Permanent Collection: As; Korean: dec/art, ptgs, gr; Hist & Cont: phot

The Wright Museum of Art had its beginnings in 1892. Over the years, the museum has obtained a large collection of Asian decorative arts, a large collection of Chinese snuff bottles, Japanese woodblock prints, Japanese sword fittings, Japanese sagemono and netsuke, Korean ceramics and Buddhist sculpture, and a wide variety of important works by major artists.

MADISON

Elvehjem Museum of Art
Affiliated Institution: University of Wisconsin-Madison
800 University Ave, Madison, WI   53706-1479

608-263-2246   www.lvm.wisc.edu
Open: 9-5 Tu-Fr 11-5 Sa, Su   *Closed:* Mo, 1/1, Thgv, 12/24, 12/25
&.: Use Murray St. entrance, elevator requires security assistance   P: University lot 46 on Lake Street and City Lake St   *Museum Shop   Group Tours   Drop-In Tours:* !
Permanent Collection: An/Grk: vases & coins; Min. Ind Ptgs: Earnest C. & Jane Werner Watson Coll; Jap: gr (Van Vleck Coll); Or: dec/arts; Russ & Soviet: ptgs (Joseph E. Davies Coll)

More than 15,000 objects that date from 2300 B.C. to the present are contained in this unique university museum collection.

ON EXHIBIT 2002

11/10/2001 to 01/06/2002   *Indian Miniatures from the Watson Collection*
17th, 18th, 19th century brightly colored miniatures

11/21/2001 to 01/06/2002   *Contemporary Prints from the Marshall Erdmann and Associates Corporate Art Collection*
Works by Close, Dill, Frankenthaler, Myers, Warhol, and Wilde normally shown at the Corporate Headquarters are brought together for the public.

01/19/2002 to 03/17/2002   *Goltzius and Tetrode (working title)*

01/20/2002 to 03/17/2002   *Xu Bing: Ten Years After (working title)*
New work by this Chinese artist who made his American debut in 1991–92

04/04/2002 to 06/16/2002   *Contemporary Studio Furniture: The Inside Story*
Thirty-five contemporary artists will focus on the expressive qualities of furniture   *Catalog*

Madison Art Center
211 State Street, Madison, WI   53703

608-257-0158   www.madisonartcenter.org
Open: 11-5 Tu-Th, 11-9 Fr, 10-9 Sa, 1-5 Su   *Closed:* Mo, Leg/Hol!
&   P: Pay   *Museum Shop   Group Tours   Historic Building*
Permanent Collection: Am: works on paper,ptgs,sculp; Jap; Mex; Cont

A museum of modern and contemporary art exhibitions including highlights from its permanent collections.   ☾ "Serenade" by Romare Bearden

MANITOWOC

Rahr-West Art Museum
610 North Eighth Street, Manitowoc, WI   54220

920-683-4501   link from www.manitowoc.org
Open: 10-4 Mo, Tu, Th, Fr, 10-8 We, 11-4 Sa-Su   *Closed:* Leg/Hol!
&   P: Free   *Museum Shop   Group Tours   Drop-In Tours   Historic Building*
Permanent Collection: Am: ptgs, dec/art 19; Or: ivory, glass; Cont: ptgs

Built between 1891 & 1893, this Victorian mansion combines with the West Wing added in 1975 and 1986. These showcase the Museum's 19th and 20th C. art, antiques while the West Gallery rotates a schedule of regional and nationally touring exhibitions. ❏ "Birch and Pine Tree No 2," by Georgia O'Keeffe ; "La Petite Boudeuse," 1888, by William Adolphe Bougereau

ON EXHIBIT 2002

11/18/2001 to 01/06/2002   *Christmas in the Mansion*

04/16/2002 to 05/31/2002   *A Carnival of Animals*
Original whimsical book illustrations from the Mazza Collection in Findlay, Ohio, both for current illustrations and historical artworks

06/16/2002 to 08/04/2002   *A History of Rock and Roll*
The high energy and exuberance of rock concerts over the past three decades. It shows the change of style, spectacle, and individuality through the eyes of one photographer   *Will Travel*

MILWAUKEE

Charles Allis Art Museum
1801 North Prospect Avenue, Milwaukee, WI   53202

414-278-8295   www.charlesallismuseum.org
Open: 1-5 We-Su   *Closed:* Mo, Tu, Leg/Hol!
Free Day: ! miscellaneous sponsored days and Crafts Fair weekend   *Adm:*   Adult: $3.00
Children: Free under 13   *Students:* $2.00   *Seniors:* $2.00
♿ P   *Group Tours:* 414-271-2513   *Drop-In Tours:* Su docent; by appt   *Historic Building   Sculpture Garden*
Permanent Collection: Ch: porcelains; Or; An/Grk; An/R; Fr: ptgs 19

With its diverse collection this museum is housed in a 1909 Tudor style house with original furnishings and art collection spanning 2,000 years   ❏ Barbizon and Hudson River school painters, Asian ceramics

ON EXHIBIT 2002

01/23/2002 to 03/10/2002   *Jens Carstensen: A Dane in Dane County*

03/20/2002 to 04/21/2002   *League of Milwaukee Artists*

05/01/2002 to 06/30/2002   *Self and Other Portraits: Wisconsin Artists*

07/10/2002 to 08/25/2002   *Richard Lazzaro Paintings*

11/01/2002 to 12/01/2002   *Wisconsin Handweavers*

12/01/2002 to 01/12/2003   *Holidays at the Allis (decorated in Tudor style)*

Institute of Visual Arts
3253 N. Downer Avenue, Milwaukee, WI   53211

414-226-5070   www.uwm.edu/SOA/inova
Open: Gal 1: 12-5 We-Su; Gal 2: 12-5 Tu-Su; Gal 3: Opens fall 2002, We-Su 12-5   *Closed:* Leg/Hol!
♿: Automatic doors in front and elevators inside   P: Meters in front of building
Permanent Collection: Am & Eur: works on paper, gr; Russ: icons; Reg: 20

The museum works to provide its audience with an artistic cultural and historical experience unlike that offered by other art institutions in Milwaukee. It shows artists who are changing the visual culture of the present and future.

ON EXHIBIT 2002

12/07/2001 to 02/25/2002   *Artists Include Bratkov and Hernandez-Diez—Photography and Roberts, Sala—Video*

03/08/2002 to 05/27/2002   *Artists Include Alaez, Allora/Guillermo Calzadilla—Installation; Brotherus—Photography; Mezzaqui, Monge, Nuenschwander —Video and Installation*

Milwaukee Art Museum
750 North Lincoln Memorial Drive, Milwaukee, WI   53202

414-224-3200   www.mam.org
Open: 10-5 Tu, We, Fr, Sa, 12-9 Th, 12-5 Su   *Closed:* 1/1, Thgv, 12/25
Adm: Adult: $5.00   *Children:* Free under 12   *Students:* $3.00   *Seniors:* $3.00
&   P   *Museum Shop*   ¶   *Group Tours:* 414-224-3825   *Historic Building   Sculpture Garden*
Permanent Collection: Cont: ptgs, sculp; Ger; Am: folk art

The Milwaukee Museum features an exceptional collection housed in a 1957 landmark building by Eero Saarinen, which is cantilevered over the Lake Michigan shoreline. A dramatic addition designed by Santiago Calatrava is scheduled to open in 2000.   € Zurburan's "St. Francis"

ON EXHIBIT 2002

10/19/2001 to 01/13/2002   *Milton Avery: The Late Paintings*
Avery pushed representation to the border of abstraction.   *Catalog   Will Travel*

Patrick & Beatrice Haggerty Museum of Art
Affiliated Institution: Marquette University
13th & Clybourn, Milwaukee, WI   53233-1881

414-288-1669   www.mu.edu/haggerty
Open: 10-4:30 Mo-Sa, 12-5 Su, 10-8 Th   *Closed:* 1/1, Easter, Thgv, 12/25
&   *Museum Shop   Group Tours:* 414-288-5915   *Sculpture Garden   Theater*
Permanent Collection: Ptgs, Drg, Gr, Sculp, Phot, Dec/Art 16-20; As, Tribal

Selections from the Old Master and modern collections are on exhibit continuously.

Villa Terrace Decorative Arts Museum
2220 North Terrace Ave, Milwaukee, WI   53202

414-271-3656   www.villaterracemuseum.org
Open: 1-5 We-Su   *Closed:* Mo, Tu, Leg/Hol!
Adm: Adult: $3.00   *Children:* Free under 13   *Students:* $2.00   *Seniors:* $2.00
&: To first floor galleries   P   *Group Tours:* 414-271-2513 by appt   *Drop-In Tours:* Su !
Historic Building   Sculpture Garden
Permanent Collection: Dec/Art; Ptgs, Sculp, Gr 15-20

Villa Terrace Decorative Arts Museum with its excellent and varied collections is located in a 1923 Italian Renaissance Style building overlooking Lake Michigan € The Garden Renaissance Project opening Spring 2002 is a recreation of a 16th-century garden. The Neptune Gate is designed in the style of Cyrus Colnik, one of the most significant iron creations in over 100 years.

ON EXHIBIT 2002

11/01/2001 to 01/06/2002   *Germanic Glass from Private Collections*

01/16/2002 to 03/03/2002   *Personal Edens: The Gardens and Film Sets of Florence Yoch*

03/13/2002 to 04/21/2002   *Gary Schirmer*

12/01/2002 to 01/12/2003   *Holidays at the Villa (decorated in Roman style)*

Paine Art Center and Arboretum
1410 Algoma Blvd, Oshkosh, WI   54901

920-235-6903
Open: 11-4 Tu-Su, 11-7 Fr extended hours apply Mem/Day-Lab/Day   *Closed:* Mo, Leg/Hol!
Adm: *Adult:* $5.00   *Children:* Free under 12   *Students:* $2.00   *Seniors:* $2.50
&   P: On-street parking   *Museum Shop*   *Group Tours:* ext 21   *Drop-In Tours:* by appt
Historic Building   *Sculpture Garden*   *Theater*
Permanent Collection: Fr & Am: ptgs, sculp, gr 19,20; Or: silk rugs, dec/art

Collections of paintings, sculpture and decorative objects in period room settings are featured in this historic 1920s Tudor Revival home surrounded by botanic gardens.   ❆ "The Bronco Buster," sculpture by Frederic Remington

Charles A. Wustum Museum of Fine Arts
2519 Northwestern Ave, Racine, WI   53404

262-636-9177   www.wustum.org
Open: 11-9 Mo-Sa, 1-5 Su   *Closed:* Leg/Hol!
&: main floor only   P: Free   *Museum Shop*   *Group Tours*   *Drop-In Tours:* by appt
Historic Building   *Sculpture Garden*
Permanent Collection: Sculp; WPA works on paper; Crafts

In an 1856 Italianate style building on acres of landscaped sculpture gardens you will find Racine's only fine arts museum. It primarily supports active, regional living artists. 4th most significant contemporary crafts collection in U.S.

John Michael Kohler Arts Center
608 New York Avenue, PO Box 489, Sheboygan, WI   53082-0489

920-458-6144   www.jmkac.org
Open: 10-5 Mo,We, Fr, 10-8; Tu, Th; 10-4 Sa, Su   *Closed:* 12/31, 1/1, Easter, Mem/Day, Thgv, 12/24, 12/25
&   P   *Museum Shop*   ❙❙   *Group Tours:* ext 110   *Drop-In Tours:* !   *Historic Building*
Sculpture Garden   *Theater*
Permanent Collection: Cont: cer; Dec/Art

This multicultural center is located in the 1860s villa of John Michael Kohler, founder of the plumbing manufacturing company with a new 100,000-square foot Arts Center. It is devoted to presenting multi-media innovative explorations in contemporary American art. Special exhibitions at the Center offer unique perspectives on art forms, artists, and various artistic concepts that have received little exposure elsewhere. The facility expansion will add 69,000 square feet with nine New Arts Galleries, a theater and studio performance space.

ON EXHIBIT 2002

10/07/2001 to 07/14/2002   *Levi Fisher Ames and Adolph Vandertie*
Wisconsin woodcarvers doing domestic and wild animals as well as mythical creatures

10/14/2001 to 01/13/2002   *Reanne Estrada: Look Closely*
Detailed soap drawings on bars of Ivory and colored glycerin soap with pencil on erasers. She adds strands of her own hair to complete.

10/21/2001 to 01/27/2002   *Teresa Serrano: Dissolving the Memories of the Home*
Sculptures based on Mexican textile traditions with an Aztec belief that the life cyle renews every 52 years

11/11/2001 to 01/27/2002   *ABCD: A Collection of Art Brut*
Selections from a Paris based organization of drawings, paintings, and sculture by asylum inmates

12/09/2001 to 02/04/2002   *Judy Fox: Premasculine/Prefeminine*
Hyperreal terracotta and hydrastone portrait sculptures of historical personages cast as children

02/01/2002 to 10/07/2002   *Masquerade*
The masquerade as an investigation of identity and social and cultural constructs

02/24/2002 to 06/09/2002   *Organic/Mechanic*
Artists who use mechanics of living organisms to explore naturally occurring systems and environments

WAUSAU

Leigh Yawkey Woodson Art Museum
700 North Twelfth Street, Wausau, WI   54403-5007

715-845-7010   www.lywam.org
Open: 9-4 Tu-Fr, 12-5 Sa-Su   *Closed:* Mo, Leg/Hol!
& P: Free   *Group Tours   Drop-In Tours:* ! 9am-4pm Tu-Fr   *Sculpture Garden*
Permanent Collection: Glass 19, 20; Studio Glass; Porcelain; Wildlife; ptgs, sculp

An English style residence surrounded by gracious lawns and gardens. A sculpture garden features permanent installations, and annually the garden exhibits 8-10 temporary pieces.

ON EXHIBIT 2002

11/10/2001 to 01/27/2002   *Gizmos, Gadgets, and Flying Frogs: The Art of William Joyce and David Weisner*
A merry romp in the imaginative and stimulating world of children's book illustration
Will Travel

02/02/2002 to 04/07/2002   *Chair Show 4*
Handmade furniture and related objects from high-tech and rustic to funk in all materials from clay and steel   *Will Travel*

04/13/2002 to 06/16/2002   *Picasso Ceramic Editions: From the Edward Weston Collection*
Picasso became intrigued with ceramics in 1946. He allowed Madoura Pottery to produce editions of 25–500. Included were dishes, plates, bowls, vases, vessels, pitchers, and plaques.
Will Travel

06/22/2002 to 08/25/2002   *From Mickey to the Grinch: Art of the Animated Film*
The art, history, and process of American animated film in animation cels, model sheets, drawings, and samples of scripts and assignment sheets. Featured will be an animation station where visitors can create their own animations.   *Will Travel*

09/07/2002 to 11/10/2002   *Birds in Art*
The 27th anniversary of this exciting exhibition   *Catalog   Will Travel*

11/16/2002 to 01/19/2003   *The Theater Posters of James McMullan*
Posters, paintings, sketches, and figure drawings for 30 staged productions to advertise and promote theatrical works of art   *Will Travel*

West Bend Art Museum
300 South 6th Ave, West Bend, WI   53095

262-334-9638   www.wbartmuseum.com
Open: 10-4:30 We-Sa, 1-4:30 Su   *Closed:* Mo, Tu, Leg/Hol!
&   P   *Group Tours   Drop-In Tours:* 8am-4:30pm   *Sculpture Garden*
Permanent Collection: Academic Art Work; Reg: 1850–1950

This community art center and museum is dedicated to the work of Wisconsin's leading artists from Euro-American settlement to 1950 and features changing exhibitions of regional, national, and international art. ℂ The colossal 1889 painting "The Flagellants" measuring approximately 14' x 26' first exhibited in the US at the 1893 Chicago World's Fair, The Columbian Exposition.

ON EXHIBIT 2002

01/02/2002 to 02/17/2002   *Preserving Our Icons: The Wisconsin Barn and its Environs, Craig Blietz, Bonnita Budysz, Steve Gerhartz*

02/20/2002 to 03/30/2002   *Jack Dowd/Larger Than Life*

04/03/2002 to 05/12/2002   *Wisconsin Watercolor Society: 50th Anniversary   Will Travel*

06/26/2002 to 08/11/2002   *Creative Thought*

08/14/2002 to 09/29/2002   *Gerrit Sinclair Retrospective*

10/02/2002 to 11/10/2002   *Ken Kwint & Karen Olsen*

11/13/2002 to 12/22/2002   *Friends of the West Bend Art Museum Annual Art Exhibition*

WYOMING

Bradford Brinton Memorial Museum
239 Brinton Road, P.O.Box 460, Big Horn, WY   82833

307-672-3173   Bradfordbrintonmemorial.com
Open: 9:30-5 daily May 15-Lab/Day, other months by appt
Adm: Adult: $3.00   *Children:* Free under 12   *Students:* $2.00   *Seniors:* $2.00
&   P   *Museum Shop   Historic Building*
Permanent Collection: Western Art; Dec/Art; Nat/Am: beadwork

Important paintings by the best known Western artists are shown in a fully furnished ranch house built in 1892 and situated at the foot of the BigHorn Mountain. ℂ "Custer's Fight on the Little Big Horn," by Frederic Remington

Nicolaysen Art Museum
400 East Collins Drive, Casper, WY   82601-2815

307-235-5247
Open: 10-5 Tu-Sa, 10-8 Th, 12-4 Su   *Closed:* Mo, 1/1, Thgv, 12/24, 12/25
Free Day: Th eve and weekends   *Adm: Adult:* $2.00   *Children:* $1.00 under 12   *Students:* $1.00   *Seniors:* $2.00
&   P   *Museum Shop   Group Tours   Drop-In Tours:* !   *Historic Building*
Permanent Collection: Reg Cont ptgs

The roots of this Museum reside in the commitment of Wyoming people to the importance of having art and culture as an integral part life. ❡ The Discovery Center, an integral part of the museum, complements the educational potential of the exhibitions

CHEYENNE

Wyoming State Museum
Barrett Building, 2301 Central Ave., Cheyenne, WY   82002

307-777-7022   www.commerce.state.wy.us/cr/wsm/index.htm
Open: 9-4:30 Tu-Sa   *Closed:* Su, Mo, Leg/Hol!
&   P: Free in lot north of Barrett bldg. Metered parking on nearby streets   *Museum Shop*
Group Tours   Sculpture Garden
Permanent Collection: 100,000 artifacts relating to Wyoming's heritage in all media

Ten galleries which tell the story of Wyoming's human and natural history. ❡ Hands on history room with interactive exhibits.

CODY

Buffalo Bill Historical Center
720 Sheridan Ave., Cody, WY   82414

307-587-4771   www.bbhc.org
Open: 7-8 daily June-Sept 19; 8-8 daily May; 8-5 daily Nov-Mar!   *Closed:* Thgv, 1/1, 12/25
Free Day: 1st Sa May   *Adm:*   *Adult:* $10.00   *Children:* 6-17 $4.00   *Students:* $8.00   *Seniors:* $6.00
&   P   *Museum Shop   Group Tours   Sculpture Garden*
Permanent Collection: Western/Art: 19,20; Am: firearms; Cultural History of the Plains Indians

The complex includes the Buffalo Bill, Plains Indian, and Cody Firearms museums as well as the Whitney Gallery which contains outstanding paintings of the American West by such artists as George Catlin, Albert Bierstadt, Frederic Remington, and contemporary artists including Harry Jackson and Fritz Scholder. ❡ The Whitney Gallery of Western Art

COLTER BAY

Grand Teton National Park, Colter Bay Indian Arts Museum
Colter Bay, WY   83012

307-739-3594
Open: 8-5 daily 5/13-6/1 & Sept, 8-8 daily 6/1-Lab/Day, closed 10/1-5/13   *Closed:* Closed 10/1-5/13
&   P   *Museum Shop*
Permanent Collection: Nat/Am: artifacts, beadwork, basketry, pottery, musical instruments

Organized into categories and themes, the Davis I. Vernon collection of Indian art housed in this museum is a spectacular assembly of many art forms including porcupine quillwork, beadwork, basketry, pottery, masks, and musical instruments. ❡ Sitting Bull's beaded blanket strip (Sioux, South Dakota, ca. 1875)

JACKSON HOLE

National Museum of Wildlife Art
PO Box 6825, Jackson Hole, WY   83002

800-313-9553   www.wildlifeart.org
Open: 9-5 daily   *Closed:* 1/1, Thgv, 12/25
Free Day: Locals free 1st Su of month   *Adm:*   *Adult:* $6.00   *Children:* Free under 6
Students: $5.00   *Seniors:* $5.00
&   P: Free   *Museum Shop*   ❙❙: cafe   *Group Tours   Drop-In Tours:* daily 11 am   *Sculpture Garden*
Permanent Collection: Wildlife Art and Artifacts

Dating from the 15th Century the collection of fine art focuses on wildlife. The museum offers special admission rates for families. ❰ Chief by Robert Bateman

ON EXHIBIT 2002

09/12/2001 to 01/15/2002   *Wyoming Wildlife Magazine Photography Contest Winners*

February 2002 to April 2002   *Norbert Wu: Photographs of Antarctica*

08/26/2002 to 10/18/2002   *A Carnival of Animals: Birds, Beasts, Bugs in Original Illustrations from Children's Books*

ROCK SPRINGS

Community Fine Arts Center
Affiliated Institution: Rock Springs Library
400, Rock Springs, WY   82901

307-362-6212
Open: 9-12 & 1-5 Mo-Fr; We 6-9; 10-12 & 6-9 Sa   *Closed:* Su, Leg/Hol !
Ġ   P   *Drop-In Tours*
Permanent Collection: Am: 19, 20

The art gallery houses the nationally acclaimed Rock Springs High School Collection, and is owned by the students. ❰ Loren McIver's "Fireplace," the first American women to exhibit at the Venice Biennial (1962).

Selected Listing of Traveling Exhibitions

American Modern, 1925–1940: Design for a New Age
01/12/2002 to 04/07/2002   Pennsylvania Academy of the Fine Arts, Philadelphia, PA
08/23/2002 to 11/17/2002   Philbrook Museum of Art Inc, Tulsa, OK

An American Anthem: 300 Years of Painting from the Butler Institute of American Art
12/15/2001 to 02/24/2002   Hunter Museum of American Art, Chattanooga, TN
12/07/2002 to 02/09/2003   Orlando Museum of Art, Orlando, FL
03/23/2002 to 06/30/2002   Yellowstone Art Museum, Billings, MT

American Impressionism: Treasures from the Smithsonian American Art Museum
11/17/2001 to 01/20/2002   Norton Museum of Art, West Palm Beach, FL
02/17/2002 to 04/14/2002   Museum of Fine Arts, Springfield, MA
06/08/2002 to 09/01/2002   High Museum of Art, Atlanta, GA

Art and Home: Dutch Interiors in the Age of Rembrandt
09/26/2001 to 01/20/2002   Newark Museum, Newark, NJ
03/02/2002 to 05/26/2002   Denver Art Museum, Denver, CO

The Art of Nathan Oliveira
02/08/2002 to 06/30/2002   San Jose Museum of Art, San Jose, CA
06/16/2002 to 09/08/2002   Neuberger Museum of Art, Purchase, NY

A Brush with History: Paintings from the Collection of the National Portrait Gallery
11/16/2001 to 01/27/2002   Speed Art Museum, Louisville, KY
02/23/2002 to 05/05/2002   Montgomery Museum of Fine Arts, Montgomery, AL
05/31/2002 to 08/11/2002   New Orleans Museum of Art, New Orleans, LA

Dancer: Photographs by Irving Penn
01/12/2002 to 05/12/2002   Whitney Museum of American Art, New York, NY
03/17/2002 to 06/16/2002   Museum of Fine Arts, Houston, Houston, TX

Eternal Egypt: Masterworks of Ancient Art from the British Museum
11/23/2001 to 02/24/2002   Brooklyn Museum of Art, Brooklyn, NY
04/12/2002 to 07/07/2002   Nelson-Atkins Museum of Art, Kansas City, MO
08/10/2002 to 11/03/2002   Fine Arts Museums of San Francisco, San Francisco, CA
12/22/2002 to 03/16/2003   Minneapolis Institute of Arts, Minneapolis, MN

From Mickey to the Grinch: Art of the Animated Film
03/02/2002 to 06/09/2002   George Walter Vincent Smith Art Museum, Springfield, MA
06/22/2002 to 08/25/2002   Leigh Yawkey Woodson Art Museum, Wausau, WI

Gerhard Richter: 40 Years of Painting
02/21/2002 to 05/21/2002   Museum of Modern Art, New York, NY
06/22/2002 to 09/15/2002   Art Institute of Chicago, Chicago, IL   60603-6110

Grandma Moses in the 21st Century
12/07/2001 to 01/27/2002   Brooklyn Museum of Art, Brooklyn, NY
02/27/2002 to 04/14/2002   Gilcrease Museum, Tulsa, OK
05/11/2002 to 07/28/2002   Columbus Museum of Art, Columbus, OH
08/17/2002 to 12/01/2002   Portland Art Museum, Portland, OR

Greuze: The Draftsman
05/14/2002 to 08/04/2002   Frick Collection, New York, NY
09/10/2002 to 12/01/2002   Getty Center, Los Angeles, CA

H. C. Westermann
02/14/2002 to 05/12/2002   Hirshhorn Museum and Sculpture Garden, Washington, DC
10/04/2002 to 01/05/2003   Menil Collection, Houston, TX

Hierophany: Tobi Kahn and the Manifestation of the Sacred
07/21/2002 to 09/15/2002   Evansville Museum of Arts & Science, Evansville, IN
11/22/2002 to 01/05/2003   Swope Art Museum, Terre Haute, IN

High Societies: Psychedelic Rock Posters of Haight-Ashbury
2002   San Diego Museum of Art, San Diego, CA
03/26/2002 to 05/19/2002   Hood Museum of Art, Hanover, NH

The Human Factor: Figuration in American Art 1950–1995
04/06/2002 to 05/26/2002   Fort Wayne Museum of Art, Fort Wayne, IN
11/17/2002 to 01/12/2003   Mitchell Gallery, Annapolis, MD

Images from the World Between: The Circus in 20th Century American Art
10/19/2001 to 01/06/2002   Wadsworth Atheneum Museum of Art, Hartford, CT
02/01/2002 to 04/14/2002   John and Mable Ringling Museum of Art, Sarasota, FL

Impressionism Transformed: The Paintings of Edmund C. Tarbell
10/13/2001 to 01/06/2002   Currier Gallery of Art, Manchester, NH
10/20/2001 to 01/13/2002   Walters Art Gallery, Baltimore, MD
02/15/2002 to 04/28/2000   Delaware Art Museum, Wilmington, DE

Imprimature: Albert Paley; Sculpture, Drawings, Graphics, and Decorative Arts
02/16/2002 to 04/14/2002 Gulf Coast Museum of Art, Largo, FL
04/01/2002 to Summer 2002   Polk Museum of Art, Lakeland, FL

Jasper Johns to Jeff Koons: Four Decades of Art from the Broad Collection
09/23/2001 to 01/06/2002   Los Angeles County Museum of Art, Los Angeles, CA
03/16/2002 to 06/03/2002   Corcoran Gallery of Art, Washington, DC
07/21/2002 to 09/20/2002   Boston Museum of Fine Arts, Boston, MA

Jose Clemente Orozco in the United States 1927–1934
2002   San Diego Museum of Art, San Diego, CA
06/08/2002 to 12/15/2002   Hood Museum of Art, Hanover, NH

Light Screens: The Leaded Glass of Frank Lloyd Wright
10/12/2001 to 01/06/2002   Grand Rapids Art Museum, Grand Rapids, MI
02/21/2002 to 04/28/2002   Allentown Art Museum, Allentown, PA

Magnificent, Marvelous, Martele: American Art Nouveau Silver from the Collection of Robert and Julie Shelton
11/10/2001 to 01/13/2002   New Orleans Museum of Art, New Orleans, LA
02/03/2002   Columbus Museum, Columbus, GA

Milk and Eggs: The American Revival of Tempera Painting, 1930–1950
03/09/2002 to 05/19/2002   Brandywine River Museum, Chadds Ford, PA
06/15/2002 to 09/01/2002   Akron Art Museum, Akron, OH

Milton Avery: The Late Paintings
10/19/2001 to 01/13/2002   Milwaukee Art Museum, Milwaukee, WI
02/16/2002 to 04/14/2002   Norton Museum of Art, West Palm Beach, FL

My Reality: Contemporary Art and the Culture of Japanese Animation
04/21/2002 to 07/23/2002   Tampa Museum of Art, Tampa, FL
09/21/2002 to 01/05/2003   Akron Art Museum, Akron, OH

Over the Line: The Art and Life of Jacob Lawrence
02/24/2002 to 05/19/2002   Grand Rapids Art Museum, Grand Rapids, MI
06/15/2002 to 09/08/2002   High Museum of Art, Atlanta, GA

A Personal Journey: The Lawrence Gussman Collection of Central African Art
09/09/2001 to 01/13/2002   Neuberger Museum of Art, Purchase, NY
02/10/2002 to 04/07/2002   Philbrook Museum of Art Inc, Tulsa, OK
06/09/2002 to 08/14/2002   National Museum of African Art, Washington, DC

Six Highlight Objects from 'Treasures from the Royal Tomb of Ur'
07/24/2001 to 03/24/2002   University of Pennsylvania Museum of Archaeology and
Anthropology, Philadelphia, PA
10/26/2002 to 01/19/2003   Michael C. Carlos Museum, Atlanta, GA

Speak Softly and Carry a Beagle: The Art of Charles Schultz
11/03/2001 to 05/05/2002   Norman Rockwell Museum at Stockbridge, Stockbridge, MA
11/15/2002 to 02/02/2003   Memphis Brooks Museum of Art, Memphis, TN

The Stuff of Dreams/Matieres de Reves: Masterworks from the Paris Musee des Arts Decoratifs
06/01/2002 to 08/11/2002   Wadsworth Atheneum Museum of Art, Hartford, CT
09/20/2002 to 01/05/2003   Birmingham Museum of Art, Birmingham, AL

Treasury of the World; Jeweled Arts of India in the Days of the Mughals
10/18/2001 to 01/13/2002   Metropolitan Museum of Art, New York, NY
06/30/2002 to 10/27/2002   Museum of Fine Arts, Houston, Houston, TX
02/24/2002 to 05/19/2002   Cleveland Museum of Art, Cleveland, OH

Wrapped in Pride: Ghanian Kente and African American Identity
10/31/2001 to 01/13/2002   Oakland Museum of California, Oakland, CA
02/23/2002 to 06/16/2002   Michael C. Carlos Museum, Atlanta, GA

Alphabetical Listing of Museums

❧

About the Author

Judith Swirsky has been associated with the arts in Brooklyn as both staff and volunteer for more than forty years. The recipient of many awards, she has held both curatorial and volunteer administration positions at The Brooklyn Museum. While Executive Director of the Grand Central Art Galleries Educational Association, she coordinated the 1989 Moscow Conference. She is now an independent curator and artists' representative. She is listed in *Who's Who of American Women*.